THE ALLYN & BACON GUIDE TO WRITING

SEVENTH EDITION

John D. Ramage
Arizona State University

John C. Bean
Seattle University

June Johnson
Seattle University

PEARSON

Boston Columbus Indianapolis New York San Francisco Upper Saddle River
Amsterdam Cape Town Dubai London Madrid Milan Munich Paris Montréal Toronto
Delhi Mexico City São Paulo Sydney Hong Kong Seoul Singapore Taipei Tokyo

Senior Acquisitions Editor: Lauren A. Finn
Senior Development Editor: Marion B. Castellucci
Executive Marketing Manager: Roxanne McCarley
Senior Supplements Editor: Donna Campion
Executive Digital Producer: Stefanie A. Snajder
Digital Editor: Sara Gordus
Content Specialist: Erin Jenkins
Project Manager: Savoula Amanatidis
Project Coordination, Text Design, and Electronic Page Makeup: Integra
Cover Design Manager: John Callahan
Cover Images: Konstantin Yolshin/Shutterstock
Photo Researcher: Integra
Senior Manufacturing Buyer: Roy L. Pickering, Jr.
Printer and Binder: Printer and Binder: R. R. Donnelley and Sons Company–Crawfordsville
Cover Printer: Lehigh-Phoenix Color Corporation–Hagerstown

Library of Congress Cataloging-in-Publication Data
Ramage, John D., author.
Allyn & Bacon guide to writing / John D. Ramage, Arizona State University, John C. Bean, Seattle University, June Johnson, Seattle University.—Seventh edition.
pages cm
Includes bibliographical references and index.
ISBN 978-0-321-91422-4
1. English language—Rhetoric—Handbooks, manuals, etc. 2. English language—Grammar—Handbooks, manuals, etc. 3. Report writing—Handbooks, manuals, etc. 4. College readers. I. Bean, John C., author. II. Johnson, June, 1953- author. III. Title: IV. Title: Allyn and Bacon guide to writing.
PE1408.R18 2015
808'.042—dc23
2013035650

6 7 8 9 10—DOC—17 16 15

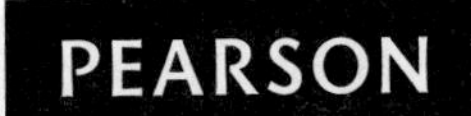

Complete Edition
ISBN-10: 0-321-91422-8; ISBN-13: 978-0-321-91422-4
Brief Edition
ISBN-10: 0-321-91442-2; ISBN-13: 978-0-321-91442-2
Concise Edition
ISBN-10: 0-321-91430-9; ISBN-13: 978-0-321-91430-9

DETAILED CONTENTS

PART 1 A RHETORIC FOR WRITERS

PART 5 WRITING FOR ASSESSMENT

PART 6 A GUIDE TO EDITING

WRITING PROJECTS

BRIEF PROJECTS

MAJOR PROJECTS

THEMATIC CONTENTS

The Allyn & Bacon Guide to Writing contains 48 readings—22 by professional writers and 26 by students. In addition, the text has more than 70 visual texts (such as advertisements, news photographs, posters, and Web sites) that can lead to productive thematic discussions.

ENERGY, ENVIRONMENT, SUSTAINABILITY, AND HEALTH

THE INTERNET, TECHNOLOGY, AND EDUCATION

VIOLENCE, PUBLIC SAFETY, AND INDIVIDUAL RIGHTS

PUBLIC POLICY AND SOCIAL ISSUES

RACE AND CLASS

GENDER

IDENTITY AND VALUES

POPULAR CULTURE, MEDIA, AND ADVERTISING

PARENTS, CHILDREN, AND FAMILY

PREFACE

Through six editions, *The Allyn & Bacon Guide to Writing* has been praised for its groundbreaking integration of composition pedagogy and rhetorical emphasis. In regular, brief, and concise editions, the text has been adopted at a wide range of two- and four-year institutions where instructors admire its appeal to students, its distinctive emphasis on reading and writing as rhetorical acts, its focus on shared problems as the starting point for academic writing, its engaging classroom activities that promote critical thinking, and its effective writing assignments. Reviewers have consistently praised the book's theoretical coherence and explanatory power, which help students produce engaged, idea-rich essays and help composition instructors build pedagogically sound, intellectually stimulating courses shaped by their own strengths, interests, and course goals.

What's New in the Seventh Edition?

While retaining the signature strengths of earlier editions, the seventh edition features the following key improvements:

- **Expanded coverage of online and multimodal composition** helps students navigate digital environments with rhetorical savvy. Although most of today's students are digital natives, their technological skills often outpace their rhetorical understanding of multimodal communication and their awareness of the legal and ethical dimensions of an interactive online environment.
  - **In Part 1, a new chapter on online and multimodal composition** (Chapter 4) teaches students to analyze the rhetorical use of words, images, and sounds in multimodal texts, to think rhetorically about the interactive Web environment, and to participate responsibly in online discourse.
  - **In Part 3, a new nuts-and-bolts chapter on composing multimodal texts** (Chapter 19) explains the design principles of multimodal composing and guides students to adapt these principles to multimodal genres including posters, speeches with presentation slides, podcasts, and videos.
  - **In each Part 2 chapter, optional Writing Projects for online or multimodal composing** allow instructors to decide the extent to which, if at all, they want to include a multimodal component in their course.
- **A completely revised chapter on analysis and synthesis** (Chapter 12) focuses on the critical thinking and writing moves students need for wrestling with multiple complex texts. This revised chapter streamlines the explanations and uses short professional readings and a new student essay, shown in

process, on the timely subject of young adults' search for identity, independence, and security in today's complicated economic and social environment.

- **A completely revised chapter on analyzing short fiction** (Chapter 11) uses engaging flash fiction stories to teach skills of literary analysis. Flash stories are ideally sized for teaching students to think critically about fiction. They contain all the elements of longer fiction but have the compactness of poems, inviting class discussion that elicits close reading.
- **Revised organization of Part 1 "A Rhetoric for Writers"** focuses students' attention more closely on the thinking moves that underlie academic writing. Instead of starting with the open to closed continuum, Chapter 1 now opens with a section restored from earlier editions on "Why Take a Writing Course?" (aimed at helping instructors persuade students of the intellectual and practical benefits of studying composition). Some of the rhetorical concepts in Part 1 have now been re-ordered. For example, Concept 1 now focuses on problem-posing as the heart of academic writing. Chapters 3 and 4 from the sixth edition have now been integrated into one chapter (Chapter 3) to make room for the new chapter on multimodal rhetoric.
- In each assignment chapter, an **"Engaging" activity** provides a classroom exercise that introduces students to the concepts and thinking skills covered in the chapter and awakens students' interest.
- **Many new examples, readings, and student essays** keep the content up-to-date and relevant. New clusters of readings, Web sites, and images focus on women in combat, the potential risk to children of increasing the role of online education, the controversy over fracking, a proposal for mandatory public service, and the problems of twenty somethings' transitioning into traditional adult roles. In Chapter 23 on citing sources a new short reading on vegetarianism provides the content for all examples.

Distinctive Pedagogical Approach of *The Allyn & Bacon Guide to Writing*

The Allyn & Bacon Guide to Writing takes a distinctive pedagogical approach that integrates composition research with rhetorical theory. It treats writing and reading both as rhetorical acts and as processes of problem posing, inquiry, critical thinking, and argument. Its aim is to evoke the kind of deep learning that allows students to transfer compositional and rhetorical skills across disciplines and professional fields. What follows are the distinctive elements of our pedagogical approach to teaching composition:

- **Focus on rhetorical reading.** An often-noted strength of *The Allyn & Bacon Guide to Writing* is its method of teaching rhetorical reading so that students can summarize complex readings and speak back to them through their own analysis and critical thinking. This skill is crucial for writing literature reviews or for doing research in any discipline that use verbal, visual, or multimodal texts as primary sources. Our instructional approach teaches students to understand the differences between print and cyberspace sources; to analyze the rhetorical occasion, genre, context, intended audience, and angle of vision of sources; to evaluate sources according to appropriate criteria; and to negotiate the World Wide Web with confidence.

- **Focus on transfer of learning into the disciplines.** Recent cognitive research shows that transfer of knowledge and skills from one course to another depends on deep rather than surface learning. *The Allyn & Bacon Guide to Writing* promotes deep learning in a variety of ways. As one example, the text emphasizes four underlying skills that novice academic writers must acquire: (1) how to pose a problem that engages targeted readers; (2) how to summarize the conversation that surrounds the problem; (3) how to produce a thesis that adds something new, challenging, or surprising to the conversation; (4) how to support the thesis with appropriate forms of reasons and evidence. Armed with knowledge of these principles (deep learning), a student entering a new discipline can ask "How does this discipline ask questions? How does it summarize the scholarly conversation surrounding this problem (literature reviews)? What constitutes evidence in this discipline?"
- **Classroom-tested assignments that guide students through all phases of the reading and writing processes and make frequent use of collaboration and peer review.** The Writing Projects promote intellectual growth and stimulate the kind of critical thinking valued in college courses. Numerous "For Writing and Discussion" exercises make it easy to incorporate active learning into a course while deepening students' understanding of concepts. The text's focus on the subject-matter question that precedes the thesis helps students see academic disciplines as fields of inquiry rather than as data banks of right answers.
- **Coverage of a wide range of genres and aims including academic, civic, and professional genres as well as multimodal, personal, and narrative forms.** By placing nonfiction writing on a continuum from closed-form prose (thesis-based) to open-form prose (narrative-based), the text presents students with a wide range of genres and aims, and clearly explains the rhetorical function and stylistic features of different genres. The text focuses on closed-form writing for entering most academic, civic, and professional conversations and on open-form writing for communicating ideas and experiences that resist closed-form structures and for creating stylistic surprise and pleasure. As new sections of this edition explain, multimodal texts combine features of closed-form and open-form prose with visual or aural elements to produce powerful new media compositions.
- **Use of reader-expectation theory to explain how closed-form prose achieves maximum clarity and how open-form prose achieves its distinctive pleasures.** Our explanations of closed-form prose (particularly Chapters 1, 2, and 17) show students why certain closed form strategies—such as identifying the problem before stating the thesis, forecasting structure, providing transitions, placing points before details, and linking new information to old information—derive from the cognitive needs of readers rather than from the rule-making penchant of English teachers. Conversely the skills

explained in Chapter 18 on open-form prose show how writers can create pleasurable surprise through purposeful disruptions and violations of the conventions of closed-form prose.

- **Full coverage of outcome goals for first-year composition from the Council of Writing Program Administrators (WPA).** The correlation of the WPA Outcomes Statement with the Seventh Edition of *The Allyn & Bacon Guide to Writing* appears on the inside back covers of the book and in the *Instructor's Resource Manual*. In addition to helping instructors plan their courses, these correlations help with program-wide internal and external assessments.

Key Features of *The Allyn & Bacon Guide to Writing*

The modular design of the text is enhanced by regularly recurring pedagogical features that promote easy navigation and consistent reinforcement of key concepts and principles.

- **An organizational structure that offers flexibility to instructors.** The modular organization gives instructors maximum flexibility in designing courses. Numbered concepts and skills are designed as mini-lessons that are easy for students to navigate and can be assigned in an order chosen by the instructor.
  - **Thirteen rhetorical "concepts" in Part 1** provide students with memorable takeaway knowledge about key concepts and principles of rhetoric. Part 1 enables students to situate texts (including visual and multimodal texts) in a rhetorical context of purpose, audience, and genre and to think critically about how any text tries to persuade its audience
  - **Writing Projects in Part 2,** arranged according to rhetorical aim, teach students the features of a genre while promoting new ways of seeing and thinking (see the inside front cover for a list of Writing Projects). Instructors can select, mix, and match assignments to fit their own course goals (or design their own assignments). The Engaging exercises for each Writing Project help students develop their skills at posing problems, generating ideas, delaying closure, valuing alternative points of view, and thinking dialectically.
  - **Modularized lessons in strategies for composing (Part 3)** teach students to develop an effective writing process while gaining expert knowledge for composing closed-form, open-form, or multimodal texts.
  - **Modularized lessons for research and writing from sources (Part 4)** teach students expert strategies for conducting academic research in a rhetorical environment. Part 4 particularly reinforces the rhetorical concepts learned in Part 1 and is closely integrated with Chapter 5's focus on summary writing and formulating strong responses to readings.
- **Clearly stated learning outcomes** at the beginning of each chapter preview the chapter's content and motivate learning by nutshelling takeaway concepts.

- **Professional and student readings on current and enduring questions** illustrate rhetorical principles, invite thematic grouping, and provide models for students' own writing.
- **"For Writing and Discussion" exercises,** which appear throughout the text, provide class-tested critical thinking activities that promote conceptual learning or active exploration of ideas.
- **The "Engaging " feature at the start of each Writing Projects chapter** helps motivate student interest in the chapter's content and reveals the thinking moves characteristic of the genre.
- **Strategies charts** present suggestions for approaching reading, writing, and research tasks in a handy format for student reference and use.
- **Framework charts showing structural options for writing assignments** help students understand the organizational features of different genres and serve as flowcharts that promote both idea generation and more purposeful ordering of ideas.
- **Peer review guidelines for major assignments** help students conduct effective peer reviews of each other's drafts.

Strategies for Using *The Allyn & Bacon Guide to Writing*

The text's organization makes it easy to design a new syllabus or adapt the text to your current syllabus. Although there are many ways to use *The Allyn & Bacon Guide to Writing,* the most typical course design has students reading and discussing selected concepts from Chapters 1–4 (Part 1) during the opening weeks. The brief, informal write-to-learn projects in these chapters can be used either for homework assignments or for in-class discussion. In the rest of the course, instructors typically assign Writing Projects chapters from the array of options available in Part 2. While students are engaged with the Writing Projects in these chapters, instructors can work in mini-lessons on the writing and research "skills" in Parts 3 and 4. Typically during class sessions, instructors move back and forth between classroom exercises related directly to the current Writing Project (invention exercises, group brainstorming, peer review workshops) and discussions focused on instructional matter from the rest of the text. (For more specific suggestions on how to select and sequence materials, see the sample syllabi in the *Instructor's Resource Manual.*)

Resources for Instructors and Students

MyWritingLab™ **Now Available for Composition.** *MyWritingLab* is an online homework, tutorial, and assessment program that provides engaging experiences to today's instructors and students. By incorporating rubrics into the writing assignments, faculty can create meaningful assignments, grade them based on their desired criteria, and analyze class performance through advanced reporting. For students who enter the course under-prepared, *MyWritingLab* offers a diagnostic test and personalized remediation so that students see improved results and instructors spend less time in class reviewing the basics. Rich multimedia resources are built in to engage students and support faculty throughout the course. Visit *www.mywritinglab.com* for more information.

Interactive Pearson eText. An e-book version of *The Allyn & Bacon Guide to Writing*, Seventh Edition, is also available in MyWritingLab. This dynamic, online version of the text is integrated into MyWritingLab to create an enriched, interactive learning experience for writing students.

CourseSmart. Students can subscribe to *The Allyn & Bacon Guide to Writing*, Seventh Edition, as a CourseSmart eText (at CourseSmart.com). The site includes all of the book's content in a format that enables students to search the text, bookmark passages, save their own notes, and print reading assignments that incorporate lecture notes.

***The Instructor's Resource Manual*, Seventh Edition,** has been revised by Susanmarie Harrington, University of Vermont. The *Instructor's Resource Manual* integrates emphases for meeting the Council of Writing Program Administrators' guidelines for outcome goals in first-year composition courses. It continues to offer detailed teaching suggestions to help both experienced and new instructors; practical teaching strategies for composition instructors in a question-and-answer format; suggested syllabi for courses of various lengths and emphases; chapter-by-chapter teaching suggestions; answers to Handbook exercises; suggestions for using the text with nonnative speakers; suggestions for using the text in an electronic classroom; transparency masters for class use; and annotated bibliographies.

PowerPoints to Accompany *The Allyn & Bacon Guide to Writing*. Ideal for hybrid or distance learning courses, the PowerPoint presentation deck offers instructors slides to adapt to their own course needs.

Accelerated Composition. Support for acceleration or immersion courses focuses on three fundamental areas: reading, writing, and grammar. Additional questions for professional and student readings help students understand, analyze, and evaluate the strategies writers employ. For each of the text's major Writing Projects, additional activities and prompts encourage students to break down the tasks involved in writing an essay into manageable chunks. Grammar support includes diagnostic, practice, instruction, and mastery assessment. Contact your Pearson representative for access through MyWritingLab or for a print workbook.

Robert Miller, Associate Professor of English at the Community College of Baltimore County, authors the reading and writing support for accelerated courses using *The Allyn & Bacon Guide to Writing*. He has been a member of CCBC's ALP steering committee since its inception and has been teaching the Accelerated Learning Program model for seven years. Professor Miller has presented on Acceleration at numerous conferences including CCCC and the Conference on Acceleration. He runs www.alp-deved.org, the national ALP Web site and writes the ALP newsletter. He also serves on the national executive board of the Council of Basic Writing.

Contact your Pearson representative for more information on resources for *The Allyn & Bacon Guide to Writing*.

Acknowledgments

We wish to thank Amy Holly of Front Range Community College for her valuable consulting help as we created the new multimodal material in the seventh edition. Amy's insightful review of the sixth edition inspired us to incorporate more in-depth treatment of multimodal texts into *The Allyn &Bacon Guide to Writing*, and her own innovative use of multimodal assignments in her courses helped stimulate our own thinking. We'd also like to thank our English Department colleague Charles Tung for the extended conversations that led to our complete revision of Chapter 11 on analyzing short fiction. As a specialist in literary theory, Charles's insights helped us develop an approach to "close reading" that will engage student interest and provide a pedagogically sound introduction to literary analysis. In addition, we would like to thank our former student and current colleague Tiffany Anderson, who in her capacity as Assistant Director of our Writing Center provided research and writing assistance for several of the issues new to this edition.

We give special thanks to the following composition scholars and instructors, who reviewed the sixth-edition text or the manuscript for the seventh edition, helping us understand how they use *The Allyn & Bacon Guide to Writing* in the classroom and offering valuable suggestions for improving the text: Larry Beason, University of South Alabama; Diane Boehm, Saginaw Valley State University; Jenna Caruso, Baker College; Christine Cucciarre, University of Delaware; Heather Salter Dromm, Northwestern State University of Louisiana; Tyler Farrell, Marquette University; Mitch Gathercole, Grand Rapids Community College; Tara Hembrough, Southern Illinois University; Thomas Patrick Henry, Utah Valley University; Guy J. Krueger, University of Mississippi; Lindsay Lewan, Arapahoe Community College; Alison Reynolds, University of Florida; Susan Roach, Purdue University Calumet; Alfred Siha, Harrisburg Area Community College; Ellen Sorg, Owens Community College; Andrea Spofford, University of Southern Mississippi; Richard S. Tomlinson, Richland Community College; and Scott Weeden, Indiana University–Purdue University Indianapolis.

Thanks also to various scholars who have written sections of *The Allyn & Bacon Guide to Writing* for previous editions and whose work remains in the seventh edition. Thanks to Tim McGee of Philadelphia University, whose work still influences our material on oral presentation. Thanks also to Alice Gillam of the University of Wisconsin–Milwaukee, who authored the chapter on self-reflective writing (Chapter 25). Finally, we wish to thank again Christy Friend of the University of South Carolina, Columbia, who wrote the chapter on essay examinations for the first edition.

We are particularly grateful to our Pearson team. We especially thank our development editor, Marion Castellucci, who has worked with us through multiple revisions and has become an invaluable part of our team. Her insight, sense of humor, professional experience, and extensive editorial knowledge have once again kept us on track and made the intense work of this revision possible. We thank our production editor, Martha Beyerlein, and have great appreciation for our editor, Lauren Finn, whose comprehensive view of the field, keen insights, and excellent people and communication skills make her a pleasure to work with.

We would also like to thank our Seattle University students who made special contributions to this edition: Michelle Eastman for her short story analysis, Claire Giordano for her classical argument, and Alex Mullen for the story board images and stills from his video production. Most of all, we are indebted to all our students, who have made the teaching of composition such a joy. We thank them for their insights and for their willingness to engage with problems, discuss ideas, and, as they compose and revise, share with us their frustrations and their triumphs. They have sustained our love of teaching and inspired us to write this book.

Finally, John Bean thanks his wife, Kit, also a professional composition teacher, whose dedication to her students as writers and individuals manifests the sustaining values of our unique profession. John also thanks his children, Matthew, Andrew, Stephen, and Sarah, who have grown to adulthood since he began writing textbooks and who continue to give him insights for writing assignments and contemporary issues. June Johnson thanks her husband, Kenneth Bube, a mathematics professor and geophysics consultant, for his insights into the fascinating intersections between learning to think mathematically and the critical thinking and development of writing knowledge and skills in composition. Finally, she thanks her daughter, Jane Ellen, who through her own college coursework in the interdisciplinary field of Environmental Studies has highlighted the importance of academic and civic writing.

John D. Ramage
John C. Bean
June Johnson

A RHETORIC FOR WRITERS

PART 1

This image shows the surrealist painting *Portrait de Famille* (1954) by American painter, artist, and writer Dorothea Tanning (1910–2012). Surrealism was an early twentieth century artistic movement that featured surprise, strange and often disturbing juxtapositions, arresting symbolism, and a blending of reality and the painter's subconscious dreams. These features make interpretation of surrealist art particularly open to speculation. What is surprising, strange, and dreamlike about this painting? What questions does a close look at the figures in this painting inspire you to ask?

1 POSING PROBLEMS: THE DEMANDS OF COLLEGE WRITING

WHAT YOU WILL LEARN

1.1 To pose subject-matter problems, in which you wrestle with the complexities of your topics.

1.2 To make decisions about your writing based on purpose, audience, and genre.

1.3 To use varying rules for "good writing" depending on the rhetorical context.

> **It seems to me, then, that the way to help people become better writers is not to tell them that they must first learn the rules of grammar, that they must develop a four-part outline, that they must consult the experts and collect all the useful information. These things may have their place. But none of them is as crucial as having a good, interesting question.**
>
> —*Rodney Kilcup, Historian*

Our purpose throughout this textbook is to help you see writers as questioners and problem posers—a view of writing that we believe will lead to your greatest growth as a college-level thinker and writer. In particular, we want you to think of writers as people who pose interesting questions or problems and struggle to work out answers or responses to them. As we show in this chapter, writers pose two sorts of problems: *subject-matter problems* (for example, Should the United States pass stricter gun-control laws?) and *rhetorical problems* (for example, Who are my readers? How much do they already care about gun control? What form and style should I use?).

We don't mean to make this focus on problems sound scary. Indeed, humans pose and solve problems all the time and often take great pleasure in doing so. Psychologists who study critical and creative thinking see problem solving as a productive and positive activity. According to one psychologist, "Critical thinkers are actively engaged with life.... They appreciate creativity, they are innovators, and they exude a sense that life is full of possibilities."* By focusing first on the kinds of problems that writers pose and struggle with, we hope to increase your own engagement and pleasure in becoming a writer.

*Stephen D. Brookfield. *Developing Critical Thinkers: Challenging Adults to Explore Alternative Ways of Thinking and Acting.* (San Francisco: Jossey-Bass, 1987): 5. Academic writers regularly document their quotations and sources. In this text sources are documented either on the page or in the Credits section at the end of the text.

Why Take a Writing Course?

Before turning directly to the notion of writers as questioners and problem posers, let's ask why a writing course can be valuable for you.

First of all, the skills you learn in this course will be directly transferable to your other college courses. Introductory courses often focus on generalized academic writing, while advanced courses in your major will introduce you to your field's specialized ways of writing and thinking. What college professors value are the kinds of questioning, analyzing, and arguing skills that this course will help you develop. You will emerge from this course as a better reader and thinker and a clearer and more persuasive writer, able to meet the demands of different academic writing situations.

Effective writing skills are also essential for most professional careers. One recent study showed that college graduates in business or professional life spend, on average, 44 percent of their time writing, including (most commonly) letters, memos, short reports, instructional materials, and professional articles and essays.

Besides the pragmatic benefits of college and career success, learning to write well can bring you the personal pleasure of a richer mental life. As we show throughout this text, writing is closely allied to thinking and to the innate satisfaction you take in exercising your curiosity, creativity, and problem-solving ability. Writing connects you to others and helps you discover and express ideas that you would otherwise never think or say. Unlike speaking, writing gives you time to think deep and long about an idea. Because you can revise writing, it lets you pursue a problem in stages, with each new draft reflecting a deeper, clearer, or more complex level of thought. In other words, writing isn't just a way to express thought; it is a way to do the thinking itself. The act of writing stimulates, challenges, and stretches your mental powers and, when you do it well, is profoundly satisfying.

With this background on why a college writing course is important, let's begin with key rhetorical concepts that will serve as the foundation for your study of writing.

CONCEPT 1.1 Subject matter problems are the heart of college writing.

1.1 Pose subject-matter problems, in which you wrestle with the complexities of your topics.

From your previous schooling, you are probably familiar with the term **thesis statement**, which is the main point a writer wants to make in an essay. However, you may not have thought much about the question that lies behind the thesis, which is the problem or issue that the writer is wrestling with. An essay's thesis statement is actually the writer's one-sentence summary answer to this question, and it is this question that has motivated the writer's thinking. Experienced writers immerse themselves in subject matter questions in pursuit of answers or solutions. They write to share their proposed solutions with readers who share their interests. Let's look more fully at the kinds of subject matter questions that initiate the writing process.

Shared Problems Unite Writers and Readers

For college professors, "a good, interesting question" is at the heart of good writing. Professors want students to become gripped by problems because they themselves are gripped by problems. For example, at a workshop for new faculty members, we asked participants to write a brief description of the question or problem that motivated their Ph.D. dissertation or a recent conference paper or article. Here is how a biochemistry professor responded:

> During periods of starvation, the human body makes physiological adaptations to preserve essential protein mass. Unfortunately, these adaptations don't work well during long-term starvation. After the body depletes its carbohydrate storage, it must shift to depleting protein in order to produce glucose. Eventually, this loss of functional protein leads to metabolic dysfunction and death. Interestingly, several animal species are capable of surviving for extensive periods without food and water while conserving protein and maintaining glucose levels. How do the bodies of these animals accomplish this feat? I wanted to investigate the metabolic functioning of these animals, which might lead to insights into the human situation.

As you progress through your college career, you will find yourself increasingly engaged with the kinds of questions that motivate your professors. All around college campuses you'll find clusters of professors and students asking questions about all manner of problems ranging from puzzles in the reproductive cycles of worms and bugs to the changing portrayal of race and gender in American films. At the heart of all these communities of writers and readers is an interest in common questions and the hope for better or different answers. Writers write because they have something new or surprising or challenging to say in response to a question. Readers read because they share the writer's interest in the problem and want to deepen their understanding.

Where Do Problems Come From?

So where do these problems come from and how can you learn to pose them? The problems that college professors value might be different from what you at first think. Beginning college students typically imagine questions that have right answers. Students ask their professors questions about a subject because they are puzzled by confusing parts of a textbook, a lecture, or an assigned reading. They hope their professors will explain the confusing material clearly. Their purpose in asking these questions is to eliminate misunderstandings, not to open up controversy and debate. Although basic comprehension questions are important, they are not the kinds of inquiry questions that initiate strong college-level writing and thinking.

The kinds of questions that stimulate the writing most valued in college are open-ended questions that focus on unknowns or invite multiple points of view. These are what historian Rodney Kilcup refers to when he says that writers should begin with a "good, interesting question" (see the epigraph to this chapter, p. 2). For Kilcup, a good question sets the writer on the path of inquiry, critical thinking, analysis, and argument.

So how does a writer get hooked on an open-ended problem? Although this "how" question is complex at a philosophical level, we can offer two relatively simple and helpful answers. Sometimes you get caught up in a question that others are already debating—an existing question that is already "out there" in a conversation in the public. Some of these "big questions" have sparked conversations for many hundreds of years: How did the universe get created? Why do good people have to suffer? Do humans have free will? Thousands of narrower subject matter questions are being discussed by communities all the time—in classroom debates, discussion threads on blog sites, or in the pages of scholarly journals or newspapers. When you advance in your major, you'll be drawn into disciplinary problems that may be new to you but not to your professors. In such cases, a problem that is already "out there" initiates your search for a possible answer and invites you to join the conversation.

But sometimes you actually initiate a conversation by posing your own problem fresh from your own brain. For example, you find your own problem whenever you see something puzzling in the natural world, note curious or unexplained features in a cultural phenomenon or artifact, or discover conflicts or contradictions within your own way of looking at the world.

In Table 1.1 we describe some of the ways that writers can become gripped by a problem that may lead to engaged writing.

TABLE 1.1 How Writers Become Gripped by a Problem

Occasion That Leads to Your Posing a Problem	Examples	Your Interior Mental State
	The problem is already "out there." *(You enter a conversation already in progress.)*	
You encounter others arguing about a problem, and you don't know where you stand.	Our class discussion has left me uncertain about whether health care should be rationed. In *To Kill a Mockingbird*, I can't decide whether Atticus Finch is a good father.	• You are equally persuaded by different views or dissatisfied with all the views. • Part of you thinks X but another part thinks Y (you feel divided).
Your gut instinct tells you that someone else is wrong, but you haven't fully investigated the issue (your instinct may be wrong).	This article's explanation of the causes for anorexia doesn't seem quite right to me. Shanita says that we should build more nuclear power plants to combat global warming, but I say nuclear power is too dangerous.	• Your skepticism or intuition pushes against someone else's view. • Your system of values leads you to views different from someone else. • *NOTE: You aren't gripped by a problem until you have seen the possible strengths of other views and the possible weaknesses of your own. You must go beyond simply having an opinion.*
Someone gives you a question that you can't yet answer.	Your boss asks you whether the company should enact the proposed marketing plan. Your history professor asks you, "To what extent does Frederick Jackson Turner's frontier hypothesis reflect a Eurocentric world view?"	• You feel overwhelmed with unknowns. • You feel that you can't begin to answer until you do more exploration and research. • You may be able to propose a few possible answers, but you aren't yet satisfied with them.

(*continued*)

TABLE 1.1 *continued*

Occasion That Leads to Your Posing a Problem	Examples	Your Interior Mental State
	You pose the problem yourself. *(You initiate the conversation.)*	
You see something puzzling in a natural or cultural phenomenon.	You note that women's fashion magazines have few ads for computers and begin wondering how you could market computers in these magazines. You notice that political activists and protesters are using social media to gain attention and gather adherents. How might social media serve purposes beyond entertainment?	• You begin puzzling about something that other people don't notice. • Your mind plays with possible explanations or new approaches. • You begin testing possible solutions or answers. (Often you want to talk to someone—to start a conversation about the problem).
You see something unexpected, puzzling, or unexplained in a poem, painting, or other human artifact.	Why is the person in this advertisement walking two dogs rather than just one? My classmates believe that Hamlet really loves Ophelia, but then how do you explain the nunnery scene where he treats her like a whore?	• You can't see why the maker/designer/artist did something in such a way. • You notice that one part of this artifact seems unexpected or incongruous. • You begin trying to explain what is puzzling and playing with possible answers.
You identify something inconsistent or contradictory in your own view of the world.	I agree with this writer's argument against consumerism, but I really want a large plasma TV. Is consumerism really bad? Am I a materialist?	• You feel unsettled by your own inconsistent views or values. • You probe more deeply into your own identity and place in the world.

In each of these cases, the problem starts to spark critical thinking. We'll examine the process of critical thinking in more detail when we discuss "wallowing in complexity" (Chapter 2, Concept 2.1).

FOR WRITING AND DISCUSSION

Finding a Problem

Background: Figure 1.1 shows a sculpture by Billie Grace Lynn that was the West Collection 2011 Grand Prize Winner. This electric/hybrid motorcycle made from cow bones, a bicycle frame, and motor is a ridable kinetic sculpture. This activist sculpture is intended to inspire people to think about reducing their consumption of meat. Lynn built a full-sized version of the Mad Cow, which runs on waste vegetable oil, and will be taking the motorcycle on a cross-country tour.

Task: Spend several minutes writing down one or more open-ended questions that emerge from looking at the photo of this sculpture. What

FIGURE 1.1 *Mad Cow Motorcycle* by Billie Grace Lynn

puzzles you about it? Consider the sculpture's title as well as its appearance and the possible effects the artist hopes to have on viewers. Then share your individual questions with classmates. Speculate about different answers to some of these questions. The best questions will lead to a genuine conversation with different points of view. (If you would like to find out more about Billie Grace Lynn, a quick Web search will yield information about her art training, philosophy of art, and other work.)

In a similar vein, your instructor may ask you to speculate and formulate thought-provoking questions about another puzzling work of art, the surreal painting *Portrait de Famille* (1954) by Dorothea Tanning, which appears on page 1.

CONCEPT 1.2 **Writers' decisions are shaped by purpose, audience, and genre.**

1.2 Make decisions about your writing based on purpose, audience, and genre.

In the introduction to this chapter, we said that writers must address two types of problems: subject matter problems and rhetorical problems. In this section we look at rhetorical problems in more detail. To begin, we'll explain in more detail what we mean by the term *rhetoric*.

What Is Rhetoric?

At the broadest level, **rhetoric** is the study of how human beings use language and other symbols to influence the attitudes, beliefs, and actions of others. One prominent twentieth-century rhetorician, Kenneth Burke, calls rhetoric "a symbolic means of inducing cooperation in beings that by nature respond to symbols." To understand what Burke means by "symbols," consider the difference in flirting behavior between peacocks and humans. When male peacocks flirt, they spread their fantastic tail feathers, do mating dances, and screech weirdly to attract females, but the whole process is governed by instinct. Peacocks don't have to choose among different symbolic actions such as buying an upscale tail from Neiman Marcus versus a knockoff tail from Walmart. Poor flirting humans, however, must make dozens of symbolic choices, all of which convey meanings to audiences. Consider, for example, the different flirting messages humans send to each other by their choice of clothes, their hairstyles, their accessories, or their song playlists. Even one's word choices (for example, street slang versus intellectual jargon), one's e-mail username (janejones@___.net versus foxychick@___.net) or one's choice of major (chemical engineering versus film studies) gives further hints of a person's identity, values, and social groups. Rhetoricians study, among other things, how these symbols arise within a given culture and how they influence others.

In a narrower sense, rhetoric is the art of making messages persuasive. Perhaps the most famous definition of rhetoric comes from the Greek philosopher Aristotle, who defined rhetoric as "the ability to see, in any particular case, all the available means of persuasion." Effective speakers or writers fruitfully begin by trying to understand their audience's values and beliefs and the kinds of arguments that different audience members might make on a given issue ("all the available means of persuasion"). If we imagine the interaction of several speakers, each proposing different points of view and each analyzing and appreciating others' viewpoints, we can see how mutual understanding might emerge. The study of rhetoric can therefore help humans construct more functional and productive communities.

At an operational level, writers can be said to "think rhetorically" whenever they are consciously aware of writing to an audience for a purpose within a genre. Let's look more closely at each of these in turn.

How Writers Think about Purpose

In this section, we want to help you think more productively about your purpose for writing. At a specific level, your purpose is to bring something new or contestable to your reader. At a more generalized level, your purpose can be expressed as a rhetorical aim. Let's look at each in turn.

Purpose as a Desire to Bring Something New or Contestable to Your Reader One powerful way to think about purpose is to focus on what is new or controversial (contestable—capable of being contested) in your paper. For most essays, you can write a one-sentence, nutshell statement about your purpose.

> My purpose is to give my readers a vivid picture of my difficult struggle with Graves' disease. [What's new: a vivid account of one person's struggle with Graves' disease.]

My purpose is to explain how Thoreau's view of nature differs in important ways from that of contemporary environmentalists. [What's new: a possibly controversial way of thinking about the difference between Thoreau and contemporary environmentalists.]

My purpose is to persuade the general public to ban the sale of assault weapons. [What's new: a contestable argument that some would say narrows the rights conveyed in the Second Amendment.]

This view of purpose will be developed further when we explain how an effective thesis statement tries to bring about some change in the reader's view of the subject (Chapter 2, Concept 2.2). Writers of closed-form prose often place explicit purpose statements in their introductions along with their thesis. In most other forms of writing, the writer uses a behind-the-scenes purpose statement to achieve focus and direction but seldom states the purpose explicitly.

Purpose as Rhetorical Aim It is also possible to think of purpose more broadly by using the concept of **rhetorical aim**. Articulating your rhetorical aim can help you clarify your relationship to your audience and identify typical ways that a piece of writing might be structured and developed. The writing projects in Part 2 of this textbook are based on six different rhetorical aims: to express, to explore, to inform, to analyze/ synthesize, to persuade, and to reflect. Table 1.2 gives you an overview of each of these rhetorical aims and sketches out how different aims typically use different approaches to subject matter, how the writer's task and relationship to readers differ according to aim, and how a chosen aim affects the writing's genre and its position on the spectrum from open to closed forms.

TABLE 1.2 Purpose as Rhetorical Aim

Rhetorical Aim	Focus of Writing	Relationship to Audience	Forms and Genres
Express or share (Chapter 6) May also include an artistic aim (Chapter 18)	Your own life, personal experiences, reflections	You share aspects of your life; you invite readers to walk in your shoes, to experience your insights.	**Form:** Has many open-form features **Sample genres:** journal, blog, personal Web site, or online profile; personal essays or literacy narratives, often with artistic features
Explore or inquire (Chapter 7)	A significant subject-matter problem that puzzles you	You take readers on your own intellectual journey by showing your inquiry process (raising questions, seeking evidence, considering alternative views).	**Form:** Follows open form in being narrative based; is thesis seeking rather than thesis supporting **Sample genres:** freewriting; research logs; articles and books focused on process of discovery

(*continued*)

TABLE 1.2 *continued*

Rhetorical Aim	Focus of Writing	Relationship to Audience	Forms and Genres
Inform or explain (Chapter 8)	Factual knowledge addressing a reader's need or curiosity	You provide knowledge that your readers need or want, or you arouse curiosity and provide new, surprising information. You expect readers to trust your authority.	**Form:** Usually has a closed-form structure **Sample genres:** encyclopedia articles; instruction booklets; sales reports; technical reports; informative magazine articles; informative Web sites
Analyze, synthesize, or interpret (Chapters 9–12)	Complex subject matter that you can break down into parts and put together in new ways for greater understanding	Using critical thinking and possibly research, you challenge readers with a new way of understanding your subject. Skeptical readers expect you to support your thesis with good particulars.	**Form:** Typically has a closed-form structure **Sample genres:** scholarly articles; experimental reports; many kinds of college research papers; public affairs magazine articles; many kinds of blogs
Persuade (Chapters 13–15)	Subject-matter questions that have multiple controversial answers	You try to convince readers, who may not share your values and beliefs, to accept your stance on an issue by providing good reasons and evidence and attending to alternative views.	**Form:** Usually closed form, but may employ many open-form features for persuasive effect **Sample genres:** letters to the editor; op-ed pieces; advocacy pieces in public affairs magazines; advocacy Web sites; researched academic arguments
Reflect (Chapter 24)	Subject matter closely connected to your interests and experience; often involves self-evaluation of an experience	Writing for yourself as well as for a reader, you seek to find personal meaning and value in an experience or course of study. You assume a sympathetic and interested reader.	**Form:** Anywhere on the closed-to-open-form continuum **Sample genres:** memoirs, workplace self-evaluations; introductory letter for a portfolio; personal essays looking back on an experience

How Writers Think about Audience

In our discussion of purpose, we have already had a lot to say about audience. What you know about your readers—their familiarity with your subject matter, their level of expertise, their reasons for reading, their values and beliefs—affects most of the choices you make as a writer.

In assessing your audience, you must first determine who that audience is—a single reader (for example, your boss), a select group (a scholarship committee; readers of a particular blog), or a general audience. If you imagine a general audience, you will need to make some initial assumptions about their views and values and about their current attitude toward your subject. Doing so creates an "implied audience," giving you a stable rather than a moving target so that you can make decisions about your own piece of writing. Once you have identified your audience, you can use the following strategies for analysis.

Strategies for Analyzing Audience

Questions to Ask about Your Audience	Reasons for Asking the Question
How busy are my readers?	• Helps you decide on length, document design, and methods of organization (see Concept 1.3 on open versus closed forms). • In workplace writing, busy readers usually appreciate tightly organized prose with headings that allow for skimming.
What are my readers' motives for reading?	• If the reader has requested the document, he or she will probably already be interested in what you say. • In most cases, you need to hook your readers' interest and keep them engaged.
What is my relationship with my readers?	• Helps you decide on a formal or informal style • Helps you select tone—polite and serious or loose and slangy
What do my readers already know about my topic? Do my readers have more or less expertise than I have, or about the same expertise?	• Helps you determine what will be old/familiar information for your audience versus new/unfamiliar information • Helps you decide how much background and context to include • Helps you decide to use or avoid in-group jargon and specialized knowledge
How interested are my readers in my topic? Do my readers already care about it?	• Helps you decide how to write the introduction • Helps you determine how to make the problem you address interesting and significant to your reader
What will be my readers' attitudes toward my thesis? Do my readers share my beliefs and values? Will they be skeptical of my argument or even threatened by it?	• Helps you make numerous decisions about tone, structure, reference to alternative views, and use of evidence • Helps you decide on the persona and tone you want to project

To appreciate the importance of audience, consider how a change in audience can affect the actual content of a piece. Suppose you want voters to approve a bond issue to build a new baseball stadium. For voters who are baseball fans, your argument can appeal to their love of the game and to the improved fan amenities in the new park (more comfortable seats, better sight lines, bigger restrooms, more food options, and so forth). But to reach non-baseball fans, you must take a different tack, appealing to values other than love of baseball. For this new audience, you might argue that the new stadium will bring new tax revenues to the city, clean up a run-down area, revitalize local businesses, or stimulate tourism. Your purpose remains the same—to persuade taxpayers to fund the stadium—but the content of your argument changes if your audience changes.

For college papers, students may think that they are writing to an audience of one—the instructor. But because instructors are captive audiences and because they often know more about the subject matter than the student writer (making it hard for the student writer to bring something "new" to the reader), they often ask students to address real audiences or to role-play addressing hypothetical audiences. They may ask you to blog for a Web audience, publish for classmates on a course Web site, write for community readers in a service learning context, or imagine writing for a particular magazine or journal. As an alternative, they may create case assignments with built-in audiences (for example, "You are an accountant in the firm of Numbers and Fudge; one day you receive a letter from..."). If your instructor does not specify an audience, you can generally assume an audience of student peers who have approximately the same level of knowledge and expertise in the field as you do, who are engaged by the question you address, and who want to read your writing and be surprised in some way.

How Writers Think about Genre

The term **genre** refers to categories of writing that follow certain conventions of style, structure, approach to subject matter, and document design. Table 1.3 shows different kinds of genres.

The concept of genre creates strong reader expectations, placing specific demands on writers. How you write any given letter, report, or article is influenced by the structure and style of hundreds of previous letters, reports, or articles written

TABLE 1.3 Examples of Genres

Personal Writing	Academic Writing	Popular Culture	Public Affairs, Civic Writing	Professional Writing	Literature
Letter	Scholarly article	Articles for magazines such as *Seventeen*, *Ebony*, or *Vibe*	Letter to the editor	Cover letter for a job application	Short story
Diary/journal	Research paper	Advertisements	Newspaper editorial	Résumé	Novel
Memoir	Scientific report	Hip-hop lyrics	Op-ed piece	Business memo	Graphic novel
Blog	Abstract or summary	Fan Web sites	Advocacy Web site	Legal brief	Play
Text message	Book review	Bumper stickers	Political blog	Brochure	Sonnet
E-mail	Essay exam	Reviews of books, films, plays, music	Magazine article on civic issue	Technical manual	Epic poem
Facebook profile	Annotated bibliography			Instruction booklet	Literary podcast
Personal essay	Textual analysis			Proposal	
Literacy narrative				Report	
Status update				Press release	
Tweet					

in the same genre. If you wanted to write for *Reader's Digest*, for example, you would have to use the conventions that appeal to its older, conservative readers: simple language, strong reliance on anecdotal evidence in arguments, high level of human interest, and choice of subject matter that reinforces the conservative values of individualism, self-discipline, and family. If you wanted to write for *Seventeen* or *Rolling Stone*, however, you would need to use quite different conventions concerning subject matter, style, and document design. Likewise, the conventions for writing for the Web (blogs, podcasts, Web pages) differ significantly from writing for print.

To illustrate the relationship of a writer to a genre, we sometimes draw an analogy with clothing. Although most people have a variety of clothing in their wardrobes, the genre of activity for which they are dressing (class, concert, party, job interview, wedding) constrains their expression of individuality. A man dressing for a job interview might express his personality through choice of tie or quality and style of business suit; he probably wouldn't express it by wearing a Hawaiian shirt and sandals. Even when people deviate from a convention, they tend to do so in a conventional way. For example, people who do not want to follow typical middle class clothing genres form their own genres of goth, grunge, or hipster. So, by analogy, if you are writing a business memo or an experimental report in APA style, you are constrained by the conventions of the genre. The concept of genre raises intriguing and sometimes unsettling questions about the relationship of the unique self to a social convention or tradition.

In the last ten years, the arrival of Web 2.0 has created a whole range of new genres. Blogs, for example, typically feature links to other Web sites and can include uploaded images, music, or videos. Whereas a print article is stable and fixed, the same article published as a blog can turn rapidly into an on-going conversation as readers post comments first to the original blogger and then to each other. A blog, then, becomes a dynamic conversation site—a genre impossible in print. Note too that if you post a response to someone else's blog, the genre of "blog response" places formidable constraints on outsiders: If you don't reveal the right insider savvy about the conversation, you can be rudely flamed. This dynamic community of readers and writers—along with the hypertext structure-makes Web genres substantially different from print genres.

See Chapter 4 for a fuller discussion of Web genres.

FOR WRITING AND DISCUSSION

Thinking about Purpose, Audience, and Genre

Suppose that you are a political science major researching Second Amendment rights. Suppose further that you generally support the right to own hunting rifles and handguns but that your research has led you to oppose ownership of assault weapons as well as high-capacity ammo clips. Through your research, you have gathered different "means of persuasion" for your position—statistical data, sociological studies of gun violence, political studies of Second Amendment controversies, comparison data with other countries, and anecdotal stories (published in newspapers or on the Web) from witnesses or surviving victims of massacre shootings. You are ready to start writing.

(*continued*)

How would your piece of writing be different under the following conditions related to purpose, audience, and genre?

1. You are an intern for your district's member of the U.S. House of Representatives. She asks you to write a well-documented argument recommending the position she should take on gun control issues.
2. You are an active citizen seriously worried about gun violence. You decide to start a blog devoted to building up public anger against easy access to assault weapons. You now need to write and post your first blog.
3. You are invited by your local newspaper to write an op-ed column on gun control. You have 500 words to make your best case.
4. You've read an argument opposing a ban on assault weapons and high-capacity ammo magazines on a blog site sponsored by the National Rifle Association. You want to post a counter-argument on this blog site—but you want to be taken seriously, not flamed.
5. You seek a broader public for your anti-assault weapon campaign. You decide to send a Twitter tweet as well as create a bumper sticker.

1.3 Use varying rules for "good writing" depending on the rhetorical context.

CONCEPT 1.3 The rules for "good writing" vary depending on rhetorical context.

So far we have said that writers must address two types of problems: subject matter problems and rhetorical problems. As we have suggested, rhetorical problems, which influence the writer's decisions about content, organization, and style, often loom as large for writers as do the subject-matter problems that drive their writing in the first place.

In this section, we focus on one important example of a rhetorical problem, an example that will interest all new college writers: Are there "rules" for good college writing? If so, what are they? In our experience, many writers come to college guided by writing rules they learned in high school: "Never use 'I' in a formal paper." "Have a thesis statement." "Use good transitions." "Put a topic sentence in every paragraph." But are these really good rules to follow? Our answer: "Sometimes yes, sometimes no." You'll be able to appreciate this answer for yourself through the following thought exercise.

A Thought Exercise: Two Pieces of Good Writing That Follow Different "Rules"

Read the following short pieces of nonfiction prose. The first is a letter to the editor written by a professional civil engineer in response to a newspaper editorial arguing for the development of wind-generated electricity. The second short piece is entitled "A Festival of Rain." It was written by the American poet and religious writer Thomas Merton, a Trappist monk. After reading the two samples carefully, proceed to the discussion questions that follow.

David Rockwood

A Letter to the Editor

1 Your editorial on November 16, "Get Bullish on Wind Power," is based on fantasy rather than fact. There are several basic reasons why wind-generated power can in no way serve as a reasonable major alternative to other electrical energy supply alternatives for the Pacific Northwest power system.

2 First and foremost, wind power is unreliable. Electric power generation is evaluated not only on the amount of energy provided, but also on its ability to meet system peak load requirements on an hourly, daily, and weekly basis. In other words, an effective power system would have to provide enough electricity to meet peak demands in a situation when the wind energy would be unavailable—either in no wind situations or in severe blizzard conditions, which would shut down the wind generators. Because wind power cannot be relied on at times of peak needs, it would have to be backed up by other power generation resources at great expense and duplication of facilities.

3 Secondly, there are major unsolved problems involved in the design of wind generation facilities, particularly for those located in rugged mountain areas. Ice storms, in particular, can cause sudden dynamic problems for the rotating blades and mechanisms which could well result in breakdown or failure of the generators. Furthermore, the design of the facilities to meet the stresses imposed by high winds in these remote mountain regions, in the order of 125 miles per hour, would indeed escalate the costs.

4 Thirdly, the environmental impact of constructing wind generation facilities amounting to 28 percent of the region's electrical supply system (as proposed in your editorial) would be tremendous. The Northwest Electrical Power system presently has a capacity of about 37,000 megawatts of hydro power and 10,300 megawatts of thermal, for a total of about 48,000 megawatts. Meeting 28 percent of this capacity by wind power generators would, most optimistically, require about 13,400 wind towers, each with about 1,000 kilowatt (one megawatt) generating capacity. These towers, some 100 to 200 feet high, would have to be located in the mountains of Oregon and Washington. These would encompass hundreds of square miles of pristine mountain area, which, together with interconnecting transmission facilities, control works, and roads, would indeed have major adverse environmental impacts on the region.

5 There are many other lesser problems of control and maintenance of such a system. Let it be said that, from my experience and knowledge as a professional engineer, the use of wind power as a major resource in the Pacific Northwest power system is strictly a pipe dream.

Thomas Merton

A Festival of Rain

1 Let me say this before rain becomes a utility that they can plan and distribute for money. By "they" I mean the people who cannot understand that rain is a festival, who do not appreciate its gratuity, who think that what has no price has no

(*continued*)

value, that what cannot be sold is not real, so that the only way to make something *actual* is to place it on the market. The time will come when they will sell you even your rain. At the moment it is still free, and I am in it. I celebrate its gratuity and its meaninglessness.

2 The rain I am in is not like the rain of cities. It fills the woods with an immense and confused sound. It covers the flat roof of the cabin and its porch with insistent and controlled rhythms. And I listen, because it reminds me again and again that the whole world runs by rhythms I have not yet learned to recognize, rhythms that are not those of the engineer.

3 I came up here from the monastery last night, sloshing through the corn fields, said Vespers, and put some oatmeal on the Coleman stove for supper. . . . The night became very dark. The rain surrounded the whole cabin with its enormous virginal myth, a whole world of meaning, of secrecy, of silence, of rumor. Think of it: all that speech pouring down, selling nothing, judging nobody, drenching the thick mulch of dead leaves, soaking the trees, filling the gullies and crannies of the wood with water, washing out the places where men have stripped the hillside! What a thing it is to sit absolutely alone, in a forest, at night, cherished by this wonderful, unintelligible, perfectly innocent speech, the most comforting speech in the world, the talk that rain makes by itself all over the ridges, and the talk of the watercourses everywhere in the hollows!

4 Nobody started it, nobody is going to stop it. It will talk as long as it wants, this rain. As long as it talks I am going to listen.

5 But I am also going to sleep, because here in this wilderness I have learned how to sleep again. Here I am not alien. The trees I know, the night I know, the rain I know. I close my eyes and instantly sink into the whole rainy world of which I am a part, and the world goes on with me in it, for I am not alien to it.

FOR WRITING AND DISCUSSION

Comparing Rockwood's and Merton's Writing

Working as a whole class or in small groups, share your answers to the following questions:

1. What are the main differences between the two types of writing?
2. Create a metaphor, simile, or analogy that best sums up your feelings about the most important differences between Rockwood's and Merton's writing: "Rockwood's writing is like . . . , but Merton's writing is like. . . ."
3. Explain why your metaphors are apt. How do your metaphors help clarify or illuminate the differences between the two pieces of writing?

Working as a whole class or in small groups, share your answers to the above questions.

Distinctions between Closed and Open Forms of Writing

Here now is our own brief analysis of the differences between these two pieces. David Rockwood's letter and Thomas Merton's mini-essay are both examples of nonfiction prose. But as these examples illustrate, nonfiction prose can vary enormously in form and style. When we give this exercise to our students, they have no trouble articulating the differences between the two pieces of writing. Rockwood's piece has an explicit thesis statement, unified and coherent paragraphs with topic sentences, evidence to support each topic sentence, and strong transitions between each paragraph. Merton's piece, in contrast, seems to ignore these rules; it is more artistic, more creative, more like a story. (Among our students, one group said that Rockwood's piece is like riding a train on a track while Merton's piece is like floating down a river on an inner tube.) One way to label these differences is to say that Rockwood's piece is thesis-based while Merton's piece is narrative-based. But another way to distinguish between them is to place them on a continuum from closed-form prose to open-form prose (see Figure 1.2).

Closed-Form Prose Rockwood's letter illustrates tightly **closed-form prose** (far left on the continuum), which we can define as writing with a hierarchical structure of points and details in support of an explicit thesis. It is characterized by unified and coherent paragraphs, topic sentences, transitions between sentences and paragraphs, and forecasting of the whole before presentation of the parts. Once Rockwood states his thesis ("Wind-generated power isn't a reasonable alternative energy source in the Pacific Northwest"), readers know the point of the essay and can predict its structure: a series of paragraphs giving reasons and evidence in support of the thesis. We say that this form is "closed" because it doesn't allow any digressions or structural surprises. Because its structure is predictable, its success depends entirely on the quality of its ideas, which must bring something new to readers or challenge them with something contestable. Closed-form prose is what most college professors expect from their students on most occasions; likewise it is often the most effective form of writing in professional and business settings. (Note that the five-paragraph essay, common in many high schools, is a by-the-numbers approach for teaching closed-form prose.)

Open-Form Prose In contrast, Merton's "A Festival of Rain" falls toward the right end of the closed-to-open continuum. **Open-form prose** resists reduction to a single, summarizable thesis. It is characterized by narrative or story-like structure, sometimes with abrupt transitions, and uses various literary techniques to make the prose memorable and powerful. Although Merton is gladdened by rain, and clearly opposes the consumer culture that will try to "sell" you the rain, it is hard to pin down exactly what he means by "festival of rain" or by rain's "gratuity and its meaninglessness." The main organizing principle of Merton's piece, like that of most open-form prose, is a story or narrative—in this case the story

FIGURE 1.2 A Continuum of Essay Types: Closed to Open Forms

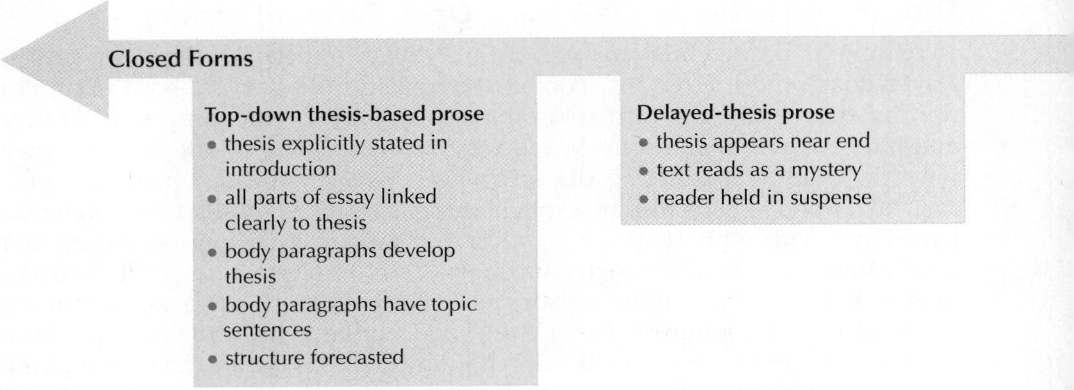

Closed Forms

Top-down thesis-based prose
- thesis explicitly stated in introduction
- all parts of essay linked clearly to thesis
- body paragraphs develop thesis
- body paragraphs have topic sentences
- structure forecasted

Delayed-thesis prose
- thesis appears near end
- text reads as a mystery
- reader held in suspense

of Merton's leaving the monastery to sleep in the rain-drenched cabin. Rather than announce a thesis and support it with reasons and evidence, Merton lets his point emerge suggestively from his story and his language. Open-form essays still have a focus, but the focus is more like a theme in fiction than like a thesis in argument. Readers may argue over its meaning in the same way that they argue over the meaning of a film or poem or novel. Consider also the extent to which Merton violates the rules for closed-form prose. Instead of using transitions between paragraphs, Merton juxtaposes narrative passages about his camping trip ("I came up here from the monastery last night...") with passages that make cryptic, interpretive comments about his experience ("The rain I am in is not like the rain of cities"). Unlike paragraphs in closed-form prose, which typically begin with topic sentences and are developed with supporting details, the paragraphs in Merton's piece have no clear hierarchical structure; paragraph four, in fact, has only twenty-nine words. Features of open-form prose often appear in personal essays, in popular magazine articles, in exploratory or reflective writing, or in character profiles that tell stories of a person's life. Open-form prose usually has an artistic or aesthetic appeal, and many examples are classified as literary nonfiction or creative nonfiction.

Flexibility of "Rules" along the Continuum

As you can see from the continuum in Figure 1.2, essays can fall anywhere along the scale. Not all thesis-with-support writing has to be top down, stating its thesis explicitly in the introduction. In some cases writers choose to delay the thesis, creating a more exploratory, open-ended, "let's think through this together" feeling before finally stating the main point late in the essay. In some cases writers explore a problem without *ever* finding a satisfactory thesis, creating an essay that seeks a thesis rather than supporting one. Because exploratory essays are aimed at deepening the reader's engagement with a question and resisting easy answers, they often include digressions, speculations, conjectures, multiple perspectives, and occasional invitations to the reader to help solve the problem. When writers reach the far right-hand position on the continuum, they no longer state an

Open Forms

Thesis-seeking prose
- essay organized around a question rather than a thesis
- essay explores the problem or question, looking at it in many ways
- writer may or may not arrive at thesis

Theme-based narrative
- often organized chronologically or has storylike elements
- often used to heighten or deepen a problem, or show its human significance
- often has an implicit theme rather than a thesis
- often violates rules of closed-form prose by using literary techniques

explicit thesis. Instead, like fiction writers, they embed their points in plot, character, imagery, and dialogue, leaving their readers to *infer* a theme from the text.

Where to Place Your Writing along the Continuum

Clearly, essays at opposite ends of this continuum operate in different ways and obey different rules. Because each position on the continuum has its appropriate uses, the writer's challenge is to determine which sort of writing is most appropriate in a given situation. Most college papers (but not all) and much professional writing are written in closed form. Thus if you were writing a business proposal, a legal brief, or an academic paper for a scholarly audience, you would typically choose a closed-form structure, and your finished product would include elements such as the following:

- An explicit thesis in the introduction
- Forecasting of structure
- Cohesive and unified paragraphs with topic sentences
- Clear transitions between sentences and between parts
- No digressions

But if you were writing, say, to express your conflicted relationship with a parent, your first discovery of evil, or your life-changing encounter with a stranger, you would probably rely on juxtaposed narratives and stories, moving toward the open end of the continuum and violating one or more of these closed-form conventions.

What is important to see is that having a thesis statement, topic sentences, good transitions, and unified and coherent paragraphs is not a mark of "good prose" but simply of "closed-form" prose. What makes closed-form prose good is the quality of its ideas. In contrast, powerful open-form prose often ignores closed-form rules. It's not that open-form prose doesn't have rules; it's that the rules are different, just as the rules for jazz are different from the rules for a classical sonata. Whether the writer chooses a closed-form or an open-form approach depends on the intended audience of the piece and the writer's purpose.

FOR WRITING AND DISCUSSION

Thinking Personally about Closed and Open Forms

Do you and your classmates most enjoy writing prose at the closed or at the more open end of the continuum? Recall a favorite piece of writing that you have done in the past. Jot down a brief description of the kind of writing this was (a personal-experience essay, a piece of workplace writing, a research paper, a blog post, a persuasive argument) and explain why you liked it. Where would you place this piece of writing on the closed-to-open continuum? Are you at your best in closed-form writing that calls for an explicit thesis statement and logical support? Or are you at your best in more open, creative, and personal forms? Share your preferences with those of classmates.

Chapter Summary

This chapter has introduced you to three useful rhetorical concepts connected to the demands of college writing.

- ***Concept 1.1 Subject matter problems are the heart of college writing.*** The starting place of college writing is a subject matter problem that interests both the writer and the reader. Writers write because they have something new, surprising, or challenging to say in response to that problem. Writers can pose their own problematic questions about a subject or become engaged in controversies or issues that are already "out there."
- ***Concept 1.2 Writers' decisions are shaped by purpose, audience, and genre.*** To articulate purpose, writers focus on what is new or contestable in their intended work or, at a more general level, consider their rhetorical aim. To think about audience, they analyze how much their readers already know about (and care about) their subject and assess their readers' values, beliefs, and assumptions. Writers attend to genre by thinking about the conventions of content, structure, and style associated with the kind of document they are writing.
- ***Concept 1.3 The rules for good writing vary according to rhetorical context.*** Good writing can vary along a continuum from closed to open forms. Closed-form prose has an explicit thesis statement, unified and coherent paragraphs with topic sentences, and good transitions. Closed-form prose is "good" only if its ideas bring something new or challenging to the reader. At the other end of the continuum, open-form prose often uses narrative techniques such as storytelling, evocative language, surprising juxtapositions, and other features that violate the conventions of closed-form prose.

Two Messages for Different Purposes, Audiences, and Genres

BRIEF WRITING PROJECT

The purpose of this brief write-to-learn assignment is to let you experience first-hand how rhetorical context influences a writer's choices. The whole assignment, which has three parts, should not be more than two double-spaced pages long.

1. ***A Text Message to a Friend.*** Write a cell phone text message to a friend using the abbreviations, capitalization, and punctuation style typically used for text messages. Explain that you are going to miss Friday's social event (movie, pizza night, dance, party) because you have to fly home to attend a funeral. Ask your friend about another time for a get-together. (Make up details as you need them.)
2. ***An E-Mail Message to a Professor.*** Compose an e-mail message to your professor explaining that you are going to miss Friday's field trip because you have to fly home to attend a funeral. You are asking how you can make up for this missed field trip. (Use the same details as in item 1.) Create a subject line appropriate for this new context.
3. ***Reflection on the Two Messages.*** Using Items 1 and 2 as illustrative examples, explain to someone who has not read Chapter 1 of this text why a difference in your rhetorical context caused you to make different choices in these two messages. In your explanation, use the terms "purpose," "audience," and "genre." Your goal is to teach your audience the meanings of these terms.

2 EXPLORING PROBLEMS, MAKING CLAIMS

WHAT YOU WILL LEARN

2.1 To "wallow in complexity" in order to determine your thesis.
2.2 To write a strong thesis that surprises readers with something new or challenging.
2.3 To begin a typical closed-form introduction with the problem, not the thesis.

> **"In management, people don't merely 'write papers,' they solve problems," said [business professor A. Kimbrough Sherman]. . . . He explained that he wanted to construct situations where students would have to "wallow in complexity" and work their way out, as managers must.**
>
> —*A. Kimbrough Sherman, Management Professor, Quoted by Barbara E. Walvoord and Lucille P. McCarthy*

In the previous chapter we explained how writers become engaged with subject matter problems, how writers think rhetorically about their purpose, audience, and genre, and how the rules for good writing vary along a continuum from closed to open forms. In this chapter we show how writers think rhetorically about their subject matter during the process of exploring a problem and determining a possible claim.* Because this chapter concerns academic writing, we focus on closed-form prose—the kind of thesis-governed writing most often required in college courses and in civic and professional life.

2.1 "Wallow in complexity" in order to determine your thesis.

CONCEPT 2.1 To determine their thesis, writers must often "wallow in complexity."

As we explained in the previous chapter, the starting point of academic writing is a "good, interesting question." At the outset, we should say that these questions may lead you toward new and unfamiliar ways of thinking. Beginning college

*In this text we use the words *claim* and *thesis statement* interchangeably. In courses across the curriculum, instructors typically use one or the other of these terms. Other synonyms for *thesis statement* include *proposition, main point,* or *thesis sentence.*

students typically value questions that have right answers. Students ask their professors questions because they are puzzled by confusing parts of a textbook, a lecture, or an assigned reading. They hope their professors will explain the confusing material clearly. Their purpose in asking these questions is to eliminate misunderstandings, not to open up controversy and debate. Although basic comprehension questions are important, they are not the kinds of inquiry questions that lead to strong college-level writing and thinking.

Instead, the kinds of questions that stimulate the writing most valued in college are open-ended questions that focus on unknowns or uncertainties (what educational researcher Ken Bain calls "beautiful problems") rather than factual questions that have single, correct answers.* Good open-ended questions invite multiple points of view or alternative hypotheses; they stimulate critical thinking and research. Our way of thinking about problems has been motivated by the South American educator Paulo Freire, who wanted his students (often poor, illiterate villagers) to become *problematizers* instead of memorizers. Freire opposed what he called "the banking method" of education, in which students deposit knowledge in their memory banks and then make withdrawals during exams. The banking method, Freire believed, left third world villagers passive and helpless to improve their situations in life. Using the banking method, students being taught to read and write might learn the word *water* through drill-and-skill workbook sentences such as, "The water is in the well." With Freire's problematizing method, students might learn the word *water* by asking, "Why is the water dirty and who is responsible?" Freire believed that good questions have stakes and that answering them can make a difference in the world.

Learning to Wallow in Complexity

This focus on important problems explains why college professors want students to go beyond simply understanding course concepts as taught in textbooks and lectures. Such comprehension is important, but it is only a starting point. As management professor A. Kimbrough Sherman explains in the epigraph to this chapter, college instructors expect students to wrestle with problems by applying the concepts, data, and thought processes they learn in a course to new situations. As Sherman puts it, students must learn to "wallow in complexity" and work their way out. To put it another way, college professors want students to "earn" their thesis. (Earning a thesis is very different from simply stating your opinion, which might not be deeply examined at all.) Because college professors value this kind of complex thinking, they often phrase essay exam questions or writing assignments as open-ended problems that can be answered in more than one way. They are looking not for the right answer, but for well-supported arguments that acknowledge alternative views. A C paper and an A paper may have

*Cognitive psychologists call these beautiful problems "ill-structured." An ill-structured problem has competing solutions, requiring the thinker to argue for the best solution in the absence of full and complete data or in the presence of stakeholders with different backgrounds, assumptions, beliefs, and values. In contrast, a "well-structured" problem eventually yields a correct answer. Math problems that can be solved by applying the right formulae and processes are well structured; they yield single, agreed upon "right answers."

the same "answer" (identical thesis statements), but the C writer may have waded only ankle deep into the mud of complexity, whereas the A writer wallowed in it and worked a way out.

What skills are required for successful wallowing? Specialists in critical thinking have identified the following:

CRITICAL THINKING SKILLS NEEDED FOR "WALLOWING IN COMPLEXITY"

- The ability to pose problematic questions
- The ability to analyze a problem in all its dimensions—to define its key terms, determine its causes, understand its history, appreciate its human dimension and its connection to one's own personal experience, and appreciate what makes it problematic or complex
- The ability (and determination) to find, gather, and interpret facts, data, and other information relevant to the problem (often involving library, Internet, or field research)
- The ability to imagine alternative solutions to the problem, to see different ways in which the question might be answered and different perspectives for viewing it
- The ability to analyze competing approaches and answers, to construct arguments for and against alternatives, and to choose the best solution in light of values, objectives, and other criteria that you determine and articulate
- The ability to write an effective argument justifying your choice while acknowledging counterarguments

We discuss and develop these skills throughout this text.

Seeing Each Academic Discipline as a Field of Inquiry and Argument

In addition to these general thinking abilities, critical thinking requires what psychologists call "domain-specific" skills. Each academic discipline has its own characteristic ways of approaching knowledge and its own specialized habits of mind. The questions asked by psychologists differ from those asked by historians or anthropologists; the evidence and assumptions used to support arguments in literary analysis differ from those in philosophy or sociology. As illustrations, here are some examples of how different disciplines might pose different questions about hip-hop:

- *Psychology:* To what extent do hip-hop lyrics increase misogynistic or homophobic attitudes in male listeners?
- *History:* What was the role of urban housing projects in the early development of hip-hop?
- *Sociology:* How does the level of an individual's appreciation for rap music vary by ethnicity, class, age, geographic region, and gender?
- *Rhetoric/Composition:* What images of urban life do the lyrics of rap songs portray?
- *Marketing and Management:* How did the white media turn a black, urban phenomenon into corporate profits?

- *Women's Studies:* What influence does hip-hop music have on the self-image of African-American women?
- *Global Studies:* How are other countries adapting hip-hop to their cultures?

As these questions suggest, when you study a new discipline, you must learn not only the knowledge that scholars in that discipline have acquired over the years, but also the processes they used to discover that knowledge. It is useful to think of each academic discipline as a network of conversations in which participants exchange information, respond to each other's questions, and express agreement and disagreement. As each discipline evolves and changes, its central questions evolve also, creating a fascinating, dynamic conversation that defines the discipline. Table 2.1 provides examples of questions that scholars have debated over the years as well as questions they are addressing today.

TABLE 2.1 Scholarly Questions in Different Disciplines

Field	Examples of Current Cutting-Edge Questions	Examples of Historical Controversies
Anatomy	What is the effect of a pregnant rat's alcohol ingestion on the development of fetal eye tissue?	In 1628, William Harvey produced a treatise arguing that the heart, through repeated contractions, causes blood to circulate through the body. His views were attacked by followers of the Greek physician Galen.
Literature	To what extent does the structure of a work of literature, for example, Conrad's *Heart of Darkness*, reflect the class and gender bias of the author?	In the 1920s, a group of New Critics argued that the interpretation of a work of literature should be based on close examination of the work's imagery and form and that the intentions of the writer and the biases of the reader were not important. These views held sway in U.S. universities until the late 1960s, when they came increasingly under attack by deconstructionists and other postmoderns, who claimed that author intentions and reader's bias were important parts of the work's meaning.
Rhetoric/ Composition	How does hypertext structure and increased attention to visual images in Web-based writing affect the composing processes of writers?	Prior to the 1970s, college writing courses in the United States were typically organized around the rhetorical modes (description, narration, exemplification, comparison and contrast, and so forth). This approach was criticized by the expressivist school associated with the British composition researcher James Britton. Since the 1980s, composition scholars have proposed various alternative strategies for designing and sequencing assignments.
Psychology	What are the underlying causes of gender identification? To what extent are differences between male and female behavior explainable by nature (genetics, body chemistry) versus nurture (social learning)?	In the early 1900s under the influence of Sigmund Freud, psychoanalytic psychologists began explaining human behavior in terms of unconscious drives and mental processes that stemmed from repressed childhood experiences. Later, psychoanalysts were opposed by behaviorists, who rejected the notion of the unconscious and explained behavior as responses to environmental stimuli.

Using Exploratory Writing to Help You Wallow in Complexity

One of the important discoveries of research in rhetoric and composition is the extent to which experienced writers use writing to generate and discover ideas. Not all writing, in other words, is initially intended as a final product for readers. The very act of writing—often without concern for audience, structure, or correctness—can stimulate the mind to produce ideas. Moreover, when you write down your thoughts, you'll have a record of your thinking that you can draw on later. In Chapter 16 we explain this phenomenon more fully, showing you how to take full advantage of the writing process for invention of ideas and revision for readers. In this section we describe five strategies of exploratory writing and talking: freewriting; focused freewriting; idea mapping; dialectic talk in person, in class discussions, or in electronic discussion boards; and playing the believing and doubting game.

Freewriting *Freewriting*, also sometimes called *nonstop writing* or *silent, sustained writing*, asks you to record your thinking directly. To freewrite, put pen to paper (or sit at your computer screen, perhaps turning *off* the monitor so that you can't see what you are writing) and write rapidly, *nonstop*, for ten to fifteen minutes at a stretch. Don't worry about grammar, spelling, organization, transitions, or other features of edited writing. The object is to think of as many ideas as possible. Some freewriting looks like stream of consciousness. Some is more organized and focused, although it lacks the logical connections and development that would make it suitable for an audience of strangers.

Many freewriters find that their initial reservoir of ideas runs out in three to five minutes. If this happens, force yourself to keep your fingers moving. If you can't think of anything to say, write, "Relax" over and over (or "This is stupid" or "I'm stuck") until new ideas emerge.

What do you write about? The answer varies according to your situation. Often you will freewrite in response to a question or problem posed by your instructor. Sometimes you will pose your own questions and use freewriting to explore possible answers or simply generate ideas.

The following freewrite, by student writer Kent Ansen, formed the starting point for his later exploration of mandatory public service. It was written in response to a class discussion of service learning. We will return to Kent's story occasionally throughout this text. You can read his final paper in Chapter 15, pages 405–414, where he proposes that the United States should require public service for all young adults. You can also read his exploratory paper (Chapter 7, pp. 159–163), which narrates the evolution of his thinking as he researched issues connected to public service programs.

KENT ANSEN'S INITIAL FREEWRITE

The class discussion of service learning was interesting. Hmmm. What do young people gain from community service? I gained a lot from my own volunteer activities in high school. They taught me about my neighbors and myself. Would it be a good idea for every American citizen to have some kind of public service experience? But that would make it mandatory. Interesting idea—mandatory community service program, sort of like the draft. Hmmm. What could it offer the country and young adults? The word that keeps catching my attention is "mandatory." The immediate connection that comes to mind is the military draft during the Vietnam War and all of the protests that went along with it. I think what really bothered people was that they didn't want to be forced to risk their lives for what they considered to be an unjust war. As a contemporary example, Israel requires a term of military service from its young citizens, although I am not sure of the particulars or of its level of support among young people and society at large. Mandatory *civil* service, on the other hand, would be controversial for different reasons. While the program would not ask people to risk their lives, it would still impose a requirement that significantly affects a person's life. I can hear the outcry already from those who oppose government involvement in citizens' choices and lives. I am not sure I disagree with them on this issue, particularly as I consider what I assume would be the high cost of a mandatory national service program and the major federal budget cuts that recently went into effect. On the other hand, when I think of how much money went into the Iraq War, I wonder why it at times seems less controversial to fund activities that tear communities apart rather than something like national service, which would probably make our communities a better place. I wonder [out of time]

Note how this freewrite rambles, moving associatively from one topic or question to the next. Freewrites often have this kind of loose, associative structure. The value of such freewrites is that they help writers discover areas of interest or rudimentary beginnings of ideas. When you read back over one of your freewrites, try to find places that seem worth pursuing. Freewriters call these places "hot spots," "centers of interest," "centers of gravity," or simply "nuggets" or "seeds." Because we believe this technique is of great value to writers, we suggest that you use it to generate ideas for class discussions and essays.

Focused Freewriting Freewriting, as we have just described it, can be quick and associational, like brainstorming aloud on paper. Focused freewriting, in contrast, is less associational and aimed more at developing a line of thought. You wrestle with a specific problem or question, trying to think and write your way into its complexity and multiple points of view. Because the writing is still informal, with the emphasis on your ideas and not on making your writing grammatically or stylistically polished, you don't have to worry about spelling, punctuation, grammar, or organizational structure. Your purpose is to deepen and extend your thinking on the problem. Some instructors will create prompts or give you specific questions to ponder, and they may call this kind of exploratory writing "focused freewriting," "learning log responses," "writer's notebook entries," or "thinking pieces."

Idea Mapping Another good technique for exploring ideas is *idea mapping*, a more visual method than freewriting. To make an idea map, draw a circle in the center of a page and write down your broad topic area (or a triggering question or your thesis) inside the circle. Then record your ideas on branches and subbranches that extend out from the center circle. As long as you pursue one train of thought, keep recording your ideas on subbranches off the main branch. But as soon as that chain of ideas runs dry, go back and start a new branch.

Often your thoughts will jump back and forth between one branch and another. This technique will help you see them as part of an emerging design rather than as strings of unrelated ideas. Additionally, idea mapping establishes at an early stage a sense of hierarchy in your ideas. If you enter an idea on a subbranch, you can see that you are more fully developing a previous idea. If you return to the hub and start a new branch, you can see that you are beginning a new train of thought.

An idea map usually records more ideas than a freewrite, but the ideas are not as fully developed. Writers who practice both techniques report that they can vary the kinds of ideas they generate depending on which technique they choose. Figure 2.1 shows a student's idea map made while he was exploring issues related to the grading system.

Dialectic Conversation Another effective way to explore the complexity of a topic is through dialectic discussions with others, whether in class, over coffee in the student union, late at night in bull sessions, or online in blogs or discussion boards.

FIGURE 2.1 Idea Map on Problems with the Grading System

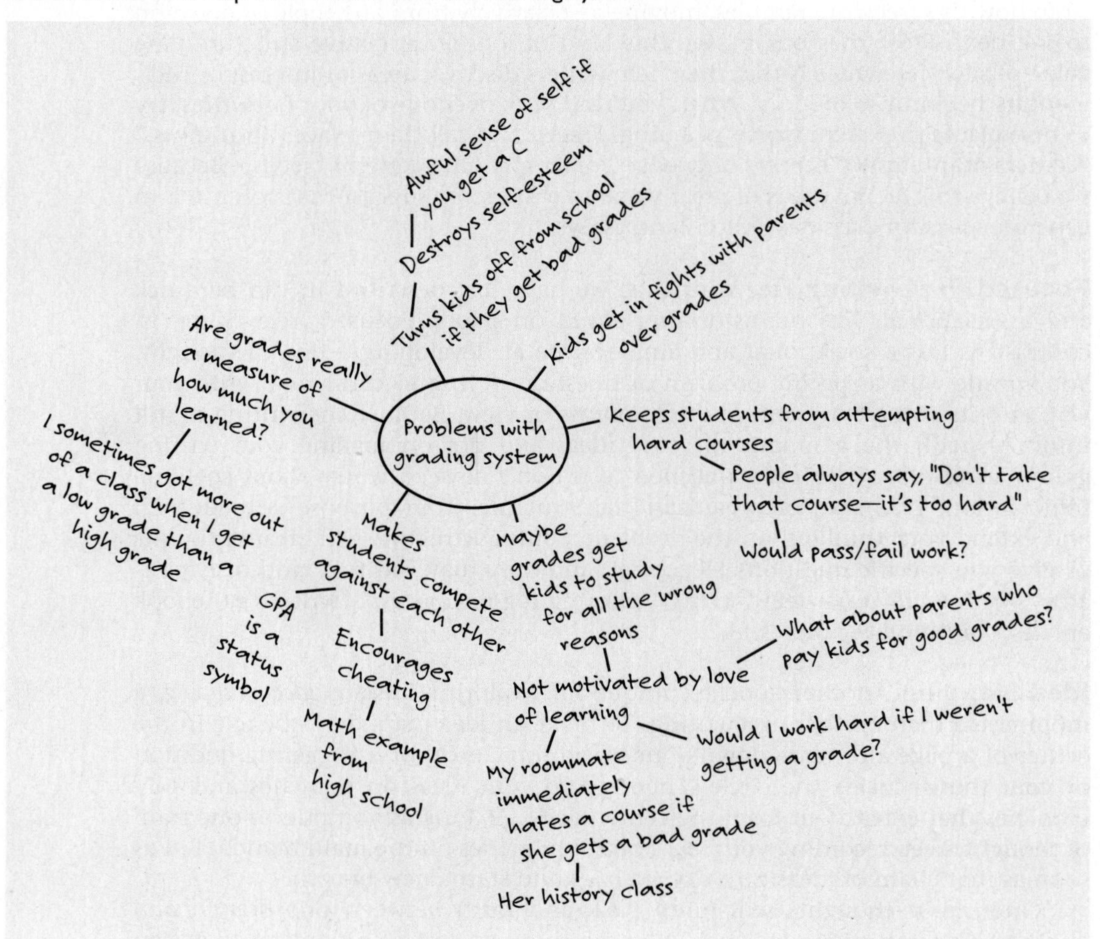

Not all discussions are productive; some are too superficial and scattered, others too heated. Good ones are *dialectic*—participants with differing views on a topic try to understand each other and resolve their differences by examining contradictions in each person's position. The key to dialectic conversation is careful listening, which is made possible by an openness to each other's views. A dialectic discussion differs from a talk show shouting match or a pro/con debate in which proponents of opposing positions, their views set in stone, attempt to win the argument. In a dialectic discussion, participants assume that each position has strengths and weaknesses and that even the strongest position contains inconsistencies, which should be exposed and examined. When dialectic conversation works well, participants scrutinize their own positions more critically and deeply, and often alter their views. True dialectic conversation implies growth and change, not a hardening of positions.

Dialectic discussion can be particularly effective online through electronic discussion boards, chat rooms, blogs, or other digital sites for informal exchange of ideas. If your goal is to generate ideas, your stance should be the exact opposite of the flamer's stance. A flamer's intention is to use brute rhetorical power (sometimes mindlessly obscene or mean, sometimes clever and humorous) to humiliate another writer and shut off further discussion. In contrast, the dialectician's goal is to listen respectfully to other ideas, to test new ways of thinking, to modify ideas in the face of other views, and to see an issue as fully and complexly as possible. If you go on to a discussion board to learn and change, rather than to defend your own position and shut off other views, you will be surprised at how powerful this medium can be.

Playing the Believing and Doubting Game One of the best ways to explore a question is to play what writing theorist Peter Elbow calls the "believing and doubting game." This game helps you appreciate the power of alternative arguments and points of view by urging you to formulate and explore alternative positions. To play the game, you imagine a possible answer to a problematic question and then systematically try first to believe that answer and then to doubt it. The game stimulates your critical thinking, helping you wallow in complexity and resist early closure.

When you play the believing side of this game, you try to become sympathetic to an idea or point of view. You listen carefully to it, opening yourself to the possibility that it is true. You try to appreciate why the idea has force for so many people; you try to accept it by discovering as many reasons as you can for believing it. It is easy to play the believing game with ideas you already believe in, but the game becomes more difficult, sometimes even frightening and dangerous, when you try believing ideas that seem untrue or disturbing.

The doubting game is the opposite of the believing game. It calls for you to be judgmental and critical, to find fault with an idea rather than to accept it. When you doubt a new idea, you try your best to falsify it, to find counterexamples that disprove it, to find flaws in its logic. Again, it is easy to play the doubting game with ideas you don't like, but it, too, can be threatening when you try to doubt ideas that are dear to your heart or central to your own worldview.

Here is how one student played the believing and doubting game with the following assertion from professional writer Paul Theroux that emphasizing sports is harmful to boys.

Just as high school basketball teaches you how to be a poor loser, the manly attitude towards sports seems to be little more than a recipe for creating bad marriages, social misfits, moral degenerates, sadists, latent rapists and just plain louts. I regard high school sports as a drug far worse than marijuana.

Believing and Doubting Paul Theroux's Negative View of Sports

Believe

1 Although I am a woman I have a hard time believing this because I was a high school basketball player and believe high school sports are *very* important. But here goes. I will try to believe this statement even though I hate it. Let's see. It would seem that I wouldn't have much first-hand experience with how society turns boys into men. I do see though that Theroux is right about some major problems. Through my observations, I've seen many young boys go through humiliating experiences with sports that have left them scarred. For example, a 7-year-old boy, Matt, isn't very athletic and when kids in our neighborhood choose teams, they usually choose girls before they choose Matt. I wonder if he sees himself as a sissy and what this does to him? I have also experienced some first-hand adverse effects of society's methods of turning boys into men. In our family, my dad spent much of his time playing football, basketball, and baseball with my brother. I've loved sports since I was very young so I was eager to play. In order to play with them, I had to play like a boy. Being told you threw or played like a girl was the worst possible insult you could receive. The phrase, "be tough" was something I heard repeatedly while I was growing up. Whenever I got hurt, my dad would say, "Be tough." It didn't matter how badly I was hurt, I always heard the same message. Today, I think, I have a very, very difficult time opening up and letting people get to know me, because for so long I was taught to keep everything inside. Maybe sports does have some bad effects.

Doubt

2 I am glad I get to doubt this too because I have been really mad at all the sports bashing that has been going on in class. I think much of what Theroux says is just a crock. I know that the statement "sports builds character" is a cliché, but I really believe it. It seems to me that the people who lash out at sports clichés are those who never experienced these aspects of athletics and therefore don't understand them. No one can tell me that sports didn't contribute to some of my best and most meaningful friendships and growing experiences. I am convinced that I am a better person because through sports I have had to deal with failure, defeat, frustration, sacrificing individual desires for the benefit of the team, and so on. After my last high school basketball game when after many years of mind games, of hating my coach one minute and the next having deep respect for him, of big games lost on my mistakes, of hours spent alone in the gym, of wondering if the end justifies the means, my coach put his arm around me and told me he was proud. Everything, all the pain, frustration, anxiety, fear, and sacrifice of the past years seemed so worthwhile. You might try to tell

me that this story is hackneyed and trite, but I won't listen because it is a part of me, and some thing you will never be able to damage or take away. I think athletes share a special bond. They know what it is like to go through the physical pain of practice time and again. They understand the wide variety of emotions felt (but rarely expressed). They also know what a big role the friendships of teammates and coaches play in an athlete's life.

We admire this writer a great deal—both for the passion with which she defends sports in her doubting section and for the courage of walking in a sports basher's shoes in the believing section. This exercise clearly engaged and stretched her thinking.

FOR WRITING AND DISCUSSION

Using Exploratory Writing and Talking to Generate Ideas

The following task is based on e. e. cummings' poem "next to of course god america I." You could do the same exercise focused on Billie Grace Lynn's sculpture (page 7) or on a puzzling phenomenon, artifact, or question supplied by your instructor.

next to of course god america i

"next to of course god america i
love you land of the pilgrims' and so forth oh
say can you see by the dawn's early my
country 'tis of centuries come and go

and are no more what of it we should worry
in every language even deafanddumb
thy sons acclaim your glorious name by gorry
by jingo by gee by gosh by gum
why talk of beauty what could be more beautiful than these heroic happy dead
who rushed like lions to the roaring slaughter
they did not stop to think they died instead
then shall the voice of liberty be mute?"

He spoke. And drank rapidly a glass of water

—*e. e. cummings*

1. ***Using freewriting, idea mapping, and dialectic discussion to stimulate thinking.*** On your own, read e. e. cummings' poem three or four times, trying to make as much sense of it as you can. Then using freewriting or idea-mapping, spend five minutes in response to this prompt: *What do you find puzzling, thought-provoking, meaningful, or disturbing about e. e. cummings' poem?* Let the ideas flow through your fingers. You are trying to

(continued)

identify aspects of the poem that you personally find puzzling or thought-provoking or that speak meaningfully to you (or against you). What is e. e. cummings trying to say or do in this poem? How does the poem affect you? As you pose questions, also explore possible ways that you might try to "answer" some of them.

Dialectic conversation: Share some of the questions or ideas raised in your freewrites or idea maps and see how the exchange with classmates inspires more ideas.

2. ***Playing "the believing and doubting game."*** On your own, play the believing/doubting game with one of the following controversial assertions or another assertion provided by your instructor. First spend at least five minutes "believing" the assertion. Then reverse directions and spend the same amount of time "doubting" the assertion.
   - My choice of clothing on any given day is an expression of my free will.
   - It is always wrong to tell a lie.
   - Athletes should be allowed to use steroids and other performance-enhancing drugs.
   - In his poem ""next to of course god america I" e. e. cummings shows that he hates America.

   Dialectic conversation. Share ideas you discovered during this process with your classmates. Also share reflections on whether (for you) playing the "believing" or the "doubting" side was more difficult and why. Which side was most helpful for extending your thinking?

2.2 Write a strong thesis that surprises readers with something new or challenging.

CONCEPT 2.2 A strong thesis statement surprises readers with something new or challenging.

The strategies for exploring ideas that we offered in the previous section can prepare you to move from posing problems to proposing your own solutions. Your answer to your subject-matter question becomes your **thesis statement**. In this section we show that a good thesis surprises its readers either by bringing something new to the reader or by pushing against other possible ways to answer the writer's question.

Thus a strong thesis usually contains an element of uncertainty, risk, or challenge. A strong thesis implies a naysayer who could disagree with you. According to composition theorist Peter Elbow, a thesis has "got to stick its neck out, not just hedge or wander. [It is] something that can be quarreled with." Elbow's sticking-its-neck-out metaphor is a good one, but we prefer to say that a strong thesis *surprises* the reader with a new, unexpected, different, or challenging view of the writer's topic. By surprise, we intend to connote, first of all, freshness or newness for the reader. Many kinds of closed-form prose don't have a sharply contestable thesis of the sticking-its-neck-out kind highlighted by Elbow. A geology report, for example, may provide readers with desired information about rock strata in an exposed cliff, or a Web page for diabetics may explain how to coordinate meals and insulin injections during a plane trip across time zones. In these cases, the information is surprising because it brings something new and significant to intended readers.

In other kinds of closed-form prose, especially academic or civic prose addressing a problematic question or a disputed issue, surprise requires an argumentative, risky, or contestable thesis. In these cases also, surprise is not inherent in the material but in the intended readers' reception; it comes from the writer's providing an adequate or appropriate response to the readers' presumed question or problem.

In this section, we present two ways of creating a surprising thesis: (1) trying to change your reader's view of your subject; and (2) giving your thesis tension.

Trying to Change Your Reader's View of Your Subject

To change your reader's view of your subject, you must first imagine how the reader would view the subject *before* reading your essay. Then you can articulate how you aim to change that view. A useful exercise is to write out the "before" and "after" views of your imagined readers:

> Before reading my essay, my readers think this way about my topic: ______________
> ____
>
> After reading my essay, my readers will think this different way about my topic:
> ____

You can change your reader's view of a subject in several ways.*

1. ***You can enlarge your reader's view.*** Writing that enlarges a view is primarily informational. It provides new ideas and data to a reader's store of knowledge about the subject. For example, suppose you are interested in the problem of storing nuclear waste (a highly controversial issue in the United States) and decide to investigate how France stores radioactive waste from its nuclear power plants. You could report your researched findings on this problem in an informative paper. (Before reading my paper, readers would be uncertain how France stores nuclear waste. After reading my paper, my readers would understand the French methods, possibly helping us better understand our options in the United States.)
2. ***You can clarify your reader's view of something that was previously fuzzy, tentative, or uncertain.*** Writing of this kind often explains, analyzes, or interprets. This is the kind of writing you do when you analyze a short story, a painting, an historical document, a set of economic data, or other puzzling phenomena or when you speculate on the cause, consequence, purpose, or function of something. Suppose you are analyzing the persuasive strategies used by various clothing ads. You are intrigued by a jeans ad that you "read" differently from your classmates. (Before reading my paper, my readers will think that this jeans ad reveals a liberated woman, but after reading my paper they will see that the ad reinforces traditional gender stereotypes.)

*Our discussion of how writing changes a reader's view of the world is indebted to Richard Young, Alton Becker, and Kenneth Pike, *Rhetoric: Discovery and Change* (New York: Harcourt Brace & Company, 1971).

3. ***You can restructure readers' whole view of a subject.*** Such essays persuade readers to change their minds or urge them to action. For example, engineer David Rockwood, in his letter to the editor, wants to change readers' views about wind power (see Chapter 1, p. 15). (Before reading my letter, readers will believe that wind-generated electricity can solve our energy crisis, but after reading my letter, they will see that the hope of wind power is a pipe dream.)

Surprise, then, is the measure of change an essay brings about in a reader. Of course, to bring about such change requires more than just a surprising thesis; the essay itself must persuade the reader that the thesis is sound as well as novel.

Giving Your Thesis Tension through "Surprising Reversal"

Another element of a surprising thesis is tension. By *tension* we mean the reader's sensation of being pulled away from familiar ideas toward new, unfamiliar ones. A strategy for creating this tension—a strategy we call "surprising reversal"—is to contrast your surprising answer to a question with your targeted audience's common answer, creating tension between your own thesis and one or more alternative views. Its basic template is as follows:

> *"Many people believe X (common view), but I am going to show Y (new, surprising view)."*

The concept of surprising reversal spurs the writer to go beyond the commonplace to change the reader's view of a topic.

One of the best ways to employ this strategy is to begin your thesis statement with an "although" clause that summarizes the reader's "before" view or the counterclaim that your essay opposes; the main clause states the surprising view or position that your essay will support. You may choose to omit the *although* clause from your actual essay, but formulating it first will help you achieve focus and surprise in your thesis. The examples that follow illustrate the kinds of tension we have been discussing and show why tension is a key requirement for a good thesis.

Question	What effect has the cell phone had on our culture?
Thesis without Tension	The invention of the cell phone has brought many advantages to our culture.
Thesis with Tension	Although the cell phone has brought many advantages to our culture, it may also have contributed to an increase in risky behavior among boaters and hikers.
Question	Do reservations serve a useful role in contemporary Native American culture?
Thesis without Tension	Reservations have good points and bad points.
Thesis with Tension	Although my friend Wilson Real Bird believes that reservations are necessary for Native Americans to preserve their heritage, the continuation of reservations actually degrades Native American culture.

In the first example, the thesis without tension (cell phones have brought advantages to our culture) is a truism with which everyone would agree and hence lacks surprise. The thesis with tension places this truism (the reader's "before" view) in an *although* clause and goes on to make a surprising or contestable assertion. The idea that the cell phone contributes to risky behavior among outdoor enthusiasts alters our initial, complacent view of the cell phone and gives us new ideas to think about.

In the second example, the thesis without tension may not at first seem tensionless because the writer sets up an opposition between good and bad points. But *almost anything* has good and bad points, so the opposition is not meaningful, and the thesis offers no element of surprise. Substitute virtually any other social institution (marriage, the postal service, the military, prisons), and the statement that it has good and bad points would be equally true. The thesis with tension, in contrast, is risky. It commits the writer to argue that reservations have degraded Native American culture and to oppose the counterthesis that reservations are needed to *preserve* Native American culture. The reader now feels genuine tension between two opposing views.

Tension, then, is a component of surprise. The writer's goal is to surprise the reader in some way, thereby bringing about some kind of change in the reader's view. As you are wallowing in complexity about your subject-matter problem, try the following strategies for bringing something new, surprising, or challenging to your targeted readers:

Strategies for Creating a Thesis with Tension or Surprise

How You Became Gripped with a Problem	Example of a Problem	Your Strategy While You "Wallow in Complexity"	Possible Thesis with Tension or Surprise
The problem is already "out there." *(You enter a conversation already in progress.)*			
You don't know where you stand on an issue.	Should health care be rationed?	Look at all sides of the issue, including all the available data, to determine where you stand based on your own examined values.	Although rationing health care at first seems inhumane, it may be the only ethical way to provide affordable health care to all citizens.
You do know where you stand on an issue but your position hasn't yet been "earned." *[You need to move from an opinion to an earned thesis.]*	Shanita says that we should build more nuclear power plants to combat global warming, but I say nuclear power is too dangerous.	Research the strengths of the opposing views and the weaknesses of your own view. (*Note: You may change your mind.*)	Although nuclear power poses danger from storage of waste or possible meltdown, the benefits of reducing greenhouse gases and cutting coal pollution outweigh the dangers.

(continued)

How You Became Gripped with a Problem	Example of a Problem	Your Strategy While You "Wallow in Complexity"	Possible Thesis with Tension or Surprise
Someone gives you a question that you can't yet answer.	Your boss asks you whether the company should enact the proposed marketing plan.	Do the research, critical thinking, and analysis needed to propose the "best solution" to the boss's question.	The marketing team's proposal, despite its creative use of advertising, is too risky to undertake at this time.
You pose the problem yourself. *(You initiate the conversation.)*			
You see something puzzling in a natural phenomenon or a cultural activity or artifact.	Why does Merton call rain "meaningless"?	Through critical thinking and research, try to figure out a plausible "best solution" to your question.	Merton's puzzling use of "meaningless" in reference to the rain can perhaps be explained by his admiration for Buddhism.
You discover something inconsistent or contradictory in your own view of the world.	I agree with Merton's argument against consumerism, but I really want a large plasma TV. Is consumerism really bad? Am I a materialist?	Reflect on your own values and beliefs; try to achieve a consistent stand with regard to enduring social or ethical issues.	Although Merton makes me consider the potential shallowness of my desire for a huge plasma TV, I don't think I'm necessarily a materialist.

FOR WRITING AND DISCUSSION

Developing Thesis Statements Out of Questions

Writers can't be asked to create thesis statements on the spot because a writer's thesis grows out of extended intellectual struggle with a problem. However, in response to a question one can often propose a hypothetical claim and treat it as a tentative thesis statement for testing. This exercise asks you to try this approach—formulate a surprising thesis statement that you could then test further through more exploration. We provide three possible questions for exploration. Your instructor might give you a different question. In formulating your claim, also imagine a targeted audience that would find your claim new, challenging, or otherwise surprising. Finally, speculate on the kinds of evidence you would need to support your thesis.

1. What can an individual do, if anything, to combat climate change? (Note: Your thesis will have no tension or surprise if you say just the obvious—take the bus or change light bulbs.)

2. What should the federal government do, if anything, to help prevent mass killings enacted with rapid-fire semi-automatic weapons?
3. What is e. e. cummings' attitude toward America in "next to of course god america i" (p. 31)?

Here is an example:

Problematic question: What can cities do to prevent traffic congestion?

One possible thesis: Although many people think that little can be done to get people out of their beloved cars, new light-rail systems in many cities have attracted former car commuters and alleviated traffic problems.

Intended audience: Residents of cities concerned about traffic congestion but skeptical about light-rail

Kinds of evidence needed to support thesis: Examples of cities with successful light-rail systems; evidence that many riders switched from driving cars; evidence that light-rail alleviated traffic problems

CONCEPT 2.3 In closed-form prose, a typical introduction starts with the problem, not the thesis.

2.3 Begin a typical closed-form introduction with the problem, not the thesis.

In Concept 2.2 we explained that in closed-form prose a writer's thesis statement is a tentative, contestable, and surprising answer to a question or problem that the writer shares with the reader. Before readers can understand or appreciate a writer's thesis, they must first know the problem or question that the thesis addresses. Typically a writer's thesis statement comes at the *end* of the introduction. What precedes the thesis is the writer's explanation of the problem that she is addressing or the conversation that she is joining. This problem-before-thesis-structure follows a principle of closed-form prose called "the old/new contract," which helps readers connect new information to previously stated old information. In closed-form prose, your thesis statement summarizes the "new information" that makes your argument surprising, new, or challenging. The "old information" that must precede the thesis is the question or problem that your thesis addresses.

See Chapter 17, pp. 433–436, where the old/new contract is explained in detail.

It follows then that a primary function of most closed-form introductions is to present the problem that you are addressing and to motivate your readers' interest in it. (If they aren't interested, they'll quit reading.) The length of the introduction is a function of how much your reader already knows and cares about your problem. The less they know or care, the more your introduction needs to provide background and answer the "so what?" question that motivates caring. Once readers are on board with you about the problem being addressed and about why the problem matters, they are prepared for your thesis statement.

A Typical Introduction

In the following example of a typical closed-form introduction, note how student writer Jackie Wyngaard first presents a question and then moves, at the end of the introduction, to her thesis statement.

Provides background on EMP

Begins to turn topic area (EMP) into a problem by showing that it has been controversial

Establishes her own purposes and expectations: She expects EMP to teach her about music history.

Implies her question: Is EMP a good place to learn about the history of rock music?

States her thesis

EMP: MUSIC HISTORY OR MUSIC TRIVIA?

Along with other college students new to Seattle, I wanted to see what cultural opportunities the area offers. I especially wanted to see billionaire Paul Allen's controversial Experience Music Project (known as EMP), a huge, bizarre, shiny, multicolored structure that is supposed to resemble a smashed guitar. Brochures say that EMP celebrates the creativity of American popular music, but it has prompted heated discussions among architects, Seattle residents, museum goers, and music lovers, who have questioned its commercialism and the real value of its exhibits. My sister recommended this museum to me because she knows I am a big music lover and a rock and roll fan. Also, as an active choir member since the sixth grade, I have always been intrigued by the history of music. I went to EMP expecting to learn more about music history from exhibits that showed a range of popular musical styles, that traced historical connections and influences, and that enjoyably conveyed useful information. However, as a museum of rock history, EMP is a disappointing failure.

Features of an Effective Introduction

Wyngaard's introduction, which shares the structure of many professionally written closed-form introductions, includes the following typical features:

- ***Topic area and context.*** Readers need early on to know the specific topic area of the paper they are about to read—in this case a paper about the Experience Music Project in Seattle rather than, say, shower mold or medieval queenship. Sometimes writers also use a startling scene or statistic as an "attention grabber" as part of the opening context.
- ***A direct or implied question.*** As soon as possible, readers need to know how the topic area gives rise to a problem, question, or issue that the writer will examine. In this case, Jackie Wyngaard implies her question: Will EMP live up to my expectations as a museum of rock history? Note that her question appears directly in her title: "EMP: Music History or Music Trivia?"
- ***An indication of how the question invites tension, has evoked controversy, or is otherwise problematic.*** Jackie indicates that the EMP has generated "heated discussions" among a range of audiences about its commercialism and the value of its exhibits. She gives the question further tension by contrasting her initial expectations with her later disappointment.
- ***An indication of how the question is significant or worth examining.*** In order to avoid a "so what?" response, writers must motivate readers' interest in the question. Somebody might say, "Who cares about EMP anyway?" Jackie's strategy is to imagine an audience who shares her interest in rock and roll music and her love of music history. These are the readers who will care whether it is worth big bucks to spend an afternoon in EMP. Readers who identify with Jackie's enthusiasm for rock history will share her engagement with the question.
- ***The writer's thesis, which brings something new to the audience.*** Once readers are hooked on the writer's question, they are ready for the writer's answer. In this case, Jackie makes the claim that EMP fails as a rock history museum.

Additional nuts-and-bolts advice for composing an effective closed-form introduction is found in Chapter 17, pp. 445–447.

For a fuller overview of how to think about introductions from a rhetorical perspective (hooking up with your reader, motivating your reader to continue reading), consider the following strategies chart:

Strategies for Introducing Your Problem to Targeted Readers

Situation	Strategies
The problem is already "out there." *(You enter a conversation already in progress.)*	*If readers are already familiar with the problem and care about it, use a mix of the following strategies:* • Provide background where needed • State the problem directly (often as a grammatical question ending with a question mark) or imply the question through context • Summarize the different points of view on the problem (or) • Summarize the particular point of view you intend to "push against" *If readers are less familiar with the problem:* • Summarize controversy in more depth • Explain why the problem is problematic (show why there are no easy answers to the problem; point out weaknesses in proposed answers; show the history of attempts to solve the problem) *If readers don't already care about the problem:* • Show why the problem is important (answer the "so what?" question) • Show how solving the problem will bring good consequences (or) • Show how answering the question will help us begin to answer a larger question

You pose the problem yourself. *(You initiate the conversation.)*	• Describe the artifact or phenomenon you are writing about and point to the specific features where you see an inconsistency, gap, or puzzle
	• State the problem directly (often as a grammatical question ending with a question mark)
	• Show how there isn't any immediate, easy answer to the question or problem or how the question can invite controversy/discussion; you can often employ a template such as the following:
	  • Some people might think..., but closer observation shows that....
	  • At first I thought..., but later I saw that....
	  • Part of me thinks..., but another part of me thinks that....
	  • I expected...; but what I actually found was....
	• Show why the problem is important (answer the "so what?" question)
	• Show how solving the problem will bring good consequences (or)
	• Show how answering this question will help us begin to answer a larger question

FOR WRITING AND DISCUSSION

Examining the Problem–Thesis Structure of Introductions

Background: Although introductions to closed-form essays don't always follow the typical structure we just described, many do. In this exercise, we invite you to analyze additional introductions.

Task: Look at the following introductions. In each case, analyze the extent to which the introduction follows or varies from the typical introductions we have described in Concept 2.3.

1. Paragraphs 1–2 of Ross Taylor's "Paintball: Promoter of Violence or Healthy Fun?" (pp. 337–339)
2. Paragraphs 1–6 of Shannon King's "How Clean and Green Are Hydrogen Fuel-Cell Cars?" (pp. 186–188)
3. Paragraphs 1–3 of Kent Ansen's "Engaging Young Adults to Meet America's Challenges: A Proposal for Mandatory National Service" (pp. 405–414)

Chapter Summary

This chapter has introduced you to three concepts that will enable you to think about your subject matter from a rhetorical perspective.

- ***Concept 2.1 To determine their thesis, writers must often "wallow in complexity."*** What typically initiates the writing process is a problematic question that invites the writer to explore the problem's complexity. To do so, experienced writers often use exploratory techniques such as freewriting, idea mapping, dialectic talk, and the believing and doubting game to generate ideas.
- ***Concept 2.2 A strong thesis surprises readers with something new or challenging.*** A good thesis tries to change the reader's view of the subject and often creates tension by pushing against alternative views.
- ***Concept 2.3 In closed-form prose, a typical introduction starts with the problem, not the thesis.*** Readers need to be engaged with the writer's question before they can understand the thesis.

BRIEF WRITING PROJECT

Playing the Believing and Doubting Game

The For Writing and Discussion exercise in Concept 2.2 (p. 32) asks you to play the believing and doubting game as a freewriting exercise. Because this game is so helpful for developing critical thinking skills and learning to wallow in complexity, we repeat it here as a brief writing assignment. Your instructor will explain whether this assignment will be graded formally (in which case grammar and organization matter) or informally (in which case you will just freewrite to explore ideas.)

Part 1. The Game. Play the believing and doubting game with one of the assertions listed here (or with another assertion provided by your instructor). Include at least one full paragraph or page (ask your instructor about length) believing the assertion and then an equivalent stretch of prose doubting the assertion. When you believe an assertion, you agree, support, illustrate, extend, and apply the idea. When you doubt an assertion, you question, challenge, rebut, and offer counterreasons and counterexamples to the assertion.

1. Grades are an effective means of motivating students to do their best work.
2. Facebook or other social media provide a good way to make new friends.
3. In recent years, advertising has made enormous gains in portraying women as strong, independent, and intelligent.
4. If there is only one kidney available for transplant and two sick persons need it, one in her thirties and one in her sixties, the kidney should go to the younger person.
5. The United States should reinstate the draft.

Part 2. Reflection. Write a reflective paragraph in which you assess the extent to which the believing and doubting game extended or stretched your thinking. Particularly, answer these questions:

1. What was difficult about this writing activity?
2. To what extent did it make you take an unfamiliar or uncomfortable stance?
3. How can believing and doubting help you wallow in complexity?

3 HOW MESSAGES PERSUADE

WHAT YOU WILL LEARN

3.1 To analyze how messages persuade through their angle of vision.
3.2 To analyze how messages persuade through appeals to *logos, ethos,* and *pathos.*
3.3 To analyze how messages persuade through style and document design.
3.4 To analyze how nonverbal texts persuade through visual rhetorical strategies.

A way of seeing is also a way of not seeing.

—Kenneth Burke, Rhetorician

The goal of this chapter is to help you analyze the rhetorical strategies that make messages persuasive. When you understand how messages achieve their effects, you will be better prepared to analyze and evaluate them and to decide whether to resist their arguments or accede to them. You'll also be better prepared to use these rhetorical strategies effectively and ethically in your own writing.

3.1 Analyze how messages persuade through their angle of vision.

CONCEPT 3.1 Messages persuade through their angle of vision.

One way that messages persuade is through their **angle of vision**, which causes a reader to see a subject from one perspective only—the writer's. Writers create an angle of vision through strategies such as the following:

- Stating point of view directly
- Selecting some details while omitting others
- Choosing words or figures of speech with intended connotations
- Creating emphasis or de-emphasis through sentence structure and organization

The writer's angle of vision—which might also be called a lens, a filter, a perspective, or a point of view—is persuasive because it controls what the reader "sees." Unless readers are rhetorically savvy, they can lose awareness that they are seeing the writer's subject matter through a lens that both reveals and conceals.

A classic illustration of angle of vision is the following thought exercise:

THOUGHT EXERCISE ON ANGLE OF VISION

Suppose you attended a fun party on Saturday night. (You get to choose what constitutes "fun" for you.) Now imagine that two people ask what you did on Saturday night. Person A is a close friend who missed the party. Person B is your parent. How would your descriptions of Saturday night differ?

Clearly there isn't just one way to describe this party. Your description will be influenced by your purpose and audience. You will have to decide:

- What image of myself should I project? (For your friend you might construct yourself as a party animal; for your parent, as a more detached observer.)
- How much emphasis do I give the party? (You might describe the party in detail for your friend while mentioning it only in passing to your parent, emphasizing instead all the homework you did over the weekend.)
- What details should I include or leave out? (Does my parent really need to know that the neighbors called the police?)
- What words should I choose? (The slang you use with your friend might not be appropriate for your parent.)

You'll note that our comments about your rhetorical choices reflect common assumptions about friends and parents. You might actually have a party-loving parent and a geeky friend, in which case your party descriptions would be altered accordingly. In any case, you are in rhetorical control; you choose what your audience "sees" and how they see it.

Recognizing the Angle of Vision in a Text

This thought exercise illustrates a key insight of rhetoric: There is always more than one way to tell a story, and no single way of telling it constitutes the whole truth. By saying that a writer writes from an "angle of vision," we mean that the writer cannot take a godlike stance that allows a universal, unfiltered, totally unbiased or objective way of knowing. Rather, the writer looks at the subject from a certain location, or, to use another metaphor, the writer wears a lens that colors or filters the topic in a certain way. The angle of vision, lens, or filter determines what part of a topic gets "seen" and what remains "unseen," what gets included or excluded, what gets emphasized or de-emphasized, and so forth. It even determines what words get chosen out of an array of options—for example, whether the writer says "panhandler" or "homeless person," "torture" or "enhanced interrogation," "universal health care" or "socialized medicine."

As an illustration of angle of vision, consider the cartoon in Figure 3.1, which shows different ways that stakeholders "see" sweatshops. For each stakeholder, some aspects of sweatshops surge into view, while other aspects remain unseen or invisible. An alert reader needs to be aware that none of these stakeholders can portray sweatshops in a completely "true" way. Stockholders and corporate leaders emphasize reduced labor costs and enhanced corporate profits and retirement portfolios while de-emphasizing (or omitting entirely) the working conditions in

FIGURE 3.1 Different Angles of Vision on "Sweatshops"

sweatshops or the plight of American workers whose jobs have been outsourced to developing countries. Consumers enjoy abundant low-cost goods made possible by sweatshops and may not even think about where or how the products are made. Opponents of sweatshops focus on the miserable conditions of sweatshop workers, their low wages, the use of child labor, and the "obscene" profits of corporations. Meanwhile, as the American union worker laments the loss of jobs in the United States, third world workers and their children may welcome sweatshops as a source of income superior to the other harsh alternatives such as scavenging in dumps or prostitution. The multiple angles of vision show how complex the issue of sweatshops is. In fact, most issues are equally complex, and any one view of the issue is controlled by the writer's angle of vision.

To get a hands-on feel for how a writer creates an angle of vision, try doing the following U. R. Riddle activity, which invites you to write a letter of recommendation for a student.

FOR WRITING AND DISCUSSION

U. R. Riddle Letter

Background: Suppose that you are a management professor who regularly writes letters of recommendation for former students. One day you receive a letter from a local bank requesting a confidential evaluation of a former student, Uriah Rudy Riddle (U. R. Riddle), who has applied for a job as a management trainee. The bank wants your assessment of Riddle's intelligence, aptitude, dependability, and ability to work with people. You haven't seen U. R. for several years, but you remember him well. Here are the facts and impressions you recall about Riddle:

- Very temperamental student, seemed moody, something of a loner
- Long hair and very sloppy dress—seemed like a misplaced street person; often twitchy and hyperactive
- Absolutely brilliant mind; took lots of liberal arts courses and applied them to business
- Wrote a term paper relating different management styles to modern theories of psychology—the best undergraduate paper you ever received. You gave it an A+ and remember learning a lot from it yourself.
- Had a strong command of language—the paper was very well written
- Good at mathematics; could easily handle all the statistical aspects of the course
- Frequently missed class and once told you that your class was boring
- Didn't show up for the midterm. When he returned to class later, he said only that he had been out of town. You let him make up the midterm, and he got an A.
- Didn't participate in a group project required for your course. He said the other students in his group were idiots.
- You thought at the time that Riddle didn't have a chance of making it in the business world because he had no talent for getting along with people.
- Other professors held similar views of Riddle—brilliant, but rather strange and hard to like; an odd duck.

You are in a dilemma because you want to give Riddle a chance (he's still young and may have had a personality transformation of some sort), but you also don't want to damage your own professional reputation by falsifying your true impressions.

Individual task: Working individually for ten minutes or so, compose a brief letter of recommendation assessing Riddle; use details from the list to support your assessment. Role-play that you have decided to take a gamble with Riddle and give him a chance at this career. Write as strong a recommendation as possible while remaining honest. (To make this exercise more complex, your instructor might ask half the class to role-play a negative angle of vision in which you want to warn the bank against hiring Riddle without hiding his strengths or good points.)

(continued)

Task for group or whole-class discussion: Working in small groups or as a whole class, share your letters. Then pick representative examples ranging from the most positive to the least positive and discuss how the letters achieve their different rhetorical effects. If your intent is to support Riddle, to what extent does honesty compel you to mention some or all of your negative memories? Is it possible to mention negative items without emphasizing them? How?

Analyzing Angle of Vision

Just as there is more than one way to describe the party you went to on Saturday night or to write about sweatshops, there is more than one way to write a letter of recommendation for U. R. Riddle. The writer's angle of vision determines what is "seen" or "not seen" in a given piece of writing—what gets slanted in a positive or negative direction, what gets highlighted, what gets thrown into the shadows. As rhetorician Kenneth Burke claims in the epigraph for the chapter, "A way of seeing is also a way of not seeing." Note how the writer controls what the reader "sees." As Riddle's former professor, you might in your mind's eye see Riddle as long-haired and sloppy, but if you don't mention these details in your letter, they remain unseen to the reader. Note too that your own terms "long-haired and sloppy" interpret Riddle's appearance through the lens of your own characteristic way of seeing—a way that perhaps values business attire and clean-cut tidiness. Another observer might describe Riddle's appearance quite differently, thus seeing what you don't see.

In an effective piece of writing, the author's angle of vision often works so subtly that unsuspecting readers—unless they learn to think rhetorically—will be drawn into the writer's spell and believe that the writer's prose conveys the "whole picture" of its subject rather than a limited picture filtered through the screen of the writer's perspective.

Contrasting Angles of Vision in Two Texts Consider the differences in what gets seen in the following two descriptions of the Arctic National Wildlife Refuge in Alaska (the ANWR), where proponents of oil exploration are locked in a fierce battle with anti-exploration conservationists. The first passage is from a pro-exploration advocacy group called Arctic Power; the second is from former President Jimmy Carter.

ARCTIC POWER'S DESCRIPTION OF THE ANWR

> On the coastal plain [of the ANWR], the Arctic winter lasts for 9 months. It is dark continuously for 56 days in midwinter. Temperatures with the wind chill can reach –110 degrees F. It's not pristine. There are villages, roads, houses, schools, and military installations. It's not a unique Arctic ecosystem. The coastal plain is only a small fraction of the 88,000 square miles that make up the North Slope. The same tundra environment and wildlife can be found throughout the circumpolar Arctic regions. The 1002 Area [the legal term for the plot of coastal plain being contested] is flat. That's why they call it a plain. [...]
>
> Some groups want to make the 1002 Area a wilderness. But a vote for wilderness is a vote against American jobs.

JIMMY CARTER'S DESCRIPTION OF THE ANWR

Rosalynn [Carter's wife] and I always look for opportunities to visit parks and wildlife areas in our travels. But nothing matches the spectacle of wildlife we found on the coastal plain of America's Arctic National Wildlife Refuge in Alaska. To the north lay the Arctic Ocean; to the south rolling foothills rose toward the glaciated peaks of the Brooks Range. At our feet was a mat of low tundra plant life, bursting with new growth, perched atop the permafrost.

As we watched, 80,000 caribou surged across the vast expanse around us. Called by instinct older than history, this Porcupine (River) caribou herd was in the midst of its annual migration. To witness this vast sea of caribou in an uncorrupted wilderness home, and the wolves, ptarmigan, grizzlies, polar bears, musk oxen and millions of migratory birds, was a profoundly humbling experience. We were reminded of our human dependence on the natural world.

Sadly, we were also forced to imagine what we might see if the caribou were replaced by smoke-belching oil rigs, highways and a pipeline that would destroy forever the plain's delicate and precious ecosystem.

—Jimmy Carter. From "Make This Natural Treasure a National Monument" from The New York Times, December 29, 2000.

How Angle of Vision Persuades To understand more clearly how angle of vision persuades, you can analyze the language strategies at work. Some strategies that writers employ consciously or unconsciously are described below.

Strategies for Constructing an Angle of Vision

Strategy	ANWR Example	U. R. Riddle Example
State your intention directly.	• Earlier passages in the preceding excepts directly state Arctic Powers' pro-drilling and Carter's anti-drilling stances.	• You might say "Riddle would make an excellent manager" or "Riddle doesn't have the personality to be a bank manager."
Select details that support your intentions; omit or de-emphasize others.	• Arctic Power writer (AP)"sees" the cold, barren darkness of the ANWR; Carter sees the beauty. • AP spotlights the people who live on the coastal plain while making the animals invisible; Carter spotlights the caribou while omitting the people. • To AP, drilling means jobs; to Carter it means destructive oil rigs.	• A positive view of Riddle would select and emphasize Riddle's good traits and de-emphasize or omit his bad ones. • A negative view would take the opposite tack.

(continued)

Strategy	ANWR Example	U. R. Riddle Example
Choose words that frame your subject in the desired way or have desired connotations.	• AP frames the ANWR as the dreary "1002 Area"; Carter frames it as a "spectacle of wildlife," a unique "delicate and precious ecosystem." • Arctic Power uses words with negative connotations ("wind chill"); Carter uses words connoting life and growth ("a mat of low tundra plant life").	• "Riddle is an independent thinker who doesn't follow the crowd" (frames him positively in value system that favors individualism). • "Riddle is a loner who thinks egocentrically" (frames him negatively in value system favoring consensus and social skills). • You could say, "Riddle is forthright" or "Riddle is rude"—positive versus negative connotations.
Use figurative language (metaphors, similes, and analogies) that conveys your intended effect.	• AP avoids figurative language, claiming objective presentation of facts. • Carter uses positive metaphors to convey ANWR's vitality (tundra "bursting with new growth") and negative metaphors for drilling ("smoke-belching oil rigs").	• To suggest that Riddle has outgrown his alienating behavior, you could say, "Riddle is a social late bloomer." • To recommend against hiring Riddle while still being positive, you could say, "Riddle's independent spirit would feel caged in by the routine of a bank."
Use sentence structure to emphasize and de-emphasize your ideas. *(Emphasize an idea by placing it at the end of a long sentence, in a short sentence, or in a main clause.)*	• AP uses short sentences to emphasize main points: "It's not pristine." It's not a unique ecosystem." "That's why they call it a plain." • Carter uses longer sentences for description, with an occasional short sentence to make a point: "We were reminded of our human dependence on the natural world."	Consider the difference between the following: • "Although Riddle had problems relating to other students, he is a brilliant thinker." • "Although Riddle is a brilliant thinker, he had problems relating to other students in the class."

3.2 Analyze how messages persuade through appeals to *logos, ethos,* and *pathos.*

CONCEPT 3.2 Messages persuade through appeals to *logos, ethos,* and *pathos.*

Another way to think about the persuasive power of texts is to examine the strategies writers or speakers use to sway their audiences toward a certain position on an issue. To win people's consideration of their ideas, writers or speakers can appeal to what the classical philosopher Aristotle called *logos, ethos,* and *pathos.*

Developing the habit of examining how these appeals are functioning in texts and being able to employ these appeals in your own writing will enhance your ability to read and write rhetorically. Let's look briefly at each:

A fuller discussion of these classical appeals appears in Chapter 13, "Writing a Classical Argument."

- **Logos *is the appeal to reason.*** It refers to the quality of the message itself—to its internal consistency, to its clarity in asserting a thesis or point, and to the quality of reasons and evidence used to support the point.
- **Ethos *is the appeal to the character of the speaker/writer.*** It refers to the speaker/writer's trustworthiness and credibility. One can often increase one's *ethos* in a message by being knowledgeable about the issue, by appearing thoughtful and fair, by listening well, and by being respectful of alternative points of view. A writer's accuracy and thoroughness in crediting sources and professionalism in caring about the format, grammar, and neat appearance of a document are part of the appeal to *ethos.*
- **Pathos *is the appeal to the sympathies, values, beliefs, and emotions of the audience.*** Appeals to *pathos* can be made in many ways. *Pathos* can often be enhanced through evocative visual images, frequently used in Web sites, posters, and magazine or newspaper articles. In written texts, the same effects can be created through vivid examples and details, through connotative language, and through empathy with the audience's beliefs and values.

To see how these three appeals are interrelated, you can visualize a triangle with points labeled *Message, Audience,* and *Writer* or *Speaker.* Rhetoricians study how effective communicators consider all three points of this *rhetorical triangle.* (See Figure 3.2.)

FIGURE 3.2 Rhetorical Triangle

Message

Logos: *How can I make my ideas internally consistent and logical? How can I find the best reasons and support them with the best evidence?*

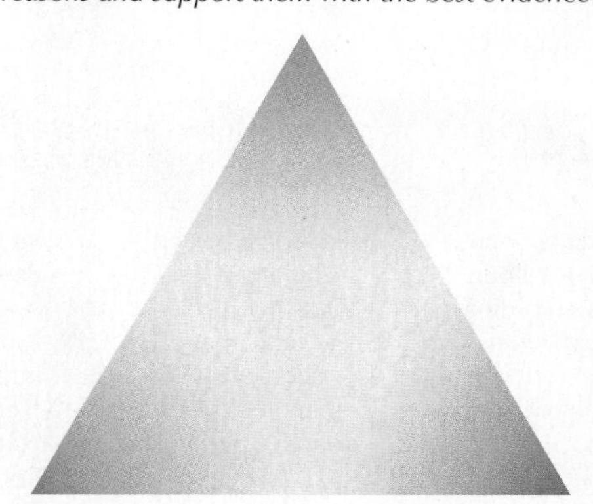

Audience

Pathos: *How can I make the readers open to my message? How can I best engage my readers' emotions and imaginations? How can I appeal to my readers' values and interests?*

Writer or Speaker

Ethos: *How can I present myself effectively? How can I enhance my credibility and trustworthiness?*

We encourage you to ask questions about the appeals to *logos, ethos,* and *pathos* every time you examine a text. For example, is the appeal to *logos* weakened by the writer's use of scanty and questionable evidence? Has the writer made a powerful appeal to *ethos* by documenting her sources and showing that she is an authority on the issue? Has the writer relied too heavily on appeals to *pathos* by using numerous heart-wringing examples? Later chapters in this textbook will help you use these appeals competently in your own writing as well as analyze these appeals in others' messages.

3.3 Analyze how messages persuade through style and document design.

CONCEPT 3.3 Messages persuade through writers' choices about style and document design.

So far we have shown how messages persuade through angle of vision and appeals to *logos, ethos,* and *pathos.* In this section we explain the persuasive power of style and document design, which are themselves factors in the creation of a message's angle of vision and contribute to its logical, ethical, or emotional appeals.

Understanding Factors That Affect Style

Style refers to analyzable features of language that work together to create different effects. As shown in Figure 3.3, style can be thought of as a mixture of four factors:

- ***Ways of shaping sentences,*** such as length or complexity of sentence structure
- ***Word choice,*** such as abstract versus concrete or formal versus colloquial
- ***Voice, or persona,*** which refers to the reader's impression of the writer as projected from the page: expert versus layperson or scholarly voice versus popular voice
- ***Tone,*** which refers to the writer's attitude toward the subject matter or toward the reader, such as cold or warm, humorous or serious, detached or passionate

FIGURE 3.3 Ingredients of Style

Ways of shaping sentences	Types of words	Voice or persona	Tone
Long/short Simple/complex Many modifiers/few modifiers Normal word order/frequent inversions or interruptions Mostly main clauses/many embedded phrases and subordinate clauses	Abstract/concrete Formal/colloquial Unusual/ordinary Specialized/general Metaphorical/literal Scientific/literary	Expert/layperson Scholar/student Outsider/insider Political liberal/conservative Neutral observer/active participant	Intimate/distant Personal/impersonal Angry/calm Browbeating/sharing Informative/entertaining Humorous/serious Ironic/literal Passionately involved/aloof

What style you adopt depends on your purpose, audience, and genre. Consider, for example, the differences in style in two articles about the animated sitcom *South Park*. The first passage comes from an academic journal in which the author analyzes how race is portrayed in *South Park*. The second passage is from a popular magazine, where the author argues that despite *South Park*'s vulgarity, the sitcom has a redeeming social value.

PASSAGE FROM SCHOLARLY JOURNAL

In these cartoons, multiplicity encodes a set of nonwhite identities to be appropriated and commodified by whiteness. In the cartoon world, obscene humor and satire mediate this commodification. The whiteness that appropriates typically does so by virtue of its mobile positioning between and through imagined boundaries contrarily shown as impassible to black characters or agents marked as black. Let me briefly turn to an appropriately confusing example of such a character in *South Park*'s scatological hero extraordinaire, Eric Cartman.... Eric Cartman's yen for breaking into Black English and interactions with black identities also fashion him an appropriator. However, Cartman's voice and persona may be seen as only an avatar, one layer of textual identity for creator Trey Parker, who may be regarded in one sense as a "black-voice" performer.

—Michael A. Chaney, "Representations of Race and Place in *Static Shock, King of the Hill,* and *South Park*"

PASSAGE FROM POPULAR MAGAZINE

Despite the theme song's chamber of commerce puffery, *South Park* is the closest television has ever come to depicting hell on earth. Its inhabitants are, almost without exception, stupid, ignorant or venal—usually all three. Its central characters are four eight-year-olds: Stan, the high-achiever, Kyle, the sensitive Jew, Kenny, whose grisly death each week prompts the tortured cry, "Oh my God! They've killed Kenny! Those bastards!" and Eric Cartman, who has become the Archie Bunker of the '90s, beloved by millions. My 12-year-old son informs me that many of his schoolmates have taken to speaking permanently in Cartman's bigoted and usually furiously inarticulate manner. A (mild) sample: any display of human sensitivity is usually met by him with the rejoinder: "Tree-hugging hippie crap!" This has led to predictable calls for *South Park*, which is usually programmed late in the evening, to be banned altogether.

—Kevin Michael Grace, "*South Park* Is a Snort of Defiance Against a World Gone to Hell"

FOR WRITING AND DISCUSSION

Analyzing Differences in Style

Working in small groups or as a whole class, analyze the differences in the styles of these two samples.

1. How would you describe differences in the length and complexity of sentences, in the level of vocabulary, and in the degree of formality?
2. How do the differences in styles create different voices, personas, and tones?

(*continued*)

3. Based on clues from style and genre, who is the intended audience of each piece? What is the writer's purpose? How does each writer hope to surprise the intended audience with something new, challenging, or valuable?
4. How are the differences in content and style influenced by differences in purpose, audience, and genre?

Your stylistic choices can enhance your appeals to *logos* (for example, by emphasizing main ideas), to *pathos* (by using words that evoke emotional responses and trigger networks of associations), and to *ethos* (by creating an appropriate and effective voice). In the rest of this section we'll show how these strategies can make your own style more effective.

Using Sentence Structure to Emphasize Main Ideas Experienced writers make stylistic choices that emphasize main ideas. For example, you can highlight an idea by placing it in a main clause rather than a subordinate clause or by placing it in a short sentence surrounded by longer sentences. We illustrated this phenomenon in our discussion of the U. R. Riddle exercise on angle of vision (pp. 45–46), where variations in sentence structure created different emphases on Riddle's good or bad points:

> Although Riddle is a brilliant thinker, he had problems relating to other students in my class. (Emphasizes Riddle's personal shortcomings.)
>
> Although Riddle had problems relating to other students in my class, he is a brilliant thinker. (Emphasizes Riddle's intelligence.)

Neither of these effects would have been possible had the writer simply strung together two simple sentences:

> Riddle had problems relating to other students in my class. He is also a brilliant thinker.

In this version, both points about Riddle are equally emphasized, leaving the reader uncertain about the writer's intended meaning (a problem of *logos*). If you string together a long sequence of short sentences—or simply join them with words like *and, or, so,* or *but*—you create a choppy effect that fails to distinguish between more important and less important material. Consider the following example:

Every Idea Equally Emphasized	Main Ideas Emphasized	Comment
I am a student at Sycamore College, and I live in Watkins Hall, and I am enclosing a proposal that concerns a problem with dorm life. There is too much drinking, so nondrinking students don't have an alcohol-free place to go, and so the university should create an alcohol-free dorm, and they should strictly enforce this no-alcohol policy.	As a Sycamore College student living in Watkins Hall, I am enclosing a proposal to improve dorm life. Because there is too much drinking on campus, there is no place for nondrinking students to go. I propose that the university create an alcohol-free dorm and strictly enforce the no-alcohol policy.	In the left-column version, every idea gets equal weight because every idea is in a main clause. In the middle-column version, subordinate ideas are tucked into phrases or subordinate clauses and the main ideas (the problem and the proposed solution) are placed in main clauses for emphasis.

Where Appropriate, Including Details Low on the Ladder of Abstraction In previous writing courses, you might have been told to use concrete, specific language or to "show, not tell." Our advice in this section follows the same spirit: to write as low on the ladder of abstraction as your context allows.

We use the metaphor of a ladder to show how words can vary along a continuum from the abstract ("harm the environment") to the more specific and concrete ("poisoning thousands of freshwater trout with toxic sludge"). As a general rule, details that are low on the ladder of abstraction provide specific factual data as evidence (appeals to *logos*) or trigger vivid images with emotional associations (appeals to *pathos*). As an illustration, consider Figure 3.4, which depicts a "ladder of abstraction" descending from abstract terms at the top toward more specific ones at the bottom.

Choosing words low on the ladder of abstraction is particularly effective for descriptive writing, where your goal is to create a vivid mental image for readers—hence the maxim "Show, don't tell." *Tell* words interpret a scene or tell readers what to feel about a scene without describing it. ("The food for the tailgate party smells wonderful.") In contrast, *show* words describe a scene through sensory details. ("The tantalizing smell of grilled hamburgers and buttered corn on the cob wafts from tailgate party barbecues, where men in their cookout aprons wield forks and spatulas and drink Budweisers.") The description itself evokes the desired effect without requiring the writer to interpret it overtly.

Of course, not all writing needs to be this low on the ladder of abstraction. Our advice, rather, is that the supporting details for a paper should come from as low on the ladder as your context allows. Even the most abstract kind of prose will move up and down between several rungs on the ladder. In closed-form prose, writers need to make choices about the level of specificity that will be most

FIGURE 3.4 Ladder of Abstraction

Level on Ladder	Clothing Example	Charity Example	Global Agriculture Example	Gendered Play Examples
High level: abstract or general	Footwear	Love your neighbor	Traditional crops versus commercial crops	Sam exhibited gendered play behavior.
Middle level	Flip flops	Help/feed the poor	Crops grown by traditional Indian farmers versus genetically engineered crops	Sam played with trucks and fire engines.
Low level: specific or concrete	Purple platform flip-flops with rhinestones	Chop vegetables for the Friday night soup kitchen dinner on 3rd Avenue	In Northern India, traditional mandua and jhangora versus genetically modified soy beans	Sam gleefully smashed his toy Tonka fire engine into the coffee table

effective based on their purpose, audience, and genre. Note the differences in the levels of abstraction in the following passages:

PASSAGE 1: FAIRLY HIGH ON LADDER OF ABSTRACTION

Point sentence

Details relatively high on ladder of abstraction

Although lightning produces the most deaths and injuries of all weather-related accidents, the rate of danger varies considerably from state to state. Florida has twice as many deaths and injuries from lightning strikes as any other state. Hawaii and Alaska have the fewest.

—*Passage from a general interest informative article on weather-related accidents*

PASSAGE 2: LOWER ON LADDER OF ABSTRACTION

Point sentence

Details at middle level on ladder

Details at lower level on ladder

Florida has twice as many deaths and injuries from lightning strikes as any other state, with many of these casualties occurring on the open spaces of golf courses. Florida golfers should carefully note the signals of dangerous weather conditions such as darkening skies, a sudden drop in temperature, an increase in wind, flashes of light and claps of thunder, and the sensation of an electric charge on one's hair or body. In the event of an electric storm, golfers should run into a forest, get under a shelter, get into a car, or assume the safest body position. To avoid being the tallest object in an area, if caught in open areas, golfers should find a low spot, spread out, and crouch into a curled position with feet together to create minimal body contact with the ground.

—*Passage from a safety article aimed at Florida golfers*

Both of these passages are effective for their audience and purpose. The first passage might be compared to a distant shot with a camera, giving an overview of lightning deaths in the United States, while the second zooms in for a more detailed look at a specific case, Florida golf courses. Sometimes, low-on-the-ladder particulars consist of statistics or quotations rather than sensory details. For example, civil engineer David Rockwood uses low-on-the-ladder numerical data about the size and number of wind towers to convince readers that wind generation of electricity entails environmental damage. Your rhetorical decisions about level of abstraction are important because too much high-on-the-scale writing can become dull for readers, while too much low-on-the-scale writing can seem overwhelming or pointless.

See Rockwood's letter to the editor on p. 15.

FOR WRITING AND DISCUSSION

Choosing Details for Different Levels on the Ladder of Abstraction

The following exercise will help you appreciate how details can be chosen at different levels of abstraction to serve different purposes and audiences. Working in small groups or as a whole class, invent details at appropriate positions on the ladder of abstraction for each of the following point sentences.

1. *Yesterday's game was a major disappointment.* You are writing an e-mail message to a friend who is a fan (of baseball, football, basketball, another sport) and missed the game; use midlevel details to explain what was disappointing.

2. *Although the game stank, there were some great moments.* Switch to low-on-the-ladder specific details to describe one of these "great moments."
3. *Advertising in women's fashion magazines creates a distorted and unhealthy view of beauty.* You are writing an analysis for a college course on popular culture; use high-to-midlevel details to give a one-paragraph overview of several ways these ads create an unhealthy view of beauty.
4. *One recent ad, in particular, conveys an especially destructive message about beauty.* Choose a particular ad and describe it with low-on-the-ladder, very specific details.

Creating a Voice Matched to Your Purpose, Audience, and Genre

College students often wonder what style—and particularly, what voice—is appropriate for college papers. For most college assignments, we recommend that you approximate your natural speaking voice to give your writing a conversational academic style. By "conversational," we mean a voice that strives to be plain and clear while retaining the engaging quality of a person who is enthusiastic about the subject. Of course, as you become an expert in a discipline, you may need to move toward a more scholarly voice. For example, the prose in an academic journal article can be extremely dense with technical terms and complex sentence structure, but expert readers in that field understand and expect this voice.

Students sometimes try to imitate a dense academic style before they have achieved the disciplinary expertise to make the style sound natural. The result can seem pretentious or phony. At the other extreme, students sometimes adopt an overly informal or street slang voice that doesn't fit an academic context. Writing with clarity and directness within your natural range will usually create the most effective and powerful voice. Consider the difference in the following examples:

Overly Academic Voice	Conversational Academic Voice	Overly Informal Voice
As people advance in age, they experience time-dependent alterations in their ability to adapt to environmental change. However, much prior research on the aging process has failed to differentiate between detrimental changes caused by an organism's aging process itself and detrimental changes caused by a disease process that is often associated with aging.	As people get older, they are less able to adapt to changes in their environment. Research on aging, however, hasn't always distinguished between loss of function caused by aging itself and loss caused by diseases common among older people.	Old folks don't adapt well to changes in their environments. Some scientists who studied the cane and walker crowd found out that it was hard to tell the difference between bad stuff caused by age versus bad stuff caused by disease.

Although the "conversational academic voice" style is appropriate for most college papers, especially those written for lower-division courses, many professors construct assignments asking you to adopt different voices and different styles. It is thus important to understand the professor's assignment and to adopt the style and voice appropriate for the assigned rhetorical situation.

Making Purposeful Choices about Document Design

Document design, which refers to the format of a text on the page including use of graphics or visual images, can have a surprising impact on the effectiveness of a message. In an academic context, writers usually produce manuscript (keyboarded pages of typed text presented electronically or in hard copy held together with a staple or folder) rather than a "camera ready" document created through desktop-publishing software. With manuscripts, your document design choices mainly concern margins, font style and size, line spacing, and headers or footers (page number, document identification, date). Generally these choices are dictated by the style guidelines of an academic discipline such as American Psychological Association (APA). If you deviate from the expected document design (for example, by using a specialty font or by designing a decorative cover page for an academic paper) you undergo the risk either of appearing unaware of academic conventions or of flaunting them to get noticed—like wearing a jumpsuit to a job interview. Attention to document design and the appearance of your manuscripts thus signals your membership in an academic or professional community. An inappropriately formatted or sloppy paper can hurt your *ethos* and may send a message that you are unprofessional.

For more on these issues, see Chapter 4 on composing in a digital environment and Chapter 10 on analyzing visual images.

In contrast, desktop-published, "camera ready" works require elaborate decisions about document design to give them a professional visual appeal ready for print or the Web. For desktop-published documents, design is closely related to genre and involves rhetorical decisions about font styles, use of space and layout, color, and graphics or images. Table 3.1 lists some of the variables associated with document design when writers move from a "manuscript" environment to a "desktop-published" or multimedia environment.

TABLE 3.1 Features of Document Design in Scholarly versus Popular Genres

Design Feature	Typical Use in Scholarly Journal	Variations in Popular Genres
Fonts	• Conservative, highly readable (Times New Roman) • Boldface for headings or occasional emphasis • Italics or underlining governed by disciplinary conventions	• Playful use of fonts in titles and introductions • Different font styles in sidebars or boxes • Larger font sizes at start of articles
Use of white space (margins, spacing, placement of titles and visuals, single versus double columns)	• Consistent use of white space in each journal article to achieve orderly effect • Table of contents often on cover • Double columns often used to maximize amount of readable prose per page	• Wide variations in use of white space • Text may be wrapped around visuals • Distinction between articles and advertisements sometimes blurred • Table of contents often buried among advertisements

TABLE 3.1 *continued*

Design Feature	Typical Use in Scholarly Journal	Variations in Popular Genres
Color	• Minimal use of color • Some color in graphics and charts to set off main ideas or highlight categories	• Playful and artistic use of color to create mood, draw eye to certain locations, create variety, or achieve desired emphasis
Visuals	• Primarily graphics or illustrations with focus on clarity and logic • Visuals are called "Tables" or "Figures"; all axes and variables are clearly labeled	• Often playful use of visuals to illustrate content or theme • Often uses drawings or photoshopped images to illustrate themes

FOR WRITING AND DISCUSSION

Analyzing Rhetorical Effect

Using examples of different kinds of published documents—scholarly articles, popular magazine articles, newspapers, pamphlets, and so forth—and images of various Web documents or multimedia products, analyze differences in document design. In each case, how is document design related to genre? How does it contribute to the document's effectiveness?

CONCEPT 3.4 Nonverbal messages persuade through visual strategies that can be analyzed rhetorically.

3.4 Analyze how nonverbal texts persuade through visual rhetorical strategies.

Just as you can think rhetorically about texts, you can think rhetorically about photographs, drawings, and other images as well as artifacts such as clothing.

Visual Rhetoric

Chapter 10 deals extensively with visual rhetoric, explaining how visual elements work together to create a persuasive effect.

The persuasive power of images shapes our impressions and understanding of events. Take, for instance, the 2010 BP oil spill in the Gulf of Mexico that pumped millions of barrels of crude oil into the Gulf for three months. Aerial photos of the spreading brown oil plumes in the water conveyed the seriousness and magnitude of the problem, which was further driven home by photos of animals coated in sticky brown oil—sea turtles, crabs, pelicans, other birds, and fish—almost unrecognizable as animals. These photos made the logical argument (*logos*) that underwater oil extraction needs more stringent regulation. They also appealed powerfully to viewers' emotions (*pathos*) in their vivid and immediate depiction of suffering and dying animals and of damage to the environment. These photos helped galvanize public opposition to expanded offshore drilling. Think also of how the images of the destruction of superstorm Sandy drove home to Americans the need to prepare for extreme weather and raised awareness of the effects of climate change. Or think of the way frequent news photos of hundreds of thousands of angry protestors in Egypt have continued to arouse American anxiety about political instability in the Middle East and Northern Africa.

What gives these images this persuasive power? For one thing, they can be apprehended at a glance, condensing an argument into a memorable scene or symbol that taps deeply into our emotions and values. Images also persuade by appealing to *logos*, *ethos*, and *pathos*. They make implicit arguments (*logos*) while also appealing to our values and emotions (*pathos*) and causing us to respond favorably or unfavorably to the artist or photographer (*ethos*). Like verbal texts, images have an angle of vision, which can be crafted by selecting, manipulating, and often photoshopping images to control what viewers see and thus influence what they think. (Note that "angle of vision" is itself a visual metaphor.) Through the location and angle of the camera, the distance from the subject, and the framing, cropping, and filtering/lighting of the image, the photographer steers us toward a particular view of the subject, influencing us to forget, at least momentarily, that there are other ways of seeing the same subject. For example, opponents of building the Keystone Pipeline linking Canada's Alberta tar sands oil with refineries in Texas used photos of contaminated sludge ponds and damaged boreal forests while supporters used up-close photos of workers benefiting from high-paying jobs.

Although images can have powerful rhetorical effects, these effects may be less controllable and more audience-dependent than those of verbal texts. Consider, for example, the photo in Figure 3.5 of a vast iceberg, a common image

FIGURE 3.5 Floating Iceberg

recently in newspapers and magazines. This photo resembles those taken by environmental photographer James Balog for his Extreme Ice Survey, documenting the recent rapid melting of glaciers around the world. (Balog's work is featured in the award-winning documentary *Chasing Ice*.) In this photo, the iceberg towers above the water and glistens in the sun. When these photographs are used in the climate change debate, the intention is to document the rapid melting of Arctic and Antarctic ice—as shown by the size of the iceberg and the vast expanse of water in which it is floating. Viewers familiar with the context of shrinking glaciers and spectacular icebergs breaking off the glaciers will interpret the *logos* of this photo as evidence for global warming, which in a matter of years is shrinking glaciers that took tens of thousands of years to form. In contrast, other viewers might find that the striking aesthetic beauty of this image distracts them from the global warming message. For them, the photographer's angle of vision and use of visual techniques have created a work of art that undermines its ability to convey scientific information in support of the global climate change crisis. Interpreted in this way, the photo could be seen to use *pathos* to attract viewers to the magnificent, strange beauty of this part of the world, perhaps as a potential part of a travel brochure. Because images are somewhat open in the way they create arguments, writers of texts that include images should anticipate viewers' possible alternative interpretations and consider the importance in many cases of contextualizing images.

For a photo of melting glaciers that participates in the climate change debate, see the image on p. 417. That photo makes different appeals to *logos*, *ethos*, and *pathos*.

For further discussion of how to use words to guide viewers' interpretation of images, see Chapter 19, Skill 19.2.

FOR WRITING AND DISCUSSION

Analyzing Images

The following exercise asks you to think about the rhetorical effects of different images of wolves and particularly about how they can create implicit arguments in the public controversy about hunting wolves in western states. The gray wolf had been on the federal Endangered Species list but was removed in 2012 when the wolf population had grown. However, "wolf wars" have flared in Montana, Wyoming, and especially Minnesota since then. Ranchers and hunters argue that wolves are too numerous and aggressive in hunting livestock and game and have lobbied for hunting permits from state governments to kill hundreds of wolves. In contrast, animal rights groups, environmental organizations, and the Ojibwe/Anishinaabe and Sioux have lobbied against these hunting permits, arguing that wolf populations should be allowed to grow in order to sustain a natural ecological system in which wolves help keep deer and other wild animal populations in balance.

Analyzing the Photos. As you imagine the use of images in Figures 3.6–3.9, explore the rhetorical effects of these images, noting how the effect may differ from person to person. In each photograph, on what details has the photographer chosen to focus? How do the details and angle of vision contribute to the dominant impression of wolves conveyed by the whole photograph? How

(*continued*)

FIGURE 3.6 Wolf in a Field of Grass

FIGURE 3.7 Four Wolves in Winter

FIGURE 3.8 Wolves with Deer Carcass

FIGURE 3.9 Wolf with Rabbit

does the photograph affect you emotionally? How does it shape your attitude toward wolves? How would you rank these images in terms of their favorable or unfavorable impression of wolves and their emotional appeal?

Using the Photos. Now imagine that you are creating a flyer for each of the following audiences and purposes. Which photo or photos would help you make the most compelling argument (consider *logos, ethos,* and *pathos*) for each group and purpose? Explain your rationale.

A. An organization consisting of hunters and ranchers has commissioned you to create a flyer that seeks to make the public more tolerant of hunting wolves now that the gray wolf has been taken off the Endangered Species list.
B. An environmental organization has asked you to create a flyer for the general public that seeks to generate appreciation for gray wolves' role in western ecosystems and to spark sympathy for them in protest against the reinstated wolf hunting permits.

The Rhetoric of Clothing and Other Consumer Items

Not only do photographs, paintings, and drawings have rhetorical power, but so do the images projected by many of our consumer choices. Consider, for example, the rhetorical thinking that goes into our choice of clothes. We choose our clothes not only to keep ourselves covered and warm but also to project visually our identification with certain social groups and subcultures. For example, if you want to be identified as a skateboarder, a preppy, a geek, a NASCAR fan, or a junior partner in a corporate law firm, you know how to select clothes and accessories that convey that identification. The way you dress is a code that communicates where you fit (or how you want to be perceived as fitting) within a class and social structure. For the most part, clothing codes are arbitrary, based on a system of differences. For example, there is no universal "truth" saying that long, baggy basketball shorts are more attractive than short basketball shorts, even though one style may feel current and the other out-of-date.

How do these symbolic codes get established? They can be set by fashion designers, by advertisers, or by trendy groups or individuals. The key to any new clothing code is to make it look different in some distinctive way from an earlier code or from a code of another group. Sometimes clothing codes develop to show rebellion against the values of parents or authority figures. At other times they develop to show new kinds of group identities.

Clothing codes are played on in conscious ways in fashion advertisements so that consumers become very aware of what identifications are signaled by different styles and brands. This aspect of consumer society is so ubiquitous that one of the marks of growing affluence in third world countries is people's attention to the rhetoric of consumer goods. Buying a certain kind of consumer good projects a certain kind of status or group or class identity. Our point, from a rhetorical perspective, is that in making a consumer choice, many people are concerned not only with the quality of the item itself but also with its rhetorical symbolism. Note that the same item can send quite different messages to different groups: A Rolex watch might enhance one's credibility at a corporate board meeting while undercutting it at a company picnic for workers.

FOR WRITING AND DISCUSSION

Clothing as Visual Arguments

Working in small groups or as a whole class, do a rhetorical analysis of the consumer items shown in Figures 3.10 through 3.13.

1. In each case, see if you can reach consensus on why these people might have chosen a particular way of dressing. How does the clothing style project a desire to identify with certain groups or to shock or reject certain groups? How do the clothing choices help establish and enhance the wearer's sense of identity?

(*continued*)

FIGURE 3.10

FIGURE 3.11

FIGURE 3.12

FIGURE 3.13

2. When you and your friends make consumer purchases, to what extent are you swayed by the quality of the item (its materials and workmanship) versus the rhetorical messages it sends to an audience (its signals about social identity and standing)?
3. How does the rhetoric of clothing extend to other consumer items such as cell phones, cars, vacations, recreational activities, home furnishings, music, and so forth?

4. Suppose that you are interviewing for a job in one or more of these job settings: barista in a coffee shop, retail sales clerk, intern at a corporate law office, or some other workplace setting of your choice. What clothing would be appropriate for your interview and why? Be as specific as possible for all items of clothing including shoes and accessories.
5. To what extent are dress codes for women more complex than those for men?

Chapter Summary

In this chapter we have looked briefly at rhetorical theory in order to explain the persuasive power of both verbal and visual texts.

- ***Concept 3.1 Messages persuade through their angle of vision.*** Any text necessarily looks at its subject from a perspective—an angle of vision—that selects and emphasizes some details while omitting or minimizing others. You can analyze writers' angle of vision by considering their direct statements of intention, their selection of details, their word choice, their figures of speech, and their manipulation of sentence structure to control emphasis.
- ***Concept 3.2 Messages persuade through appeals to* logos, ethos, *and pathos.*** *Logos* refers to the power of the writer's reasons and evidence; *pathos* to the way the writer connects to the reader's sympathies, emotions, values, and beliefs; and *ethos* to the way the writer portrays himself or herself as trustworthy and credible.
- ***Concept 3.3 Messages Persuade through Writers' Choices about Style and Document Design*** Stylistic features such as sentence structure, word choice, voice, and tone work together to create different rhetorical effects. An effective style highlights key ideas, moves down the ladder of abstraction for details, and establishes an appropriate voice. Document design also contributes to a message's effect. Academic articles generally adopt a conservative design while more popular genres approach design playfully and artistically.
- ***Concept 3.4 Nonverbal messages persuade through visual strategies that can be analyzed rhetorically.*** Like verbal texts, visual texts have an angle of vision created by the way the image is framed and by the perspective from which it is viewed. Images also make implicit arguments (*logos*), appeal to the viewer's emotions and values (*pathos*), and suggest the creator's character and trustworthiness (*ethos*). One can also analyze consumer choices (clothing, jewelry, cars) rhetorically because such choices make implicit arguments about the consumer's desired identity.

Two Contrasting Descriptions of the Same Scene

BRIEF WRITING PROJECT

This brief writing project is a write-to-learn task that will help you appreciate how writers construct an "angle of vision" (see Concept 3.1) through selection of low-on-the-ladder details, word choice, and other means.

Write two descriptions of the same scene. Here is the catch. Your two descriptions must illustrate contrasting angles of vision. Your first description must convey a favorable impression of the scene, making it appear pleasing or attractive. The second description must convey a negative or unfavorable impression, making the scene appear unpleasant or unattractive. Both descriptions must contain only factual details and must describe exactly the same scene from the same location at the same time. It's not fair, in other words, to describe the scene in sunny weather and then in the rain or otherwise to alter factual details. Each description should be one paragraph long (approximately 125–175 words).

To get into the spirit of this unusual assignment, you need to create a personal rationale for why you are writing two opposing descriptions. You might think of yourself being in two different moods so that you look at the scene first through your "happy glasses" and then through your "sad glasses." Or you could simply think of yourself as a word wizard consciously trying to create, in the spirit of a game, two different effects on readers for two different rhetorical purposes.

Once you have chosen your scene, you'll need to observe and take notes in preparation for writing the focused descriptions of the scene. You need to compose descriptions that are rich in sensory detail (low on the ladder of abstraction)—sights, sounds, smells, textures, even on occasion tastes—all contributing to a dominant impression that gives the description focus.

You can train yourself to notice sensory details by creating a two-column sensory chart and noting details that appeal to each of the senses. Then try describing them, first positively (left column) and then negatively (right column). One student, observing a scene in a local tavern, made these notes in her sensory chart:

Positive Description	**Negative Description**
	Taste
salted and buttered popcorn	salty, greasy popcorn
frosty pitchers of beer	half-drunk pitchers of stale, warm beer
big bowls of salted-in-the-shell peanuts on the tables	mess of peanut shells and discarded pretzel wrappers on tables and floor
	Sound
hum of students laughing and chatting	din of high-pitched giggles and various obnoxious frat guys shouting at each other
the jukebox playing oldies but goodies from the early Beatles	jukebox blaring out-of-date music

Student Example

We conclude with a student example of this assignment.

DESCRIPTION 1—POSITIVE EFFECT

Light rain gently drops into the puddles that have formed along the curb as I look out my apartment window at the corner of 14th and East John. Pedestrians layered in sweaters, raincoats, and scarves and guarded with shiny rubber boots and colorful umbrellas sip their steaming hot triple-tall lattes. Some share smiles and pleasant exchanges as they hurry down the street, hastening to work where it is warm and dry. Others, smelling the aroma of French roast espresso coming from the coffee bar next to the bus stop, listen for the familiar rumbling sound that will mean the 56 bus has arrived. Radiant orange, yellow, and red leaves blanket the sidewalk in the areas next to the maple trees that line the road. Along the curb a mother holds the hand of her toddler, dressed like a miniature tugboat captain in yellow raincoat and pants, who splashes happily in a puddle.

DESCRIPTION 2—NEGATIVE EFFECT

A solemn grayness hangs in the air, as I peer out the window of my apartment at the corner of 14th and East John. A steady drizzle of rain leaves boot-drenching puddles for pedestrians to avoid. Bundled in rubber boots, sweaters, coats, and rain-soaked scarves, commuters clutch Styrofoam cups of coffee as a defense against the biting cold. They lift their heads every so often to take a small sip of caffeine, but look sleep-swollen nevertheless. Pedestrians hurry past each other, moving quickly to get away from the dismal weather, the dull grayness. Some nod a brief hello to a familiar face, but most clutch their overcoats and tread grimly on, looking to avoid puddles or spray from passing cars. Others stand at the bus stop, hunched over, waiting in the drab early morning for the smell of diesel that means the 56 bus has arrived. Along the curb an impatient mother jerks the hand of a toddler to keep him from stomping in an oil-streaked puddle.

4 MULTIMODAL AND ONLINE COMMUNICATION

WHAT YOU WILL LEARN

4.1 To analyze the rhetorical use of words, images, and sounds in multimodal texts.

4.2 To think rhetorically about the interactive Web environment with shifting audiences, purposes, genres, and authorial roles.

4.3 To participate responsibly in online discourse by understanding intellectual property rights and by constructing an ethical persona.

Everything is a remix.

—*Kirby Ferguson, filmmaker*

We examined the rhetorical power of images in Chapter 3 (Concept 3.4). In this chapter we expand our discussion of visual rhetoric to include a range of **multimodal texts**, by which we mean any text that supplements words with another mode of communication such as images, sounds, or even the rhetorical use of page design. The word *multimodal* combines the concepts of "multi" (more than one) and "modality" (a channel, medium, or mode of communication). The use of multimodal texts has increased dramatically in the digital age, but multimodal texts that combine words and images have a long history. Medieval scriptures often had vivid religious scenes painted in the margins (called "illuminations"), and Charles Darwin's field notes combine words with carefully drawn images of flora and fauna. Many of the multimodal compositions in this text combine words and images in ways that require no digital technology—see the poster arguing that high heel shoes are harmful to feet (p. 168) or the advocacy ad arguing that black kids are more likely than white kids to go to prison (p. 390).

What is new in the digital age is the predominance of online multimodal texts with full-color images, videos, animations, and sounds as well as embedded hyperlinks that allow readers to jump from one location to another. The resulting interactive Web environment differs substantially from print text—usually black letters on white paper—that you read linearly from left to right, top to bottom. How to think rhetorically about this interactive multimodal environment is the subject of this chapter. It is one thing to post a video of cute kittens or funny golf swings on YouTube; it is quite another thing to compose a purposeful multimodal text that effectively uses rhetorical principles to move an audience. Moreover, Web environments complicate our understanding of audiences, purposes, genres, and authors while also raising legal issues about intellectual property and ethical issues about online etiquette and personas.

CONCEPT 4.1 **Composers of multimodal texts use words, images, and sounds rhetorically to move an audience.**

4.1 Analyze the rhetorical use of words, images, and sounds in multimodal texts.

Research suggests that Internet surfers view a Web page for only a second or two before they move on to something else. Effective Web communicators have to negotiate this competitive, short-attention-span environment by hooking audiences quickly and then keeping them engaged with high-level content.

Hooking Audiences with Images and "Nutshell" Text

Readers on the Web typically don't read from beginning to end as they might in a print text. They jump from page to page, influenced by multisensory stimuli urging them to pause on an image, scan a verbal text, or click on a link. Texts in multimodal forms are layered, shuffled, combined, and recombined in ways that make it difficult for authors to predict how readers will navigate a Web site or what they will choose to read or view.

In such a busy environment, composers often use images for immediate appeals to *pathos*. Because Web composers have but a split second to hook the reader's interest, they often use emotion-evoking or interest-arousing images, which have an immediacy that verbal texts can't match, as we explained in Concept 3.4. Such images invoke in audiences a kind of non-rational investment in a subject, an investment that precedes attention to a page's more logical appeals often conveyed by words. For an illustration of how Web composers use images to hook readers, see our rhetorical analysis of competing Web sites about fracking in Chapter 21 (pp. 535–542).

Another way to attract a reader's attention is through pithy "nutshell" sentences that convey the "take away" point of a page. These nutshell sentences, often highlighted by a different color, enlarged font, or placement in a call-out box, are the multimodal equivalent of a thesis statement or paragraph topic sentence in purely verbal text. Because long chunks of text look deadly dull on a screen, skilled Web composers produce easily readable, concise texts that are often broken up by spacing, text boxes, or bullets. Often, too, Web composers use the journalistic inverted pyramid, so that the opening paragraph of a story summarizes the whole story. The goal of nutshell sentences and inverted pyramids is to send readers the complete take-away message of a text quickly in case the reader jumps to something else. In our discussion of fracking Web sites, we note nutshell sentences such as the following: "Keep North Carolina Frack-Free"; "We pay $86 million in taxes—just another way oil or natural gas companies keep our country running on more than just energy"; or "Can you light your tap water on fire?"

Holding Readers through Strong Content

Once readers are hooked by a site, they will continue only if the site delivers good content—that is, only if it gives them something new, challenging, surprising, or otherwise interesting or entertaining. Sometimes this content is conveyed entirely through verbal text to be read on the screen. But often the content is presented in multimodal texts such as audio podcasts, slide shows set to music, videos of lectures containing PowerPoint or Prezi slides, animations, or videos produced with rhetorical sophistication to make a point. Because simple videos can be made with smartphone and digital cameras and relatively easy-to-learn editing programs, many students are trying their hand at this powerful new genre. Although it is beyond the scope of this text to discuss the technology of video-making, we can introduce you to the rhetorical thinking that underlies an effective video.

Designing Video Narratives that Move Viewers

An effective video calls for a full range of visual analysis. A video can be paused at any moment to freeze single frames, each of which can be analyzed rhetorically as a still image using the strategies introduced in Concept 3.4 and developed more fully in Chapter 10, "Analyzing Images." In the "play" mode, however, videos add the dimension of motion (narration, movement through time) as well as the power of sound (dialogue, background sounds, music, voice-over) to achieve desired effects.

Visually, a video makes its narrative impact along two channels. First, a video's "story" is told through the narrative action and dialogue—the content of the video. But the story is also told through the visual grammar deployed through camera placement and technique. Teachers of video production say that beginning camera users tend to photograph the action from one camera position only— usually a distance or mid-distance shot—that requires minimal editing. In contrast, experienced videographers shoot from several positions and purposely use cutting and splicing techniques to narrate the action through the perspective of different camera positions. They choose each position for a rhetorical purpose in order to emphasize some parts of the action and deemphasize others. Their goal is to *design* or *compose* a video sequence that has a narrative arc and shape. Film scholars have shown that camera positions can generally be classified into three types:

- *Establishing shots,* which set the narrative in a context showing location and setting.
- *Reaction shots,* which show a close-up, often of a face, to register a character's emotional reaction.
- *Point of view shots,* which look at a scene through the eyes of one of the characters.

These three kinds of shots are illustrated in Figure 4.1, which shows still frames from a student video of an urban gardener gathering eggs from her backyard chicken coop. The first image is an establishing shot showing the chicken coop, some chickens, and the woman lifting the coop door to retrieve the day's eggs.

Establishing shot

Point of view shot

Reaction shot

FIGURE 4.1 Urban Gardener Video

Next we see a point of view shot (looking through the woman's eyes) of the eggs up close including the woman's hand grasping one of the eggs. Finally, we see a reaction shot showing the woman's smiling face expressing happiness for the eggs and gratitude toward her hens. These different camera positions create a brief narrative arc of the urban gardener's anticipation and satisfaction at getting eggs from her free range backyard chickens.

FOR WRITING AND DISCUSSION

Analyzing a Video Sequence

Watch and then analyze a short video assigned by your instructor or chosen by yourself. The video should use different camera positions as well as sounds for rhetorical effect.

1. ***Analyzing editing choices:*** After playing the whole clip several times, pause the video at each of the edits where the camera position shifts.

(continued)

Consider the following questions: How does the videographer use establishing, point of view, and reaction shots to achieve a desired effect on viewers? What is the rhetorical purpose of each camera position? What is emphasized in each camera position? How does the sequence create a thematic point or meaning?

2. ***Analyzing still frames:*** Pause the video on several frames that can be analyzed rhetorically like a photograph. How is the scene framed? How is it lighted or filtered? What is the camera angle and distance? What is the subject matter of the scene? If the scene contains people, what is the rhetorical effect of the characters' clothing and accessories, hairstyle, gestures, poses, and positioning? How would you analyze the scene in terms of gender, social class, or implied values?

See Chapter 10, pp. 229–235, for advice on how to analyze a still image.

3. ***Analyzing sound:*** Finally, play the clip again, this time paying attention to sounds. If the video includes music, what is the effect of the musical choices? If the clip has a voice-over, what is the effect of the choices about gender, vocal register, accent, pacing, and so forth? What sounds are emphasized in the video? What sounds might have been filtered out?

4.2 Think rhetorically about the interactive Web environment with shifting audiences, purposes, genres, and authorial roles.

CONCEPT 4.2 Online environments are rhetorically interactive with shifting audiences, purposes, genres, and authorial roles.

Consider the difference between reading a print version of a news story and the same newspaper's online version. Here is the headline from a recent front page print story in a city newspaper: "**INTRUDER TERRIFIES STUDENTS.**" According to the print story, a man wearing a trench coat and eating an ice cream cone entered a classroom at a local university and "frightened students with his bizarre behavior." When the intruder refused to leave the classroom, the professor called campus security and dismissed the class. According to the newspaper, campus security was slow to respond; meanwhile, students were terrified as they watched the man "talking incoherently and turn[ing] over tables and other classroom furniture." Once campus security arrived, the man was arrested and booked into the county jail. (He was unarmed.)

If you read the story only in the print version, you would think the campus barely escaped a disaster. But how accurate was the story? In the newspaper's online version, the same story was accompanied by comment posts from students who were in the classroom at the time. Many of these posts contradicted the newspaper's story, saying that the intruder was odd, but not threatening, that campus security arrived within one minute of being called, and that students, rather than fleeing the classroom in terror, lingered out of curiosity. One commenter said that the intruder seemed to be enjoying his ice cream cone. Another said that he couldn't have possibly tipped over tables because the classroom furniture was fixed to the floor. Whereas the newspaper's "angle of vision" portrayed the incident as frightening and dangerous, the posts portrayed it collectively as a bizarre but harmless encounter with a possibly mentally ill street person. Within a day, more than a hundred posts contributed to the story. The ensuing discussion thread evolved from concerns about what happened in the classroom to a larger conversation about the best way to respond to threats. One respondent said it was lucky that no one in the class carried a concealed weapon because an armed student might have killed the intruder (or accidentally shot a classmate), turning a harmless incident into a tragedy. The discussion thread was then dominated by heated exchanges over the advisability of armed citizens.

Our point in recounting this episode is that the Web creates an interactive participatory news environment very unlike that of traditional print newspapers and news magazines. Because Web readers are often Web writers, content published online can receive reader responses within minutes. These responses in turn can alter the way readers read the original content so that the "message" itself begins to evolve. This participatory environment has many implications for reading online communication rhetorically.

Shifting and Evolving Rhetorical Contexts Online

We can see the rhetorical implications of an online environment if we return for a moment to the rhetorical triangle (audience, writer, message) that we introduced in Concept 3.2 , page 48. Consider how an online environment destabilizes each point of the triangle.

Shifting Audiences When you publish something online (say an e-mail or a Yelp! restaurant review), who are your readers? In some cases, you might think you can identify your audience precisely. If you send an e-mail, for example, you assume that your audience is the person addressed. But sometimes recipients forward e-mails without your knowledge or consent, or sometimes, to your great embarrassment, you might hit "reply all" when you intended to hit "reply." Moreover, e-mails are always stored somewhere on servers and may be leaked by a whistleblower or read by attorneys who subpoena them in legal proceedings. (Almost every week produces news stories of scandals or lawsuits initiated by leaked e-mails.) Likewise you might believe your Facebook audience is limited to "friends" only. However, unless you set your privacy codes very narrowly, one of your friends can "like" or "share" one of your posts, sending it to a whole new network of that person's friends. One of your posts or pictures may well be viewed by hundreds of strangers including your boss or your teacher. (And we know, of course, that "friends" on a Facebook site are often not really friends at all, and sometimes not even acquaintances.)

Variability of audiences occurs in different ways if you write a blog, upload a video to YouTube, or create your own Web site. In such cases, you cast your net for readers or viewers, probably hoping for a large audience. Although a given post can sometimes go viral by spreading exponentially through social media, often you are thankful for a small readership that you hope will grow. Sometimes your post may be read by audiences that you didn't intend to target—people who disagree with you, for example—and these people may forward your work to a largely hostile audience. At other times, however, online communities often work paradoxically to shut off outside readers by creating "insider" discussion threads that reinforce insider views and make outsiders feel unwelcome. Sometimes, in fact, members of these communities will flame an outsider who posts unwittingly on a thread. The community thus tries to stabilize its audience through self-policing, but in the process often limits a real exchange of communication across differences. Wise online writers, we believe, will in most cases try to enlarge their audiences rather than limit them. This desire to reach more readers puts the burden on the writer to use the appeals of *logos*, *pathos*, and *ethos* to draw in readers rather than shut them out.

Shifting Writers Just as the Web environment destabilizes our conception of "audience," so can it destabilize the concept of "writer." Online environments often blur the concept of the single, authoritative writer by creating texts written by communities. Through wikis, for example, writers who may not even know each other can build collaborative texts that cannot be identified with any individual writer. Although wiki writers don't produce texts in quite the way that bees build a hive—as if some group mind generates the words and makes the rhetorical decisions rather than an individual—the text seems to emerge collaboratively without a controlling lead author. In an analogous way, discussion threads on blog sites can be said to blur the individual writer. Although an originating blogger may have a strong individual identity, the responses posted by readers bring other voices to the original blogger's message, creating a kind of larger and more complex "co-created" message. We saw this phenomenon in our example of the news story about the ice-cream cone eating classroom intruder: That story's "truth content" was not controlled by the original author (the news reporter) but by the collective weight of all readers who posted responses to the story. Finally, the concept of the writer is blurred by the anonymity created by the use of pseudonyms or avatars, which often make it difficult to identify texts with the actual human author.

Evolving Messages Very few pieces of content published on the Web are stable or permanent. Items appear and quickly disappear. An author can post a story or article on a Web site, make corrections or revisions, and then quickly repost the altered version. (This impermanence explains why academic conventions for citing and documenting sources sometimes require you to indicate the date on which you viewed the site.) Also readers often don't read Web texts linearly from beginning to end in the stabilizing way they read print-based text. Rather they are apt to click on embedded hyperlinks, jumping from text to text. Thus a message will be perceived differently by different readers according to their pathway through it. Messages evolve in still another way within threaded discussion sites where the reader's view of the subject is gradually modified by the cumulative impact of all the posts. Moreover, even an individual writer's view might evolve as the discussion continues. A given writer who expresses one view early on in a thread may express a quite different view later.

Online Variations in Purposes, Genres, and Authorial Roles

Another way to think rhetorically about online communication is to consider how a writer's choice of genre or medium affects the writer's purpose and authorial role. To see what we are talking about, consider the following thought experiment:

THOUGHT EXPERIMENT

> Suppose that next year you plan to do something unusual (take a road trip, do a service project in an impoverished area, live in a foreign country) and want to keep your friends posted about your activities. How could you best do so? An old technology approach would be to send them postcards once a week. New technology approaches include e-mail (you could set up an address list), Facebook (you already have "friends" established), tweets, or a personal blog. How would each choice influence your role and purpose in constructing a message? How would each choice affect the size and composition of your audience? Which would you choose and why?

When we discuss this thought experiment with our own students, they reveal many variables among these choices. They surmise that the blog invites the most serious, reflective, and in-depth writing. Writers would be apt to compose a blog in a word-processing program, revise and proof it, and then post it to the blog site. Their purpose would be to bring interesting insights and points of view to willing readers. In contrast, the least reflective genres or media would be tweets (requiring "sound bites" with 140 or fewer characters) or old-technology postcards, which have limited space and have traditionally invited clichés such as "wish you were here" or "check out the pic on the back—we were there yesterday." In between is e-mail, which hypothetically could be as reflective as a blog, but is more likely to be breezier and less formal—probably composed in the e-mail program itself and limited in length.

Another important variable concerns audience. Our students surmise that the blog is apt to have the fewest readers among your friends. Your friends would have to know about it and be motivated to find and read it. However, the blog is the most apt to attract outside readers if your subject matter and style were interesting and if enough initial readers "liked" you and began spreading the word. In contrast, e-mail has a captive audience, but raises awkward decisions about whom to include in your mailing list. Sending an e-mail seems to tell recipients that your message is worth their time. Some might resent having an e-mail from you every day, yet feel obligated at least to skim it. Others might be excited to follow your every word. Tweets have different audiences still. If your friends just want quick updates on your travels, then tweets serve that purpose well. Friends can follow you on Twitter as they like without having to log into a blog or get annoyed with your clogging their e-mail inbox. The worst option for reaching a wide audience, everyone agrees, is the old technology postcard, which requires you to write to each recipient separately in long hand, address the postcard, add a stamp, and mail it.

Of special consideration is Facebook. Our students think most people would use Facebook to post photographs of a trip and to send brief sound bite messages, but they would not use Facebook as a way to share the reflections that would be put into a blog. Facebook seems to invite triviality more than depth.

FOR WRITING AND DISCUSSION

How Do You Read and Write the Web?

In small groups or as a whole class, share how you currently use the Web for reading and writing. When you are online, what do you typically view or read? Do you use social media? How? Do you post photos on Flickr? Have you ever uploaded a video on YouTube? Have you ever tweeted? Do you use e-mail? (If so, how do you use it differently from text messaging on a phone?) Have you ever blogged? Created a Web site? Created a multimodal text? Have you ever responded to a blog or otherwise posted on a discussion thread? Have you ever written an online review? Have you ever contributed to a wiki? Your goal here is to share the various ways that you and members of your class read and write on the Web.

Maintaining Appropriate Online Privacy

As we have suggested, the Internet goes on forever. Therefore, it is important that writers are careful about what personal information they bring into the cyber universe. What writers publish in their early teens may come back to haunt them as they pursue careers later in life. Even the youngest writers must remember that the persona they cultivate in their earliest online publications will continue to exist online for decades to come. One good strategy is to follow the Parent/Boss/Teacher Rule. Before posting something online, ask yourself, is this something I would want my parent/boss/teacher to see? If the answer is no, there's a good chance it might pose problems for you later.

That said, we also want to emphasize that sharing online is not a bad thing. Quite the contrary, the willingness of ordinary people to share information and perspectives online has made the Internet a powerful tool for democracy. Individuals feel less isolated when they can interact with interested readers. When you are willing to share your views and knowledge online—honestly, albeit carefully—you contribute to increased democratic interaction around the globe. This kind of sharing ranges from the most mundane Facebook posts to more sophisticated participation in blog sites devoted to political or social issues. Online chat rooms can blossom into fully-formed support groups that help people overcome adversities and promote justice.

4.3 Participate responsibly in online discourse by understanding intellectual property rights and by constructing an ethical persona.

CONCEPT 4.3 Responsible participation in online discourse requires understanding intellectual property rights and constructing an ethical persona.

To understand concerns about "intellectual property," consider the student-produced scientific poster that reports a student team's findings about gender stereotypes in Mickey Mouse versus SpongeBob Squarepants cartoons (p. 226). In the upper corners of their original poster, the students included a downloaded image of a smiling SpongeBob Squarepants as well as an iconic image of Mickey

Mouse. Our reproduction of the poster in this text omits these images because the copyright owners refused to grant us permission to use them. Probably these corporate copyright owners would grant a "fair use" exception to students who download the images for a one-time class project that wasn't later posted to the Web, but they would certainly not grant this exception to a textbook company.

We say "probably" in the preceding sentence about student use of copyrighted images because "fair use" exceptions to copyright laws are continually being tested in court and often remain uncertain and evolving. Intellectual property laws often seem undemocratic to digital natives who consider downloading and remixing of Web materials as artistic "sharing." Many Web authors in fact seem uninterested in intellectual property rights. They may not even take credit for their work, choosing to publish under a pseudonym or by first name only. A growing community of Web authors, committed to what has come to be called the "creative commons," embrace a view of originality as **remixing**—combining or editing existing materials to produce something new. According to filmmaker Kirby Ferguson, who advocates for the creative commons, "Everything is a remix" (see the epigraph to this chapter).

It's no wonder that for many students traditional rules about intellectual property or plagiarism seem opposed to their own personal experience in reading and writing online. They've grown up in a digital culture marked by video sharing sites such as Flickr and YouTube and by "blurred authorship" media that includes CNN iReports (where every citizen is a news reporter with a camera) and shows like *Ridiculousness* or *Tosh.O,* which cite their video sources by first name only if at all. This is a culture of sampling, remixing, and mashups, where it seems impossible to mark off someone's "intellectual property." Nevertheless, the issue of intellectual property and plagiarism is real as evidenced by disputes about plagiarism in print texts or disputes in the music industry, where the desire of individuals to download songs for free on the Web conflicts with the rights of artists to profit financially from their intellectual work.

Understanding Issues of Copyright, Fair Use, and Creative Commons Licenses

Although it takes a lawyer to understand the intricacies of copyright law, ethical students need to be familiar with the issues surrounding intellectual property:

See also the discussion of plagiarism in Chapter 22, pp. 556–560

- ***Copyright laws*** The right to protection of one's intellectual property is guaranteed in the U.S. Constitution and, like patent law that protects inventions, is essential for providing financial reward to creative people for their work. Copyright laws cover nonfiction articles and books, fictional works including plays and poems, film scripts, paintings, drawings, photographs, videos, music, dance, sculpture, print or digital designs, computer programs, and any other kind of intellectual or creative work. Copyright laws are particularly enforced in commercial situations to prevent one person from using a second person's work for financial gain without the second person's knowledge and permission. Copyright laws tend to see "borrowing" as "stealing."
- ***Fair use*** Fair use doctrine specifies occasions where someone can use another person's work without permission. Fair use, however, always requires

citation and attribution—that is, the person must identify work done by others, credit that work, and cite the source from which the borrowed material was obtained. For multimodal projects produced for a class assignment, fair use doctrine usually allows students one-time use of copyrighted material, but it does not allow the student to "publish" the project on the Web.

- ***Creative commons*** The digital age has given rise to a highly democratic community of writers and artists who have formed what is called a "creative commons." (To learn more, type "creative commons" into your Web search engine.) These writers and artists wish to make their works freely available for downloading and remixing so long as the purposes are non-commercial and the borrowers properly acknowledge and cite their sources. A well known creative common site for images is Flickr, which allows you to use images for free without having to obtain written permission from the copyright holder. You must, however, cite the source according to the level of restrictions specified for each image on the Flickr site.

Using Images and Sound Ethically in Your Multimodal Projects

The ethics of multimodal production involves three principles: Get permission from any persons whom you photograph or audio-record; compile a complete bibliography of all borrowed texts, images, and sounds that you use in your work; and follow all intellectual property laws as they apply to your particular situation, rhetorical context, and source.

Obtaining Permission The first two of these principles apply in all situations. Anytime you take your own photographs, shoot your own videos, or audio-record sounds or voices, you need permission from the people being photographed or audio-recorded. (If they are under 18 years of age, you must get a parent's permission.)

Bibliographic instructions for documenting sources are shown on pp. 563–576 (MLA) and 577–583 (APA).

Compiling a Complete Bibliography You must also be meticulous in citing the source of all material that you borrow from others—verbal text from other people's work (see discussion of plagiarism, pp. 556–560); images, videos, or music downloaded from the Web; photographs scanned into your own files; your own CD or vinyl music collections; and so forth.

When you submit a multimodal project, include a complete bibliography of all sources. In videos or photo galleries, you can include the bibliography in final credits or as a final slide.

Following Intellectual Property Law The third of these principles requires you to negotiate the distinction between copyright law, which requires permission from the copyright holder, and possible exceptions to copyright law allowed by "fair use" or the creative commons. If you produce a multimodal project for a course assignment and submit it as a one-time class project in print form (a brochure, a poster), on a jump drive or CD, or on a password protected course Web site, then your project may meet the criteria for fair use. If you publish your project on the Web, however, full national and international copyright law is apt to apply. You will need to consult your instructor for guidance.

Creating an Ethical Online Persona

In addition to ethical use of sources, online ethics includes other considerations. As we all know, sometimes people say—or write—things they don't really mean. And sometimes the anonymity of the Web (if we compose under a pseudonym or an avatar) can bring out our dark sides, leading to mean-spirited flaming, to name-calling, or even to cyber-bullying. In many cases, it is not our dark sides that we later regret expressing, but simply our impolite or non-respectful selves. For example, we may create offensive stereotypes of political opponents—stereotypes that may play well on a Web site that attracts mostly like-minded people, but that may be deeply offensive to readers you weren't anticipating. Thus, given the instantaneous and global nature of the Web, writers can easily publish something online they might later regret. Because writing online is not usually restrained by editorial oversight, authors must become their own editors—not only for thought-intensive blog posts but for the most hastily composed tweet, status update, or e-mail.

In our view, it is not okay to write something offensive online and imagine that no one on the other side is affected by what you say. The democratic potential of the Web depends on promoting communication across differences rather than shutting people off into their own self-selected portion of the Web. You can be an agent for change simply by creating an online persona who listens to others respectfully and advances conversations with politeness and integrity. (For what we might call "problematic personae," see the cartoon in Figure 4.2.)

FIGURE 4.2 Problematic Online Personae

We end this chapter by inviting you to think more fully about your own online persona. If you compose regularly on the Web, you will find it all too easy to move in and out of "multiple personalities." Writers may take on a different persona for each different writing situation—a persona for their Facebook presence, a different persona for writing product reviews, a still different persona for blogging or for posting comments on someone else's blog. However, we suggest that it is good for new Web writers to avoid "multiple personality disorder." Writers will be taken more seriously in the long run if they build toward an overall body of work characterized by a consistent, respectful, and sustainable persona.

Chapter Summary

This chapter has introduced you to three rhetorical concepts useful for analyzing and producing multimodal and other online texts.

- ***Concept 4.1 Composers of multimodal texts use words, images, and sounds rhetorically to move an audience.*** Online communication is typically hyperlinked and multimodal so that it is difficult for authors to predict how viewers will navigate their work. Web communicators have to hook audiences quickly and then keep them engaged with high level content. Effective messages often combine verbal text with rhetorically effective images and sounds that make immediate appeals to *pathos, logos,* and *ethos*. Effective videos combine the rhetorical power of still images with the storytelling effect of moving images and sound.
- ***Concept 4.2 Online environments are rhetorically interactive with shifting audiences, purposes, genres, and authorial roles.*** Online communication frequently destabilizes all three points of the rhetorical triangle—audience, writer, and message. Audiences for online texts can shift rapidly because a reader can forward messages to new readers or post a message to a new site. The "writer" of on online text can be blurred through communally produced wiki texts or through the anonymity of pseudonyms and avatars. Online messages are ephemeral, frequently revised, and nuanced through the cumulative effect of posted reader responses. Also different genres and media (such as e-mail, blogs, Facebook, or Twitter) invite different purposes and authorial roles.
- ***Concept 4.3 Responsible participation in online discourse requires understanding of intellectual property rights and the construction of an ethical online persona.*** Because online environments celebrate sampling and remixing while blurring boundaries of intellectual property, responsible Web communicators must respect copyright laws, understand when fair use exceptions may be permissible, and appreciate the democratic value of creative commons sites. Additionally, multimodal texts must be accompanied by a complete bibliography of all borrowed texts, images, and sounds. Finally, responsible Web communicators should try to create a respectful, consistent online persona that promotes dialog across differences.

Option 1: Description and Reflection on Your Online Communications

Consider recent examples of your own online communications (writing a blog, posting comments on a blog or news site, posting a product or book review, maintaining a Facebook page, collaborating on a Wiki, sending a tweet, or even sending e-mails). Consider also any responses you may have received from these communications.

- Part 1. Describe one or more of these communications. What was the occasion? What was your purpose or motivation? Who was your targeted audience? What was the content of the message (in summary form)? What effort went into the communication in terms of planning or drafting? What responses did you receive, if any?
- Part 2. Reflect on these online experiences based on the ideas and concepts in this chapter. How much did you think about audience and purpose as you composed your communication? What persona were you conscious of trying to convey? What kind of audience response did you anticipate or hope for? What kinds of insights into your experience have you gotten from this chapter? How might the concepts in this chapter influence your online communications from here on?

Option 2: Description and Reflection on Your Creation of a Multimodal Composition

If you have ever created a multimodal text (involving any combination of verbal text, images, video, or sound), either for a class or for personal reasons, this brief assignment asks you to describe your creation and reflect on it.

- Part 1. Describe the multimodal text that you created—for example, a poster or brochure, a research report that incorporated graphs and images, a podcast, a video, a slideshow set to music, and so forth). Describe your multimodal creation. What was its core message? What was its rhetorical context—your purpose, and audience? What were you trying to accomplish with this multimodal text?
- Part 2. Reflect on why you designed it the way you did and on the responses that you received. Particularly explain the challenges of creating this text and the effect you wanted this text to have on your audience. Think about the concepts in this chapter and explain which ones particularly relate to the challenges you faced and the degree of success you had with this text.

WRITING PROJECTS

PART 2

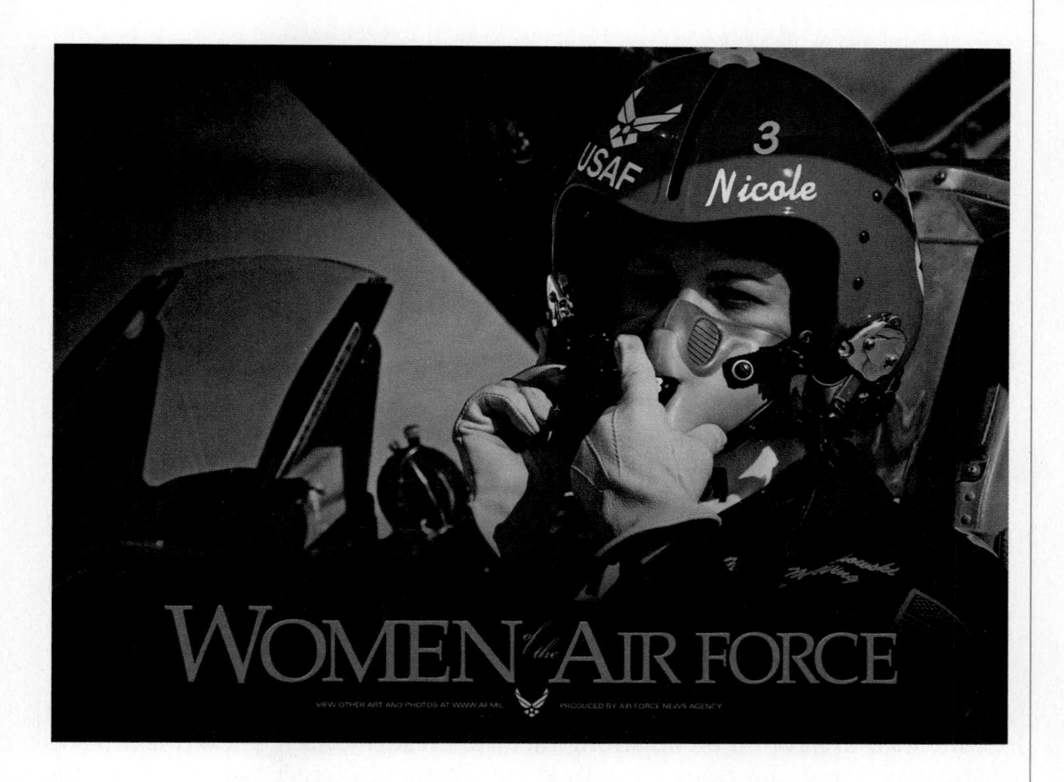

This U.S. Air Force poster represents a strong voice in the ongoing national discussion of women's role in the military. In 2013, the Pentagon lifted the ban on women in combat, recognizing their active role and high performance in modern irregular warfare. However, opponents continue to argue that women lack the fitness and stamina to keep up with men and that they compromise the standards and morale of fighting units. Examine the image of this woman carefully—how she looks and what she is doing. To what extent does this poster support gender equality, the argument that women can play key roles in combat operations? To what extent does it complicate our response to the issue of women's leadership roles in modern warfare? This poster speaks back to the readings on women in combat in Chapter 13, pages 340–353.

5 READING RHETORICALLY

The Writer as Strong Reader

WHAT YOU WILL LEARN

5.1 To carefully read a text, analyze its parts and their functions, and summarize its ideas.

5.2 To write strong responses to texts by interacting with them, either by agreeing with, questioning, or actively challenging them.

Many new college students are surprised by the amount, range, and difficulty of reading they have to do in college. Every day they are challenged by reading assignments ranging from scholarly articles and textbooks on complex subject matter to primary sources such as Plato's dialogues or Darwin's *Voyage of the Beagle.*

To interact strongly with challenging texts, you must learn how to read them both with and against the grain. When you read *with the grain* of a text, you see the world through its author's perspective, open yourself to the author's argument, apply the text's insights to new contexts, and connect its ideas to your own experiences and personal knowledge. When you read *against the grain* of a text, you resist it by questioning its points, raising doubts, analyzing the limits of its perspective, or even refuting its argument.

We say that readers read *rhetorically* when they are aware of the effect a text is intended to have on them. Strong rhetorical readers analyze how a text works persuasively, and they think critically about whether to accede to or challenge the text's intentions. The two writing projects in this chapter, both of which demand rhetorical reading, introduce you to several of the most common genres of academic writing: the **summary**, and various kinds of **strong response essays**, which usually incorporate a summary of the text to which the writer is responding. This chapter will help you become a more powerful reader of academic texts, prepared to take part in the conversations of the disciplines you study.

Engaging Rhetorical Reading

Imagine that you are investigating different strategies that individual Americans might take to protect the environment. In doing your research, you have encountered Michael Pollan's 2008 article, "Why Bother?" from the *New York Times Magazine.*

Pollan, a professor of journalism at the University of California Berkeley Graduate School of Journalism, is known for his popular books on reforming our food production system for the benefit of humans, animals, and the environment: *The Omnivore's Dilemma: A Natural History of Four Meals* (2007), *In Defense of Food: An Eater's Manifesto* (2009), and *Food Rules* (2010). Shortly we'll ask you to read Pollan's article, but before you do so, respond to the following opinion survey, using a 1 to 5 scale, with 1 meaning "strongly agree" and 5 meaning "strongly disagree."

Item	Strongly agree	Agree	Neutral	Disagree	Strongly disagree
1. Global warming is a very serious problem.	1	2	3	4	5
2. Going green in my own lifestyle will have no effect on climate change—the magnitude of the problem is too great.	1	2	3	4	5
3. The only way to make a real difference in climate change is through hugely expensive actions taken by governments and businesses.	1	2	3	4	5
4. The best way to combat global warming is for individual Americans to go green in their own consumer choices.	1	2	3	4	5
5. Environmentally conscious people should change the way they eat.	1	2	3	4	5

Once you have finished rating your degree of agreement with these statements, please read Pollan's article on pages 114–119. (We'll refer to Pollan's article regularly throughout this chapter.) As you read, use whatever note-taking, underlining, or highlighting strategies you normally use when reading for a class. When you have finished reading, please explore how this article may have influenced your ideas about what we might do to combat global warming.

ON YOUR OWN

1. In three or four sentences, summarize Michael Pollan's main points.
2. Freewrite a response to these questions: In what way has Pollan's article caused me to reconsider one or more of my answers to the survey above? From my perspective, what are the most insightful or provocative points in the article? If I were engaging Pollan in conversation, which of his views would I agree with? Where would I raise questions, doubts, or counterarguments?

IN CONVERSATION

1. To help you become more aware of your thinking processes as you read, compare your note-taking strategies with those of your classmates. How many people wrote marginal notes, underlined, or highlighted passages? Did people highlight the same passages or different ones? Why did you write or mark what you did?

2. What passages did you and your classmates choose as important? How did this article influence people's thinking about the impact of individual actions and lifestyles on climate change? As a result of reading Pollan's article, are you more apt to try growing some of your own vegetables either now or in the future?

5.1 Understanding Rhetorical Reading

5.1 Carefully read a text, analyze its parts and their functions, and summarize its ideas.

In this section, we explain why college-level reading is often difficult for new students and offer suggestions for improving your reading process based on the reading strategies of experts.

What Makes College-Level Reading Difficult?

The difficulty of college-level reading stems in part from the complexity of new subject matter. Whatever the subject—from international monetary policies to the intricacies of photosynthesis—you have to wrestle with new and complex materials that might perplex anyone. But in addition to the daunting subject matter, several other factors contribute to the difficulty of college-level reading:

- ***Vocabulary.*** Many college-level readings contain unfamiliar technical language such as the economic terms *assets*, or *export subsidy* or the philosophic terms *hermeneutics* or *Neo-Platonism*. Even nontechnical readings and civic writing for the general public can contain unfamiliar terms. For example, in the Pollan article, the literary term *doppelgänger* or the ecological terms *feedback loops* or *pollution-trading systems* may have given you pause. In academia, words often carry specialized meanings that evoke a whole history of conversation and debate that may be inaccessible, even through a specialized dictionary. Good examples might be *postmodernism, string theory,* or *cultural materialism.* You will not fully understand these terms until you are initiated into the disciplinary conversations that gave rise to them.
- ***Unfamiliar rhetorical context.*** As we explained in Part 1, writers write to an audience for a purpose arising from some motivating occasion. Knowing an author's purpose, occasion, and audience may clarify confusing parts of a text. For example, Pollan's article was published in the *New York Times Magazine,* which attracts a liberal, well-educated audience. Pollan assumes that his audience already takes climate change seriously. In fact, they may be so overwhelmed with the problem that they are ready to give up. His purpose is to motivate them to action. A text's internal clues can sometimes help you fill in the rhetorical context, but often you may need to do outside research.
- ***Unfamiliar genre.*** You will encounter a range of genres such as textbooks, trade books, scholarly articles, scientific reports, historical documents, newspaper articles, op-ed pieces, and so forth. Each of these makes different demands on readers and requires a different reading strategy.
- ***Lack of background knowledge.*** Writers necessarily make assumptions about what their readers already know. For example, Pollan makes numerous references to popular culture (Al Gore's *An Inconvenient Truth*; "the Ed Begley Jr.

treatment"; "imported chops at Costco") or to general liberal arts knowledge (references to the economist Adam Smith or to the recent history of Communist Czechoslovakia and Poland). The more familiar you are with this cultural background, the more you will understand Pollan's argument on first reading.

FOR WRITING AND DISCUSSION

Appreciating the Importance of Background Knowledge

The importance of background knowledge is easily demonstrated any time you dip into past issues of a newsmagazine or try to read articles about an unfamiliar culture. Consider the following passage from a 1986 *Newsweek* article. How much background knowledge do you need before you can fully comprehend this passage? What cultural knowledge about the United States would a student from Ethiopia or Indonesia need?

> Throughout the NATO countries last week, there were second thoughts about the prospect of a nuclear-free world. For 40 years nuclear weapons have been the backbone of the West's defense. For almost as long American presidents have ritually affirmed their desire to see the world rid of them. Then, suddenly, Ronald Reagan and Mikhail Gorbachev came close to actually doing it. Let's abolish all nuclear ballistic missiles in the next 10 years, Reagan said. Why not all nuclear weapons, countered Gorbachev. OK, the president responded, like a man agreeing to throw in the washer-dryer along with the house.
>
> What if the deal had gone through? On the one hand, Gorbachev would have returned to Moscow a hero. There is a belief in the United States that the Soviets need nuclear arms because nuclear weapons are what make them a superpower. But according to Marxist-Leninist doctrine, capitalism's nuclear capability (unforeseen by Marx and Lenin) is the only thing that can prevent the inevitable triumph of communism. Therefore, an end to nuclear arms would put the engine of history back on its track.
>
> On the other hand, Europeans fear, a nonnuclear United States would be tempted to retreat into neo-isolationism.
>
> —Robert B. Cullen*

Working in small groups or as a class, identify words and passages in this text that depend on background information or knowledge of culture for complete comprehension.

Using the Reading Strategies of Experts

In Chapter 16, we describe the differences between the writing processes of experts and those of beginning college writers. There are parallel differences between the reading processes of experienced and inexperienced readers, especially when they encounter complex materials. In this strategies chart we describe some expert reading strategies for any kind of college-level material.

*From "Dangers of Disarming" by Robert B. Cullen and Scott Sullivan from Newsweek, October 27, 1986.

Strategies for Reading Like an Expert

Strategies	What to Do	Comments
Reconstruct the rhetorical context.	Ask questions about purpose, audience, genre, and motivating occasion.	If you read an article that has been anthologized (as in the readings in this textbook), note any information you are given about the author, publication, and genre. Try to reconstruct the author's original motivation for writing.
Take notes.	Make extensive marginal notes as you read.	Expert readers seldom use highlighters, which encourage passive, inefficient reading.
Get in the dictionary habit.	Look up words whose meaning you can't get from context.	If you don't want to interrupt your reading, check off words to look up when you are done.
Match your reading speed to your goals.	Speed up when skimming or scanning for information. Slow down for complete comprehension or detailed analysis.	Robert Sternberg, a cognitive psychologist, discovered that novice readers tend to read everything at about the same pace, no matter what their purpose. Experienced readers know when to slow down or speed up.
Read a complex text in a "multidraft" way.	Read a text two or three times. The first time, read quickly, skimming ahead rapidly, looking at the opening sentences of paragraphs and at any passages that sum up the writer's argument or clarify the argument's structure. Pay particular attention to the conclusion, which often ties the whole argument together.	Rapid "first-draft reading" helps you see the text's main points and structure, thus providing background for a second reading. Often, experienced readers reread a text two or three times. They hold confusing passages in mental suspension, hoping that later parts of the essay will clarify earlier parts.

Reading with the Grain and against the Grain

For an explanation of the believing and doubting game, see Chapter 2, Concept 2.1.

The reading and thinking strategies that we have just described enable skilled readers to interact strongly with texts. Your purpose in using these strategies is to read texts both *with the grain* and *against the grain*, a way of reading that is analogous to the believing and doubting game we introduced in Chapter 2. This concept is so important that we have chosen to highlight it separately here.

When you read with the grain of a text, you practice what psychologist Carl Rogers calls "empathic listening," in which you try to see the world through the author's eyes, role-playing as much as possible the author's intended readers by adopting their beliefs and values and acquiring their background knowledge. Reading with the grain is the main strategy you use when you summarize a text, but it comes into play also when you develop a strong response. When making with-the-grain points, you support the author's thesis with your own arguments and examples, or apply or extend the author's argument in new ways.

When you read against the grain of a text, you question and perhaps even rebut the author's ideas. You are a resistant reader who asks unanticipated questions, pushes back, and reads the text in ways unforeseen by the author. Reading against the grain is a key part of creating a strong response. When you make against-the-grain points, you challenge the author's reasoning, sources, examples, or choices of language. You present alternative lines of reasoning, deny the writer's values, or raise points or specific data that the writer has omitted. Strategies for thinking with the grain and against the grain are shown in the following chart, along with particular occasions when each is helpful.

Strategies for Reading with and against the Grain

Reading with the Grain	Reading against the Grain
• Listen to the text, follow the author's reasoning, and withhold judgment. • Try to see the subject and the world from the author's perspective. • Add further support to the author's thesis with your own points and examples. • Apply the author's argument in new ways.	• Challenge, question, and resist the author's ideas. • Point out what the author has left out or overlooked; note what the author has *not* said. • Identify what assumptions, ideas, or facts seem unsupported or inaccurate. • Rebut the author's ideas with counterreasoning and counterexamples.
Occasions When Most Useful	**Occasions When Most Useful**
• In writing summaries, you listen to a text without judgment to identify the main ideas. • In writing analyses, you seek to understand a text to determine points to elaborate on and discuss. • In synthesizing ideas from sources, you determine what ideas to adopt and build on. • In writing arguments, you inhabit an author's viewpoint to deepen your understanding of an issue and to understand alternative views so you can represent them fairly.	• In writing an initial strong response, you determine the ways in which your beliefs, values, and views might be different from the author's. • In writing analyses, you identify limitations in the author's view. • In synthesizing, you determine which ideas to reject, replace, or go beyond. • In writing arguments, you develop refutations and rebuttals to the author's views.

Strong readers develop their ability to read in both ways—with the grain and against the grain. Some readers prefer to separate these approaches by first reading a text with the grain and then rereading it with more against-the-grain resistance. Throughout the rest of this chapter, we show you different ways to apply these strategies in your reading and writing.

Understanding Summary Writing

A **summary** (often called an **abstract**) is a condensed version of a text that extracts and presents main ideas in a way that does justice to the author's intentions. As fairly and objectively as possible, a summary states the main ideas of a longer text, such as an article or even a book. Although the words "summary" and "abstract" are often used interchangeably, the term "abstract" is usually used for a stand-alone summary at the head of a published article. Scholars often present "abstracts" of their own work (that is, a summary of their argument) for publication in a conference program.

Usefulness of Summaries

Students often report later in their academic careers how valuable summary writing skills are. Summary writing fosters a close engagement between you and the text and demonstrates your understanding of it. By forcing you to distinguish between main and subordinate points, summary writing is a valuable tool for improving your reading comprehension. Summary writing is also useful in other ways. For example, summaries at the beginning of articles, in prefaces to books, and on book jackets help readers determine if they want to read the article or book. To participate in conferences, your professors—and perhaps you also—send abstracts of proposed papers to conference committees in hopes of getting the paper accepted for presentation. Engineers and business executives place "executive summaries" at the beginning of proposals of major reports. In the "literature review" section of scientific papers, summaries of previous research are used to demonstrate gaps in knowledge that the present researchers will try to fill. Finally, writing summaries is a particularly important part of research writing, where you often present condensed views of other writers' arguments, either in support of your own view or as alternative views that you are analyzing or responding to.

The Demands that Summary Writing Makes on Writers

Even though summaries are short, they are challenging to write. You must distinguish between the main and subordinate points in a text, and you must provide even coverage of the text. You must also convey clearly the main ideas—ideas that are often complex—in a limited number of words. Often, summaries are written to certain specifications, say, one-tenth of the original article, or 200 words, or 100 words.

One of the biggest challenges of summarizing is framing the summary so that readers can easily tell your own ideas from those of the author you are summarizing. Often, you are incorporating a summary into a piece of writing as a basis of your own analysis or argument, so this distinction is particularly important. You make this distinction by using frequent **attributive tags** (sometimes called "signal phrases") such as "Pollan claims," "according to Pollan," or "Pollan says"; by putting quotation marks around any passages that use the writer's original wording; and by citing the article using the appropriate documentation style. Typically, writers also introduce the summary with appropriate contextual information giving the author's name and perhaps also the title and genre (in research writing, this information is repeated in the "Works Cited" or "References" list). The first sentence of the summary typically presents the main idea or thesis of the entire article. Here is an example summary of the Pollan article using MLA citation and documentation style.

Chapter 22 provides additional instruction in summarizing, paraphrasing, and quoting sources. It also explains how to incorporate sources smoothly into your own writing and avoid plagiarism.

Summary of "Why Bother?"

In "Why Bother?" published in the *New York Times Magazine*, environmental journalist Michael Pollan asks why, given the magnitude of the climate change problem, any individual should bother to go green, and argues that an individual's actions can bring multiple rewards for individuals, society, and the environment. Explaining that "the warming and the melting" (115) are occurring much faster than earlier models had predicted, Pollan acknowledges the apparent powerlessness of individuals to make a difference. Not only are we uncertain what actions to take to preserve the planet, but we realize that whatever we do will be offset by growing carbon emissions from emerging nations. Our actions will be "too little too late" (115). He asserts that our environmental problem is a "crisis of lifestyle"—"the sum total of countless little everyday choices" (116) made possible by cheap fossil fuel, which has led to our increasingly specialized jobs. Nevertheless, to counteract our practical and moral distance from the environment caused by this specialization, Pollan urges individuals to go green. Although he concedes that "'laws and money'" (116) are necessary, he still believes that individual actions may be influential by setting off a "process of viral social change" (118). A particularly powerful act, he claims, is to convert yards into vegetable gardens. Growing your own vegetables, he argues, will help us overcome "specialization," eat locally, reduce carbon emissions, get healthy exercise, reconnect with neighbors, and restore our relationship with the earth. (227 words)

Identification of the article, journal, and author

Gives overview summary of whole article

Attributive tag

Short quotations from article, MLA documentation style; number in parentheses indicates page number of original article where quotation is found

Bibliographic citation for Pollan's article using MLA style. In a formal paper, the "Works Cited" list begins on a new page at the end of the paper.

Work Cited

Pollan, Michael. "Why Bother?" *New York Times Magazine* 20 Apr. 2008: 19+. Rpt. in *The Allyn and Bacon Guide to Writing.* John D. Ramage, John C. Bean, and June Johnson. 7th ed. New York: Pearson, 2015, 114–19. Print.

Note in this example how the use of attributive tags, quotation marks, and citations makes it easy to tell that the writer is summarizing Pollan's ideas rather than presenting his own. Note too the writer's attempt to remain neutral and objective and not to impose his own views. To avoid interjecting your own opinions, you need to choose your verbs in attributive tags carefully. Consider the difference between "Smith argues" and "Smith rants" or between "Brown asserts" and "Brown leaps to the conclusion that...." In each pair, the second verb, by moving beyond neutrality, reveals the writer's judgment of the author's ideas.

In an academic setting, then, think of summaries as short, tightly written pieces that retain an author's main ideas while eliminating the supporting details. In the writing projects for this chapter, we'll explain the strategies you can use to write a good summary. The following chart lists the criteria for incorporating a summary effectively into your own prose.

CRITERIA FOR AN EFFECTIVE SUMMARY INCORPORATED INTO YOUR OWN PROSE

- Represents the original article accurately and fairly.
- Is direct and concise, using words economically.
- Remains objective and neutral, not revealing the writer's own ideas on the subject, but, rather, only the original author's points.
- Gives the original article balanced and proportional coverage.
- Uses the writer's own words to express the original author's ideas.
- Distinguishes the summary writer's ideas from the original author's ideas by using attributive tags (such as "according to Pollan" or "Pollan argues that").
- Uses quotations sparingly, if at all, to present the original author's key terms or to convey the flavor of the original.
- Is a unified, coherent piece of writing in its own right.
- Cites and documents the text the writer is summarizing and any quotations used according to an appropriate documentation system.

FOR WRITING AND DISCUSSION

Determining What Is a Good Summary

This exercise asks you to work with the "Criteria for an Effective Summary Incorporated into Your Own Prose" (above) as you analyze the strengths and weaknesses of three summaries of the same article: "Protect Workers' Rights" by Bruce Raynor, published in the *Washington Post* on September 1, 2003. Imagine three student writers assigned to summarize this editorial in approximately 200 words. The first of the summaries below we have rated as excellent. Read the excellent summary first and then determine how successful the other summaries are.

SUMMARY 1 (AN EXCELLENT SUMMARY OF THE RAYNOR ARTICLE)

In Bruce Raynor's op-ed article "Protect Workers' Rights," originally published in the *Washington Post* on September 1, 2003, union official Raynor argues that workers everywhere are threatened by the current rules of globalization that allow corporations and governments to seek out the cheapest and least regulated labor around the world. Using the example of the Pillowtex Corporation that recently shut down its plant in Kannapolis, North Carolina, he shows how ending manufacturing that has played a long and major role in the economies of towns leaves workers without severance pay, medical insurance, money to pay taxes and mortgages, and other options for employment. According to Raynor, in the last three years, millions of jobs have been lost in all branches of American manufacturing. While policymakers advise these workers to seek education to retool for white-collar jobs, Raynor points out that fields such as telemarketing and the computer industry are also losing millions of jobs. Furthermore, outsourcing has caused a drop in wages in the United States. The same dynamic of jobs moving to countries with cheaper and less stringent safety and health regulation has recently caused Mexican and Bangladeshi workers to lose their jobs to Chinese workers. Raynor concludes with a call to protect the rights of workers everywhere by rewriting the "rules for the global economy" (A25). (214 words)

Work Cited

Raynor, Bruce. "Protect Workers' Rights." *Washington Post* 1 Sept. 2003: A25. Print.

SUMMARY 2

The closing of the Pillowtex Corporation's factories in the United States represents a loss of sixteen textile plants and about 6,500 jobs, according to Bruce Raynor, president of UNITE, a union of textile workers.

The workers left in Kannapolis, North Carolina, former home of one of the largest Pillowtex plants, are experiencing financial problems as they are unable to buy medical insurance, pay their taxes or mortgages or find other jobs.

Raynor argues that the case of the Pillowtex workers is representative of workers in other industries such as metals, papers, and electronics and that "this is the longest decline since the Great Depression" with about three million jobs gone in the last three years.

He then explains that white-collar jobs are not safe either because millions of jobs in telemarketing, claims adjusting, and even government are predicted to go overseas in the next five years. Furthermore, Raynor states that the possibility of outsourcing jobs leads to lowering of wages within the United States, as "outsourcing has forced down hourly wage rates by 10 percent to 40 percent for many U.S. computer consultants" (A25).

However, according to Raynor, the developing countries like Mexico and Bangladesh that have acquired manufacturing jobs are also threatened by countries like China who can offer employees who are willing to work for even lower wages and under worse conditions.

(*continued*)

Raynor concludes that "a prosperous economy requires that workers be able to buy the products that they produce" (A25) and that workers everywhere need to be protected. (251 words)

Work Cited

Raynor, Bruce. "Protect Workers' Rights." *Washington Post* 1 Sept. 2003: A25. Print.

SUMMARY 3

In his article "Protect Workers' Rights," Bruce Raynor, president of UNITE, a textile workers' union, criticizes free trade and globalization for taking away workers' jobs. Using the Pillowtex Corporation's closing of its plant in Kannapolis, North Carolina, as his prime example, Raynor claims that outsourcing has destroyed the economy of this town and harmed workers across the United States. Raynor threatens that millions of white-collar jobs are also being lost and going to be lost in the next five years. Raynor complains that the whole national and global economy is falling apart and is going to get worse. He implies that the only solution is to keep jobs here in the United States. He maintains that workers around the world are also suffering when factories are moved from one developing country to another that has even more favorable conditions for the corporations. Raynor naively fails to factor in the role of consumers and the pressures on corporations into his defense of workers' rights. Clearly, Raynor loves unions and hates corporations; he probably fears that he is going to lose his own job soon. (183 words)

Understanding Strong Response Writing

We have said that the summary or abstract is an important academic genre and that summary writing is an essential academic skill. Equally important is strong response writing in which you identify and probe points in a text, sometimes by examining how a piece is written and often by inserting your own ideas into the text's conversation. "Strong response" is an umbrella term that incorporates a wide variety of ways that you can speak back to a text. In all cases, you are called on to do your own critical thinking by generating and asserting your own responses to the text.

In this section we will explain four different genres of strong response writing:

- Rhetorical critique
- Ideas critique
- Reflection
- Blended version of all three of these

Strong Response as Rhetorical Critique

A strong response as **rhetorical critique** analyzes a text's rhetorical strategies and evaluates how effectively the author achieves his or her intended goals. When writing a rhetorical critique, you discuss how a text is constructed, what rhetorical strategies it employs, and how effectively it appeals to *logos*, *ethos*, and *pathos*. In other words, you closely analyze the text itself, giving it the same close attention that an art critic gives a painting, a football coach gives a game video, or a biologist gives a cell formation. The close attention can be with the grain, noting the effectiveness of the text's rhetorical strategies, or against the grain, discussing what is ineffective or problematic about these strategies. Or an analysis might point out both the strengths and weaknesses of the text's rhetorical strategies.

For example, suppose that you are writing a rhetorical critique of an article from a conservative business journal advocating oil exploration in the Arctic National Wildlife Refuge (ANWR). You might analyze the article's rhetorical strategies by asking questions like these:

- How is the argument shaped to appeal to a conservative, business-oriented audience?
- How has the writer's angle of vision influenced the selection of evidence for his or her argument?
- How does the writer make himself or herself seem credible to this audience?

You would also evaluate the *logos* of the argument:

- How sound is the logic of the argument?
- Is the evidence accurate and current?
- What are the underlying assumptions and beliefs on which the argument is based?

Rhetorical critiques are usually closed-form, thesis-driven essays. The essay has a thesis that captures the writer's overall assessment of the text and maps out the specific points that the writer will develop in the analysis. When you are writing a rhetorical critique, your goal is to find a few rhetorical points that you find particularly intriguing, important, or disturbing to discuss and probe. Typically, your analysis zeroes in on some key features that you, the writer, find noteworthy. In the following strategies chart, we suggest the kinds of questions you can ask about a text to construct a rhetorical critique.

Question-Asking Strategies for Writing a Rhetorical Critique

Ask Questions about Any of the Following:	Examples
Audience and purpose: • Who is the intended audience? • What is the writer's purpose? • How well does the text suit its particular audience and purpose?	Examine how Michael Pollan writes to the well-educated audience of the *New York Times Magazine*, who are aware of climate change debates and most likely concerned about the problems ahead. Consider how Pollan writes to move these readers beyond good intentions to action. Examine how the text's structure, language, and evidence support this purpose.

(*continued*)

Ask Questions about Any of the Following:	Examples
Influence of genre on the shape of the text: • How has the genre affected the author's style, structure, and use of evidence?	Examine how the genre of the feature editorial for a highbrow magazine accounts for the length, structure, and depth of Pollan's argument. Examine how his references to political and intellectual figures (Al Gore, then Vice President Cheney, Adam Smith, Wendell Berry, and so forth) carry weight in this magazine's investigation of contemporary issues.
Author's style: • How do the author's language choices and sentence length and complexity contribute to the impact of the text?	Examine how Pollan's casual and cordial connections with readers (use of "I," "you," and "we"), his urgency, and his use of questions contribute to the article's effect.
Appeal to *logos*, the logic of the argument: • How well has the author created a reasonable, logically structured argument?	Examine how well Pollan uses logical points to support his claim and make his claim persuasive.
Use of evidence: • How reputable, relevant, current, sufficient, and representative is the evidence?	Examine how Pollan uses references to scientific articles, newspaper accounts, and his own experiences to develop his points.
Appeal to *ethos* and the credibility of the author: • How well does the author persuade readers that he/she is knowledgeable, reliable, credible, and trustworthy?	Examine how Pollan conveys his knowledge of environmentalism, economics, and social trends. Examine the effects of genre and style in creating this *ethos*. Examine whether this *ethos* is effective for readers who are not familiar with Pollan's other writing, are skeptical of climate change, or are less in tune with environmental activism.
Appeal to *pathos*: • How well does the writer appeal to readers' emotions, sympathies, and values?	Examine how Pollan seeks to tap his audience's values and feelings. Consider how he conveys his familiarity with the everyday choices and decisions facing his readers.
Author's angle of vision: • How much does the author's angle of vision or interpretive filter dominate the text, influencing what is emphasized or omitted?	Examine how Pollan's angle of vision shapes his perspective on climate change, his choice of activist solutions, and his development of solutions. Consider how Pollan's reputation as the author of a number of books on food system reform influences his focus in this argument.

For a rhetorical critique, you would probably not choose all of these questions but would instead select three or four to highlight. Your goal is to make insightful observations about how a text works rhetorically and to support your points with examples and short quotations from the text.

Strong Response as Ideas Critique

A second kind of strong response, the **ideas critique**, focuses on the ideas at stake in the text. Rather than treat the text as an artifact to analyze rhetorically (as in a rhetorical critique), you treat it as a voice in a conversation—one perspective on an issue or one solution to a problem or question. Your strong response examines how the ideas of the original author mesh or conflict with your own. Based on your own critical thinking, personal experiences, and research, to what extent do you agree or disagree with the writer's thesis? A with-the-grain reading of a text would support all or some of the text's ideas, while also supplying additional evidence or extending the argument, perhaps applying it in a new context. An against-the-grain reading would challenge the writer's ideas, point out flaws and holes in the writer's thinking, and provide counterexamples and rebuttals. You might agree with some ideas and disagree with others in the text. In any case, in an ideas critique you speak back to the text from your own experience, background, reading, and thoughtful wrestling with the writer's ideas.

As an example, let's return to the article from the conservative business journal on drilling for oil in the ANWR. For an ideas critique, you would give your own views on oil exploration in the ANWR to support or challenge the writer's views, to raise new questions, and otherwise to add your voice to the ANWR conversation.

- You might supply additional reasons and evidence for drilling.
- You might oppose drilling in the ANWR by providing counterreasoning and counterexamples.
- You might propose some kind of synthesis or middle ground, where you would allow drilling in the ANWR but only under certain conditions.

When you write an ideas critique you are thus joining an important conversation about the actual subject matter of a text. Because much academic and professional writing focuses on finding the best solution to complex problems, this kind of strong response is very common. Usually this genre requires closed-form, thesis-governed prose. The following strategies chart suggests questions you can ask about a text to enter into its conversation of ideas.

Question-Asking Strategies for Writing an Ideas Critique

Questions to Ask	Examples
Where do I agree with this author? (with the grain)	Consider how you might amplify or extend Pollan's ideas. Build on his ideas by discussing examples where you or acquaintances have tried to change your lifestyle to lower carbon emissions. Show how these changes might have inspired others to do so.

(continued)

Questions to Ask	Examples
What new insights has this text given me? (with the grain)	Explore Pollan's ideas that the environmental crisis is at heart a "crisis of lifestyle" or that specialization leads to a disjuncture between our everyday acts and their environmental consequences. Explore Pollan's argument that individual actions may lead to a social revolution. Think of how your eating habits or relationship to gardens has or could contribute to reform.
Where do I disagree with this author? (against the grain)	Challenge Pollan's assumptions about the magnitude of the problem. Challenge Pollan's idea that individuals can make a difference. Challenge his assumptions that technological solutions won't work because we still will face a crisis of lifestyle. Challenge the practicality and value of his main solution—growing gardens.
What points has the author overlooked or omitted? (against the grain)	Recognize that Pollan overlooks the constraints that would keep people from gardening. Consider that Pollan chooses not to focus on problems of overpopulation, water shortage, or economic disruption caused by environmentalism.
What new questions or problems has the text raised? (with or against the grain)	Explain how Pollan minimizes the economic impact of environmental action and downplays the role of government and business. Consider how we might need to "change the system" rather than just change ourselves. Consider his apparent lack of interest in technological solutions to the energy crisis.
What are the limitations or consequences of this text? (with or against the grain)	Consider ways that Pollan excludes some of his readers even while reaching out to others. Consider how Pollan, given his books on food and his passion for replacing industrial food production with local food, has written a predictable argument. Consider what new ideas he brings to his readers.

Because critiques of ideas appear in many contexts where writers search for the best solutions to problems, this kind of thinking is essential for academic research. In writing research papers, writers typically follow the template "This other writer has argued A, but I am going to argue B." Often the writer's own view (labeled "B") results from the writer's having wrestled with the views of others. Because this kind of dialectic thinking is so important to academic and professional life, we treat it further in Chapter 7 on exploratory writing, in Chapter 12 on analysis and synthesis, and in Chapter 13 on classical argument. Each of these chapters encourages you to articulate alternative views and respond to them.

Strong Response as Reflection

A third kind of strong response is often called a "reflection" or a "reflection paper." (An instructor might say, for example, "Read Michael Pollan's article on climate change and write a reflection about it.") Generally, a **reflection** is an introspective genre; it invites you to connect the reading to your own personal experiences, beliefs, and values. In a reflection paper, the instructor is particularly interested in how the reading has affected you personally—what memories it has triggered, what personal experiences it relates to, what values and beliefs it has challenged, what dilemmas it poses, and so forth. A **reflection paper** is often more exploratory, open-ended, musing, and tentative than a rhetorical critique or an ideas critique, which is usually closed form and thesis governed.

To illustrate, let's consider how you might write a reflection in response to the article in the conservative business journal on drilling for oil in the ANWR. One approach might be to build a reflection around a personal conflict in values by exploring how the reading creates a personal dilemma:

- You might write about your own wilderness experiences, musing about the importance of nature in your own life.
- But at the same time, you might reflect on the extent to which your own life depends on cheap oil and acknowledge your own reluctance to give up owning a car.

In short, you want pristine nature and the benefits of cheap oil at the same time. Another quite different approach might be to reflect on how this article connects to discussions you are having in your other courses, say, the economic cost of individuals' and companies' going green. Here are some strategies you can use to generate ideas for a reflective strong response:

Question-Asking Strategies for Writing a Reflective Strong Response

Questions to Ask	Examples
What personal memories or experiences does this text trigger?	Explore how Pollan's article evokes memories of your own frustrations about or successes with "green" living. Have you ever tried to change your habits for environmental reasons? If so, how did you go about doing it? Would your changes have met Berry's and Pollan's criteria for a change of "lifestyle"?
What personal values or beliefs does this text reinforce or challenge?	Explore the extent to which you can or can't identify with Pollan, Al Gore, and others who are proclaiming the seriousness of climate change and advocating changes in lifestyle. To what extent does Pollan as a person of conviction spark your admiration?
What questions, dilemmas, or problems does this text raise for me?	Explore how Pollan has challenged readers to take actions that may be difficult for them. For instance, you may have arrived at other solutions or know groups or organizations that are contributing positively in other ways. Perhaps Pollan's level of commitment or his particular approach to living green disturbs you in some way.

(continued)

Questions to Ask	Examples
What new insights, ideas, or thoughts of my own have been stimulated by this text?	Explore any moments of enlightenment you had while reading Pollan. For example, perhaps his focus on individual action rather than on "laws and money" seems problematic to you. Perhaps there are other causes besides the environment that spur you to concern or to action. Perhaps you are now interested in exploring what inspires people to make major changes in how they live.

As you can tell from these questions, a reflective strong response highlights your own personal experiences and beliefs in conversation with the text. Whereas the focus of a rhetorical critique is on analyzing the way the text works rhetorically and the focus of an ideas critique is on taking a stance on the ideas at stake in the text, a reflective response focuses on the personal dimension of reading the text. Reflections call for a degree of self-disclosure or self-exploration that would be largely absent from the other kinds of strong responses.

Strong Response as a Blend

It should be evident that the boundaries among the rhetorical critique, ideas critique, and reflection overlap and that a strong response could easily blend features of each. In trying to decide how to respond strongly to a text, you often don't have to confine yourself to a pure genre but can mix and match different kinds of responses. You can analyze and critique a text's rhetorical strategies, show how the text challenges your own personal values and beliefs, and also develop your own stance on the text's ideas. In writing a blended response, you can emphasize what is most important to you, while not limiting yourself to only one approach.

Before we turn to the writing project for this chapter, we show you an example of a student's summary/strong response that is a blend of rhetorical critique, ideas critique, and personal reflection. Note that the essay begins by conveying the writer's investment in environmental conservation. It then summarizes Pollan's article. Following the summary, the student writer states his thesis, followed by his strong response, which contains both rhetorical points and points engaging Pollan's ideas.

Kyle Madsen (student)

Can a Green Thumb Save the Planet?

A Response to Michael Pollan

When I was a child, our household had one garbage can, in which my family and I would deposit all of our cardboard, plastic, glass, and paper waste. No one on my block had ever heard of recycling or using energy saving bulbs, and we never considered turning down our thermostats during the frozen winters and ice storms that swept our region from November to March. It wasn't that we didn't care about what we were doing to our environment. We just didn't know any better. However, once I got to college all that changed. My university's policies requested that students separate glass bottles and pizza boxes from plastic candy wrappers and old food containers. Thanks in large part to the chilling success of Al Gore's documentary *An Inconvenient Truth*, many of my old neighbors were starting to catch on as well, and now my home town is as devoted to its recycling as any major metropolitan area. Still, even though we as a country have come a long way in just a few years, there is a long way to go. Environmental journalist Michael Pollan in his article "Why Bother?" for the *New York Times Magazine* examines why working to slow the threat of climate change is such a daunting task.

Introduces topic/problem and shows writer's investment in caring for the environment

Identifies Pollan's article and Pollan's purpose

In "Why Bother?" Michael Pollan explores how we have arrived at our current climate change crisis and argues why and how we should try to change our individual actions. Pollan sums up the recent scientific evidence for rapid climate change and then focuses on people's feeling overwhelmed in the face of this vast environmental problem. He presents his interpretation of how we have contributed to the problem and why we feel powerless. Pollan asserts that the climate-change crisis is "the sum total of countless everyday choices" made by consumers globally and that it is "at its very bottom a crisis of lifestyle—of character, even" (116). Our reliance on "cheap fossil fuel" has contributed to both the problem and to our sense of helplessness. In the final part of his article, Pollan concedes that "laws and money" (90) are necessary to create change, but he still advocates acting on our values and setting an example, which might launch a green social revolution. According to Pollan, "The idea is to find one thing to do in your life that does not involve spending or voting . . . that will offer its own rewards" (93). He concludes by encouraging readers to plant gardens in order to reduce carbon emissions, to lessen our "sense of dependence and dividedness" (93)—to empower ourselves to contribute positively to our environment.

Summary of Pollan's article

Although Pollan has created an argument with strong logical, ethical, and emotional appeals, his very dominant angle of vision—seen in his assumptions, alarmist language, and exclusive focus on garden-growing—may fail to win neutral readers. I also think Pollan's argument loses impact by not discussing more realistic alternatives such as pursuing smart consumerism and better environmental education for children.

Thesis statement focused on rhetorical points here

Second part of thesis focused on ideas critique

Pollan builds a forceful case in his well-argued and knowledgeable interpretation of our climate-change problem as a "crisis of lifestyle—of character, even" (116). His frank confrontation of the problem of how to motivate people is compelling, especially when he admits the contrast between "the magnitude of the problem" and the "puniness" of individual action (114). Pollan both deepens his argument and constructs a positive *ethos* by drawing on the ideas of environmental ethicist Wendell Berry and classical economist Adam Smith to explain how modern civilization has developed through the division of labor (specialization), which has brought us many advantages but also cut us off from community and environmental responsibility. In this part of his argument, Pollan helps readers understand how our dependence on cheap oil and our lifestyle choices have enhanced our roles as limited, specialized producers and ma-

With-the-grain rhetorical point focused on the logos and ethos of Pollan's argument

(*continued*)

Brief reflective comment

jor consumers. Pollan's development of his theory of the "cheap-energy mind" (117) and his reasonable support of this idea are the strongest part of his argument and the most relevant to readers like me. I have thought that we have become small cogs in an overbearing machine of consumption and only larger cogs such as the government can have enough influence on the overall system to make change happen. From time to time, I have wondered what I as one person could really do. This sense of insignificance, which Pollan theorizes, has made me wait until my regular light bulbs burned out before considering replacing them with energy-efficient ones.

With-the-grain rhetorical point focused on the pathos *of Pollan's argument*

Another strength of Pollan's argument is the way he builds bridges to his audience through his appeals to *pathos.* He understands how overwhelmed the average person can feel when confronted with the climate-change problem. Pollan never criticizes his readers for not being as concerned as he is. Instead he engages them in learning with him. He explores with readers the suggestion of walking to work, a task on par with light bulb changing, when he writes, even if "I decide that I am going to bother, there arises the whole vexed question of getting it right. Is eating local or walking to work really going to reduce my carbon footprint?" (114–15). By asking questions like these, he speaks as a concerned citizen who tries to create a dialogue with his audience about the problem of climate change and what individuals can do.

Against-the-grain rhetorical point focused on angle of vision

However, despite his outreach to readers, Pollan's angle of vision may be too dominant and intense for some readers. He assumes that his *New York Times Magazine* readers already share his agreement with the most serious views of climate change held by many scientists and environmentalists, people who are focusing on the "truly terrifying feedback loops" (115) in weather and climate. He also assumes that his readers hold similar values about local food and gardening. This intense angle of vision may leave out some readers. For example, I am left wondering why gardening is more effective than, say, converting to solar power. He also tries to shock his readers into action with his occasional alarmist or overly dramatic use of language. For example, he tries to invoke fear: "Have you looked into the eyes of a climate scientist recently? They look really scared" (115). However, how many regular people have run-ins with climate scientists?

Transition to ideas critique, an against-the-grain point critiquing Pollan's ideas—Pollan doesn't acknowledge the impracticality of expecting people to grow their own vegetables.

In addition, after appearing very in tune with readers in the first part of his argument, in the final part he does not address his readers' practical concerns. He describes in great detail the joys of gardening—specifically how it will connect readers not only to the earth, but to friends and neighbors as well—yet he glosses over the amount of work necessary to grow a garden. He writes, "Photosynthesis still works so abundantly that in a thoughtfully organized vegetable garden (one planted from seed, nourished by compost from the kitchen and involving not too many drives to the gardening center), you can grow the proverbial free lunch" (118). However, not everyone has a space for a garden or access to a public one to grow tomatoes themselves, and it takes hours of backbreaking labor to grow a productive vegetable garden—hardly a free lunch. Average Americans work upwards of sixty hours per week, so it is unrealistic to expect them to spend their free time working in a garden. In not addressing readers' objections to gardening or suggesting other ways to mend our cheap oil values, I think Pollan proposes simply another situation for semi-concerned individuals to again say, "Why bother?"

Also, besides gardens, I think Pollan could emphasize other avenues of change such as sustainable consumerism. In different places in the article, he mentions that individuals can use their consumer lifestyles to achieve a more sustainable way of life, but he chooses to insist that gardening be the main means. I would have liked him to discuss how we as consumers could buy more fuel-efficient cars, avoid plastic packaging, drink tap water, and buy products from green industries. This "going green" trend has already taken root in many of America's top industries—at least in their advertising and public relations campaigns. We can't leave a Starbucks without inadvertently learning about what they are doing to offset global warming. But we consumers need to know which industries really are going green in a significant way so that we can spend our shopping dollars there. If Pollan is correct, environmentally conscientious consumers can demand a change from the corporations they rely on, so why not use the same consumerism that got us into this mess to get us out?

Another point critiquing Pollan's ideas. Madsen proposes sustainable consumerism as an alternative to gardening.

Besides sustainable consumerism, I think we should emphasize the promotion of better environmental education for our children. Curriculum in K–12 classrooms presented by teachers rather than information from television or newspapers will shape children's commitment to the environment. A good example is the impact of Recycle Now, an organization aimed at implementing recycling and global awareness in schools. According to Dave Lawrie, a curriculum expert featured on their Web site, "Recycling at school is a hands-on way to show pupils that every single person can help to improve the environment. Everyone in our school has played a part in making a difference." With serious education, kids will learn the habits of respecting the earth, working in gardens, and using energy-saving halogen bulbs, making sustainability and environmental stewardship a way of life.

Another point addressing Pollan's ideas—environmental education in the schools as an alternative to gardening.

While Pollan is correct in pushing us into action now, asking Americans to grow a garden, when changing a light bulb seems daunting, is an unrealistic and limited approach. However, Pollan persuasively addresses the underlying issues in our attitudes toward the climate crisis and works to empower readers to become responsible and involved. Whether it be through gardening, supporting green businesses, or education, I agree with Pollan that the important thing is that you learn to bother for yourself.

Short conclusion bringing closure to the essay.

Works Cited

Lawrie, Dave. "Bringing the Curriculum to Life." School Success Stories. *RecycleNow* 11 Nov. 2009. Web. 28 Feb. 2010.

Pollan, Michael. "Why Bother?" *New York Times Magazine* 20 Apr. 2008: 19+. Rpt. in *The Allyn and Bacon Guide to Writing*. John D. Ramage, John C. Bean, and June Johnson. 7th ed. New York: Pearson, 2015. 114–19. Print.

Citation of works cited in the essay using MLA format

In the student example just shown, Kyle Madsen illustrates a blended strong response that includes both a rhetorical critique of the article and some of his own views. He analyzes Pollan's article rhetorically by pointing out both the persuasive features of the argument and the limiting angle of vision of a worried environmentalist and extremely committed gardening enthusiast. He seconds some of Pollan's points with his own examples, but he also reads Pollan against the grain by suggesting how Pollan's word choice and fixation on gardening as a solution prevent him from developing ideas that might seem more compelling to some readers.

WRITING PROJECT — A Summary

5.2 Write strong responses to texts by interacting with them, either by agreeing with, questioning, or actively challenging them.

Write a summary of an article assigned by your instructor for an audience who has not read the article. Write the summary using attributive tags and providing an introductory context as if you were inserting it into your own longer paper (see the model on p. 89). The word count for your summary will be specified by your instructor. Try to follow all the criteria for a successful summary listed on page 90, and use MLA documentation style, including a Works Cited entry for the article that you are summarizing. (Note: Instead of an article, your instructor may ask you to summarize a longer text such as a book or a visual-verbal text such as a Web page or an advocacy brochure. We address these special cases at the end of this section.)

Generating Ideas: Reading for Structure and Content

Once you have been assigned an article to summarize, your first task is to read it carefully a number of times to get an accurate understanding of it. Remember that summarizing involves the essential act of reading with the grain as you figure out exactly what the article is saying. In writing a summary, you must focus on both a text's structure and its content. In the following steps, we recommend a process that will help you condense a text's ideas into an accurate summary. As you become a more experienced reader and writer, you'll follow these steps without thinking about them.

Step 1: The first time through, read the text fairly quickly for general meaning. If you get confused, keep going; later parts of the text might clarify earlier parts.

Step 2: Read the text carefully paragraph by paragraph. As you read, write gist statements in the margins for each paragraph. A *gist statement* is a brief indication of a paragraph's function in the text or a brief summary of a paragraph's content. Sometimes it is helpful to think of these two kinds of gist statements as "what it does" statements and "what it says" statements.* A "what it does" statement specifies the paragraph's function—for example, "summarizes an opposing view," "introduces another reason," "presents a supporting example," "provides

*For our treatment of "what it does" and "what it says" statements, we are indebted to Kenneth A. Bruffee, *A Short Course in Writing*, 2nd ed. (Cambridge, MA: Winthrop, 1980).

statistical data in support of a point," and so on. A "what it says" statement captures the main idea of a paragraph by summarizing the paragraph's content. The "what it says" statement is the paragraph's main point, in contrast to its supporting ideas and examples.

When you first practice detailed readings of a text, you might find it helpful to write complete *does* and *says* statements on a separate sheet of paper rather than in the margins until you develop the internal habit of appreciating both the function and content of parts of an essay. Here are *does* and *says* statements for selected paragraphs of Michael Pollan's article on climate change activism.

Paragraph 1: *Does:* Introduces the need for environmental action as a current problem that readers know and care about and sets up the argument. ***Says:*** We as individuals often wonder if our small, minor actions are worth doing in light of the magnitude of the climate change problem.

Paragraph 2: *Does:* Explores another reason why individuals may doubt whether individual actions could make a difference. ***Says:*** People willing to change their lifestyles to combat climate change may be discouraged by the increase in a carbon-emissions lifestyle in other parts of the world such as China.

Paragraph 8: *Does:* Expresses an alternative view, partially concedes to it, and asserts a counterview. ***Says:*** Although big money and legislation will be important in reversing climate change, the problem at its heart is a "crisis of lifestyle—of character" (116), and therefore will require the effort of individuals.

Paragraph 18: *Does:* Presents and develops one of Pollan's main reasons that concerned individuals should take personal action to fight climate change. ***Says:*** Setting an example through our own good environmental choices could exert moral influence here and abroad, on individuals and big business.

Writing a *says* statement for a paragraph is sometimes difficult. You might have trouble, for example, deciding what the main idea of a paragraph is, especially if the paragraph doesn't begin with a closed-form topic sentence. One way to respond to this problem is to formulate the question that you think the paragraph answers. If you think of chunks of the text as answers to a logical progression of questions, you can often follow the main ideas more easily. Rather than writing *says* statements in the margins, therefore, some readers prefer writing *says* questions. *Says* questions for the Pollan text may include the following:

- What are some of the biggest obstacles that discourage people from undertaking individual actions to fight climate change?
- Despite our excuses not to act, why is individual action still necessary?
- How is the problem of climate a "crisis of lifestyle"?
- What are the reasons we should "bother"?
- Why is growing one's own vegetable garden a particularly powerful individual act?

No matter which method you use—*says* statements or *says* questions—writing gist statements in the margins is far more effective than underlining or highlighting in helping you recall the text's structure and argument.

Step 3: Locate the article's main divisions or parts. In longer closed-form articles, writers often forecast the shape of their essays in their introductions or use their conclusions to sum up main points. For example, Pollan's article uses some forecasting and transitional statements to direct readers through its parts and main points. The article is divided into several main chunks as follows:

- Introductory paragraphs, which establish the problem to be addressed and describe the reasons that people don't take action to help slow climate change (paragraphs 1–5)
- Two short transitional paragraphs (a one-sentence question and a two-word answer) stating the author's intention to call for individual action in spite of the obstacles. These two paragraphs prepare the move into the second part of the article (paragraphs 6 and 7).
- A paragraph conceding to the need for action beyond the individual (laws and money) followed by a counterclaim that the climate change problem is a "crisis of lifestyle" (paragraph 8)
- Eight paragraphs developing Pollan's "crisis of lifestyle" claim, drawing on Wendell Berry and explaining the concepts of specialization and the "cheap-energy mind" that have led us into both the climate change problem and our feelings of inadequacy to tackle it (paragraphs 9–16)
- A transitional paragraph conceding that reasons against individual action are "many and compelling," but proposing better ways to answer the "why bother" question (paragraph 17)
- Two paragraphs developing Pollan's reasons for individual action—how individuals will influence each other and broader communities and lead to "viral social change" (paragraphs 18–19)
- Two paragraphs elaborating on the possibility of viral social change based on analogy to the end of Communism in Czechoslovakia and Poland and to various ways individuals might make significant changes in their lifestyles (paragraphs 20–21)
- Five paragraphs detailing Pollan's choice for the best solution for people to reduce their carbon emissions and make a significant environmental statement: grow gardens (paragraphs 22–26)

Instead of listing the sections of your article, you might prefer to make an outline or tree diagram of the article showing its main parts.

Drafting and Revising

Once you have determined the main points and grasped the structure of the article you are summarizing, combine and condense your *says* statements into clear sentences that capture the gist of the article. These shortened versions of your *says* statements will make up most of your summary, although you might mention the structure of the article to help organize the points. For example, you might say, "[Author's name] makes four main points in this article.... The article concludes with a call to action...." Because representing an article in your own words in a greatly abbreviated form is a challenge, most writers revise their sentences to find the clearest, most concise way to express the article's ideas accurately. Choose and use your words carefully to stay within your word limit.

The procedures for summarizing articles can work for book-length texts and visual-verbal texts as well. For book-length texts, your *does* and *says* statements may cover chapters or parts of the book. Book introductions and conclusions as well as chapter titles and introductions may provide clues to the author's thesis and subthesis to help you identify the main ideas to include in a book summary. For verbal-visual texts such as a public affairs advocacy ad, product advertisement, Web page, or brochure, examine the parts to see what each contributes to the whole. In your summary, help your readers visualize the images, comprehend the parts, and understand the main points of the text's message.

Plan to create several drafts of all summaries to refine your presentation and wording of ideas. Group work may be helpful in these steps.

FOR WRITING AND DISCUSSION

Finding Key Points in an Article

If the whole class or a group of students is summarizing the same article, brainstorm together and then reach consensus on the main ideas that you think a summary of that article should include to be accurate and complete. Then reread your own summary and check off each idea.

When you revise your summary, consult the criteria on page 90 in this chapter as well as the Questions for Peer Review that follow.

Questions for Peer Review

In addition to the generic peer review questions explained in Skill 16.4, ask your peer reviewers to address these questions:

1. In what way do the opening sentences provide needed contextual information and then express the overall thesis of the text? What information could be added or more clearly stated?
2. How would you evaluate the writer's representation and coverage of the text's main ideas in terms of accuracy, balance, and proportion? What ideas have been omitted or overemphasized?
3. Has the writer treated the article fairly and neutrally? If judgments have crept in, where could the writer revise?
4. How could the summary use attributive tags more effectively to keep the focus on the original author's ideas?
5. Has the writer used quotations sparingly and cited them accurately? Has the writer translated points into his or her own words? Has the writer included a Works Cited?
6. Where might the writer's choice of words and phrasing of sentences be revised to improve the clarity, conciseness, and coherence of the summary?

WRITING PROJECT

A Summary/Strong Response Essay

In response to a text assigned by your instructor, write a "summary/strong response" essay that incorporates a 150–250-word summary of the article. In your strong response to that reading, speak back to its author from your own critical thinking, personal experience, values, and, perhaps, further reading or research. Unless your instructor assigns a specific kind of strong response (rhetorical critique, ideas critique, or reflection), write a blended response in which you are free to consider the author's rhetorical strategies, your own agreement or disagreement with the author's ideas, and your personal response to the text. Think of your response as your analysis of how the text tries to influence its readers rhetorically and how your wrestling with the text has expanded and deepened your thinking about its ideas. As you work with ideas from the text, remember to use attributive tags, quotation marks for any quoted passages, and MLA documentation to distinguish your own points about the text from the author's ideas and language.

Exploring Ideas for Your Strong Response

Earlier in the chapter we presented the kinds of strong responses you may be asked to write in college. We also provided examples of the questions you can ask to generate ideas for different kinds of strong response. Your goal now is to figure out what you want to say. Your first step, of course, is to read your assigned text with the grain, listening to the text so well that you can write a summary of its argument. Use the strategies described in the previous writing project to compose your summary of the assigned text.

After you have written your summary, which demonstrates your full understanding of the text, you are ready to write a strong response. Because your essay cannot discuss every feature of the text or every idea the text has evoked, you will want to focus on a small number of points that enable you to bring readers a new, enlarged, or deepened understanding of the text. You may decide to write a primarily with-the-grain response, praising, building on, or applying the text to a new context, or a primarily against-the-grain response, challenging, questioning, and refuting the text. If your strong response primarily agrees with the text, you must be sure to extend it and apply the ideas rather than simply make your essay one long summary of the article. If your strong response primarily disagrees with the text and criticizes it, you must be sure to be fair and accurate in your criticisms. Here we give you some specific rereading strategies that will stimulate ideas for your strong response, as well as an example of Kyle Madsen's marginal response notes to Pollan's article (Figure 5.1).

See Chapter 1, Concept 1.2, for a discussion of audience analysis.

Strategies for Rereading to Stimulate Ideas for a Strong Response

Strategies	What to Do	Comments
Take notes.	Make copious marginal notes while rereading, recording both with-the-grain and against-the-grain responses.	Writing a strong response requires a deep engagement with texts. For example, in Figure 5.1, observe how Kyle Madsen's notes incorporate with-the-grain and against-the-grain responses and show him truly talking back to and interacting with Pollan's text.
Identify "hot spots" in the text.	Mark all hot spots with marginal notes. After you've finished reading, find these hot spots and freewrite your responses to them in a reading journal.	By "hot spot" we mean a quotation or passage that you notice because you agree or disagree with it or because it triggers memories or other associations. Perhaps the hot spot strikes you as thought provoking. Perhaps it raises a problem or is confusing yet suggestive.
Ask questions.	Write several questions that the text caused you to think about. Then explore your responses to those questions through freewriting, which may trigger more questions.	Almost any text triggers questions as you read. A good way to begin formulating a strong response is to note these questions.
Articulate your difference from the intended audience.	Decide who the writer's intended audience is. If you differ significantly from this audience, use this difference to question the author's underlying assumptions, values, and beliefs.	Your gender, age, class, ethnicity, sexual orientation, political and religious beliefs, interests, values, and so forth, may cause you to feel estranged from the author's imagined audience. If the text seems written for straight people and you are gay, or for Christians and you are a Muslim or an atheist, or for environmentalists and you grew up in a small logging community, you may well resist the text. Sometimes your sense of exclusion from the intended audience makes it difficult to read a text at all.

Michael Pollan

Why Bother?

Why bother? That really is the big question facing us as individuals hoping to do something about climate change, and it's not an easy one to answer. I don't know about you, but for me the most upsetting moment in *An Inconvenient Truth* came long after Al Gore scared the hell out of me, constructing an utterly convincing case that the very survival of life on earth as we know it is threatened by climate change. No, the really dark moment came during the closing credits, when we are asked to . . . change our light bulbs. That's when it got really depressing. The immense disproportion between the magnitude of the problem Gore had described and the puniness of what he was asking us to do about it was enough to sink your heart.

But the drop-in-the-bucket issue is not the only problem lurking behind the "why bother" question. Let's say I do bother, big time. I turn my life upside-down, start biking to work, plant a big garden, turn down the thermostat so low I need the Jimmy Carter signature cardigan, forsake the clothes dryer for a laundry line across the yard, trade in the station wagon for a hybrid, get off the beef, go completely local. I could theoretically do all that, but what would be the point when I know full well that halfway around the world there lives my evil twin, some carbon-footprint *doppelgänger* in Shanghai or Chongqing who has just bought his first car (Chinese car ownership is where ours was back in 1918), is eager to swallow every bite of meat I forswear and who's positively itching to replace every last pound of CO2 I'm struggling no longer to emit. So what exactly would I have to show for all my trouble?

A sense of personal virtue, you might suggest, somewhat sheepishly. But what good is that when virtue itself is quickly becoming a term of derision? And not just on the editorial pages of the *Wall Street Journal* or on the lips of the vice president, who famously dismissed energy conservation as a "sign of personal virtue." No, even in the pages of the *New York Times* and the *New Yorker*, it seems the epithet "virtuous," when applied to an act of personal environmental responsibility, may be used only ironically. Tell me: How did it come to pass that virtue—a quality that for most of history has generally been deemed, well, a virtue—became a mark of liberal softheadedness? How peculiar, that doing the right thing by the environment—buying the hybrid, eating like a locavore—should now set you up for the Ed Begley Jr. treatment.

Marginal notes (left): This idea is very direct and clear. / Short sentence sounds casual. / Another very informal statement. / Good word choice? Sounds prejudiced and alarmist. / This paragraph shows Pollan's liberal perspective.

Marginal notes (right): Informal speech. / Sounds like Pollan is talking to readers. / How I felt when I saw this film. / Helpful examples. / Look up this word. / Exaggerated statement? / Former Vice President Cheney? / What's the definition of this term?

FIGURE 5.1 Kyle Madsen's Marginal Response Notes

FOR WRITING AND DISCUSSION

Practicing Strong Response Reading Strategies

What follows is a short passage by writer Annie Dillard in response to a question about how she chooses to spend her time. This passage often evokes heated responses from our students.

> I don't do housework. Life is too short.... I let almost all my indoor plants die from neglect while I was writing the book. There are all kinds of ways to live. You can take your choice. You can keep a tidy house, and when St. Peter asks you what you did with your life, you can say, "I kept a tidy house, I made my own cheese balls."

Individual task: Read the passage and then briefly freewrite your reaction to it.

Group task: Working in groups or as a whole class, develop answers to the following questions:

1. What values does Dillard assume her audience holds?
2. What kinds of readers are apt to feel excluded from that audience?
3. If you are not part of the intended audience for this passage, what in the text evokes resistance?

Articulate Your Own Purpose for Reading

Although you usually read a text because you are joining the author's conversation, you might occasionally read a text for an entirely different purpose from what the author intended. For example, you might read the writings of nineteenth-century scientists to figure out what they assumed about nature (or women, or God, or race, or capitalism). Or suppose that you examine a politician's metaphors to see what they reveal about her values, or analyze *National Geographic* for evidence of political bias. Understanding your own purpose will help you read deeply both with and against the grain.

Writing a Thesis for a Strong Response Essay

A thesis for a strong response essay should map out for readers the points that you want to develop and discuss. These points should be risky and contestable; your thesis should surprise your readers with something new or challenging. Your thesis might focus entirely on with-the-grain points or entirely on against-the-grain points, but most likely it will include some of both. Avoid tensionless thesis statements such as "This article has both good and bad points."

See Chapter 2, Concept 2.2, for a discussion of surprising thesis statements.

Here are some thesis statements that students have written for strong responses in our classes. Note that each thesis includes at least one point about the rhetorical strategies of the text.

EXAMPLES OF SUMMARY/STRONG RESPONSE THESIS STATEMENTS

- In "The Beauty Myth," Naomi Wolf makes a very good case for her idea that the beauty myth prevents women from ever feeling that they are good enough; however, Wolf's argument is geared too much toward feminists to be persuasive for a general audience, and she neglects to acknowledge the strong social pressures that I and other men feel to live up to male standards of physical perfection.
- Although Naomi Wolf in "The Beauty Myth" uses rhetorical strategies persuasively to argue that the beauty industry oppresses women, I think that she overlooks women's individual resistance and responsibility.
- Although the images and figures of speech that Thoreau uses in his chapter "Where I Lived, and What I Lived For" from *Walden* wonderfully support his argument that nature is spiritually renewing, I disagree with his antitechnology stance and with his extreme emphasis on isolation as a means to self-discovery.
- In "Where I Lived, and What I Lived For" from *Walden*, Thoreau's argument that society is missing spiritual reality through its preoccupation with details and its frantic pace is convincing, especially to twenty-first century audiences; however, Thoreau weakens his message by criticizing his readers and by completely dismissing technological advances.
- Although the booklet *Compassionate Living* by People for the Ethical Treatment of Animals (PETA) uses the design features of layout, color, and image powerfully, its extreme examples, its quick dismissal of alternative views, and its failure to document the sources of its information weaken its appeal to *ethos* and its overall persuasiveness.

FOR WRITING AND DISCUSSION

Examining Thesis Statements for Strong Response Critiques

Working individually or in groups, identify the points in each of the thesis statements in the preceding section and briefly state them. Think in terms of the ideas you are expecting the writers to develop in the body of the essay. As a follow-up to this exercise, you might share in your groups your own thesis statements for your strong response essays. How clearly does each thesis statement lay out points that the writer will probe? As a group, discuss what new, important perspectives each thesis statement promises to bring to readers and how each thesis suits a rhetorical critique, ideas critique, or some combination of these.

Shaping and Drafting

A possible framework for a summary/response essay is shown in Figure 5.2. Most strong response essays call for a short contextualizing introduction to set up your analysis. In the essay on pages 98–101, student writer Kyle Madsen begins by reflecting on personal and societal changes in environmental

FIGURE 5.2 Framework for a Summary/Strong Response Essay

Introduction (usually one paragraph)	• Introduces the topic/problem/question that the article (or book, chapter, or piece) addresses • Conveys the writer's investment in the author's topic • Provides rhetorical context of the article and its question, and identifies the author and the author's title and purpose
Summary (one paragraph)	• Summarizes the article, chapter, or book, giving a balanced, accurate, concise, and neutral presentation of its main points
Thesis statement (forms its own paragraph or comes at the end of the summary)	• Presents the two or more rhetorical or ideas points that the writer will analyze and discuss in the body of the essay • Establishes the writer's perspective on the author's text • Often maps out the analysis and critique to follow, giving readers a clear sense of the direction and scope of the essay
Body section 1 (one or more paragraphs)	• Develops the first rhetorical or ideas point with examples from the text • Explains and discusses this point in a thorough critique with the writer's own perspective (and perhaps knowledge and personal experience, for an ideas critique)
Body section 2 (one or more paragraphs	• Develops the second rhetorical or ideas point with examples from the text • Explains and discusses this point in a thorough critique with the writer's own perspective (and perhaps knowledge and personal experience, for an ideas critique)
Body section 3, 4, etc., on additional rhetorical or ideas points (one or more paragraphs per main point)	• Continues the critique and analysis by explaining writer's ideas with examples and elaboration until all points in the thesis statement are fleshed out
Conclusion (usually a short paragraph)	• Might briefly recap the writer's points, but summarizes these ideas only if the essay is long and complex • Wraps up the critique and analysis to leave readers thinking about both the author's piece and the writer's strong response
Work Cited	• Gives an appropriate citation in MLA format for the text discussed in the paper and any other sources mentioned in the essay (often only one source to list)

awareness and then raises the question that Pollan will address: What challenges confront us in changing how we live? Student writer Stephanie Malinowski (pp. 121–123) uses a similar strategy. She begins by tapping into her readers' experiences with outsourcing, and then poses the question that

Thomas Friedman addresses in his op-ed piece: Should Americans support or question the practice of outsourcing?

Both student writers introduce the question addressed by the article they are critiquing, and both include a short summary of the article that gives readers a foundation for the critique before they present the points of the article they will address in their strong responses.

Each of the thesis statements in the preceding section as well as Kyle's and Stephanie's thesis statements identifies and maps out two or more points that readers will expect to see developed and explained in the body of the essay. In a closed-form, thesis-driven strong response, readers will also expect the points to follow the order in which they are presented in the thesis. If your strong response is primarily a rhetorical critique, your evidence will come mainly from the text you are analyzing. If your strong response is primarily an ideas critique, your evidence is apt to come from personal knowledge of the issue or from further reading or research. If your strong response is primarily reflective, much of your evidence will be based on your own personal experiences and inner thoughts. A blended response, of course, can combine points from any of these perspectives.

Each point in your thesis calls for a lively discussion, combining general statements and specifics that will encourage readers to see this text your way. Just as you do in your summary, you must use attributive tags to distinguish between the author's ideas and your own points and responses. In addition, you must document all ideas gotten from other sources as well as place all borrowed language in quotation marks or block indentations according to MLA format and include a Works Cited in MLA format. Most strong response essays have short conclusions—just enough commentary to bring closure to the essay.

Revising

In a summary/strong response essay, you may want to work on the summary separately before you incorporate it into your whole essay. Use the peer review questions for summaries (p. 90) for that part of your essay. You will definitely want to get feedback from readers to make your strong response as clear, thorough, and compelling as possible.

Questions for Peer Review

In addition to the generic peer review questions explained in Skill 16.4, ask your peer reviewers to address these questions:

1. How appealingly do the title and introduction of the essay set up the topic of critique, convey the writer's interest, and lay a foundation for the summary of the article and the writer's thesis?
2. How could the writer's thesis statement be clearer in presenting several focused points about the text's rhetorical strategies and ideas?
3. How could the body of the strong response follow the thesis more closely?

4. Where do you, the reader, need more clarification or support for the writer's points? How could the writer develop with-the-grain or against-the-grain points more appropriately?
5. Where could the writer work on the effectiveness of attributive tags, quotations, and documentation?

Multimodal or Online Options

WRITING PROJECT

1. **Summary/Strong Response to a Blog Post** Identify a blogger with a reputation for substantial, serious, in-depth analysis or commentary. Select a recent post from your chosen blogger (recent enough that the "comments" feature for this post is still open). Write a summary/strong response critique of your chosen post, and post your critique to the "comments" section of the blog, adapting your response to the conventions of responses on this site. Although all respondents will have read the original blog, a short summary of its argument will help frame your own response. Your goal is to contribute significantly to the conversation initiated by the blogger's original post.
2. **Online Book Review** Write a summary/strong response critique of a book and "publish" it as an online book review for a site such as Amazon or Goodread. Typically, online customer reviews are likely to be much shorter than an academic essay, so you need to plan the points you want to highlight. Writers contributing to these public online forums should be aware of their ethical responsibility. Customer reviews are a powerful marketing tool that can boost or hurt authors' sales and success. Take this responsibility seriously: Consider your *ethos* as a careful, insightful reader and insightful critic and make your review lively, interesting, and fair.

For understanding rhetorical issues connected to online and multimodal compositions, see Chapter 4, pp. 66–80.

Readings

Our first reading for this chapter is the article by Michael Pollan, which forms the basis of the examples for this chapter and is best read before you read the chapter.

Michael Pollan

Why Bother?

1 **Why bother?** That really is the big question facing us as individuals hoping to do something about climate change, and it's not an easy one to answer. I don't know about you, but for me the most upsetting moment in *An Inconvenient Truth* came long after Al Gore scared the hell out of me, constructing an utterly convincing case that the very survival of life on earth as we know it is threatened by climate change. No, the really dark moment came during the closing credits, when we are asked to... change our light bulbs. That's when it got really depressing. The immense disproportion between the magnitude of the problem Gore had described and the puniness of what he was asking us to do about it was enough to sink your heart.

2 But the drop-in-the-bucket issue is not the only problem lurking behind the "why bother" question. Let's say I do bother, big time. I turn my life upside-down, start biking to work, plant a big garden, turn down the thermostat so low I need the Jimmy Carter* signature cardigan, forsake the clothes dryer for a laundry line across the yard, trade in the station wagon for a hybrid, get off the beef, go completely local. I could theoretically do all that, but what would be the point when I know full well that halfway around the world there lives my evil twin, some carbon-footprint *doppelgänger* in Shanghai or Chongqing who has just bought his first car (Chinese car ownership is where ours was back in 1918), is eager to swallow every bite of meat I forswear and who's positively itching to replace every last pound of CO2 I'm struggling no longer to emit. So what exactly would I have to show for all my trouble?

3 A sense of personal virtue, you might suggest, somewhat sheepishly. But what good is that when virtue itself is quickly becoming a term of derision? And not just on the editorial pages of the *Wall Street Journal* or on the lips of the vice president,* who famously dismissed energy conservation as a "sign of personal virtue." No, even in the pages of the *New York Times* and the *New Yorker,* it seems the epithet "virtuous," when applied to an act of personal environmental responsibility, may be used only ironically. Tell me: How did it come to pass that virtue—a quality that for most of history has generally been deemed, well, a virtue—became a mark of liberal softheadedness? How peculiar, that doing the right thing by the environment—buying the hybrid, eating like a locavore—should now set you up for the Ed Begley Jr.* treatment.

4 And even if in the face of this derision I decide I am going to bother, there arises the whole vexed question of getting it right. Is eating local or walking to work really

* Jimmy Carter was the Democratic president (1977–1981) who supported environmental policies, world peace, and human rights.
* Pollan is referring to Dick Cheney, who served as George W. Bush's vice president from 2001 to 2009.
* Ed Begley, Jr., is a prominent television star who has his own green living reality TV show, *Living with Ed.* Begley has explored such topics as tapping the energy produced by people using exercise equipment.

going to reduce my carbon footprint? According to one analysis, if walking to work increases your appetite and you consume more meat or milk as a result, walking might actually emit more carbon than driving. A handful of studies have recently suggested that in certain cases under certain conditions, produce from places as far away as New Zealand might account for less carbon than comparable domestic products. True, at least one of these studies was co-written by a representative of agribusiness interests in (surprise!) New Zealand, but even so, they make you wonder. If determining the carbon footprint of food is really this complicated, and I've got to consider not only "food miles" but also whether the food came by ship or truck and how lushly the grass grows in New Zealand, then maybe on second thought I'll just buy the imported chops at Costco, at least until the experts get their footprints sorted out.

5 There are so many stories we can tell ourselves to justify doing nothing, but perhaps the most insidious is that, whatever we do manage to do, it will be too little too late. Climate change is upon us, and it has arrived well ahead of schedule. Scientists' projections that seemed dire a decade ago turn out to have been unduly optimistic: the warming and the melting is occurring much faster than the models predicted. Now truly terrifying feedback loops threaten to boost the rate of change exponentially, as the shift from white ice to blue water in the Arctic absorbs more sunlight and warming soils everywhere become more biologically active, causing them to release their vast stores of carbon into the air. Have you looked into the eyes of a climate scientist recently? They look really scared.

6 So do you still want to talk about planting gardens?

7 I do.

8 Whatever we can do as individuals to change the way we live at this suddenly very late date does seem utterly inadequate to the challenge. It's hard to argue with Michael Specter*, in a recent *New Yorker* piece on carbon footprints, when he says:

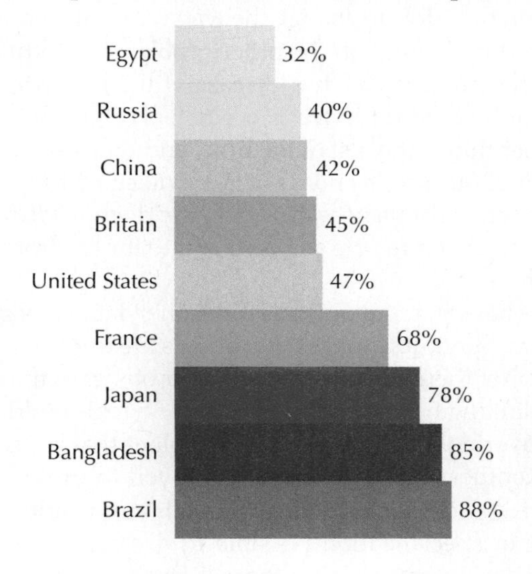

High Anxiety?
Percentage of people by country who view global warming as a "very serious" problem.

*Michael Specter is a staff writer for the *New Yorker* and a national science reporter, who has most recently written a book, *Denialism*, about people's refusal to accept scientific evidence.

"Personal choices, no matter how virtuous [N.B.!], cannot do enough. It will also take laws and money." So it will. Yet it is no less accurate or hardheaded to say that laws and money cannot do enough, either; that it will also take profound changes in the way we live. Why? Because the climate-change crisis is at its very bottom a crisis of lifestyle—of character, even. The Big Problem is nothing more or less than the sum total of countless little everyday choices, most of them made by us (consumer spending represents 70 percent of our economy), and most of the rest of them made in the name of our needs and desires and preferences.

9 For us to wait for legislation or technology to solve the problem of how we're living our lives suggests we're not really serious about changing—something our politicians cannot fail to notice. They will not move until we do. Indeed, to look to leaders and experts, to laws and money and grand schemes, to save us from our predicament represents precisely the sort of thinking—passive, delegated, dependent for solutions on specialists—that helped get us into this mess in the first place. It's hard to believe that the same sort of thinking could now get us out of it.

10 Thirty years ago, Wendell Berry, the Kentucky farmer and writer, put forward a blunt analysis of precisely this mentality. He argued that the environmental crisis of the 1970s—an era innocent of climate change; what we would give to have back *that* environmental crisis!—was at its heart a crisis of character and would have to be addressed first at that level: at home, as it were. He was impatient with people who wrote checks to environmental organizations while thoughtlessly squandering fossil fuel in their everyday lives—the 1970s equivalent of people buying carbon offsets to atone for their Tahoes and Durangos. Nothing was likely to change until we healed the "split between what we think and what we do." For Berry, the "why bother" question came down to a moral imperative: "Once our personal connection to what is wrong becomes clear, then we have to choose: we can go on as before, recognizing our dishonesty and living with it the best we can, or we can begin the effort to change the way we think and live."

11 For Berry, the deep problem standing behind all the other problems of industrial civilization is "specialization," which he regards as the "disease of the modern character." Our society assigns us a tiny number of roles: we're producers (of one thing) at work, consumers of a great many other things the rest of the time, and then once a year or so we vote as citizens. Virtually all of our needs and desires we delegate to specialists of one kind or another—our meals to agribusiness, health to the doctor, education to the teacher, entertainment to the media, care for the environment to the environmentalist, political action to the politician.

12 As Adam Smith and many others have pointed out, this division of labor has given us many of the blessings of civilization. Specialization is what allows me to sit at a computer thinking about climate change. Yet this same division of labor obscures the lines of connection—and responsibility—linking our everyday acts to their real-world consequences, making it easy for me to overlook the coal-fired power plant that is lighting my screen, or the mountaintop in Kentucky that had to be destroyed to provide the coal to that plant, or the streams running crimson with heavy metals as a result.

13 Of course, what made this sort of specialization possible in the first place was cheap energy. Cheap fossil fuel allows us to pay distant others to process our food for us, to entertain us and to (try to) solve our problems, with the result that there is very

little we know how to accomplish for ourselves. Think for a moment of all the things you suddenly need to do for yourself when the power goes out—up to and including entertaining yourself. Think, too, about how a power failure causes your neighbors—your community—to suddenly loom so much larger in your life. Cheap energy allowed us to leapfrog community by making it possible to sell our specialty over great distances as well as summon into our lives the specialties of countless distant others.

14 Here's the point: Cheap energy, which gives us climate change, fosters precisely the mentality that makes dealing with climate change in our own lives seem impossibly difficult. Specialists ourselves, we can no longer imagine anyone but an expert, or anything but a new technology or law, solving our problems. Al Gore asks us to change the light bulbs because he probably can't imagine us doing anything much more challenging, like, say, growing some portion of our own food. We can't imagine it, either, which is probably why we prefer to cross our fingers and talk about the promise of ethanol and nuclear power—new liquids and electrons to power the same old cars and houses and lives.

15 The "cheap-energy mind," as Wendell Berry called it, is the mind that asks, "Why bother?" because it is helpless to imagine—much less attempt—a different sort of life, one less divided, less reliant. Since the cheap-energy mind translates everything into money, its proxy, it prefers to put its faith in market-based solutions—carbon taxes and pollution-trading schemes. If we could just get the incentives right, it believes, the economy will properly value everything that matters and nudge our self-interest down the proper channels. The best we can hope for is a greener version of the old invisible hand. Visible hands it has no use for.

16 But while some such grand scheme may well be necessary, it's doubtful that it will be sufficient or that it will be politically sustainable before we've demonstrated to ourselves that change is possible. Merely to give, to spend, even to vote, is not to do, and there is so much that needs to be done—without further delay. In the judgment of James Hansen, the NASA climate scientist who began sounding the alarm on global warming 20 years ago, we have only 10 years left to start cutting—not just slowing—the amount of carbon we're emitting or face a "different planet." Hansen said this more than two years ago, however; two years have gone by, and nothing of consequence has been done. So: eight years left to go and a great deal left to do.

17 Which brings us back to the "why bother" question and how we might better answer it. The reasons not to bother are many and compelling, at least to the cheap-energy mind. But let me offer a few admittedly tentative reasons that we might put on the other side of the scale:

18 If you do bother, you will set an example for other people. If enough other people bother, each one influencing yet another in a chain reaction of behavioral change, markets for all manner of green products and alternative technologies will prosper and expand. (Just look at the market for hybrid cars.) Consciousness will be raised, perhaps even changed: new moral imperatives and new taboos might take root in the culture. Driving an S.U.V. or eating a 24-ounce steak or illuminating your McMansion like an airport runway at night might come to be regarded as outrages to human conscience. Not having things might become cooler than having them. And those who did change the way they live would acquire the moral standing to demand changes in behavior from others—from other people, other corporations, even other countries.

19 All of this could, theoretically, happen. What I'm describing (imagining would probably be more accurate) is a process of viral social change, and change of this kind, which is nonlinear, is never something anyone can plan or predict or count on. Who knows, maybe the virus will reach all the way to Chongqing and infect my Chinese evil twin. Or not. Maybe going green will prove a passing fad and will lose steam after a few years, just as it did in the 1980s, when Ronald Reagan took down Jimmy Carter's solar panels from the roof of the White House.

20 Going personally green is a bet, nothing more or less, though it's one we probably all should make, even if the odds of it paying off aren't great. Sometimes you have to act as if acting will make a difference, even when you can't prove that it will. That, after all, was precisely what happened in Communist Czechoslovakia and Poland, when a handful of individuals like Václav Havel and Adam Michnik resolved that they would simply conduct their lives "as if" they lived in a free society. That improbable bet created a tiny space of liberty that, in time, expanded to take in, and then help take down, the whole of the Eastern bloc.

21 So what would be a comparable bet that the individual might make in the case of the environmental crisis? Havel himself has suggested that people begin to "conduct themselves as if they were to live on this earth forever and be answerable for its condition one day." Fair enough, but let me propose a slightly less abstract and daunting wager. The idea is to find one thing to do in your life that doesn't involve spending or voting, that may or may not virally rock the world but is real and particular (as well as symbolic) and that, come what may, will offer its own rewards. Maybe you decide to give up meat, an act that would reduce your carbon footprint by as much as a quarter. Or you could try this: determine to observe the Sabbath. For one day a week, abstain completely from economic activity: no shopping, no driving, no electronics.

22 But the act I want to talk about is growing some—even just a little—of your own food. Rip out your lawn, if you have one, and if you don't—if you live in a high-rise, or have a yard shrouded in shade—look into getting a plot in a community garden. Measured against the Problem We Face, planting a garden sounds pretty benign, I know, but in fact it's one of the most powerful things an individual can do—to reduce your carbon footprint, sure, but more important, to reduce your sense of dependence and dividedness: to change the cheap-energy mind.

23 A great many things happen when you plant a vegetable garden, some of them directly related to climate change, others indirect but related nevertheless. Growing food, we forget, comprises the original solar technology: calories produced by means of photosynthesis. Years ago the cheap-energy mind discovered that more food could be produced with less effort by replacing sunlight with fossil-fuel fertilizers and pesticides, with a result that the typical calorie of food energy in your diet now requires about 10 calories of fossil-fuel energy to produce. It's estimated that the way we feed ourselves (or rather, allow ourselves to be fed) accounts for about a fifth of the greenhouse gas for which each of us is responsible.

24 Yet the sun still shines down on your yard, and photosynthesis still works so abundantly that in a thoughtfully organized vegetable garden (one planted from seed, nourished by compost from the kitchen and involving not too many drives to the garden center), you can grow the proverbial free lunch—CO2-free and dollar-free.

This is the most-local food you can possibly eat (not to mention the freshest, tastiest and most nutritious), with a carbon footprint so faint that even the New Zealand lamb council dares not challenge it. And while we're counting carbon, consider too your compost pile, which shrinks the heap of garbage your household needs trucked away even as it feeds your vegetables and sequesters carbon in your soil. What else? Well, you will probably notice that you're getting a pretty good workout there in your garden, burning calories without having to get into the car to drive to the gym. (It is one of the absurdities of the modern division of labor that, having replaced physical labor with fossil fuel, we now have to burn even more fossil fuel to keep our unemployed bodies in shape.) Also, by engaging both body and mind, time spent in the garden is time (and energy) subtracted from electronic forms of entertainment.

25 You begin to see that growing even a little of your own food is, as Wendell Berry pointed out 30 years ago, one of those solutions that, instead of begetting a new set of problems—the way "solutions" like ethanol or nuclear power inevitably do—actually beget other solutions, and not only of the kind that save carbon. Still more valuable are the habits of mind that growing a little of your own food can yield. You quickly learn that you need not be dependent on specialists to provide for yourself—that your body is still good for something and may actually be enlisted in its own support. If the experts are right, if both oil and time are running out, these are skills and habits of mind we're all very soon going to need. We may also need the food. Could gardens provide it? Well, during World War II, victory gardens supplied as much as 40 percent of the produce Americans ate.

26 **But there are sweeter** reasons to plant that garden, to bother. At least in this one corner of your yard and life, you will have begun to heal the split between what you think and what you do, to commingle your identities as consumer and producer and citizen. Chances are, your garden will re-engage you with your neighbors, for you will have produce to give away and the need to borrow their tools. You will have reduced the power of the cheap-energy mind by personally overcoming its most debilitating weakness: its helplessness and the fact that it can't do much of anything that doesn't involve division or subtraction. The garden's season-long transit from seed to ripe fruit—*will you get a load of that zucchini?!*—suggests that the operations of addition and multiplication still obtain, that the abundance of nature is not exhausted. The single greatest lesson the garden teaches is that our relationship to the planet need not be zero-sum, and that as long as the sun still shines and people still can plan and plant, think and do, we can, if we bother to try, find ways to provide for ourselves without diminishing the world.

Our next two readings address outsourcing, the practice of moving jobs from developed countries like the United States to developing countries with cheaper workforces. This affects available jobs for U.S. college graduates and workers as well as the progress and vitality of the economies of many countries. Outsourcing continues to spark fiery debates about U.S. job creation and unemployment, about the distribution of benefits and harm, and about global economic competition.

The second reading is an op-ed by journalist Thomas L. Friedman, published in the *New York Times*. Friedman is known for his pro–free trade enthusiasm and his books on globalization, *The Lexus and the Olive Tree* (1999), *The*

World Is Flat: A Brief History of the Twenty-First Century (2005), *Hot, Flat, and Crowded* (2008), and *That Used To Be Us* (2012). "Thinking Critically" questions have been omitted so that you can do your own independent thinking in preparation for writing your summary/strong response essay.

Thomas L. Friedman*

30 Little Turtles

1 Indians are so hospitable. I got an ovation the other day from a roomful of Indian 20-year-olds just for reading perfectly the following paragraph: "A bottle of bottled water held 30 little turtles. It didn't matter that each turtle had to rattle a metal ladle in order to get a little bit of noodles, a total turtle delicacy. The problem was that there were many turtle battles for less than oodles of noodles."

2 I was sitting in on an "accent neutralization" class at the Indian call center 24/7 Customer. The instructor was teaching the would-be Indian call center operators to suppress their native Indian accents and speak with a Canadian one—she teaches British and U.S. accents as well, but these youths will be serving the Canadian market. Since I'm originally from Minnesota, near Canada, and still speak like someone out of the movie "Fargo," I gave these young Indians an authentic rendition of "30 Little Turtles," which is designed to teach them the proper Canadian pronunciations. Hence the rousing applause.

3 Watching these incredibly enthusiastic young Indians preparing for their call center jobs—earnestly trying to soften their t's and roll their r's—is an uplifting experience, especially when you hear from their friends already working these jobs how they have transformed their lives. Most of them still live at home and turn over part of their salaries to their parents, so the whole family benefits. Many have credit cards and have become real consumers, including of U.S. goods, for the first time. All of them seem to have gained self-confidence and self-worth.

4 A lot of these Indian young men and women have college degrees, but would never get a local job that starts at $200 to $300 a month were it not for the call centers. Some do "outbound" calls, selling things from credit cards to phone services to Americans and Europeans. Others deal with "inbound" calls—everything from tracing lost luggage for U.S. airline passengers to solving computer problems for U.S. customers. The calls are transferred here by satellite or fiber optic cable.

5 I was most taken by a young Indian engineer doing tech support for a U.S. software giant, who spoke with pride about how cool it is to tell his friends that he just spent the day helping Americans navigate their software. A majority of these call center workers are young women, who not only have been liberated by earning a decent local wage (and therefore have more choice in whom they marry), but are using the job to get M.B.A.'s and other degrees on the side.

*Thomas L. Friedman. "30 Little Turtles" from The New York Times, February 29, 2004.

6 I gathered a group together, and here's what they sound like: M. Dinesh, who does tech support, says his day is made when some American calls in with a problem and is actually happy to hear an Indian voice: "They say you people are really good at what you do. I am glad I reached an Indian." Kiran Menon, when asked who his role model was, shot back: "Bill Gates—[I dream of] starting my own company and making it that big." I asked C. M. Meghna what she got most out of the work: "Self-confidence," she said, "a lot of self-confidence, when people come to you with a problem and you can solve it—and having a lot of independence." Because the call center teams work through India's night—which corresponds to America's day—"your biological clock goes haywire," she added. "Besides that, it's great."

7 There is nothing more positive than the self-confidence, dignity and optimism that comes from a society knowing it is producing wealth by tapping its own brains—men's and women's—as opposed to one just tapping its own oil, let alone one that is so lost it can find dignity only through suicide and "martyrdom."

8 Indeed, listening to these Indian young people, I had a déjà vu. Five months ago, I was in Ramallah, on the West Bank, talking to three young Palestinian men, also in their 20's, one of whom was studying engineering. Their hero was Yasir Arafat. They talked about having no hope, no jobs and no dignity, and they each nodded when one of them said they were all "suicide bombers in waiting."

9 What am I saying here? That it's more important for young Indians to have jobs than Americans? Never. But I am saying that there is more to outsourcing than just economics. There's also geopolitics. It is inevitable in a networked world that our economy is going to shed certain low-wage, low-prestige jobs. To the extent that they go to places like India or Pakistan—where they are viewed as high-wage, high-prestige jobs—we make not only a more prosperous world, but a safer world for our own 20-year-olds.

Our third reading is a summary/strong response essay by student writer Stephanie Malinowski in response to the Friedman article. It follows primarily a "rhetorical critique" strategy for the strong response.

Stephanie Malinowski

Questioning Thomas L. Friedman's Optimism in "30 Little Turtles"

1 You are struggling to fix a problem that arises when you are downloading new computer software on to your computer. You're about to give up on the whole thing when an idea hits you: call the software company itself to ask for assistance. Should you be surprised when the person who answers the phone to help you is based in India? Should Americans support or question outsourcing?

2 In "30 Little Turtles," an op-ed piece that appeared in the *New York Times* on February 29, 2004, journalist and foreign affairs columnist Thomas L. Friedman argues that outsourcing call center jobs from the Western world to India is transforming the lives of

Indian workers and benefiting geopolitics. Friedman supports his argument by detailing his experience visiting a call center in India. He claims that the Indians working to serve Canadian and American markets are happy with how their work has improved their lives. Friedman points out that the working Indian women feel liberated now that they are making a decent wage and can afford such things as a college education. He describes Indian workers' view of their jobs, using words such as "self-confidence" and "independence." At the end of his article, Friedman states that he doesn't favor Indian employment over American employment but that outsourced jobs in countries like India or Pakistan create both prosperity and global security. Although Friedman's article clearly conveys to its audience how some Indian workers are benefiting from outsourcing, his argument relies heavily on personal experience and generalizations. I also think his condescending attitude hurts his argument, and he concludes his article too abruptly, leaving readers with questions.

3 Friedman succeeds in portraying the positive side of outsourcing to his *New York Times* readers who may be questioning the rationale for outsourcing. Friedman interviews the recipients of American jobs to see outsourcing from their perspective and enlightens Americans trying to understand how outsourcing is benefiting workers in other countries. Friedman's opening is vivid and captures the readers' interest by detailing his experience inside an Indian call center. He quotes the Indian workers expressing the joys of working for American and Canadian people. These workers testify to the financial and personal gains these jobs have brought. One woman says that she feels good about her job and herself "when people come to you with a problem and you can solve it" (121). The article is so full of optimism that the reader can't help but empathize with the Indians and feel happy that outsourcing has transformed their lives. Through these emotional appeals, Friedman succeeds in making readers who may have big reservations about outsourcing think about the human dimension of outsourcing.

4 However, Friedman also makes large generalizations based on his few personal experiences, lessening the credibility of his article. The first sentence of the article reads, "Indians are so hospitable." So are *all* Indians "so hospitable"? Friedman seems to make this generalization about national character based on the fact that he was applauded by a room full of Indians after reading a tongue twister paragraph in a perfect Canadian accent. I can see why Friedman appreciates his warm reception, but "feel good" moments can hardly provide evidence for the soundness of global economic policies. Friedman generalizes further about what he sees and hears in the call center room. He talks about the Indian employees in these terms: "All of them seem to have gained self-confidence and self-worth" (120). From this single observation, Friedman makes the assumption that almost every Indian working an outsourcing job must be gaining, and that the overall experience has done wonders for their lives. However, other articles that I have read have mentioned that call center work is basically a dead-end job and that $200 a month is not a big salary. Later in his conclusion, Friedman states that "we make not only a more prosperous world, but a safer world for our own 20-year-olds" (121). Can this conclusion

be drawn from one visit to a call center where Indians expressed gratitude for their outsourcing work?

5 An even bigger problem with Friedman's article is the condescending way in which he describes the Indian workers. I think he portrays the culture as being incompetent before the American and Canadian outsourcing jobs came to improve their accents and their lives. One statement that conveys condescension is this remark: "Watching these incredibly enthusiastic young Indians preparing for their call center jobs—earnestly trying to soften their t's and roll their r's—is an uplifting experience . . ." (120). This passage reminds me of the delight and pride of parents witnessing their children's growth milestones. Friedman is casting the accent neutralization of the Indian workers as overcoming a barrier in order to reach success. Friedman's condescending tone is apparent again when he restates the words of one American caller to an Indian worker, "They say you people are really good at what you do. I am glad I reached an Indian" (121). I see Friedman's reason for including this quote; he wants the reader to know that Indian workers are being valued for their work. However, the words that the American uses, which Friedman deliberately chooses to include in his article, "you people," suggest that Indians are a whole other kind of people different from American workers in their skills. Friedman's condescension also appears when he says that these are "low-wage, low-prestige jobs" (121). This remark is full of problems because it puts down the Indians taking the jobs and the Americans who have lost them, and it misrepresents the outsourcing scene that now includes many highly skilled prestigious jobs.

6 I also think that Friedman weakens his article by concluding abruptly and introducing new ideas to readers that leave them with unanswered questions. Friedman asks the reader, "What am I saying here? That it's more important for young Indians to have jobs than Americans?" (121). This point seems like a relevant question to investigate, but its weakness is that Friedman never even mentions any place in his article the loss that American workers are experiencing. At the end of the article, readers are left with questions. For example, the last sentence reads, "we make not only a more prosperous world, but a safer world for our own 20-year-olds" (121). Although Friedman is implying that outsourcing improves our relationships with other countries and enhances our national safety, nowhere in the article does he substantiate this claim. He seems to have thrown this statement into the conclusion just to end the article on a happy note.

7 Giving a human face to outsourcing is a good idea; however, Friedman does not support his main argument well, and this article comes across as a simplistic, unexplored view of outsourcing. I and other readers are left needing to look for answers to serious questions about outsourcing elsewhere.

Work Cited

Friedman, Thomas L. "30 Little Turtles." *New York Times* 29 Feb. 2004. Rpt. in *The Allyn & Bacon Guide to Writing.* John D. Ramage, John C. Bean, and June Johnson. 7th ed. New York: Pearson, 2015. 120–21. Print.

THINKING CRITICALLY

about "Questioning Thomas L. Friedman's Optimism in '30 Little Turtles'"

1. What rhetorical points has Stephanie Malinowski chosen to analyze in her strong response essay?
2. What examples and quotations from Friedman's article work particularly well as support for her points? Where might she have included more support?
3. Where does Stephanie use attributive tags effectively?
4. If you were to write a rhetorical critique of Friedman's article, what points would you select to analyze?
5. If you were to write an ideas critique, what would you choose to focus on? Where would you agree and disagree with Friedman?

WRITING AN AUTOBIOGRAPHICAL NARRATIVE

6

WHAT YOU WILL LEARN

6.1 To explain open-form strategies for autobiographical writing.
6.2 To compose an effective autobiographical essay or literacy narrative.

This chapter focuses on the rhetorical aim "writing to express or share." Its writing projects ask you to write an autobiographical narrative about something significant in your own life. But rather than state the significance up front in a thesis, you let it unfold in storylike fashion. This narrative structure places autobiographical writing at the open end of the closed-to-open-form continuum, making it more like a nonfiction "short story" than a traditional academic essay. Consequently, we will refer to Chapter 18, "Strategies for Writing Open-Form Prose," on several occasions in this chapter.

Autobiographical writing can help us explore, deepen, and complicate our perceptions of the world. In addition to telling stories to convey the complexity and significance of an event, we use stories to reveal something about ourselves. The writing projects for this chapter address two genres of narrative writing: an **autobiographical narrative** on any significant event or moment in your life or a **literacy narrative** centered on the writer's experience with language, reading, writing, school, teachers, or education. Both kinds use the narrative strategies of plot, character, and setting to develop tension, move the story forward, and give it significance. Good autobiographical narrative does not depend on having an exciting life with highly dramatic moments. On the contrary, some of the most memorable autobiographical and literacy narratives relate ordinary experiences in a way that reveals the writer's new ways of understanding that serve to deepen, darken, or expand our view of the world.

Engaging Autobiographic Narrative

One of the premises of this book is that good writing is rooted in the writer's perception of a problem that the writer tries to address or resolve in some way. Problems are at the center not only of thesis-based writing but also of narrative writing. In effective narration, the problem usually takes the form of a *contrary*, two or more things in opposition—ideas, characters, expectations, forces, worldviews, or whatever. Three kinds of contraries that frequently form the plots of autobiographical narratives are the following:

1. ***Old self versus new self.*** The writer perceives changes in himself or herself as a result of some transforming or breakthrough moment or event.
2. ***Old view of person X versus new view of person X.*** The writer's perception of a person (favorite uncle, childhood hero, scary teacher) changes as a result of some revealing moment; the change in the narrator's perception of person X also indicates growth in the narrator's self-perception.
3. ***Old values versus new values that threaten, challenge, or otherwise disrupt the old values.*** The writer confronts an outsider (or a new, unfamiliar situation such as a class or a learning task) that challenges his or her worldview, or the writer undergoes a crisis that creates a conflict in values.

Another way to look at contraries is to imagine a scene that has a "moment of revelation." In considering a significant experience for a narrative, think of *significant* not as "unusual" or "exciting" but as "revealing" or "conveying new and unexpected meaning or insight." Thought of in this way, a "moment of revelation" in a story might be a gesture, a remark, a smile, a way of walking or tying a shoe, the wearing of a certain piece of clothing, or the carrying of a certain object in a purse or pocket. Try inventing a short scene in which a gesture, smile, or brief action reverses one character's feelings about, or understanding of, another character.

1. You thought that Maria had led a sheltered life until ____________________.
2. You thought Mr. Watson was a racist until ____________________.
3. Marco (Jillian) seemed the perfect date until ____________________.

Here is an example:

> My dad seemed unforgivingly angry at me until he suddenly smiled, turned my baseball cap backward on my head, and held up his open palm for a high five. "Girl, if you don't change your ways, you're going to be as big a high school screw-up as your old man was."

ON YOUR OWN

Think of turning point moments in your life that might fit one or more of the typical plots just described: old self versus new self; old view of person X versus new view of person X; old values versus new values that threaten, challenge, or otherwise disrupt the old values. Choose one of these moments and freewrite about it for several minutes. See if you can identify a scene that would suggest a "moment of revelation."

IN CONVERSATION

Share your ideas with classmates. Your goal is to begin seeing that each person's life is a rich source of stories.

Understanding Autobiographical Writing

6.1 Explain open-form strategies for autobiographical writing.

Autobiographical writing includes telling descriptions of places and people and events that happen through time. However, the spine of good autobiographical writing is a key moment or event, or a series of key moments or events, that shape or reveal the author's emerging character or growth in understanding.

Autobiographical Tension: The Opposition of Contraries

Key events in autobiography are characterized by a clash of opposing values or points of view. These oppositions are typically embodied in conflicts between characters or in divided feelings within the narrator. The contraries in a story can often be summed up in statements such as these:

> My teacher thought I had a low IQ, but she didn't know that I was afraid to read or why.
>
> The job that bored me and made all my muscles ache rescued me from a hopeless summer.
>
> Although I broke all Miller King's football records after he lost his arm in a car accident, I realized that he was a better person than I was. (See "Phantom Limb Pain," pp. 137–138.)
>
> The school that I had dreamed of attending turned into a nightmarish prison.

An autobiographical piece without tension is like an academic piece without a surprising thesis. No writing is more tedious than a pointless "and then" narrative that rambles on without tension. You can read such a narrative in Chapter 18 in our discussion of "The Stolen Watch" to illustrate the difference between a "story" and an "*and then* chronology." It is a good example of what *not* to do for this assignment.

See Chapter 18, pp. 475–487. Contrast "The Stolen Watch," pp. 476–477, with "No Cats in America?", pp. 139–140.

Like the risky thesis statement in closed-form writing, the opposition of contraries creates purpose and focus for open-form writing. It functions as an organizing principle, helping the writer determine what to include or omit. It also sets a direction for the writer. When a story is tightly wound and all the details contribute to the story line, the tension moves the plot forward as a mainspring moves the hands of a watch. The tension is typically resolved when the narrator experiences a moment of recognition or insight, vanquishes or is vanquished by a foe, or changes status.

How Literary Elements Work in Autobiographical Narratives

The basic elements of a literary narrative that work together to create a story are plot, character, setting, and theme.

The Importance of Plot By **plot** we mean the basic action of the story, including the selection and sequencing of scenes and events. Often stories don't open with the earliest chronological moment; they may start *in medias res* ("in the middle of things") at a moment of crisis and then flash backward to fill in earlier details that explain the origins of the crisis. What you choose to include in your story and where you place it are concerns of plot. The amount of detail you choose to devote to each scene is also a function of plot. How a writer varies the amount of detail in each scene is referred to as a plot's *pacing*.

Plots typically unfold in the following stages: (a) an arresting opening scene; (b) the introduction of characters and the filling in of background; (c) the building of tension or conflict through oppositions embedded in a series of events or scenes; (d) the climax or pivotal moment when the tension or conflict comes to a head; and (e) reflection on the events of the plot and their meaning.

To help you recognize story-worthy events in your own life, consider the following list of pivotal moments that have figured in numerous autobiographical narratives:

- Moments of enlightenment or coming to knowledge
- Passages from one realm to the next: from innocence to experience, from outsider to insider or vice versa, from novice to expert, from what you once were to what you now are
- Confrontation with the unknown
- Moments of crisis or critical choice in struggle against nature or against societal pressure
- Problems maintaining relationships without compromising your own growth or denying your own needs
- Problems accepting limitations and necessities
- Contrasts between common wisdom and your own unique knowledge or experience

The Importance of Character Who might be the characters in your autobiographical story? The answer depends on the nature of the tension that moves your story forward. Characters who contribute significantly to that tension or who represent some aspect of that tension with special clarity belong in your story. Whatever the source of tension in a story, a writer typically chooses characters who exemplify the narrator's fears and desires or who forward or frustrate the narrator's growth in a significant way.

Sometimes writers develop characters not through description and sensory detail but through dialogue. Particularly if a story involves conflict between people, dialogue is a powerful means of letting the reader experience that conflict directly. The following piece of dialogue, taken from African-American writer Richard Wright's classic autobiography *Black Boy*, demonstrates how a skilled writer can let dialogue tell the story, without resorting to analysis and abstraction. In the following scene, young Wright approaches a librarian in an attempt to get a book by Baltimore author and journalist H. L. Mencken from a whites-only public library. He has forged a note and borrowed a library card from a sympathetic white coworker and is pretending to borrow the book in his coworker's name.

> "What do you want, boy?"
>
> As though I did not possess the power of speech, I stepped forward and simply handed her the forged note, not parting my lips.
>
> "What books by Mencken does he want?" she asked.
>
> "I don't know ma'am," I said avoiding her eyes.
>
> "Who gave you this card?"

"Mr. Falk," I said.

"Where is he?"

"He's at work, at the M— Optical Company," I said. "I've been in here for him before."

"I remember," the woman said. "But he never wrote notes like this."

Oh, God, she's suspicious. Perhaps she would not let me have the books? If she had turned her back at that moment, I would have ducked out the door and never gone back. Then I thought of a bold idea.

"You can call him up, ma'am," I said, my heart pounding.

"You're not using these books are you?" she asked pointedly.

"Oh no ma'am. I can't read."

"I don't know what he wants by Mencken," she said under her breath.

I knew I had won; she was thinking of other things and the race question had gone out of her mind.

—Richard Wright, *Black Boy*

It's one thing to hear *about* racial prejudice and discrimination; it's another thing to *hear* it directly through dialogue such as this. In just one hundred or so words of conversation, Wright communicates the anguish and humiliation of being a "black boy" in the United States in the 1920s.

Another way to develop a character is to present a sequence of moments or scenes that reveal a variety of behaviors and moods. Imagine taking ten photographs of your character to represent his or her complexity and variety and then arranging them in a collage.

The Importance of Setting Your choice of settings also depends on how much a description of place helps readers understand the conflict or tension that drives the story. When you write about yourself, what you notice in the external world often reflects your inner world. In some moods you are apt to notice the expansive lawn, beautiful flowers, and swimming ducks in the city park; in other moods you might note the litter of paper cups, the blight on the roses, and the scum on the duck pond. The setting typically relates thematically to the other elements of a story. In "No Cats in America?" (pp. 139–140), for example, the author contrasts his parents' parties in the Philippines, replete with music and dancing, firecrackers, a mahjong gambling room, and exotic food and drink such as homemade mango juice and coconut milk, with the American school lunchroom where he opened his Tupperware lunchbox filled with fish and bagoong. The contrast of these settings, especially when the author's American classmates laugh at his lunch, embodies the story's tension.

The Importance of Theme The word *theme* is difficult to define. Themes, like thesis statements, organize the other elements of the essay. But a theme is seldom stated explicitly and is never proved with reasons and factual evidence. Readers ponder—even argue about—themes, and often different readers are affected very differently by the same theme. Some literary critics view theme as simply a different way of thinking about plot. To use a phrase from critic Northrop Frye, a plot is "what happened" in a story, whereas the theme is "what happens" over and over again in this story and others like it. To illustrate this distinction, we summarize student writer Patrick José's autobiographical narrative "No Cats in America?", one of the essays in the Readings section of this chapter, from a plot perspective and from a theme perspective:

> Plot Perspective It's the story of a Filipino boy who emigrates with his family from the Philippines to the United States when he is in the eighth grade. On the first day of school, he is humiliated when classmates snicker at the lunch his mother packed for him. Feeling more and more alienated each day, he eventually proclaims, "I hate being Filipino!"
>
> Theme Perspective It's the story of how personal identity is threatened when people are suddenly removed from their own cultures and immersed into new ones that don't understand or respect difference. The story reveals the psychic damage of cultural dislocation.

As you can see, the thematic summary goes beyond the events of the story to point toward the larger significance of those events. Although you may choose not to state your theme directly for your readers, you need to understand that theme to organize your story. This understanding usually precedes and guides your decisions about what events and characters to include, what details and dialogue to use, and what elements of setting to describe. But sometimes you need to reverse the process and start out with events and characters that, for whatever reason, force themselves on you, and then figure out your theme after you've written for a while. In other words, theme may be something you discover as you write.

Special Features of Literacy Narratives

A literacy narrative is a subset of autobiographical narrative: It uses the elements of a story to recount a writer's personal experience with language in all its forms—reading and writing, acquiring a second language, being an insider or outsider based on literacy level and cultural context—or with learning how to learn in general through experiences inside and outside of school. The academic and public fascination with literacy narratives has grown out of—and contributed to—contemporary discussions about cultural diversity in the United States and the connections between literacy and cultural power.

Literacy narratives are a frequently encountered and important genre. For example, one of the most famous literacy narratives is by Frederick Douglass, the ex-slave and abolitionist leader who describes learning to read and write as the key to his liberation from slavery. Another well-known literacy narrative is by Zitkala-Ša (Gertrude Bonnin), a Native American woman who exposes the forceful assimilation tactics employed by missionary schools to separate Native American children from their tribes in the late nineteenth and early twentieth centuries. Perhaps the most famous literacy narrative is by Helen Keller, who recounts the moments when an understanding of language broke through the isolation created by her blindness and deafness. More recently, literacy narratives by immigrants from many cultures have explored the role of education in thwarting or encouraging their integration into American society.

Writing a literacy narrative in college classes can help students explore their adjustment to college, link their earlier learning experiences to the literacy demands of college courses, and take ownership of their own education.

Thinking about your own literacy experiences compels you to ponder your educational path and your own ideas of the purpose of education. In contemplating the way that ethnic, economic, gender, class, and regional considerations have shaped your own learning to read and write, you will experience the pleasure of self-discovery and cultural insight.

Literacy narratives resemble other autobiographical narratives in their open-form structure and their inclusion of some or all of these literary features: a plot built on tension and presented as well-sequenced scenes, vivid descriptions of settings, well-drawn characters, dialogue, and theme. Like other autobiographical narratives, literacy narratives rely on vivid, concrete language to make settings and dramatic moments come alive for readers. While literacy narratives share many elements with other autobiographical narratives, they differ in their attention to the following features:

DISTINCTIVE FEATURES OF LITERACY NARRATIVES

- A focus on a writer's experience with language, reading, writing, schooling, teachers, or some other important aspect of education
- A focus on bringing an insight about the significance of learning, language, reading, or writing to readers through an implied theme (although this theme might be explicitly stated, most likely at the end of the narrative)
- A focus on engaging readers and connecting them to an understanding of the writer's educational/learning experience, prompting them to think about their own educational experiences and larger questions about the purpose and value of education

FOR WRITING AND DISCUSSION

Analyzing Features of Literacy Narratives

Read the following passages that depict key moments in two students' literacy experiences, and answer the questions about them that direct your attention to specific features.

EXCERPT FROM MEGAN LACY'S LITERACY NARRATIVE

...I was placed in the remedial reading group. Our books had red plastic covers while the other kids had books with yellow covers that looked gold to me. When it was reading time, the rest of the red group and I congregated around a rectangular wood table where Mrs. Hinckley would direct each of us to read a passage from the story aloud. The first time this happened, my stomach dropped. Even the remedial kids were sounding out the words, but I had no idea what those symbols on the page meant.

When my turn came, I muttered meekly, "I can't...."

"Don't say 'can't' in my classroom!" Mrs. Hinckley snapped. Then, more gently, she said, "Just sound it out...."

I did as she recommended and could hardly believe what was happening. I was reading. I felt superhuman with such a power. After that moment, I read to my mom every night....

(*continued*)

EXCERPT FROM JEFFREY CAIN'S LITERACY NARRATIVE

In the Walla Walla Public Library, I remember the tomato soup colored carpet, the bad oil paintings of pioneers fording the Columbia River, the musty smell, the oak card catalog with brass knobs, the position of the clock when I first read Jerzi Kosinski's *The Painted Bird.*

"Just read it," my sister-in-law said. "I know you don't read much fiction, but just read this one," she pleaded.

Reluctantly, at first, I turned the pages. But each word covertly seduced me; slowly the odyssey of the dark-skinned gypsy affected my spirit like an exotic opiate, until Lehki's painted bird lay pecked to death on the ground. The image haunted my conscience for days. During some of my more restless nights, I was chased like the characters by Nazis through the Black Forest.

Who was this Kosinski? Why did his book affect me this way? How and why did he write like this? Did all writers write like Kosinski?

The novel incited a series of questions that forced me to begin writing notes and summarizing my thoughts. I began a reading journal and my development as a writer shadowed my habits as a reader. . . .

1. What literacy experiences have Megan and Jeffrey chosen to focus on?
2. How do Megan and Jeffrey use the narrative elements of plot, setting, and concrete, specific language to involve their readers in their experiences?
3. Based on these excerpts, how would you articulate the theme of each piece?
4. What educational memories of your own are triggered by these excerpts?

WRITING PROJECT

6.2 Compose an effective autobiographical essay or literacy narrative.

Autobiographical or Literacy Narrative

Option 1: Autobiographical Narrative

Write a narrative essay about something significant in your life using the literary strategies of plot, character, and setting. Develop your story through the use of contraries, creating tension that moves the story forward and gives it significance. You can discuss the significance of your story explicitly, perhaps as a revelation, or you can imply it. (The readings at the end of this chapter illustrate different options.) Use specific details and develop contraries that create tension.

Option 2: Literacy Narrative

Write a narrative essay that focuses on your experiences with language, reading, writing, or education. You could explore positive or negative experiences in learning to read or write, breakthrough moments in your development as a literate person, or some educational experiences that have shaped your identity as a person or student. Incorporate the literary elements of plot, character, setting, theme, and descriptive language in the telling of your story. Think of your task as finding new significance for yourself in these experiences and sharing your discoveries with your readers in ways that hold their interest and bring them new understanding.

Both these options call for a story. In Chapter 18, we argue that a narrative qualifies as a story only when it depicts a series of connected events that create for the reader a sense of tension or conflict that is resolved through a new understanding or change in status. Your goal for this assignment is to write a story about your life or literacy experiences that fulfills these criteria. The suggestions that follow will help you.

Generating and Exploring Ideas

As you generate and explore ideas, your goal is to develop a plot—a significant moment or insight arising out of contrariety—that you can develop with the storytelling strategies of open-form prose. If you are still searching for ideas, the following questions might help:

QUESTIONS FOR AN AUTOBIOGRAPHICAL NARRATIVE

- ***Questions arising from your achievement of a new status*** (winning/losing a competition, passing/failing an important test, making/not making the team). If you failed, what did you learn from it or how did it shape you? If you succeeded, did the new status turn out to be as important as you had expected it to be?
- ***Questions arising from challenges to your normal assumptions about life or from your failure to fit or fulfill others' expectations of you*** (encounter with persons from a different culture or social class; your discovery that you have stereotyped someone or have been stereotyped; your difficulty in living up to someone's expectations of you)
- ***Questions arising from conflicts of values or failure to live up to values*** (a time when a person who mattered to you rejected you or let you down, or a time when you rejected or let down someone who cared for you; a time when you were irresponsible or violated a principle or law and thereby caused others pain—for example, shoplifting, leaving work early, or being drunk; a time when you were criticized unjustly or given a punishment you didn't deserve)

ADDITIONAL QUESTIONS FOR A LITERACY NARRATIVE

- ***Questions about adjusting to college or educational challenges*** (unexpected problems with reading and writing encountered in college, or earlier in middle school or high school; discovery of holes or weaknesses in your education; educational issues related to your "difference"—ethnic, class, physical/mental, sexual orientation—from the norm)
- ***Questions about your experiences with language*** (issues arising from learning a second language; from being bilingual; from speaking a

nonstandard dialect; from having a speech or hearing impairment or a learning disability; from preferring math or art or athletics or video games rather than reading and writing)

- ***Questions about influential (or inhibiting) teachers or mentors*** (influence of people who have helped or hindered your literacy development; people who have changed your view of yourself as a reader or writer)
- ***Questions about literacy and social status or citizenship*** (issues connected to literacy and cultural power or economic success; the role of education in preparing you for local, national, or global citizenship)

Shaping and Drafting Your Narrative

Once you've identified an event about which you'd like to write, you need to develop ways to show readers what makes that event particularly story-worthy. In thinking about the event, consider the following questions:

Question-Asking Strategies to Help Shape and Draft Your Narrative

Element of the Narrative	Questions to Ask
How to Start	• What are the major contraries or tensions in this story? • What events and scenes portraying these contraries might you include in your narrative? • What insights or meaning do you think your story suggests? How would you articulate for yourself the theme of your narrative? • How might you begin your narrative?
How to Think about and Develop Characters and Setting	• What characters are important in this story? • How will you portray them—through description, action, dialogue? • What settings or scenes can you re-create for readers? • What particulars or physical details will make the setting, characters, and conflicts vivid and memorable?
How to Think about and Develop the Plot	• How might you arrange the scenes in your story? • What would be the climax, the pivotal moment of decision or insight?
How to Conclude Your Narrative	• What resolution can you bring to the tensions and conflicts in your story? • How can you convey the significance of your story? What will make it something readers can relate to? • How can the ending of your narrative leave readers thinking about larger human issues and concerns?

When stuck, writers often work their way into a narrative by describing in detail a vividly recalled scene, person, or object. You may not be able to include all the descriptive material, but in the act of writing exhaustively about this one element, the rest of the story may begin to unfold for you, and forgotten items and incidents may resurface. In the course of describing scenes and characters, you will probably also begin reflecting on the significance of what you are saying. Try freewriting answers to such questions as "Why is this important?" and "What am I trying to do here?" Then continue with your rough draft. Remember that it is the storyteller's job to put readers into the story by providing enough detail and context for the readers to see why the event is significant.

Revising

Testing your narrative out on other readers can give you valuable feedback about your effectiveness in grabbing and holding their interest and conveying an insight. Plan to write several drafts of your narrative.

Questions for Peer Review

In addition to the generic peer review questions explained in Skill 16.4, ask your peer reviewers to address these questions:

OPENING AND PLOT

1. How could the title and opening paragraphs more effectively hook readers' interest and prepare them for the story to follow?
2. How might the writer improve the tension, structure, or pacing of the scenes?
3. How could the writer improve the connections between scenes or use a different organization such as a collage of scenes or flashbacks to enhance the clarity or drama of the narrative?

CHARACTERIZATION

4. Where might the writer provide more information about characters or describe them more fully?
5. Where might the writer use dialogue more effectively to reveal character?

SETTING, THEME, AND LANGUAGE

6. How might the writer make the setting more vivid and connected to the action and significance of the story?
7. What insight or revelation do you get from this story? How could the narrative's thematic significance be made more memorable or powerful?
8. Where do you find examples of specific language? Where could the writer use more concrete language?

WRITING PROJECT

Multimodal or Online Options

For advice on producing multimedia compositions, see Chapter 19.

1. ***Personal Narrative as Podcast*** Tell your personal narrative or literacy narrative orally as a story suitable for radio or other oral settings. Produce a podcast and consider posting it online.
2. ***Personal Narrative as Video Photo Essay*** If your narrative lends itself to a visual telling, you can combine voice with images in a video photo essay. Tell your story orally through voice-over, but illustrate your narrative with photographs or drawings connected to your story. These might be actual photographs of the events depicted in your narrative or new photographs that you have taken or found (or drawings that you make) that enhance your story. Consider posting your video photo essay online.
3. ***Personal Essay in Graphic Novel Format*** If you have interest in drawing, consider transforming your personal narrative or literacy narrative into the style and format of a graphic novel. The drawings can add a powerful visual dimension to your narrative.

Our first reading is by Kris Saknussemm, a poet and fiction writer. He is the author of the dystopian, futuristic novel *Zanesville* (2005) and the contemporary novel *Reverend America* (2011). His poems and short stories have appeared in literary magazines around the country, including *The Boston Review, New Letters, The Antioch Review,* and *ZYZZYVA*. This selection is taken from his autobiographical work in progress.

Kris Saknussemm

Phantom Limb Pain

1 When I was thirteen my sole purpose was to shed my baby fat and become the star halfback on our football team. That meant beating out Miller King, the best athlete at my school. He was my neighbor and that mythic kid we all know—the one who's forever better than we are—the person we want to be.

2 Football practice started in September and all summer long I worked out. I ordered a set of barbells that came with complimentary brochures with titles like "How to Develop a He-Man Voice." Every morning before sunrise I lumbered around our neighborhood wearing ankle weights loaded with sand. I taught myself how to do Marine push-ups and carried my football everywhere so I'd learn not to fumble. But that wasn't enough. I performed a ceremony. During a full moon, I burned my favorite NFL trading cards and an Aurora model of the great quarterback Johnny Unitas in the walnut orchard behind our house, where Miller and I'd gotten into a fight when we were seven and I'd burst into tears before he even hit me.

3 Two days after my ceremony, Miller snuck out on his older brother's Suzuki and was struck by a car. He lost his right arm, just below the elbow. I went to see him the day after football practice started—after he'd come back from the hospital. He looked pale and surprised, but he didn't cry. It was hard to look at the stump of limb where his arm had been, so I kept glancing around his room. We only lived about 200 feet away, and yet I'd never been inside his house before. It had never occurred to me that he would also have on his wall a poster of Raquel Welch from *One Million Years* B.C.

4 I went on to break all his records that year. Miller watched the home games from the bench, wearing his jersey with the sleeve pinned shut. We went 10–1 and I was named MVP, but I was haunted by crazy dreams in which I was somehow responsible for the accident—that I'd found the mangled limb when it could've been sewn back on—and kept it in an aquarium full of vodka under my bed.

5 One afternoon several months later, toward the end of basketball season, I was crossing the field to go home and I saw Miller stuck going over the Cyclone fence—which wasn't hard to climb if you had both arms. I guess he'd gotten tired of walking around and hoped no one was looking. Or maybe it was a matter of pride. I'm sure I was the last person in the world he wanted to see—to have to accept assistance from. But even that challenge he accepted. I helped ease him down the fence, one diamond-shaped hole at a time. When we were finally safe on the other side, he said to me, "You know, I didn't tell you this during the season, but you did all right. Thanks for filling in for me."

6 We walked home together, not saying much. But together. Back to our houses 200 feet apart. His words freed me from my bad dreams. I thought to myself, how many things I hadn't told him. How even without an arm he was more of a leader. Damaged but not diminished, he was still ahead of me. I was right to have admired him. I grew bigger and a little more real from that day on.

THINKING CRITICALLY
about "Phantom Limb Pain"

Perhaps the first thing the reader realizes about Saknussemm's narrative is that the climactic event—one boy helping another climb down a Cyclone fence—is a small action; however, it has a big psychological and emotional meaning for the narrator. The events leading to this moment have prepared us to understand the writer's revelation of his new relationship to his rival. Saknussemm's last paragraph comments on the preceding narrative, making connections and pulling out threads of meaning.

1. Saknussemm chooses to leave a lot unsaid, depending on his readers to fill in the gaps. Why do you suppose that he had never been inside Miller King's house before? Why does he feel "somehow responsible for the accident"? What details does Saknussemm use to sketch in Miller's admirable traits?
2. What examples can you find in this narrative of revelatory words, memory-soaked words, and other concrete words low on the ladder of abstraction? Where does Saknussemm use words that *show* what is happening in the narrative instead of simply telling readers?
3. In closed-form prose, writers seldom use sentence fragments. In open-form prose, however, writers frequently use fragments for special effects. Note the two fragments in Saknussemm's final paragraph: "But together. Back to our houses 200 feet apart." Why does Saknussemm use these fragments? What is their rhetorical effect?
4. Part of Saknussemm's style in this narrative is to use understatement and minimalistic language while also using words that resonate with multiple meanings. For example, he lets readers imagine what Miller would look like trying to climb the Cyclone fence with one arm. However, some phrases and words are figurative and symbolic. What does Saknussemm mean by the phrases "grew bigger" and "a little more real" in his final sentence? How do the ideas of size and of reality versus illusion play a role in this narrative and relate to the theme?

See Skill 18.2 for a discussion of concrete language including revelatory words and memory-soaked words. See Chapter 3, Concept 3.3, for a discussion of *show* words and *tell* words.

For a different approach to narrative, consider student writer Patrick José's "No Cats in America?" Unlike Saknussemm's narrative, José's includes plentiful description. Note also how José creates tension through contrasts in his narrative: between an ideal image of America and a factual image, between life in the Philippines and life in California.

Patrick José (student)

No Cats in America?

1 "There are no cats in America." I remember growing up watching *An American Tail* with my sisters and cousins. Ever since I first saw that movie, I had always wanted to move to America. That one song, "There Are No Cats in America," in which the Mousekewitz family is singing with other immigrating mice, had the most profound effect on me. These were Russian mice going to America to find a better life—a life without cats. At first, I thought America really had no cats. Later, I learned that they meant that America was without any problems at all. I was taught about the American Dream with its promise of happiness and equality. If you wanted a better life, then you better pack up all your belongings and move to America.

2 However, I loved living in the Philippines. My family used to throw the best parties in Angeles City. For a great party, you need some delicious food. Of course there would be lechon, adobo, pancit, sinigang, lumpia, and rice. We eat rice for breakfast, lunch, and dinner, and rice even makes some of the best desserts. (My mom's bibingka and puto are perfect!) And you mustn't forget the drinks. San Miguel and Coke are usually sufficient. But we also had homemade mango juice and coconut milk. And a party wouldn't be a party without entertainment, right? So in one room, we had the gambling room. It's usually outside the house. Everybody would be smoking and drinking while playing mahjong. And sometimes, others would play pepito or pusoy dos. Music and dancing is always a must. And when there are firecrackers, better watch out because the children would go crazy with them.

3 Then one day, a mixed feeling came over me. My dad told us that he had gotten a job... in California. In the span of two months, we had moved to America, found a small apartment, and located a small private Catholic school for the kids. We did not know many people in California that first summer. We only had ourselves to depend on. We would go on car trips, go to the beach, cook, play games. In August, I thought we were living the American Dream.

4 But at the end of summer, school began. I was in the eighth grade. I had my book bag on one shoulder, stuffed with notebooks, folder paper, calculators, a ruler, a pencil box, and my lunch. I still can remember what I had for lunch on the first day of school—rice and tilapia and, in a small container, a mixture of vinegar, tomatoes, and bagoong. My mom placed everything in a big Tupperware box, knowing I eat a lot.

5 When I walked into the classroom, everyone became quiet and looked at me. I was the only Filipino in that room. Everyone was white. We began the day by introducing ourselves. When it got to my turn, I was really nervous. English was one of the courses that I took in the Philippines, and I thought I was pretty proficient at it. But when I first opened my mouth, everyone began to laugh. The teacher told everyone to hush. I sat down, smiling faintly not understanding what was so funny. I knew English, and yet I was laughed at. But it had nothing to do with the language. It was my accent.

6 Some students tried to be nice, especially during lunch. But it didn't last long. I was so hungry for my lunch. I followed a group of students to the cafeteria and

sat down at an empty table. Some girls joined me. I didn't really talk to them, but they asked if they could join me. As I opened my Tupperware, I saw their heads turn away. They didn't like the smell of fish and bagoong. The girls left and moved to another table of girls. From the corner of my eye I saw them looking and laughing at me. I tried to ignore it, concentrating on eating my lunch as I heard them laugh. In the Philippines, the only way to eat fish and rice is with your hands. But that was in the Philippines. My manners were primitive here in America. I was embarrassed at the smell, was embarrassed at the way I ate, was embarrassed to be me.

7 When I got home, I lied to my parents. I told them school was great and that I was excited to go back. But deep down, I wanted to go back to the Philippines. When lunch came the next day, I was hungry. In my hand was my lunch. Five feet away was the trash. I stood up, taking my lunch in my hands. Slowly, I walked my way towards the trashcan, opened the lid, and watched as my lunch filled the trashcan. Again, I told my parents I enjoyed school.

8 When my grades began to suffer, the teacher called my parents and scheduled an appointment. The next day, my parents came to the classroom, and when they started talking to the teacher I heard laughter in the background. It humiliated me to have my classmates hear my parents talk.

9 That night, my parents and I had a private discussion. They asked why I lied to them. I told them everything, including my humiliation. They told me not to worry about it, but I pleaded for us to return to the Philippines. My parents said no. "Living here will provide a better future for you and your sisters," they said. Then the unexpected came. I didn't know what I was thinking. I yelled to them with so much anger, "I hate being Filipino!" Silence filled the room. Teardrops rolled down my cheeks. My parents were shocked, and so was I.

10 I went to my room and cried. I didn't mean what I said. But I was tired of the humiliation. Lying on my bed, with my eyes closed, my mind began to wander. I found myself in the boat with the Mousekewitz family singing, "There are no cats in America." If only they knew how wrong they were.

THINKING CRITICALLY
about "No Cats in America?"

Patrick José lets the reader infer his essay's significance from the details of the narrative and from their connection to the framing story of the fictional mice and cats.

1. How do the settings help you understand José's theme at different points in the narrative?
2. What would you say is the narrative's climax or pivotal moment?
3. José's title, first paragraph, and last paragraph are about a children's movie that features the Mousekewitz's song proclaiming that there are no cats in America. How does the "no cats" image function both as part of the underlying tension

of this narrative and as a symbolic vehicle for conveying the theme of José's essay? What is the insight that José has achieved at the end?

4. During a rough draft workshop, José asked his peer reviewers whether he should retain his description of parties in the Philippines, which he thought was perhaps unconnected to the rest of the narrative. His classmates urged him to keep those details. Do you agree with their advice? Why?
5. For Filipinos and Filipinas, the specific names of foods and party games would be rich examples of memory-soaked words. For other readers, however, these names are foreign and strange. Do you agree with José's decision to use these specific ethnic names? Why?

See Skill 18.2 for a discussion of the power of memory-soaked words.

Our final reading, a literacy narrative, is by student writer Stephanie Whipple.

Stephanie Whipple (student)

One Great Book

1 When first asked to remember my earliest experiences with reading, I thought of my favorite books as a young teen, and I was excited to explore how they shaped the person that I am today. However, upon trying to remember the very first books that I ever read as a child, some quite negative and frankly painful memories were brought to the surface.

2 When I was a little girl living in Memphis, Tennessee, I was a well-behaved bright child who never had trouble learning at a good pace or working with other children. In what I am guessing was my first grade class I remember being so excited when I found out that that year I was going to learn to read. My entire life, my mother and both of my older sisters have all loved reading. I was so excited to be able to read with them and join the big girls' conversations about the books that they were reading.

3 My very first vivid memory of reading was in the playroom of our house in Memphis. I was sitting with my father reading *The Poky Little Puppy* with him, and my younger brother, who had just started kindergarten, was playing with his Nerf gun.

4 "Okay, Steph. Start with this word." My dad points to the first word on the page.

5 "Ff...i...fi—"

6 "Five!" My little brother pops his little freckled face over my shoulder.

7 "Stevie, Steph and I are reading this first. You can read it after her" says my father turning to me. "Go ahead Steph."

8 "Five...li...lit—"

9 "Little puppies!" yells Stevie from right behind me.

10 I turn away from the book, discouraged.

11 "Stephen!" says our father sternly. "Let Stephanie read. She knows the words; she just has to think about it for a little while. Go play over there and we will read a book when she is done." My Dad turns to me and smiles.

12 "Five little puppies... d... dug... a... h... h—"

13 "A hole under the fence!" My brother is behind me again, and I cannot believe that he is smarter than I am. He is only in kindergarten. You're not even supposed to start learning words until the first grade! I drop *The Poky Little Puppy* and run to my mommy, telling myself that reading is stupid, and I don't want to learn how anymore. Drawing and doing other arts and crafts are much more fun anyway, and Stevie can't even draw a bunny!

14 I was by no means a slow learner; Steve was just an exceptionally fast learner when it came to reading. He knew how to read whole chapter books before any of his peers could even read *The Poky Little Puppy.* However, the fact that my little brother could read better than I could made me feel stupid and I lost all of my previous enthusiasm about books.

15 Both of my parents desperately tried to get me to like reading. They were always sure to separate my brother and me when they were helping me with my reading, but I had shut down. My mom always tried to read to me before bed, but I told her that I hated books. Instead I wanted her to make up stories and tell them to me, or tell me stories about when she was a little girl. I had made up my mind that I hated reading. If I didn't like it, I wouldn't have to be good at it. So, I did just as much reading as my teacher and my parents forced me to do, but that was it. When my brother was reading every word of *Calvin and Hobbes* comics and needing no help from my father, I was coloring Calvin's hair pink and turning Hobbes into a purple tiger with big black sunglasses on.

16 I continued to dislike reading for years. As I got older, I never finished any of the chapter books that I was required to read for school, and I certainly never read the other books that my mother was constantly trying to get me to read. I remember her telling me, "If you just find one book that you really love, you will love reading forever. I promise." My response was always, "Mom, reading is boring. I'm not a nerd." I wanted to spend my spare time playing with my friends and making friendship bracelets, not reading *A Wrinkle in Time* like my dorky little brother.

17 My parents have since told me that my not liking to read broke their hearts. My dad felt like it was his fault for reading with me around my brother. They did not know what to do, and they were convinced that I would go through my entire life without ever enjoying a good book.

18 One rainy summer day when I was about fourteen years old, however, all of this changed. My family and I were at our mountain house in the Poconos and the weather was too bad to go out on the boat or play outside, so I was bored. I approached my mom to ask her to play a game with me while she was sitting on our screened-in porch reading. She told me that she bought me a book that she loved when she was my age, and suggested that she read some of it to me just to see if I might like it. I don't know if it was out of utter boredom, being worn down by my mom constantly nagging me to read, or just out of really wanting to spend time with my mother, but I agreed. The book was about a little girl named Francie who was extremely poor and lived in a city that I was completely unfamiliar with, but I still related to her. I loved Francie, and after my mom finished reading the first chapter to me and left to go to the store, I continued reading the book and didn't put it down until it was time for dinner.

I loved reading! When I was not reading, I was thinking about Francie and hoping that everything would turn out all right for her. The book had opened up a whole new world for me in which a family could be so poor and have almost none of the things that I was accustomed to, but still be happy and full of love and warmth and hope. I spent the whole week reading my book and discussing it with my mom and sisters.

19 I do not remember the next good book or even the next five good books that my mother gave me and I enthusiastically poured myself into. However, to this day whenever anyone mentions *A Tree Grows in Brooklyn*, or I see the movie on TV, or I read about another character named Frances or Francie, I get a warm feeling in my heart, and I thank God for my mother and her persistence. Without my mom, and without that one great book, I might not be the person and the reader that I am today. If anyone ever tells me that they do not like reading, I smile and tell them, "If you just find one book that you really love, you will love reading forever. I promise."

THINKING CRITICALLY
about "One Great Book"

1. In this literacy narrative, how does Stephanie Whipple create tension and establish the main conflicts?
2. In her desire to engage readers with her characters and setting, Stephanie chooses to use the present tense rather than the past tense for her early scene about reading. Do you find this choice effective? (It violates the normal rules about needless shifting of tense.) How else does she try to engage readers in her characters and setting?
3. This piece leads up to a moment of breakthrough and new insight about the significance of reading. How does Stephanie use story elements rather than straight exposition to convey her transformation in her attitude toward literature?
4. In much of this narrative, Stephanie includes words that are specific and descriptive—that is, low on the ladder of abstraction. What passages are vivid and memorable?
5. This piece is fairly straightforward, yet it points to some deeper themes about learning. What new understanding about children and reading does Stephanie want readers to grasp?

7 WRITING AN EXPLORATORY ESSAY OR ANNOTATED BIBLIOGRAPHY

WHAT YOU WILL LEARN

7.1 To pose a significant and problematic research question.

7.2 To explore your problem and narrate your thinking process in an exploratory essay.

7.3 To think about your problem dialectically, find relevant sources, and take effective research notes.

7.4 To summarize and critique your research sources in an annotated bibliography.

In Part 1, we explained how writers wrestle with subject-matter problems. During exploration, experienced writers often redefine their problem, discover new ideas, and alter or even reverse their initial thesis. In contrast, inexperienced writers often truncate this process, closing off the period of exploratory thinking. Asserting a thesis too soon can prevent writers from acknowledging an issue's complexity, whereas dwelling with a question invites writers to contemplate multiple perspectives, entertain new ideas, and let their thinking evolve. In this chapter, we introduce two genres of writing built on exploratory thinking:

- An **exploratory essay** narrates a writer's thinking process while doing research. The essay recounts your attempt to examine your question's complexity, explore alternatives, and arrive at a solution or answer. Because an exploration often requires research, many instructors pair this project with Part 4, "A Rhetorical Guide to Research."
- An **annotated bibliography** summarizes and briefly critiques the research sources a writer used while exploring a problem. It encourages exploration and inquiry, provides a "tracing" of your work, and creates a guide for others interested in your research problem.

Engaging Exploratory Writing

Through our work in writing centers, we often encounter students disappointed with their grades on essay exams or papers. "I worked hard on this paper," they tell us, "but I still got a lousy grade. What am I doing wrong? What do college professors want?"

To help you think about this question, read the following two essays written for a freshman placement examination in composition at the University of Pittsburgh, and then formulate your own response to the questions that follow.* The essays were written for this assignment:

Describe a time when you did something you felt to be creative. Then, on the basis of the incident you have described, go on to draw some general conclusions about "creativity."

ESSAY A

I am very interested in music, and I try to be creative in my interpretation of music. While in high school, I was a member of a jazz ensemble. The members of the ensemble were given chances to improvise and be creative in various songs. I feel that this was a great experience for me, as well as the other members. I was proud to know that I could use my imagination and feelings to create music other than what was written.

Creativity to me means being free to express yourself in a way that is unique to you, not having to conform to certain rules and guidelines. Music is only one of the many areas in which people are given opportunities to show their creativity. Sculpting, carving, building, art, and acting are just a few more areas where people can show their creativity.

Through my music I conveyed feelings and thoughts which were important to me. Music was my means of showing creativity. In whatever form creativity takes, whether it be music, art, or science, it is an important aspect of our lives because it enables us to be individuals.

ESSAY B

Throughout my life, I have been interested and intrigued by music. My mother has often told me of the times, before I went to school, when I would "conduct" the orchestra on her records. I continued to listen to music and eventually started to play the guitar and the clarinet. Finally, at about the age of twelve, I started to sit down and to try to write songs. Even though my instrumental skills were far from my own high standards, I would spend much of my spare time during the day with a guitar around my neck, trying to produce a piece of music.

Each of these sessions, as I remember them, had a rather set format. I would sit in my bedroom, strumming different combinations of the five or six chords I could play, until I heard a series which sounded particularly good to me. After this, I set the music to a suitable rhythm (usually dependent on my mood at the time), and ran through the tune until I could play it fairly easily. Only after this section was complete did I go on to writing lyrics, which generally followed along the lines of the current popular songs on the radio.

*For our discussion of the creativity assignment, we are indebted to David Bartholomae, "Inventing the University," *When Writers Can't Write: Studies in Writer's Block and Other Composing Process Problems*. Ed. Mike Rose. New York, Guilford Press, 1985: pp. 273–85.

At the time of the writing, I felt that my songs were, in themselves, an original creation of my own; that is, I, alone, made them. However, I now see that, in this sense of the word, I was not creative. The songs themselves seem to be an oversimplified form of the music I listened to at the time.

In a more fitting sense, however, I *was* being creative. Since I did not purposely copy my favorite songs, I was, effectively, originating my songs from my own "process of creativity." To achieve my goal, I needed what a composer would call "inspiration" for my piece. In this case the inspiration was the current hit on the radio. Perhaps, with my present point of view, I feel that I used too much "inspiration" in my songs, but, at the time, I did not.

Creativity, therefore, is a process which, in my case, involved a certain series of "small creations" if you like. As well, it is something the appreciation of which varies with one's point of view, that point of view being set by the person's experience, tastes, and his own personal view of creativity. The less experienced tend to allow for less originality, while the more experienced demand real originality to classify something a "creation." Either way, a term as abstract as this is perfectly correct, and open to interpretation.

ON YOUR OWN

Note the major differences between Essay A and Essay B. What might cause college professors to rate one essay higher than the other?

IN CONVERSATION

Compare your responses with those of other class members. As a group, make suggestions about what the writer of the weaker essay has to do to produce an essay more like the stronger.

7.1 Understanding Exploratory Writing

7.1 Pose a significant and problematic research question.

Even though academic readers usually expect thesis-driven arguments, both exploratory essays and annotated bibliographies are frequently encountered. Exploratory essays exist in embryo in the research or lab notebooks of scholars. For students, both the exploratory essay and the annotated bibliography serve as an intermediate stage in the research process. Student Kent Ansen's exploratory paper and annotated bibliography in this chapter are products of the exploratory phase of his research about mandatory public service, which later resulted in a researched argument. You can compare his exploratory essay with the final thesis-driven argument in Chapter 15 (pp. 405–414).

The essential move for exploratory thinking and writing is to keep a problem alive through consideration of multiple solutions or points of view. The thinker identifies a problem, considers a possible solution or point of view, explores its strengths and weaknesses, and then moves on to consider another possible solution or viewpoint. The thinker resists closure—that is, resists settling too soon on a thesis.

To show a mind at work examining multiple solutions, let's return to the two student essays you examined in the previous Engaging activity (pp. 145–146). The fundamental difference between Essay A and Essay B is that the writer of Essay B treats the concept of "creativity" as a true problem. Note that the writer of Essay A is satisfied with his or her initial definition:

> Creativity to me means being free to express yourself in a way that is unique to you, not having to conform to certain rules and guidelines.

The writer of Essay B, however, is *not* satisfied with his or her first answer and uses the essay to think through the problem. This writer remembers an early creative experience—composing songs as a twelve-year-old:

> At the time of the writing, I felt that my songs were, in themselves, an original creation of my own; that is, I, alone, made them. However, I now see that, in this sense of the word, I was not creative. The songs themselves seem to be an oversimplified form of the music I listened to at the time.

This writer distinguishes between two points of view: "On the one hand, I used to think *x*, but now, in retrospect, I think *y*." This move forces the writer to go beyond the initial answer to think of alternatives.

The key to effective exploratory writing is to create a tension between alternative views. When you start out, you might not know where your thinking process will end up; at the outset you might not have formulated an opposing, countering, or alternative view. Using a statement such as "I used to think..., but now I think" or "Part of me thinks this..., but another part thinks that..." forces you to find something additional to say; writing then becomes a process of inquiry and discovery.

The second writer's dissatisfaction with the initial answer initiates a dialectic process that plays one idea against another, creating a generative tension. In contrast, the writer of Essay A offers no alternative to his or her definition of creativity. This writer presents no specific illustrations of creative activity (such as the specific details in Essay B about strumming the guitar) but presents merely space-filling abstractions ("Sculpting, carving, building, art, and acting are just a few more areas where people can show their creativity"). The writer of Essay B scores a higher grade, not because the essay creates a brilliant (or even particularly clear) explanation of creativity; rather, the writer is rewarded for thinking about the problem dialectically.

We use the term **dialectic** to mean a thinking process often associated with the German philosopher Hegel, who said that each thesis ("My act was creative") gives rise to an antithesis ("My act was not creative") and that the clash of these opposing perspectives leads thinkers to develop a synthesis that incorporates some features of both theses ("My act was a series of 'small creations'"). You initiate dialectic thinking any time you play Elbow's believing and doubting game or use other strategies to place alternative possibilities side by side.

Essay B's writer uses a dialectic thinking strategy that we might characterize as follows:

1. Sees the assigned question as a genuine problem worth puzzling over.
2. Considers alternative views and plays them off against each other.

3. Looks at specific examples and illustrations.
4. Continues the thinking process in search of some sort of resolution or synthesis of the alternative views.
5. Incorporates the stages of this dialectic process into the essay.

These same dialectic thinking habits can be extended to research writing where the researcher's goals are to find alternative points of view on the research question, to read sources rhetorically, to consider all the relevant evidence, to search for a resolution or synthesis of alternative views, and to use one's own critical thinking to arrive at a thesis.

FOR WRITING AND DISCUSSION

Keeping a Problem Open

1. Working individually, read each of the following questions and write out the first plausible answer that comes to your mind.
   - Why on average are males more attracted to video games than females? Are these games harmful to males?
   - Have online social networks such as Facebook improved or harmed the lives of participants? Why?
   - The most popular magazines sold on college campuses are women's fashion and lifestyle magazines such as *Glamour*, *Elle*, and *Cosmopolitan*. Why do women buy these magazines? Are these magazines harmful?
2. As a whole class, take a poll to determine the most common first-response answers for each of the questions. Then explore other possible answers and points of view. The goal of your class discussion is to postulate and explore answers that go against the grain of or beyond the common answers. Try to push deeply into each question so that it becomes more complex and interesting than it may at first seem.
3. How would you use library and Internet research to deepen your exploration of these questions? Specifically, what keywords might you use in a database search? What databases would you use?

WRITING PROJECT

An Exploratory Essay

7.2 Explore your problem and narrate your thinking process in an exploratory essay.

Choose a question, problem, or issue that genuinely perplexes you. At the beginning of your essay, explain why you are interested in this problem, why you think it is significant, and why you have been unable to reach a satisfactory answer. Then write a first-person, chronologically organized narrative account of your thinking process as you investigate your question through research, talking with others, and doing your own reflective thinking. Your goal is to examine your question, problem, or issue from a variety of perspectives, assessing the strengths and weaknesses of different positions and points of view. Your goal is not to answer your question but to report on the process of wrestling with it.

This assignment asks you to dwell on a problem—and not necessarily to solve that problem. Your problem may shift and evolve as your thinking progresses. What matters is that you are actively engaged with your problem and demonstrate why it is problematic.

Generating and Exploring Ideas

Your process of generating and exploring ideas is, in essence, the *subject matter* of your exploratory essay. This section will help you get started and keep going.

Posing Your Initial Problem

If your instructor hasn't assigned a specific problem to be investigated, then your first step is to choose one that currently perplexes you. Perhaps a question is problematic for you because you haven't yet had a chance to study it (Should the United States turn to nuclear power for generating electricity?). Maybe the available data seem conflicting or inconclusive (Should women younger than fifty get annual mammograms?). Or, possibly, the problem or issue draws you into an uncomfortable conflict of values (Should we legalize the sale of organs for transplant?).

The key to this assignment is to choose a question, problem, or issue *that truly perplexes you.* (Your instructor may limit the range of topics you can choose.) Here are several exercises to help you think of ideas for this essay:

- Make a list of issues or problems that both interest and perplex you within the range of subjects specified by your instructor. Then choose two or three and freewrite about them for five minutes or so. Use as your model Kent Ansen's freewrite on pages 26–27, which marked the origin of his exploratory paper for this chapter. Share your questions and your freewrites with friends and classmates because doing so often stimulates further thinking and discovery.
- A particularly valuable kind of problem to explore for this assignment is a current public controversy. Often such issues involve disagreements about facts and values that merit open-ended exploration. This assignment invites you to explore and clarify where you stand on such public issues as gay marriage, immigration, health care reform, energy policies, government responses to terrorism, and so forth. Make a list of currently debated public controversies that you would like to explore. Share your list with classmates and friends.

Formulating a Starting Point

After you've chosen a problem, you are ready to write a first draft of your introduction in which you identify your chosen problem and show why you are interested in it, why you find it perplexing, and why it is significant. You might start out with a sharp, clearly focused question (Should the United States build a fence between the United States and Mexico?). Often, however, formulating a focused question will turn out to be part of the *process* of writing the paper. Instead of a single, focused question, you might start with a whole cluster of related questions swimming in your head. That's fine too because you can still explain why you are interested in this cluster of questions.

The goal of your introduction is to hook your reader's interest in your chosen problem. Often the best way to do so is to show why you yourself became interested in it. For example, Kent Ansen opens his exploratory essay by recalling his experience with volunteer work and his discussion with older friends who are questioning their majors and their futures (see p. 160). He then introduces the questions he wants to investigate—how could mandatory public service benefit the country and youth and should it be installed as a requirement for all youth?

7.3
Think about your problem dialectically, find relevant sources, and take effective research notes.

Taking "Double-Entry" Research Notes

After you have formulated your initial problem, you are ready to start your research. As you read, take purposeful notes, as explained in Skill 21.1 in Part 4, "A Rhetorical Guide to Research." Whereas novice researchers often avoid taking notes and instead create a pile of photocopied or downloaded-and-printed articles, experienced researchers use note taking as a discipline to promote strong rhetorical reading. We recommend "double-entry" notes in which you use one column for taking notes on a source and another column for recording your own thinking about the source. When you have finished taking notes in the first column, write a "strong response" to the source in the second column, explaining how the source advanced your thinking, raised questions, or pulled you in one direction or another.

What follows is Kent Ansen's double-entry research notes for one of the articles he used in his exploratory essay. When you read both his exploratory essay in this chapter and his final researched argument in Chapter 15, you'll be able to see how he used this article at a crucial place in his research.

Kent's Double-Entry Research Log Entry for the Opinion Piece in the *Chronicle of Philanthropy*

Date of entry so you can reconstruct chronological order →

February 8

Bibliographic citation following assigned format, in this case MLA →

Rosenman, Mark. "A Call for National Service." *Chronicle of Philanthropy* 2007: 38. *Proquest*. Web. 8 Feb. 2013.

Rhetorical notation about genre, purpose, audience →

Editorial in the journalistic style in the opinion section of a magazine for "the nonprofit world"

Reading notes in column 1 on content of the source →

Include full quotations if you won't keep a copy of the full source →

Reading Notes	Strong Response Notes
—Begins with the current political discussions about national service as voluntary or compulsory. Expresses Rosenman's view that compulsory national service might be good for citizen participation in public policy. Identifies a problem that as tax and fee payers only "we are reduced to little more than consumers of government services, to being government's customers."	*—Rosenman's point is a good one, but I think as voters and campaigners for candidates we also have a role as citizens. This quotation could be useful.*

—Argues that people have to own their government and get in there and do work.

—Says that "[m]andatory national service would change the relationship of people to their government and vice versa" and would lead to greater accountability required of leaders.

—This point makes sense and is a compelling moral argument. Makes me think of how a volunteer army keeps us from having the kind of stakes in our government's decisions as we did when we had a military draft.

Strong response notes in column 2 show reactions to the source

—Moves into a section on the urgency of citizen involvement in deteriorating conditions, loss of economic status for poor and middle class, money spent on wars, and so forth.

—I wish Rosenman could have offered more examples and maybe some statistics.

—Mentions low voter turnout.

—Could give more details.

—Develops the reasons supporting his main claim by discussing his points: people would make a connection between policies and their effects; observing "constituencies poorly served by government" would increase people's involvement in government; service would connect Americans across typical barriers "by race, class, ethnicity, religion, geography, perhaps even age."

—This thinking is useful in presenting one angle on my question. In my volunteer work I often saw how government service could be improved—made me want to do something.

—Rosenman then briefly discusses the practical dimensions of his view—how to make a mandatory national service plan work. He mentions two-year service, stipends or salary, and credit toward education. He says that schools should make service an important part of the curriculum to build character and citizens....

—I am glad he devotes some space to practical considerations. However, I wonder if I would have found my high school volunteering as effective if the school made me do it?

—He acknowledges that any employees who might have their jobs taken by community-service workers should be given new opportunities, maybe training the service workers.

—Good idea to confront this objection to mandatory public service.

[Kent's research log continued to cover the whole article.]

Part of Kent's strong response summary:
Very useful article, not scholarly but clear in the argument it asserts. I will use this source to represent the liberal perspective on mandatory public service. Rosenman is a public service professor at Union Institute and University and clearly has a strong background in this issue. This article provides a broad-strokes approach and overview of the pro–national service position. I will want to give more depth to this view and also examine arguments against it.

Shaping and Drafting

Your exploratory essay records the history of your researching and thinking process (what you read or whom you talked to, how you responded, how your thinking evolved). Along the way you can make your narrative more colorful and grounded by including your strategies for tracking down sources, your conversations with friends, your late-night trips to a coffee shop, and so forth. What you will quickly discover about this exploratory assignment is that it forces you actually to do the research. Unless you conduct your research in a timely fashion, you won't have any research process to write about.

Exploratory essays can be composed in two ways—what we might call the "real-time strategy" and the "retrospective strategy."

Strategies for Composing an Exploratory Essay

Strategies	Advantages
Real-time strategy. Compose the body of the essay during the actual process of researching and thinking.	Yields genuine immediacy—like a sequence of letters or e-mails sent home during a journey.
Retrospective strategy. Look back over your completed research notes and then compose the body of the essay.	Allows for more selection and shaping of details and yields a more artistically designed essay.

In either case, the goal when writing with an exploratory aim is to reproduce the research and thinking process, taking the readers on the same intellectual and emotional journey you have just traveled. The exploratory essay has the general organizational framework shown in Figure 7.1.

There are a number of keys to writing successful exploratory papers. As you draft, pay particular attention to the following:

- ***Show how you chose sources purposively and reflectively rather than randomly.*** As you make a transition from one source to the next, help your reader see your thought processes. Note the following examples of bridging passages that reveal the writer's purposeful selection of sources:

  At this point, I decided I should investigate more thoroughly the drawbacks of mandatory national service, so I turned to an online *Time* article that was a direct response to Stengel: Michael Kinsley's "National Service? Puh-lease" (from Kent Ansen's essay, para. 7, p. 162).

  After reading Friedman's views of how globalization was changing lives in India and China, I realized that I needed to *talk* to some students from these countries, so I grabbed my backpack and headed to the International Student Center.

- ***Give your draft both open-form and closed-form features.*** Because your exploratory paper is a narrative, it follows an unfolding, open-form structure. Many of your paragraphs should open with chronological transitions such as "I *started* by reading," "*Early the next morning,* I headed for the library to...," "On the *next* day, I decided," or "*After* finishing...I *next* looked at...." At the same time, your summaries of your sources and your strong responses to them should be framed within closed-form structures with topic sentences and logical transitions: "This article, in raising objections to genetic screening of embryos, began changing my views about new advances in reproductive technology. Whereas before I felt..., now I feel...."

FIGURE 7.1 Framework for an Exploratory Essay

Introduction (one or more paragraphs)	• Establishes that your question is complex, problematic, and significant • Shows why you are interested in it • Presents relevant background You can begin with your question or build up to it, using it to end your introductory section.
Body section 1 on first source	• Introduces your first source and shows why you started with it • Provides rhetorical context and information about the source • Summarizes the source's content and argument • Offers your strong response to this source, frequently including both with-the-grain and against-the-grain points • Talks about what this source contributes to your understanding of your question: What did you learn? What value does this source have for you? What is missing from this source that you want to consider? Where do you want to go from here?
Body section 2 on second source	• Repeats the process with a new source selected to advance the inquiry • Explains why you selected this source (to find an alternative view, pursue subquestions, find more data, and so forth) • Summarizes the source's argument • Provides a strong response • Shows how your cumulative reading of sources is shaping your thinking or leading to more questions
Body sections 3, 4, 5, etc., on additional sources	• Continues the process
Conclusion	• Wraps up your intellectual journey and explains where you are now in your thinking and how your understanding of your problem has changed • Presents your current answer to your question based on all that you have read and learned so far, or explains why you still can't answer your question, or explains what further research you might do
Works Cited or References list	• Includes a complete list of citations in MLA or APA format, depending on your assignment

- ***Show yourself wrestling with ideas.*** Readers want to see how your research stimulates your own thinking. Throughout, your paper should show you responding strongly to your sources. Here is a good example from Kent's paper on mandatory public service.

However, Rosenman did not offer any concrete evidence in support of his claims. Instead, his philosophical approach helped me understand some of the moral arguments—essentially, that public service can make us better people who live in better communities—but these arguments would not convince people who value small government and dislike government intrusion on personal freedom. I was particularly drawn to the idea that national service would make people feel more invested in their government. I wondered if I could locate any evidence showing that community service led people to become more personally involved in working on our country's problems.

Although you might feel that sentences that show your mind talking its way through your research will sound too informal, they actually work well in exploratory essays to create interest and capture your critical thinking.

Revising

Because an exploratory essay describes the writer's research and thinking in chronological order, most writers have little trouble with organization. When they revise, their major concern is to improve their essay's interest level by keeping it focused and lively. Often drafts need to be pruned to remove extraneous details and keep the pace moving. Frequently, introductions can be made sharper, clearer, and more engaging. Peer reviewers can give you valuable feedback about the pace and interest level of an exploratory piece. They can also help you achieve the right balance between summarizing sources and showing the evolution of your own thinking. As you revise, make sure you use attributive tags and follow proper stylistic conventions for quotations and citations.

Questions for Peer Review

In addition to the generic peer review questions explained in Skill 16.4, ask your peer reviewers to address these questions:

POSING THE PROBLEM

1. In the introduction, how has the writer tried to show that the problem is interesting, significant, and problematic? How could the writer engage you more fully with the initial problem?
2. How does the writer provide cues that his/her purpose is to explore a question rather than argue a thesis? How might the opening section of the draft be improved?

NARRATING THE EXPLORATION

3. Is the body of the paper organized chronologically so that you can see the development of the writer's thinking? Where does the writer provide chronological transitions?
4. Part of an exploratory essay involves summarizing the argument of each new research source. Where in this draft is a summary of a source particularly clear and well developed? Where are summary passages either undeveloped or unclear or too long? How could these passages be improved?
5. Another part of an exploratory paper involves the writer's strong response to each source. Where in this draft is there evidence of the writer's own critical thinking and questioning? Where are the writer's ideas particularly strong and effective? Where are the writer's own ideas undeveloped, unclear, or weak?

6. Has the writer done enough research to explore the problem? How would you describe the range and variety of sources that the writer has consulted? Where does the writer acknowledge how the kinds of sources shape his or her perspective on the subject? What additional ideas or perspectives do you think the writer should consider?

An Annotated Bibliography

WRITING PROJECT

7.4 Summarize and critique your research sources in an annotated bibliography.

Create an annotated bibliography that lists the research sources you have used for your exploratory project. Because annotated bibliographies can vary in the number, length, and kinds of entries, follow guidelines provided by your instructor. Some instructors may also require a critical preface that explains your research question and provides details about how you selected the bibliographic sources.

What Is an Annotated Bibliography?

Bibliographies are alphabetized lists of sources on a given topic, providing readers with the names of authors, titles, and publication details for each source. Unlike a plain list of sources, an **annotated bibliography** also includes the writer's "annotation" or commentary on each source. These annotations can be either *summary-only* or *evaluative.*

- A **summary-only annotation** provides a capsule of the source's contents without any additional comments from the bibliography's author.
- An **evaluative annotation** adds the author's critique or assessment of the work, including comments about the source's rhetorical context, its particular strengths or weaknesses, and its usefulness or value.

Whichever type is used, the length of the annotation is a function of its audience and purpose. Brief annotations comprise only a few sentences (one standard approach—to be described later—uses three sentences) while longer annotations can be up to 150 words. Brief annotations are most common when the annotated bibliography has numerous entries; longer annotations, which allow for fuller summaries and more detailed analyses, are often more helpful for readers but can make an annotated bibliography too long if there are many sources.

Annotated bibliographies serve several important functions. First, writing an annotated bibliography engages researchers in exploratory thinking by requiring that they read sources rhetorically like experts, entering critically into scholarly conversations. Annotated bibliographies can also be valuable time-saving tools for new researchers in a field. By providing overview information about potential sources, they help new researchers determine whether a particular source might be useful for their own purposes. Think of source annotations as analogous to short movie reviews that help you select your next film. (What's this movie about? How good is it?) Additionally, annotated bibliographies can establish the writer's *ethos* by showing the depth, breadth, and competence of the writer's research. (A good annotated bibliography proves that you have read and thought about your sources.)

Features of Annotated Bibliography Entries

Each entry has two main parts, the bibliographic citation and the annotation. The **bibliographic citation** should follow the conventions of your assigned documentation style such as the Modern Language Association (MLA) or the American Psychological Association (APA).

An **evaluative annotation** (the most common kind) typically includes three elements. In a three-sentence evaluative annotation, each element is covered in one sentence.

- ***Rhetorical information,*** including the source's rhetorical context, particularly its genre and (if not implied by the genre) its purpose and audience. Is this source a scholarly article? An op-ed piece? A blog? What is the author's purpose and who is the intended audience? Are there any political biases that need to be noted?
- ***A summary of the source's content.*** In some cases, a writer simply lists what is covered in the source. Whenever possible, however, summarize the source's actual argument. (Note: In a *summary-only* annotation, this summary is the only element included.)
- ***The writer's evaluation of the source.*** What are the source's particular strengths or weaknesses? How useful is the source for specific purposes? How might the writer use the source for his or her research project? (Or, if the annotated bibliography comes at the end of the project, how did the writer use the source?)

Examples of Annotation Entries

Here are examples of different kinds of annotations based on Kent Ansen's research notes for one of his sources (see pp. 150–151):

SUMMARY-ONLY ANNOTATION

Rosenman, Mark. "A Call for National Service." *Chronicle of Philanthropy* 2007: 38. *Proquest.* Web. 8 Feb. 2013.

Rosenman argues that compulsory national service would engage Americans directly with the urgent problems facing our nation, shifting Americans from being passive consumers of government services to active stakeholders who demand accountability from elected officials. He suggests that compulsory service would promote empathy for the poor and marginalized, create awareness of the real world impacts of public policy, and inspire a sense of shared responsibility for the results. He also provides some practical considerations for how to make compulsory service work.

EVALUATIVE ANNOTATION

Rosenman, Mark. "A Call for National Service." *Chronicle of Philanthropy* 2007: 38. *Proquest.* Web. 8 Feb. 2013.

The article is a call to action directed at nonprofit leaders, urging them to build bipartisan support for compulsory national service and providing tips on how to make their proposals effective. It was published in the opinion section of the *Chronicle of Philanthropy*, which provides news and information to influence philanthropic professionals who likely already support an expansion of national service. The author argues that compulsory national service would engage Americans directly with the urgent problems facing the nation, shifting a disengaged and passive public to an active, engaged citizenry capable of holding the government accountable for its response. The article provides a good overview of the basic arguments and assumptions that support mandatory service and is helpful in understanding how people who already believe in national service think about its value and impact. However, its claims lack specific evidence and therefore read mostly as assumptions, which weakens the persuasive power of the piece and its usefulness as backing for the call for national service.

THREE-SENTENCE EVALUATIVE ANNOTATION

Rosenman, Mark. "A Call for National Service." *Chronicle of Philanthropy* 2007: 38. *Proquest*. Web. 8 Feb. 2013.

This persuasive argument aims to help nonprofit leaders make an effective public policy case for compulsory national service. Rosenman argues that by connecting Americans with real-world problems and the people negatively affected by them, compulsory service would create active, responsive citizens who hold government accountable for results. This source provides some good general suggestions for how to make compulsory national service work and asserts many of the common arguments in support of it, although its claims are mostly assumptions unsupported by evidence.

Writing a Critical Preface for Your Annotated Bibliography

Scholars who publish annotated bibliographies typically introduce them with a critical preface that explains the scope and purpose of the bibliography. When you write a critical preface for your own annotated bibliography, you have a chance to highlight your critical thinking and show the purposeful way that you conducted your research. Typically the critical preface includes the following information:

- A contextual overview that shows the purpose of the annotated bibliography and suggests its value and significance for the reader
- The research question posed by the author
- The dates during which the bibliography was compiled
- An overview of the number of items in the bibliography and the kinds of material included

A student example of an annotated bibliography with a critical preface is found in the Readings section of this chapter (pp. 165–167).

Shaping, Drafting, and Revising

The key to producing a good annotated bibliography is to take good research notes as you read. Compare the various versions of the above annotations with Kent Ansen's research notes (pp. 150–151). Before composing your annotated bibliography, make sure that you understand your instructor's preferences for the number of entries required and for the length and kinds of annotations. Arrange the bibliography in alphabetical order as you would in a "Works Cited" (MLA format) or "References" (APA format) list.

The specific skills needed for an annotated bibliography are taught in various places in this text. If you are having problems with aspects of an annotated bibliography, you can find further instruction as follows.

Problems With	Where to Find Help
Formatting the citations.	Refer to Skill 23.3 for MLA style, and Skill 23.4 for APA style.
Describing the rhetorical context and genre.	Review Skill 21.1, and reread Chapter 1, Concept 1.2.
Writing a summary.	Read Chapter 5, pages 88–90, on summary writing; read also Skill 22.2.
Writing an evaluation.	Use the strategies for strong response in Chapter 5, pages 92–98, and also Skills 21.1–21.3.

Questions for Peer Review

The following questions are based on the assumption that your instructor requires evaluative annotations and a critical preface. Adjust the questions to fit a different assignment.

CRITICAL PREFACE

1. Where does the writer explain the following: The purpose and significance of the bibliography? The research question that motivated the research? The dates of the research? The kinds of sources included?
2. How could the critical preface be improved?

BIBLIOGRAPHIC CITATIONS

3. Does each citation follow MLA or APA conventions? Pay particular attention to the formatting of sources downloaded from a licensed database or from the Web.
4. Are the sources arranged alphabetically?

ANNOTATIONS

5. Where does each annotation include the following: Information about genre or rhetorical context? A capsule summary of the source's contents? An evaluative comment?
6. Identify any places where the annotations are confusing or unclear or where the writer could include more information.
7. How could one or more of the annotations be improved?

Multimodal or Online Options

Speech with Visual Aids (Flip Chart, PowerPoint, Prezi) Deliver your exploratory paper as a formal speech supported with visual aids. You can imagine an occasion for a short speech in which the audience is interested in your exploratory process while you wrestled with an interesting and engaging problem. If you use PowerPoint or Prezi slides to illustrate your exploration, you can include slides showing how you found sources (screen shots of search results or database abstracts). If you used any online sources such as blogs or videos, you might use hyperlinks to show these to your audience also. Pay equal attention to the construction and delivery of your speech and to the multimodal design of the visual aids. Your goal is to reproduce for your audience the narrative of your thinking process, particularly the moments that advanced or complicated your thinking.

Readings

Our first reading is an exploratory essay by student writer Kent Ansen on mandatory public service for young adults. After completing the exploratory essay, Kent continued his research, writing a proposal argument on the benefits of instigating a mandatory public service. Kent's final argument is our sample MLA student research paper and appears in Chapter 15 (pp. 405–414).

Kent Ansen (Student)

Should the United States Establish Mandatory Public Service for Young Adults?

1 During high school, I volunteered at an afterschool tutoring program in a poor neighborhood near my school. My guidance counselor stressed the importance of volunteer work in strong college applications, which was my primary motivation for volunteering. The more I volunteered, though, the more I began to see evidence of the two-way benefits of volunteer work. The program I volunteered with connected community members to a number of resources, such as food and healthcare benefits, and organized community cleanups and neighborhood celebrations. At the same time, I diversified my resume and had memorable experiences that gave me a different view of the community I lived in and people who were struggling with issues like poverty and hunger.

2 This experience was in the back of my mind during some recent conversations I had with friends who are college seniors. As they make plans for their lives after graduation, some of them are questioning the value of their majors as they face the competitive job market. Others are not sure what they want to do, even after four years of focused study in a particular field. I have heard a lot of buzz about volunteer programs like AmeriCorps and Jesuit Volunteer Corps, which place volunteers in needy communities for a year in exchange for a living stipend and the opportunity to gain work experience. In fact, the tutoring program I volunteered with was run by an AmeriCorps team. This type of volunteer work seems like a valuable opportunity for our generation, often referred to as the "Lost Generation" because of our struggles to settle on career paths and find direction, find jobs at all, and achieve stability in our lives. I have even heard of proposals to bring back the draft, not necessarily for military service but for national service on a broader scale. While mandatory public service would probably be controversial, it might benefit the country and youth in numerous ways. Pondering what I could gain from a mandatory year working on a national service project, I decided to pose the following question for this exploratory paper: Should the United States require a year of national service for all its young adults?

3 To begin, I wanted to familiarize myself with current national service programs in the United States. First, I wanted to have a good grasp of the range of work that AmeriCorps workers do, so I consulted the AmeriCorps website. According to this site, team-based projects focus on service in five areas: "natural and other disasters,

infrastructure improvement, environmental stewardship and conservation, energy conservation, and urban and rural development." Another part of the site spelled out this work even more concretely, explaining that participants can "tutor and mentor disadvantaged youth, fight illiteracy, improve health services, build affordable housing, teach computer skills, clean parks and streams, manage or operate after-school programs, and help communities respond to disasters…." AmeriCorps also supports the work of nonprofit organizations such as Habitat for Humanity and the Red Cross.

4 I then did several Google searches using search terms such as "national public service," "mandatory public service," and "AmeriCorps." These searches gave me a quick overview of the issues. The first lead I followed in depth was an article from a fact-checking website run by the Annenberg Corporation, which explained a proposed bill in the House and the Senate aimed at expanding national service (Robertson). Called the GIVE Act ("Generations Invigorating Volunteerism and Education") this bill expands national service organizations like AmeriCorps and funds increased participation to include 250,000 volunteers by 2014. Currently, 75,000 people participate in national service programs, so the GIVE Act represents a drastic increase in participation. Notably, the GIVE Act is not a bill for mandatory national service. It seems heavily reliant on expanding the current AmeriCorps program, which places volunteers in a variety of different volunteer settings in nonprofit and public agencies in exchange for a living stipend and an education award to pay for student loans or future educational opportunities. The GIVE Act helped me understand the scale of our current national service system. I was encouraged that the GIVE Act has strong bipartisan support. It suggests that there is public support for an expansion of national service.

5 To understand what an expanded national service program would look like, I wanted to find out if anyone had ever proposed a model. From my notes on my original Google searches, I found a 2007 article from *Time* entitled "A Time to Serve" (Stengel), which I then located in print in our library. Stengel describes a ten-point plan for creating universal national service, including a cabinet-level Department of National Service and the government purchase of a "baby bond" for each American baby (56). This bond would mature to around $19,000 by the time the baby reached young adulthood. This money could then be accessed if the person committed to a year of national service. The plan also includes ideas for a rapid response corps for disasters like Hurricane Katrina and for creating a national service academy. In addition to offering practical suggestions about how a national service program would work, Stengel argues that "a republic, to survive, [needs] not only the consent of the governed but also their active participation," asserting that "free societies do not stay free without the involvement of their citizens" (51).

6 This article made me confident that mandatory national public service was feasible, but I also began to realize why many people might object to mandatory service. It is one thing to recruit more young adults to volunteer for public service. It is another thing to require them to do so through a draft-like process. But then I noted that this article does not actually advocate *mandatory* national service. Instead it's calling for the "compelling idea that devoting a year or more to national service, whether military or civilian, should become a countrywide rite of passage" (55) or a socially perpetuated norm, not a government-mandated one. It seems like a nation powered

by a socially conscious momentum rather than a national service law would inspire more pride in and ownership of the service experience. Yet, would the people who might most benefit from doing public service actually volunteer if they weren't compelled to serve? For these people, national service could be incredibly transformative, but they might miss out on these opportunities if service were optional.

7 At this point, I decided I should investigate more thoroughly the drawbacks of mandatory national service, so I turned to an online *Time* article that was a direct response to Stengel: Michael Kinsley's "National Service? Puh-lease." (I Googled Michael Kinsley and discovered that he is a widely known conservative writer.) Kinsley uses a sarcastic tone to raise several problems with a mandatory national service plan or voluntary plans with strong incentives to participate. He argues that Stengel's proposal for a $19,000 bond that a person could access after completing a year of service would appeal to poor people more than rich people. In effect, the rich would simply buy their way out of public service. He also notes the hypocrisy of using social pressure and government incentives to encourage participation and then calling it "volunteerism." He sees Stengel's proposal as an infringement on personal freedom and on free markets. Arguing that people are willing to do any job for the right amount of money, Kinsley wonders why we would force someone to work for drastically less than a traditional employee would be paid when there is already a supply of workers in the market willing to do the same job for reasonable pay. Instead of making someone happy by providing a decently paying job, Stengel's proposal would put poor people out of work and force volunteers to work unhappily at minimum wage. For me, Kinsley's most powerful point was a reference to George Orwell's novel *1984*, which he uses to paint a picture of people forced into doing jobs that they would otherwise not take. Kinsley is also worried that volunteer work would be "make-work," meaning bureaucrats would spend time finding trivial ways to keep all the volunteers busy.

8 While I think Kinsley vastly underestimates the value of community service, I do understand his concern that forcing people to volunteer could undermine its impact. For me, though, a larger problem is putting volunteers to work on projects that require a lot of care when the volunteers themselves may not feel the intrinsic motivations and empathy required to deliver good service because they were forced into the role rather than choosing it for themselves. His article made me consider exactly how our democracy and the market do and should work together to create a socially-optimal reality. I agree that mandating service is problematic in a country that values freedom, but I also agree that many young Americans seem to take our democracy for granted. I understand Kinsley's point that mandatory service would interfere with market solutions to problems. Yet my understanding of government is that it exists to provide goods and services that the market fails to provide on its own. If the market is failing poor people, why should we rely on it to provide the solutions? Again, the conflict seems to come back to values, in this case the disagreements between those who value market solutions and those who value government intervention.

9 I decided I needed to pursue the perspective of someone who values government intervention and found Mark Rosenman's 2007 article "A Call for National Service," which I located in the journal *Chronicle of Philanthropy* using the *Proquest*

Complete database. Rosenman's main argument is that military or civilian national service "may be invaluable for getting Americans more involved in their government and more concerned about influencing public policy." He argues that through this direct service, citizens become more involved in government-provided services and "would more likely demand accountability from their elected leaders." Rosenman is concerned that we have become citizens whose only responsibility to government is to pay taxes and user fees, which makes us customers who passively take from government without investing effort to maintain and manage our democracy. Becoming more involved through national service will help restore citizens to being "owners" of government.

10 Overall, I found Rosenman's argument compelling, even though it did not help me resolve the conflict between those who value market solutions and those who value government intervention. His thoughts on active versus passive citizens echoed some of the points raised by "A Time to Serve" and got me excited about the idea of using national service to reinvigorate our levels of public engagement. However, Rosenman did not offer any concrete evidence in support of his claims. Instead, his philosophical approach helped me understand some of the moral arguments—essentially, that public service can make us better people who live in better communities—but these arguments would not convince people who value small government and dislike government intrusion on personal freedom. I was particularly drawn to the idea that national service would make people feel more invested in their government. I wondered if I could locate any evidence showing that community service led people to become more personally involved in working on our country's problems.

11 At this point, I realized it would be helpful to gain the perspectives of young adults who had volunteered for public service. I decided to look more closely at the AmeriCorps website and discovered a link to a page of quotations from AmeriCorps members who served with Rise, an organization in Minnesota that helps people with disabilities and other problems become self-sufficient ("Americorps Testimonials"). Several alumni noted the learning opportunities offered by AmeriCorps such as better understanding of the kinds of problems experienced by vulnerable populations and the difficulty of getting help. Several alumni noted how AmeriCorps provided opportunities for professional development and gave them work skills and leadership experiences that would transfer to future careers. Others noted how inspired they were by the people they worked with, both clients and coworkers.

12 These testimonials highlighted how impactful a year of service can be for individuals professionally and socially. I became convinced again that community service nurtures personal growth and civic engagement. Through helping others, AmeriCorps members are also able to help themselves—some even note they gain so much more than they give. This seemed like direct evidence of the two-way benefits I had experienced as a volunteer in high school and highlighted the potential value of service opportunities in light of the challenges young adults are facing today. However, I reminded myself that these testimonials did not constitute a random sample of AmeriCorps volunteers and didn't provide evidence that every volunteer (much less somebody forced to serve) would experience the same benefits.

13 The testimonials highlighted the anecdotal evidence of the benefits of national service. However, I wanted to find out whether there were any empirical studies that showed these benefits. On the "Research and Evaluation" section of the AmeriCorps website, I found a report issued by Abt Associates, an independent social policy and research firm, titled "Serving Country and Community: A Longitudinal Study of Service in AmeriCorps" (Jastrzab et al.). The study examines the impacts on participants' civic engagement, education, employment and life skills by surveying members upon entering and completing a term of service, including some follow-up three years after enrollment in AmeriCorps. This study found that participation in AmeriCorps had positive impacts on civic engagement and employment outcomes. In comparison to a control group not enrolled in service, alumni across AmeriCorps programs demonstrated statistically significant gains in basic work skills. Additionally, civic engagement behavior and attitudes were positively affected. Participation in AmeriCorps led to higher community-based activism and to a greater belief that communities could identify and solve problems. This study seemed to corroborate the AmeriCorps testimonials, providing evidence of the benefits of national service in terms of greater civic engagement.

14 Looking back over my research, I think the rewards of national service to individual volunteers and the communities they serve are clear. However, I continue to worry about the feasibility of making national service a mandatory program. As I end this exploratory paper, I still have some more research and thinking to do before I am ready to start my proposal argument. I am leaning in the direction of supporting mandatory public service. I am convinced that such service will benefit America's communities and also help the "Lost Generation" find themselves through learning more about our country's problems and developing valuable job skills. But the clincher for me—if I go in the direction I am leaning—is that mandatory public service would get Americans more involved in their government.

Works Cited

AmeriCorps. 2012. Web. 9 Feb. 2013.

"AmeriCorps Testimonials." *Rise: A Partnership that Works*. Rise, 2012. Web. 9 Feb. 2013.

Jastrzab, JoAnn, et al. "Serving Country and Community: A Longitudinal Study of Service in AmeriCorps." *Corporation for National and Community Service*. Abt Associates, Apr. 2007. Web. 10 Feb. 2013.

Kinsley, Michael. "National Service? Puh-lease." *Time Lists*. Time, 30 Aug. 2007. Web. 8 Feb. 2013.

Robertson, Lori. "Mandatory Public Service." *FactCheck.org*. Annenberg Public Policy Center, 31 Mar. 2009. Web. 6 Feb. 2013.

Rosenman, Mark. "A Call for National Service." *Chronicle of Philanthropy* 2007: 38. *Proquest*. Web. 8 Feb. 2013.

Stengel, Richard. "A Time to Serve." *Time* 10 Sept. 2007: 48–67. Print.

THINKING CRITICALLY

about "Should the United States Establish Mandatory Public Service for Young Adults?"

1. How does Kent show that his personal experience contributed to his interest in his chosen question?
2. Earlier in this chapter, we suggested ways to organize and strengthen an exploratory essay. Where do you see Kent including the following features: (a) A blend of open-form narrative moves with closed-form focusing sentences? (b) A purposeful selection of sources? (c) A consideration of the rhetorical context of his sources—that is, an awareness of the kinds of sources he is using and how the genre of the source influences its content? (d) Reflective/critical thinking that shows his strong response to his sources? (e) His dialectical thinking and critical evaluation of his sources?
3. Trace the evolution of Kent's ideas in this paper. How does his thinking change?
4. Read Kent's argument in favor of mandatory public service for young adults on pages 405–414. What new research did he do for his final argument? How do you see the exploratory paper contributing to Kent's argument in the final paper? How do differences in purpose (exploration versus persuasion) lead to different structures for the two papers?
5. What are the strengths and weaknesses of Kent's exploration of mandatory public service?

Our next reading is an excerpt from Kent's annotated bibliography based on the same research he did for his exploratory paper. We have used Kent's research for both examples so that you can compare an exploratory paper with an annotated bibliography. His original annotated bibliography contained six entries. We have printed three of these, along with his critical preface. Additionally, the evaluative annotated bibliography entry for the Rosenman article is shown on pages 156–157.

Kent Ansen (student)

Should the United States Establish Mandatory Public Service for Young Adults?

An Annotated Bibliography

Critical Preface

1 Today, national service programs like AmeriCorps seem to be gaining the attention of young adults who are facing a hostile job market and are unsure about their futures. I have also noticed some proposals to create a kind of draft that would extend

beyond military service to require terms of civil service from young adults, putting them to work on projects that meet basic needs like hunger and poverty. These plans are always controversial, especially in America, where we value freedom of choice. With this research project, I set out to explore the following questions: Should the United States require a year of national service from all its young adults? How would a plan of this scale be feasible? These questions are particularly important during a time of scarce resources, Congressional budget battles, growing social and economic divisions among our citizens, and general public mistrust of government. The country seems to be reevaluating the optimal level of citizen involvement in public life and where we should invest public resources.

2 I conducted this research over several days in early February 2013. My research included a variety of sources: a scholarly research study, two articles from a popular newsmagazine, an article from an online non-profit-sector journal, two webpages that provided program overviews and background information, a fact-checking website, and a nonprofit webpage of testimonials from national service participants. This research helped me better understand our current system of national service opportunities and see how this system could be expanded. The testimonials and the scholarly research study by Jastrzab et al. also highlighted the impacts national service has on individual participants. Several of these sources (particularly Rosenman and Kinsley) illuminated the different values, beliefs, and assumptions that drive disagreements about mandatory national service. Ultimately, these sources convinced me that our nation and young adults could greatly benefit from expanding national service, although I remain concerned about the feasibility of implementing a mandatory plan.

Annotated Bibliography

Jastrzab, JoAnn, et al. "Serving Country and Community: A Longitudinal Study of Service in AmeriCorps." *Corporation for National and Community Service*. Abt Associates, Apr. 2007. Web. 10 Feb. 2013.

This scholarly research report examines the impacts of AmeriCorps participation on participants' attitudes and behavior related to civic engagement, education, employment and life skills. The findings of the study were mixed. Surveys of participants initially and up to three years after enrolling in AmeriCorps revealed generally positive gains, particularly in measures of civic engagement, but the findings were not always statistically significant and revealed no impacts in educational outcomes. This study is helpful in providing statistically significant data on the positive impacts AmeriCorps participation can have on participants' future attitudes and behavior and provides some evidence of an important claim that national service increases lifelong civic engagement. However, it does not identify the impacts of mandatory service, as AmeriCorps enrollment is voluntary.

Kinsley, Michael. "National Service? Puh-lease." *Time Lists*. Time, 30 Aug. 2007. Web. 8 Feb. 2013.

This op-ed written by a popular conservative writer offers a direct response to and critique of Stengel's proposal for universal national service. Kinsley scornfully addresses the Baby Boomer generation Stengel represents, chastising their attempts to force national service on young people from the safety of retirement. He opposes universal service on the following grounds: (1) service cannot be both universal and voluntary, which jeopardizes freedom of choice and undermines the virtue of volunteerism, (2) capitalism and our system of voting and taxation, when functioning well, properly respond to social needs, and (3) there is not enough work to go around, so a universal corps would end up doing unimportant work. This article provides a clear, well-reasoned conservative perspective on the problems with mandatory national service.

Stengel, Richard. "A Time to Serve."*Time* 10 Sept. 2007: 48-67. Print.

This article from a popular news magazine argues that the next president and the US more broadly should take action to make national service a central part of American culture because a healthy republic requires not only the consent but the active participation of its citizens. It outlines a 10-point plan for how to institute universal national service by expanding the existing network of opportunities (like AmeriCorps) and creating new corps in education, health, environmental work, and disaster response. The article proposes using baby bonds that mature during young adulthood and increasing private investment to pay for the expansion. The proposal and 10-point plan are particularly valuable in illustrating how to make service work on a universal scale while simultaneously emphasizing why voluntary service motivated by a shared culture is superior to a mandatory plan.

THINKING CRITICALLY

about "Should the United States Establish Mandatory Public Service for Young Adults? An Annotated Bibliography"

1. Explain how Kent includes the three common elements of an evaluative annotation (genre/rhetorical context, summary of content, evaluation) in each of his annotations.
2. Compare Kent's annotated bibliography with his exploratory essay (pp. 160–164), noting differences between the way each source is described in the bibliography versus the essay. What insights do you get from the exploratory essay that are missing from the bibliography? What information about the sources comes through more clearly in the bibliography than in the essay?
3. How might Kent use information and points in this annotated bibliography in his researched argument?

8 WRITING AN INFORMATIVE (AND SURPRISING) ESSAY OR REPORT

WHAT YOU WILL LEARN

8.1 To explain the rhetorical concerns, features, and strategies of effective informative writing.

8.2 To write an informative report or a surprising reversal informative essay.

As a reader, you regularly encounter writing with an informative aim, ranging from the instruction booklet for a new coffee maker to a Wikipedia article on Jimi Hendrix. Informative documents include instruction manuals, encyclopedias, cookbooks, and business reports as well as informative magazine and Web articles. In some informative prose, visual representations of information can be more important than the prose itself.

A useful way to begin thinking about informative writing is to place it in two categories according to the reader's motivation for reading. In the first category, readers are motivated by an immediate need for information (setting the clock on a new microwave) or by curiosity about a subject (the rise of the impressionistic movement in painting). Informative writing in this category does not necessarily contain a governing thesis statement. Documents are organized effectively, of course, but they often follow a chronological order, a step-by-step order, or a topic-by-topic order. The writer provides factual information about a subject without necessarily shaping the information to support a thesis.

In contrast, the second category of informative writing, which is aimed at readers who may not be initially interested in the subject matter, *is* thesis-based. The writer's purpose is to bring readers new, unanticipated, or surprising information. Because readers are not initially motivated by curiosity or by a need to know, the writer's first task is to hook readers' interest and motivate their desire to continue reading. An excellent strategy for creating this motivation is the technique of "surprising reversal," which we explain later.

Engaging Informative (and Surprising) Writing

Consider this informational poster on the dangers of high heel shoes. We found this poster from a link in a Web article about orthopedic foot problems, but it could just as easily have appeared as a wall poster in a doctor's office or a gym (but probably not in a women's shoe store!). Take a moment to analyze this poster rhetorically.

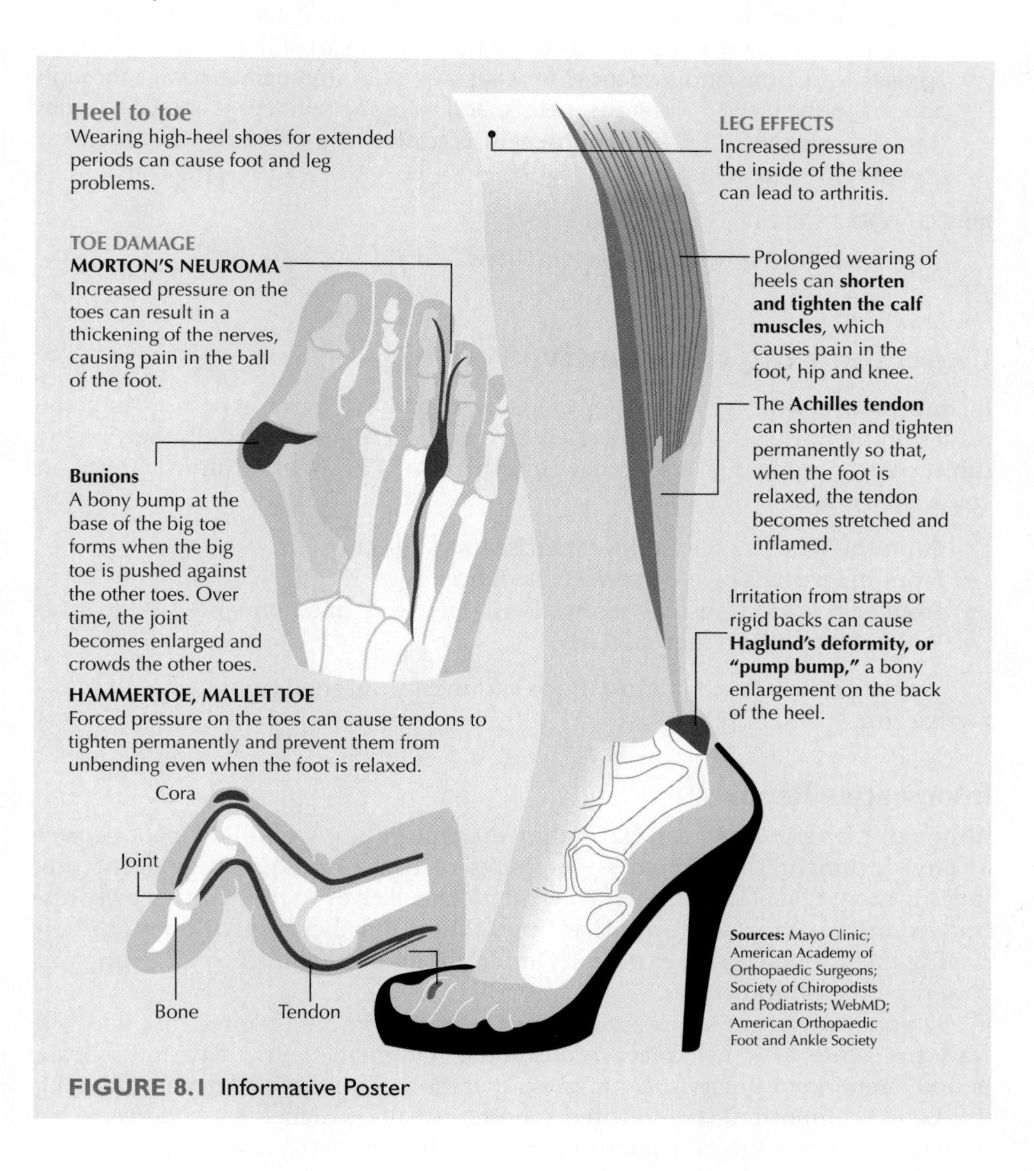

FIGURE 8.1 Informative Poster

ON YOUR OWN

1. How long did it take you to realize the purpose of the poster? What features of the poster most helped you realize its intentions? How effective is the poster at conveying the dangers of high heels in ways that are compelling and easy to understand?
2. Instead of a poster, the designer could have presented the same information in a short magazine article without an image. How might the poster be more effective than a prose-only article in reaching its intended audience?
3. To what extent does the design of the poster (drawing, text, location of text, font types and sizes, and so forth) contribute to the *logos* of the message through appeals to reasons and evidence? In what way does it generate *pathos* through appeals to the viewers' interests, beliefs, and values? How does it appeal to *ethos* (the viewer's sense that the information is trustworthy and believable, coming from a respected authority or source)?

IN CONVERSATION

Share your answers to the above questions.

8.1 Understanding Informative Writing

8.1 Explain the rhetorical concerns, features, and strategies of effective informative writing.

In informative writing, the writer is assumed to have more expertise than the reader on a given subject. The writer's aim is to enlarge the reader's view of the subject by bringing the reader new information. The writer's information can come from a variety of sources:

- From the writer's preexisting expertise in a subject
- From the writer's own personal experiences
- From field research such as observations, interviews, questionnaires, and so forth
- From library or Internet research

We turn now to a closer look at two commonly assigned genres with an informative aim.

Informative Reports

Although the term *report* can have numerous meanings, we will define a **report** as any document that presents the results of a fact-finding or data-gathering investigation. Sometimes report writers limit themselves to presenting newly discovered information, while at other times they go further by analyzing or interpreting the information to explain its implications and significance or to uncover patterns of cause and effect.

Reports of various kinds are among the most common genres that you will read and write as a workplace professional. Often managers have to prepare periodic reports to supervisors on sales, operations, expenses, or team productivity. Equally important are solicited reports, usually assigned by supervisors to individuals or task forces, requesting individuals to investigate a problem, gather crucial information, and report the results.

Characteristics of a Report The text of a report should be concise, with a tightly closed-form structure often broken into sections marked by headings. Individual points might be bulleted. Numeric data are usually displayed in graphs or tables. Long reports usually include a cover page and a table of contents and often begin with an "executive summary" that condenses the main findings into a paragraph.

The Introduction to a Report How you write the introduction to a report depends on the audience you are addressing. In some cases a report is aimed at general readers and published in, say, a popular magazine. In such cases, you must arouse your readers' interest and provide necessary background, just as you would do in most closed-form introductions. Kerri Ann Matsumoto's "How Much Does It Cost to Go Organic?" (p. 185) is a student example of an informative report written for a magazine audience. (Note how Matsumoto "desktop-published" her essay in two-column format to look like a magazine article.)

In other cases, the report is solicited (say, by a supervisor); it is aimed at a specific reader who is already interested in the information and is waiting for you to provide it. In this case, the report is often written as a memorandum. Instead of a title, short reports usually have an informative "subject line" that identifies the report's topic and purpose. The introduction typically creates a brief context for the report, states its purpose, and maps its structure. Here is an example of an introduction:

PROTOTYPE INTRODUCTION FOR A SOLICITED REPORT

To: Ms. Polly Carpenter, Business Manager
From: Ralph Hiner
Subject: Projected costs for the new seed catalog

As you requested, I have researched the projected costs for the new seed catalog. This memo provides background on the marketing plan, itemizes projected expenses, and presents an overall figure for budget planning.

The following exercise will give you a taste of workplace report writing. Suppose that you are a marketing researcher for a company that designs and produces new video games. One day you receive the following memo from your manager:

To: You
From: Big Boss
Subject: Information about gender differences in video game playing

The marketing team wants to investigate differences in the amount of time male and female college students spend playing video games and in the kinds of video games that each gender enjoys. I want you to conduct appropriate research at local colleges using questionnaires, interviews, and focus groups. Specifically, the marketing team wants to know approximately how many minutes per week an average college male versus a college female spends playing video games. Also investigate whether there is any difference in the kinds of games they enjoy. We need your report by the end of the month.

FOR WRITING AND DISCUSSION

For guidance on developing a questionnaire, see Chapter 9, pp. 200–203.

Producing a Solicited Report

1. Assume that your classroom is a "focus group" for your investigation. As a class, create an informal questionnaire to gather the information that you will need for your report.
2. Give the questionnaire to the class and tabulate results.
3. Working individually or in small groups, prepare a memo to Big Boss reporting your results.

Informative Essay Using the Surprising-Reversal Strategy

Another commonly encountered genre is an informative essay aimed at providing readers with unexpected or surprising information that they hadn't been seeking. In this section, we focus on a specific version of this kind of essay—a thesis-based informative article aimed at general audiences. Because readers are assumed not to be looking for this information—perhaps they are casually surfing the Web or browsing through the pages of a magazine—the writer's rhetorical challenge is to arouse the reader's curiosity and then to keep the reader reading by providing interesting new information. The writer's first task is to hook the reader on a question and then to provide a surprising thesis that gives shape and purpose to the information. A good way to focus and sharpen the thesis, as we will show, is to use the "surprising-reversal" strategy.

"All About" Versus "Thesis-Governed" Informative Writing To appreciate the difference between "all about" and "thesis-governed" informative writing, let's return to the multimodal poster on the dangers of high heels (page 169). A simple Web search for "high heels" yields a number of "all about" informative articles on high heels—articles on the history of high heels, informative stories about celebrity's fashion choices, and commercial sites featuring fashion footware. But the poster enters this conversation with an against-the-grain message, employing a surprising reversal strategy: "Most people associate high heels with fashionable feminine beauty, but this poster shows that wearing high heels can damage the legs and feet." Every aspect of this poster supports the thesis announced in the title: "Wearing high heels for an extended period can cause feet and leg problems." The image of the leg in high heels makes a visual appeal to viewers interested in heels and fashion; only when they get closer to the poster and note its title and text do they realize that the poster offers unexpected information.

Surprising-Reversal Pattern **Surprising reversal**, as we explained in Chapter 2, Concept 2.2, is our term for a strategy in which the writer's thesis pushes sharply against a counterthesis. This structure automatically creates a thesis with tension focused on a question or problem. Because of its power to hook and sustain readers, surprising-reversal essays can be found in many publications, ranging from easy-reading magazines to scholarly journals. Here are some examples of the surprising-reversal pattern:

Commonly Held, Narrow, or Inaccurate View	New, Surprising Information
Pit bulls are aggressive and dangerous pets that responsible owners should avoid.	The bad reputation of pit bulls is based on wrong information; in kind households, pit bulls can be gentle and loving pets.
Athletes' use of performance enhancing drugs leads to dangerous health consequences in later life.	When taken and used under a doctor's supervision, performance enhancing drugs are often safe and cause no future damage.
Native Americans used to live in simple harmony with the earth.	Many American Indians used to "control" nature by setting fire to forests to make farming easier or to improve hunting.
Having fathers present in the delivery room helps the mother relax and have an easier birth.	Having fathers present in delivery rooms may reduce the amount of oxytocin produced by the mother and lead to more caesarian sections.

A similar pattern is often found in scholarly academic writing, which typically has the following underlying shape:

Whereas some scholars say X, I am going to argue Y.

Because the purpose of academic research is to advance knowledge, an academic article almost always shows the writer's new view against a background of prevailing views (what other scholars have said). This kind of tension is what often makes thesis-based writing memorable and provocative.

The writer's surprising information can come from personal experience, field research, or library/Internet research. If a college writer bases an informative piece on research sources and documents them according to academic conventions, the magazine genre doubles as an effective college research paper by combining academic citations with a tone and style suitable for general readers. Shannon King's article on hydrogen cars (p. 186–188) is an example of a student research paper written in magazine article style.

"Surprise" as a Relative Term When using the surprising-reversal strategy, keep in mind that *surprise* is a relative term based on the relationship between you and your intended audience. You don't have to surprise everyone in the world, just those who hold a mistaken or narrow view of your topic. The key is to imagine an audience less informed about your topic than you are. Suppose, as an illustration, that you have just completed an introductory economics course. You are less informed about economics than your professor, but more informed about economics than persons who have never had an econ class. You might therefore bring surprising information to the less informed audience:

> The average airplane traveler thinks that the widely varying ticket pricing for the same flight is chaotic and silly, but I can show how this pricing scheme makes perfect sense economically. [written to the "average airplane traveler," who hasn't taken an economics course]

This paper would be surprising to your intended audience, but not to the economics professor. From a different perspective, however, you could also write about economics to your professor because you might know more than your professor about, say, how students struggle with some concepts:

> Many economics professors assume that students can easily learn the concept of "elasticity of demand," but I can show why this concept was particularly confusing for me and my classmates. [written to economics professors who aren't aware of student difficulties with particular concepts]

Additionally, your surprising view doesn't necessarily have to be diametrically opposed to the common view. Perhaps you think the common view is *incomplete* or *insufficient* rather than *dead wrong*. Instead of saying, "View X is wrong, whereas my view, Y, is correct," you can say, "View X is correct and good as far as it goes, but my view, Y, adds a new perspective." In other words, you can also create surprise by going a step beyond the common view to show readers something new.

WRITING PROJECT

Informative Report

8.2 Write an informative report or a surprising reversal informative essay.

Write a short informative report based on data you have gathered from observations, interviews, questionnaires, or library/Internet research. Your report should respond to one of the following scenarios or to a scenario provided by your instructor:

- Your boss runs a chain of health food stores that sell high-nutrition smoothies. Because sales have been flat, she wants to create an advertising campaign to attract more customers to her smoothie bars. She has heard that the boutique coffee drinks sold at coffee shops such as Starbucks are actually high in calories and fat. She has asked you to research the nutritional information on coffee drinks. She would also like you to compare the fat/calorie content of various coffee drinks to that of cheeseburgers, fries, and milkshakes sold at fast-food restaurants. She's hoping that the information you provide will help her launch a campaign to lure customers from coffee shops to her smoothie bars. Write your report in the form of a memorandum to your boss, providing the requested information in a closed-form, crisply presented style.
- You are doing a service-learning project for a health maintenance organization. Your manager is worried about hearing loss in young people,

possibly caused by listening to loud music through earbuds plugged into iPods or MP3 players. Your manager asks you to write a short informative article, suitable for publication in the HMO's newsletter, that reports on research on hearing loss due to earbuds. Write your report for a general audience who read the HMO newsletter for helpful health information.

Generating and Exploring Ideas

Your initial goal is to use effective research strategies to find the requested information. If your report draws on library/Internet research, consult Part 4 of this textbook. If your report draws on field research, consult Chapter 9 on gathering and analyzing data. Particularly helpful will be pages 198–203, on using questionnaires and interviews. For displaying numerical information in graphs or tables, consult Skill 17.9.

Shaping and Drafting

Although there is no one correct way to organize an informative report, such reports typically have the structure shown in Figure 8.2. Kerri Ann Matsumoto's essay on the cost of organic food (p. 185), aimed at general audiences, exhibits this typical structure. Her title and introduction announce her research question and engage her readers' interest (how much does it cost to buy organic food versus non-organic food?). The body of the paper then explains her process (she did

FIGURE 8.2 Framework for an Informative Report

Title	• For a report addressed to a general audience, an interest-grabbing title • For a solicited report, an informative subject line
Introduction (one to several paragraphs)	• For general audiences, provides background and context and arouses interest • For a solicited report, refers to the request, explains the purpose of the report, and maps its structure
Body section 1 (brief)	• Explains your research process and the sources of your data
Body section 2 (major)	• Provides the information in a logical sequence • Uses closed-form organizational strategies • Displays numeric data in graphs or tables referenced in the text
Conclusion	• Suggests the significance of the information provided

comparison pricing for a chicken stir-fry for a family of four at an organic and a non-organic store); presents her findings in both words and graphics (organic foods cost more); and suggests the significance of her research (helps readers sort out the advantages of organic foods versus the advantages of spending the extra money in other ways).

Revising

As you revise, make sure that your graphics (if you used them) and your words tell the same story and reinforce each other. As you edit, try to achieve a clear, concise style that allows your intended audience to read quickly. For workplace reports, show your respect for the busy business environment that places many simultaneous demands on managers. When you have a near-final draft, exchange it with a classmate for a peer review.

Questions for Peer Review

In addition to the generic peer review questions explained in Skill 16.4, ask your peer reviewers to address these questions:

1. If the report is solicited, does the document have a professional appearance (memo format, pleasing use of white space, appropriate use of headings)? Do the subject line and opening overview passage effectively explain the report's occasion, purpose, and structure?
2. If the report is aimed at a general audience, does it follow the manuscript style and document design specified by the instructor? Do the title and introduction provide context and motivate reader interest?
3. Does the writer explain how the research was conducted?
4. Is the report clear, concise, and well organized? How might the presentation of the information be improved?
5. If the report uses graphics, are the graphics referenced in the text? Are they clear, with appropriate titles and labels? How might they be improved?

WRITING PROJECT

Informative Essay Using the Surprising-Reversal Strategy

Using personal experience, field research, or library/Internet research, write an informative magazine article using a surprising-reversal strategy in a tone and style suitable for general readers. Your task is to arouse your readers' curiosity by posing an interesting question, summarizing a common or expected answer to the question, and then providing new, surprising information that counters or "reverses" the common view. You imagine readers who hold a mistaken or overly narrow view of your topic; your purpose is to give them a new, surprising view.

Depending on the wishes of your instructor, this assignment can draw either on personal experience or on research. Shannon King's "How Clean and Green Are Hydrogen Fuel-Cell Cars?" (pp. 186–188) is an example of a researched essay that enlarges the targeted audience's view of a subject in a surprising way. Although it is an example of a short academic research article, it is written in a relaxed style suitable for magazine publication.

For this assignment, try to avoid issues calling for persuasive rather than informative writing. With persuasive prose, you imagine a resistant reader who may argue back. With informative prose, you imagine a more trusting reader, one willing to learn from your experience or research. Although you hope to enlarge your reader's view of a topic, you aren't necessarily saying that your audience's original view is wrong, nor are you initiating a debate. For example, suppose a writer wanted to develop the following claim: "Many of my friends think that having an alcoholic mother would be the worst thing that could happen to you, but I will show that my mother's disease forced our family closer together." In this case the writer isn't arguing that alcoholic mothers are good or that everyone should have an alcoholic mother. Rather, the writer is simply offering readers a new, unexpected, and expanded view of what it might be like to have an alcoholic mother.

Generating and Exploring Ideas

If you do field research or library/Internet research for your article, start by posing a research question. As you begin doing initial research on your topic area, you will soon know more about your topic than most members of the general public. Ask yourself, "What has surprised me about my research so far? What have I learned that I didn't know before?" Your answers to these questions can suggest possible approaches to your paper. For example, Shannon King began her research believing that fuel-cell technology produced totally pollution-free energy. She didn't realize that one needs to burn fossil fuels in order to produce the hydrogen. This initial surprise shaped her paper. She decided that if this information surprised her, it should surprise others also.

What follows are two exercises you can try to generate ideas for your paper.

Individual Task to Generate Ideas

Here is a template that can help you generate ideas by asking you to think specifically about differences in knowledge levels between you and various audiences.

> I know more about X [topic area] than [specific person or persons].

For example, you might say, "I know more about [computer games/gospel music/the energy crisis] than [my roommate/my high school friends/my parents]." This exercise helps you discover subjects about which you already have expertise compared to other audiences. Likewise, you can identify a subject that interests you, do a couple of hours of research on it, and then say: "Based on just this little amount of research, I know more about X than my roommate." Thinking in this way, you might be able to create an intriguing question that you could answer through your research.

Small-Group Task to Generate Ideas

Form small groups. Assign a group recorder to make a two-column list, with the left column titled "Mistaken or Narrow View of X" and the right column titled "Groupmate's Surprising View." Using the surprising-reversal strategy, brainstorm ideas for article topics until every group member has generated at least one entry for the right-hand column. Here are several examples:

Mistaken or Narrow View of X	Groupmate's Surprising View
Being an offensive lineman in football is a no-brain, repetitive job requiring size and strength, but only enough intelligence and athletic ability to push people out of the way.	Jeff can show that being an offensive lineman is a complex job that requires mental smarts as well as size, strength, and athletic ability.
Pawnshops are disreputable places.	Samantha's uncle owns a pawnshop that is a wholesome family business that serves an important social function.
To most straight people, *Frankenstein* is a monster movie about science gone amuck.	Cody can show how to the gay community, *Frankenstein* holds a special and quite different meaning.

To help stimulate ideas, you might consider topic areas such as the following:

- ***People:*** computer programmers, homeless people, cheerleaders, skateboarders, gang members, priests or rabbis, reality show stars, feminists, mentally ill or developmentally disabled persons.
- ***Activities:*** washing dishes, climbing mountains, wrestling, modeling, gardening, living with a chronic disease or disability, owning a certain breed of dog, riding a subway at night, posting status updates on Facebook, entering a dangerous part of a city.
- ***Places:*** particular neighborhoods, specific buildings or parts of buildings, local attractions, junkyards, college campuses, places of entertainment, summer camps.
- ***Other similar categories:*** groups, events, animals and plants, gadgets, and so forth; the list is endless.

Next, go around the room, sharing with the entire class the topics you have generated. Remember that you are not yet committed to writing about any of these topics.

Shaping, Drafting, and Revising

A surprising-reversal informative essay has the features and organization shown in Figure 8.3.

To create the "surprising-reversal" feel, it's important to delay your thesis until after you have explained your audience's common, expected answer to your

FIGURE 8.3 Framework for an Informative Essay Using the Surprising-Reversal Strategy

Introduction (one to several paragraphs)	• Engages readers' interest in the writer's question • Provides background and context
Body section 1 (brief)	• Explains the common or popular answer to the writer's question
Body section 2 (major)	• Provides a delayed thesis—the writer's surprising answer to the question • Supports the thesis with information from personal experience or research • Displays numeric data in graphs or tables referenced in the text
Conclusion	• Suggests the significance of the writer's new perspective on the question

opening question. This delay in presenting the thesis creates an open-form feel that readers often find engaging. Shannon King's research paper on hydrogen cars (pp. 186–188) has this surprising-reversal shape.

As a way of helping you generate ideas, we offer the following five questions. Following each question, we speculate about what King might have written if she had used the same questions to help her get started on her essay.

1. ***What question does your essay address?*** (King might have asked, "Will hydrogen fuel-cell automobiles solve our nation's energy and pollution crises?")
2. ***What is the common, expected, or popular answer to this question held by your imagined audience?*** (King might have said, "Most people believe that hydrogen fuel-cell cars will solve our country's pollution and energy crises.")
3. ***What examples and details support your audience's view?*** Expand on these views by developing them with supporting examples and details. (King might have noted her research examples praising fuel-cell technology, such as Mercedes Benz experimental fuel cell cars or money being poured into fuel cell research by Japan or the European Union.)
4. ***What is your own surprising view?*** (King might have said, "Although hydrogen fuel-cell cars are pollution free, getting the hydrogen in the first place requires burning fossil fuels.")
5. ***What examples and details support this view? Why do you hold this view? Why should a reader believe you?*** Writing rapidly, spell out the evidence that supports your point. (King would have done a freewrite about her research discoveries that hydrogen has to be recovered from carbon-based fossils or from electrolysis of water—all of which means continued use of pollution-causing fossil fuels.)

After you finish exploring your responses to these five trigger questions, you will be well on your way to composing a first draft of your article. Now finish writing your draft fairly rapidly without worrying about perfection.

Once you have your first draft on paper, the goal is to make it work better, first for yourself and then for your readers. If you discovered ideas as you wrote, you may need to do some major restructuring. Check to see that the question you are addressing is clear. If you are using the surprising-reversal strategy, make sure that you distinguish between your audience's common view and your own surprising view. Apply the strategies for global revision explained in Chapter 16.

Questions for Peer Review

In addition to the generic peer review questions explained in Skill 16.4, ask your peer reviewers to address these questions:

1. What is the question the paper addresses? How effective is the paper at hooking the reader's interest in the question?
2. Where does the writer explain the common or popular view of the topic? Do you agree that this is the common view? How does the writer develop or support this view? What additional supporting examples, illustrations, or details might make the common view more vivid or compelling?
3. What is the writer's surprising view? Were you surprised? What details does the writer use to develop the surprising view? What additional supporting examples, illustrations, or details might help make the surprising view more vivid and compelling?
4. Is the draft clear and easy to follow? Is the draft interesting? How might the writer improve the style, clarity, or interest level of the draft?
5. If the draft includes graphics, are they effective? Do the words and the visuals tell the same story? Are the visuals properly titled and labeled? How might the use of visuals be improved?

WRITING PROJECT

Multimodal or Online Options

For advice on producing multimodal compositions see Chapter 19.

1. **Informative Poster** Along the lines of the poster in Figure 8.1 on page 169, make a poster that conveys new or surprising information about a popular or unpopular activity, consumer item, or phenomenon such as a food, a diet plan, an exercise, a sport, or a fad. Make your poster visually interesting, clear, and useful. Give credit to any sources that you use.
2. **An Informative Video** Create a short video informing new students about some aspect of your college or university that you think students would benefit from knowing and that you believe your college or uni-

versity does not adequately explain from students' perspective. Possible examples include the following: how to use the Writing Center; how to start an intramural team; how to get help with your computer; how to prepare for finals; how to dispute a grade. Make your video visually interesting and useful; if you use excerpts from interviews keep them short, focused, and lively. Your purpose is to helpfully inform other students.

3. **Pechakucha 20/20 Presentation** Pick an area of knowledge in which you are an insider with more expertise than most of your classmates (growing tomatoes, bee keeping, backpacking, playing the flute, babysitting, shooting free throws, baking pies, repairing bicycles, playing video games, knowing the best coffee houses). Create an informative pechakucha presentation that shares with audiences some of your insider knowledge. Such a presentation gives you 20 images, each projected on a screen for 20 seconds. You'll need to time your informative speech to fit the rhythm of your slide show.

Readings

Our first reading, by student writer Theresa Bilbao, is a short informative essay of the kind often found in popular print or online magazines. The absence of formal documentation and the inclusion of an illustration reflect a typical style of journalistic writing. For this assignment, the instructor asked for an accompanying reflective piece explaining the sources used in the article.

Theresa Bilbao (student)

Spinning Spider Webs from Goat's Milk—The Magic of Genetic Science

1 Today when we hear about genetically modified organisms (GMOs), we often think of food products. We have heard of corn or soybeans containing a spliced gene from a bacterium that makes the plant resistant to herbicides. We have even heard of tomatoes containing a spliced gene from a flounder to make it resistant to cold weather.

2 But now comes something even stranger. A research team led by molecular biologist Dr. Randy Lewis from Utah State University is splicing a spider gene into the DNA of female goats. Don't worry. We aren't talking about miniature eight-legged goats hanging from your ceiling on silk threads or of big floppy-eared spiders munching on clover in a farmer's pasture. These goats are like other goats in every possible way except for one tiny thing: Their milk contains a protein that can be extracted and converted into spider silk.

3 Professor Lewis's team is pursuing the vast potential of spider silk ranging from stronger fishing line or surgical sutures to improved airbags in vehicles. According to a Utah State press release about Professor Lewis's research, spider silk can produce structures that are "simultaneously feather-light, incredibly strong, more elastic than

nylon and moisture proof." Scientists have long been amazed at the unusual properties of spider silk. Historically, it has been used to bind wounds, but now technology can convert spider silk into binding elements for repairing torn ligaments or for making superfine sutures for eye surgery.

4 Spider silk is also highly sticky and can adhere to almost any surface. According to Professor Lewis, "Spiders successfully attach webs to rocks, trees and other surfaces right next to water in very humid environments. We're trying to see if we can produce this material synthetically, test its adhesive properties and duplicate its function." These properties of spider silk have even caught the attention of the United States Navy, the source of one of Professor Lewis's grants. "The Navy," says Professor Lewis, "envisions a kind of super, one-sided Velcro-type fastener that would attach to surfaces underwater." The Navy is also interested in possible military applications including super light bulletproof vests.

5 So why do scientists need goats to produce spider silk? For one thing, it is impossible to breed spiders in the volume needed to produce enough silk for industrial uses. They are very territorial and tend eat each other. Professor Lewis's team solved this problem by splicing the silk-making gene from a golden orb spider into the DNA of female goats in a way that causes the silk protein to be expressed into the goat's milk. After the goat has the spider gene in her DNA, she needs to get pregnant, give birth, and then start lactating. (The baby goats are removed from the mother and fed from another goat milk source.) The goats produce the same spider silk substance as the spiders—except it can be extracted in large quantities, turned into stringlike filaments, and wrapped on a roller. Professor Lewis says that about four drops of the liquid protein extracted from the milk can produce about four meters of silk string.

6 It will be many years yet until the spider-goat process yields large-scale industrial applications but the biotechnological science is advancing rapidly. Professor Lewis also reassures those interested in his work that no goats are ever harmed in this process and that they lead normal goat lives.

THINKING CRITICALLY

about "Spinning Spider Webs from Goat Milk"

1. This essay was written for an assignment calling for a 500–600 word informative piece in "easy reading" style on a science or technology topic for a popular magazine or Web site. What features of style and format give this essay a journalistic feel rather than a formal academic feel?

2. Theresa Bilbao assures readers that no goats were harmed through their genetic modification either physically or psychologically. However, she doesn't mention anything about the ethical or "theological" implications of this kind of research. Her essay sparked disagreement among her classmates about whether the spider-goat research was ethical. Assume this article appeared on a Web site. If you were going to post a reader comment on the essay, what would you say?

Our second reading, by student writer Kerri Ann Matsumoto (p. 185), is formatted to look like a popular magazine article.

THINKING CRITICALLY
about "How Much Does It Cost to Go Organic?"

1. In our teaching, we have discovered that students appreciate the concept of genre more fully if they occasionally "desktop-publish" a manuscript to look like a magazine article, a poster, or a brochure rather than a standard double-spaced academic paper. If Kerri Ann had been an actual freelance writer, she would have submitted this article double-spaced with attached figures, and the magazine publisher would have done the formatting. How does document design itself help signal the document's genre? To what extent has Kerri Ann made this article *sound* like a popular magazine article as well as look like one?
2. Do you think Kerri Ann used graphics effectively in her essay? How might she have revised the graphics or the wording to make the paper more effective?
3. Do you think it is worth the extra money to go organic? How would you make your case in an argument paper with a persuasive aim?

How Much Does It Cost to Go Organic?

Kerri Ann Matsumoto

Organic foods, grown without pesticides, weed killers, or hormone additives, are gaining popularity from small privately owned organic food stores to large corporate markets. With the cost of living rising, how much can a family of four afford to pay for organically grown food before it becomes too expensive?

To find out more information about the cost of organic foods, I went to the Rainbow Market, which is a privately owned organic food store, and to a nearby Safeway. I decided to see what it would cost to create a stir-fry for a family of four. I estimated that the cost of organic vegetables for the stir-fry would cost $3.97. Non-organic vegetables for the same stir-fry, purchased at Safeway, would cost $2.37. If we imagined our family eating the same stir fry every night for a year, it would cost $1,499 for organic and $865 for non-organic for a difference of $584.

After pricing vegetables, I wanted to find out how much it would cost to add to the stir-fry free-range chicken fed only organic feeds, as opposed to non-organic factory farmed chicken. For good quality chicken breasts, the organic chicken was $6.99 per pound and the non-organic was $3.58 per pound. Projected out over a year, the organic chicken would cost $5,103 compared to $2,613 for non-organic chicken.

Comparative Cost of Ingredients in an Organic Versus Non-Organic Stir-Fry

	Vegetables per day	Chicken per day	Total per day	Total per year
Organic	$3.97	$13.98	$17.95	$6552
Non-Organic	$2.37	$7.16	$9.53	$3478

If we add the cost of chicken and vegetables together (see the table and the graph), we can compute how much more it would cost to feed our family of four organic versus non-organic chicken stir-fry for a year.

My research shows that over the course of one year it will cost $6,552 per year to feed our family organic stir-fry and $3,478 for non-organic for a difference of $3,074. If a family chose to eat not only organic dinner, but also all organic meals, the cost of food would sharply increase.

Before going to the Rainbow Market I knew that the price of organic foods was slightly higher than non-organic. However, I did not expect the difference to be so great. Of course, if you did comparison shopping at other stores, you might be able to find cheaper organic chicken and vegetables. But my introductory research suggests that going organic isn't cheap.

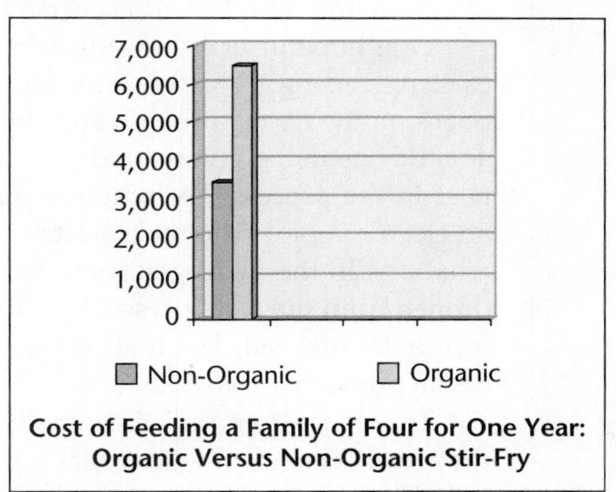

Cost of Feeding a Family of Four for One Year: Organic Versus Non-Organic Stir-Fry

Is it worth it? Many people today have strong concerns for the safety of the foods that they feed to their family. If you consider that organic vegetables have no pesticides and that the organic chicken has no growth hormone additives, the extra cost may be worth it. Also if you are concerned about cruelty to animals, free-range chickens have a better life than caged chickens. But many families might want to spend the $3,074 difference in other ways. If you put that money toward a college fund, within ten years you could save over $30,000. So how much are you willing to pay for organic foods?

The next reading, by student writer Shannon King, is a short academic research paper using the surprising-reversal strategy. Shannon's paper uses research information to enlarge her readers' understanding of hydrogen fuel-cell vehicles by showing that hydrogen fuel is not as pollution-free as the general public believes.

Shannon King (student)

How Clean and Green Are Hydrogen Fuel-Cell Cars?

1 The United States is embroiled in a controversy over energy and pollution. We are rapidly using up the earth's supply of easily accessible fossil fuels. Only a decade ago, one energy expert, Paul Roberts, believed, as did many others, that serious oil shortages would start occurring by 2015, when the world's demand for oil would outstrip the world's capacity for further oil production. However, as we approach 2015, oil suppliers have avoided shortages by extracting less accessible oil found in shale, tar sands, or deep ocean floors. As a result, oil extraction now causes even more pollution, greenhouse gasses, and environmental destruction. With signs of climate change emerging faster than anticipated, the need to reduce carbon emissions has spurred efforts to limit fossil fuels, especially in the cars we drive.

2 One hopeful way of addressing fossil fuel use is to develop hydrogen fuel-cell cars. According to Karim Nice and Jonathan Strickland, the authors of the fuel-cell pages on the *HowStuffWorks* Web site, a fuel cell is "an electrochemical energy conversion device that converts hydrogen and oxygen into water, producing electricity and heat in the process." A hydrogen-fueled car is therefore an electric car, powered by an electric motor. The car's electricity is generated by a stack of fuel cells that act like a battery. In the hydrogen fuel cell, the chemicals that produce the electricity are hydrogen from the car's pressurized fuel tank, oxygen from the air, and special catalysts inside the fuel cell. The fuel cell releases no pollutants or greenhouse gases. The only waste product is pure water.

3 To what extent will these pollution-free fuel cells be our energy salvation? Are they really clean and green? Many people think so. The development of hydrogen fuel cells has caused much excitement. I know people who say we don't need to worry about running out of oil because cars of the future will run on water. For example, Mercedes-Benz spokesman Ray Burke described the use of Mercedes fuel-cell vehicles at the U.S. Tennis Open, praising Mercedes-Benz' commitment to "exploring new ways of innovative eco mobility" ("Automotive"). Another example of excitement regarding hydrogen fuel-cell vehicles is featured on the Web site for the Hydrogen Fuel Cell Institute. It includes a picture of a crystal-clear, blue-sky landscape with a large letter headline proclaiming, "A bold dream, too long overlooked, might have the power to transform energy systems." At the bottom of the picture are the words, "Offering potential promise of clean & abundant power, Hydrogen and Fuel Cells might one day help to reduce our reliance on oil and minimize emissions of pollution and greenhouse gas emissions *(Hydrogen Fuel Cell Institute*). Many national governments are also pursuing the dream of hydrogen fuel-cell vehicles that will not spout out carbon emissions. Recently, Japan has opted to try out fuel cells in both homes and

vehicles (Jean), while the European Union is subsidizing research into fuel cells, budgeting almost a billion euros over six years (De Colvenaer and Castel).

4 But what I discovered in my research is that hydrogen is not as green as most people think. Although hydrogen fuel cells appear to be an environmentally friendly alternative to fossil fuels, the processes for producing hydrogen actually require the use of fossil fuels. The problem is that pure hydrogen doesn't occur naturally on earth. It has to be separated out from chemical compounds containing hydrogen, and that process requires other forms of energy. What I discovered is that there are only two major ways to produce hydrogen. The first is to produce it from fossil fuels by unlocking the hydrogen that is bonded to the carbon in coal, oil, or natural gas. The second is to produce it from water through electrolysis, but the power required for electrolysis would also come mainly from burning fossil fuels. These problems make hydrogen fuel-cell cars look less clean and green than they first appear.

5 One approach to creating hydrogen from fossil fuels is to use natural gas. According to Matthew L. Wald, writing in a *New York Times* article, natural gas is converted to hydrogen in a process called "steam reforming." Natural gas (made of hydrogen and carbon atoms) is mixed with steam (which contains hydrogen and oxygen atoms) to cause a chemical reaction that produces pure hydrogen. But it also produces carbon dioxide, which contributes to global warming. According to Wald, if fuel-cell cars used hydrogen from steam reforming, they would emit 145 grams of global warming gases per mile compared to the 374 grams an ordinary gas-powered car would emit. The good news is that using hydrogen power would cut carbon emissions by more than half. The bad news is that these cars would still contribute to global warming and consume natural gas. Moreover, Wald suggests that the natural gas supply is limited and that natural gas has many better, more efficient uses than being converted to hydrogen.

6 The next likely source of hydrogen is to produce it directly from water using an electrolyzer. Wald explains that the electrolyzer uses an electrical current to break down water molecules into hydrogen and oxygen atoms. Creating hydrogen through electrolysis sounds like a good idea because its only waste product is oxygen. But the hazardous environmental impact is not in the electrolysis reaction, but in the need to generate electricity to run the electrolyzer. Wald claims that if the electricity to run the electrolyzer came from a typical coal-fired electrical plant, the carbon dioxide emissions for a fuel-cell car would be 17 percent worse than for today's gasoline-powered cars. One solution would be to run the electrolyzer with wind-generated or nuclear-powered electricity. But wind power would be able to produce only a small fraction of what would be needed, and nuclear power brings with it a whole new set of problems, including disposal of nuclear waste.

7 Another nonpolluting energy source is solar energy, which scientists from the United States and Switzerland have used in a solar reactor to create the hydrogen for fuel cells ("Sunlight Helps"). However, Donald Anthrop, professor emeritus in environmental studies at San Jose State University, argues that solar—the clean energy solution to hydrogen fuel production—is impractical. He claims that to supply the amount of hydrogen fuel needed for California's goal of 80 percent fuel-cell vehicles, solar panels would cover about 1.2 million acres of land—a space far larger

than Yosemite National Park. Another way of seeing the power requirements for hydrogen-fuel production, according to Anthrop, is to picture the power as equal to one-third of the total nuclear energy produced in the United States.

8 Although there seem to be various methods of producing hydrogen, the current sources being considered do not fulfill the claim that hydrogen fuel-cell technology will end the use of fossil fuels or eliminate greenhouse gases. The problem is not with the fuel cells themselves but with the processes needed to produce hydrogen fuel. I am not arguing that research and development should be abandoned, and I hope some day that the hydrogen economy will take off. But what I have discovered in my research is that hydrogen power is not as clean and green as I thought.

Works Cited

Anthrop, Donald F. "Faulty Engineering Driving Air Board's Hydrogen Hypothesis." *Contra Costa Times* [Walnut Creek, CA] 8 Apr. 2012: A:15. *ProQuest*. Web. 11 Apr. 2013.

"Automotive; Mercedes-Benz of Long Beach Confirm, Mercedes-Benz Is Leading the USTA's Green Mission at 2010 US Open." *Transportation Business Journal* 19 Sep. 2010. *ProQuest*. Web. 11 Apr. 2013.

De Colvenaer, Bert, and Claire Castel. "The Fuel Cells and Hydrogen Joint Undertaking (FCH JU) in Europe." *International Journal of Low-Carbon Technologies* 7:1 (2012): 5–7. *Academic Search Complete*. Web. 11 Apr. 2013.

Hydrogen Fuel Cell Institute. Wilder Foundation, 2013. Web. 12 Apr. 2013.

Jean, Grace V. "Hydrogen Fuel Cells to Power Homes, Vehicles in Japan." *National Defense* 93:657 (2008): 54. *ProQuest*. Web. 6 Apr. 2013.

Nice, Karim, and Jonathan Strickland. "How Fuel Cells Work." *HowStuffWorks.com*. HowStuffWorks, 2013. Web. 17 Apr. 2013.

Roberts, Paul. "Running Out of Oil—and Time." Common Dreams News Center, 7 Mar. 2004. ProQuest. Web. 30 Apr. 2013.

"Sunlight Helps Power New Reactor." *Investor's Business Daily* [Los Angeles] 30 Dec. 2010:A2 *ProQuest*. Web. 11 Apr. 2013.

Wald, Matthew L. "Will Hydrogen Clear the Air? Maybe Not, Some Say." *New York Times* 12 Nov. 2003: C1. *ProQuest*. Web. 17 Apr. 2013.

THINKING CRITICALLY
about "How Clean and Green Are Hydrogen Fuel-Cell Cars?"

1. Explain Shannon King's use of the surprising-reversal strategy. What question does she pose? What is the common answer? What is her surprising answer? How effectively does she use research data to support her surprising answer?

2. The line between information and persuasion is often blurred. Some might argue that Shannon's essay has a persuasive aim that argues against hydrogen fuel-cell cars rather than an informative aim that simply presents surprising information about hydrogen production. To what extent do you agree with our classification of Shannon's aim as primarily informative rather than persuasive? Can it be both?

Our final reading is a press release from the National Association for the Advancement of Colored People (NAACP), an influential African-American civil rights organization founded in 1909. The press release announces the publication of an informational report documenting how the environmental and health hazards of coal-fired power plants fall disproportionately on poor communities with an above average percentage of minority citizens. The report itself is too long to be published in a textbook, but is easily retrieved on NAACP's Web site. The press release summarizes the main findings from the report itself ("Coal Blooded: Putting Profits Before People").

NAACP Report Reveals Disparate Impact of Coal-Fired Power Plants

NAACP Press Release

November 16, 2012

"Coal Blooded" ranks plants, power companies on environmental justice scale

1 (Washington, DC)—The NAACP and its allies today released a research report titled Coal Blooded: Putting Profits before People, which documents the health, economic and environmental impacts of coal pollution on those who can least afford it—low income communities and communities of color.

2 Coal Blooded ranks 378 coal-fired power plants in the nation based on their Environmental Justice Performance. The score is based on both toxic emissions and demographic factors—including race, income, and population density. The six million Americans living near coal plants have an average income of $18,400, compared with $21,857 nationwide, and 39% are people of color.

3 "Coal pollution is literally killing low-income communities and communities of color," stated NAACP President and CEO Benjamin Todd Jealous. "There is no disputing the urgency of this issue. Environmental justice is a civil and human rights issue when our children are getting sick, our grandparents are dying early, and mothers and fathers are missing work."

4 In addition to the rankings, Coal Blooded lays out a framework for individuals, organizations, and policymakers to make a just transition from coal to other energy sources. The recent closure of two coal-fired power plants in Chicago is used as a case study. The report also ranks coal power companies on their Environmental Justice Performance.

5 "We are committed to preserving the livelihood of our communities, our country and our climate," stated NAACP Director of Climate Justice Programs Jacqueline Patterson. "Old, dirty coal plants are poisoning our environment, and emissions controls are simply not sufficient. We need to transition from coal and replace plants with profitable, clean energy alternatives."

6 "This report will help put a human face on the life and death issue of coal pollution," stated Executive Director of the Indigenous Environmental Network Tom

Goldtooth. "Clean coal is an oxymoron. Toxic emissions are harmful to people living nearby coal plants, and also contribute to the devastating effects of climate change."

7 "Coal Blooded is a chance to show the world how dirty these plants are, and to highlight the impact they have on our communities," stated Executive Director of the Little Village Environmental Justice Organization Kimberly Wasserman, who was instrumental in the shutdown of Fisk and Crawford Generating Stations in Chicago. "It is exciting to see people come together and speak up on this important issue."

8 Pollutants emitted by coal plants have been linked to asthma attacks, lung inflammation, chronic bronchitis, irregular heart conditions, and birth defects. According to the Clean Air Task Force, coal pollution is estimated to cause 13,200 premature deaths and 9,700 hospitalizations per year across the United States.

9 The full report can be found on the NAACP's website.

THINKING CRITICALLY

about "NAACP Report Reveals Disparate Impact of Coal-Fired Power Plants"

1. This press release is an informative piece based on the research report "Coal Blooded: Putting Profits Before People" as well as on interviews with officials from the NAACP and other organizations. To what extent does the press release by itself convince you that the environmental impact of coal-powered plants disproportionately harms people of color and low income people? How does it try to appeal to *logos*, *pathos*, and *ethos*? How much would it inspire readers to click on the report itself?
2. As we noted in the critical thinking questions for Shannon King's essay on hydrogen vehicles, it is often hard to mark the point when a primarily informational piece moves from an informative aim to a persuasive aim. The NAACP report begins with an informative aim—gathering and reporting information about 378 coal-fired plants based on toxic emissions of the plants and on demographic information about the communities close to the plants. However, the second half of the report takes on a more persuasive aim, arguing for a shift from a coal-fired to a green energy economy. To what extent does the press release combine informative and persuasive aims?

ANALYZING FIELD RESEARCH DATA

9

WHAT YOU WILL LEARN

9.1 To pose an empirical question about a phenomenon that interests you.

9.2 To collect relevant data through observation, interviews, or a questionnaire.

9.3 To present your findings in the form of an APA (American Psychological Association) research report.

Field research—which uses strategies such as questionnaires, interviews, or direct observation—is one of the most powerful methods that scholars use to investigate our world. If you plan to major in the social or physical sciences or in professional fields such as business, nursing, or education, this chapter will introduce you to a common genre of scientific writing—the empirical research report. If your major is in the humanities, this chapter will familiarize you with ways that scientists and other professionals gather and interpret research data as they investigate empirical questions.

Engaging the Analysis of Field Research Data

Suppose you want to find out whether there is any difference in the exercise habits of male versus female college students. You might hypothesize that there are no differences in the percentage of male versus female students who exercise regularly or in the amount of time spent exercising by men versus women. However, you might speculate that the kinds of exercise vary by gender. For example, you might hypothesize that male students spend more time than females on muscle-building activities such as weight training or on pickup team sports such as basketball or touch football. Conversely, you might hypothesize that female students select exercises aimed at weight loss, muscle toning, and psychological well-being.

Before you read this chapter, take a few moments to imagine how you might design and conduct a research study that would confirm or disconfirm your hypothesis. Suppose your research question is this: "Are there gender differences in the exercise habits of male versus female college students?" Suppose further that you decide to use a questionnaire for your field research.

ON YOUR OWN

1. What questions would you place on the questionnaire? Try writing down some of the questions you might ask. (You'll see that it is harder to create a good questionnaire than you might at first imagine.)
2. Suppose on two successive days you gave one of your questionnaires to all students entering your college library and tabulated the results. Would this population constitute a random sample of students at your institution? Why or why not?
3. Do you think that your study is ethical? Might some students feel embarrassed or even harmed by this study if their answers were made public? Is it anyone's business how much a person exercises? How might safeguards be built into your study to minimize the chances of any person being made to feel uncomfortable?

IN CONVERSATION

Share your answers to the above questions. As a class exercise, try working in pairs or small groups to make a first draft of a questionnaire. Also try to figure out how you would tabulate and report your results.

9.1 Pose an empirical question about a phenomenon that interests you.

Understanding the Analysis of Field Research Data

The Structure of an Empirical Research Report

A framework chart for a typical research report is shown in Figure 9.1. Formatting conventions call for section headings so that readers can quickly find the sections labeled "Introduction," "Method," "Results," and "Discussion." What is noteworthy about this structure is that the main sections of a research report follow the logic of the scientific method, as the following explanation suggests.

Introduction (Stage 1: Posing the question) Scientists begin by posing a research question and formulating their own hypothetical answer based on their initial theories, assumptions, hunches, and reasoning. The "Introduction" section of the research report corresponds to this stage: It describes the research question, explains its significance, and reviews previous scientific research addressing the same or a similar question. (Note: The writing projects for this chapter do not ask you to do a literature review.) Typically, the introduction ends with the scientist's hypothesis predicting what the observed data will show.

Method (Stage 2: Collecting data) Scientists develop a method for collecting the data needed to confirm or disconfirm the hypothesis. The materials and methods used to conduct the research, along with operational definitions of any key terms, are described in detail in the "Method" section of the report. The Method section is like a recipe that allows future researchers to replicate the research process exactly. It also allows peer reviewers to look for possible flaws or holes in the research design.

Results (Stage 3: Determining results) Scientists examine the collected data carefully. The findings are reported in the "Results" section, usually displayed in

FIGURE 9.1 Framework for an Empirical Research Report*

(Title Page)	• For format of an APA title page and body of research report, see pages 217–224 • Gives title of paper and author's name; short version of title appears flush left, the page number in the upper right-hand corner on this and all subsequent pages
ABSTRACT	• Provides a 120-word or less summary of paper (research question, methods, major findings, significance of study)
INTRODUCTION	• Explains the problem to be investigated • Shows importance and significance of the problem • *Reviews previous studies examining the same problem (called a "literature review") and points to conflicts in these studies or to unknowns meriting further investigation*† • Poses the determinate research question(s) to be investigated • Presents the researcher's hypothesis
METHOD	• Describes how the study was done (enables future researchers to replicate the study exactly) • Often has subheadings such as "Participants," "Materials," and "Procedure" • Often provides operative definitions of key concepts in the problem/hypothesis
RESULTS	• Presents the researcher's findings or results • Often displays findings in figures, charts, or graphs as well as describes them in words • Usually does not present raw data or behind-the-scenes mathematics; data focus on composite results • *Presents statistical analysis of data to show confidence levels and other advanced statistical implications or meanings*†
DISCUSSION	• Presents the researcher's analysis of the results • Interprets and evaluates the collected data in terms of the original research question and hypothesis • Speculates on causes and consequences of the findings • Shows applications and practical or theoretical significance of the study • Usually includes a section pointing out limitations and possible flaws in the study and suggests directions for future research
REFERENCES	• Bibliographic listing of cited sources • For format of APA references, see Skill 23.4, and page 224.
APPENDICES	• Provides place to include questionnaires or other materials used in study

*Based on guidelines in *Publication Manual of the American Psychological Association*, 6th ed., Washington, DC: APA, 2010, pp. 21–59.

†*Italicized sections are not required for the writing project in this chapter.*

tables or graphs as well as described verbally. To help determine the extent to which researchers can have confidence in the gathered data, expert researchers perform a variety of statistical tests that show, among other things, whether the results might be attributable simply to chance. (The writing projects for this chapter do not require statistical tests.)

Discussion (Stage 4: Analyzing results) Finally, scientists interpret and analyze their findings, drawing conclusions about what the findings mean and how the research advances knowledge. This stage of the scientific process corresponds to the "Discussion" section of the research report. Typically, the Discussion section also points to limitations and flaws in the research design and suggests directions for future research.

Other Sections In addition to the four main sections, research reports often include an abstract of 120 words or less that summarizes the research problem, research design, results, and major implications of the study. The abstract allows readers at a glance to get a basic understanding of the research. At the end of the report, a "References" section lists bibliographic details about any cited sources. Finally, scientists can add, in the "Appendices" section, copies of questionnaires used, interview questions asked, or special calculations that might interest readers.

How Readers Typically Read a Research Report

What is unusual about research reports is that readers typically don't read them in a linear fashion. The advantage of a well-marked structure is that readers can skim a report first and then, if they're interested, read it carefully in an order that meets their needs. Readers will typically skim the Introduction to understand the problem under investigation and then skip directly to the Discussion section, where the researcher's findings are analyzed in depth. Readers with special interest in the question being investigated may then go back to read the Introduction, Method section, and Results section in detail to evaluate the soundness of the research design and the accuracy and reliability of the data. Some readers may follow a different order. For example, researchers primarily interested in developing new research designs might read the Method section first to learn how the research was conducted. Our point is that the conventional format of a research report allows readers to tailor their reading practices to their own interests.

We will now go back through the sections of a research report, offering you suggestions for doing the kinds of thinking needed at each stage of the research process.

Posing Your Research Question

When you pose your research question for this writing project, you need to appreciate the difference between the broad, open-ended questions we have emphasized throughout this text and the very narrow questions that scientists use when doing empirical studies. Scientists, of course, pose big, open-ended questions all the time: What is the origin of the universe? What is the role of nature versus nurture in human gender behavior? But when they conduct actual research, scientists transform these big, speculative, indeterminate questions into narrow determinate questions. By "determinate," we mean questions that can be answered either with yes or no or with a single fact, number, or range of numbers. The kinds of determinate questions that scientists typically ask can be placed in five categories in ascending order of complexity (see Table 9.1).*

FOR WRITING AND DISCUSSION

Generating Research Questions

This exercise encourages you to brainstorm ideas for your own research question. The goal here is not to settle on a research question but to get a feeling for the range of options you might choose for your own investigation.

Background: The following list shows how students might use the five categories in Table 9.1 to frame questions about the exercise habits of college students.

CATEGORIES OF RESEARCH QUESTIONS APPLIED TO STUDY OF EXERCISE HABITS

1. ***Existence Questions ("Does X exist in domain Y?"):*** Does "yoga" appear as an exercise choice among the respondents to this questionnaire?
2. ***Measurement Questions ("How large/small/fast/much/many/bright is X?"):*** On average, how many hours per week do female (and male) college students devote to physical exercise? Or, what percentage of females (and males) report five or more hours per week of physical exercise?
3. ***Comparison Questions ("Is X greater/less than Y or different from Y?"):*** Do a higher percentage of male college students than female college students report five or more hours per week of physical exercise?
4. ***Correlation Questions ("If X varies, does Y vary?"):*** Do students who report studying more than thirty hours per week exercise more than students who report studying fewer than thirty hours per week?
5. ***Experimental Questions ("Does a variation in X cause a variation in Y?"):*** Will an experimental group of students asked to keep an exercise log exercise more regularly than a control group of students who do not keep such a log?

Individual task: Spend ten minutes thinking of possible ideas for your own research project. Try using the five categories of questions to stimulate your thinking, but don't worry whether a question exactly fits one category or another. Remember to ask determinate questions that can be answered by yes/no or by a single number, percentage, or range of numbers.

Group task: Working in small groups or as a whole class, share your initial ideas, using your classmates' proposed research questions to stimulate more of your own thinking. Your goal is to generate a wide range of possible research questions you might like to investigate.

*Table 9.1 is based on an unpublished paper by psychologist Robert Morasky, "Model of Empirical Research Question." Morasky's model was used for the section on "Asking Empirical Research Questions for Science" in John C. Bean and John D. Ramage, *Form and Surprise in Composition: Writing and Thinking Across the Curriculum* (New York: Macmillan, 1986), pp. 183–189.

TABLE 9.1 Asking Determinate Research Questions

Question Type	Explanation	Natural Science Example	Social Science Example	Question That You Might Ask for This Chapter's Writing Project
1. *Existence Questions:* "Does X exist in domain Y?"	Researchers simply want to determine if a given phenomenon occurs or exists in a given domain	Do fragments of fungi exist in Precambrian sediments?	Do racial stereotypes exist in current world history textbooks?	Do advertisements for computers appear in women's fashion magazines?
2. *Measurement Questions:* "How large/small/fast/much/many/bright is X?"	Researchers want to measure the extent to which something occurs (percentages) or the degree or size of a phenomenon	How hot is the surface of Venus?	What percentage of homeless persons suffer from mental illness?	What percentage of children's birthday cards currently displayed at local stores contain gender stereotyping?
3. *Comparison Questions:* "Is X greater/less than Y or different from Y?"	Researchers want to study how two events, groups, or phenomena differ according to some measure	Is radiation from Io greater in volcanic areas than in nonvolcanic areas?	Is the incidence of anorexia greater among middle-class women than among working-class women?	Do humanities majors report fewer study hours per week than nonhumanities majors?
4. *Correlation Questions:* "If X varies, does Y vary?"	Researchers determine whether differences in X are accompanied by corresponding differences in Y	Does the aggression level of male rats vary with testosterone levels in their blood?	Do students' evaluations of their teachers vary with the grades they expect to receive for the course?	Does students' satisfaction with university food services vary with their family size?
5. *Experimental Questions:* "Does a variation in X cause a variation in Y?"	Researchers move beyond correlations to try to determine the direct causes of a certain phenomenon	If male rats are forced into stress situations to compete for food, will the level of testosterone in their blood increase?	Will preschool children taken shopping after watching TV commercials for high-sugar cereals ask for such cereals at a higher rate than children in a control group who did not see the commercials?	Will persons shown a Monsanto ad promoting biotech corn reveal a more favorable attitude toward genetically modified foods than a control group not shown the ad?

**Direct experiments can be difficult to design and conduct in some of the social sciences. Also, experimental questions often raise ethical issues whenever experiments place human subjects in psychological stress, cause physical pain and suffering to laboratory animals, or otherwise bring harm to individuals. See pages 207–208 for further discussion of ethical issues in research.*

Collecting Data through Observation, Interviews, or Questionnaires

9.2
Collect data through observation, interviews, or a questionnaire.

Once you have formulated your research question, you need to develop a plan for collecting the needed data. In this section, we give you suggestions for conducting your research through direct observation, interviews, or questionnaires.

Using Observation to Gather Information The key to successful observation of human behavior or other natural phenomena is having a clear sense of your purpose combined with advance preparation. We offer the following practical strategies for carrying out observational research:

Strategies for Using Observation to Collect Data

Strategies	What to Do	Comments
Determine the purpose and scope of your observation.	Think ahead about the subject of your observation and the details, behaviors, or processes involved. Make a list.	Some phenomena can be observed only once; others can be observed regularly. If you plan on a series of observations, the first one can provide an overview or baseline, while subsequent observations can enable you to explore your subject in more detail or note changes over time.
Make arrangements ahead of time.	In making requests, state clearly who you are and what the purpose of your observation is. Be cordial in your requests and in your thanks after your observations.	If you need to ask permission or get clearance for your observation, be sure to do so long before you plan to start the observation.
Take clear, usable notes while observing.	Bring note-taking materials—either a laptop or plenty of paper, a clipboard or binder with a hard surface for writing, and good writing utensils. Document your notes with exact indications of location, time, and names and titles of people (if relevant).	Make sure that your notes are easy to read and well labeled with helpful headings.
Go through your notes soon afterward.	Fill in gaps and elaborate where necessary. You might then write a first draft while your observations are still fresh in your mind.	Don't let too much time go by, or you will not be able to reconstruct details or recapture thoughts you had while observing.

Here are two examples of how students have used direct observation to conduct research:

- A student wanting to know how often people violated a "Do Not Walk on the Grass" sign on her campus observed a lawn for one week during mornings between classes and counted persons who took a shortcut across the grass rather than followed the sidewalks. She also recorded the gender of shortcut-takers to see if there were any gender differences in this behavior.
- A student research team hypothesized that episodes of the cartoon *SpongeBob SquarePants* would contain fewer gender stereotypes than episodes of a 1930s Mickey Mouse cartoon. The researchers watched the cartoons in one-minute segments and for each segment recorded the presence of behaviors that they categorized as stereotypical or nonstereotypical male behavior and stereotypical or nonstereotypical female behavior. (You can read their research report and their poster in the Readings section of this chapter.)

Conducting Interviews Interviews can be an effective way to gather field research information. They can range from formal interviews lasting thirty or more minutes to quick, informal interviews. As an example of informal interviews, consider the hypothetical case of a researcher investigating why customers at a local grocery store choose to buy or not buy organic vegetables. This researcher might ask persons buying vegetables if they would be willing to be briefly interviewed. (The researcher would need to be very polite, keep the interviews brief, and get the store manager's permission in advance.)

In other kinds of field research studies, you might rely on longer, formal interviews with persons whose background or knowledge is relevant to your research question. Although asking a busy professional for an interview can be intimidating, many experts are generous with their time when they encounter a student who is interested in their field. To make interviews as useful as possible, we suggest several strategies.

Strategies for Conducting an Interview

Strategies	What to Do	Comments
	Before the Interview	
Consider your purpose.	Determine what you hope to learn from the interview. Think about your research question and the aim of the paper you are planning to write.	This thinking will help you focus the interview.

Strategies	What to Do	Comments
Learn about your subject.	Research important subjects related to your research question and the person you will be interviewing. Although you needn't become an expert, you should be conversant about your subject.	Ideally, interviews should give you knowledge or perspectives unavailable in books or articles.
Formulate your questions.	Develop a range of questions, including short-answer questions like the following: How long have you been working in this field? What are the typical qualifications for this job?	Be as thorough with your questions as possible. Most likely you will have only one chance to interview this person. Avoid yes-or-no questions that can stall conversation with a one-word answer.
	Create open-ended questions, which should be the heart of your interview. For example: What changes have you seen in this field? What solutions have you found to be the most successful in dealing with . . . ? What do you see as the causes of . . . ? Questions framed in this way will elicit the information you need but still allow the interviewee to answer freely.	Avoid leading questions. The more you lead the interviewee to the answers you want, the less valid your research becomes.
Gather your supplies.	If you plan to record the interview, be sure to get your interviewee's permission, and spend time familiarizing yourself with recording equipment. Bring a laptop, tablet, smartphone, or pad of paper to take notes.	Using a recorder allows you to focus your attention on the substance of the interview. Most likely, you will want to take notes even if you are recording.
	During the Interview	
Manage your time.	Arrive on time. Also agree to a time limit for the interview and stick to it. (If necessary, you can request a second interview, or your interviewee may be willing to stay longer.)	You will show a lack of professionalism if you are not particularly careful to respect the interviewee's time.
Be courteous.	Thank the interviewee for his or her time. During the interview, listen attentively. Don't interrupt.	Your attitude during the interview can help set up a cordial and comfortable relationship between you and the person you are interviewing.

(continued)

Strategies	What to Do	Comments
Take notes.	Take down all the main ideas and be accurate with quoted material. Don't hesitate to ask if you are unsure about a fact or statement or if you need to double-check what the person intended to say.	If you are recording the interview, you can double-check quotations later.
Be flexible.	Ask your questions in a logical order, but also be sensitive to the flow of the conversation. If the interviewee rambles away from the question, don't jump in too fast.	You may learn something valuable from the seeming digression. You may even want to ask unanticipated questions if you have delved into new ideas.
	After the Interview	
Go through your notes soon afterward.	No matter how vivid the words are in your mind, take time *very* soon after the interview to go over your notes, filling in any gaps, or to transcribe your tape.	What may seem unforgettable at the moment is all too easy to forget later. Do not trust your memory alone.

Using Questionnaires In constructing a questionnaire, your goal is to elicit responses that are directly related to your research question and that will give you the data you need to answer the question. The construction of a questionnaire—both its wording and its arrangement on the page—is crucial to its success. As you design your questionnaire, imagine respondents with only limited patience and time. Keep your questionnaire clear, easy to complete, and as short as possible, taking care to avoid ambiguous sentences. Proofread it carefully, and pilot it on a few volunteer respondents so that you can eliminate confusing spots. Some specific examples of types of questions often found on questionnaires are shown in Figure 9.2.

When you have designed the questions you will ask, write an introductory comment that explains the questionnaire's purpose. If possible, encourage responses by explaining why the knowledge gained from the questionnaire will be beneficial to others. Make your completed questionnaire as professionally attractive and easy to read and fill out as possible. As an example, Figure 9.3 shows a questionnaire, introduced with an explanatory comment, prepared by a student investigating the parking problems of commuter students on her campus.

When you distribute your questionnaire, try to obtain a random sample. For example, if you assessed student satisfaction with a campus cafeteria by passing out questionnaires to those eating in the cafeteria at noon on a particular day, you might not achieve a random sampling of potential cafeteria users. You would miss those

FIGURE 9.2 Types of Questions Used in Questionnaires

1. Fixed-choice question

Compared to other campuses with which you are familiar, this campus's use of alcohol is (mark one):

—— greater than other campuses'
—— less than other campuses'
—— about the same as other campuses'

2. Open-ended question

How would you say alcohol use on this campus compares to other campuses?

Comment: Fixed-choice questions are easier to tabulate and report statistically; open-ended questions can yield a wider variety of insights but are impractical for large numbers of respondents.

3. Question with operationally defined rather than undefined term

Undefined term: Think back over the last two weeks. How many times did you engage in binge drinking?
Operationally defined term: Think back over the last two weeks. How many times have you had four or more drinks in a row?

Comment: An "operational definition" states empirically measurable criteria for a term. In the first version of the question, the term "binge drinking" might mean different things to different persons. Moreover, respondents are apt to deny being binge drinkers given that it is an unflattering categorization. In the revised question, the term "binge drinking" is replaced with an observable and measurable behavior; respondents are more apt to give an honest response.

4. Category question

What is your current class standing?

—— freshman
—— sophomore
—— junior
—— senior
—— other (please specify)

Comment: In category questions, it is often helpful to have an "Other" category for respondents who do not fit neatly into any of the other categories.

5. Scaled-answer question

This campus has a serious drinking problem (circle one):

strongly agree	agree	neither agree nor disagree	disagree	strongly disagree
5	4	3	2	1

How much drinking goes on in your dormitory on Friday or Saturday nights?

a lot   some   not much   none

Comment: Although scaled-answer questions are easy to tabulate and are widely used, the data can be skewed by the subjective definitions of each respondent (one person's "a lot" may be another person's "not much").

FIGURE 9.3 Example of a Questionnaire

Dear Commuter Student:
I am conducting a study aimed at improving the parking situation for commuter students. Please take a few moments to complete the following questionnaire, which will provide valuable information that may lead to specific proposals for easing the parking problems of commuters. If we commuter students work together with the university administration, we may be able to find equitable solutions to the serious parking issues we face. Please return the questionnaires to the box I have placed at the south entrance to the Student Union Building.

1. When do you typically arrive on campus?
   Before 8 A.M. ______
   Between 8 A.M. and 9 A.M. ______
   Between 9 A.M. and noon ______
   During noon hour ______
   Between 1 P.M. and 5 P.M. ______
   Between 5 P.M. and 7 P.M. ______
   After 7 P.M. ______
2. How frequently do you have problems finding a place to park?
   Nearly every day ____
   About half the time ____
   Occasionally ____
   Almost never ____
3. When the first lot you try is full, how long does it typically take you to find a place to park (for those who buy a commuter parking permit)?
   Less than 10 minutes ___
   10–15 minutes ___
   More than 15 minutes ___
4. For those who use street parking only, how long does it take you to find a place to park?
   Less than 10 minutes ___
   10–15 minutes ___
   More than 15 minutes ___
5. Do you currently carpool?
   Yes ____
   No ____
6. The university is considering a proposal to raise parking fees for single-driver cars and lower them for car pools. If you don't currently carpool, how difficult would it be to find a car-pool partner?
   Impossible ___
   Very difficult ___
   Somewhat difficult ___
   Fairly easy ___
7. If finding a car-pool partner would be difficult, why?
   Few fellow students live in my neighborhood ___
   Few fellow students match my commuting hours ___
   Other ___
8. What suggestions do you have for improving the parking situation for commuter students?

who avoid the cafeteria because they hate it; also, the distribution of noon users of the cafeteria might be different from the distribution of breakfast or dinner users. Another problem with sampling is that people who feel strongly about an issue are more likely to complete a questionnaire than those who don't feel strongly. The student who prepared the parking questionnaire, for example, is likely to get a particularly high rate of response from those most angry about parking issues, and thus her sample might not be representative of all commuter students.

In some situations, random sampling may be unfeasible. For the assignment for this chapter, check with your instructor whether a "convenience sample" would be acceptable (for example, you would pass out questionnaires to persons in your dorm or in your class as a matter of convenience, even though these persons would not represent a random sample of the larger population).

FOR WRITING AND DISCUSSION

Developing a Research Plan

Write a possible research question that you might investigate for your project. Working individually, consider ways that you might use one of the research methods just discussed—observation, interviews, or questionnaires—to answer your question. Begin designing your research plan, including procedures for observations or formulation of questions for your questionnaire or interviews. Then, working in small groups or as a whole class, share your brainstorming. Your goal is to develop the beginnings of a research plan. Help each other talk through the stages of a possible investigation.

Reporting Your Results in Both Words and Graphics

Once you have completed your research and tabulated your findings, you are ready to write the "Results" section of your paper, which reports your findings in words often supplemented with tables and graphs. In reporting results, your aim is to create a scientific *ethos* that is objective and unbiased. Your purpose is to help readers understand your findings concisely and clearly. Do not report raw data. Rather, create composite results by tabulating totals or calculating averages and report these results in words and in appropriate graphics. Try to report your data in such a way that readers can quickly see whether the data support or do not support your hypothesis. For help on creating appropriate graphics for displaying your data, see Skill 17.9, which explains how to create reader-effective tables, pie charts, line graphs, and bar graphs.

Once you have created effective graphics, you then need to integrate them into your own text, making sure that your words and graphics tell the same story in a clear, easy-to-follow manner. Skill 17.9 also provides guidance on integrating graphics into a paper.

FIGURE 9.4 Example of an Unclear Student Graphic

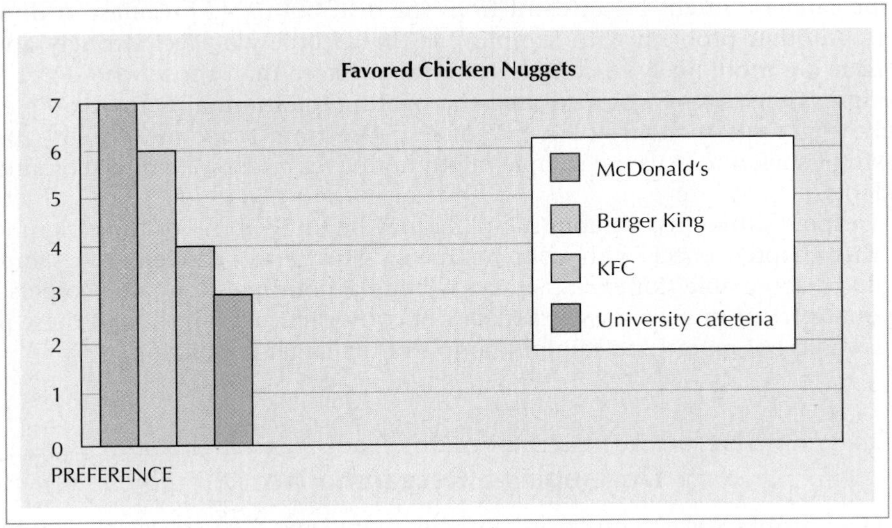

FOR WRITING AND DISCUSSION

Revising a Poor Graph

Background: A frequent problem with graphics designed by inexperienced writers is unclear purpose (What is this graphic supposed to show? What is its story?). Often this confusion comes from a missing or incomplete title, from missing or misleading labels for the *x*- and *y*-axes, or from inclusion of extraneous information.

Your task: Working in small groups or as a whole class, explain what is confusing about the graphic in Figure 9.4. The writer's purpose is to explain respondents' answers to the question, "Which fast-food restaurant produces the best chicken nuggets?" How might you redesign the graphic to tell the story more clearly?

Analyzing Your Results

The "Discussion" section of a research report is devoted to the writer's analysis of the results. This section most resembles a thesis-governed essay addressing an open-ended problem. Think of your Discussion section as answering the following questions: What do my results mean? What do we learn from them? How are these results important or significant?

The Discussion section should open with a thesis statement that indicates whether your findings support or do not support your original hypothesis and that summarizes or forecasts the other main points of your analysis. Here is an example of how a thesis statement from a professional research report entitled

"Marital Disruption and Depression in a Community Sample" is connected to the research problem in the Introduction:

RESEARCH QUESTION AND HYPOTHESIS FROM INTRODUCTION

Research question: Researchers have long known that recently divorced persons tend to show high degrees of depression, but the direction of causation is unknown: Does divorce cause depression or does depression cause divorce?

Hypothesis: Marital disruption contributes to higher levels of depression in recently divorced persons.

Early in the Discussion section, the authors create an explicit thesis statement that directly responds to the hypothesis:

THESIS STATEMENT FROM THE "DISCUSSION" SECTION

According to the results, marital disruption does in fact cause a significant increase in depression compared to pre-divorce levels within a period of three years after the divorce.

Although there are no formulas for the Discussion section of a research report, most reports contain the following four conventional features:

1. Identification of significant patterns and speculation about causes
2. Implications and significance of the results
3. Limitations of the study
4. Suggestions for further research

Let's look at each in turn.

Identification of Significant Patterns and Speculation about Causes The first part of a Discussion section often points out patterns within the results that bear directly on the researcher's hypothesis. For example, in studying exercise habits of college students, you might find that, contrary to your hypothesis, women exercise more than men. Depending on other findings derived from your questionnaire, you might note additional patterns—for example, that persons claiming to be on a diet exercise more than those who don't or that persons who are regular runners tend to spend more time studying than do persons who play lots of pickup team sports.

The discovery of significant patterns leads naturally to speculation about causes. Understanding how a certain event or condition leads to other events or conditions contributes to our knowledge of the world and often may have practical consequences for improving the world or our situation in it. As you contemplate questions raised by your research, consider the following ways that data may suggest causality:

- ***Causality induced from a recurring pattern:*** If numerous observations reveal a recurring pattern, you may be justified in inducing causality. For example, psychologists attempting to understand the causes of anorexia have discovered that many (but not all) anorexics come from perfectionist, highly work-oriented homes that emphasize duty and responsibility. This frequently recurring element is thus a suspected causal factor leading to anorexia.

- ***Causality hypothesized from correlations:*** **Correlation** is a statistical term indicating the probability that two events or phenomena will occur together. For example, various studies have shown a correlation between creativity and left-handedness. (The percentage of left-handed people within a sample of highly creative people is considerably higher than the percentage of left-handed people in the general population.) But does being left-handed cause a person to be more creative? Or does some other factor cause both left-handedness and creativity? The presence of this puzzling correlation leads scientists to speculate about its causes and to design further research that might pin down an answer.
- ***Causality demonstrated through experimental control of variables:*** In some cases, scientists try to resolve causal questions through direct experiment. By controlling variables and testing them one at a time, scientists can sometimes isolate causal factors quite precisely. For example, through experimentation, scientists now know that a particular bacterium causes typhoid fever and that particular antibiotics will kill that bacterium.

FOR WRITING AND DISCUSSION

Analyzing Results

Working in small groups or as a whole class, speculate on possible explanations for each of the following phenomena:

1. White female teenagers are seven times more likely to smoke than African-American female teenagers (a finding based on several professional studies).
2. When asked about the "car of their dreams," ninety-one percent of students polled listed an SUV, luxury car, or high-performance sports car. Only three percent specifically mentioned a fuel-conserving vehicle such as a hybrid.

Implications and Significance of the Results Another typical portion in the Discussion section focuses on the implications and significance of your research—the "So what?" question. What is important about this research? How does it advance our knowledge? What, if any, are its practical applications? For example, the discovery that white female teenagers smoke at a higher rate than African-American female teenagers could lead to speculation on ways to reduce teenage smoking among white females or offer clues into the psyches of white versus African-American women. (One theory proposed in the scientific literature is that white women are more obsessed with weight and body image than African-American women and see smoking as a way to suppress appetite.) Or, to take our other example, the study showing that only three percent of students mentioned a fuel-conserving car as their "dream car" could lead to speculation on how consumer preferences might be changed to promote the goal of environmental preservation.

Limitations of the Study Another common feature of the Discussion section is the researcher's skeptical analysis of his or her own research methods and data. It may seem counterintuitive that authors would explicitly point out problems with their own research, but this honesty is part of the scientific *ethos* aimed at advancing knowledge. By nature, scientists are skeptical and cautious. Typically, authors go out of their way to mention possible flaws and other limitations of their studies and to caution other scholars against overgeneralizing from their research. They might refer to problems in sample size or duration of the study, flaws in the research design that might contaminate results, possible differences between an experimental group and a control group, or lack of statistical confidence in the data.

Your own research for this assignment will probably exhibit a number of problems that would limit other researchers' confidence in your findings. To increase your own *ethos* as a scientific writer, you should make these objections yourself as part of the Discussion section.

Suggestions for Further Research At the conclusion of their Discussion sections, researchers often suggest avenues for future research. Typically they show how their own research raises new questions that could be profitably explored. You might try this approach at the conclusion of your own Discussion section by mentioning one or more questions that you think would be the logical next steps for researchers interested in your area of study.

Following Ethical Standards

When research involves human subjects, researchers must scrupulously adhere to ethical standards. In the past, there have been horrible cases of unethical research using human subjects. Among the most notorious are Nazi medical experiments on Jews in concentration camps and the Tuskegee syphilis study in which four hundred low-income African-American males with syphilis were denied treatment—even though a cure for syphilis had been discovered—because the researchers wanted to continue studying the progress of the untreated disease.

As a response to problems like these, scientific bodies have established strict ethical guidelines for research using human subjects. Today, almost all colleges and universities have Institutional Review Boards that provide oversight for such research. In the case of your own research, for example, consider how certain items on a questionnaire might cause stress to a potential respondent or be considered an invasion of his or her privacy. It's one thing to ask persons if they prefer a Mac to a PC; it is quite another to ask them if they have ever cheated on an exam or gotten drunk at a party. As a general rule, the kind of first-time research that you do for this writing project will not require oversight from your university's Institutional Review Board, but you should nevertheless adhere to the following guidelines:

- ***Obtain informed consent***. Explain to potential respondents the purpose of your research, your methods for collecting data, and the way your data will be used. In the case of interviews, reach agreement on whether the respondent will be named or anonymous. Obtain direct permission for recording the session.

- ***Explain that participation in your study is voluntary***. Do not apply any kind of personal or social pressure that would make it difficult for a respondent to say no.
- ***In the case of questionnaires, explain that no respondent will be individually identified and that results will be reported as statistical aggregates***. If possible, ensure that all responses are anonymous to you (don't try to identify handwriting or otherwise match responses to an identified individual). If such anonymity is impossible (for example, you might be conducting an oral survey), then assure the respondent that you will keep all answers confidential.
- ***If any of your respondents are minors, check with your instructor because human-subject regulations are particularly strict in such instances***. Parents or guardians generally have to give consent for interviews with their children.

WRITING PROJECT

9.3

Present your findings in the form of an APA research report.

Empirical Research Report

The assignment for this project is a modified version of a standard empirical research report. We have omitted advanced features that would be required of upper-division science majors, such as a statistical analysis of the data or a review of previous research.

> Write a scientific report in APA style that presents and analyzes your research findings in response to an empirical question about a phenomenon, behavior, or event. Your research can be based on direct observations, interviews, or questionnaires. Your report should have a title page and abstract, followed by the four main sections of a research report: Introduction, Method, Results, and Discussion. Also include a "References" page if you cite any sources.

An example of a student empirical research report written for this writing project is found on pages 217–224. In the Introduction section of this report, the student researchers present a brief review of the literature based on readings in gender identity that the instructor had used in class for this unit. In most cases, you will not be expected to have a similar section in your report.

Generating Ideas for Your Empirical Research Report

In addition to the ideas presented earlier in this chapter, here are some suggestions for possible research projects:

- Using a questionnaire to gather evidence, investigate students' usage patterns or levels of satisfaction with some aspect of student services on your campus (for example, computer labs, security escorting service, student newspaper, recreational facilities in the student union, study skills workshops).

- Using direct observation, investigate the degree of gender stereotyping in randomly selected children's birthday cards from a local card store or supermarket. Or investigate adherence to road rules at a chosen intersection, testing variables such as car type, weather conditions, time of day, amount of traffic, and so forth.
- Using interviews or a questionnaire, investigate the way students spend their time during a typical week (for example, studying, watching television, playing video games, logging onto Facebook, playing recreational sports, working, and so forth). You might also try to determine whether there are differences in these patterns depending upon factors such as gender, major, GPA, ethnicity, career aspirations, job status, part time/full time, or commuter/residential.

Designing Your Empirical Study and Drafting the Introduction and Method Sections

To design your study, you'll need to begin with a determinate research question that can be answered with yes/no or with a number, range of numbers, or percentage. Review pages 194–196 on asking a determinate research question.

We recommend that you write a draft of your Introduction and your Method section *before* you do the actual research. Drafting these sections first not only gets them out of the way but helps you think through your whole research process. Drafting your Introduction helps you understand your purpose more clearly and serves to clarify your research question and hypothesis. Drafting the Method section helps you plan exactly the steps you will take to do the research. If your research uses a questionnaire, make sure that it is carefully designed, tested on a few volunteers, and revised before you start distributing it. Many research projects are ruined when the researcher discovers that the questionnaire had ambiguous questions or didn't ask the right questions.

Doing the Research and Writing the Rest of the Report

Your next step is to do the research, record your raw numbers, and do the calculations needed for creating composite numbers that answer your research question. What follows is brief advice on drafting the rest of the report.

- ***Writing the Results section:*** This section simply presents your results both in words and in graphics. Refer to Skill 17.9 for advice on how to reference graphs and tables.
- ***Writing the Discussion section:*** Novice science writers often have trouble determining what goes in the Results section versus the Discussion section. The Results section answers the question, "What are my findings?" In contrast, the Discussion section addresses the question, "What do my findings mean?" It is the place where you bring your own critical thinking to bear on your results, creating your own thesis and argument. Reread page 205 to understand the typical features of a Discussion section.

- ***Writing the Abstract:*** When you have finished your draft, write a summary (no more than 120 words) of your report. In a few sentences indicate the broad problem you were investigating and the narrower purpose of your research; state your research question and your hypothesis. Then briefly describe your methods. In the last half of the abstract, describe your results and the extent to which they support your hypothesis. Conclude by suggesting the significance and implications of your research.

Revising Your Report

Because a scientific report follows a conventional structure, you should check your draft against the framework chart on page 193 (Figure 9.1). Make sure you have placed the right type of material in the appropriate section. Inside each section, revise for effective transitions, conciseness, and clarity. Getting feedback from peers can be very helpful.

Questions for Peer Review

In addition to the generic peer review questions explained in Skill 16.4, ask your peer reviewers to address these questions:

TITLE AND ABSTRACT

1. Can the title be improved to better focus the paper and pique reader interest?
2. Can the abstract be improved for accuracy, coverage, or clarity? Where does it state the research question and hypothesis? Briefly summarize the methods? Briefly state the results? Discuss the significance of the results?

INTRODUCTION

1. Where does the writer present the research question(s) and hypothesis(es)? Are these clear and focused?
2. Where does the writer suggest the importance or significance of the research question? What overall suggestions might you make to improve the introduction?

METHOD

1. Will the writer's method provide the data necessary to answer the research question?
2. If you had to replicate the writer's research, where might you have problems? How could the Methods section be improved?

RESULTS

1. Are the writer's results clearly stated in both words and graphics? Are there any graphics that need more explanation?
2. Are the graphics well designed? What suggestions might you have for improving the titles, labels, legends, and overall design of graphics?

DISCUSSION

1. Where is the thesis statement that shows whether the research supports the hypothesis? Can you suggest ways to improve the thesis?
2. Where does the writer: (a) Identify significant patterns in the data and speculate about possible causes? (b) Show the significance and importance of the study? (c) Describe the limitations of the study? (d) Suggest ideas for future research or next steps? How might the Discussion section be improved?

Multimodal and Online Options

WRITING PROJECT

Publish the results of your empirical research project as a scientific poster suitable for display at an undergraduate research conference. Your poster should combine visual and verbal elements to hook participants' interest in your project, show your research question and results, and provide a frame for further personal discussion of your research. Explanations of the scientific poster as a genre as well as instructions on how to produce one are shown in Chapter 19, pp. 497–498. An example of a student-produced poster is found in the readings section, page 226.

Readings

The readings include a professional research report, a student research report in APA style, and a student example of a scientific poster. The first reading is a short empirical report published in the "Clinical and Program Notes" section of the peer-reviewed *Journal of American College Health.* This article should be accessible to you even though you may need to skip over the statistical analysis in the "Results" section. Because the article is short, the discussion section is labeled "Comment" rather than "Discussion."

LeAnne M. Forquer, Ph.D.; Adrian E. Camden, B.S.;
Krista M. Gabriau, B.S.; C. Merle Johnson, Ph.D.*

Sleep Patterns of College Students at a Public University

Abstract. Objective: The authors' purpose in this study was to determine the sleep patterns of college students to identify problem areas and potential solutions. **Participants**: A total of 313 students returned completed surveys. **Methods**: A sleep survey was e-mailed to a random sample of students at a North Central university. Questions included individual sleep patterns, problems, and possible influencing factors. **Results**: Most students reported later bedtimes and rise times on weekends than they did on weekdays. More than 33% of the students took longer than 30 minutes to fall asleep, and 43% woke more than once nightly. More than 33% reported being tired during the day. The authors found no differences between freshmen, sophomores, juniors, seniors, and graduate students for time to fall asleep, number of night wakings, or total time slept each night. **Conclusions**: Many students have sleep problems that may interfere with daily performance, such as driving and academics. Circadian rhythm management, sleep hygiene, and white noise could ameliorate sleep difficulties.

Keywords: college students, night wakings, sleep, sleep aids, sleep deprivation

1

Adolescents and young adults, including college students, appear to be one of the most sleep-deprived groups in the United States.[1–3] Individuals in this age group require about 9 hours of sleep each night; however, most receive only 7 to 8 hours.[1] This sleep deprivation can have detrimental effects on performance, including driving[4] and academics.[5] According to Carskadon,[1] 55% of sleep-related accidents involve individuals younger than 25 years. In a survey by the American College Health Association[5] involving students from 33 universities across the United States, researchers examined the top impediments to academic performance. Both men (23%) and women (25%) rated sleep difficulties as the third most common impediment, after stress and illness such as colds, flu, or sore throats. In this study we examined college students' sleep patterns to identify problem areas and potential solutions.

**At the time of the study, all authors were with the Department of Psychology at Central Michigan University in Mount Pleasant.*

Methods

Participants

2 Graduate and undergraduate students from a North Central university participated in an e-mail survey. We randomly selected these students from the approximately 20,000 currently enrolled. The Dean of Students approved the release of their university-issued e-mail addresses by the Registrar's office. The university's institutional review board approved this project.

Measures

3 To identify students' potential problem areas and factors influencing these problems, we conducted a sleep survey that included questions from the Pittsburgh Sleep Quality Index[6] and the Sleep Hygiene Test.[7]

Procedure

4 We attached the survey to an e-mail that explained the study's purpose. We sent this e-mail to the university-issued e-mail addresses of students randomly selected to participate. All information was confidential; only a number identified participants. Students who decided to participate were instructed to complete the attached survey and return it via e-mail or campus mail. We sent all participants a reminder 2 weeks later with another copy of the survey. We conducted the study during the beginning of the spring semester, when sleep deprivation should be lowest.

Results

5 We e-mailed surveys to 2,024 students; 44 of the surveys could not be delivered and 241 were completed. We e-mailed a second survey 2 weeks later, and this time 43 could not be delivered and 72 more were completed. A total of 313 students returned completed surveys, although 23 more surveys were returned without attachments. The sample of participating students was 62% female, 90% Caucasian, 93% unmarried, and 87% undergraduate; their mean age was 21.4 years ($SD = 4.3$). Most participants (90%) had roommates, including spouses (7%). Demographics were representative of the university.

6 The survey asked the students about their typical sleep patterns (see Table 1). When asked about their typical sleeping situation, most participants reported sleeping with roommates, although in separate beds. Bedtimes on weekends were more than 1 hour later and rise times were more than 2 hours later; thus, most participants slept more on weekend nights ($M = 8.6$ hours, $SD = 1.5$) than they did on weekdays ($M = 7.2$ hours, $SD = 1.2$). Furthermore, women averaged 8 hours of sleep compared with 7.7 for men ($F[1, 312] = 5.27$, $p < .01$). Participants took an average of 25 minutes to fall asleep ($SD = 20$). An analysis of variance showed that women averaged 27.3 minutes to fall asleep, compared with 21.2 for men ($F[1, 312] = 6.93$, $p < .01$). We observed no sex differences in the number of night wakings ($M = 1.7$, $SD = 1$), nor any class differences (freshmen through graduate students) in the number of night wakings, time to fall asleep, or hours of nightly sleep. The most common reasons for night wakings included hearing noise from others (41%), going to the bathroom (40%), and being worried about something (33%).

TABLE 1 Participants' Sleep Patterns

Pattern	Value
Typical sleeping situation (%)	
Roommate in different room	41
Share a room	31
Share a bed	16
Alone	12
Mean bedtime (AM)	
Weekday	12:24
Weekend	1:54
Mean rise time (AM)	
Weekday	8:12
Weekend	10:30
Why do you awaken during the night? (Check all that apply)	
Noise from others	41
Need to go to bathroom	40
Worried about something	33
Bad dreams	20
Pain	9
Muscle spasms	7
Do you typically use sound to help you sleep? (%)	
Yes	47
No	53
If yes, what type of sound do you use? (%)	
Fan	55
Music	34
Humidifier	22
Television	8
Sound machine	3
Do you use any other aids to help you sleep? (%)	
Yes	10
No	90
If yes, what aids do you use? (%)	
Medication	60
Reading	13
Relaxation exercises	13
Earplugs	7
Alcohol	3

Note. The standard deviations for mean bedtimes and mean rise times are as follows: bedtime. $SD = 1.4$ and $SD = 1.6$, respectively, weekday and weekend; rise time, $SD = 1.4$ and $SD = 2.0$, respectively, weekday and weekend.

7 When asked what a typical night's sleep consisted of, most participants answered that they slept all night (26%), had 1 waking (26%), or had 2–3 wakings (21%). The participants were also asked about sleep aids; half reported using sounds such as fans or music. Less common sleep aids included medication (6%). When asked how they felt during waking hours, 58% of participants reported being tired in the morning but okay once they got going. However, more than 33% reported that they started out energetic and then got tired or were tired all day.

Comment

8 College students reported later bedtimes and wake times on weekends than on weekdays. Of the participants, 33% took more than 30 minutes to fall asleep and 43% woke more than once a night. These data suggest sleep difficulties consistent with research of the National Sleep Foundation,[8] which reported that more than 40% of Americans have difficulty falling asleep or have night wakings.

9 Our results support American College Health Association[5] survey findings on college students' sleep difficulties, including long sleep latencies, short sleep time, and frequent night waking. Sleep problems may be worse than these self-reported responses, as students may give socially desirable answers such as not noting sexual encounters or alcohol abuse before bedtime. Thus, this survey may be limited by underreporting.

10 Improving sleep may enhance academic performance. Possible strategies include circadian rhythm management, sleep hygiene, and white noise.[1,9,10] The circadian rhythm is the 24-hour day–night cycle that influences quantity and quality of sleep.[9] The more stable and consistent this circadian rhythm, the better a person sleeps. This implies that individuals should go to bed and wake at the same time every day, including on weekends.[10] Clearly, students in this sample disrupted circadian rhythms when weekday sleep is compared with weekend sleep. Improvements in sleep hygiene—including limiting naps to less than 1 hour, using beds only for sleeping (no reading, TV, or homework), and making sure the bedroom is comfortable[9,10]—also promote sleep. White noise, which is continuous sound covering the entire range of human hearing from 20 to 20,000 Hertz (or approximations to white noise such as fans or humidifiers), also could improve sleep.[9,10] College students need to address sleep problems with better sleep management, which may improve academic performance and driving.

Note

For comments and further information, address correspondence to Dr LeAnne M. Forquer, Division of Counselor Education and Psychology, Delta State University, Box 3142, Cleveland, MS, USA 38733. (e-mail: lforquer@deltastate.edu).

References

1. Carskadon MA. *Adolescent Sleep Patterns: Biological, Social, and Psychological Influences*. New York: Cambridge University; 2002.
2. Pilcher JJ, Walters AS. How sleep deprivation affects psychological variables related to college students' cognitive performance. *J Am Coll Health*. 1997;46:121–126.
3. Tsai L, Li S. Sleep patterns in college students: gender and grade differences. *J Psychosom Res*. 2004;56:231–237.

4. Subramanian R. *Motor Vehicle Traffic Crashes as a Leading Cause of Death in the US, 2002*. http://nhtsa.gov/people/crash/LCOD/Index.htm. Accessed April 27, 2005.
5. American College Health Association. The American College Health Association–National College Heatlh Assessment (ACHA–NCHA), spring 2003 reference group report. *J Am Coll Health*. 2005;53:199–210.
6. Buysse DJ, Reynolds CF, Monk TH, et al. The Pittsburgh Sleep Quality Index: a new instrument for psychiatric practice and research. *Psychiatry Res*. 1989;28:193–213.
7. *Sleep Hygiene Test–Abridged*. http://www.discoveryhealth.queendom.com/sleep_hygiene_abridged_access.html. Accessed September 22, 2004.
8. National Sleep Foundation. *The Basics of Sleep*. http://www.harvestmoonstudio.com/assets/SLEEP_HTML/pub_newsmaker.htm. Accessed September 28, 2005.
9. Breus M. *Sleep Dos and Don'ts: Sleep Hygiene Solutions for Better Sleep*. http://my.webmd.com/content/Article/62/71839.htm. Accessed June 2, 2005.
10. Dement WC. *How To Sleep Well*. http://www.stanford.edu/~dement/howto.html. Accessed June 2, 2005.

THINKING CRITICALLY
about "Sleep Patterns of College Students at a Public University"

1. The introduction to this article doesn't state its research question directly, even though a question is clearly implied. In your own words, what is the question these researchers are asking? How does the introduction try to show readers that the question is significant and worth researching?
2. The first paragraph of the methods section states that the dean of students approved the release of e-mail addresses and that the institutional review board approved the project. Why do the researchers need to provide this information? Without an approval process, what unethical behaviors might arise from research like this?
3. The results of the survey (see "Results" section) are reported in two different ways: in linear prose and also in Table 1, where the "value" column represents percentages of respondents. How does the material in the prose section differ from the material in Table 1? What principles of selection or development explain the material highlighted in the prose section?
4. The last sentence of the introduction promises that this report will "identify problem areas and potential solutions." How does the "Comment" section fulfill this promise? What are the key sleep problems identified in the report? What are the potential solutions? Are you convinced? Would this report cause you to try changing your sleep behavior in any way?

Our second reading, which was written for this chapter's writing project, was jointly authored by a team of three students. We have reproduced it in manuscript format to illustrate the form and documentation style of the APA (American Psychological Association) system for research papers. For further explanation of APA style, see Skill 22.4.

Running head: GENDER STEREOTYPES 1

Include shortened title and page number on each page. On p. 1, include "Running head"

A Comparison of Gender Stereotypes in *SpongeBob SquarePants* and a 1930s Mickey Mouse Cartoon

Lauren Campbell, Charlie Bourain, and Tyler Nishida

Center title and authors.

APA Style

Brief abstract summarizes paper and appears on a separate page.

Abstract

Researchers in gender identity have continually argued whether gender differences are biological or social. Because television is a prime place for teaching children gender differences through socialization, we studied the extent of gender stereotyping in two 1930s Mickey Mouse cartoons and two recent *SpongeBob SquarePants* cartoons. We analyzed the cartoons in one-minute increments and recorded the number of gender stereotypical and gender-non-stereotypical actions in each increment. Our results confirmed our hypothesis that *SpongeBob SquarePants* would have fewer gender stereotypes than Mickey Mouse. This study is significant because it shows that in at least one contemporary cartoon males and females have a range of acceptable behaviors that go beyond traditional gender stereotypes.

GENDER STEREOTYPES 3

A Comparison of Gender Stereotypes in *SpongeBob SquarePants* and a 1930s Mickey Mouse Cartoon

Repeat title before body of paper.

Researchers in gender identity have long argued over the role of biology versus culture in causing gendered behavior. Pinker (2005) has argued that biology plays a more significant role in gender identity. In contrast, Barres (2006) has argued that culture plays the more significant role in gender identity. Proponents of socialization over biology have shown that cultural influences begin at a very young age. For example, Clearfield and Nelson (2006) show that mothers are more verbal and nurturing towards girls but are more focused on promoting independence and use more commands with boys.

Also of interest are the effects of media and popular culture on children and adults. A large part of a child's life is spent watching cartoons; therefore we believe it is important to find how much of a role gender stereotypes play in the media. In response to this question, we have examined data about gender stereotypes from two different kinds of children's cartoons. The first is a recent, somewhat controversial cartoon called *SpongeBob SquarePants*. The other is a popular 1930s Mickey Mouse cartoon.

Double-space all text.

The purpose of our study is to see if there is a difference in the extent of gender stereotypes between *SpongeBob SquarePants* and the earlier Mickey Mouse cartoon. We asked the following research question: To what extent has *SpongeBob SquarePants* rejected or reinforced gender stereotypes compared to the Mickey Mouse cartoon? Our hypothesis is that *SpongeBob SquarePants* will show fewer gender stereotypes than the older Mickey Mouse cartoon. We believe this because SpongeBob SquarePants has been attacked by some conservative religious groups as a gay character (Kirkpatrick, 2005). We hypothesize that this characterization comes from the cartoon's male characters' not exhibiting stereotypical male behaviors. In contrast, we believe that the older Mickey Mouse cartoon will show Mickey exhibiting stereotypical male behavior and Minnie stereotypical female behavior.

Use italics for titles.

Center section headings in bold.

Reference tables in text.

Methods

To analyze the cartoons, we developed four specific categories for coding the data: Stereotypical Female Action, Stereotypical Male Action, Non-Stereotypical Female Action, and Non-Stereotypical Male Action. For each category we developed certain criteria that can be viewed in Table 1.

We watched two episodes of each cartoon (obtained from the Internet) in one-minute intervals. After each minute, we stopped the cartoon and waited for each team member to record his or her analysis. We all watched the same episodes at the same time, but recorded our data separately and later compiled the data after the last episode had been watched.

Here is a representative example of how we applied our coding scheme: In one one-minute segment from *SpongeBob SquarePants*, SpongeBob and

Table 1

Coding Criteria for Gender Stereotypes

Category	Criteria for Making Category Decision
Stereotypical Female Action	Female character behaves in a timid, submissive, or passive way; breaks into tears; shows caring, nurturing, empathic, or motherly behavior; dresses in stereotypical way (frilly clothes, dresses, feminine accessories)
Stereotypical Male Action	Male character behaves in an aggressive, fearless, or competitive way; is cocky or taunting; shows physical strength; dresses in stereotypical male way
Non-Stereotypical Female Action	Female character exhibits stereotypical male behavior
Non-Stereotypical Male Action	Male character exhibits stereotypical female behavior

his friend Patrick decide to lift weights. While lifting weights, SpongeBob infuriates a body building fish who is much bigger and stronger than SpongeBob. SpongeBob runs away in fear while his friend Sandy (the female squirrel) stands up to the mean body building fish. She then makes sure SpongeBob is okay before she returns to lifting weights. We coded this example as containing a stereotypical male action (body building fish), a non-stereotypical male action (SpongeBob showing fear), a stereotypical female action (Sandy expressing concern for others), and non-stereotypical female actions (Sandy challenging the fish and also lifting weights).

Results

Our results (see Figure 1) show that the Mickey Mouse cartoon had a higher percentage of stereotypical male and female actions than did *SpongeBob SquarePants*, which had an almost equal amount of non-stereotypical and stereotypical gendered actions.

Reference figures in text.

As shown in Figure 1, female actions in *SpongeBob SquarePants* were 59% gender stereotypical and 40% gender non-stereotypical while in Mickey Mouse female actions were 84% gender stereotypical and only 16% gender non-stereotypical. Similarly, male actions in *SpongeBob SquarePants* were 48% gender stereotypical and 52% gender non-stereotypical, while in Mickey Mouse male actions were 87% gender stereotypical and 12% gender non-stereotypical.

Discussion

Our hypothesis that *SpongeBob SquarePants* will have fewer gender stereotypes than the Mickey Mouse cartoon was confirmed. The data show that overall *SpongeBob SquarePants* is the more gender-neutral cartoon, showing balance between non-stereotypical and stereotypical actions, while Mickey Mouse showed strong gender stereotypes.

The study we have done is important because it shows that *SpongeBob SquarePants* does not reveal gender stereotyping in the

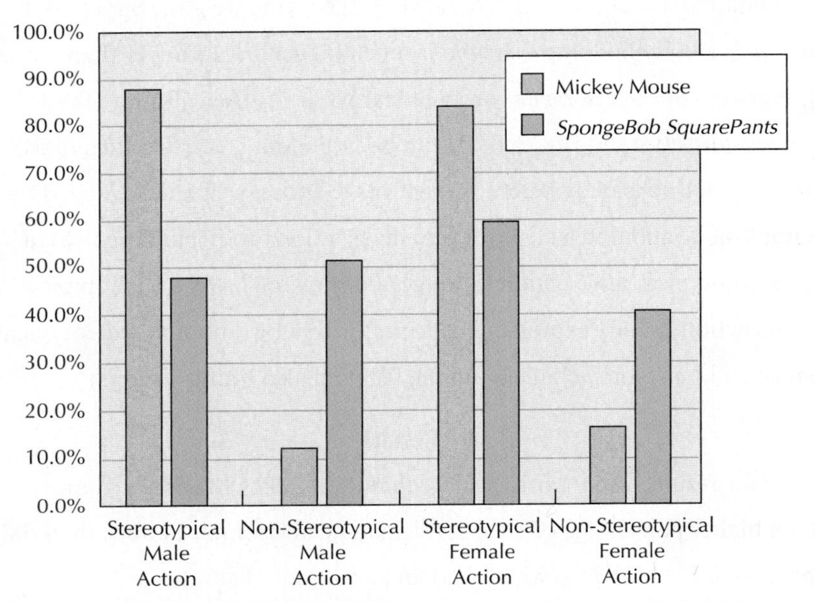

Figure 1 Stereotypical Behaviors by Gender in *SpongeBob SquarePants* and Mickey Mouse.

stereotypical ways exhibited in the Mickey Mouse cartoon. In *SpongeBob SquarePants*, almost every gender stereotypical action (like SpongeBob acting tough or macho) was followed by a gender non-stereotypical action (like SpongeBob crying). This was not the case for Mickey Mouse, where there were many more gender stereotypical actions (for instance, Mickey Mouse rescuing Minnie Mouse) than gender non-stereotypical actions (for instance, Mickey Mouse quivering in fear).

The trends found in the *SpongeBob SquarePants* and Mickey Mouse cartoons suggest to us that these cartoons reveal ways that society's view of gender is evolving. In *SpongeBob SquarePants*, the greater variation and complexity of behavior may reflect such cultural and social changes as women and mothers in the workforce, stay-at-home dads raising the kids, shared household responsibilities, women in the military, and nontraditional families. These recent social and cultural changes have complicated our culture's views of gender, and we speculate that it is these less rigid gender restrictions that we glimpse in *SpongeBob SquarePants*. However, there is still a cultural war going on over gender roles in the media. Our class's discussion of advertising showed that the media in the 21st century still promote gender stereotypes, and the continuation of these stereotypes could explain why *SpongeBob SquarePants* has been controversial and has come under attack from cultural conservatives.

A potential limitation of our study could be that we didn't observe enough episodes of the two cartoons to get a representative sample. Another limitation was our difficulty in deciding how to code continuous actions that lasted more than one minute. For example, in a one-minute segment, *SpongeBob SquarePants* characters would exhibit many different actions, while actions in Mickey Mouse would last longer. For example, there might be a chase scene in which Mickey exhibited the same male action for several minutes or a scene where Minnie cried for several minutes. Should we count the chase scene or the crying scene as one action or as several because it continued across one-minute increments? We decided to count the same continuous action as several actions. Making another choice might have changed our data.

For future studies, researchers could ask questions like the following: Do other modern cartoons follow the trend of *SpongeBob SquarePants*? New research could compare *SpongeBob SquarePants* with other recent cartoons like *The Justice League* or *Jimmy Neutron* to see if they follow *SpongeBob SquarePants*' gender-neutral tendencies. If we believe that gender stereotyping is harmful, furthering the research on gender stereotypes in the media could help identify how to promote a more gender-neutral society in the future.

APA Style

Center page heading.

Use initials for first names.

Place date after author's name.

Italicize publication names.

Use initial cap for article titles.

Check that everything cited in report is in References list (except personal communications).

GENDER STEREOTYPES 8

References

Barres, B. A. (2006, July 13). Does gender matter? *Nature, 442*, 133–136.

Clearfield, M., & Nelson, N. (2006, January). Sex differences in mothers' speech and play behavior with 6-, 9-, and 14-month-old infants. *Sex Roles, 54*(1/2), 127–137.

Kirkpatrick, D. (2005, January 20). Conservatives pick soft target: A cartoon sponge. *The New York Times*. Retrieved from http://www.nytimes.com

Pinker, S. (2005, February 7). The science of difference. Sex ed. *The New Republic Online*. Retrieved from http://www.tnr.com

THINKING CRITICALLY

about "A Comparison of Gender Stereotypes in *SpongeBob SquarePants* and a 1930s Mickey Mouse Cartoon"

1. Explain how this paper follows the genre conventions for a scientific report.
2. To what extent do you think the authors' research design was effective? Are you persuaded that *SpongeBob SquarePants* has moved away from gender stereotypes?
3. This research project was part of a class unit on issues in gender identity that included the readings by Pinker, Barres, and Clearfield and Nelson referred to in the introduction. What does this brief "review of the literature" add to the paper?
4. The authors located the reference to Kirkpatrick on their own. How does the use of this source contribute to the paper?
5. How might the authors expand their speculations about causes of new approaches to gender in cartoons and their ideas about the significance of the study? How has this study inspired you to think about gender and cartoons?

Our final reading is the poster created by the authors of the *SpongeBob SquarePants* paper for presentation at a poster session (see p. 226).

THINKING CRITICALLY

about "*SpongeBob SquarePants* Has Fewer Gender Stereotypes than Mickey Mouse"

1. To what extent does this poster present the same scientific content as the complete research report? If you attended a conference, would you rather listen to a fifteen-minute talk by the authors or view their poster and ask them questions? Why?
2. How does this poster employ the "sound-bite" principle by using minimal text connected to visual elements?
3. In what ways do you think this poster is effective? What questions would you want to ask the creators of this poster?

SpongeBob SquarePants Has Fewer Gender Stereotypes than Mickey Mouse

Lauren Campbell, Charlie Bourain, and Tyler Nishida

Introduction

Television cartoons may influence children's learning of gender stereotypes. Knowing how a contemporary cartoon portrays gender stereotypes would help us understand messages children receive.

Objective

We wanted to see if there is a difference in gender stereotypes between *SpongeBob SquarePants* and a 1930s Mickey Mouse cartoon.

Method

We analyzed cartoons in one-minute increments.

We coded behavior in four categories:

- *Stereotypical female* [timid, passive, tearful; caring, motherly; wearing frilly clothes, accessories]
- *Stereotypical male* [aggressive, fearless, competitive; cocky; showing physical strength; wearing typical male clothing]
- *Non-stereotypical female* [female exhibiting stereotypical male action]
- *Non-stereotypical male* [male exhibiting stereotypical female action]

Results

More Non-Stereotypical Behavior for Males and Females in SpongeBob

- *SpongeBob SquarePants* has almost equal ratio of stereotypical and non-stereotypical behaviors for both males and females (49%/51% for males; 59%/41% females)
- Mickey Mouse has mostly stereotypical behaviors (88%/12% for males; 84%/16% for females)

Discussion

SpongeBob SquarePants showed males and females engaged in wider range of behavior with fewer gender stereotypes than Mickey Mouse.

- *SpongeBob SquarePants* intermixed gender stereotypical action (SpongeBob acting tough, Sandy being nurturing) and non-stereotypical behavior (SpongeBob crying, Sandy rescuing SpongeBob)
- Mickey Mouse had mostly gender stereotypical actions (Mickey rescuing Minnie, who is in tears).

These differences may match changes in culture since 1930s (women's movement, working women, stay-at-home dads) and may explain why *SpongeBob SquarePants* has been attacked by cultural conservatives.

ANALYZING IMAGES

10

WHAT YOU WILL LEARN

10.1 To analyze the persuasive effects of images and how these effects are created.

10.2 To respond to visual images as a more informed citizen and perceptive cultural critic.

10.3 To write a comparative analysis of two visual texts.

This chapter asks you to think about three major kinds of communication through images—documentary or news photos, paintings, and advertisements—to increase your visual literacy skills. By **visual literacy**, we mean your awareness of the importance of visual communication and your ability to interpret or make meaning out of images by examining their context and visual features. We focus on the ways that images influence our conceptual and emotional understanding of a phenomenon and the ways that they validate, reveal, and construct the world.

This chapter invites you to analyze images in order to understand their rhetorical and experiential effects. To **analyze** means to divide or dissolve the whole into its parts, examine these parts carefully, look at the relationships among them, and then use this understanding of the parts to better understand the whole—how it functions, what it means. As Chapter 1 explains (Concept 1.2), when you analyze, your goal is to raise interesting questions about the image or object being analyzed—questions that perhaps your reader hasn't thought to ask—and then to provide tentative answers, supported by points and details derived from your own close examination.

The ability to analyze visual texts rhetorically is important because we are surrounded by glamorous and disturbing images from photojournalism, the Internet, billboards, newspapers, television, and magazines—images that, as one critic has stated, "have designs on us," yet we may not fully understand how they affect us.

Engaging Image Analysis

To introduce you to image analysis, we provide an exercise that asks you to interact with several news photographs on the issue of immigration reform.

Immigration reform is one of the most complex issues facing the United States today; the problem is particularly acute with respect to immigrants from Mexico and Central America, who are drawn to the United States by employment opportunities. U.S. citizens benefit from immigrants' inexpensive labor, which helps keep the prices of services and goods low. In addition to a sizable Mexican-American citizenry, more than ten million illegal immigrants currently live in the United States. All these factors give rise to a number of controversial questions: Should the United States increase border security and focus on building impassable barriers? Should it deport illegal immigrants or explore routes to making them citizens? Should it crack down on employers of illegal immigrants or should it implement a guest worker program to legitimize immigrant labor?

Public debate about immigration issues is particularly susceptible to manipulation by the rhetorical appeal of images. Examine these news photos and consider their rhetorical effects.

FIGURE 10.1 Wall between Tijuana, Mexico, and the United States

FIGURE 10.2 Immigrants Crossing the Border Illegally

FIGURE 10.3 Protestors Marching for Compassionate Treatment of Immigrants

FIGURE 10.4 Immigrants Saying Their Citizenship Pledge

ON YOUR OWN

1. What objects, people, or places stand out in each photo? Does the photo look candid or staged, taken close-up or from a distance? How do the angle of the photo (taken from below or above the subject) and the use of color contribute to the effect?
2. What is the dominant impression conveyed by each photo?
3. Examine how the similarities and differences among the four photos convey different rhetorical impressions of immigrants, Latino culture, or the role of immigrants and ethnic diversity in U.S. culture.

IN CONVERSATION

Share your responses to the photos and then speculate about how you might use these photos to enhance the persuasiveness of particular claims. Choose one or two photos to support or attack each claim below and explain what the photo could contribute to the argument.

1. The United States should install stricter border security using physical barriers, increased border patrols, and more visa checks.
2. The United States should offer amnesty and citizenship to immigrants who are currently in the United States illegally.

Understanding Image Analysis: Documentary and News Photographs

10.1
Analyze the persuasive effects of images and how these effects are created.

Documentary and news photos are aimed at shaping the way we think and feel about an event or cultural/historical phenomenon. For example, consider the newspaper photos, TV news footage, or Internet videos of the billowing clouds of smoke and ash from the collapsing World Trade Center towers on September 11, 2001. Figures 10.5, 10.6, and 10.7 present three well-known documentary images of this event, taken from three different positions and at three slightly different moments as the event unfolded.

Although all three photos convey the severity of the terrorist attack, each has a different impact. Figure 10.5 records the event shortly before the north tower collapsed and just after the south tower was struck by the second plane, marked in the photo by the red flames. The sheer magnitude and horror of the moment-by-moment action unfolding before our eyes evoked shock, anger, and feelings of helplessness in Americans.

In contrast to the first image, which was taken from a distance below the towers, Figure 10.6 was taken by a police detective in a helicopter searching for survivors on the roof of the north tower before it collapsed. This photo suggests the apocalyptic explosion and implosion of a contemporary city. The destruction pictured here is too massive to be an ordinary event such as a fire in a major building, and yet the streams of ash and smoke don't reveal exactly what is happening.

Another well-publicized view of this event is that of the firefighters on the ground, seen in Figure 10.7. Here the firefighters, risking their lives while trying to rescue the people in the towers, have come to symbolize the self-sacrifice, courage, and also vulnerability of the human effort in the face of such colossal

FIGURE 10.5 Terrorist Attack on the World Trade Center

FIGURE 10.6 World Trade Center Attack Seen from the Air

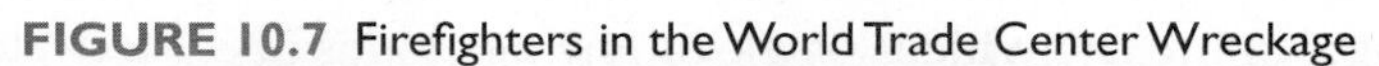

FIGURE 10.7 Firefighters in the World Trade Center Wreckage

destruction. This image also suggests the terror and suspense of a science-fiction-like conflict. All three photos, while memorializing the same event, have different specific subjects, angles of vision, and emotional and mental effects.

The rest of this section introduces you to the ways that photographers think about their use of the camera and the effects they are trying to achieve.

Angle of Vision and Credibility of Photographs

Although the word "documentary" is associated with an objective, transparent, unmediated glimpse of reality, the relationship of documentary photography to its subject matter has always been complex. Historians are now reassessing early documentary photographs, exploring the class and race agendas of the photographers in the kinds of scenes chosen, the photographers' stance toward them, and the wording of the narratives accompanying the photographs. In other words, despite a photograph's appearance of capturing a moment of reality (whose reality?), its effect is always influenced by the photographer's rhetorical angle of vision conveyed through the framing and focusing power of the camera. Perhaps now more than ever, we are aware that the photographer's purpose and techniques actually shape the reality that viewers see. (Think of the multiple cameras tracking a football game and replaying a touchdown from different angles, often creating very different impressions of a particular play.)

The photographer's power to shape reality is enhanced by various strategies for making "unnatural" photographs seem "natural" or "real." For example, photographs can be manipulated or falsified in the following ways:

- staging images (scenes that appear spontaneous but are really posed)
- altering images (airbrushing, reshaping body parts)
- selecting images or parts of images (cropping photographs so that only certain parts are shown)
- mislabeling images (putting a caption on a photograph that misrepresents the image)
- constructing images (putting the head of one person on the body of another)

Research has revealed that many famous photographs were tampered with. As early as the Civil War, composite photos of generals were created by combining heads, bodies, and scenery and inserting figures into scenes. Today this manipulation is also conducted by amateur photographers using photo-editing software. The potential for altering images gives us additional reasons for considering the active role of the photographer and for investigating the credibility and purpose behind images.

How to Analyze a Documentary Photograph

Photographs are always created and interpreted within a social, political, and historical context—the original context in which the photograph was made and viewed and your own context as a current viewer and interpreter. At play are the assumptions, values, and cultural knowledge of the photographer, the original viewers, and the later viewers. Also at play are the sites in which the photograph is viewed—whether in an original news story, a museum, an upscale art exhibit, an expensive coffee-table book, a documentary film, an Internet site, or a textbook. These sites invite us to respond in different ways. For example, one site may call us to social action or deepen our understanding of an event, while another aims to elicit artistic appreciation or to underscore cultural differences.

Examining the Rhetorical Contexts of a Photo A first step in analyzing a documentary photograph is to consider its various rhetorical contexts. The following chart will help you ask illuminating questions.

Strategies for Analyzing the Rhetorical Contexts of Documentary Photographs

Context	Questions to Ask
Photographer's purpose and context in making the photograph	• What was the photographer's original intention/purpose in making the image (to report an event, convey information, persuade viewers to think about the event or people a certain way)? • What was the original historical, cultural, social, and political context in which the photograph was taken?
Original context for displaying the photograph	• Where was the photograph originally viewed (news story, photo essay, scientific report, public exhibit, advocacy Web site)? • How does the original title or caption, if any, reflect the context and shape impressions of the image?
Cultural contexts for interpreting the photograph	• How does the photograph's appearance in a particular place influence your impression of it? • How does your own cultural context differ from that of original viewers? • What assumptions and values do you bring to the context?

Examining the Effects of a Photo on a Viewer In addition to considering the contexts of photographs, we can explore how photographs achieve their effects—that is, how they move us emotionally or intellectually, how they imply arguments and cause us to see the subject in a certain way. An image might soothe us or repel us; it might evoke our sympathies, trigger our fears, or call forth a web of interconnected ideas, memories, and associations.

Before you begin a detailed analysis of a photograph, you will find it helpful to explore the photograph's immediate impact.

- What words come to mind when you view this photograph?
- What is the mood or overall feeling conveyed by the photo?
- Assuming that photographs "have designs on us," what is this photograph trying to get you to feel, think, do, or "see"?

The following chart will help you examine a photograph in detail in order to analyze how it achieves its persuasive effects.*

Strategies for Analyzing the Persuasive Effects of Photographs and Other Images

What to Examine	Some Questions to Ask about Rhetorical Effect
Subject matter: People in portraits: Portraits can be formal or informal and can emphasize character or social role. The gaze of the human subjects can imply power through direct eye contact and deference or shyness through lack of eye contact.	Is the emphasis on identity, character, and personality, or representative status (wife of wealthy merchant, king, soldier, etc.), or symbolic (an image of wisdom, daring, etc.)? What do details of clothing and setting (a room's furnishings, for example) reveal about historical period, economic status, national or ethnic identity?
Subject matter: People in scenes: Scenes can make a statement about everyday life or capture some aspect of a news event or crisis.	What is the relationship of the people to each other and the scene? Can you re-create the story behind the scene? Does the scene look natural/realistic or staged/aesthetically attractive?
Subject matter: Landscape or nature: Scenes can focus on nature or the environment as the dominant subject.	If the setting is outdoors, what are the features of the landscape: urban or rural, mountain or desert? What aspects of nature are shown? If people are in the image, what is the relationship between nature and the human figures? What vision of nature is the artist constructing—majestic, threatening, hospitable, tamed, orderly, wild?

(continued)

*We are indebted to Terry Barrett, Professor Emeritus of Art Education at Ohio State University, for his formulation of questions, "Looking at Photographs, Description and Interpretation," and to Claire Garoutte, Associate Professor of Photography at Seattle University, for informing our discussion of context in analyzing documentary photographs.

What to Examine	Some Questions to Ask about Rhetorical Effect
Distance from subject: Close-ups tend to increase the intensity of the image and suggest the importance of the subject. Long shots tend to blend the subject into the environment.	Are viewers brought close to the subject or distanced from it? How does the distance from the subject contribute to the effect of the photo or painting?
Angle and orientation: The vantage point from which the photograph was taken and the positioning of the photographer to the subject determine the effect of images. Low angle makes the subject look larger. High angle makes the subject look smaller. A level angle implies equality. Front views tend to emphasize the persons in the image. Rear views often emphasize the scene or setting.	How does the angle influence what you see? Why do you think this angle was chosen? How would the photograph have changed if it had been taken from another angle?
Framing: Framing determines what is inside the image and what is closed off to viewers; it's a device to draw the attention of viewers.	How does the framing of the image direct your attention? What is included and what is excluded from the image? How does what the photo or painting allows you to see and know contribute to its effect? Why do you think this particular frame was chosen?
Light: The direction of the light determines the shadows and affects the contrasts, which can be subtle or strong. Lighting has different effects if it is natural or artificial, bright, soft, or harsh.	How does the light reveal details? What does the direction of the light contribute to the presence of shadows? How do these shadows affect the mood or feeling of the photo?
Focus: Focus refers to what is clearly in focus or in the foreground of the photo versus what is blurry. The range between the nearest and farthest thing in focus in the photo is referred to as the depth of field.	What parts of the image are clearly in focus? Are any parts out of focus? What effect do these choices have on viewers' impression of the image? How great is the depth of field and what effect does that have?

What to Examine	Some Questions to Ask about Rhetorical Effect
Scale, space, and shape: Size/scale and shape affect prominence and emphasis. Size and scale can be natural, minimized, or exaggerated. Use of space can be shallow, deep, or both. Both positive shapes and voids can draw viewers' attention.	How do the scale, space, and shape of objects direct viewers' attention and affect a feeling or mood? Are shapes geometric and angular or flowing and organic? Are shapes positive such as objects, or negative such as voids?
Use of repetition, variety, and balance: Repetition of elements can create order, wholeness, and unity. Variety can create interest. Balance can create unity and harmony.	What elements are repeated in this image? What variety is present, say, in shapes? Does the visual weight of the photo seem to be distributed evenly on the sides, top, and bottom? What roles do repetition, variety, and balance play in the impression created by the photo?
Line: Lines can be curved and flowing, straight, or disjointed and angular. Lines can be balanced/symmetrical, stable, and harmonious, or disjointed and agitated.	Does the use of line create structure and convey movement/action or calm/stasis? How does the use of line control how viewers look at the photo or painting?
Color: Choice of black and white can reflect the site of publication, the date of the photo, or an artistic choice. Colors can contribute to the realism and appeal; harmonious colors can be pleasing; clashing or harsh colors can be disturbing.	How many colors are used? What is the relationship of the colors? Which colors dominate? Are the colors warm and vibrant or cool, bright, or dull? How are light and dark used? How does the use of color direct viewers' attention and affect the impression of the image? What emotional response do these colors evoke?

Sample Analysis of a Documentary Photograph

To illustrate how a documentary photograph can work on the viewer's mind and heart, we show you our own analysis of a photo titled *The Fall of the Berlin Wall* (Figure 10.8), taken by photojournalist Peter Turnley in 1989. At the time, the Berlin Wall, which separated communist East Berlin from democratic West Berlin, symbolized the oppression of communism. In 1987 President Ronald Reagan appealed to Mikhail Gorbachev, president of the Union of Soviet Socialist Republics, saying in a famous speech, "Mr. Gorbachev, tear down this wall." When the border opened in November 1989, marking the end of communist rule in Eastern Europe, East Berliners flooded into West Berlin, sparking weeks of celebration. Peter Turnley is a world-famous American photojournalist whose photos of major world events have appeared on the covers of *Newsweek* as well as international magazines. This photograph appeared in a 1996 exhibit (and

FIGURE 10.8 Fall of the Berlin Wall, 1989, by Peter Turnley

later a book) entitled *In Time of War and Peace* at the International Center of Photography in New York.

This documentary photograph of a celebratory scene following the opening of the Berlin Wall in 1989 uses elements of framing, orientation, focus, balance, and color to convey the dominant impression of a life-changing explosion of energy and emotion triggered by this significant event. This distance photo is divided into three horizontal bands—the sky, the wall, and the celebratory crowd—but the focal point is the yelling, triumphant German youth sitting astride the wall, wearing jeans, a studded belt, and a black jacket. The graffiti indicate that the photo was taken from the West Berlin side (East Berliners were not permitted to get close to the wall), and the light post between the two cranes was probably used to illuminate the no-man zone on the communist side.

Every aspect of the photograph suggests energy. In contrast with the mostly homogeneous sky, the wall and the crowd contain many diverse elements. The wall is heavily graffitied in many colors, and the crowd is composed of many people. The wall looks crowded, tattered, and dirty, something to be torn down rather than cleaned up. Most of the graffiti consist of tags, people's response to the ugly obstruction of the wall; West Berliners had no power to destroy the wall, but they could mark it up. The slightly blurred crowd of heads suggests that the people are in motion. At first it is hard to tell if they are angry protesters storming the wall or celebrators cheering on the German youth. The photograph captures this dual emotion—anger and joy—all at once.

At the center of the photograph is the German youth, whose dark jacket makes him stand out against the light blue sky. A few days earlier the wall had fenced him in (at that time, it would have been unthinkable even to approach the wall lest he be shot by border guards). Now he rides the wall like an American cowboy at a rodeo. He has conquered the wall. He has become transformed from prisoner to liberator. His cowboy gesture, reflecting European fascination with American cowboy movies, becomes the symbol of the ideological West, the land of freedom, now the wave of the future for these reunited countries. He holds in his hand a tool (a hammer or chisel?) used to chip away the wall symbolically, but the position of his arm and hand suggests a cowboy with a pistol.

What makes this photograph so powerful is the distance. Had Turnley used a telescopic lens to focus on the German youth up close, the photograph would have been about the youth himself, a personal story. But by placing the youth into a larger frame that includes the crowd, the long expanse of ugly wall, and the cranes and lamppost behind the wall, Turnley suggests both the enormous public and political nature of this event and the implications for individual lives. The youth appears to be the first of the energized crowd to demonstrate the conquering of the powerful barrier that had shaped so many German lives for almost three decades. Thus the composition of this photo packs many layers of meaning and symbolism into its depiction of this historic event.

FOR WRITING AND DISCUSSION

Exploring a Photograph's Compositional Elements and Rhetorical Effect

In the last eight years, documentary photographs have played a key role in persuading audiences that climate change is a serious threat that must be addressed through stricter carbon dioxide emission limits and investments in clean energy. One recurring image shows mountains with receding or disappearing glaciers. An example is the photograph on page 417 at the beginning of Part 3.

1. Working in groups or individually, describe and interpret this photo using questions from the strategies chart for analyzing the context, composition, and rhetorical effects of photos (pp. 233–235). What is the dominant impression conveyed by this photograph?
2. Then using the Internet, search for another photograph that is currently being used in the public discussion of climate change (for example, a photograph employed by environmentalists to fight climate change on an advocacy Web site). Analyze its context, composition, and rhetorical effect.
3. If you were writing to underscore to young voters the seriousness of climate change, which photograph—the one on page 417, the one you found on the Internet, or another—would you choose and why?

Understanding Image Analysis: Paintings

10.2 Respond to visual images as a more informed citizen and perceptive cultural critic.

When you analyze a painting, many of the strategies used for analyzing documentary photographs still apply. You still look carefully at the subject matter of the painting (the setting, the people or objects in the setting, the arrangement in space, the clothing, the gaze of persons, the implied narrative story, and so forth). Likewise, you consider the painter's distance from the subject, the angle of orientation, the framing, and other features that paintings share with photographs. Additionally, your analysis of paintings will be enriched if you consider, as you did with documentary photographs, the context in which the painting was originally created and originally viewed as well as your own cultural context and place of viewing.

But painters—by means of their choice of paints, their brushstrokes, their artistic vision, and their methods of representation—often do something quite different from photographers. For example, they can paint mythological or imaginary subjects and can achieve nonrepresentational effects not associated with a camera such as a medieval allegorical style or the striking distortions of Cubism. Also, the long history of painting and the ways that historical periods influence painters' choices of subject matter, medium, and style affect what viewers see and feel about paintings. Background on the artist, historical period, and style of paintings (for example, Baroque, Impressionism, Expressionism, and Cubism) can be found in sources such as the Oxford Art Online database. In analyzing paintings, art critics and historians often contrast paintings that have similar subject matter (for example, two portraits of a hero, two paintings of a biblical scene, two landscapes) but that create very different dominant impressions and effects on viewers.

How to Analyze a Painting

Just as with photographs, you should ground your interpretation of a painting in close observation. Many of the elements introduced in the strategies chart on pages 233–235 for analyzing photographs can apply or be adapted to the analysis of paintings. In addition, you will want to examine the following elements of the paintings you are analyzing.

Strategies for Analyzing the Particular Elements of Paintings

Elements to Analyze	Questions to Ask about Rhetorical Effect
Design and shape of the painting: The width to height, division into parts, and proportional relationship of parts influence the impression of the painting.	What is the viewer's impression of the shape of the painting and the relationship of its parts? How does line organize the painting? Is the painting organized along diagonal, horizontal, or vertical lines?
Medium, technique, and brushstrokes: The material with which the painting is made (for example, pen and ink, tempera/water colors, charcoal, oil paints on paper or canvas) and the thickness and style of brushstrokes determine the artistic effect.	In what medium is the artist working? How does the medium contribute to the impression of the painting? Are brushstrokes sharp and distinct or thick, layered, or fused? Are they delicate and precise or vigorous? What effect does the awareness or lack of awareness of brushstrokes have on the appearance of the painting?

Sample Analysis of a Painting

As an example of a visual analysis of a painting, we offer an interpretation of a famous painting by Pierre-Auguste Renoir (1841–1919), a French Impressionist painter of the late nineteenth century. The French Impressionists were recognized for their refusal to paint old themes; their embrace of scenes of modern society, especially the city and suburbs; and their experimentation with light and brushstrokes as a way to capture fleeting impressions. Figure 10.9 shows Renoir's oil painting *La Loge* (The Theater Box), which he painted as his main contribution to the first exhibit of Impressionist paintings in 1874. Impressionist paintings were considered too *avant garde* to be displayed at the conservative state-controlled Salon, which was the official arbiter and channel of the work of established French artists.

Renoir's *La Loge* depicts social life in nineteenth-century urban society as an occasion to act out social roles. This painting of a man and a woman elegantly dressed in a theater box at the opera, a popular social spot of the period, suggests that attending the theater/opera entailed displaying one's wealth, being seen, and inspecting others as much as it did watching a performance. This painting focuses intensely on two members of the audience and specifically on the woman, who catches and holds our gaze. While the man in the background is looking at someone in the audience through his opera glasses, the woman looks directly at viewers and invites their attention.

FIGURE 10.9 Renoir's *La Loge* (1874)

Renoir has compelled viewers to dwell on this woman by a number of his choices in this painting. He has chosen to paint her in a tightly framed close-up image, which the slightly off-center woman dominates. Her face and eyes convey the impression that she and the viewer are staring at each other, while in the shadows the man's eyes are blocked by his opera glasses. Thus this painting combines the woman's portrait with a scene at the opera, even though most of the setting, the theater box, is excluded from the painting. (We know we are at the opera because of the painting's title and the man's and woman's accessories.) There seems to be a story behind the scene: What is the man looking at and why is he not noticing the woman as we, the viewers, are compelled to do? This depiction of a moment seems to be less a shared experience of relationship and more a site for performance: men engaged in looking, women inviting the gaze of others.

Another choice Renoir has made to focus viewers' attention on the woman is his striking use of color. In this painting, the color palette is not large—white, black, brown/gold/sepia, with her red lips and red flowers on her bodice. The white of her face and her upper body is the brightest, suggesting light shining on her. Renoir also highlights the woman with short, thick brushstrokes, which give her shimmering, elegant dress texture and the impression of silk, velvet, and lace. As additional signs of wealth, she wears earrings, a gold bracelet, a flower in her hair, and a flower at her bosom. The stark contrast of the black and white in her dress, the white of her face, and the red of her lips—and the agitated diagonal but converging lines of the stripes of her dress that, along with her arms angled out from her body, shape her into a diamond—all work to direct viewers' eyes to her bosom and most of all to her face. Although the expression of the woman is calm, smiling in mild amusement or subtle emotion, the painting captures intensity, perhaps excitement or anticipation, through the sharp contrast of the red, white, and black. The piece is fairly still, and yet we are transfixed by this woman's eyes and lips. With the complex interaction of artistic elements in this painting, Renoir has invited viewers to experience an exciting scene of privileged nineteenth-century urban life.

FOR WRITING AND DISCUSSION

Contrasting the Compositional Features of Two Paintings

This exercise asks you to apply the analysis strategies presented on pages 238 and 233–235 to examine the pastel painting *Carousel* by Camille Pissarro shown in Figure 10.10 and to contrast it with Renoir's painting in Figure 10.9. Camille Pissarro (1830–1903) was also a French Impressionist who regularly exhibited his works in Impressionist exhibitions. He painted *Carousel* in 1885; the medium is pastel on paper mounted on board.

Your task: Working individually or in groups, analyze Pissarro's painting and then find some striking points of commonality or difference with the Renoir painting that you think merit discussion.

- Begin by applying the strategies for analyzing photographic images and paintings on pages 233–235 and 238.
- After you have analyzed the visual features of the paintings, consider why Pissarro titled his painting *Carousel.*

FIGURE 10.10 *Carousel* by Camille Pissarro (1885)

- Finally, what are the thematic differences between these two paintings? How do these paintings, both Impressionistic images of well-dressed women at leisure, create similar or different effects on viewers? What view or feeling about life or about the artists' worlds is conveyed in each painting? What way of seeing or thinking are these paintings persuading you to adopt?

Understanding Image Analysis: Advertisements

The images in advertisements are fascinating to analyze. Like other images, they employ the rhetorical strategies we described in the section on documentary photographs. Often, the ad's words (called the "copy") also contribute to its rhetorical effect. Moreover, ads make a more direct and constant demand on us than do documentary photographs and paintings. Advertising, a multibillion-dollar global industry whose business is communicating across a wide range of media to stimulate the purchase of products or services, comes to us in multiple forms: not just as slick, glamorous magazine ads, but also as direct mail, billboards, radio and television commercials, e-advertisements, banners, pop-ups, and spam. Figures 10.11 and 10.12, a billboard and a bus ad, illustrate the ordinary ubiquity of ads. Because of advertising's powerful role in shaping our culture and influencing our self-images, we have good reason to analyze the rhetorical strategies of advertisers.

FIGURE 10.11 A Billboard Ad

FIGURE 10.12 Ad on a City Bus

FOR WRITING AND DISCUSSION

Examining the Appeal of Ads

Think about the images and words in the two car insurance ads in Figures 10.11 and 10.12.

1. What do you notice most about the images and copy in these ads?
2. What is the appeal of these ads?
3. How are these ads designed to suit their contexts, a billboard and a bus panel? Why would they be less suitable for a magazine?

How Advertisers Think about Advertising

Although cultural critics frequently focus on ads as manipulative messages that need to be decoded to protect unwary consumers, we confess that we actually enjoy ads, appreciate how they hold down the consumer cost of media, and admire their often-ingenious creativity. (We suspect that others secretly enjoy ads also: Think of how the Super Bowl is popular both for its football and for its ads.) In this section, we take a look at advertising from a marketer's point of view in order to deepen your awareness of an ad's context and the many behind-the-scenes decisions and negotiations that produced it. Whether marketing professionals design an individual ad or a huge marketing campaign, they typically begin by asking questions.

Who Is Our Target Audience? At the outset, marketers identify one or more target audiences for their product or service. They often use sophisticated psychological research to identify segments of the population who share similar values, beliefs, and aspirations and then subdivide these categories according to age, gender, region, income level, ethnicity, and so forth. Think of the different way you'd pitch a product or service to, say, Wal-Mart shoppers versus Neiman Marcus shoppers, steak eaters versus vegans, or skateboarders versus geeks.

How Much Media Landscape Can We Afford? While identifying their target audience, marketers also consider how much terrain they can afford to occupy on the enormous media landscape of billboards, newspapers, magazines, mailing lists, Internet pop-ups, mobile ads, TV and radio commercials, posters, naming rights for sports stadiums, T-shirts, coffee mugs, product placements in films, sandwich boards, or banners carried across the sky by propeller airplanes. Each of these sites has to be rented or purchased, with the price depending on the perceived quality of the location and the timing. For example, a thirty-second TV commercial during the 2013 Super Bowl cost $3.8 million, and a one-time, full-page ad in a nationally circulated popular magazine can cost up to $500,000 or more. Overall, advertisers hope to attain the best possible positioning and timing within the media landscape at a price they can afford.

What Are the Best Media for Reaching Our Target Audience? A marketer's goal is to reach the target audience efficiently and with a minimum of overflow—that is, messages sent to people who are not likely buyers. Marketers are keenly aware of both media and timing: Note, for example, how daytime TV is dominated by ads for payday loans, exercise equipment, or technical colleges, while billboards around airports advertise rental cars. Women's fashion magazines advertise lingerie and perfume but not computers or life insurance, while dating services advertise primarily through Internet ads.

Is Our Goal to Stimulate Direct Sales or to Develop Long-Term Branding and Image? Some ads are intended to stimulate retail sales directly: "Buy two, get one free." In some cases, advertisements use information and argument to show how their product or service is superior to that of their competitors. Most advertisements, however, involve parity products such as soft drinks, deodorants, breakfast cereals, or toothpaste. (*Parity products* are roughly equal in quality among competitors and so can't be promoted through any rational or scientific proof of superiority.) In such cases, advertisers' goal is to build brand loyalty based on a long-lasting relationship with consumers. Advertisers, best thought of as creative teams of writers and artists, try to convert a brand name appearing on a cereal box or a pair of jeans to a field of qualities, values, and imagery that lives inside the heads of its targeted consumers. Advertisers don't just want you to buy Nikes rather than Reeboks but also to see yourself as a Nike kind of person, who identifies with the lifestyle or values conveyed in Nike ads.

Mirrors and Windows: The Strategy of an Effective Advertisement

A final behind-the-scenes concept that will help you analyze ads is the marketers' principle of *"mirrors and windows,"* a psychological and motivational strategy to associate a product with a target audience's dreams, hopes, fears, desires, and wishes (often subconscious).

- ***The mirror effect*** refers to the way in which the ad mirrors the target audience's self-image, promoting identification with the ad's message. The target audience has to say, "I am part of the world that this ad speaks to. I have this problem (pimples, boring hair, dandelions, cell phone service without enough bars)."
- ***The window effect*** provides visions of the future, promises of who we will become or what will happen if we align ourselves with this brand. The ad implies a brief narrative, taking you from your ordinary self (mirror) to your new, aspirational self (window).

For example, the acne product Proactiv Solutions uses a very common mirrors/windows strategy. Proactiv infomercials create the mirror effect by featuring regular-looking teenagers with pimples and the window effect by using a gorgeous actress as endorsing spokesperson: If I use Proactiv Solutions, ordinary "me" will look beautiful like Jessica Simpson.

But the mirrors and windows principle can be used in much more subtle and creative ways. Consider the brilliance of the Geico insurance gecko ads promoting what advertisers call "a resentful purchase"—that is, something you need to have but that doesn't give you material pleasure like a new pair of shoes or money in a savings account. Insurance, a hassle to buy, is also associated with fear—fear of needing it, fear of not having it, fear of not being able to get it again if you ever use it. In this light, think of the Geico campaign featuring the humorous, big-eyed gecko (friendly, cute) with the distinctive cockney voice (working-class swagger). When this chapter was being written, Geico billboards were sprouting up all over the country (see Figure 10.13), while large-print ads were appearing in popular magazines along with numerous TV and radio commercials. Here are some of the particular advantages of the gecko for Geico's layered advertising campaign across many media:

- ***"Gecko" sounds like "Geico."*** In fact, this sound-alike feature was the inspiration for the campaign.
- ***The gecko is identifiable by both sight and sound.*** If you see a print ad or a billboard, you remember what the voice sounds like; if you hear a radio ad, you remember what the gecko looks like; on TV or YouTube, you get both sight and sound.
- ***The gecko is cheap.*** The cost of the computer simulations that produce the gecko is minimal in comparison to the royalties paid to celebrities for an advertising endorsement.

FIGURE 10.13 Geico Gecko Billboard Ad

- ***The gecko is ethnically/racially neutral.*** Marketers didn't have to decide whether to choose a white versus black versus Asian spokesperson, yet a person of any race or nationality can identify with the little lizard. (Think Kermit the Frog on *Sesame Street.*) Feminist critics, however, might rightly ask why the gecko has to be male.
- ***The gecko is scandal-proof.*** When in 2010 the Tiger Woods imbroglio ruined the golfer's public image, the huge insurance company Accenture, along with TagHauer watches and other companies, had to drop his endorsement ads, forcing them at great expense to create new advertising campaigns and to lose media visibility in the interim.

Yet we must still ask why the gecko is a good advertising device for an insurance company. How does the gecko campaign incorporate mirrors and windows? Let's start with the mirror effect. It is easy to identify with the Geico ads because everyone has to buy insurance and because everyone wants to save money. (The gecko's main sales pitch is that Geico will save you 15 percent.) Moreover, our long cultural history of identifying with animated characters (*Sesame Street, ET*) makes it easy to project our own identities onto the gecko. Additionally, the cockney voice makes the gecko a bit of an outsider, someone breaking into corporate culture through sheer bravado. (Many people think of the gecko's accent as Australian more than cockney, giving the lizard a bit of sexy, macho Crocodile Dundee appeal.)

The ads also create a window effect, which comes from the way the gecko humanizes the insurance company, removing some of the fear and anxiety of buying insurance. You don't think of the gecko as *selling* you the insurance so much as *buying* it for you as your agent, hopping right up on the corporate desk and demanding your rights. Geico becomes a fun company, and you as consumer picture yourself going away with a pile of saved money. Recent ads have added another symbolic feature to the gecko—a pair of glasses—which makes him seem intellectual and responsible, more serious and grown-up. Meanwhile, another Geico campaign, the talking-money ad (see the billboard ad in Figure 10.11), extends the concept of a humorous, friendly creature, like the gecko, that turns Geico insurance into a savings, not an expense.

FOR WRITING AND DISCUSSION

Designing Ads

This exercise asks you to apply these marketing concepts to designing your own ad. Imagine you are an advertising professional assigned to the Gloopers account. Gloopers is a seaweed (kelp)-based snack treat (a fiction, but pretend it is real) that is very popular under another name in Japan. It was introduced earlier in the American market and failed miserably—what sort of a treat is seaweed? But now, you have laboratory evidence that Gloopers provides crucial nutritional benefits for growing bodies and that it is a healthy alternative to junk food. Many food companies would kill for the endorsement of nutritious content that you now have to work with, but the product is still made out of gunky seaweed. Working in groups or individually, develop a campaign for this product by working out your answers to the following questions:

- Who is your target audience? (Will you seek to appeal to parents as well as children?)
- What is your core message or campaign concept? (Think of a visual approach, including a mirror and window appeal, and perhaps a tagline slogan.)
- What is the best positioning in the media landscape for this campaign?
- How will you build a brand image and brand loyalty?

How to Analyze an Advertisement

In addition to thinking about the decision making behind an ad, when you analyze a print ad you need to ask three overarching questions:

1. How does the ad draw in the target audience by helping them identify with the ad's problematic situation or story (mirror effect)?
2. How does the ad create a field of values, beliefs, and aspirations that serve as windows into a more fulfilled life?
3. How do the ad's images and words work together to create the desired persuasive effects?

For the images in an ad, all the strategies we have already described for documentary photographs and for paintings continue to apply—for example, angle of vision, framing, and so forth. (Review the strategies chart on pp. 233–235.) With many ads you also have to factor in the creative use of words—puns, connotations, and intertextual references to other ads or cultural artifacts. Note that in professionally created ads, every word, every punctuation mark, and every visual detail down to the props in the photograph or the placement of a model's hands are consciously chosen.

The following strategies chart focuses on questions particularly relevant to print ads.

Strategies for Analyzing the Compositional Features of Print Ads

What to Do	Some Questions to Ask
Examine the settings, furnishings, and all other details.	• Is the room formal or informal; neat, lived-in, or messy? • How is the room furnished and decorated? • If the setting is outdoors, what are the features of the landscape: urban or rural, mountain or meadow? • Why are particular animals or birds included? (Think of the differences between using a crow, a hummingbird, or a parrot.)
Consider the social meaning of objects.	• What is the emotional effect of the objects in a den: for example, duck decoys and fishing rods versus computers and high-tech printers? • What is the social significance (class, economic status, lifestyle, values) of the objects in the ad? (Think of the meaning of a groomed poodle versus a mutt or a single rose versus a fuchsia in a pot.)
Consider the characters, roles, and actions.	• Who are these people and what are they doing? What story line could you construct behind the image? • Are the models regular-looking people, "beautiful people," or celebrities? • In product advertisements, are female models used instrumentally (depicted as mechanics working on cars or as consumers buying cars) or are they used decoratively (bikini-clad and lounging on the hood of the latest truck)?

(*continued*)

What to Do	Some Questions to Ask
Observe how models are dressed, posed, and accessorized.	• What are the models' facial expressions? • What are their hairstyles and what cultural and social significance do they have? • How well are they dressed and posed?
Observe the relationships among actors and among actors and objects.	• How does the position of the models signal importance and dominance? • Who is looking at whom? • Who is above or below, in the foreground or background?
Consider what social roles are being played out and what values appealed to.	• Are the gender roles traditional or nontraditional? • Are the relationships romantic, erotic, friendly, formal, uncertain? • What are the power relationships among characters?
Consider how document design functions and how the words and images work together.	• What features of document design (variations of font style and size, placement on the page, formal or playful lettering) stand out? • How much of the copy is devoted to product information or argument about superiority of the product or service? • How much of the copy helps create a field of values, beliefs, aspirations? • How do the words contribute to the "story" implied in the visual images? • What is the style of the language (for example, connotations, double entendres, puns)?

Sample Analysis of an Advertisement

With an understanding of possible photographic effects and the compositional features of ads, you now have the background knowledge needed to begin doing your own analysis of ads. Many of the most dramatic and effective ads now come to us in the form of billboards and television commercials. To show you how such ads can be analyzed, let's examine the acclaimed General Electric Cloud commercial that first aired in 2008. Most people think of General Electric as a company that produces consumer electronics and appliances (refrigerators, dishwaters, etc.); however, GE, one of the largest multinational corporations in the world, actually has divisions focused on energy, technology infrastructure, and consumer industrial products as well. In 2005, in a push to be recognized as a green company, GE initiated its Ecoimagination campaign and has since increased its presence in wind power, solar panels, desalination, and water purification technology. GE's positioning of itself as a green company invested in water reuse solutions is the back story as well as the subtext of the GE Cloud commercial. You can see the forty-eight second commercial on YouTube.

From its first frame, this ad plays on imagination and pulls viewers into a highly romanticized industrial fantasy of the water cycle in which workers in the clouds perform the purification processes of nature. In the first several frames, white buckets sail through the air above green fields to the clouds, where they are received by male and female workers dressed in perfectly white uniforms, wearing white gloves, white hair coverings, and white hardhats. The sequence of frames that follows depicts the synchronized process of these workers feeding the water from earth through enormous bellows, which vaporize it and then condense it through a giant wringer, like those once used for laundry. Then a scientist-technician examines a test tube of this water and pronounces it pure so that the brigade of workers in an assembly line in the clouds can pass buckets of the water to other technicians, who pour it into a vast watering can structure. As thunder crashes, the watering can tips and the purified water falls to earth as rain. In the final few seconds of the commercial, a voice-over interprets the action of the narrative: "Just as nature reuses water, GE water technologies turn billions of gallons into clean water every year. Rain or shine." The final frame shows a glimpse of these actual industrial processes, and the ad ends with the "Ecoimagination" logo.

Our students in film studies noticed how this ad exemplifies the intense dynamism of commercials with the camera constantly moving, zooming in and out, and panning left or right. These movements reflect the time constraints and attention spans commercials must accommodate. The rapidly moving images are tied together by the color palette—mostly whites and grays—and the consistent pace of rapidly changing frames.

Our students also noted that this ad affects viewers first through its multiple, fantastical, and powerful appeals to *pathos*, which arouse viewers' curiosity with a narrative that does not directly declare its product or its purpose. Why is the setting for this ad the clouds? Why are the characters in the ad dressed in technicians' uniforms that are scrupulously white? What exactly are these workers producing? One curiosity-arousing appeal to *pathos* derives from the "heavenly" associations conveyed through the gorgeous images of billowing clouds and radiant sun beams outlining and shining through them and the predominance of white, the color of purity. These images conjure up paintings of heaven in which the figures in the sky are angels or good souls entering the afterlife. These associations suggest that there is something supernatural and divine about this scene, a message underscored by the Creedence Clearwater Revival song "Have You Ever Seen the Rain?" sung by the winsome voice of Julu Stulbach. In this case, a familiar classic song, charged with personal associations and emotional power, is rendered in a new arrangement, making it particularly evocative. The song with its lyrics about "the calm before the storm" adds a seriousness and builds on the audience's fascination with weather—what causes it and how could we control it? A second, more playful appeal to *pathos* is generated by the white-uniformed workers who tap viewers' familiarity with science fiction and children's fantasy stories in their resemblance to the uniformed Umpa-Lumpa factory workers in the film *Willy Wonka and the Chocolate Factory*. These workers signal, as do their counterparts in fiction and film, that readers are in an imagined world but one that comments on the real world. A third appeal to *pathos* carries the mirror effect of the commercial. In depicting these workers as purposeful, industrious, coordinated, and effective, the ad prompts viewers to admire the hard work and indirectly see themselves as dedicated team players engaged in a project to accomplish some important task.

This analysis of the ad's appeals to *pathos* reveals why GE chose to romanticize and fantasize rather than be realistic and direct. If we ask, "Why not take viewers on a tour of a wastewater treatment plant?", the answer dawns on us. A wastewater treatment plant with its giant steel rakes and grates, with scraps of toilet paper and even condoms caught in the prongs, and its various holding tanks for different stages of processing sewage, would interest only a small portion of the audience—and perhaps disgust others—while limiting water technologies to one process. Similarly, the actual technology and plants for industrial cleanup might bore many viewers, who are more interested in product than in process. Instead, the fantastical and associational appeals of the ad can deliver a larger hopeful message while shaping a positive and memorable image of the company.

All these appeals to *pathos* build the company's *ethos* and brand recognition and prepare viewers to absorb the subtly conveyed core message of the ad: Not only is GE good for the environment in the care it takes with resources like water, but GE also possesses the power of nature, and equipped with human ingenuity, knowledge, and ecoimagination, GE's water technologies can solve the world's water problems. The ad, through its window effect, comforts viewers with a sense of the world in which tough problems such as available clean water are faced and solved by the wonders of technology. The dirty process of recycling is now connected with cleanliness, purity, and ample supply of water. The ad inspires appreciation and confidence in GE's know-how and technological capabilities that are as good as, if not better than, nature itself. After all, GE can process billions of gallons of water a year and can do it whether it is raining or sunny.

FOR WRITING AND DISCUSSION

Analyzing an Ad from Different Perspectives

The Axe Apollo men's cologne ad that aired during the 2013 Super Bowl is part of a recent campaign that features traditional culture heroes—lifeguards and firefighters—in competition with another culture hero, the astronaut. Go to YouTube to see the ad with its story line of a shark-endangered, bikini-clad woman rescued by a handsome, buff lifeguard. The audience's expected narrative—rescued girl falls in love with lifeguard—is thwarted, strangely and humorously, by the out-of-nowhere appearance of the geeky, uniformed astronaut. What makes this strange ad effective? You may want to watch the entire ad several times to aid you in your analysis.

1. ***Campaign and analysis.*** After watching this ad, analyze its rhetorical effect and appeal by using the strategies suggested in the charts on pages 233–235 and 247–248 as well as ideas presented throughout this section (target audience, choice of medium, brand building, mirror-and-window strategy, and compositional features).
2. ***Focus on camera techniques.*** Think especially in terms of camera shifts and framing, angle and orientation, distance from the subject, and focus. How do these visual techniques contribute to the narrative and the overall impact of the ad?
3. ***Cultural criticism.*** Reexamine the ad from the perspective of gender, class, ethnicity, and historical moment. Think about the relationships among the characters and focus on the gender roles. To what extent does this ad break or reinforce traditional notions of gender, race, and class? Consider also our particular historical moment. India and China are strengthening their educational systems in math, science, and technology as they look to the development of their space programs; meanwhile funding for the U.S. space program has not kept pace with its robust start in the 1960s and 1970s. Speculate on the cultural relevance of this campaign at this historical moment.
4. ***Cultural criticism continued.*** Compare the view of heroism and gender in the Axe Apollo ad with that of the Air Force recruitment poster on page 81. To what extent does the woman as expert, solo pilot in the Air Force poster reverse the stereotype of the bikini-clad woman in the Axe Apollo ad? What strategies do advertisers use to appeal simultaneously to both power and femininity in their portrayals of female leaders?

Analysis of Two Visual Texts

WRITING PROJECT

10.3
Write a comparative analysis of two visual texts.

Choose two documentary/news photographs, two paintings, or two advertisements to analyze in a closed-form essay. Your two visual texts should have enough in common to facilitate meaningful comparisons. Show these images in your essay (if you are analyzing videos, you'll need to show screen captures), but also describe your two visual texts in detail to highlight what you want viewers to see and to provide a foundation for your analysis. For this closed-form analysis, choose several key points of contrast as the focus. Your thesis statement should make a claim about key differences in the way that your chosen visual texts establish their purposes and achieve their persuasive effects.

Exploring and Generating Ideas for Your Analysis

For the subject of your analysis, your instructor may allow you to choose your own images or may provide them for you. If you choose your own, be sure to follow your instructor's guidelines. In choosing your visual texts, look for some important commonality that will enable you to concentrate on similarities and differences in your analysis:

- ***Documentary or news photographs.*** Analyze two photographs of an event from magazines with different political biases; two news photographs from articles addressing the same story from different angles of vision; or two images on Web sites presenting different perspectives on a recent controversial issue such as industrial farming or the war against terrorists.
- ***Paintings.*** Find two paintings with similar subject matter but different dominant impressions or emotional impacts.
- ***Print ads or television (YouTube) ads.*** Look for two ads for the same product (for example, cars, perfume, watches, shampoo) that are aimed at different target audiences or that make appeals to noticeably different value systems.

No matter what type of visual texts you are using, we suggest that you generate ideas and material for your analysis by using the question-asking strategies presented earlier in this chapter (see the strategies charts on pp. 233-235 and 247–248).

To help you generate more ideas, go detail by detail through your images, asking how the rhetorical effect would be different if some detail were changed:

- How would this documentary photo have a different effect if the homeless man were lying on the sidewalk instead of leaning against the doorway?
- Why did the artist blur images in the background rather than make them more distinct?
- What if the advertisers had decided the model should wear jogging shorts and a tank top instead of a bikini? What if the model were a person of color rather than white?

Shaping and Drafting Your Analysis

Your closed-form essay should be fairly easy to organize at the big-picture level, but each part will require its own organic organization depending on the main points of your analysis. At the big-picture level, you can generally follow a structure like the one shown in Figure 10.14.

If you get stuck, we recommend that you write your rough draft rapidly, without worrying about gracefulness or correctness, merely trying to capture your initial ideas. Many people like to begin with the description of the two visual texts and then write the analysis before writing the introduction and conclusion. After you have written your draft, put it aside for a while before you begin revising.

FIGURE 10.14 Framework for an Analysis of Two Visuals

Introduction	• Hooks readers' interest; • Gives background on the two visual texts you are analyzing; • Sets up the similarities; • Poses the question your paper will address; • Ends with initial mapping in the form of a purpose or thesis statement.
General description of your two visual texts (ads, photographs, paintings)	• Describes each visual text in turn.
Analysis of the two visual texts	• Analyzes and contrasts each text in turn, using the ideas you generated from your observations, question asking, and close examination.
Conclusion	• Returns to the big picture for a sense of closure; • Makes final comments about the significance of your analysis.

Revising

Most experienced writers make global changes in their drafts when they revise, especially when they are doing analytical writing. The act of writing a rough draft generally leads to the discovery of more ideas. You may also realize that some of your original ideas aren't clearly developed or that the draft feels scattered or disorganized.

We recommend that you ask your classmates for a peer review of your draft early in the revising process to help you enhance the clarity and depth of your analysis.

Questions for Peer Review

In addition to the generic peer review questions explained in Skill 16.4, ask your peer reviewers to address these questions:

1. How well do the title, introduction, and thesis set up an academic analysis?
2. Where does the writer capture your interest and provide necessary background information? How might the writer more clearly pose the question to be addressed and map out the analysis?
3. Where could the writer describe the visual texts more clearly so that readers can "see" them?
4. How has the writer established the complexity of the texts and their commonalities and differences?
5. How well has the writer used the questions about angle of vision, artistic techniques, and compositional features presented in this chapter to achieve a detailed and insightful analysis of the texts? Where could the writer add more

specific details about settings, props, posing of characters, facial expressions, manners of dress, story line, and so forth?

6. In what ways could the writer improve this analysis by clarifying, deepening, expanding, or reorganizing the analysis? How has the writer helped you understand something new about these two texts?

WRITING PROJECT

Multimodal or Online Options

1. **Museum Audioguide Podcast** Many art museums feature portable audioguide recorders that prompt viewers to pause in front of exhibits to hear an analysis of the painting or photograph. Assume that your chosen images (if you have selected two paintings or two documentary photographs) are exhibited side by side at a museum as part of a featured display. Create a podcast describing and analyzing the exhibits. You can assume that your audience will be looking at the exhibit as you talk. For advice on preparing a podcast, see Skill 19.3.
2. **Lecture with Visual Aids** Assume that for a global outreach program you have been invited to present an analysis of two ad campaigns for the same product or company as this product or company is marketed in different cultures. For example, how are Coca Cola products advertised in China? How is MacDonald's advertised in Central America? Prepare a lecture with PowerPoint or Prezi slides that you can record on video and upload to YouTube. Your slides can hone in on certain features of the ads as you talk. For advice on preparing oral presentations with visual aids, see Skill 19.3.

Our first two readings argue different perspectives on the ethics of photographing injuries and victims' suffering in disasters. The readings refer to victims of the massive 2010 Haiti earthquake, and the same issue resurfaced in news coverage of the 2013 Boston Marathon bombing. The first reading is an op-ed by Clark Hoyt, public editor of the *New York Times*. For background, you can do a Web search of photographs of the Haiti disaster as well as explore the *New York Times'* gallery of photos.

Clark Hoyt*

Face to Face with Tragedy

1 It was hard to look at some of the pictures of suffering and death caused by the earthquake in Haiti—and impossible to turn away.

2 The top of one front page in the *Times* was dominated by a woman, her hand to her cheek, as if in shock, walking past partially covered corpses lined up along a dirty curb. The next day, an even larger photograph at the top of page 1 showed a man covered in gray dust, lying alone, dead, statue-like, on a stretcher made from a piece of tattered cardboard spread over a crude ladder. Inside that same paper, the Friday after the disaster, was a gruesome scene from the central morgue in Port-au-Prince: a man mourning the death of his 10-month-old daughter, lying in her diaper atop a pile of bodies.

3 Some readers were offended at these scenes and even more graphic pictures on the paper's Web site, calling them exploitive and sensationalistic. "The numerous photographs printed in the *Times* showing the dead strewn about the streets of Port-au-Prince are unnecessary, unethical, unkind and inhumane," wrote Randy Stebbins of Hammond, La. Christa Robbins of Chicago said, "I feel that the people who have suffered the most are being spectacularized by your blood-and-gore photographs, which do not at all inform me of the relief efforts, the political stability of the region or the extent of damage to families and infrastructure." She spoke for several readers when she added, "If this had happened in California, I cannot imagine a similar depiction of half-clothed bodies splayed out for the camera. What are you thinking?"

4 But other readers were grateful for the shocking pictures, even as they were deeply troubled by them. Mary Louise Thomas of Palatka, Fla., said a different photo of the baby, lying on her dead mother, caused her to cry out, "Oh, my God!" and to sob for an hour. "But run from it? Never," she said. People repelled by such images "should really try staring truth in the face occasionally and try to understand it," she wrote.

5 Mary Claire Carroll of Richmond, Vt., asked, "How else can you motivate or inspire someone like me to donate money" to help out in Haiti? Her son, she added, thinks Americans "are too sheltered and protected from the real world."

6 Every disaster that produces horrific scenes of carnage presents photographers and their editors with the challenge of telling the unsanitized truth without crossing into the offensive and truly exploitive. In 2004, when a giant undersea earthquake

*Clark Hoyt. "Face to Face with Tragedy" from The New York Times, January 23, 2010.

unleashed a tsunami that killed tens of thousands along Indian Ocean coastlines, the *Times* ran a dramatic front-page photo of a woman overcome with grief amid rows of dead children, including her own. Some readers protested, but the newspaper's first public editor, Daniel Okrent, concluded that the paper was right to publish the picture. It told the story of the tsunami, he said.

7 I asked Kenneth Irby, leader of the visual journalism group at the Poynter Institute in Florida, for his assessment of the pictures from Haiti. Irby brings unusual perspectives to the task. He is a veteran photojournalist and an ordained minister, the pastor of an African Methodist Episcopal church in Palmetto, Fla. His wife's best friend is Haitian, and her family was still unaccounted for when we talked last week. "I think the *Times* coverage has been raw, truthful and tasteful," he told me, defending even the most graphic images.

8 Irby, who has been in touch with photographers in Haiti, said survivors want the world to see what has happened. "The actual loved ones, the bereaved, implore the journalists to tell their stories," he said.

9 That is exactly what Damon Winter told me. He is the *Times* photographer who took the pictures that elicited most of the protests to me and much praise on the paper's Web site. Winter, who won a Pulitzer Prize last year for his coverage of the Obama presidential campaign, was the first *Times* staff photographer on the scene, flying from New York to the Dominican Republic and then into Haiti aboard a chartered helicopter. He had never been to Haiti or covered a natural disaster.

10 "I have had so many people beg me to come to their home and photograph the bodies of their children, brothers, sisters, mothers, fathers," he said. "There are so many times that I have to apologize and say that I cannot, that I have photographed so many bodies already, and I think it breaks their hearts because they so desperately want people to know what has happened to them, what tremendous pain they are in, and that they desperately need help." Winter said it was important "that I do whatever I can to try and make our readers understand just how dire the situation is here."

11 Jessie De Witt, an international photo editor, said Winter sent the paper 26 pictures on his first day in Haiti, including the picture of the bodies along the curb that wound up on the front page. He sent 65 the next day, including the mourning father and the dead man on the stretcher. De Witt and her colleagues think carefully about photo selections. A picture of a dog eyeing a corpse is out, as are stacks of bodies without context. And they think about juxtaposition: an Armageddon-like scene of people scrambling for supplies from a ruined store was played against a quieter picture of people waiting patiently for medical treatment.

12 Michele McNally, the assistant managing editor in charge of photography, said she was going through all the photos from all sources, and Winter's photos of the single dead man and the grieving father "stopped me in my tracks." Bill Keller, the executive editor, said editors considered both for the front page, but chose the lone body, played big, because it was dramatic and there was "an intimacy that causes people to pause and dwell on the depth of the tragedy." Looking at one person, instead of many, "humanizes it," he said.

13 I asked McNally about Robbins's contention that such pictures would not appear in the paper if the victims were somewhere in the United States. If such pictures

existed, she said, she would run them. When Hurricane Katrina hit New Orleans, the *Times* did publish a front-page picture of a body floating near a bridge where a woman was feeding her dog. But despite Katrina's toll, there were relatively few such images in the paper. Irby said that authorities in the United States are generally quick to cordon off disaster scenes.

14 Just as a picture of a grieving mother told the story of the tsunami in 2004, the disturbing images of the last two weeks have been telling the story of Haiti, and the *Times* is right to publish them. As Patricia Lay-Dorsey, a reader from Detroit, put it, Winter's "camera was my eye as much as it was his. And every one of his photos told the truth."

THINKING CRITICALLY
about "Face to Face with Tragedy"

1. According to Clark Hoyt, what are the ethical and rhetorical problems that photojournalists face in photographing disasters like the Haiti earthquake? Who are the different stakeholders in this controversy?
2. On page 232 in this chapter, we discussed the importance of the photographer's purpose and of the cultural, social, historical, and political context of the photograph. What claims does Hoyt make for the purpose and context of the published images of human suffering in Haiti?
3. Research the coverage of the Haiti earthquake in one of the prominent general news commentary sources such as *Newsweek, Time, USA Today*, or a leading newspaper's or online news site's archives. What images appear the most often? How did the captions for these images shape your impression of them?
4. What intellectual and emotional impact did these images have on you?

Our second reading, an op-ed piece by Manoucheka Celeste, a doctoral candidate in the Department of Communication at the University of Washington, was published in the *Seattle Times* on January 26, 2010.

Manoucheka Celeste

Disturbing Media Images of Haiti Earthquake Aftermath Tell Only Part of the Story

1 As a Haitian, former journalist and media scholar, [I found] the earthquake in Haiti... both personally devastating and intellectually challenging.

2 The first earthquake to hit Haiti in more than 200 years was unbelievable, unexpected and unprecedented. The devastation is clear with more than 200,000 lives lost. The damage is real. As we saw, people around the world responded quickly and generously.

3 This catastrophe presented an opportunity for media to respond in an unprecedented way. Some news outlets arrived before relief workers and doctors. We watched the horrors as they happened. I hoped that this was the moment when those of us trained in journalism would do something remarkable: Bring news of an unimaginable event in a way that disrupted the sensational and stereotypical ways that people in the "Third World" are represented.

4 What we got instead was much less humane. Videos of dead bodies, including children and the elderly, filled our television screens. For those of us who tuned in for information about friends and families, it was and is unbearable and despicable. Coverage went from sensational to ridiculous as CNN compared the literacy rates of Haiti and the United States. This was irrelevant as it continued to represent Haiti as a failed state.

5 The focus on poverty, with the repeated tagline "the poorest country in the Western Hemisphere" and references to crime and unrest, make it hard for viewers to imagine any other aspect of life in Haiti. People were called looters for taking food from collapsed buildings after not having eaten for days, framing their survival as a crime. The humanity needed in this moment is clearly missing.

6 Media scholars have long connected media coverage with public opinion, cultivating our attitudes and creating and reinforcing stereotypes. It is predominantly people of color who are shown negatively in news and entertainment. While the images mobilized some to help, they are damaging in the long term as they become ingrained in how we imagine Haitians. For many this is the first and last contact they will have with this population. The images matter as Haitians are shown as less than human. In mass media when images of Haiti and various countries in the African continent are shown, blackness becomes associated with helplessness, danger, poverty and hopelessness.

7 In the most disgusting moment in broadcast history, Pat Robertson proclaimed that Haiti had it coming because of its "deal with the devil," linking Haiti to "godlessness." What Robertson didn't consider was that "godlessness" was used as an excuse to kill and colonize peoples throughout history in the name of God, including Haiti, which, incidentally, is a heavily Christian country.

8 The question that plagues me and hopefully all audiences is: Who is able to die with dignity? In recent media history, there are few, but increasing instances where dead Americans are shown. From Columbine to Sept. 11, we rightfully protect the dead and rarely dare show them on television or in newspapers. Yet, the increasing presence of graphic and emotionally charged images, especially in broadcast media makes it seem normal or desirable.

9 This earthquake, despite the amazing pain that it has caused to so many, presents an unprecedented opportunity. Viewers and readers can demand that in people's darkest hour or once they lose their lives that they are treated with dignity.

10 We want the story without sensationalism and reinforcement of stereotypes. We want the media to value the lives of people who are "not us." As I waited for eight days to hear that my own mother and grandmother in Port-au-Prince are safe, I wanted to hold on to good memories of the person who brought me into the world and the one who taught me to be generous and tenacious. Let's seize the opportunity of this horrific tragedy to demand better from our news sources: dignity for everyone.

THINKING CRITICALLY

about "Disturbing Media Images of Haiti Earthquake Aftermath Tell Only Part of the Story"

1. In her criticism of the media's use of "graphic and emotionally charged images," how does Manoucheka Celeste argue against the main perspective that Hoyt endorses?
2. Celeste's op-ed piece examines the role of viewers' knowledge, values, and assumptions in interpreting photos in news stories. What historical, political, and racial elements does Celeste underscore?
3. For the photographs of the Haiti disaster that you located and viewed, argue that they either simplified and distorted the issues or pushed them toward complexity and depth. In your mind, what does it mean to treat the human subjects of photographs with "dignity"?
4. How do the views of photography argued in these two readings relate to the gory images of victims of the Boston Marathon bombings in April 2013? What should the public see? What is responsible, ethical visual coverage of events like this? What images from this event had powerful emotional impact?

Our final reading is student Lydia Wheeler's analytical essay written for the writing project in this chapter. It analyzes two documentary photos focused on economic hardship and displacement. One photo, taken by photographer Stephen Crowley, accompanied a *New York Times* story about a mother and her daughters in the 2008 recession caused by the collapse of the housing bubble in the United States. The subject, Isabel Bermudez, was subsisting on food stamps unable to find a job; previously she had supported her daughters with a six-figure salary. Then the market collapsed, she lost her job, and shortly afterward she lost her house. The second photo is a famous image taken in 1936 in Nipoma, California, during the Great Depression. The photo is part of the *Migrant Mother* series by photographer Dorothea Lange. Lydia decided to examine the original newspaper contexts for these photographs and to approach them as depictions of women's experiences of economic crisis.

Lydia Wheeler (student)

Two Photographs Capture Women's Economic Misery

1 During economic crises, the hardship of individuals is often presented to us as statistics and facts: number of bankruptcies, percentage of the population living below the poverty line, and foreclosures or unemployment rates. Although this numerical data can be shocking, it usually remains abstract and impersonal. In contrast, photographers such as Stephen Crowley and Dorothea Lange help us visualize the human suffering involved in the economic conditions, skillfully evoking the emotional, as

well as the physical, reality of their subjects. Crowley's color photograph, first published January 2, 2010, in a *New York Times* article titled "Living on Nothing but Food Stamps," is captioned "Isabel Bermudez, who has two daughters and no cash income." Lange's black and white photograph was commissioned by the Resettlement Agency to document Americans living in the Great Depression; she originally captioned it *Destitute pea pickers in California; a 32 year old mother of seven children. February 1936.* However, in March of the same year, the *San Francisco Times* published Lange's photograph in an article demanding aid for workers like Florence Owens Thompson, the central subject of the picture. Once published, the photograph became famous and was nicknamed *Migrant Mother.* A close look at these two photos shows that through their skillful use of photographic elements such as focus, framing, orientation, and shape, Stephen Crowley and Dorothea Lange capture the unique emotional and physical realities of their subjects, eliciting compassion and admiration, respectively.

2 Stephen Crowley's photograph of a mother sitting in a room, perhaps the dining room of her house, and her young daughter standing and reaching out to comfort her sets up contrasts and tensions that underscore loss and convey grief. The accompanying article explains that Isabel Bermudez, whose income from real estate once amply supported her family, now has no income or prospect for employment and relies entirely on food stamps. A careful examination of Crowley's photograph implies this loss by hinting that Bermudez's wealth is insecure.

3 The framing, distance, and focus of Crowley's photograph emphasize this vanished wealth and the emotional pain. The image is a medium close up with its human

Isabel Bermudez, who has two daughters and no cash income, by Stephen Crowley

Destitute pea pickers in California; a 32 year old mother of seven children [*Migrant Mother*] by Dorothea Lange

subjects to the side, surrounding them with empty space and hints of expensive furnishings. While part of the foreground is sharply focused, the background is blurry and unfocused. There is a suggestion that the room is spacious. Further, the high, decorative backs of the room's chairs, the repetitive design decorating the bookshelf on the frame's left, and the houseplant next to the bookshelf show that the room is well furnished, even luxurious. Bermudez and her daughter match their surroundings in being elegantly dressed. Bermudez looks across the room as if absorbed in her troubles; her daughter looks intently at her. Viewers' eyes are drawn to Bermudez's dark dress and her pearl necklace and earrings. However, the ostensible comfort of Bermudez and her surroundings starkly contrasts with her grief.

4 Crowley heightens this contrast and tension through the subjects' orientation and the space between them. The space between Bermudez and her daughter is one of the photograph's dominant features, but it contains only out-of-focus objects in the background. Neither figure is centered in the photo; neither looks at the camera. Consequently, the viewers' attention moves back and forth between them, creating a sense of uneasiness. The meaning of this photo is focused not on what Bermudez has but on what she has lost.

5 Crowley also evokes sympathy and compassion for his subjects with his choice of angle, scale, and detail. The photograph's slightly high angle makes viewers look down—literally—on Bermudez, making her appear vulnerable and powerless and reinforcing the pathos. The most striking bid for compassion is the tears streaming down Bermudez's well made-up face. The contrast between her tidy appearance and the tear tracks on her face suggest overwhelming sadness. The poignancy of her apparent breakdown is heightened by her somber daughter's attempt to wipe away the tears on her mother's face. Crowley's decisions regarding *Isabel's* composition create an image that is highly disturbing.

6 In contrast to Crowley's photograph, Lange's *Migrant Mother*—through its content, focus, frame, rhythm, and angle—conveys long-standing poverty. Yet through this image of inescapable poverty pressing upon its subjects, it evokes admiration for this mother.

7 Lange's frame and focus generate much of the intensity of *Migrant Mother.* This photo is also a medium close up, but Lange's frame is tight with no open space. The lack of this openness cramps Lange's subjects and creates a claustrophobic feel intensified by the number of subjects shown—four to *Isabel's* two. There is almost no background. The subjects filling the foreground are crowded and sharply focused. The contrast between crowded foreground and empty background exaggerates the former and adds a touch of loneliness to *Migrant Mother;* this mother has no resources besides herself. Additionally, the subjects of *Migrant Mother* almost epitomize poverty: Their hair is messy and uncombed, their skin dirt-stained. Even their clothes are worn—from the hem of Thompson's frayed sleeve to the smudges on her baby's blanket, Lange's photograph shows that Thompson can barely afford functional items.

8 *Migrant Mother's* circular lines also create a sense of sameness, stagnation, and hopelessness. Thompson's face draws viewers' eyes as the dominant feature, and Lange has ringed it with several arcs. The parentheses of her standing children's bodies, the angle of her baby in its blanket, and the arc of her dark hair form a ring that hems Thompson in and creates a circular path for the eyes of viewers. Seen with the obvious destitution of Lange's subjects, this repetition is threatening and grimly promises that it will be difficult, if not impossible, for this family to escape its poverty.

9 Like Crowley's *Isabel,* the impact of Lange's *Migrant Mother* derives from both the tragedy of her subjects' situation and their reactions. Lange uses angle and scale to generate sympathy and admiration for Thompson's strength. Once again we see a slightly high angle highlighting the subjects' vulnerability, which Lange reinforces with the slender necks of Thompson's children and a glimpse of her brassiere.

However, Lange then contrasts this vulnerability with Thompson's strength, fostering viewers' admiration rather than compassion. *Migrant Mother's* scale, for example, exaggerates rather than diminishes Thompson's size: the photograph's frame focuses viewers' attention on the mother, who looks large, compared to her children. Additionally, Lange's subject literally supports the bodies of the children surrounding her. Unlike Bermudez, Thompson sits tall as a pillar of strength for her vulnerable children. Even her expression—worried but dry eyed—fosters admiration and respect in viewers. By juxtaposing Thompson's vulnerability with her strength, Lange creates a photograph that conveys both its subjects' poverty and their stoicism in facing the Great Depression.

10 Lange and Crowley guide viewer's reactions to their photographs through careful control of the elements that influence our emotional responses to their work. Though they both show women in economic crises, these artists are able to convey the distinct realities of their subjects' situations and consequently send viewers away in different emotional states: one of compassion, one of admiration. The fame and veneration of Lange's *Migrant Mother* is a testament to her ability to evoke desired emotions. The photograph was exhibited at the Museum of Modern Art in 1941 and again in 1955, and was co-opted by countless movements since it was first published. Whether Crowley's *Isabel* will achieve similar fame for epitomizing this generation's economic crisis remains to be seen, but both photographs certainly succeed in delivering strong, lasting emotional statements.

THINKING CRITICALLY
about "Two Photographs Capture Women's Economic Misery"

1. What photographic elements has Lydia chosen to emphasize in her analysis of each of these photos?
2. What parts of Lydia's analysis help you see and understand these photos with greater insight? Do you agree with her choice of important elements and her analysis of their effects?
3. If you were analyzing these photos, what features would you choose to compare and stress?

11 ANALYZING SHORT FICTION

WHAT YOU WILL LEARN

11.1 To explain strategies for reading short stories literarily.

11.2 To pose an interpretive question about a flash fiction story and write an analytical argument in response using textual detail for support.

The genre of the short story has existed for a long time. In this chapter, we'll focus on a very short form of short story—often called "flash fiction"—which is becoming increasingly popular in the digital age. **Flash fiction** is the most common current name for stories with fewer than 1000 words and in many cases fewer than 500 words. (Other commonly encountered names include "sudden fiction" and "nanofiction."). Flash fiction lovers have created a vigorous market for stories that can be read on a single computer screen or on a smartphone while waiting for a bus. Flash fiction stories contain all the elements of longer fiction—plot, character, setting, metaphoric language, and imagery—all working together to express a theme. The analytical skills you learn in this chapter can be applied to fiction of any length.

Engaging Literary Analysis

Both fiction and creative nonfiction invite us into a world created by a complex, layered use of language that asks us to read *literarily* rather than *literally.* When you read something **literally**, you attempt to reduce its meaning to one clear set of statements without ambiguity. When you read something **literarily**, you value ambiguity, perceive possible layers of meanings within the text, and enlist your imagination to fill in gaps and bring the story to life. This multiplicity of possible readings partially accounts for the interpretive pleasures of reading a literary work.

To appreciate what we mean by reading literarily, read the following flash fiction story and then explore your answers to the questions that follow. (We will discuss this story in depth as this chapter proceeds.)

Alison Townsend
The Barbie Birthday

Girls learn how to be women not from their dolls but from the women around them.

Yona Zeldis McDonough, *The Barbie Chronicles*

The first gift my father's girlfriend gave me was the Barbie I wanted. Not the original—blond, ponytailed Barbie in her zebra-striped swimsuit and matching cat-eye shades— but a bubble-cut brunette, her hair a color the box described as "Titian," a brownish-orange I've never seen since. But I didn't care. My hair was brown too. And Barbie was Barbie, the same impossible body when you stripped off her suit, peeling it down over those breasts without nipples, then pulling it back up again. Which was the whole point, of course.

There must have been a cake. And ten candles. And singing. But what I remember is how my future stepmother stepped from the car and into the house, her auburn curls bouncing in the early May light, her suit of fuchsia wool blooming like some exotic flower, just that, then Barbie—whom I crept away with afterwards, stealing upstairs to play with her beneath a sunny window in what had been my parents' bedroom.

She likes me; she really likes me, I thought, recalling Shirley's smile when I opened the package. As I lifted the lid of Barbie's narrow, coffin-like box, she stared up at me, sloe-eyed, lids bruised blue, lashes caked thick with mascara, her mouth stuck in a pout both seductive and sullen. Alone, I turned her over and over in my hands, marveling at her stiff, shiny body—the torpedo breasts, the wasp waist, the tall-drink-of-water legs that didn't bend, and the feet on perpetual tiptoe, their arches crimped to fit her spike-heeled mules as she strutted across the sunny windowsill.

All Barbie had to do was glance back once and I followed, casting my lot with every girl on every block in America, signing on for life. She was who I wanted to be, though I couldn't have said then, anymore than I could have said that Barbie was sex without sex. I don't think my stepmother-to-be knew that either, just that she wanted to please me, the eldest daughter who remembered too much and who had been too shy to visit. My mother had been dead five months, both her breasts cut off like raw meat. But I yearned for the doll she'd forbidden, as if Barbie could tell me what everything meant—how to be a woman when I was a girl with no mother, how to dress and talk, how to thank Shirley for the hard, plastic body that warmed when I touched it, leading me back to the world.

ON YOUR OWN

1. What does the story suggest or imply about the value of Barbie dolls or about the role of Barbie dolls for girls growing up?
2. What does it suggest or imply about the relationship of daughters to mothers or stepmothers?

3. The narrator calls the box that the Barbie comes in "coffin-like." What effect does this image have on your interpretation of the story?
4. What are some more puzzling questions that you might pose about this story?

IN CONVERSATION

Share individual responses to the previous questions and try to reach class consensus on the answers.

11.1 Explain strategies for reading short stories literarily.

Understanding Literary Analysis

Reading fiction is pleasurable only if you use your own imagination to bring the text to life. To exercise your imagination fully, you must read closely and actively, connecting the dots created by the author's words into an imaginary movie in your mind. To illustrate what we mean by reading imaginatively, observe how your mind works differently when you read the following six-word short story (allegedly by Ernest Hemingway) versus a six-word declarative sentence:

> **Story**: For sale: Baby shoes. Never worn.
> **Declarative sentence**: Baby shoes are on sale tomorrow.

If you are like most readers, you processed these two examples differently. The story invites readers to slow down, to fill in gaps, to create their own mental images of a plot with characters. These six words, sequenced as three idea-bearing units or elements, invite readers to imagine a couple who were expecting a baby and, during the pregnancy, bought baby shoes in anticipation of happy days ahead. Then, before this anticipation could be fulfilled, they must have lost the baby. Now they are selling the shoes, perhaps trying to reach closure by wiping away the memories. The last two words of the story, "Never worn," produce the kind of layered multiple meanings characteristic of literature. On the one hand, "never worn" (or "never used") is simply the way people advertise a secondhand item that it is actually new—a way of upping the price. On the other hand, the two words startle us with the realization that the baby didn't live, evoking our sadness that tiny feet never touched these tiny shoes. The story works only if we help make it work. In contrast, the declarative sentence simply states a fact that requires little imaginative energy from us.

The difference between closed-form and open-form prose is introduced in Chapter 1, pp. 17–18; see also Chapter 17 on closed-form prose and Chapter 18 on open-form prose.

Critical Elements of a Literary Text

Short stories belong to the category of open-form prose, which uses literary strategies such as plot, character, setting, imagery, metaphor, and theme to create meaning in ways different from that of thesis-governed closed-form prose. To analyze a short story, you will need first to become familiar with the literary elements of open-form prose as explained in Chapter 18 and elaborated in more detail in Chapter 6 on writing an autobiographical essay. What follows is a brief summary of the ideas developed in Chapters 18 and 6.

Criteria for a Story A story depicts chronological events that are connected causally or thematically to create a sense of tension that is resolved through action, insight, or understanding. When you analyze a short story, you'll need to identify the story's sources of tension or ambiguity and try to see how they are resolved or left open. These tensions and possible resolutions are primary contributors to the story's theme—that is, to its meaning or significance, the reader's sense that the story says something to us that matters. A story thus differs from an "and then" narrative that simply recounts events chronologically without point or significance. But the meaning of the story can't be summed up in a single statement. It has layers of meanings or, to use metaphors from sound rather than space, various pitches, resonances, or echoes that cause us to hear within the sound chamber of the text different combinations of sounds rather single notes. These layers or resonances are relevant to an interpretation of the story because of the relational "connectedness" that distinguishes stories from "and then" chronologies. When you analyze a short story, you are often trying to show how different aspects of the story are connected.

The difference between an "and then" narrative and a story is explained in Chapter 18, pp. 476–479.

Literary Elements The tensions and resolutions of a story are realized within a time frame in which the actions of the story (its plot) are performed by characters within settings. Much of literary analysis looks at the relationships of these formal elements of a story. For an overview of the formal elements of plot, character, setting, and theme see Chapter 6 on writing an autobiographical essay.

The discussion of formal elements is on pp. 127–130. See also Chapter 18, where we analyze Kris Saknussemm's "Phantom Limb Pain" (pp. 137–138).

Ambiguity and Layered Meanings In Chapter 18, we explain that open-form prose often evokes ambiguity whereas closed-form prose usually tries to avoid it. Ambiguity allows us to hold in tension several different layers or resonances of meaning at once. The word "ambiguity" comes from the Latin word "ambi" meaning "both ways" and "agere" meaning "to lead or drive." Ambiguous words, metaphorically speaking, lead us two ways at once. Within an ambiguous word or phrase, two or more meanings may be echoing simultaneously. Often ambiguities are sparked by figurative language such as similes or metaphors. If we say "A great football coach is a chess master," our minds are lead in the direction of football and chess simultaneously. The passage doesn't mean literally that great football coaches are great chess players, but it invites us to consider how football strategy and chess strategy share similar elements.

See Chapter 18, Skill 18.4 "Tap the power of metaphors and other tropes."

Historical and Cultural Contexts

Another aspect of literary analysis is the role played by internal and external context (historical and cultural context). Also, just as figurative language can trigger multiple meanings, so can internal contexts within a story. The following humorous example illustrates how context can cause words to go "two ways at once." Consider what happens to the apparently unambiguous phrase "Some people just need a pat on the back" when it is put in an unexpected context, as in the following example found on a T-shirt:

Now the "pat on the back" must be read ironically not as an affectionate sign of support but as a shove off a cliff. The humor resides in the tension between two different ways of reading the same line. Similarly, a simple statement such as "You look nice," can echo with different meanings depending on context. We can imagine contexts in which a speaker might be genuinely sincere (you really do look nice), ironic (actually you look hideous), or awkwardly conflicted (you look tired and stressed out, but I'm trying to be kind).

In addition to internal context, external context—when a story is written and the historical/cultural moment it depicts—can be important external contexts. How does a piece of fiction reflect its historical and cultural context? "The Barbie Birthday" obviously joins a cultural conversation about the role of Barbie dolls in socializing American girls into womanhood. Its external context is signified immediately in the title (readers know who "Barbie" is from knowing about the culture) and by the quotation from *The Barbie Chronicles,* which is a book devoted entirely to the cultural debate about Barbie. Based on this external context, we expect the story to make its own contribution to this conversation.

A Process for Analyzing a Short Story

When you analyze a short story, we recommend that you begin by rereading it carefully several times. The shorter the story, the more you can reread it, keeping in mind the critical elements of a literary text that we have just described. You can then use the following sequence of strategies to help you discover ideas for your analysis.

Write a Plot Summary Your first task should be simply to articulate what happens in the story at a literal level. A good strategy is to write your own plot summary of the story. Later, when you analyze the story, you will be showing why the story itself is much richer and more complex than the plot summary alone. Here is our plot summary of "The Barbie Birthday."

> The narrator recalls that on her tenth birthday her father's girlfriend, Shirley, gave her a Barbie doll. She particularly remembers the moment that Shirley stepped from

her car into the house and met the narrator, apparently for the first time. The narrator loved every feature of this Barbie doll and played with it in her parents' bedroom. Near the end of the story we learn that the narrator's mother had been dead for five months. The mother had died of breast cancer and had forbidden her daughter to have a Barbie.

Pose Possible Interpretive Questions Your goal now is to switch from reading literally to reading literarily, trying to figure out how all the elements of the story "connect" and contribute to the story's theme. That is, before you can fully and persuasively argue what you believe the story expresses or suggests at the thematic level, you must first explore the elements that the story uses to convey that theme. You are looking for puzzling elements of the story—parts or layers or resonances that don't at first seem to fit or that strike you as perhaps significant but you can't figure out why. Because the thesis of academic prose typically addresses a problem, your first step is to identify an interpretive problem arising from the text. The following strategies charts will guide you through the critical elements of literary analysis helping you pose interpretive questions or problems. The last column shows our own problem-posing questions based on "The Barbie Birthday."

Strategies for Posing Questions about Formal Features of a Short Story

Formal Feature	Possible Questions to Ask	Illustrations from "The Barbie Birthday"
Character	Who are the main characters in the story? What are each character's values? Which characters are flat and which are round? Which characters change and which are static? What is the significance of any changes? Are any of the characters ambiguous or hard to figure out? If so, why?	How are Shirley's values different from the dead mother's values? How does the narrator change from her ten-year-old self to her adult self? How does the narrator's attitude toward Barbies change?
Plot	What puzzling things happen in the story? What tensions or conflicts develop? Are there any turning points? Do the events occur in chronological order, or is time sequence distorted and, if so, why? Does the action take place in one place, or is there movement from one location to another? Is this switch in locality significant (see also "setting")?	Why does Shirley give the girl a bubble cut brunette Barbie rather than a blond, pony-tailed Barbie? Why does the child worry whether Shirley "likes her"? Does the Barbie gift create a turning point in the narrator's life? Why do the events occur out of chronological order (we hear about the dead mother late in the story, not at the beginning)?

(*continued*)

Formal Feature	Possible Questions to Ask	Illustrations from "The Barbie Birthday"
Point of view	Is the narration first person or third person? Is the narrator omniscient (knows the inner thoughts of all characters) or limited (knows the thoughts and actions of one character but sees other characters only through the eyes of the first character)? Is the narrator reliable, or is the narrator's blindness or bias part of the narrative's plot? How does your awareness of point of view affect the way you read the narrative? With whom do readers sympathize?	The point of view is complex—an older, wiser, first-person narrator looks back on an event when she was ten. The narrator's point of view toward Barbies seems different from that of the ten-year-old. To what extent does the adult narrator still feel sympathy for her ten-year-old's view?
Setting	What are the physical characteristics of the setting? Are these used metaphorically? Do the settings shift as the narrative progresses? How does setting contribute to ambiguities, echoes, or resonances in the story? How does your awareness of time and place affect the way you read the narrative?	Almost all the description focuses on the Barbie rather than setting, but the setting might be important. Why does the main character play in her parents' bedroom rather than, say, her own bedroom?
Imagery, metaphor, and other figurative language	Imagery, metaphors, and other figurative language often trigger resonances or layers of meaning. What are the dominant images in the story? What figures of speech occur in certain passages? What patterns do you find in the use of images, metaphors, or other figures of speech? What do you understand to be the purpose or meaning of these patterns?	Why is the box Barbie comes in described as "coffin-like"? Why does the narrator choose "bruised blue" to describe Barbie's eyelids? What is the significance of the metaphor "warmed" in the last sentence? What is the significance of the difference between Barbie's "torpedo breasts" and the dead mother's breasts "cut off like raw meat"?
Language, tone, style	What is the significance of the author's language and style (sentence length, word choice, grammatical complexity, abstract versus concrete language)? Does the style change as the narrative progresses? Are different characters associated with differences in style/language? Is the style or tone ironic? Why?	The narrator as adult seems to use words that would not have occurred to the ten-year old—such as "torpedo breasts" or "breasts cut off like raw meat." What is suggested by the gap between the adult narrator's language and the language used by the child? Is the narrator ironic in saying that the Barbie led "me back into the world"?

Strategies for Posing Questions about the Contexts of a Short Story

Context	Possible Questions to Ask	Illustrations from "The Barbie Birthday"
Internal context	How does the relationship between characters or the timing of an event cause us to see ambiguities or "double meanings" in what characters say or think? How does context help us read between the lines at certain points?	A Barbie doll seems like an ordinary gift that many girls would receive on their tenth birthdays. How does the context of this gift—given to her by her future stepmother—have special significance? How does the context deepen our understanding of her concern whether Shirley "likes me"? Does the Barbie fill a void left by the dead mother?
Story's time period(s)	When is the time period of the author or of the story? What background knowledge about that time period is needed and relevant?	A Google search shows that Barbies were first marketed in 1959 and that some had bendable legs starting in 1965. The *Barbie Chronicles* was published in 1999. The narrator's adult time period is after 1999, but the ten-year-old's birthday may have occurred in the early 60s.
Relevant cultural debates and anxieties	To what extent does the story participate in cultural debates occurring at the time of its publication? How does the narrative try to influence the readers' view of something? How does the narrative reflect cultural concerns and anxieties?	Why does the story open with a quotation from *The Barbie Chronicles*? What view of Barbie dolls does the story try to persuade us toward? Another relevant context is cultural anxiety about breast cancer or about stability of marriage. The father already seems to have replaced his wife with his new girlfriend, Shirley. But can Shirley replace the narrator's mother? Can the Barbie replace the mother?

Strategies for Putting It All Together: Posing Questions about Theme and Significance

	Possible Kinds of Questions to Ask	Illustrations from "The Barbie Birthday"
Tensions, conflicts	What are the chief tensions or conflicts in the story? What values or world views are in conflict? What cultural anxieties are reflected in the story? What cultural debates does the story join?	The chief tensions are between the contrasting views of Barbie dolls and contrasting role models for a young girl. What view of Barbie dolls emerges from this story? What view of mothers or of role models for girls emerges?

(*continued*)

	Possible Kinds of Questions to Ask	Illustrations from "The Barbie Birthday"
Resolution	To what extent are these tensions resolved? Does the story argue a position inside a cultural debate? Is there a single-view resolution or does the resolution try to hold in tension two or more contrasting views?	The ending of the story at first seems to resolve in favor of Barbies because the child's touch warms the plastic and brings the child back into the world. But does the overall impact argue against Barbies? What is the story's final resolution of the tension?
Theme, significance	What does the story seem to be "about" in terms of ideas or of shared human issues, problems, or questions? Does the story make any arguments about good versus bad values, right versus wrong behavior, or meaningful versus trivial pursuits? What views of power or justice emerge from the story? To what extent does the title give us any hints about theme?	What is this story saying about womanhood and motherhood? Was it good or bad that Shirley gave the narrator a Barbie? What does the story say about death and loss and about the process of filling a spot left by an absent mother? What is the significance of the title, "The Barbie Birthday," which puts more emphasis on the Barbie than on the narrator?

Conduct Your Own Analysis and Write Your Interpretive Argument It is now time to "wallow in complexity" by further engaging your own critical thinking. Your goal is to work out some of your own answers to your interpretive questions. But recognize that you aren't looking for "right answers," just for plausible answers that you could support by reference to specific details in the text. One of the pleasures of literary analysis is the extent to which critics disagree about how to read a text. As in all academic writing, you will need to be aware of alternative interpretations and assume a skeptical audience who will read the story differently from the way you do.

Sample Analysis of "The Barbie Birthday"

To illustrate what a literary analysis might look like, we show you our own analysis of "The Barbie Birthday." To fit the genre of an academic paper, we give our analysis the following title: "Barbie Dolls and Young Girls: Probing the Value of Barbie in Townsend's 'The Barbie Birthday.'" Note how our introductory paragraph highlights an interpretive problem and then presents our thesis.

Alison Townsend's short story "The Barbie Birthday" tells the story of a young girl's pleasure over receiving a Barbie doll for her tenth birthday. The opening epigraph from *The Barbie Chronicles* draws attention to the cultural significance of Barbie and raises questions about the role Barbie dolls play in the life of young girls. Does the story reinforce a feminist rejection of Barbie for the way the Barbie culture objectifies women, as some readers might claim? Or does it treat Barbie more sympathetically? We argue that the tensions in this story between two views of Barbie are not fully resolved.

The major tension in this story is between two views of Barbie. One view is closely identified with the father's girlfriend, Shirley, who is the pro-Barbie woman. Through the Barbie birthday gift, Shirley initiates her relationship with this motherless ten-year-old girl. Shirley, the story suggests, resembles a Barbie doll in her fashionable appearance. Like the doll, Shirley has auburn hair similar to Barbie's "brownish-orange" hair. Shirley's outfit, as the narrator remembers it as she "stepped from the car" into the house, has the style and trendiness of the outfits made for Barbie. (And as all girls know, Barbie's fashionable wardrobe and endless accessories are her main attraction.)

The other view of Barbie comes from the girl's mother, who died five months previously of breast cancer and had forbidden her daughter to have one of these dolls. We wonder whether the mother had always objected to Barbies because of their materialism and sexual objectification of women, or whether her objection emerged during her battle with breast cancer when she lost all control of her own body and beauty, and therefore of her ability to guide her daughter through the Barbie stage of emerging womanhood. The story leaves this question unanswered; however, it is clear that the young girl, in gratefully accepting this present on her tenth birthday, "sign[s] on for life," to this culturally approved version of womanhood, along with "every girl on every block in America" (265). The young girl eagerly receives the doll as a toy and as a guide to identity—"as if Barbie could tell me what everything meant—how to be a woman when I was a girl with no mother " (265).

The tension between two views of Barbie also resides in the disjunction between the ten-year-old's thrill at getting a Barbie and the older narrator's interpretation of this incident from her adult perspective. The young girl's pleasure is twofold. The first pleasure comes from the doll itself. After opening the package, she is soon delighting in dressing and undressing her, which, as she says, "was the whole point, of course" (265). She plays with Barbie, using the "sunny windowsill" in her parents' room as a stage for Barbie to "strut." She is resuming former play habits, and the familiar sunny spot seems comforting and pleasurable. An equally important pleasure, the story suggests, is the girl's realization that her father's girlfriend cares about her and will become a positive part of her life, filling the void left by the dead mother: "*She likes me; she really likes me,* I thought, recalling Shirley's smile when I opened the package" (265). Barbie represents both a cherished toy and a token of a new relationship that will be important for the young narrator in her loneliness over the loss of her mother.

However, interwoven with this positive view of Barbie are hints of death, darkness, and criticism. Whereas the ten-year-old loved her Barbie, the adult narrator, looking back, subtly associates the Barbie with a funeral and death: "As I lifted the lid of Barbie's narrow, coffin-like box, she stared up at me, sloe-eyed, lids bruised blue" (265). The doll seems to have rigor mortis with its "stiff and shiny" body, its bruised eyelids, its mouth that was "stuck in a pout," and its "legs that didn't bend" (265). The child in the moment of pleasure is unaware of the questions and meanings raised by the Barbie, as her happy play with Barbie indicates. However, the older narrator now links the Barbie image not with the bouncing, auburn-curled Shirley but with a bruised, sloe-eyed cadaver. The adjective "sloe-eyed" transfers to the doll the qualities of sloe, i.e., dark purple plums or blackthorn fruit with a sour taste. If the narrator as a young girl thinks Barbie can teach her "how to dress and talk" in a culturally sanctioned way, the older, wiser narrator perceives this toy as an unrealistic, warped, and dangerous image of womanhood: "feet on perpetual tiptoe," "the torpedo breasts [without nipples], the wasp waist" (265). She also underscores the irony of an image of female beauty that had proved to be so fragile and destructible in the dying mother with her breasts "cut off like raw meat" (265). The gift of this forbidden toy seems to accentuate the absence of the mother, who would have guided her daughter differently from the way that Shirley (and the dominant culture) did.

The story further asks readers to accept a degree of irresolution in this tension between Barbie as a wonderful toy and Barbie as an image of death. Although the older narrator sees the wisdom in the mother's prohibition of Barbie's false and shallow vision of womanhood, she acknowledges Barbie's value. This ambiguity is powerfully conveyed in the last lines of the story when she describes Barbie as "the hard plastic body that warmed when I touched it, leading me back to the world" (265). The body is "hard" and "plastic"—lifeless and fake—and yet this Barbie plays a vital role in this girl's life. Pulling her out of her grief and reconnecting her to the present, the doll warms to her touch and revives her interest in life.

In its various powerful tensions, this story refuses simple answers about the value of Barbie dolls and their effects on young girl's budding womanhood. With its title—"The Barbie Birthday"—the story emphasizes both the culturally iconic doll and the girl's taking one more step toward assuming her grown-up identity. Ultimately, we argue that in its tensions and ambiguities, this story offers insight into the cultural confusion facing young girls as they grapple with distorted but appealing images of femininity represented by Barbie dolls and harsh realities facing women, including young mothers whose bodies and lives are destroyed by cancer.

WRITING PROJECT

An Analytical Essay about a Short Story

11.2 Pose an interpretive question about a flash fiction story and write an analytical argument in response using textual detail for support.

Pose an interpretive question about a short story and respond to it analytically, showing your readers where and how the text of the story supports your interpretation. Use the introduction of your essay to pose your interpretive question, showing how it is both problematic and significant. Your one-sentence summary answer to that question will serve as your thesis statement. Your task in this assignment is not to discover the right way to interpret the text, but to show why your reading is plausible and can be supported by textual detail.

Although this assignment asks you to analyze an open-form short story, the essay you produce should be closed-form academic prose. Before you give your thesis, make clear what question you are putting to the text and why. It is this question that will engage your readers' interest and make them look forward to your analysis. Then, in the body of your paper, use your close reading of key scenes and passages to support your interpretation. You should be aware of alternative readings and imagine a skeptical audience. Without necessarily disputing the alternative interpretations, concentrate on showing your readers how you arrived at *your* interpretation and why you think that your interpretation can deepen your readers' appreciation of the story. A student example of an analytical essay written to your assignment is Michelle Eastman's analysis of "Forsythia" in the readings section of this chapter.

The readings in this chapter include two flash fiction stories as well as a student analysis of one of the stories—"Forsythia."

Generating and Exploring Ideas

Eastman's essay is on pp. 280–281. Jacquelyn Kolosov's "Forsythia" is on pp. 278–279.

We suggest that you follow the process that we explained in our own analysis of "The Barbie Birthday."

Write a Plot Summary Begin by writing your own plot summary. The act of simply saying what happens in the story can urge you to ponder the function of the material that makes the whole story richer and more complex than the plot summary itself.

Pose Possible Interpretive Questions Return to the strategies chart we used for posing possible questions about "The Barbie Birthday" (pp. 269–272). In the third column of the chart we posed questions about the Barbie story. Use these as models for possible questions you can pose about the story that you are analyzing. As you pose questions, let your mind play with possible ways you might answer them. Especially rich ones are questions that also puzzle your classmates or that lead to disagreements during discussions. Your goal is to begin seeing how all parts of the story "connect."

See our summary of "The Barbie Birthday" on pp. 268–269.

Choosing Your Problematic Question and Exploring Your Answer

You're now ready to choose the question that will initiate your essay and to explore your answer. If you have posed a number of different questions about your story, identify the one that seems the most significant, interesting, and manageable to you, realizing that one of the principles of effective open-form prose is "connectedness"—that is, all the story's details, if read *literarily*, contribute in some way to the story's theme and meaning.

Shaping, Drafting, and Revising

As you write your first draft, follow the general principles for composing and revising closed-form prose, Literary analysis is a form of academic argument that follows a problem-thesis pattern, as shown in the Framework for a Literary Analysis Essay (Figure 11.1).

After you have produced a good rough draft, let it sit for a while. Then try it out on readers, asking them to respond to the following questions for peer review. Based on your readers' advice, begin revising your draft, making it as clear as possible for your readers. Remember to start with the big issues and major changes and then work your way down to the smaller issues and minor changes.

FIGURE 11.1 Framework for a Literary Analysis Essay

Introduction (one to several paragraphs)	• Poses your question about the text • Shows why your question is interesting, problematic, and significant • Presents relevant background about the story • Presents your thesis statement—a one-sentence answer to your question
Body (several paragraphs)	• Develops and supports your thesis using textual details and quotations and argument • Summarizes and responds to alternative interpretations (if not done in the introduction)
Conclusion	• Returns to your question and suggests why your answer is significant • Addresses the larger implications of your interpretation

Questions for Peer Review

In addition to the generic peer review questions provided in Skill 16.4, ask your peer reviewers to address these questions:

INTRODUCTION

1. Does the title arouse interest and forecast the problem to be addressed? How might the author improve the title?
2. How effectively does the introduction capture your interest, explain the question to be addressed, and suggest why it is both problematic and significant?
3. Does the introduction conclude with the writer's thesis? Is the thesis surprising? How might the author improve the introduction?

ANALYSIS AND INTERPRETATION

1. How is the essay organized? Does the writer helpfully forecast the whole, place topic sentences at the head of paragraphs (points before supporting details), use transitions, and follow the old/new contract as explained in Chapter 17? How might the author improve or clarify the organization?
2. Where does the author quote from the story (or use paraphrase or other specific references to the text)? How is each of the author's points grounded in the text? Where does the author do a particularly good job of reading *literarily* through attention to plot, character, setting, figurative language, and so forth? What passages not cited might better support the argument? What recommendations do you have for improving the author's use of supporting details?
3. Where do you disagree with the author's analysis? What aspects of the story are left unexplained? What doesn't fit?

WRITING PROJECT

Multimodal or Online Options

1. **Post to an Online Flash Fiction Site** If you do a web search for "flash fiction," you will find numerous sites, many of which have a "comments" function where you can post your own analysis of a selected short story. Your goal is to find a flash fiction piece that invites analysis, and post a comment that goes beyond the typical "liked it" or "didn't like it" response. Use strategies from this chapter to advance readers' understanding of the story and deepen their appreciation. Such a post would typically be shorter than the analyses modeled in this chapter, but it should have enough depth to make an engaging contribution to the way readers experience the story.
2. **Podcast Reading** Choose a flash fiction story and do a podcast reading of it as you imagine the author might read it. Read the story expressively to make readers engage with the story and think about it. Then using the strategies from the chapter to examine how the story achieves its effects, give a brief commentary about several of its important literary features.

Readings

Our first reading is "Forsythia" by Jacquelyn Kolozov. It was first published in 2006 in the literary magazine *Pisgah Review*. Kolozov is the author of several young adult novels.

Jacqueline Kolosov

Forsythia

1 Miranda pulls the old Chevy into the drive. A neat row of daffodils and grape iris border the front walk. Here, too, forsythia blooms, the spiraling branches like captured sunshine. Beyond, the house is white-washed brick.

2 When Grace Wickersham steps onto the porch, Miranda's hands instinctively curve around her swelling belly. "Please come in." Grace's voice is husky, nervous.

3 This is only the second time they've met.

4 Inside, Miranda takes in the room in one long sweep. In the corner, there is an overstuffed sofa covered with red poppies. On the sofa a big, gray dog lies drowsing.

5 Grace's husband. Matt, enters with a plate of cookies and three glasses of juice. Miranda smiles at the bright drink chock full of vitamins. Surely she is the reason why they're drinking orange juice at three o'clock in the afternoon.

6 Crumbs fall into their laps as they circle around the subject that has brought them together. How could she possibly tell them that at night she lies awake thinking about keeping him, for she's sure he is a boy? In bed, with the curtains drawn back, the sky becomes a magician's cape, and the edges of reality are softened.

7 Morning restores the sharp outlines. In the kitchen, her mother's face is a grid of gray planes, and she is wearing the catsup stained factory uniform that always smells of sweat and tomatoes.

8 "We have two extra bedrooms upstairs," Grace Wickersham says, her eyes meeting Miranda's. "The one beside ours will be the baby's room. The other is for guests."

9 "What Grace is trying to say is we'd like you to be our guest for the remainder of the pregnancy," Matt adds. "We'd like to help you in any way we can."

10 Miranda is reminded of the neat rows of daffodils, the forsythia, their delicate branches swaying in the breeze. "Thank you," she says, "but I live at home with my mother and my sister Kate."

11 "We didn't mean to imply—" Matt says, fiddling with the ice in his glass.

12 "Do you think I could see the baby's room?" Miranda asks.

13 "I'll wait down here," Matt says, as the two women move toward the staircase.

14 Grace opens the door.

15 It is everything a child's room should be. The walls are a warm, honey gold. There is a border of crayon-bright sunflowers and frogs running along the floor. A refinished crib sits beside the window; beside it, a rocker.

16 "I spent the past month getting the room ready," Grace says.

17 Miranda nods, unable to imagine how it would feel to be an expectant mother painting flowers and animals on the walls of a room in her own home, then sitting down in the rocker to admire her handiwork, a cup of tea warming her hands.

18 "Would you like to see the extra room?" Grace asks her then.

19 "All right."

20 Down the hallway, Grace opens another neatly painted door, and Miranda beholds a double bed, heaped with pillows. A single dresser holds a crystal vase filled with forsythia. White lace curtains adorn the windows. The room is exactly what Miranda would have chosen for herself.

21 "We thought it would be nice to get to know each other better," Grace tells her.

22 Miranda watches the play of sunlight in Grace's long auburn hair. She would like to take the silver-backed brush from the dresser and run it through Grace's hair. She would like to tell Grace that the baby's father is on a scholarship at the University of Michigan. He, too, comes from one of the factory towns, but he managed to get out. Miranda doesn't even know when she will see him again.

23 What she does know is she cannot move into this sunny room. If she were to enter into the inner spaces of this life, how would she ever find the strength to say goodbye?

24 On the drive back to Ipswich, Miranda listens to Bruce Springsteen sing about love and amusement parks. The song brings back the summer her father took her and her sister to a carnival. Miranda's front tooth was loose, and as they walked through the fairgrounds, she kept wiggling it with her tongue. She wanted to loosen it, but she didn't want it to fall out there. Miranda was afraid of losing that tooth, afraid of missing out on the tooth fairy's visit.

25 Miranda's father held her hand and Kate's. They passed the Ferris wheel with its Lifesaver-colored lights, the shooting gallery with its toys. Even with her small hand in his, Miranda hadn't felt secure.

26 Her father, a very tall man with rough, reddish whiskers, looked down. "What's the matter, little mouse?" he asked. "Aren't you having fun? You're supposed to be having fun."

27 After that, Miranda tried hard to have fun. She wanted to please her father. She wanted to show him that she was a good girl.

28 That next summer when the carnival returned, Miranda had already lost half a dozen more teeth. And that next summer, her father was already gone.

29 When Miranda told her mother that she was going to have a baby, her mother stayed silent for a long time, her hopes and fears interlaced as tightly as her hands. "I just don't want you to wind up like me," her mother said finally. "I want you to have more choices in your life."

30 Miranda understood what her mother was saying. Don't become a woman with a high school diploma, a job at the catsup factory, a mortgage on a ramshackle house, two daughters, and no husband.

31 *And yet*, Miranda thinks, *you did your best.*

32 Miranda nears the Ipswich exit and recalls the daffodils and the forsythia, the hopping frogs and sunflowers, the white wicker rocker, and understands—deep within herself, where her baby stirs—that, by giving up her child to them, she won't be doing her best for him, but she will be doing the best she can.

33 And this, she knows, *this* will have to be enough.

Our second reading is an analysis of "Forsythia" by student writer Michelle Eastman. This analysis was written for the assignment in this chapter.

Michelle Eastman (student)

Unconditional Love and the Function of the Rocking Chair in Kolosov's "Forsythia"

1 In Jacqueline Kolosov's short story "Forsythia" Miranda decides to give her baby up for adoption after thinking about the details of the adoptive family's home. An important feature in the home is the rocking chair in the baby's bedroom, first mentioned when Miranda notes that the bedroom with its rocker "is everything a child's room should be" (278). At the end of the story—as the final detail about the house—the rocker is described more fully as "white wicker" (279). What function does this rocking chair serve in the story? Miranda's repeated mention of the rocker suggests that is it more than simply a piece of furniture. I believe that the chair represents domestic security and suggests a mother's unconditional love for her child. But it also reminds Miranda of her status as an outsider and of the different direction her life is heading. The rocker is what allows her to realize that she cannot keep her baby. By giving the baby to Grace and Matt, Miranda hopes that her son will have the unconditional love that is missing from her own life.

2 At first, the rocker in the baby's room represents Miranda's awareness of how different her economic and social status is from that of Grace and Matt. Miranda is "unable to imagine how it would feel to be an expectant mother painting flowers and animals on the walls of a room in her own home, then sitting down in the rocker to admire her handiwork, a cup of tea warming her hands" (278). To be able to take that kind of time and care in preparing for a baby implies having the resources to do so, resources that Miranda lacks. Grace and her husband Matt live in a house that is carefully put together with its "neatly painted door[s]" for the upstairs bedrooms, the "warm honey gold" walls of the baby's room, the "double bed, heaped with pillows" in the guest room along with a vase of flowers and "[w]hite lace curtains"—all surrounded by "forsythia blooms...like captured sunshine" (278, 279). There is even a "big gray dog...drowsing" on the sofa (278).

3 In contrast, Miranda lives in a "ramshackle" house and pictures her mother, whose face is like a "grid of gray planes," "wearing the catsup-stained factory uniform that always smells of sweat and tomatoes" (279). Like Miranda, her mother does not have a husband (he seems to have abandoned the family years before), so the mother has to support her children by herself with her limited factory worker's pay. Miranda has no clue about whether her boyfriend will be a part of her life, so like her mother she does not have someone to provide financial and parental support to her and her child. While Miranda does fantasize about keeping the child, a part of her also wants to escape her mother's fate.

4 The rocker thus represents the economic security and domestic stability of the Wickersham's middle-class, two-parent family. Miranda's own life is represented

instead by the ups and downs of a Ferris wheel at a carnival. Prompted by the "Bruce Springsteen song about love and amusement parks" Miranda remembers a childhood visit to a carnival with her father (279). Miranda recalls how she was afraid of losing her tooth and how she did not feel "secure" holding her father's hand (279). Her insecurity stems from the notion that when her father asks what the problem is he tells her that she "is supposed to be having fun," which Miranda takes to mean that she must try "to have fun" to be "a good girl" in order "to please" him (279). Miranda's efforts to gain her father's approval show that she feels his love is conditional based on his approval of her behavior. A couple of years later, Miranda's father himself disappears from the family's life. Miranda's insecurity connects back to the Wickersham's invitation to live with them during the remainder of her pregnancy. Whatever love she would feel in the Wickersham household would also be conditional based on her ability to give them a baby. Her stay would be only temporary, and then she would disappear from the Wickersham's lives.

5 Although Miranda is unable to feel security and love in her own life, she still hopes that her baby might find unconditional love in the Wickersham's home. The interconnection between mother and child is represented by the "white wicker" rocker. The rocker represents the interconnection between mother and child because it would be a primary place where Grace would bond with her baby, rocking her child to sleep. A wicker rocker represents this interconnection metaphorically because wicker furniture is made of interwoven strands of wood. These strands create a whole piece of furniture much in the way that mother and child are interconnected. (Although the idea might seem far-fetched, perhaps Kolosov chooses the name "Wickersham" to connect with "wicker.") The white wicker rocking chair thus has two different meanings for Miranda. For her, the rocker represents temporary conditional love. But for the baby it represents the unconditional love promised by Grace and Matt.

6 The white wicker rocker helps us understand Miranda's final decision. If she keeps her baby, she will "wind up" like her mother, "a woman with a high school diploma, a job at the catsup factory, a mortgage on a ramshackle house, two daughters, and no husband" (279). But if she gives the baby to the Wickersham's she might be able to free herself from her mother's fate while also giving a better life to the baby. She perhaps feels guilty that she is not giving her own unconditional love to her child. Maybe that is why she thinks she is not "doing her best" (279). But she is "doing [(courageously, I think)] the best she can" (279).

THINKING CRITICALLY ABOUT

"Unconditional Love and the Function of the Rocking Chair in Kolosov's 'Forsythia'"

1. The assignment in this chapter asks for an essay that poses a problematic and significant interpretive question. Has Michelle Eastman been successful in articulating a problematic question and demonstrating its importance in her understanding of the story? What other problematic questions might someone pose about "Forsythia"?

2. What is Eastman's thesis? Does her thesis adequately respond to the question? Does she supply enough details to support her analysis?
3. To what extent do you agree with Eastman's analysis of this story? Do you think the story portrays Grace and Matt as ideal adoptive parents who will love Miranda's baby unconditionally? Eastman believes that Miranda's decision to give up the baby for adoption is "courageous." Do you agree with her?
4. What do you think Eastman does especially well in this essay? What recommendations would you have for improving the essay?

Our final reading, "After," by Bill Konigsberg, first appeared in *Sudden Flash Youth: 65 Short Stories*, published by Persea Books in 2011. Konigsberg is currently a full-time fiction writer but in an earlier life was an award winning sportswriter for the Associated Press and for ESPN.com. In 2002 he won a GLAAD media award for his essay "Sports World Still a Struggle for Gays."

Bill Konigsberg
After

1 After, get in your car and drive. Turn up the heat. Blare music. Something with screeching guitars that drowns out any thought. Thinking is bad, after.

2 Watch the streetlights whiz by in your peripheral vision, and let their blurs trickle down the sides of your eyes. Think of them like tears. They are as close as you'll allow. You know that. You know.

3 Remember how you felt during, how you turned everything off, how you let your mind leave. You thought about, of all things, the white Tonka truck you used to love as a kid. You used to sleep with it. When the paint chipped, you had your mom take you to the hobby store to buy paint so you could touch it up. The white color you used wasn't quite right, but you loved that truck like it was your best friend.

4 Be careful not to go through a red light. Last time, you sped past a red on Broadwater. You were lucky no car was crossing the other way, or else you'd be dead. Yeah, real lucky. At home under your denim sheets that night, you'd wondered if maybe you'd forgotten about that light on purpose. In a flash, it could have been all over, and in the warmth of your bed you shuddered, thinking about what it would have felt like. After.

5 Slow down your driving. Stop on a yellow. Feel your forehead. Smooth. No blood. When they pushed your head into the side of the table, you thought maybe it would puncture, leave a scar. They were smarter than that. Both times, they only left marks under your clothes.

6 Mikey watched. So did Ethan. Your dad used to pick Mikey up and drive him to school with you, when you were in middle school, and you would sit in the back seat, texting dirty words to each other and seeing who cracked up first. Ethan used to come over after school and you'd wrestle. Mikey stopped talking to you when the rumor started. You're not sure, but Ethan may have started the rumor.

7 You simply don't know how anyone else could know about Joey. Ethan, he saw you guys. At Rimrock Mall. Joey is different, way. Ethan saw you together, and the next day at school was the first time. This was the second. You wonder if your pride can take a third without erupting in some dangerous way. You think possibly not.

8 Your elbow burns, bad. Last time they used lighters, burnt the hairs along your forearm. It scared you more than anything else. This time, a lit cigarette. Under your clothes. You don't want any marks that will last. You want to be a blank slate when you finally escape Billings, escape high school. Tabula rasa.

9 Pass the police station off Grand and 13th and ponder what would happen if you stopped there, pulled up your shirt sleeve, explained. Coach Donahue would freak. That's not what baseball players do. They don't squeal on teammates, they don't go all soft, and anyway, what good could come of it? If they arrested all those kids, you'd be the one who had them arrested. Everyone would hate you.

10 Besides, your family. You remember the time over dinner your dad made the joke about Coaches versus Cancer, a popular college basketball tournament.

11 "I'll take cancer," he said, and you cracked up because it was in such bad taste and your mom was sitting there staring at him, her mouth wide open. Then, somehow, the conversation turned political, and your dad's mustache twitched as he cut into his steak, and he said something you'd never forget.

12 "Tell you what, Ricky. You ever get the urge to come home and tell us you're gay, do me a favor. Have cancer instead. Tell me you have cancer."

13 You think of the burn on the tip of your elbow like a cancer splotch. What do they call them? Lesions. Maybe tonight you'll take your shirt off and show him your elbow and tell him it's cancer. He'll be so relieved. Family values.

14 Think about calling Joey. He's the one person who would get it. Think of his voice like caramel, glance in the rearview mirror, and catch yourself smiling, which surprises you. You expected a grimace, but the caramel voice in your imagination melted some of the anguish away. You will. You'll call him tonight. There are some things you can change, and some you guess you can't. Like in a million years. Caramel soothes burns. Burns don't ruin caramel.

15 Pull up to your house, turn off the headlights, and close your eyes for the moment before you pull the key from the ignition. Hold your breath. Count to ten.

16 The pain throbs in your elbow. You think about your mom and calamine lotion. When you were a kid. You wonder if you could just show her, no words, no explanations, and get her to sit on the side of the tub and rub calamine lotion on your elbow. That's what you want. You're sixteen, and you want your mom to stop what she's doing and soothe you, make it all better.

17 Step out of the car, head up the walkway, fumble for your key. Go for a blank expression when you open the door, and Mom is sitting there, on the couch, eating a bowl of Cheerios.

18 "Welcome home," she'll say, smiling, and the calamine dreams will fade away. Because you know. The price would be too high. After.

12 ANALYZING AND SYNTHESIZING IDEAS

WHAT YOU WILL LEARN

12.1 To explain the thinking moves involved in writing analysis and synthesis essays.

12.2 To analyze texts with different perspectives and synthesize their ideas to present a new perspective of your own.

Many college courses require synthesis essays in which you will be asked to explore connections and contradictions among groups of texts and to work your way to your own perspective through a series of essential thinking and writing moves. You will need first to formulate a synthesis question that connects your chosen or assigned texts. You will then need to summarize the texts accurately, analyze the main commonalities and disagreements among them, and, through your own critical thinking, arrive at your own perspective on the synthesis question.

Engaging Analysis and Synthesis

This exercise introduces you to the main thinking moves required for analysis and synthesis. The subject for the short articles that follow—"boomerang kids," the new social phenomenon of young adults in their twenties and thirties who live with parents while they are looking for jobs or starting their careers—is also explored by the student writing in this chapter. The first reading, "Ground Rules for Boomerang Kids" by John Miley*, appeared in the June 2012 edition of *Kiplinger's Personal Finance*. The second reading is a review of Katherine Newman's book *The Accordian Family: Boomerang Kids, Anxious Parents, and the Private Toll of Global Competition*, which appeared in *Publishers Weekly* on August 29, 2011. After reading these short pieces, develop answers to the questions that follow.

*John Miley. "Ground Rules for Boomerang Kids: It's okay to help, but don't coddle", from Kiplinger's Personal Finance, June 1, 2012.

John Miley

Ground Rules for Boomerang Kids

It's Okay to Help, but Don't Coddle

Suzanne Bernier is one of the lucky ones. Just before graduating from Brandeis University in 2010, she landed a job at a medical software company. Yet after graduation, the frugal 24-year-old moved back in with her parents. "I wanted to save as much money as possible," she says. More than one-fifth of people ages 25 to 34 live in multi-generational homes, the highest level since the 1950s, reports Pew Research. The hospitality helps boomerangers stay positive in tough times. More than three-fourths of people ages 25 to 34 who have lived at home are upbeat about their future finances, according to Pew. Laying ground rules can help prevent a clash of the generations. "Put a game plan together with expectations," says Linda Leitz, a certified financial planner in Colorado. Parents who open their homes should establish a time limit for the stay and get regular progress reports. The child should pay rent, save money or pay off debt. Don't subsidize a lavish lifestyle. If kids can't contribute money, consider requiring household chores instead. Parents should gradually turn up the heat, Leitz says. Raise the cost of rent by a certain date, for example, even if your plan is to make a gift of the money when your child departs. The comfort of home shouldn't be cushy enough to erode financial independence.

Publishers Weekly

Book Review

Review of *The Accordion Family* by Katherine Newman

Newman examines the proliferation of "accordion families," in which children continue to live with their parents late into their 20s and 30s. It's a phenomenon that spans cultures and continents, and Newman's inquiry takes her around the world to examine how family structures are responding to societal changes. She examines how high unemployment rates, the rise of short-term employment, staggered birth rates, longer life expectancies, and the high cost of living have affected the younger generation's transition to adulthood. While in Spain and Italy the new family dynamics mark a change from the past, they are more easily accepted than they are in Japan, where expectations for maturity and developmental milestones are more socially fixed. Newman's interviews with parents and their cohabitating children reveal how the definition of "adulthood" is changing, from the possession of external markers (a marriage, a home) to a psychological state, an understanding of one's place in the world and one's responsibilities. While the book fails to provide a prescription to the accordion family, it does provide an alternative when Newman looks north to strong welfare states like Sweden and Denmark, where the government subsidizes housing and provides grants to help young adults transition more easily, a place that the U.S. can look "to see what can be done, and at what cost, to insure the orderly transition of the generations."

ON YOUR OWN

Jot down responses to the following questions:

1. How would you summarize the main points of each piece in one or two sentences?
2. What rhetorical features (about audience, purpose, genre, angle of vision) stand out for you in each piece?
3. List ideas that the two pieces have in common.
4. List any contradictions or disagreements you see in these pieces' views of boomerang kids.
5. Freewrite your own responses to these readings, exploring what questions they raise for you or personal experiences or views you have about this subject.

IN CONVERSATION

In groups or as a class, share your responses, looking for points in the readings that many people found important.

12.1 Explain the thinking moves involved in writing analysis and synthesis essays.

Understanding Analysis and Synthesis

Synthesis, which is a way of seeing and coming to terms with complexities, is an extension of and counterpart to analysis. When you **analyze** something, you break it down into its parts to see the relationships among them. When you **synthesize**, you take one more step, putting parts together in some new fashion. The cognitive researcher Benjamin Bloom schematized "synthesis" as the fifth of six levels of thinking processes, ranked in order of complexity and challenge: knowledge, comprehension, application, analysis, synthesis, and evaluation. Bloom defined *synthesis* as the "putting together of constituent elements or parts to form a whole requiring original creative thinking." Recent educational theorists have revised Bloom's hierarchy to place synthesis at the top, relabeling it "creating" rather than synthesizing: remembering, understanding, applying, analyzing, evaluating, and creating.* This revision emphasizes the creative aspect of synthesis through which you arrive at your own revelations ("Aha!" moments) based on new ways of seeing something or on your creating a new idea or product.

A second useful way to look at synthesis is as a dialectical critical thinking process. Throughout this text, we have explained that college writing involves posing a significant question that often forces you to encounter clashing or contradictory ideas. Such conflicts intrigued the German philosopher Hegel, who posited that thinking proceeds dialectically when a thesis clashes against an antithesis, leading the thinker to formulate a synthesis encompassing dimensions of both the original thesis and the antithesis. When you write to synthesize ideas, your thinking exemplifies this dialectical process.

Synthesis is an especially important component of academic research writing, where you use synthesis to carve out your own thinking space on a question while sifting through the writings of others. Synthesis, then, is the skill of wrestling with ideas from different texts and sources and creatively forging a new

*Benjamin Bloom, *Taxonomy of Educational Objectives: Handbook I: Cognitive Domain* (New York: David McKay, 1956).

whole out of potentially confusing parts. It is the principal way you enter into a conversation on a social, civic, or scholarly issue.

Posing a Significant Synthesis Question

As we have shown throughout this text, most academic and professional writing begins with the posing of a problem. Writing a synthesis essay follows the same principle. The need to synthesize ideas usually begins when you are given or pose a problematic question that sends you off on an intellectual journey through a group of texts. The synthesis question focuses your attention by directing you to look for ways that a group of texts are connected and ways that they differ in their approaches to a particular problem or issue. A synthesis question helps you zero in on a problem that these texts address or that you are trying to solve through exploring these texts. Your goal is to achieve your own informed view on that question, a view that reflects your intellectual wrestling with the ideas in your sources and in some way integrates ideas from these sources with your own independent thinking.

Although synthesis writing appears in college courses across the curriculum, the set-up of these assignments varies. Sometimes instructors will specify the question and the texts that you are to explore whereas at other times you will be asked to articulate your own synthesis question and choose your texts. The following examples show typical synthesis assignments that you might encounter in different disciplines, with both the synthesis questions and the texts provided in each case.

Texts to Be Analyzed	Possible Synthesis Questions
Environmental Studies Course	
A chapter from Gary Chamberlain's *Troubled Waters: Religion, Ethics, and the Global Water Crisis* (2008) A chapter from Charles Fishman's *The Big Thirst: The Secret Life and Turbulent Future of Water* (2011) "College Issues" video "Student Activism 101" on the Bottled Water Matters Web site Maude Barlow, "Address to the UN General Assembly on Need to Conserve Water" (2009)	• Who owns our water? Should water be a human right or a commodity? • Who should have control of water sources and management—corporations or governments representing citizens? • What are the best solutions to providing safe drinking water in water-stressed areas of the world? • What are the main points of disagreement in the bottled water controversy?
Introductory Sociology Course on Global Culture	
Samuel P. Huntington's article "The Clash of Civilizations?" *Foreign Affairs* (1993) Jan Nederveen Pieterse's "Globalization and Culture: Three Paradigms" in *Readings in Globalization: Key Concepts and Major Debates* edited by George Ritzer and Zeynep Atalay (2010) Helena Norberg-Hodge's *Ancient Futures: Learning from Ladakh* (1991) Tony Karon, "What Soccer Means to the World" *Time* (2004)	• What are the power dynamics of cultural globalization? • Can cultural exchange be an instrument for promoting global understanding, cooperation, and peace? • How is increasing global cultural contact affecting cultural diversity?

Synthesis Writing as an Extension of Summary/Strong Response Writing

Chapter 5 introduced you to writing summaries of texts and responding strongly to them through critique of their rhetorical strategies and ideas. These skills are the basis of synthesis writing as well. In writing a synthesis essay, you use both with-the-grain and against-the-grain thinking. You listen carefully to texts as you summarize them to determine their main points. You also conduct—at least informally in your exploratory stages—a critique of both the rhetorical features and the ideas of these texts. This analysis builds the platform from which you create a synthesis of ideas—that is, from which you begin your own independent thinking based on the synthesis question that ties your texts together.

A synthesis essay differs from a summary/strong response essay in that a synthesis essay extends the process to more texts with the aim of bringing them into conversation with each other. A synthesis essay shows how you have taken apart, made sense of, assessed, and recombined the ideas of these texts in an integration of ideas all your own that creates a new vision of the subject. A synthesis essay most likely incorporates the following features:

TYPICAL FEATURES OF A SYNTHESIS ESSAY

- A statement of the synthesis question that shows your interest in the texts and presents this question as problematic and significant
- Short summaries of these texts to give your readers a sense of the readings you are working with
- A thesis that indicates how you have analyzed and synthesized the readings to arrive at a new perspective
- Your analysis of key points in these texts, determined in part by the synthesis question
- Your new view, which combines ideas gathered from readings with your own independent ideas

The student example of a synthesis essay by Rosie Evans at the end of this chapter shows you how these parts are developed in a complete essay (pp. 305–308).

WRITING PROJECT — A Synthesis Essay

12.2 Analyze texts with different perspectives and synthesize their ideas to present a new perspective of your own.

Write a synthesis essay that meets the following criteria:

- Addresses a synthesis question that your instructor provides or that you formulate for yourself
- Summarizes and analyzes the views of at least two writers on this question
- Shows how you have wrestled with different perspectives on the question and have synthesized these ideas to arrive at your own new view of the question

Ideas for Synthesis Questions and Readings

Readings and Images Options for This Assignment

Synthesis Questions	Possible Readings and Images
What contemporary social and economic conditions are complicating young people's transition to adulthood? What actions can families take to help young adults with this transition?	• John Miley, "Ground Rules for Boomerang Kids: It's Okay to Help but Don't Coddle," pp. 284–285 • Publishers' Weekly, "Review of *The Accordion Family: Boomerang Kids, Anxious Parents, and the Private Tool of Global Competition* by Katherine Newman," p. 285
What ethical issues should be considered by news media in documenting human tragedy in disastrous events?	• Clark Hoyt, "Face to Face with Tragedy," pp. 254–256 • Manoucheka Celeste, "Disturbing Media Images of Haiti Earthquake Aftermath Tell Only Part of the Story," pp. 257–258
Should women be accepted as equals in military combat?	• Air Force Recruitment, "Women of the Air Force," (poster) p. 81 • Megan H. MacKenzie, "Let Women Fight," pp. 341–347 • Mackubin Thomas Owens, "Coed Combat Units: A Bad Idea on All Accounts," pp. 348–353 • Gary Varvel, "Combat Barbie: New Accessories," (editorial cartoon), p. 354
Should the United States increase, curb, or more stringently regulate oil companies' practice of hydraulic fracturing (fracking) to obtain natural gas?	• Josh Fox, *Gasland,* (photos), p. 507 • Web page for Energy from Shale: Arkansas, pp. 537 • Web page for Americans Against Fracking, pp. 537 • Graphic drawing showing safety provisions for and problems with fracking wells, pp. 541

Understanding the Components of Synthesis Thinking and Writing

A synthesis essay involves summarizing, analyzing, and synthesizing. A productive way to move through these stages is to break your process into a series of incremental thinking and writing steps in order to show how your wrestling with the ideas in the texts has influenced your own thinking. Consider these strategies as your toolkit to use when you are asked to write essays involving analysis and synthesis.

In the sections that follow, we explain each of these thinking and writing steps in more detail, show you examples, and give you strategies to do them. Our examples come from the idea-generating strategies used by student writer Rosie Evans, whose final synthesis essay is shown on pages 305–308. Her essay, written for this assignment, asks the question, "What are the causes of the delayed-adulthood trends we see within Generation Y and how should society respond?" Rosie analyzed and synthesized two texts:

- Robin Marantz Henig, "What Is It about 20- Somethings?" from the *New York Times Magazine*, August 18, 2010
- A blog post by ScammedHard! "What's Wrong with 20-Somethings?" posted on the Web on August 20, 2010

Although we have not reprinted these two texts, Rosie's summaries and exploratory pieces will familiarize you with their content. (You can also look them up on the Web yourself.)

Summarizing Your Texts to Explore Their Ideas

Instructions on how to write a summary are found on pp. 89–90.

Depending on your instructor's specific assignment, the texts you are working with will most likely be magazine articles, op-ed pieces, blogs, scholarly articles, or book chapters. As a starting point for grappling with each author's ideas, we recommend that you compose careful summaries of each text. Writing summaries prompts you to read each text with the grain, adopting each text's perspective and walking in each author's shoes. When you summarize a text, you try to achieve an accurate, thorough understanding of it by stating its main ideas in a tightly distilled format. It is often a good idea to create a full paragraph summary of each reading to give you space to cover the main ideas of the article or chapter. Later, for your essay itself, your instructor may give you a word limit for your summaries and may ask you to shorten them to make more room in your essay for your analysis and synthesis.

Instructions on how to use attributive tags are found in Skill 21.3.

What follows are student Rosie Evans's summaries of the two readings she used in her synthesis essay. Notice how she uses attributive tags to show that she is representing the authors' ideas, not her own, and notice the neutral, nonjudgmental approach she takes.

Rosie Evans's Summary of Robin Marantz Henig's Article

In her *New York Times Magazine* article "What Is It about 20-Somethings?" Robin Marantz Henig explores psychology professor Jeffrey Arnett's claim that twenty-somethings are experiencing a new life stage called "emerging adulthood." For Arnett, this is a time for twentysomethings to explore their possibilities and identities, but this exploration also brings uncertainty, instability, and fear. He argues that these experiences are meaningful even though twentysomethings can seem lazy and directionless. Arnett thinks we should devote more resources to supporting them during this time. Henig links Arnett's claims to scientific findings that brains are not fully developed until the mid-twenties and suggests that Millennials' transition to adulthood may be limited because their brains haven't fully matured. She also wonders if changing cultural norms about traditional signs of adulthood, like marriage and financial independence, have removed pressure on twentysomething brains to assume adult functioning earlier in life. If brain development or emerging adulthood are really causing Millennials to delay adulthood, then Henig thinks some of our social institutions, like education and health care, should change to offer better support. She imagines expanding programs like AmeriCorps to help young people explore their interests and options before choosing a career. She acknowledges some drawbacks to providing more time for twentysomething to become self-supporting adults such as the drain on their parents' long-term financial security. Although she never firmly settles on a cause of Generation Y's delayed adulthood, she ultimately seems drawn to the idea of Arnett's emerging adults who use their twenties to become better-prepared adults.

Rosie Evans's Summary of Scammed Hard!'s Blog Post

In response to Henig, blogger Scammed Hard! argues in "What's Wrong with 20-Somethings?" that the economy is to blame for Generation Y's struggles. While agreeing that the brain is constantly changing, he characterizes Arnett's theory of emerging adulthood as a psychology professor's attempt to gain professional distinction by inventing a new theory. Referencing twentysomethings like Alexander the Great and Winston Churchill, he argues that our ancestors would not have achieved the success they did if emerging adulthood were a real life stage. Instead, he blames Baby Boomers for creating the conditions that killed the ambition and creativity of Generation Y. According to Scammed Hard!, the Boomers promoted the comfort of a middle-class lifestyle, encouraged dangerous levels of student debt, and then wrecked the economy. By setting high expectations and then limiting the possibility of meeting those expectations, they have destroyed this generation's incentives for hard work and sacrifice needed to succeed in America today. Scammed Hard! believes that although drifting through the twenties may provide Generation Y with a fun distraction, it does not prepare them with the skills and motivation to respond to our serious economic problems. Scammed Hard! notes that this reality endangers our shared welfare by failing to create a new generation of productive workers contributing to tax revenue. Most dangerous of all in the eyes of this blogger is characterizing Generation Y's shared strife as a positive new life stage, diverting attention from the urgent economic problems that drive this generation's reality.

FOR WRITING AND DISCUSSION

Summarizing Your Texts

Begin by writing a 200-250 word summary of each of your texts. Then confirm your decisions about main ideas by working in small groups or as a whole class to list the ideas that must be included in a summary of each piece for the summary to be accurate and complete. What points do you agree are secondary and can be left out?

Analyzing Your Texts

After writing summaries to achieve a solid grasp of the content of your texts, the next key thinking step is to analyze your texts. When you analyze a text, you examine its parts and features, what it says and how it says it. This examination, unlike a more neutral summary, involves your own pondering, questioning, weighing, and wrestling with ideas in the texts. Now your independent observations and sense of what is important come into play. In the process of analyzing your texts, you should consider what rhetorical features are important in each text, how these texts relate to your synthesis question, and how these texts express similar and different views.

These rhetorical terms are explained in Chapter 1 (Concept 1.2) and Chapter 3, (Concept 3.2)

Instructions on how to write a rhetorical critique of a text are found in Chapter 5 on pp. 92–95.

Analyzing the Rhetorical Features of Your Texts

In order to understand how your texts work rhetorically, you should analyze the rhetorical strategies. What do you observe and think is important about the way your texts handle purpose, audience, genre, angle of vision, the use of appeals to *logos, ethos,* and *pathos,* and the use of evidence? Seek out background information on the author of a text and on the publication and genre (for instance, whether it's a scholarly book, journal, popular magazine, or a blog). Applying the following questions in your analysis of each text will help you reach a deeper understanding of how the text conveys its ideas.

QUESTIONS TO ASK TO EXAMINE RHETORICAL FEATURES IN EACH TEXT

- Who is the author? To whom is the author writing and why? What is the motivating occasion?
- How do the publication and genre of the text influence the author's choices about structure and language?
- What angle of vision shapes the text and accounts for what is included, emphasized, and excluded?
- How logically developed and consistent is this text? Is the author's argument well supported with relevant evidence?
- How fair, reliable, knowledgeable, and authoritative does the author appear to be?

- How well does the author appeal to readers' emotions, imaginations, and values?
- Do you share the values of the author or of his or her intended audience?

Rosie Evans's informal rhetorical analyses of her texts show her exploratory thinking.

Rosie Evans's Rhetorical Analysis of Henig's Article

Writer comments on the author's purpose.

Henig's article poses a set of related questions about Millennials and then tries to answer them by exploring psychological studies, neuroscience research, case studies, and survey data. The piece is written for a general audience; the readership of *The New York Times Magazine* is typically educated and liberal. However, the article is not directed at the Millennials themselves. Instead, it addresses their parents and society at large, who may feel responsible for causing and even solving the generation's problems. Henig aims to raise awareness about the twentysomething experience, explore the possible causes, and convince readers about the importance of the questions she raises and the solutions we choose. In my research, I discovered that the popularity of this article led her to write a book on the topic with her twentysomething daughter. I thought this suggested her investment in the topic as a mother witnessing her daughter or her daughter's friends adrift in their twenties.

Writer comments on the audience and publication.

Writer discusses the author's purpose.

Writer shares background information about the author.

Henig is a science writer, so she discusses the science and psychology of emerging adulthood in a balanced, reasoned way and uses survey data as evidence. For example, she explains a Purdue University survey that provides information about how much parents help their twentysomething children. Then, she uses the survey findings to suggest that the gap between the resources of low-income and high-income emerging adults probably grows during this time. Henig also carefully examines Arnett's claims and points out his contradictions. She questions how emerging adulthood could be a new life stage when not every twentysomething experiences it. She is concerned that Arnett uses one case study to represent all low-income Millennials and wants more evidence of their experiences. Henig's use of evidence and the problems she identifies with some of the information she finds help build trust with her readers.

Writer discusses the author's use of evidence.

However, what her article lacks is the voice of the twentysomethings themselves. The details of the twentysomething experience are revealed by academics' studies and experts' observations. When we finally meet a Millennial at the end of the article, her words and experiences are interpreted for us by her caregivers at a mental-health treatment facility. As the talking heads fret over the experiences of Generation Y, I wonder how the so-called emerging adults feel about all of this? In examining the Millennials' problems, I think Henig should have included them in the conversation.

Writer identifies gaps in the author's article, commenting on the limitations of the angle of vision and raising her own question.

Rosie Evans's Rhetorical Analysis of Scammed Hard!'s Blog Post

Writer identifies the angle of vision and tone of the blog author.

Writer shares her speculations about the author's background.

In contrast, Scammed Hard! is writing as a Millennial, and he is angry! In his post, he identifies as an "older (young) curmudgeon," and the tagline of his blog, "Sold down the river for a law school dream," hints that he is a disillusioned law student or graduate. He is probably writing from the "scam blog" movement, a loose band of law school students and graduates who feel cheated by the high cost of school and the limited availability of jobs. The blog post reads as more of a stream-of-consciousness rant than a carefully-reasoned argument, but the writer's anger itself is convincing. You can feel his outrage at the economic realities crippling his generation and at Henig's willingness to consider a psychological explanation for their problems.

Writer discusses how the blog genre influences the depth and shape of this argument.

Writer points out the weaknesses of this blog post as persuasive writing and the blog author's limited audience appeal.

Posting anonymously on a blog, with its typical informal format, gives Scammed Hard! greater freedom of expression. For example, he uses sarcasm to show his disgust with Arnett and Henig, whom he calls "academic puffs and their pals at the *NYT*." But this sarcasm is also an example of his failure to build trust with his readers. Readers from the older generations whom he blames for the current state of affairs would probably be offended by his tone and aggression. He also sometimes treats Henig unfairly, assigning meaning to her work that I do not think she intended. He rarely supports his claims, and when he does, he uses underdeveloped anecdotes (like name-dropping Alexander the Great). The unbalanced nature of his work, combined with his sarcastic tone, is unlikely to convince readers who do not already agree with his views, no matter how large a role the economy plays in delaying adulthood for Millennials.

FOR WRITING AND DISCUSSION

Analyzing the Rhetorical Strategies in Your Texts

Use the questions in the chart on pages 292–293 to analyze the rhetorical features of your selected texts. You may choose to list the features as bullet points or write out paragraph descriptions. In small groups or as the whole class, discuss the features that you listed. Which features particularly give you a deeper understanding of the texts?

Analyzing the Main Themes and Similarities and Differences in Your Texts' Ideas

After you understand how your texts work rhetorically, you are ready to analyze closely how each text addresses your synthesis question and to envision these texts in conversation. At this stage in your thinking, your main task is to identify main issues, ideas, or themes that surface in your texts. Then from closely examining the ideas in each individual text, you can move to looking for similarities and differences among your texts. This process of thinking—using comparison and contrast—will help you clarify your understanding of each reading, but it will also help you see the texts in relationship to your synthesis question and in relationship to each other. As you consider the ideas and underlying values and assumptions of each author, think about how each text offers answers to your synthesis question and where these answers coincide and where they clash. The following questions can guide your thinking and help you generate ideas for the analysis part of your synthesis essay.

QUESTIONS TO ASK TO HELP YOU EXPLORE SIMILARITIES AND DIFFERENCES IN YOUR TEXTS

- What main ideas or themes related to your synthesis question do you see in each text?
- What similarities and differences do you see in the way the authors choose to frame the issues they are writing about? How do their theses (either implied or stated) differ?
- What are the main similarities and differences in their angles of vision?
- What commonalities and intersections related to your synthesis question do you see in their ideas? What contradictions and clashes do you see in their ideas?
- What similarities and differences do you see in the authors' underlying values and assumptions?
- What overlap, if any, is there in these authors' examples and uses of terms?
- On the subject of your synthesis question, how would Author A respond to Author B?

In the following example of Rosie Evans's exploratory analysis of ideas in her texts, note that she has restated her synthesis question and identified similarities among her texts. Note also how she begins to organize comparisons by points, to make analytical connections among them, and to push herself to think out exactly where these authors agree and differ.

Synthesis Question: What are the causes of the delayed-adulthood trends we see within Generation Y and how should society respond?

SIMILARITIES BETWEEN THE TWO ARTICLES:

- Both authors acknowledge that Generation Y's problems are not unique to their generation, and both use Baby Boomer experiences in the 60s and 70s as evidence.
- Despite the similarities between Generation Y and the Baby Boomers, both authors seem to think that Generation Y's problems are worse.

- Both authors find Arnett's theory limited by the fact that the emerging adult experience is more common among the privileged and therefore not universal.
- Both authors accept the evidence that brains continue to develop into the mid- and late-twenties.

Rosie has also articulated what she considers to be important differences between the ideas in her two texts.

Differences between the Two Articles

Henig	Scammed Hard!
• Henig explores in-depth how psychology and brain science offer explanations for the Millennials' unsettled condition.	• Scammed Hard! does not accept psychological or neurological explanations and finds that these theories divert attention from the true causes.
• Henig believes the economy exacerbated trends already present in Millennials and would point to evidence of Generation Y's trends beginning before the Great Recession.	• Scammed Hard! believes the economy is the primary cause of the Millennials' drifting and blames the Baby Boomers for wrecking economic opportunity for Millennials.
• Henig suggests that if emerging adulthood is a new life stage, then social services should adapt to expand opportunities for Millennials to support themselves while simultaneously exploring their identities.	• Scammed Hard! implies that if the economy is the problem, then fixing it will address the Millennials' problems. He would be frustrated if resources were diverted from fixing the economy to encouraging Millennial self-exploration.
• Henig agrees with Arnett that Millennials may appear lazy and directionless and suggests that experiences in their twenties might help them make better choices later in life.	• Scammed Hard! thinks the Baby Boomers have ruined Millennials' work ethic with high expectations that reality cannot match. He seems to find Millennials lazy, but does not blame them.
• Henig finds evidence of parental support among both low-income and privileged Millennials, but also finds that privileged Millennials receive more benefits. These findings show how emerging adulthood, if it exists, is problematic because it widens the resource gap.	• Scammed Hard! believes that the lack of evidence of emerging adulthood in low-income Millennials falsifies Arnett's theory.

FOR WRITING AND DISCUSSION

Generating Points about Themes, Shared Ideas, and Differences

Working on your own, identify main issues or themes in your assigned or chosen texts. Then explore the similarities and differences in their ideas. You may find that using bullets for your points helps you picture your points clearly, or you may want to write out your ideas in a draft form. Then working in small groups or as a whole class, review the accuracy and importance of these similarities and differences. To deepen your analysis, discuss this question: How do each author's purposes, assumptions, and values account for the similarities and differences you have identified?

Synthesizing Ideas From Your Texts

One of your biggest challenges in writing a synthesis essay is to move beyond summary and analysis to synthesis. A successful synthesis essay incorporates ideas from your texts and yet represents your own independent, creative thinking, showing evidence of the dialectic process.

Generating Ideas of Your Own

As you synthesize ideas, you put ideas together in new combinations and you demonstrate how the texts you have analyzed have informed and influenced the development of your own views. To move to synthesis, you need to think about how the differing perspectives of each text have led you to new realizations that you want to contribute to the conversation of these texts. As you begin to formulate your synthesis views, you will also need to reassert your personal/intellectual investment in the conversation of the texts. You will need to take ownership of the ideas and to emerge with a clearer sense of your own views. You may also want to consider which text—in your mind—makes the most significant contribution to the question you are exploring. You may want to evaluate the texts to determine which has influenced your thinking the most and why. The following questions can help you generate your own views.

QUESTIONS TO HELP YOU DEVELOP YOUR OWN VIEWS

- Do I have any knowledge from my personal experiences that is influencing my response to these texts?
- What do I agree with and disagree with in the texts I have analyzed?
- If I find one author's perspective more valid, accurate, interesting, or useful than another's, why is that?
- How have these texts changed my perception and understanding of an issue, question, or problem? (You might want to use these prompts: "I used to think ____________, but now I think ____________." "Although these texts have persuaded me that ____________, I still have doubts about ____________.")
- What is my current view on the synthesis question that connects my texts and that all my texts explore?
- Related to my synthesis question, what new, significant questions do these texts raise for me? What do I now see as the main controversies?
- How would I position myself in the conversation of the texts?

To illustrate this step in writing a synthesis essay, we show you Rosie Evans's wrestling with the ideas in both texts and with her own experiences as she begins to work out her position. You may find that several of these questions resonate more with you than others, and you may choose to probe your responses to those particular questions.

Rosie Evans's Exploration of Her Personal Connections to Her Texts and the Synthesis Question

Writer chooses to explore the personal experience that led to her interest in the synthesis question.

My older sister always seemed to succeed easily. She was high school valedictorian and mastered a long list of academic and leadership achievements in college. After she graduated, though, she seemed to drift. After several years of volunteer work and traveling, she returned home during the height of the Great Recession to live with our parents and work a retail job. My parents and other adults who expected success and greatness from her were baffled. I saw her frustration and even signs of depression as she worked a job she was overqualified for and struggled to afford health insurance while averaging 25 hours per week at $10 per hour. At the time, I felt sorry for her and suspected that she just didn't know what she was supposed to do without the structure of school and a clear definition of success to strive for. I sympathized with my parents, who were frustrated by her moping around the house and staying out late with friends while they footed her grocery bills and paid for her car insurance.

Writer shows how the texts have influenced her thinking.

She discusses her attraction to one of her text's ideas.

She discusses how the texts opened up new avenues of thought for her.

She shows how the texts have moved her to an enlarged view of the synthesis question and to ask more questions.

Both Henig's and ScammedHard!'s articles caused me to consider other causes of my sister's struggles. I related to Scammed Hard!'s piece because I could hear my sister's voice in his angry exclamations. She definitely feels cheated by our parents, who raised us to believe if we studied hard and earned a Bachelor's degree, professionals would be begging us to work for them. It seems clear that the Great Recession changed the economic reality Millennials face once they graduate, perhaps permanently, and that they feel underprepared for the uncertain future. However, I had never considered that brain development had anything to do with it. Although I am not totally persuaded that "emerging adulthood" exists, Henig's article convinced me that the state of the economy alone cannot have caused Millennials' delayed adulthood. Like Henig, I wonder how changing cultural norms impact the pathways our brains choose for us. Henig at one point mentions that the Baby Boomer generation of "helicopter parents" might actually be pleased to be so needed by their children this late in life. Other articles I've skimmed offer deeper studies on the psychology of emerging adults, isolating variables like Millennials' relationships with their parents and their social support structures to understand their experiences as emerging adults. I wonder how much parents' willingness and capacity to help their children enables Millennials to postpone the traditional markers of adulthood? If my sister hadn't had the option to spend three years traveling and volunteer teaching and then return home to my parents' couch, would she have harnessed her talents and grown up earlier?

Taking Your Position in the Conversation: Your Synthesis

After you have discovered what you think about the texts you have analyzed—what ideas you accept and reject, what new questions you have formulated, how your ideas have been modified and transformed through your analysis of your texts—you need to find a way to pull your ideas together. How do you want to enter the conversation of your synthesis question and your texts? What two or three main synthesis points would you like to develop? How will you respond to the ideas you have presented in your analysis and build on them in your own independent way? Your synthesis view should be the fruit of your intellectual work, a perspective that you have come to after analyzing the ideas of other authors and pondering them reflectively and keenly. Here are some questions that can help you articulate the points that you want to develop in your essay.

QUESTIONS TO HELP YOU FORMULATE AND DEVELOP YOUR SYNTHESIS VIEWS

- What discoveries have I made after much thought?
- What are the most important insights I have gotten from these readings?
- What is my intellectual or personal investment with the synthesis question at this point?
- Where can I step out on my own, even take a risk, in my thinking about the ideas discussed in these texts?
- What new perspective do I want to share with my readers?

In the following passage, we show you Rosie Evans's step toward integrating her own ideas with ideas from her texts as she inserts her voice into the conversation about Millennials.

I think both authors make strong cases for what they think is causing Millennials to delay adulthood, Scammed Hard! with his impassioned experiential case and Henig with her willingness to seek out and carefully examine evidence. They have convinced me that the unsettled state of Millennials is far too complex to have one isolated cause. Rather, it is the result of numerous factors: a shift in cultural expectations and parent-child relationships, economic realities created by the previous generation, and even twentysomethings' brains' responses to these changing circumstances. This high level of complexity is the very reason why identifying problems and agreeing on solutions are so difficult. What is the relationship between individuals and their parents? What role does the economic damage of decades of irresponsible policies play? How should social services respond to the increasingly accepted idea that young adulthhood experiences dramatic brain development? Rather than grapple with all these factors, I think many people fret over Millennials' mental health and argue over who deserves blame. Society at large seems guilty of the same inaction they see in the Millennials.

Writer tentatively offers two main synthesis points.

First synthesis point: no simple or single cause of Millennials' problems.

However, I don't think the Millennials are as inert as adults—and even these authors—seem to think they are. My sister worked very hard to survive on a retail salary while trying to navigate a home life she had left many years earlier. What she gave up on, though, was seeking out other opportunities, instead channeling her energy into surviving her immediate situation. When she faced the job market for a second time after earning a graduate degree, she submitted over fifty job applications, participated in multiple rounds of interviews for a total of eight positions, and was finally offered a part-time job she probably could have done without her graduate degree. She had gone from living a life where hard work led to success to a life where hard work led to a cycle of rejection and more hard work. Because of this, she feels powerless and trapped. How can we expect Millennials to stay motivated under such circumstances? It seems as though everyone needs to adjust their expectations, adults and Millennials alike.

Second synthesis point: writer speaks back to her texts: need to examine who Millennials really are and look at their individual experiences before generalizing about them.

These points incorporate writer's personal knowledge with ideas from the texts.

FOR WRITING AND DISCUSSION

Generating and Developing Your Synthesis Points

In light of the ideas you have developed through your exploratory analysis of your texts, explore your own views of your synthesis question by freewriting in response to the questions on page 299. What do you want to say in your own voice to show the connections you have made and the new insights you now have? What risky, surprising, or new views could you bring to your readers? Share your ideas with a writing partner or a group and explain why these points interest you.

Shaping and Drafting

Your main project in shaping and drafting your synthesis essay is to move from the kernels of good ideas that you generated in your thinking and early writing stages to a focused, fully developed, and logically organized discussion of these ideas. Focusing and organizing your ideas for a synthesis essay are both challenging writing tasks. We offer some strategies for developing the analysis and synthesis sections of your essay and then for formulating a thesis that will direct and hold together your essay.

Strategies for Shaping the Analytical Section of Your Essay

What to Consider in Planning the Analysis Section of Your Essay	Questions and Decisions
• Your analysis section, usually one-half to two-thirds of your essay, lays the foundation for your synthesis. • This section discusses several ways that your texts relate to your synthesis question.	• How many analytical points do you want to develop? • What are these points?
• Your analysis section should show that you have wallowed in the complexity of your texts. • It may include points about the rhetorical features of your texts (as in a rhetorical critique), and it may include points about the ideas (as in an ideas critique). • It should map out and explain a number of important similarities and differences in your texts.	Consider developing answers to these questions: • How do your texts frame the problem? How do they present different angles of vision? Where do they intersect in their perspectives and approaches? How do they argue and support their views with evidence? • How rhetorically effective are these texts? • What do the authors do to make their readers think?

Strategies for Shaping the Synthesis Section of Your Essay	
What to Consider in Planning the Synthesis Section of Your Essay	**Questions and Decisions**
• Your essay should build to your synthesis section, typically one-third to one-half of your essay.	• How can you best show where the texts and their authors promote your own independent thinking? • What synthesis points do you want to explore and discuss?
• The synthesis section of your essay should show your informed, independent thinking. • It should show how you have worked your way to a new understanding and created your own view.	• What new insights have you developed through studying these texts? • What new perspectives have you gained through the contrast and/or clash of different ideas? • How much or how little have these texts changed your views and why?

Writing a Thesis for a Synthesis Essay

In a synthesis essay, your thesis statement is particularly important and challenging to write. It sets up your readers' expectations, promising an illuminating view of the texts you have worked with. It should reflect earnest intellectual work, promise insights achieved through serious reflection, present your own original connection of ideas, and contain some element of risk and newness. Avoid bland, noncontestable thesis statements such as "These articles have both good and bad points."

You will probably want to work back and forth between formulating your thesis statement and drafting the analysis and synthesis sections of your essay. We recommend that you map out a rough thesis, draft your essay, and then revise and sharpen your thesis. For a synthesis essay, it is sometimes difficult to write a one-sentence, high-level thesis statement that encompasses both your analysis and your synthesis points. In such cases, you can write two lower-level, more specific thesis statements—one for your analysis section and one for your synthesis section—and simply join them together. What is important is that your thesis forecasts your main analysis and synthesis points and creates a map for your readers. The following examples illustrate these different options.

LOW-LEVEL, TWO-SENTENCE THESIS

Although both authors identify the negative impacts of Generation Y's delayed adulthood and call for society's urgent attention and action, Henig highlights the positive opportunities while Scammed Hard! focuses on the economic dangers. Both articles helped me understand why it is complicated to identify causes and propose solutions and nurtured my conviction that any workable solution must offer Millennials an active role in crafting society's response.

HIGH-LEVEL, ONE-SENTENCE THESIS

Both Henig's more psychological approach to the problems of Millennials and Scammed Hard!'s economic critique and their suggestions for solutions have led me to examine more closely the causes of Millennials' problems and to endorse a more complex explanation and a solution that involves active participation of Millennials themselves.

Organizing a Synthesis Essay

The biggest organizational decision you have to make in writing a synthesis essay is how much to summarize your texts and how to incorporate these summaries into your essay. Your decision should be guided by your audience's familiarity with the texts you are discussing and the complexity of the points you are making. Two ways of organizing a synthesis essay are shown in Figure 12.1.

Framework 1

Introduction and summary of both texts (several paragraphs)	• Presents the synthesis question and hooks readers • Summarizes the texts (unless your instructor posits that readers have already read the texts, in which case you can omit the summaries or reduce them to one or two sentences each) • Presents your thesis, which maps out your main analytical and synthesis points (Your thesis might come at the end of the paragraphs with your summaries or in a mini-paragraph of its own.)
Analytical section	• Includes paragraphs discussing and developing your analytical points
Synthesis section	• Includes paragraphs discussing and developing your synthesis points
Concluding paragraph	• Reiterates the values and limitations of the texts you have analyzed • Pulls together your new insights • Leaves readers thinking about your views

Framework 2

Introduction	• Presents the synthesis question and hooks readers • Presents your thesis, which maps out your main analytical and synthesis points
Summary/analysis of first text	• Summarizes the first text • Analyzes the first text
Summary/analysis of second text	• Summarizes the second text • Analyzes the second text, perhaps with connections and differences with the first text
Synthesis section	• Develops several main synthesis points
Concluding paragraph	• Reiterates values and limitations of the texts you have analyzed • Pulls together your new insights • Leaves readers thinking about your views

FIGURE 12.1 Two Frameworks for a Synthesis Essay

Revising

As you revise your synthesis essay, make sure that you have set up the synthesis question effectively. Then work on clarifying and developing your analytical points while striving for an engaging style. Also consider how to make your synthesis views more clearly reflect your own wrestling with the texts' ideas. Think about finding the most interesting ways to show how these texts have enlarged and deepened your own views.

Questions for Peer Review

In addition to the generic peer review questions explained in Skill 16.4, ask your peer reviewers to address these questions:

INTRODUCTION, SUMMARIES OF THE TEXTS, AND THESIS

1. What works well about the writer's presentation of the synthesis question that connects the texts under examination? How could the writer better show this question's significance and problematic nature?
2. Where could the writer's summaries of the texts be expanded, condensed, or clarified? Where would the summaries be better located in the essay to help readers?
3. How could the thesis be made more focused, risky, and clear in setting up the writer's analytical and synthesis points?

ANALYTICAL SECTION OF THE ESSAY

1. How could the writer's analytical points more clearly compare and contrast the authors' values, assumptions, angles of vision, or rhetorical strategies in addressing the synthesis question?
2. What further textual evidence could the writer add to develop these analytical points and make them more interesting or comprehensive?

SYNTHESIS SECTION OF THE ESSAY

1. How could the writer's synthesis points more clearly demonstrate the writer's thoughtful interaction with these texts?
2. What examples or other specifics could the writer include to develop these synthesis points more effectively?
3. How could the writer conclude this essay more effectively to leave readers with a new perspective on the texts and on the underlying question?

WRITING PROJECT

Multimodal or Online Options

Online Discussion On a class discussion board, class blog, or wiki space, post your own summaries of several readings your class has done and then include your own synthesis of these readings, exploring several points of similarity and difference. Share your own perspective of the way these readings have shaped your thinking. You may also want to respond to the synthesis discussions that others have posted.

The reading for this chapter is Rosie Evans's final synthesis essay, which developed out of the exploratory writing and thinking steps described earlier. The specifics of Rosie's assignment are provided on pages 289–290.

Rosie Evans (student)

Boomerang Kids: What Are the Causes of Generation Y's Growing Pains?

My older sister always seemed to succeed easily—that is, until she graduated from college. She went from high school valedictorian and university academic leader to perpetual volunteer and wandering world traveler. When the economy collapsed during the Great Recession, she returned home to live with our parents and work a retail job, confounding the many adults who expected great accomplishments from her. As it turns out, my sister's experience is not isolated but rather represents the experience of a larger cohort, those born roughly between 1980 and 2000. This generation is delaying life choices that traditionally signaled adulthood—like marriage, parenthood, or establishing a career—choosing instead to travel and experiment with different jobs. Many from this generation end up returning to live at home and/or relying on their parents for financial support, putting stress on their family relationships and their own mental health. The numerous labels attached to this generation—Millennials, Generation Y, the Lost Generation, boomerang kids, the Peter Pan generation, emerging adults, accordion families—show that our society is struggling to name and define exactly what is happening and what to do about it. What are the causes of the delayed-adulthood trends we see within Generation Y and how should society respond?

Opens with writer's investment and introduces the context for the issue, showing why it is problematic, and leads into the synthesis question.

States the synthesis question.

One point of view on this question comes from Robin Marantz Henig's 2010 *New York Times Magazine* article "What Is It About 20-Somethings?" Henig, a science writer, explores possible psychological and neurological explanations for Generation Y's delayed adulthood. She examines psychology professor Jeffrey Arnett's claim that twentysomethings are experiencing a new life stage called "emerging adulthood" in which they explore their possibilities and identities while also dealing with the instability, uncertainty, and fear that exploration brings. Rather than seeing Millennials as lazy and directionless, Arnett sees them as having meaningful experiences leading to better decisions about the kinds of lives they want to lead as adults. Henig links Arnett's claims to scientific findings that brains are not fully developed until the mid-twenties and suggests that immature brains might contribute to Millennials' delaying of adulthood. She also wonders if changing cultural norms about traditional signs of adulthood have removed pressure on twentysomething brains to achieve adult functioning earlier in life. If these claims are true, Henig suggests that our social institutions, like education and health care, should change to offer better support to Millennials as they transition to adulthood.

Introduces the first text and summarizes it.

In response to Henig's article, blogger Scammed Hard! argues in his post "What's Wrong with 20-Somethings?" that the economy is to blame for Generation Y's

Introduces the second text and summarizes it.

struggles. While agreeing that the brain is constantly changing, he dismisses Arnett's theory of emerging adulthood as a bogus psychological theory designed to give its inventor professional distinction. Instead, Scammed Hard! blames Generation Y's struggles on Baby Boomers' destruction of the economy combined with their promotion of dangerous levels of student debt and their encouragement of a comfortable middle-class lifestyle. By setting high expectations and then making those expectations impossible to fulfill, Boomers have destroyed Generation Y's incentives for hard work and sacrifice. Scammed Hard! believes that although drifting toward adulthood may provide Millennials with a fun distraction, it does not prepare them with the skills and motivation needed to find success in a destroyed economy.

Thesis statement with analytical points and synthesis points.

Although both authors identify the negative impacts of GenerationY's delayed adulthood and call for society's urgent attention and action, Henig highlights the positive opportunities while Scammed Hard! focuses on the economic dangers. Both articles helped me understand why it is complicated to identify causes and propose solutions and nurtured my conviction that any workable solution must offer Millennials an active role in crafting society's response.

Analysis: compares and contrasts ideas in both texts and develops similarities in ideas.

Both Henig and Scammed Hard! acknowledge that the current trends among Millennials are not unique to this generation (after all, the Baby Boomers themselves went through a hippie period). Nevertheless, they acknowledge that the problem of delayed adulthood is more widespread and troubling today. Using survey data, Henig compares the average age of marriage and the percentage of twentysomethings living at home in the 70s and today to show that delayed adulthood is more prevalent now. Scammed Hard! argues that even hippies eventually had to settle down and make productive contributions to society. Both authors worry about the long-term impacts to our society as Millennials take longer to reach adulthood and become innovative, industrious, taxpaying members of society.

Continuation of analysis section: writer analyzes differences in views.

Writer brings in rhetorical points to explain the differences.

Analyzes and elaborates on differences.

Continuation of analysis section focusing on the differences in the ideas in the two texts.

Writer brings in rhetorical points to explain the differences.

While both authors accept the science on brain development, they disagree on the role it plays in causing the Millennials' problems. Henig uses the psychological research to suggest that it might be time for society to enact policies that enrich "the cognitive environment of people in their 20s" in order to better shape their brains for the demands of adulthood. As a science writer and parent of a Millennial, Henig constructs a balanced, reasoned discussion that builds trust with her readers—other parents and the larger society who may feel responsible for causing and solving the Millennials' problems. In contrast, Scammed Hard's refuses to "write off the problems my generation faces as merely 'normal stages of development.'" He thinks that focusing on a new "life stage" diverts attention from the urgent economic problems that drive this generation's reality and account for Millennials' anger, depression, and humiliating inability to support themselves. Writing as a Millennial from the "scam blog" movement, a loose band of law school students and graduates who feel cheated by the high cost of education and the limited availability of jobs, Scammed Hard! effectively employs his outrage to make a compelling argument for economic causes of Generation Y's problems. He believes that the Boomers' decision to outsource jobs, lend irresponsibly, and encourage student debt led to the catastrophic economic collapse that has limited Millennials' financial independence, whereas Henig thinks the economy has merely accelerated trends that already existed among Millennials before the Great Recession.

The differences in how each author views the causes of Generation Y's problems affect their proposed solutions. Henig thinks we should devote our resources to modifying and expanding social services that support Millennials of all income levels as their brains and identities develop. In contrast, Scammed Hard! urges Baby Boomers to fix the economy and calls on everyone to mobilize to create better incentives for hard work and innovation among the younger generation.

Writer discusses how different perspectives on the problem lead to different proposed solutions.

Henig's discussion of emerging adulthood raised some important questions for me. She mentions that the Boomer generation of "helicopter parents" might actually be pleased to be so involved in their children's lives. I wonder how much parents' willingness and capacity to help their children enables Millennials to delay adulthood. If my sister hadn't had the parent-subsidized option to spend three years volunteering and traveling and then return home to our parents' couch, would she have harnessed her talents and grown up earlier? And if mostly privileged Millennials are the ones choosing to delay adulthood, does it make sense to devote even more resources to this already well-supported group? Or should the social support systems be expanded to provide low-income Millennials similar opportunities for financial security and self-exploration?

Transition to synthesis section:

Synthesis point: writer explains how Henig's ideas have raised questions of personal interest and importance.

After reading these articles, I am convinced that Generation Y's delayed adulthood is the result of many complex causes, not just one. These factors include shifts in cultural expectations for young adults, evolving parent-child relationships, collapse of the job market, and other economic realities created by the previous generation, and maybe also the effects of not-yet-mature twentysomething brains. The factors also likely reinforce each other, strengthening their collective impact. For example, perhaps Baby Boomer parents are subconsciously trying to cover up their guilt over the state of the economy by lifting their children's financial burdens. Also, because it is more culturally acceptable to marry later in life and medically possible to have kids during middle age, perhaps Millennials don't worry about a career because they do not yet need financial security for starting a family. Rather than tackle the complex causes of the problems, I sense that established adults find it easier to fret over Millennials' mental health and argue over who is to blame, making society at large guilty of the same inaction they accuse Millennials of.

Synthesis point: writer asserts her own perspective, showing how her analysis of the texts has informed her own views.

However, when I think about my sister, I can't agree that Millennials are as inert as adults seem to think they are. What concerns me about the perspectives on Millennials is how often older generations view them as passive actors in their own lives. I think Millennials work a lot harder and more courageously than people realize and make active, intentional choices as best they can under the circumstances. Henig's piece, for all its measured evidence in its ten pages, fails to offer the authentic perspective of a Millennial voice. She should have talked to my sister, who worked very hard to survive on a retail salary while trying to navigate a home life she had left behind years earlier. However, as my sister devoted most of her energy to survival, she gave up on seeking other opportunities for herself. I think this happened because of her disappointment as she transitioned between life where hard work led to success and life where hard work led to a cycle of rejection and more hard work. When she faced the job market for a second time after earning a graduate degree, she submitted over fifty job applications, participated in multiple rounds of interviews for a total of eight

Synthesis point discusses the writer's own view.

Synthesis point asserts writer's independent thinking.

Elaborates on the connections the writer is making and delineates her differences from the two authors' ideas.

Writer integrates personal experience with ideas from the two texts.

positions, and was finally offered a part-time job she probably could have done without her graduate degree. This situation—certainly not unique among Millennials—made her feel powerless and trapped, because she wants to be making successful, valuable contributions to society.

Synthesis point discusses the writer's own view.

I believe a real solution to Millennials' problems must be multifaceted if it is going to significantly impact the numerous interrelated causes. But more importantly, an effective solution will be one that creates a partnership with Millennials, listens to *them*, and offers them an active role in the response. It is a challenge I think all of their experiences and self-reflection have prepared them for. And it will align with their desires to participate, rather than watch, as the economy, and maybe even adulthood, pass them by.

Conclusion with final connections.

Henig and Scammed Hard! offer differing perspectives on the causes and solutions to Generation Y's delayed adulthood. I encourage them, and anyone else who is serious about making changes to the systems and social structures that have created an America in which it is difficult to grow up, to begin by connecting with the Millennials themselves. They might find that Generation Y is full of ideas, creativity, and possibility waiting to be unleashed.

Complete citation of texts in MLA format.

Works Cited

Henig, Robin Marantz. "What Is It About 20-Somethings?" *The New York Times Magazine*, 18 Aug. 2010. Web. 15 Dec. 2013.

"What's Wrong with 20-Somethings?"*Scammed Hard!*, 20 Aug. 2010. Web. 15 Dec. 2013.

WRITING A CLASSICAL ARGUMENT

13

WHAT YOU WILL LEARN

13.1 To explain the theory and rhetorical principles underlying effective arguments.

13.2 To write a classical argument that offers reasons and evidence in support of your position while also summarizing and responding to opposing views.

On many occasions in your academic or civic life you will be asked to take a stand on an issue, to support your stand persuasively with reasons and evidence, and to respond ethically to opposing or alternative views. The need for argument arises whenever members of a community disagree about the best solution to a problem or the best answer to a question. Classical rhetoricians believed that the art of arguing is essential for good citizenship. If disputes can be resolved through exchange of perspectives, negotiation of differences, and flexible seeking of the best solutions to a problem, then nations won't have to resort to war or individuals to fisticuffs.

Engaging Classical Argument

The following thought exercise, which involves ethical treatment of animals, introduces you to an issue that invites classical argument. References to this thought exercise will recur as the chapter progresses. Your initial position may reflect what social scientists call your personal *ideology*—that is, a network of basic values, beliefs, and assumptions that tend to guide a person's view of the world. However, if you adopt an open-minded, truth-seeking attitude, your initial position may evolve as the argumentative conversation progresses. In fact, the conversation may even cause changes in some of your basic beliefs, since ideologies aren't set in stone and since many of us have unresolved allegiances to competing ideologies that may be logically inconsistent (for example, a belief in freedom of speech combined with a belief that hate speech should be banned). In this thought exercise we ask you to record your initial views and then to keep track of how your views may change during further reflection or ensuing class discussions.

Situation

A bunch of starlings build nests in the attic of a family's house, gaining access to the attic through a torn vent screen. Soon the eggs hatch, and every morning at sunrise the family is awakened by the sound of birds squawking and wings beating against rafters as the starlings fly in and out of the house to feed the hatchlings. After losing considerable early morning sleep, the family repairs the screen. Unable to get in and out, the parent birds are unable to feed their young. The birds die within a day.

Question at issue

Was the family's action an instance of cruelty to animals (that is, was their decision to repair the screen ethically justifiable or not)?

ON YOUR OWN

1. Freewrite your initial response to this question. Explain why you think the family's act was or was not ethical.
2. We initially framed this issue as an after-the-fact yes/no question: Is the family guilty of cruelty to animals? But we can also frame it as an open-ended, before-the-fact question: "What should the family have done about the starlings in the attic?" Suppose you are a family member discussing the starlings at dinner, prior to the decision to fix the vent screen. Make a list of your family's other options and try to determine whether one of these options would have been better than fixing the vent screen. Why?

IN CONVERSATION

1. Working in small groups or as a whole class, share your individual responses to these questions and then try to reach a group consensus on the issues: Was fixing the screen an instance of cruelty to animals? What other alternatives, if any, might have been ethically preferable?
2. If class discussion caused some students' views to evolve or change, how and why?

13.1 Explain the theory and rhetorical principles underlying effective arguments.

Understanding Classical Argument

What Is Argument?

The study of argumentation involves two components: truth seeking and persuasion:

- By *truth seeking,* we mean a diligent, open-minded, and responsible search for the best course of action or solution to a problem, taking into account all the available information and alternative points of view.
- By *persuasion,* we mean the art of making a claim* on an issue and justifying it convincingly so that the audience's initial resistance to your position is overcome and they are moved toward your position.

*By long-standing tradition, the thesis statement of an argument is often called its "claim."

These two components of argument seem paradoxically at odds: Truth seeking asks us to relax our certainties and be willing to change our views; persuasion asks us to be certain, to be committed to our claims, and to get others to change their views. We can overcome this paradox if we dispel two common but misleading views of argument. The most common view is that argument is a fight as in "I just got into a horrible argument with my roommate." This view of argument as a fist-waving, shouting match in which you ridicule anyone who disagrees with you (popularized by radio and television talk shows and the Internet) entirely disregards argument as truth seeking, but it also misrepresents argument as persuasion because it polarizes people, rather than promoting understanding, new ways of seeing, and change.

Another common but misleading view is that argument is a pro/con debate modeled after high school or college debate matches. Although debating can be an excellent way to develop critical thinking skills, it misrepresents argument as a two-sided contest with winners and losers. Because controversial issues involve many different points of view, not just two, reducing an issue to pro/con positions distorts the complexity of the disagreement. Instead of thinking of *both* sides of an issue, we need to think of *all* sides. Equally troublesome, the debate image invites us to ask, "Who won the debate?" rather than "What is the best solution to the question that divides us?" The best solution might be a compromise between the two debaters or an undiscovered third position. The debate image tends to privilege the confident extremes in a controversy rather than the complex and muddled middle.

From our perspective, the best image for understanding argument is neither "fight" nor "debate" but the deliberations of a committee representing a wide spectrum of community voices charged with finding the best solution to a problem. From this perspective, argument is both a *process* and a *product*. As a process, argument is an act of inquiry characterized by fact-finding, information gathering, and consideration of alternative points of view. As a product, it is someone's contribution to the conversation at any one moment—a turn taking in a conversation, a formal speech, or a written position paper such as the one you will write for this chapter. The goal of argument as process is truth seeking; the goal of argument as product is persuasion. When members of a diverse committee are willing to argue persuasively for their respective points of view but are simultaneously willing to listen to other points of view and to change or modify their positions in light of new information or better arguments, then both components of argument are fully in play.

We cannot overemphasize the importance of both truth seeking and persuasion to your professional and civic life. Truth seeking makes you an informed and judicious employee and a citizen who delays decisions until a full range of evidence and alternative views are aired and examined. Persuasion gives you the power to influence the world around you, whether through letters to the editor or blogs on political issues or through convincing position papers for professional life. Whenever an organization needs to make a major decision, those who can think flexibly and write persuasively can wield great influence.

Having introduced you to argument as both process and product, we now turn to the details of effective argumentation. To help orient you, we begin by describing the typical stages that mark students' growth as arguers.

Stages of Development: Your Growth as an Arguer

We have found that when we teach argument in our classes, students typically proceed through identifiable stages as their argumentative skills increase. While these stages may or may not describe your own development, they suggest the skills you should strive to acquire.

- ***Stage 1: Argument as personal opinion.*** At the beginning of instruction in argument, students typically express strong personal opinions but have trouble justifying their opinions with reasons and evidence and often create short, undeveloped arguments that are circular, lacking in evidence, and insulting to those who disagree. The following freewrite, written by a student first confronting the starling case, illustrates this stage:

  > The family shouldn't have killed the starlings because that is really wrong! I mean that act was disgusting. It makes me sick to think how so many people are just willing to kill something for no reason at all. How are these parents going to teach their children values if they just go out and kill little birds for no good reason?!! This whole family is what's wrong with America!

  This writer's opinion is passionate and heartfelt, but it provides neither reasons nor evidence why someone else should hold the same opinion.

- ***Stage 2: Argument structured as claim supported by one or more reasons.*** This stage represents a quantum leap in argumentative skill because the writer can now produce a rational plan containing point sentences (the reasons) and particulars (the evidence). The writer who produced the previous freewrite later developed a structure like this:

  The family's act constituted cruelty to animals

  - because the starlings were doing minimal harm.
  - because other options were available.
  - because the way they killed the birds caused needless suffering.

- ***Stage 3: Increased attention to truth seeking.*** In Stage 3 students become increasingly engaged with the complexity of the issue as they listen to their classmates' views, conduct research, and evaluate alternative perspectives and stances. They are often willing to change their positions when they see the power of other arguments.
- ***Stage 4: Ability to articulate the unstated assumptions underlying their arguments.*** As we show later in this chapter, each reason in a writer's argument is based on an assumption, value, or belief (often unstated) that the audience must accept if the argument is to be persuasive. Often the writer needs to state these assumptions explicitly and support them. At this stage students identify and analyze their own assumptions and those of their intended audiences. Students gain increased skill at accommodating alternative views through refutation or concession.
- ***Stage 5: Ability to link an argument to the values and beliefs of the intended audience.*** In this stage students are increasingly able to link their arguments to their audience's values and beliefs and to adapt structure and

tone to the resistance level of their audience. Students also appreciate how delayed-thesis arguments or other psychological strategies can be more effective than closed-form arguments when addressing hostile audiences.

The rest of this chapter helps you progress through these stages. Although you can read the remainder in one sitting, we recommend that you break your reading into sections, going over the material slowly and applying it to your own ideas in progress. Let the chapter's concepts and explanations sink in gradually, and return to them periodically for review. This section on "Understanding Classical Argument" comprises a compact but comprehensive course in argumentation.

Creating an Argument Frame: A Claim with Reasons

Somewhere in the writing process, whether early or late, you need to create a frame for your argument. This frame includes a clear question that focuses the argument, your claim, and one or more supporting reasons. Often your reasons, stated as *because* clauses, can be attached to your claim to provide a working thesis statement.

Finding an Arguable Issue At the heart of any argument is an **issue,** which we can define as a question that invites more than one reasonable answer and thus leads to perplexity or disagreement. This requirement excludes disagreements based on personal tastes, where no shared criteria can be developed ("Baseball is more fun than soccer"). It also excludes purely private questions because issues arise out of disagreements in communities.

Issue questions are often framed as yes/no choices, especially when they appear on ballots or in courtrooms: Should gay marriage be legalized? Should the federal government place a substantial tax on gasoline to elevate its price? Is this defendant guilty of armed robbery? Just as frequently, they can be framed openly, inviting many different possible answers: What should our city do about skateboarders in downtown pedestrian areas? How can we best solve the energy crisis?

It is important to remember that framing an issue as a yes/no question does not mean that all points of view fall neatly into pro/con categories. Although citizens may be forced to vote yes or no on a proposed ballot initiative, they can support or oppose the initiative for a variety of reasons. Some may vote happily for the initiative, others vote for it only by holding their noses, and still others oppose it vehemently but for entirely different reasons. To argue effectively, you need to appreciate the wide range of perspectives from which people approach the yes/no choice.

How you frame your question necessarily affects the scope and shape of your argument itself. In our exploratory exercise we framed the starling question in two ways: (1) Was the family guilty of cruelty to animals? and (2) What should the family have done about the starlings? Framed in the first way, your argument would have to develop criteria for "cruelty to animals" and then argue whether the family's actions met those criteria. Framed in the second way, you could argue for your own solution to the problem, ranging from doing nothing (waiting for the birds to grow up and leave, then fixing the screen) to climbing into the attic and drowning the birds so that their deaths are quick and painless. Or you could word the question in a broader, more philosophical way: When are humans justified in killing animals? Or you could focus on a subissue: When can an animal be labeled a "pest"?

FOR WRITING AND DISCUSSION

Identifying Arguable Issues

1. Working individually, make a list of several communities that you belong to and then identify one or more questions currently being contested within those communities. (If you have trouble, check your local campus and city newspapers or an organizational newsletter; you'll quickly discover a wealth of contested issues.) Then share your list with classmates.
2. Pick two or three issues of particular interest to you, and try framing them in different ways: as broad or narrow questions, as open-ended or yes/no questions. Place several examples on the chalkboard for class discussion.

Stating a Claim Your **claim** is the position you want to take on the issue. It is your brief, one-sentence answer to your issue question:

> The family was not ethically justified in killing the starlings.
> The city should build skateboarding areas with ramps in all city parks.
> The federal government should substantially increase its taxes on gasoline.

You will appreciate argument as truth seeking if you find that your claim evolves as you think more deeply about your issue and listen to alternative views. Be willing to rephrase your claim to soften it or refocus it or even to reverse it as you progress through the writing process.

Articulating Reasons

Your claim, which is the position you take on an issue, needs to be supported by reasons and evidence. A **reason** (sometimes called a "premise") is a subclaim that supports your main claim. In speaking or writing, a reason is usually linked to the claim with such connecting words as *because, therefore, so, consequently,* and *thus.* In planning your argument, a powerful strategy for developing reasons is to harness the grammatical power of the conjunction *because;* think of your reasons as *because* clauses attached to your claim. Formulating your reasons in this way allows you to create a thesis statement that breaks your argument into smaller parts, each part devoted to one of the reasons.

For advice on how much of your supporting argument you should summarize in your thesis statement, see skill 17.4 on effective introductions.

Suppose, for example, that you are examining the issue "Should the government legalize hard drugs such as heroin and cocaine?" Here are several different points of view on this issue, each expressed as a claim with *because* clauses:

ONE VIEW

Cocaine and heroin should be legalized

- because legalizing drugs will keep the government out of people's private lives.
- because keeping these drugs illegal has the same negative effects on our society that alcohol prohibition did in the 1920s.

ANOTHER VIEW

Cocaine and heroin should be legalized

- because taking drug sales out of the hands of drug dealers would reduce street violence.
- because decriminalization would cut down on prison overcrowding and free police to concentrate on dangerous crime rather than on finding drug dealers.
- because elimination of underworld profits would change the economic structure of the underclass and promote shifts to socially productive jobs and careers.

STILL ANOTHER VIEW

The government should not legalize heroin and cocaine

- because doing so will lead to an increase in drug users and addicts.
- because doing so will send the message that it is okay to use hard drugs.

Although the yes/no framing of this question seems to reduce the issue to a two-position debate, many different value systems are at work here. The first pro-legalization argument, libertarian in perspective, values maximum individual freedom. The second argument—although it too supports legalization—takes a community perspective valuing the social benefits of eliminating the black market drug-dealing culture. In the same way, individuals could oppose legalization for a variety of reasons.

FOR WRITING AND DISCUSSION

Generating *Because* Clauses

Working in small groups or as a whole class, generate a list of reasons for and against one or more of the following yes/no claims. State your reasons as *because* clauses. Think of as many *because* clauses as possible by imagining a wide variety of perspectives on the issue.

1. The school year for grades 1 through 12 should be lengthened to eleven months.
2. The federal government should place a substantial tax on gasoline.
3. The United States should adopt a single-payer, government-financed healthcare system like that of Canada.
4. Playing violent video games is a harmful influence on teenage boys. [or] Women's fashion and style magazines (such as *Glamour* or *Seventeen*) are harmful influences on teenage girls.
5. The war on terror requires occasional use of "enhanced interrogation techniques" on some detainees.

Articulating Underlying Assumptions

So far, we have focused on the frame of an argument as a claim supported with one or more reasons. Shortly, we will proceed to the flesh and muscle of an argument, which is the evidence you use to support your reasons. But before turning to evidence, we need to look at another crucial part of an argument's frame: its *underlying assumptions*.

What Do We Mean by an Underlying Assumption? Every time you link a claim with a reason, you make a silent assumption that may need to be articulated and examined. Consider this argument:

> The family was justified in killing the starlings because starlings are pests.

To support this argument, the writer would first need to provide evidence that starlings are pests (examples of the damage they do and so forth). But the persuasiveness of the argument rests on the underlying assumption that it is okay to kill pests. If an audience doesn't agree with that assumption, then the argument flounders unless the writer articulates the assumption and defends it. The complete frame of the argument must therefore include the underlying assumption.

Claim: The family was justified in killing the starlings.
Reason: Because starlings are pests.
Underlying assumption: It is ethically justifiable to kill pests.

It is important to examine the underlying assumption that connects any reason to its claim *because you must determine whether your audience will accept that assumption. If not, you need to make it explicit and support it.* Think of the underlying assumption as a general principle, rule, belief, or value that connects the reason to the claim. It answers your reader's question, "Why, if I accept your reason, should I accept your claim?"*

Here are a few more examples:

Claim with reason: Women should be allowed to join combat units because the image of women as combat soldiers would help society overcome gender stereotyping.
Underlying assumption: It is good to overcome gender stereotyping.

Claim with reason: The government should not legalize heroin and cocaine because doing so will lead to an increase in drug users.
Underlying assumption: It is bad to increase the number of drug users.

Claim with reason: The family was guilty of cruelty to animals in the starling case because less drastic means of solving the problem were available.
Underlying assumption: A person should choose the least drastic means to solve a problem.

*Our explanation of argument structure is influenced by the work of philosopher Stephen Toulmin, who viewed argument as a dynamic courtroom drama where opposing attorneys exchange arguments and cross-examinations before a judge and jury. Although we use Toulmin's strategies for analyzing an argument structure, we have chosen not to use his specialized terms, which include *warrant* (the underlying assumption connecting a reason to a claim), *grounds* (the evidence that supports the claim), *backing* (the evidence and subarguments that support the warrant), *conditions of rebuttal* (all the ways that skeptics could attack an argument or all the conditions under which the argument wouldn't hold), and finally *qualifier* (an indication of the strength of the claim). However, your instructor may prefer to use these terms and in that case may provide you with more explanation and examples.

FOR WRITING AND DISCUSSION

Identifying Underlying Assumptions

Identify the underlying assumptions in each of the following claims with reasons.

1. Cocaine and heroin should be legalized because legalizing drugs will keep the government out of people's private lives.
2. The government should raise gasoline taxes because the higher price would substantially reduce gasoline consumption.
3. The government should not raise gasoline taxes because the higher price would place undue hardship on low-income people.
4. The government should not raise gasoline taxes because other means of reducing gasoline consumption would be more effective.
5. The government is justified in detaining suspected terrorists indefinitely without charging them with a crime because doing so may prevent another terrorist attack.

Using Evidence Effectively

Inside your arguments, each of your reasons (as well as any underlying assumptions that you decide to state explicitly and defend) needs to be supported either by subarguments or by evidence. By "evidence" we mean facts, examples, summaries of research articles, statistics, testimony, or other relevant data that will persuade your readers to accept your reasons. Note that evidence always exists within a rhetorical context; as a writer you select and shape the evidence that will best support your position, knowing that skeptics may point to evidence that you did not select. Evidence is thus not the same as "proof"; used ethically, evidence presents the best case for your claim without purporting to be the whole truth.

Evidence can sometimes come from personal experience, but in most cases it comes from your own field or library research. The kinds of evidence most often used in argument are the following:

Factual Data Factual data can provide persuasive support for your arguments. (Keep in mind that writers always select their facts through an angle of vision, so the use of facts doesn't preclude skeptics from bringing in counterfacts.) Here is how evolutionary biologist Olivia Judson used factual data to support her point that malaria-carrying mosquitoes cause unacceptable harm to human lives and wealth.

> Each year, malaria kills at least one million people and causes more than 300 million cases of acute illness. For children worldwide, it's one of the leading causes of death. The economic burden is significant too: malaria costs Africa more than $12 billion in lost growth each year. In the United States, hundreds of millions of dollars are spent every year on mosquito control.

Examples An example from personal experience can often be used to support a reason. Here is how student writer Ross Taylor used personal experience to argue that paintball is safe even though accidents can happen. (You can read his complete essay on pp. 337–339.)

I admit that paintball can be dangerous and that accidents do happen. I personally had a friend lose an eye after inadvertently shooting himself in the eye from a very close range. The fact of the matter is that he made a mistake by looking down the barrel of a loaded gun and the trigger malfunctioned. Had he been more careful or worn the proper equipment, he most likely would have been fine. During my first organized paintball experience I was hit in the goggles by a very powerful gun and felt no pain. The only discomfort came from having to clean all the paint off my goggles after the game. When played properly, paintball is an incredibly safe sport.

Besides specific examples like this, writers sometimes invent hypothetical examples, or *scenarios,* to illustrate an issue or hypothesize about the consequences of an event. (Of course, you must tell your reader that the example or scenario is hypothetical.)

Summaries of Research Another common way to support an argument is to summarize research articles. Here is how a student writer, investigating whether menopausal women should use hormone replacement therapy to combat menopausal symptoms, used one of several research articles in her paper. The student began by summarizing research studies showing possible dangers of hormone replacement therapy. She then made the following argument:

Another reason not to use hormone replacement therapy is that other means are available to ease menopausal symptoms such as hot flashes, irritability, mood changes, and sleep disturbance. One possible alternative treatment is acupuncture. One study (Cohen, Rousseau, and Carey) revealed that a randomly selected group of menopausal women receiving specially designed acupuncture treatment showed substantial decreases in menopausal symptoms as compared to a control group. What was particularly persuasive about this study was that both the experimental group and the control group received acupuncture, but the needle insertion sites for the experimental group were specifically targeted to relieve menopausal symptoms whereas the control group received acupuncture at sites used to promote general well-being. The researchers concluded that "acupuncture may be recommended as a safe and effective therapy for reducing menopausal hot flushes as well as contributing to the reduction in sleep disruptions" (299).*

Statistics Another common form of evidence is statistics. Here is how one writer used statistics to argue that the federal government should raise fuel-efficiency standards placed on auto manufacturers:

There is very little need for most Americans to drive huge SUVs. One recent survey found that 87 percent of four-wheel-drive SUV owners had never taken their SUVs off-road (Yacobucci)... . By raising fuel-efficiency standards, the government would force vehicle manufacturers to find a way to create more earth-friendly vehicles that would lower vehicle emissions and pollution. An article entitled "Update:

*The examples in this section use the MLA (Modern Language Association) style for documenting sources. See Chapter 23 for full explanations of how to use both the MLA and APA (American Psychological Association) systems for citing and documenting sources. The complete bibliographic information for this article would be found in the "Works Cited" pages alphabetized under "Cohen."

What You Should Know Before Purchasing a New Vehicle" states that for every gallon of gasoline used by a vehicle, 20 to 28 pounds of carbon dioxide are released into the environment. This article further states that carbon dioxide emissions from automobiles are responsible for 20 percent of all carbon dioxide released into the atmosphere from human causes.

Just as writers select facts, examples, and research studies according to their angle of vision, so do they select and shape numerical data. In the above example, the writer focuses on the environmental harm caused by vehicles, especially SUVs. But you must always read statistics rhetorically. For example, the same statistical "fact" can be framed in different ways. There is a difference in focus and feel between these two ways of using the same data:

- "20 percent of human-caused CO_2 emissions come from automobiles" [puts automobiles in the foreground]
- "Although cars do cause some pollution, a full 80 percent of human-caused CO_2 emissions come from sources other than cars." [puts automobiles in the background]

Testimony Writers can also use expert testimony to bolster a case. The following passage from a student essay arguing in favor of therapeutic cloning uses testimony from a prominent physician and medical researcher. Part of the paragraph quotes this expert directly; another part paraphrases the expert's argument.

> As Dr. Gerald Fischbach, Executive Vice President for Health and Biomedical Sciences and Dean of Medicine at Columbia University, said in front of a United States Senate subcommittee: "New embryonic stem cell procedures could be vital in solving the persistent problem of a lack of genetically matched, qualified donors of organs and tissues that we face today." Fischbach goes on to say that this type of cloning could also lead to the discovery of cures for diseases such as ALS, Parkinson's disease, Alzheimer's disease, diabetes, heart disease, cancer, and possibly others.

Rather than provide direct research evidence that stem cell cloning might one day lead to cures for diseases, the writer draws on testimony from the dean of a prestigious medical school. Opponents of stem cell research might draw on other experts, selecting those who are skeptical of this claim.

Subarguments Sometimes writers support reasons not directly through data but through sequences of subarguments. Sometimes these subarguments develop a persuasive analogy, hypothesize about consequences, or simply advance the argument through a chain of connected points. In the following passage, taken from a philosophic article justifying torture under certain conditions, the author uses a subargument to support one of his main points—that a terrorist holding victims hostage has no "rights":

> There is an important difference between terrorists and their victims that should mute talk of the terrorist's "rights." The terrorist's victims are at risk unintentionally, not having asked to be endangered. But the terrorist knowingly initiated his actions. Unlike his victims, he volunteered for the risks of his deed. By threatening to kill for profit or idealism, he renounces civilized standards, and he can have no complaint if civilization tries to thwart him by whatever means necessary.

Rather than using direct empirical evidence, the author supports his point with a subargument showing how terrorists differ from victims and thus relinquish their claim to rights.

Evaluating Evidence: The STAR Criteria

To make your arguments as persuasive as possible, apply to your evidence what rhetorician Richard Fulkerson calls the STAR criteria (**S**ufficiency, **T**ypicality, **A**ccuracy, and **R**elevance),* as shown in the chart on this page.

It is often difficult to create arguments in which all your evidence fully meets the STAR criteria. Sometimes you need to proceed on evidence that might not be typical, verifiable, or as up-to-date as you would like. In such cases, you can often increase the effectiveness of your argument by qualifying your claim. Consider the difference between these two claims:

- ***Strong claim:*** Watching violent TV cartoons increases aggressive play behavior in boys.
- ***Qualified claim:*** Watching violent TV cartoons can increase aggressive play behavior in some boys.

To be made persuasive, the strong claim requires substantial evidence meeting the STAR criteria. In contrast, the qualified claim requires less rigorous evidence, perhaps only an example or two combined with the results of one study.

The STAR Criteria for Evaluating Evidence

STAR Criteria	Implied Question	Comments
Sufficiency	Is there enough evidence?	If you don't provide enough evidence, skeptical audiences can dismiss your claim as a "hasty generalization." To argue that marijuana is not a harmful drug, you would probably need more evidence than the results of one study or the testimony of a healthy pot smoker.
Typicality	Are the chosen data representative and typical?	If you choose extreme or rare-case examples, rather than typical and representative ones, your audience might accuse you of cherry-picking your data. Testimony from persons whose back pain was cured by yoga may not support the general claim that yoga is good for back pain.
Accuracy	Are the data accurate and up-to-date?	Providing recent, accurate data is essential for your own *ethos* as a writer. Data from 1998 on homelessness or inaccurately gathered data may be ineffective for a current policy argument.
Relevance	Are the data relevant to the claim?	Even though your evidence is accurate, up-to-date, and representative, if it's not pertinent to the claim, it will be ineffective. For example, evidence that nuclear waste is dangerous is not relevant to the issue of whether it can be stored securely in Yucca Mountain.

*Richard Fulkerson, *Teaching the Argument in Writing,* Urbana: National Council of Teachers of English, 1996, pp. 44–53. In this section we are indebted to Fulkerson's discussion.

As you gather evidence, consider also its source and the extent to which your audience will trust that source. While all data must be interpreted and hence are never completely impartial, careful readers are aware of how easily data can be skewed. Newspapers, magazines, blogs, and journals often have political biases and different levels of respectability. Generally, evidence from peer-reviewed scholarly journals is more highly regarded than evidence from secondhand sources. Particularly problematic is information gathered from Internet Web sites, which can vary widely in reliability and degree of bias.

See Skill 21.2 for advice on evaluating sources for reliability and bias. See Skill 21.3 for help on evaluating Web sites.

Addressing Objections and Counterarguments

Having looked at the frame of an argument (claim, reasons, and underlying assumptions) and at the kinds of evidence used to flesh out the frame, let's turn now to the important concern of anticipating and responding to objections and counterarguments. In this section, we show you an extended example of a student's anticipating and responding to a reader's objection. We then describe a planning schema that can help you anticipate objections and show you how to respond to counterarguments, either through refutation or concession. Finally, we show how your active imagining of alternative views can lead you to qualify your claim.

Anticipating Objections: An Extended Example In our earlier discussions of the starling case, we saw how readers might object to the argument "The family was justified in killing the starlings because starlings are pests." What rankles these readers is the underlying assumption that it is okay to kill pests. Imagine an objecting reader saying something like this:

> It is *not* okay to get annoyed with a living creature, label it a "pest," and then kill it. This whole use of the term *pest* suggests that humans have the right to dominate nature. We need to have more reverence for nature. The ease with which the family solved their problem by killing living things sets a bad example for children. The family could have waited until fall and then fixed the screen.

Imagining such an objection might lead a writer to modify his or her claim. But if the writer remains committed to that claim, then he or she must develop a response. In the following example in which a student writer argues that it is okay to kill the starlings, note (1) how the writer uses evidence to show that starlings are pests; (2) how he summarizes a possible objection to his underlying assumption that killing pests is morally justified; and (3) how he supports his assumption with further arguments.

STUDENT ARGUMENT DEFENDING REASON AND UNDERLYING ASSUMPTION

The family was justified in killing the starlings because starlings are pests. Starlings are nonindigenous birds that drive out native species and multiply rapidly. When I searched "starlings pests" on Google, I discovered thousands of Web sites dealing with starlings as pests. Starlings are hated by farmers and gardeners because huge flocks of them devour newly planted seeds in spring as well as fruits and berries at harvest. A flock of starlings can devastate a cherry orchard in a few days. As invasive nesters, starlings can also damage attics by tearing up insulation and defecating

Claim with reason

Evidence that starlings are pests

on stored items. Many of the Web site articles focused on ways to kill off starling populations. In killing the starlings, the family was protecting its own property and reducing the population of these pests.

Summary of a possible objection

Many readers might object to my argument, saying that humans should have a reverence for nature and not quickly try to kill off any creature they label a pest. Further, these readers might say that even if starlings are pests, the family could have waited until fall to repair the attic or found some other means of protecting their property without having to kill the baby starlings. I too would have waited until fall if the birds in the attic had been swallows or some other native species without starlings' destructiveness and propensity for unchecked population growth. But starlings should be compared to rats or mice. We set traps for rodents because we know the damage they cause when they nest in walls and attics. We don't get sentimental trying to save the orphaned rat babies. In the same way, we are justified in eliminating starlings as soon as they begin infesting our houses.

Response to the objection

In the preceding example, we see how the writer uses evidence to support his reason and then, anticipating readers' objection to his underlying assumption, summarizes that objection and provides a response to it. One might not be convinced by the argument, but the writer has done a good job of trying to support both his reason (starlings are pests) and his underlying assumption (it is morally justifiable to kill at least some pests).

Using a Planning Schema to Anticipate Objections In the previous example, the student's arguing strategy was triggered by his anticipation of reader objections. Note that a skeptical audience can attack an argument by attacking either a writer's reasons or a writer's underlying assumptions. This knowledge allows us to create a planning schema that can help writers develop a persuasive argument. This schema encourages writers to articulate their argument frame (claim, reason, and underlying assumption) and then to imagine what kinds of evidence or arguments could be used to support both the reason and the underlying assumption. Equally important, the schema encourages writers to anticipate counterarguments by imagining how skeptical readers might object to the writer's reason or underlying assumption or both. To create the schema, simply make a chart with slots for each of these elements. Here is how another student writer used this schema to plan an argument on the starling case:

CLAIM WITH REASON

The family showed cruelty to animals because the way they killed the birds caused needless suffering.

UNDERLYING ASSUMPTION

If it is necessary to kill an animal, then the killing should be done in the least painful way possible.

EVIDENCE TO SUPPORT REASON

First I've got to show how the way of killing the birds (starving them slowly) caused the birds to suffer. I've also got to show that this way of killing was needless since other means were available such as calling an exterminator who would remove the birds and either relocate them or kill them painlessly. If no other alternative was available, someone should have crawled into the attic and found a painless way to kill the birds.

EVIDENCE/ARGUMENTS TO SUPPORT UNDERLYING ASSUMPTIONS

I've got to convince readers it is wrong to make an animal suffer if you don't have to. Humans have a natural antipathy to needless suffering—our feeling of unease if we imagine cattle or chickens caused to suffer for our food rather than being cleanly and quickly killed. If a horse is incurably wounded, we put it to sleep rather then let it suffer. We are morally obligated to cause the least pain possible.

WAYS SKEPTICS MIGHT OBJECT

How could a reader object to my reason? A reader might say that the starlings didn't suffer much (baby birds don't feel pain). A reader might also object to my claim that other means were available: They might say there was no other way to kill the starlings. Poison may cause just as much suffering. Cost of exterminator is prohibitive.

How could a reader object to my underlying assumption? Perhaps the reader would say that my rule to cause the least pain possible does not apply to animal pests. In class, someone said that we shouldn't worry about the baby starlings any more than we would worry about killing baby rats. Laws of nature condemn millions of animals each year to death by starvation or by being eaten alive by other animals. Humans occasionally have to take their place within this tooth-and-claw natural system.

How many of the ideas from this schema would the writer use in her actual paper? That is a judgment call based on the writer's analysis of the audience. If this student's target audience includes classmates who think it is morally okay to kill pests by the most efficient means possible, then she should summarize her classmates' argument fairly and then try to convince them that humans are ethically called to rise above tooth-and-claw nature.

FOR WRITING AND DISCUSSION

Creating Argument Schemas

Working individually or in small groups, create a planning schema for the following arguments. For each claim with reason: (a) imagine the kinds of evidence needed to support the reason; (b) identify the underlying assumption; (c) imagine a strategy for supporting the assumption; and (d) anticipate possible objections to the reason and to the assumption.

1. ***Claim with reason:*** We should buy a hybrid car rather than an SUV with a HEMI engine because doing so will help the world save gasoline. (Imagine this argument aimed at your significant other, who has his or her heart set on a huge HEMI-powered SUV.)
2. ***Claim with reason:*** Gay marriage should be legalized because doing so will promote faithful, monogamous relationships among lesbians and gay men. (Aim this argument at supporters of traditional marriage.)
3. ***Claim with reason:*** The war in Iraq was justified because it rid the world of a hideous and brutal dictator. (Aim this argument at a critic of the war.)

Responding to Objections, Counterarguments, and Alternative Views

We have seen how a writer needs to anticipate alternative views that give rise to objections and counterarguments. Surprisingly, one of the best ways to approach counterarguments is to summarize them fairly. Make your imagined reader's best case against your argument. By resisting the temptation to distort a counterargument, you demonstrate a willingness to consider the issue from all sides. Moreover, summarizing a counterargument reduces your reader's tendency to say, "Yes, but have you thought of...?" After you have summarized an objection or counterargument fairly and charitably, you must then decide how to respond to it. Your two main choices are to rebut it or concede to it.

Rebutting Opposing Views When rebutting or refuting an argument, you can question the argument's reasons and supporting evidence or the underlying assumptions or both. In the following student example, the writer summarizes her classmates' objections to abstract art and then analyzes shortcomings in their argument.

> Some of my classmates object to abstract art because it apparently takes no technical drawing talent. They feel that historically artists turned to abstract art because they lacked the technical drafting skills exhibited by Remington, Russell, and Rockwell. Therefore these abstract artists created an art form that anyone was capable of and that was less time consuming, and then they paraded it as artistic progress. But I object to the notion that these artists turned to abstraction because they could not do representative drawing. Many abstract artists, such as Picasso, were excellent draftsmen, and their early pieces show very realistic drawing skill. As his work matured, Picasso became more abstract in order to increase the expressive quality of his work. *Guernica* was meant as a protest against the bombing of that city by the Germans. To express the terror and suffering of the victims more vividly, he distorted the figures and presented them in a black and white journalistic manner. If he had used representational images and color—which he had the skill to do—much of the emotional content would have been lost and the piece probably would not have caused the demand for justice that it did.

Conceding to Opposing Views In some cases, an alternative view can be very strong. If so, don't hide that view from your readers; summarize it and concede to it.

Making concessions to opposing views is not necessarily a sign of weakness; in many cases, a concession simply acknowledges that the issue is complex and that your position is tentative. In turn, a concession can enhance a reader's respect for you and invite the reader to follow your example and weigh the strengths of your own argument charitably. Writers typically concede to opposing views with transitional expressions such as the following:

admittedly	I must admit that	I agree that	granted
even though	I concede that	while it is true that	

After conceding to an opposing view, you should shift to a different field of values where your position is strong and then argue for those new values. For example, adversaries of drug legalization argue plausibly that legalizing drugs would increase the number of users and addicts. If you support legalization, here is how you might deal with this point without fatally damaging your own argument:

> Opponents of legalization claim—and rightly so—that legalization will lead to an increase in drug users and addicts. I wish this weren't so, but it is. Nevertheless, the other benefits of legalizing drugs—eliminating the black market, reducing street crime, and freeing up thousands of police from fighting the war on drugs—more than outweigh the social costs of increased drug use and addiction, especially if tax revenues from drug sales are plowed back into drug education and rehabilitation programs.

The writer concedes that legalization will increase addiction (one reason for opposing legalization) and that drug addiction is bad (the underlying assumption for that reason). But then the writer redeems the case for legalization by shifting the argument to another field of values (the benefits of eliminating the black market, reducing crime, and so forth).

Qualifying Your Claim The need to summarize and respond to alternative views lets the writer see an issue's complexity and appreciate that no one position has a total monopoly on the truth. Consequently, writers often need to qualify their claims—that is, limit the scope or force of a claim to make it less sweeping and therefore less vulnerable. Consider the difference between the sentences "After-school jobs are bad for teenagers" and "After-school jobs are often bad for teenagers." The first claim can be refuted by one counterexample of a teenager who benefited from an after-school job. Because the second claim admits exceptions, it is much harder to refute. Unless your argument is airtight, you will want to limit your claim with qualifiers such as the following:

perhaps	maybe
in many cases	generally
tentatively	sometimes
often	usually
probably	likely
may *or* might (*rather than* is)	

You can also qualify a claim with an opening *unless* clause ("*Unless* your apartment is well soundproofed, you should not buy such a powerful stereo system").

Seeking Audience-Based Reasons

Much of the advice that we have presented so far can be consolidated into a single principle: Seek "audience-based reasons." By **audience-based reasons**, we mean reasons that depend on underlying assumptions, values, or beliefs that your targeted audience already holds. In such cases, you won't need to state and defend your underlying assumptions because the audience already accepts them. A good illustration comes from civil engineer David Rockwood's argument against wind power that we used in Chapter 1, page 15. Rockwood's targeted readers are environmentalists who have high hopes for wind-generated electricity. Rockwood's final reason opposing wind power is that constructing thousands of wind towers will damage the pristine mountain environment. To environmentalists, this reason is powerful because its underlying assumption ("Preserving the environment is good") appeals to their values.

When you plan your argument, seek audience-based reasons whenever possible. Suppose, for example, that you are advocating the legalization of heroin and cocaine. If you know that your audience is concerned about street crime, then you can argue that legalization of drugs will make the streets safer.

We should legalize drugs *because doing so will make our streets safer:* It will cut down radically on street criminals seeking drug money, and it will free up narcotics police to focus on other kinds of crime.

Audience-based reason: Underlying assumption is that making our streets safer is a good thing—a value the audience already holds.

For another group of readers—those concerned about improving the quality of life for youths in inner cities—you might argue that legalization of drugs will lead to better lives for people in poor neighborhoods.

We should legalize drugs *because doing so will improve the lives of inner-city youth* by eliminating the lure of drug trafficking that tempts so many inner-city youth into crime.

Audience-based reason: Its underlying assumption is that it is good to improve the lives of inner-city youth.

Or if your audience is concerned about high taxes and government debt, you might say:

We should legalize drugs *because doing so will help us balance federal and state budgets*: It will decrease police and prison costs by decriminalizing narcotics; and it will eliminate the black market in drugs, allowing us to collect taxes on drug sales.

Audience-based reason: Assumes that it is a good thing to balance federal and state budgets.

In contrast, if you oppose legalizing drugs, you could appeal to those concerned about drug addiction and public health by using the following audience-based reason:

We should not legalize drugs *because doing so will increase the number of drug addicts and make drug use seem socially acceptable.*

Audience-based reason: Appeals to the underlying assumption that increasing the number of drug addicts and making drugs socially acceptable are bad things.

In each case, you move people toward your position by connecting your argument to their beliefs and values.

Appealing to *Ethos* and *Pathos*

When the classical rhetoricians examined ways that orators could persuade listeners, they focused on three kinds of proofs: *logos,* the appeal to reason; *ethos,* the appeal to the speaker's character; and *pathos,* the appeal to the emotions and the sympathetic imagination. We introduced you to these appeals in Chapter 3, Concept 3.2, because they are important rhetorical considerations in any kind of writing. Understanding how arguments persuade through *logos, ethos,* and *pathos* is particularly helpful when your aim is persuasion. So far in this chapter we have focused on *logos*. In this section we examine *ethos* and *pathos*.

***Appeals to* Ethos** A powerful way to increase the persuasiveness of an argument is to gain your readers' trust. You appeal to *ethos* whenever you present yourself as credible and trustworthy. For most readers to accept your argument, they must perceive you as knowledgeable, trustworthy, and fair. In the following chart, we suggest ways to enhance your argument's *ethos:*

Strategies for Enhancing Your Argument's *Ethos*

What to Do	Explanation
Be knowledgeable by doing your homework.	Your credibility is enhanced when readers are convinced that you know your subject thoroughly.
Use evidence responsibly.	If you cherry-pick your evidence, you may be perceived as a propagandist rather than as a thoughtful arguer who recognizes complexity.
Be fair to alternative views.	If you scorn or misrepresent opposing views, you will win favor only with those who already agree with you. If you are a good listener to others, they will be more apt to listen to you.
Search for values and assumptions you can share with your audience.	You will build bridges toward skeptical readers, rather than alienate them, if you can highlight shared assumptions or values. Use audience-based reasons where possible.
Show that you care about your issue; show also why your readers should care about it.	By showing why the issue matters both to you and your readers, you portray yourself as a person of integrity rather than as someone playing an argumentative game.

***Appeals to* Pathos** Besides appealing to *logos* and *ethos,* you might also appeal to what the Greeks called *pathos*. Sometimes *pathos* is interpreted narrowly as an appeal to the emotions and is therefore devalued on the grounds that arguments should be rational rather than emotional. Although appeals to *pathos* can sometimes be irrational and irrelevant ("If you don't give me at least a B in this course, I will lose my scholarship and break my ill grandmother's heart"), they can also arouse audience interest and deepen understanding of an argument's human dimensions. The following chart suggests ways to increase *pathos* in your arguments:

Strategies for Enhancing Your Argument's *Pathos*

What to Do	Explanation	Example
Include storylike anecdotes.	Specific stories often create more emotional appeal than abstract statistics or generalizations.	In promoting health care reform, President Obama often told stories of persons made bankrupt by an illness or deprived of care because of a preexisting condition. On many occasions, he spoke of his own mother's fight with insurance companies as she lay dying of cancer.
Choose words with emotional or values-laden connotations.	Connotations of words often carry heavy emotional impact.	Opponents of health care reform talked about the Democrats' bill as "being jammed down people's throats"; supporters used words like "safety net," "compassion," or "care for children in poverty."
Where appropriate, use vivid language low on the ladder of abstraction.	Specific words paint pictures that have emotional appeal.	"The homeless man is huddled over the sewer grate, his feet wrapped in newspapers. He blows on his hands, then tucks them under his armpits and lies down on the sidewalk with his shoulders over the grate, his bed for the night." *[creates sympathy for the homeless]* "Several ratty derelicts drinking wine from a shared sack caused shoppers to avoid going into the store." *[creates sympathy for shoppers rather than the homeless]*
If the genre permits, include visuals with emotional impact.	Photographs or other visuals, including dramatic graphs or charts, can have a strong emotional appeal.	Articles promoting the environment often include photographs of smoke-belching factories or of endangered animals (often emphasizing their beauty or cuteness); often charts can have emotional appeals—such as a graph portraying dramatic increases in coal-fired electricity plants.

A Brief Primer on Informal Fallacies

We'll conclude our explanation of classical argument with a brief overview of the most common informal fallacies. Informal fallacies are instances of murky reasoning that can cloud an argument and lead to unsound conclusions. Because they can crop up unintentionally in anyone's writing, and because advertisers and hucksters often use them intentionally to deceive, it is a good idea to learn to recognize the more common fallacies.

Post Hoc, Ergo Propter Hoc *("After This, Therefore Because of This")* This fallacy involves mistaking sequence for cause. Just because one event happens before another event doesn't mean the first event caused the second. The connection may be coincidental, or some unknown third event may have caused both of these events.

Example When the New York police department changed its policing tactics in the early 1990s, the crime rate plummeted. But did the new police tactics cause the decline in crime? (Many experts attributed the decline to other causes.) Persons lauding the police tactics ("Crime declined because the NYPD adopted new tactics") were accused of the *post hoc* fallacy.

Hasty Generalization Closely related to the *post hoc* fallacy is the hasty generalization, which refers to claims based on insufficient or unrepresentative data. Generally, persuasive evidence should meet the STAR criteria that we explained on page 320. Because the amount of evidence needed in a given case can vary with the audience's degree of skepticism, it is difficult to draw an exact line between hasty and justified generalizations.

Example The news frequently carries stories about vicious pit bulls. Therefore all pit bills must be vicious. [or] This experimental drug has been demonstrated safe in numerous clinical trials [based on tests using adult subjects]. Therefore this drug is safe for children.

False Analogy Arguers often use analogies to support a claim. (We shouldn't go to war in Iraq because doing so will lead us into a Vietnam-like quagmire.) However, analogical arguments are tricky because there are usually significant differences between the two things being compared as well as similarities. (Supporters of the war in Iraq argued that the situation in Iraq in 2002 was very different from that in Vietnam in 1964.) Although it is hard to draw an exact line between a false analogy and an acceptable one, charges of false analogy are frequent when skeptical opponents try to refute arguments based on analogies.

Example Gun control will work in the United States because it works in England. [or] It's a mistake to force little Johnnie to take piano lessons because you can't turn a reluctant child into a musician any more than you can turn a tulip into a rose.

Either/Or Reasoning This fallacy occurs when a complex, multisided issue is reduced to two positions without acknowledging the possibility of other alternatives.

Example Either you are pro-choice on abortion or you are against the advancement of women in our culture.

Ad Hominem *("Against the Person")* When people can't find fault with an argument, they sometimes attack the arguer, substituting irrelevant assertions about that person's character for an analysis of the argument itself.

Example We should discount Senator Jones's argument against nuclear power because she has huge holdings in oil stock.

Appeals to False Authority and Bandwagon Appeals These fallacies offer as support the fact that a famous person or "many people" already support it. Unless the supporters are themselves authorities in the field, their support is irrelevant.

Example Buy Freeble oil because Joe Quarterback always uses it in his fleet of cars. [or] How can abortion be wrong if millions of people support a woman's right to choose?

Non Sequitur *("It Does Not Follow")* This fallacy occurs when there is no evident connection between a claim and its reason. Sometimes a *non sequitur* can be repaired by filling in gaps in the reasoning; at other times, the reasoning is simply fallacious.

Example I don't deserve a B for this course because I am a straight-A student.

Circular Reasoning This fallacy occurs when you state your claim and then, usually after rewording it, you state it again as your reason.

Example Marijuana is injurious to your health because it harms your body.

Red Herring This fallacy refers to the practice of raising an unrelated or irrelevant point deliberately to throw an audience offtrack. Politicians often employ this fallacy when they field questions from the public or press.

Example You raise a good question about my support of companies' outsourcing jobs to find cheaper labor. Let me tell you about my admiration for the productivity of the American worker.

Slippery Slope The slippery slope fallacy is based on the fear that one step in a direction we don't like inevitably leads to the next step with no stopping place.

Example If we allow embryonic stem cells to be used for medical research, we will open the door for full-scale reproductive cloning.

A Classical Argument

Write a position paper that takes a stand on a controversial issue. Your introduction should present your issue, provide background, and state the claim you intend to support. In constructing your claim, strive to develop audience-based reasons. The body of your argument should summarize and respond to opposing views as well as present reasons and evidence in support of your own position. You will need to choose whether to summarize and refute opposing views before or after you have made your own case. Try to end your essay with your strongest arguments. Try also to include appeals to *pathos* and to create a positive, credible *ethos*.

WRITING PROJECT

13.2
Write a classical argument that offers reasons and evidence in support of your position while also summarizing and responding to opposing views.

We call this assignment a "classical" argument because it is patterned after the persuasive speeches of ancient Greek and Roman orators. A framework chart showing the generic structure of a classical argument is shown in Figure 13.1. Although there are many other ways to persuade audiences, the classical approach is a particularly effective introduction to persuasive writing.

FIGURE 13.1 Framework for a Classical Argument

INTRODUCTION	• Attention-grabber (often a memorable scene) • Explanation of issue and needed background • Writer's thesis (claim) • Forecasting passage
PRESENTATION OF WRITER'S POSITION	• Main body of essay • Presents and supports each reason in turn • Each reason is tied to a value or belief held by the audience
SUMMARY OF OPPOSING VIEWS	• Summary of views differing from writer's (should be fair and complete)
RESPONSE TO OPPOSING VIEWS	• Refutes or concedes to opposing views • Shows weaknesses in opposing views • May concede to some strengths
CONCLUSION	• Brings essay to closure • Often sums up argument • Leaves strong, lasting impression • Often calls for action or relates topic to a larger context of issues

Generating and Exploring Ideas

The tasks that follow are intended to help you generate ideas for your argument. Our goal is to help you build up a storehouse of possible issues, explore several of these possibilities, and then choose one for deeper exploration before you write your initial draft.

Finding an Issue If you are having trouble finding an arguable issue for this writing project, consider the following strategies:

Strategies for Finding an Arguable Issue

What to Do	Explanation
Make an inventory of various communities you belong to.	See the exercise on page 333. Communities can range from the local (family, dorm, campus) to the state, nation, and world.
Brainstorm contested issues in these communities.	Start off with a fairly large list and then narrow it down according to your personal interest, current knowledge level, and degree of engagement.
On a few of these issues, explore the causes of disagreement.	Ask questions like these: What is at the heart of the disagreement? Disagreement about facts? About beliefs and values? About benefits versus costs?
Then explore your own point of view.	Ask: What is my position on the issue and why? What are alternative points of view? What is at stake?
Determine how much research you'll need to do.	If your issue requires research (check with your instructor), do a bibliographic search and enough skim reading to determine the kinds of arguments surrounding your issue, the kinds of evidence available, and the alternative views that people have taken.
Choose your issue and begin your research.	Your goal is to "wallow in complexity" in order to earn your thesis and create a knowledgeable *ethos*. Note: Some issues allow you to argue from personal experience (see Ross Taylor's argument on paintball, pp. 337–339). Again, check with your instructor.
Brainstorm claims and reasons on various sides of the issue.	State your own claim and possible *because* clause reasons in support of your claim. Do the same thing for one or more opposing or alternative claims.

Conduct an In-Depth Exploration Prior to Drafting

The following set of tasks is designed to help you explore your issue in depth. Most students take one or two hours to complete these tasks; the time will pay off, however, because most of the ideas that you need for your rough draft will be on paper.

1. Write out the issue your argument will address. Try phrasing your issue in several different ways, perhaps as a yes/no question and as an open-ended question. Try making the question broader, then narrower. Finally, frame the question in the way that most appeals to you.

See the discussion of issue questions on p. 313.

2. Now write out your tentative answer to the question. This will be your beginning thesis statement or claim. Put a box around this answer. Next, write out one or more different answers to your question. These will be alternative claims that a neutral audience might consider.
3. Why is this a controversial issue? Is there insufficient evidence to resolve the issue, or is the evidence ambiguous or contradictory? Are definitions in dispute? Do the parties disagree about basic values, assumptions, or beliefs?
4. What personal interest do you have in this issue? How does the issue affect you? Why do you care about it? (Knowing why you care about it might help you get your audience to care about it.)
5. What reasons and evidence support your position on this issue? Freewrite everything that comes to mind that might help you support your case. This freewrite will eventually provide the bulk of your argument. For now, freewrite rapidly without worrying whether your argument makes sense. Just get ideas on paper.
6. Imagine all the counterarguments your audience might make. Summarize the main arguments against your position and then freewrite your response to each of the counterarguments. What are the flaws in the alternative points of view?
7. What kinds of appeals to *ethos* and *pathos* might you use to support your argument? How can you increase your audience's perception of your credibility and trustworthiness? How can you tie your argument to your audience's beliefs and values?
8. Why is this an important issue? What are the broader implications and consequences? What other issues does it relate to? Thinking of possible answers to these questions may prove useful when you write your introduction or conclusion.

Shaping and Drafting

Once you have explored your ideas, create a plan. Here is a suggested procedure:

Begin your planning by analyzing your intended audience. You could imagine an audience deeply resistant to your views or a more neutral, undecided audience acting like a jury. In some cases, your audience might be a single person, as when you petition your department chair to waive a requirement in your major. At other times, your audience might be the general readership of a newspaper, church bulletin, or magazine. When the audience is a general readership, you need to imagine from the start the kinds of readers you particularly want to sway. Here are some questions you can ask:

- ***How much does your audience know or care about your issue?*** Will you need to provide background? Will you need to convince them that your issue is important? Do you need to hook their interest? Your answers to these questions will particularly influence your introduction and conclusion.
- ***What is your audience's current attitude toward your issue?*** Are they deeply opposed to your position? If so, why? Are they neutral and undecided? If so, what other views will they be listening to?
- ***How do your audience's values, assumptions, and beliefs differ from your own?*** What aspects of your position will be threatening to your audience? Why? How does your position on the issue challenge your imagined reader's worldview or identity? What objections will your audience raise toward your argument? Your answers to these questions will help determine the content of your argument and alert you to the extra research you may have to do to respond to audience objections.
- ***What values, beliefs, or assumptions about the world do you and your audience share?*** Despite your differences with your audience, where can you find common links? How might you use these links to build bridges to your audience?

Your next step is to plan an audience-based argument by seeking audience-based reasons or reasons whose underlying assumptions you can defend. Here is a process you can use:

1. Create a skeleton, tree diagram, outline, or flowchart for your argument by stating your reasons as one or more *because* clauses attached to your claim. Each *because* clause will become the head of a main section or *line of reasoning* in your argument.
2. Use the planning schema on pages 315–316 to plan each line of reasoning. If your audience accepts your underlying assumption, you can concentrate on supporting your reason with evidence. However, if your audience is apt to reject the underlying assumption for one of your lines of reasoning, then you'll need to state it directly and argue for it. Try to anticipate audience objections by exploring ways that an audience might question either your reasons or your underlying assumptions.
3. Using the skeleton you created, finish developing an outline or tree diagram for your argument. Although the organization of each part of your argument will grow organically from its content, the main parts of your classical argument should match the framework chart shown on page 331 (Figure 13.1).

This classical model can be modified in numerous ways. A question that often arises is where to summarize and respond to objections and counterarguments. Writers generally have three choices: One option is to handle opposing positions before you present your own argument. The rationale for this approach is that skeptical audiences may be more inclined to listen attentively to your argument if they have been assured that you understand their point of view. A second option is to place this material after you have presented your argument. This approach is effective for neutral audiences who don't start off with strong opposing views. A final option is to intersperse opposing views throughout your argument at appropriate moments. Any of these possibilities, or a combination of all of them, can be effective.

Another question often asked is, "What is the best way to order one's reasons?" A general rule of thumb when ordering your own argument is to put your strongest reason last and your second-strongest reason first. The idea here is to start and end with your most powerful arguments. If you imagine a quite skeptical audience, build bridges to your audience by summarizing alternative views early in the paper and concede to those that are especially strong. If your audience is neutral or undecided, you can summarize and respond to possible objections after you have presented your own case.

Revising

As you revise your argument, you need to attend both to the clarity of your writing (all the principles of closed-form prose described in Chapter 17) and also to the persuasiveness of your argument. As always, peer reviews are valuable, and especially so in argumentation if you ask your peer reviewers to role-play an opposing audience.

Questions for Peer Review

In addition to the generic peer review questions explained in Skill 16.4, ask your peer reviewers to address these questions:

INTRODUCTION

1. How could the title be improved so that it announces the issue, reveals the writer's claim, or otherwise focuses your expectations and piques interest?
2. What strategies does the writer use to introduce the issue, engage your interest, and convince you that the issue is significant and problematic? What would add clarity and appeal?
3. How could the introduction more effectively forecast the argument and present the writer's claim? What would make the statement of the claim more focused, clear, or risky?

ARGUING FOR THE CLAIM

1. Consider the overall structure: What strategies does the writer use to make the structure of the paper clear and easy to follow? How could the structure of the argument be improved?
2. Consider the support for the reasons: Where could the writer provide better evidence or support for each line of reasoning? Look for the kinds of evidence for each line of reasoning by noting the writer's use of facts, examples,

statistics, testimony, or other evidence. Where could the writer supply more evidence or use existing evidence more effectively?

3. Consider the support for the underlying assumptions: For each line of reasoning, determine the assumptions that the audience needs to grant for the argument to be effective. Are there places where these assumptions need to be stated directly and supported with arguments? How could support for the assumptions be improved?
4. Consider the writer's summary of and response to alternative viewpoints: Where does the writer treat alternative views? Are there additional alternative views that the writer should consider? What strategies does the writer use to respond to alternative views? How could the writer's treatment of alternative views be improved?

CONCLUSION

1. How might the conclusion more effectively bring completeness or closure to the argument?

WRITING PROJECT

Multimodal or Online Options

1. **Speech with Visual Aids (Flip Chart, PowerPoint, Prezi)** Deliver your classical argument as a formal speech supported with visual aids. You can imagine an occasion for a short speech limited to 3–5 minutes (modeled, say, after public hearings) or a longer presentation such as a TED talk. Pay equal attention to the construction and delivery of your speech and to the multimodal design of the visual aids.
2. **Persuasive Poster or Advocacy Ad** Create a one-page poster or advocacy ad that captures your argument in a highly condensed verbal/visual form. Consider how you will use all the features of visual argument—type sizes and fonts, layout, color, and images and graphics—to grab the attention of your audience and drive home your claim.
3. **Video** Create a short video aimed at moving neutral or opposing audiences toward your point of view. Use the resources of music, voice, words, and images to reach audiences who might not be expected to read your print argument. Conversely, create a video aimed at increasing the enthusiasm of people who already support your position. Your goal is to call them to action in some way (donate funds, vote, participate in a rally or strike).
4. **T-shirt or Bumper Sticker as Part of a Campaign Plan** Imagine a full-fledged campaign advocating your position on an issue. Design a T-shirt or bumper sticker in support of your claim.

For advice on producing multimedia compositions see Chapter 19. For an example of a student speech with PowerPoint slides, see Chapter 15, pp. 402–404

Our first reading, by student writer Ross Taylor, aims to increase appreciation of paintball as a healthy sport. An avid paintballer, Ross was frustrated by how many of his friends and acquaintances didn't appreciate paintball and had numerous misconceptions about it. The following argument is aimed at those who don't understand the sport or those who condemn it for being dangerous and violent.

Ross Taylor (student)

Paintball:

Promoter of Violence or Healthy Fun?

1 Glancing out from behind some cover, I see an enemy soldier on the move. I level my gun and start pinching off rounds. Hearing the incoming fire, he turns and starts to fire, but it is far too late. His entire body flinches when I land two torso shots, and he falls when I hit his leg. I duck back satisfied with another good kill on my record. I pop up again, this time to scan for more enemy forces. Out of the corner of my eye I see some movement and turn to see two soldiers peeking out from behind a sewer pipe. I move to take cover again, but it's futile. I feel the hits come one by one hitting me three times in the chest and once on the right bicep before I fall behind the cover. I'm hit. It's all over—for me at least. The paintball battle rages on as I carefully leave the field to nurse my welts, which are already showing. Luckily, I watch my three remaining teammates trample the two enemy soldiers who shot me to win the game. This is paintball in all its splendor and glory.

2 Paintball is one of the most misunderstood and generally looked down upon recreational activities. People see it as rewarding violence and lacking the true characteristics of a healthy team sport like ultimate Frisbee, soccer, or pickup basketball. Largely the accusations directed at paintball are false because it is a positive recreational activity. Paintball is a fun, athletic, mentally challenging recreational activity that builds teamwork and releases tension.

3 Paintball was invented in the early 1980s as a casual activity for survival enthusiasts, but it has grown into a several hundred million dollar industry. It is, quite simply, an expanded version of tag. Players use a range of CO_2 powered guns that fire small biodegradable marbles of paint at approximately 250–300 feet per second. The result of a hit is a small splatter of oily paint and a nice dark bruise. Paintball is now played nationwide in indoor and outdoor arenas. Quite often variants are played such as "Capture the Flag" or "Assassination." In "Capture the Flag" the point is to retrieve the heavily guarded flag from the other team and return it to your base. The game of "Assassination" pits one team of "assassins" against the "secret service." The secret service men guard an unarmed player dubbed the "president." Their goal is get from point A to point B without the president's getting tagged. Contrary to popular belief, the games are highly officiated and organized. There is always a referee present. Barrel plugs are required until just before a game begins and must be reinserted as soon as the game ends. No hostages may be taken. A player catching another off guard at close range must first give the player the opportunity to surrender. Most importantly

there is no physical contact between players. Punching, pushing, or butt-ending with the gun is strictly prohibited. The result is an intense game that is relatively safe for all involved.

4 The activity of paintball is athletically challenging. There are numerous sprint and dives to avoid being hit. At the end of a game, typically lasting around 20 minutes, all the players are winded, sweaty, and ultimately exhilarated. The beginning of the game includes a mad dash for cover by both teams with heavy amounts of fire being exchanged. During the game, players execute numerous strategic moves to gain a tactical advantage, often including quick jumps, dives, rolls, and runs. While undercover, players crawl across broad stretches of playing field often still feeling their bruises from previous games. These physical feats culminate in an invigorating and physically challenging activity good for building muscles and coordination.

5 In addition to the athletic challenge, paintball provides strong mental challenge, mainly the need for constant strategizing. There are many strategic positioning methods. For example, the classic pincer move involves your team's outflanking an opponent from each side to eliminate his or her mobility and shelter. In the more sophisticated ladder technique, teammates take turns covering each other as the others move onward from cover to cover. Throughout the game, players' minds are constantly reeling as they calculate their positions and cover, their teammates' positions and cover, and their opponents' positions and strength. Finally, there is the strong competitive pull of the individual. It never fails to amaze me how much thought goes into one game.

6 Teamwork is also involved. Paintball takes a lot of cooperation. You need special hand signals to communicate with your teammates, and you have to coordinate, under rapidly changing situations, who is going to flank left or right, who is going to charge, and who is going to stay back to guard the flag station. The importance of teamwork in paintball explains why more and more businesses are taking their employees for a day of action with the intent of creating a closer knit and smooth-functioning workplace. The value of teamwork is highlighted on the Web site of a British Columbia facility, Action and Adventure Paintball, Ltd, which says that in paintball,

> as in any team sport, the team that communicates best usually wins. It's about thinking, not shooting. This is why Fortune 500 companies around the world take their employees to play paintball together.

An advantage of paintball for building company team spirit is that paintball teams, unlike teams in many other recreational sports, can blend very skilled and totally unskilled players. Women like paintball as much as men, and the game is open to people of any size, body type, and strength level. Since a game usually takes no more than seven to ten minutes, teams can run a series of different games with different players to have lots of different match-ups. Also families like to play paintball together.

7 People who object to paintball criticize its danger and violence. The game's supposed danger gets mentioned a lot. The public seems to have received the impression that paintball guns are simply eye-removing hardware. It is true that paintball can lead to eye injuries. An article by medical writer Cheryl Guttman in a trade magazine for ophthalmologists warns that eye injuries from paintball are on the rise. But the fact

is that Guttman's article says that only 102 cases of eye injuries from paintballs were reported from 1985 to 2000 and that 85 percent of those injured were not wearing the required safety goggles. This is not to say that accidents don't happen. I personally had a friend lose an eye after inadvertently shooting himself in the eye from a very close range. The fact of the matter is that he made a mistake by looking down the barrel of a loaded gun and the trigger malfunctioned. Had he been more careful or worn the proper equipment, he most likely would have been fine. During my first organized paintball experience I was hit in the goggles by a very powerful gun and felt no pain. The only discomfort came from having to clean all the paint off my goggles after the game. When played properly, paintball is an incredibly safe sport.

8 The most powerful argument against paintball is that it is inherently violent and thus unhealthy. Critics claim paintball is simply an accepted form of promoting violence against other people. I have anti-war friends who think that paintball glorifies war. Many new parents today try to keep their kids from playing cops and robbers and won't buy them toy guns. These people see paintball as an upgraded and more violent version of the same antisocial games they don't want their children to play. Some people also point to the connections between paintball and violent video games where participants get their fun from "killing" other people. They link paintball to all the other violent activities that they think lead to such things as gangs or school shootings. But there is no connection between school shootings and paintball. As seen in Michael Moore's *Bowling for Columbine,* the killers involved there went bowling before the massacre; they didn't practice their aim by playing paintball.

9 What I am trying to say is that, yes, paintball is violent to a degree. After all, its whole point is to "kill" each other with guns. But I object to paintball's being considered a promotion of violence. Rather, I feel that it is a healthy release of tension. From my own personal experience, when playing the game, the players aren't focused on hurting the other players; they are focused on winning the game. At the end of the day, players are not full of violent urges, but just the opposite. They want to celebrate together as a team, just as do softball or soccer teams after a game. Therefore I don't think paintball is an unhealthy activity for adults. (The only reason I wouldn't include children is because I believe the pain is too intense for them. I have seen some younger players cry after being shot.) Paintball is simply a game, a sport, that produces intense exhilaration and fun. Admittedly, paintball guns can be used in irresponsible manners. Recently there have been some drive-by paintballings, suggesting that paintball players are irresponsible and violent. However, the percentage of people who do this sort of prank is very small and those are the bad apples of the group. There will always be those who misuse equipment. For example, baseball bats have been used in atrocious beatings, but that doesn't make baseball a violent sport. So despite the bad apples, paintball is still a worthwhile activity when properly practiced.

10 Athletic and mentally challenging, team-building and fun—the game of paintball seems perfectly legitimate to me. It is admittedly violent, but it is not the evil activity that critics portray. Injuries can occur, but usually only when the proper safety equipment is not being used and proper precautions are ignored. As a great recreational activity, paintball deserves the same respect as other sports. It is a great way to get physical exercise, make friends, and have fun.

THINKING CRITICALLY
about "Paintball: Promoter of Violence or Healthy Fun?"

1. Before reading this essay, what was your own view of paintball? To what extent did this argument create for you a more positive view of paintball? What aspects of the argument did you find particularly effective or ineffective?
2. How effective are Ross's appeals to *ethos* in this argument? Does he create a persona that you find trustworthy and compelling? How does he do so or fail to do so?
3. How effective are Ross's appeals to *pathos*? How does he appeal to his readers' values, interests, and emotions in trying to make paintball seem like an exhilarating team sport? To what extent does he show empathy with readers when he summarizes objections to paintball?
4. How effective are Ross's appeals to *logos*? How effective are Ross's reasons and evidence in support of his claim? How effective are Ross's responses to opposing views?
5. What are the main strengths and weaknesses of Ross's argument?

Our next three readings address the ongoing controversy over whether women belong in active combat units, fighting in the U.S. military forces. Although a decision was made by Secretary of Defense Leon Panetta to lift the ban on women in combat in 2013, various positions on this issue continue to be debated, perhaps because it touches so many other areas: national security; the history, present conditions, and symbolism of the military; assumptions about men's and women's physical capacities and psychological make-up, among others.

Our first reading is by Dr. Megan H. Mackenzie who researches and writes in the areas of feminist security studies, international relations, gender and the military, and the aftermath of war. Her book *Female Soldiers in Sierra Leone: Sex, Security, and Post-Conflict Development* was published in 2012. She is a lecturer in the Department of Government and International Relations at the University of Sydney (Australia). She has also held a post-doctoral fellowship at the Belfer Center for International Security and the Women and Public Policy Program at Harvard University. This article appeared in *Foreign Affairs,* a well-established and influential journal on international affairs and foreign policy, in the November-December 2012 issue, just before Secretary Panetta lifted the ban on women in combat.

Megan H. Mackenzie

Let Women Fight

1 Today, 214,098 women serve in the U.S. military, representing 14.6 percent of total service members. Around 280,000 women have worn American uniforms in Afghanistan and Iraq, where 144 have died and over 600 have been injured. Hundreds of female soldiers have received a Combat Action Badge, awarded for actively engaging with a hostile enemy. Two women, Sergeant Leigh Ann Hester and Specialist Monica Lin Brown, have been awarded Silver Stars—one of the highest military decorations awarded for valor in combat—for their service in Afghanistan and Iraq.

2 Yet the U.S. military, at least officially, still bans women from serving in direct combat positions. As irregular warfare has become increasingly common in the last few decades, the difference on the ground between the frontline and support roles is no longer clear. Numerous policy changes have also eroded the division between combat and noncombat positions. More and more military officials recognize the contributions made by female soldiers, and politicians, veterans, and military experts have all begun actively lobbying Washington to drop the ban. But Congress has not budged.

3 Proponents of the policy, who include Duncan Hunter (R-Calif.), former chair of the House Armed Services Committee, and former Senator Rick Santorum (R-Pa.), rely on three central arguments: that women cannot meet the physical requirements necessary to fight, that they simply don't belong in combat, and that their inclusion in fighting units would disrupt those units' cohesion and battle readiness. Yet these arguments do not stand up to current data on women's performance in combat or their impact on troop dynamics. Banning women from combat does not ensure military effectiveness. It only perpetuates counterproductive gender stereotypes and biases. It is time for the U.S. military to get over its hang-ups and acknowledge women's rightful place on the battlefield.

Women in a Man's World

4 Women have long served in various auxiliary military roles during wars. Further, the 1948 Women's Armed Services Integration Act created a permanent corps of women in all the military departments. This was considered a step forward at the time, but it is also the origin of the current combat ban. The act limited women's number to two percent of total service members and formally excluded them from combat duties. The exclusion policy was reinforced in 1981, when the U.S. Supreme Court ruled that the all-male draft did not constitute gender-based discrimination since it was intended to increase combat troops and women were already restricted from combat.

5 Despite this restriction, the share of women in the U.S. armed forces increased in the 1980s and 1990s, from 8.5 percent to 11.1 percent, as a result of the transition to an all-volunteer force in 1973 and high demand for troops. Today, the air force is the most open service for women. Women have been flying in combat aircrafts since 1993, and they now make up 70 of the 3,700 fighter pilots in the service.

6 In the rest of the military, restrictions on women have also been slipping for some time, albeit more slowly, due to an increase in female enlistment and the public's growing sensitivity to equal labor rights. In January 1994, a memorandum from then Secretary of Defense Les Aspin rescinded the "risk rule" barring women from any positions that could expose them to direct combat, hostile fire, or capture; the rule was replaced by the "direct ground combat assignment rule," which more narrowly tailored the restriction to frontline combat positions.

7 Recent policy changes have also blurred the distinction between combat and support roles. In 2003, the army began reorganizing units and increasing the number of brigades within each division. Under this system, forward support companies, which provide logistical support, transportation, and maintenance to battalions, are now grouped together on the same bases as combat units. Since women are permitted to serve in such support units, a major barrier designed to keep them away from combat has almost vanished.

8 The assignment of women to combat-related tasks has further undermined the strength of the ban. Beginning in 2003, for example, so-called Lioness teams were deployed to assist combat units in Iraq searching women for weapons and explosives. Drawing from this model, the military created several other female-only units in 2009, including "female engagement teams." In their first year of operation, these teams conducted over 70 short-term search-and-engagement missions in Afghanistan. Paying lip service to the exclusion policy, the military specified that these units could not contribute to hunt-and-kill foot patrols and should stay at combat bases only temporarily. In practice, however, this meant that female soldiers were required to leave their combat bases for one night every six weeks before immediately returning. Not only did this practice put women at risk with unnecessary travel in an insecure environment; it also exemplifies the waste and hardship that the preservation of the formal ban imposes on the military.

9 Meanwhile, the U.S. military is finding different ways to recognize the fact that women now fight in the country's wars. Members of forward support companies and female engagement teams now receive combat pay, also known as "hostile fire" or "imminent danger" pay, acknowledging the threats women regularly face. And 78 percent of the deaths of female U.S. service members in Iraq were categorized as hostile, yet another sign of how American women in uniform regularly put their lives at risk.

10 In light of all these changes, in 2011 the Military Leadership Diversity Commission recommended that the Department of Defense remove all combat restrictions on women. Although the total number of jobs closed to women is now relatively low, at 7.3 percent, the commission found that "exclusion from these occupations has a considerable influence on advancement to higher positions" and that eliminating the exclusion is essential "to create a level playing field for all service members who meet the qualifications." Echoing this sentiment, Senator Kirsten Gillibrand (D-N.Y.) introduced the Gender Equality in Combat Act in 2012, which seeks the termination of the ground combat exclusion policy. In addition, Command Sergeant Major Jane Baldwin and Colonel Ellen Haring, both of the Army Reserve, filed a lawsuit in May against the secretary of defense and the army's secretary, assistant secretary, and deputy chief of staff claiming that the exclusion policy violates their constitutional rights.

Responding to growing scrutiny, the Pentagon's press secretary, George Little, announced on February 9, 2012, that the Department of Defense would continue to remove restrictions on women's roles. Since then, the military has made a slew of policy revisions and commissioned a series of reviews. In May 2012, for example, the army opened up more than 14,000 combat-related jobs to women. Much of this increase, however, came from officially recognizing the combat-related nature of the jobs conducted by medics and intelligence officers, among others, positions that are already open to women. More substantially, the Marine Corps announced in April 2012 that for the first time, women can enroll and train, but not yet serve, as infantry combat officers. The army has also opened six new combat-related occupational specialties to women. In June 2012, Cicely Verstein became the first woman to serve in one of these newly opened combat support roles when she enlisted as a Bradley Fighting Vehicle systems maintainer. Women such as Verstein can now operate with combat arms units in select positions, yet they are still technically restricted from infantry and special operations roles.

12 Although the ban still exists on paper, the military is finding various ways to lift it in practice, and so the complete repeal of the policy would not constitute a radical change in operational terms. But it would be an acknowledgment of the contributions that women are already making to U.S. military operations. As Anu Bhagwati, a former Marine captain and now executive director of the Service Women's Action Network, explained in a BBC News interview, "Women are being shot at, are being killed overseas, are being attached to all of these combat arms units.... The [combat exclusion] policy has to catch up to reality." Indeed, all soldiers, female as well as male, have been given extensive combat training since 2003, when the army altered its basic training procedures in response to the growth of irregular warfare in Afghanistan and Iraq. The main obstacle that remains for women who want to serve their country is an outmoded set of biased assumptions about their capabilities and place in society.

Why Women Can Keep Up

13 The argument that women are not physically fit for combat is perhaps the most publicized and well-researched justification for their exclusion from fighting units. In her 2000 book, *The Kinder, Gentler Military,* the journalist Stephanie Gutmann summarized the position this way: "When butts drop onto seats, and feet grope for foot pedals, and girls of five feet one (not an uncommon height in the ranks) put on great bowl-like Kevlar helmets over a full head of long hair done up in a French braid, there are problems of fit — and those picayune fit problems ripple outward, eventually affecting performance, morale, and readiness."

14 This argument continues to receive a significant amount of attention in the United States, despite the fact that other militaries across the world have found that with proper training and necessary adaptations, women can complete the same physical tasks as men. In the 1970s, the Canadian military conducted trials that tested women's physical, psychological, and social capacity for combat roles. The results informed the final decision of the Canadian Human Rights Tribunal to remove Canada's female combat exclusion. After similar tests, Denmark also lifted its combat ban in the late 1980s.

15 The physical fitness argument, which tends to focus on differences between average male and female bodies, is also undermined by the fact that women who join

the military tend to be more fit than the average American. Additional training and conditioning further decrease the gap between female and male service members, and evidence indicates that women usually benefit substantially from fitness-training programs. More to the point, performance is not necessarily determined by gender; it is determined by other attributes and by an individual's determination to reach physical prowess. To put it bluntly, there are physically fit, tough women who are suitable for combat, and weak, feeble men who are not.

16 The U.S. armed services would do a better job recognizing this were it not for the fact that, as critics have pointed out, the military's physical standards were created to measure male fitness, not job effectiveness. As Matthew Brown, a U.S. Army colonel and director of the Arizona Army National Guard, found in a U.S. Army War College study, "There is no conclusive evidence that all military members, regardless of occupational specialty, unit assignment, age or gender, should acquire the same level of physical fitness." The U.S. General Accounting Office (now the Government Accountability Office) also admitted in a 1998 report that physical fitness tests are not necessarily a useful gauge of operational effectiveness, explaining, "fitness testing is not aimed at assessing the capability to perform specific missions or military jobs." To be sure, men and women have different types of bodies, but growing research points to the limitations of having a single male-centered standard for fitness and equipment. Recently, for example, the army has moved to design body armor for women rather than force them to continue wearing equipment that restricts their movement and cuts into their legs because it was designed for men. With proper training and equipment, women can contribute to missions just as well as men.

Breaking Up the Band of Brothers

17 Even though the physical argument does not hold up to scrutiny, many in the military establishment continue to instinctively oppose the idea of women serving in combat roles. In a 1993 *New York Times* article, General Merrill McPeak, former chief of staff of the air force, admitted that he had "a culturally based hang-up." "I can't get over this image of old men ordering young women into combat," he said. "I have a gut-based hang-up there. And it doesn't make a lot of sense in every way. I apologize for it." This belief had earlier been spelled out in the 1992 report of the Presidential Commission on the Assignment of Women in the Armed Forces, which was established by George H. W. Bush to review the combat exclusion. The commission identified several factors related to having women serve in combat roles that could negatively impact troop dynamics, including the "real or perceived inability of women to carry their weight without male assistance, a 'zero privacy' environment on the battlefield, interference with male bonding, cultural values and the desire of men to protect women, inappropriate male/female relationships, and pregnancy—particularly when perceived as a way to escape from combat duty."

18 While campaigning for the Republican presidential nomination this year, Santorum, the former senator, echoed these concerns, arguing that "instead of focus[ing] on the mission, [male soldiers] may be more concerned about protecting...a [female solider] in a vulnerable position." Others fear that men will not be able to restrain themselves sexually if forced to fight and work in close proximity to

women. The conservative Independent Women's Forum strongly supports the ban because of the "power of the sex drive when young women and men, under considerable stress, are mixed together in close quarters."

19 Even as these false assumptions about the inherent nature of men and women persist, many in the military and the general public have changed their minds. In 2010, Admiral Mike Mullen, then chairman of the U.S. Joint Chiefs of Staff, said, "I know what the law says and I know what it requires, but I'd be hard pressed to say that any woman who serves in Afghanistan today or who's served in Iraq over the last few years did so without facing the same risks as their male counterparts." Similarly, Bhagwati contends that "as proven by ten years of leading troops in combat in Iraq and Afghanistan, there are women that are physically and mentally qualified to succeed ... and lead infantry platoons." Meanwhile, a 2011 survey conducted by ABC News and *The Washington Post* found that 73 percent of Americans support allowing women in combat.

20 Despite such shifts in opinion, defenders of the status quo argue that lifting the ban would disrupt male bonding and unit cohesion, which is thought to build soldiers' confidence and thereby increase combat readiness and effectiveness. In 2007, Kingsley Browne, a former U.S. Supreme Court clerk and the author of *Co-ed Combat: The New Evidence That Women Shouldn't Fight the Nations Wars,* argued that "men fight for many reasons, but probably the most powerful one is the bonding—'male bonding'—with their comrades.... Perhaps for very fundamental reasons, women do not evoke in men the same feelings of comradeship and 'followership' that men do." These comments betray the widely held fear that women would feminize and therefore reduce the fighting potential of the military. The Israeli military historian Martin van Creveld has echoed this sentiment, writing, "As women enter them, the armed forces in question will become both less willing to fight and less capable of doing so." And as Anita Blair, former assistant secretary of the navy, warned, "The objective for many who advocate a greater female influence in the armed services is not so much to conquer the military as conquer manhood: they aim to make the most quintessentially masculine of our institutions more feminine." By such lights, women fundamentally threaten the unified masculine identity of the military and could never properly fill combat roles because they are inherently incapable of embodying the manly qualities of a soldier.

21 This argument is intuitive and plausible. It is also dead wrong. It assumes that a key objective of the military is enhancing masculinity rather than national security and that unit bonding leads to better task performance. In fact, a 1995 study conducted by the U.S. Army Research Institute for the Behavioral and Social Sciences found that "the relation between cohesiveness and performance is due primarily to the 'commitment to the task' component of cohesiveness, and not the 'interpersonal attraction' or 'group pride' components of cohesiveness." Similarly, a 2006 study in Armed Forces and Society, written by the scholars Robert MacCoun, Elizabeth Kier, and Aaron Belkin, concluded that "all of the evidence indicates that military performance depends on whether service members are committed to the same professional goals, not on whether they like one another."

22 There is significant evidence that not only male bonding but any sort of closeness can actually hinder group performance. In a 1998 study on demographics and

leadership, the group management experts Andrew Kakabadse and Nada Kakabadse found that "excessive cohesion may create a harmful insularity from external forces," and they linked high cohesion to "high conformity, high commitment to prior courses of actions, [and a] lack of openness." In her analysis of gender integration in the military, Erin Solaro, a researcher and journalist who was embedded with combat troops in Afghanistan and Iraq, pointed out that male bonding often depended on the exclusion or denigration of women and concluded that "cohesion is not the same as combat effectiveness, and indeed can undercut it. Supposedly 'cohesive' units can also kill their officers, mutiny, evade combat, and surrender as groups."

23 The mechanisms for achieving troop cohesion can also be problematic. In addition to denigrating women, illegal activities, including war crimes, have sometimes been used as a means for soldiers to "let off steam" and foster group unity. In sum, there is very little basis on which to link group cohesion to national security.

Strength in Diversity

24 Over the last century, the military has been strengthened when attitudes have been challenged and changed. Despite claims in the 1940s that mixed-race units would be ineffective and that white and black service members would not be able to trust one another, for example, integration proceeded without any major hiccups. A 2011 study of the impacts of racial integration on combat effectiveness during the Korean War found that integration "resulted in improvements in cohesion, leadership and command, fighting spirit, personnel resources and sustainment that increased the combat effectiveness." Initial research indicates that mixed-gender units could provide similar benefits.

25 Leora Rosen, a former senior analyst at the National Institute of Justice, found that when women were accepted into mixed-gender units, the groups' effectiveness actually increased. Similarly, a 1993 RAND Corporation paper summarizing research on sexual orientation and the U.S. military's personnel policy found that diversity "can enhance the quality of group problem-solving and decision-making, and it broadens the group's collective array of skills and knowledge." These conclusions are supported by a 1993 report by the General Accounting Office, which found that "members of gender-integrated units develop brother-sister bonds rather than sexual ones.... Experience has shown that actual integration diminishes prejudice and fosters group cohesiveness more effectively than any other factor." The same report also found that gender homogeneity was not perceived by soldiers to be a requirement for effective unit operations.

26 It should come as no surprise that elements of the military want uniformity in the ranks. The integration of new groups always ruffles feathers. But the U.S. military has been ahead of the curve in terms of the inclusion of most minority groups. It was the first federal organization to integrate African Americans. And with the repeal of the "don't ask, don't tell" (DADT) policy, the military now has more progressive policies toward gay employees than many other U.S. agencies. In fact, DADT was repealed despite the fact that there are no federal laws preventing employment discrimination on the basis of sexual orientation.

27 In September 2012, one year after the repeal of DADT, a study published by the Palm Center found that the change "has had no overall negative impact on military

readiness or its component dimensions, including cohesion, recruitment, retention, assaults, harassment or morale." The research also found that overall, DADT'S "repeal has enhanced the military's ability to pursue its mission." Previous claims about the negative impact that gay service members might have on troop cohesion mirror those currently used to support the female combat exclusion.

28 Unlike the military's treatment of other groups, its current policies toward women are much more conservative than those of other federal and state government bodies. Women who choose military service confront not only restricted career options but also a higher chance of harassment, discrimination, and sexual violence than in almost any other profession. The weak record on addressing these issues gives the impression that the military is an unwelcome place and an unsafe career choice for women. In an interview with National Public Radio in 2011, Sergeant Kayla Williams, who served in Iraq, explicitly linked the combat exclusion and harassment: "I believe that the combat exclusion actually exacerbates gender tensions and problems within the military because the fact that women can't be in combat arms jobs allows us to be portrayed as less than fully soldiers." Fully integrating women could therefore begin to address two major issues for the U.S. military: enhancing diversity and equality and also weakening the masculine culture that may contribute to harassment.

29 Unsubstantiated claims about the distracting nature of women, the perils of feminine qualities, and the inherent manliness of war hardly provide a solid foundation on which to construct policy. Presumably, some levels of racism and homophobia also persist within the military, yet it would be absurd, not to mention unconstitutional, for the U.S. government to officially sanction such prejudices. The U.S. military should ensure that it is as effective as possible, but it must not bend to biases, bigotry, and false stereotypes.

30 Just as when African Americans were fully integrated into the military and DADT was repealed, lifting the combat ban on women would not threaten national security or the cohesiveness of military units; rather, it would bring formal policies in line with current practices and allow the armed forces to overcome their misogynistic past. In a modern military, women should have the right to fight.

THINKING CRITICALLY
about "Let Women Fight"

1. What are Megan Mackenzie's main reasons for ending the ban on women in combat and where in her argument does she introduce them? What examples of Mackenzie's use of evidence to support these reasons are particularly effective in developing the logos of her argument?
2. Mackenzie devotes part of her argument to a full engagement with the assumptions about and objections to women's participation in active combat roles. How does she address the opposing views that target women's physical limitations? How does she employ evidence from the United States and other countries and seek to reframe the issue?

3. Another major portion of her argument focuses on the cultural values and views inhibiting women's participation in active combat. What cultural objections does she address? How does her probing of these assumptions and objections help her respond to them?
4. How does Mackenzie use the precedent of mixed-race units and sexual diversity to extend and strengthen her argument? What positive outcomes does she predict for the full inclusion of women in the military?
5. Throughout this argument, how does Mackenzie's *ethos* as an authority on women's involvement in military forces contribute to the impact of her argument?

Our next piece on women in combat is written by Mackubin Thomas Owens, a military historian, decorated veteran of the Vietnam War, and editor of *Orbis*, the journal of the Foreign Policy Institute. He writes extensively for conservative publications such as *The Wall Street Journal*, *National Review*, and *The Weekly Standard*, and in 2011 published his book *US Civil-Military Relations After 9/11: Renegotiating the Civil-Military Bargain*. He holds a doctorate in politics and a masters in economics and is widely known for his objections to women in combat. This editorial appeared in *The Weekly Standard* on February 4, 2013, several weeks after the Pentagon's decision to end the ban on women in combat.

Mackubin Thomas Owens

Coed Combat Units

A Bad Idea on All Counts

1 For over two decades, I have been arguing against the idea of placing American women in combat or in support positions associated with direct ground combat. I base my position on three factors. First, there are substantial physical differences between men and women that place the latter at a distinct disadvantage when it comes to ground combat. Second, men treat women differently than they treat other men. This can undermine the comradeship upon which the unit cohesion necessary to success on the battlefield depends. Finally, the presence of women leads to double standards that seriously erode morale and performance. In other words, men and women are not interchangeable.

Physical Differences

2 The average female soldier, sailor, airman, and Marine is about five inches shorter than her male counterpart and has half the upper body strength, lower aerobic capacity (at her physical peak between the ages of 20 and 30, the average woman has the aerobic capacity of a 50-year-old male), and 37 percent less muscle mass. She has a lighter skeleton, which means that the physical strain on her body from carrying the heavy loads that are the lot of the infantryman may cause permanent damage.

3 But can't these differences be reduced? In the past, gender politics has made it difficult—if not impossible—to ascertain exactly what can be done to improve the performance of women, because advocates of gender equity understand that the establishment of objective strength criteria would have a deleterious effect on their demand to open the infantry to women. Several years ago, the Army attempted to establish such strength standards and pretests for each military occupational specialty, but those efforts were abandoned when studies showed that not enough women would meet the standards proposed for many Army jobs. Funding subsequently was denied for a study about remedial strength training for women.

4 Anatomical differences between men and women are as important as strength differences. A woman cannot urinate standing up. Most important, she tends, particularly if she is under the age of 30 (as are 60 percent of female military personnel) to become pregnant.

5 Indeed, each year, somewhere between 10 and 17 percent of servicewomen become pregnant. In certain locales, the figure is even higher. Former senator James Webb noted that when he was secretary of the Navy in 1988, 51 percent of single Air Force and 48 percent of single Navy women stationed in Iceland were pregnant. During pregnancy (if she remains in the service at all), a woman must be exempted from progressively more routine duties, such as marching, field training, and swim tests.

After the baby is born, there are more problems, as exemplified by the many thousand uniformed-service mothers, none of whom fairly could be called a frontline soldier.

6 Women also suffer a higher rate of attrition than men from physical ailments, and because of the turnover, are a more costly investment. Women are four times more likely to report ill, and the percentage of women being medically nonavailable at any time is twice that of men. If a woman can't do her job, someone else must do it for her.

7 If one doesn't believe me, perhaps one should look at an article by a Marine officer, Captain Katie Petronio, in the *Marine Corps Gazette,* the Corps's professional journal ("Get Over It! We Are Not All Created Equal"). She noted the physical deterioration she suffered during her deployment to Afghanistan as a combat engineer officer:

> It was evident that stress and muscular deterioration was affecting everyone regardless of gender; however, the rate of my deterioration was noticeably faster than that of male Marines and further compounded by gender-specific medical conditions. At the end of the 7-month deployment ... I had lost 17 pounds and was diagnosed with polycystic ovarian syndrome (which personally resulted in infertility, but is not a genetic trend in my family), which was brought on by the chemical and physical changes endured during deployment. Regardless of my deteriorating physical stature, I was extremely successful during both of my combat tours, serving beside my infantry brethren and gaining the respect of every unit I supported. Regardless, I can say with 100 percent assurance that despite my accomplishments, there is no way I could endure the physical demands of the infantrymen whom I worked beside as their combat load and constant deployment cycle would leave me facing medical separation long before the option of retirement. I understand that everyone is affected differently; however, I am confident that should the Marine Corps attempt to fully integrate women into the infantry, we as an institution are going to experience a colossal increase in crippling and career-ending medical conditions for females. [www.mca-marines.org/gazette/article/get-over-it-we-are-not-all-created-equal]

Men and Women

8 The key to success on the battlefield is unit cohesion, which all research has shown to be critically important. Advocates of opening combat specialties to women have tried to change the definition of cohesion over the years, but the best remains that of the 1992 report of the Presidential Commission on the Assignment of Women in the Armed Forces: "the relationship that develops in a unit or group where (1) members share common values and experiences; (2) individuals in the group conform to group norms and behavior in order to ensure group survival and goals; (3) members lose their identity in favor of a group identity; (4) members focus on group activities and goals; (5) unit members become totally dependent on each other for the completion of their mission or survival; and (6) group members ... meet all the standards of performance and behavior in order not to threaten group survival."

9 The glue of unit cohesion is what the Greeks called *philia*—friendship, comradeship, or brotherly love. In *The Warriors: Reflections on Men in Battle,* J. Glenn Gray described the importance of *philia:* "Numberless soldiers have died, more or less willingly, not for country or honor or religious faith or for any other abstract good, but

because they realized that by fleeing their post and rescuing themselves, they would expose their companions to greater danger. Such loyalty to the group is the essence of fighting morale… . Comrades are loyal to each other spontaneously and without any need for reasons."

10 The Greeks identified another form of love: *eros.* Unlike *philia, eros* is individual and exclusive. *Eros* manifests itself as sexual competition, protectiveness, and favoritism. The presence of women in the close confines of a combat unit unleashes *eros* at the expense of *philia.* As the late Charles Moskos, the great military sociologist, once commented, "when you put men and women together in a confined environment and shake vigorously, don't be surprised if sex occurs. When the military says there can be no sex between a superior and a subordinate, that just flies in the face of reality. You can't make a principle based on a falsehood." Mixing the sexes and thereby introducing *eros* into an environment based on *philia* creates a dangerous form of friction in the military.

11 The destructive effect on unit cohesion of amorous relationships can be denied only by ideologues. Does a superior order his or her beloved into danger? If he or she demonstrates favoritism, what are the consequences for unit morale and discipline? What happens when jealousy rears its head? These are questions of life and death.

12 Feminists contend that these manifestations of *eros* are the result only of a lack of education and insensitivity to women, and can be eradicated through indoctrination. But all the social engineering in the world cannot change the fact that men treat women differently than they treat other men.

Double Standards

13 The physical differences between men and women have, unfortunately, all too often caused the military to, in effect, discard the very essence of *philia:* fairness and the absence of favoritism. This is the crux of the problem. As Webb has observed, "In [the military] environment, fairness is not only crucial, it is the coin of the realm." The military ethos is dependent on the understanding that the criteria for allocating danger and recognition, both positive and negative, are essentially objective.

14 Favoritism and double standards are deadly to *philia* and the associated phenomena—cohesion, morale, discipline—that are critical to the success of a military organization. Not surprisingly, double standards generate resentment on the part of military men, which in turn leads to cynicism about military women in general, including those who have not benefited from a double standard and who perform their duties with distinction.

15 The military has created two types of double standards. The first is the tendency to allow women, but not men, to take advantage of sexual differences. For instance, morale, trust, and cohesion have suffered from the perception among military men that women can use pregnancy to avoid duty or deployments. A very contentious debate over favoritism arose some years ago over the claim that some women had been permitted to advance in flight training with performances that would have caused a man to wash out.

16 The second type of double standard is based on differing physical requirements. Last week, after Secretary of Defense Leon Panetta announced that the ban on women in combat would be lifted, my good friend, retired Air Force general Charlie Dunlap, a

former JAG and the director of Duke Law School's Center on Law, Ethics and National Security, weighed in: "Secretary Panetta's decision to lift the ban on women serving in certain combat roles makes sense so long as there is no lowering of the physical or other standards required for the new positions."

17 The trouble is that the desire for equal *opportunity* is, in practice, usually translated into a demand for equal *results.* Consequently, there has been a watering down of standards to accommodate the generally lower physical capabilities of women. This has had two consequences.

18 First, standards have been reduced so much that, in many cases, service members no longer are being prepared for the strenuous challenges they will face in the fleet or field. Second—and even more destructive of morale and trust—is the fact that when the requirement can't be changed and the test cannot be eliminated, scores are "gender normed" to conceal the differences between men and women. All the services have lower physical standards for women than for men. Two decades ago, the U.S. Military Academy identified 120 physical differences between men and women, not to mention psychological ones, that resulted in a less rigorous overall program of physical training at West Point in order to accommodate female cadets.

19 For instance, the "USMA Report on the Integration and Performance of Women at West Point," prepared for the Defense Advisory Committee on Women in the Services in February 1992, revealed that scores for physically demanding events were gender

normed at the academy: A woman could receive an A for the same performance that would earn a man a D. Navy women can achieve the minimum score on the physical readiness test by performing 11 percent fewer sit-ups and 53 percent fewer push-ups and by running 1.5 miles 27 percent more slowly than men. There is immense political pressure to prevent women from failing to meet even these reduced standards.

20 To argue against women in combat is not to deny the significant contributions women have made to the nation's defense. For the last century, women have served honorably, competently, and bravely during this country's wars. It is my experience that the vast majority of women in today's armed forces are extremely professional and want nothing to do with the two extremes of feminism that Jean Bethke Elshtain described several years ago in *Real Politics: At the Center of Everyday Life* and that the military spends time and effort trying to appease: the "feminist victimization wing" and the "repressive androgynists."

21 I doubt that there is a huge push on the part of female soldiers and Marines to join the infantry. Captain Petronio makes the same point. The impetus comes instead from professional feminists still living in the 1970s and a small number of female officers who believe that serving in the infantry will increase the likelihood that they will become generals. But the Pentagon itself points out that military women are already promoted at rates equal to or faster than men.

22 In short, there is no reason for this change. It doesn't make the military stronger, and risks making it weaker by undermining the factors crucial for combat effectiveness.

THINKING CRITICALLY
about "Coed Combat Units"

1. What claim about women in combat does Owens make in this argument and what reasons does he offer in support of this claim?
2. How effective is Owens's reasoning and use of evidence? Think especially about his employment of the testimony of a woman Marine officer, Captain Katie Patronio, as she relates her personal experience and response to the stress of active duty.
3. What authorities, government reports, and numerical data does Owens enlist to support his reasons? How persuasive do you find these, for instance, the data about the lowered physical standards for women?
4. To what extent does Owens address the alternative views to his position against women? Where does he concede points? How rhetorically effective is his engagement with alternative views?
5. Thinking about the depth and complexity of Megan Mackenzie's argument, what points of Mackenzie's would you say Owens's argument calls into question? What points of hers does he fail to address?

Our final selection on this issue is a cartoon. Gary Varvel is a part-time teacher and editorial cartoonist for the *Indianapolis Star,* who previously worked as the chief artist for the *Indianapolis News*. Varvel identifies himself as a conservative cartoonist and his work is syndicated with Creators Syndicate.

Gary Varvel

Combat Barbie: New Accessories

THINKING CRITICALLY
about "Combat Barbie"

1. What are the details of this cartoon? What does it literally depict?
2. This cartoon participates in two major cultural debates. The first controversy focuses on Barbie dolls and the socialization of girls: Are Barbie dolls good toys for young girls? What do they teach about femininity, sexuality, and women's roles? In thinking about this controversy, it is helpful to know that since her creation in 1959, Barbie has had between eighty and over a hundred "careers" or "jobs," meaning that clothing and accessories for different careers have come with the doll: airline pilot, rock star, doctor, firefighter,

business executive, among others, and a variety of military jobs—army, air force, navy, and marine. The second controversy is the ongoing discussion—despite the 2013 Pentagon ruling—over whether it is appropriate for women to be part of active combat units. What does this cartoon contribute to these two controversies?

3. What is the significance that this doll is "Made by the Pentagon" and not by Mattel? What details in this cartoon suggest the cultural/social perspective Varvel is taking on the Pentagon's decision to end the ban on women in combat? In other words, what argument do you think Varvel is making in this cartoon?

Our last reading is by student writer Claire Giordano, who wrote this paper for an argument assignment like the one in this chapter. In challenging the national enthusiasm for the expansion of online courses, Claire Giordano draws on her research and her experience and knowledge as an Environmental Studies major.

Claire Giordano (student)

Virtual Promise: Why Online Courses Will Not Adequately Prepare Us for the Future

1 In 2012 more than 6.7 million students took at least one online course (Sloan Consortium). Proponents of online education hope that such courses will improve the current educational system, but this potential is undermined by the problems of reliance on technology. A 2013 Kaiser Family Foundation Survey found that children and teens spend more than 53 hours using digital media every week (Toppo). Educational programs that place more people behind more computers may not be the best way to improve education for the future, and we as a country seem to be at a critical decision-making point of whether to increase technology's role in our lives. At this historical moment, I, as an Environmental Studies major concerned about my education and the well-being of the environment around me, believe the costs and consequences of online education must be evaluated based on how well they prepare us for future engagement with the world. Although many people have great expectations for the possibilities of online courses, their negative repercussions ultimately outweigh the supposed benefits. Online courses are not the best way to educate students because these virtual classes are more expensive, promote inequality by requiring technology that is inaccessible to many of our fellow citizens, inhibit the full development of our critical thinking skills, and further entrench our reliance on technology.

2 The optimism surrounding online courses arises from the belief that they will make higher education less expensive and more accessible and thus alleviate education inequality. From this perspective, the opportunities, flexibility, and lower costs of online courses outweigh their potential drawbacks. For example, Dr. Hershey Friedman, a business professor at Brooklyn College, who is widely published on the

use of technology and media in education, supports the expansion of online education. He states that online courses ease the financial burden on both the student and the university and provide flexible schedules, which allow students to engage in other activities (H. Friedman).

3 However, while these ideas sound good, they have fundamental problems with cost and accreditation. For example, one of the most common arguments in favor of virtual courses cites the cost effectiveness. The problem with this claim, though, is that it oversimplifies the issue. There are currently many models for online education that students could choose, from Massive Open Online Courses (MOOCS) that don't provide credit to programs that do grant credit. Within this range of possibilities, the programs that offer accreditation are the only ones students could use in the job market and in reality do not save us substantial amounts of money. A study by Tamara Battaglino et al. found that the average per pupil cost to a university for a full online education ranges from $6,400 to $10,200, which translates into a higher cost to students that is in some cases close to the rates of a traditional education (4). With these figures in mind, I cannot see why we would advocate for a course of education that is not only unacceptable in most of the job market but that also does not substantially reduce costs to make the classes more accessible.

4 Proponents who mistakenly believe that online education is cheaper also believe that its widespread accessibility will alleviate education inequalities. Thomas Friedman, who is a Pulitzer Prize winning journalist for the *New York Times*, believes that online courses will reduce poverty by granting all citizens equal access to the best education possible (T. Friedman 1). This hope for accessibility nurtures a vision of universities "as central informational hubs that offer learning and knowledge and skills for anyone around the globe willing to absorb them" (Lagos 1). This image is quite compelling, and I will admit that arguments like Friedman's are appealing, especially when I consider students in similar situations like that of my sister, who has recently been overwhelmed with health problems and has missed a semester of high school and is still struggling to catch up in her classes. For students like her, online courses could be a godsend, giving them equal access to material and classes otherwise inaccessible.

5 However, the problem with believing that online courses create equality is that credit-bearing courses are too expensive and require technology that is simply not available to everyone. Many people struggling with poverty are not computer and Web users. This fundamental inequality is illustrated by the FCC's Broadband Access Report, which found that 119 million Americans do not have access to broadband Internet as a result of poverty or deficient wireless infrastructure. This problem was especially pronounced in rural areas, where 25% lacked access (Brodkin). The implications of this exclusion are explained clearly by Cynthia L. Selfe, who is a Distinguished Professor of the Humanities at The Ohio State University and the first female English teacher to receive the EDUCOM Medal for innovative computer use. She explains that the push for technological literacy by the government and businesses "disguises the fact that technology is not available to everyone in this country or to every student in our schools...and directs our attention from the realization that, in America, technology supports social divisions along race, class, and gender" (Selfe xxi). In light of this

statement, it is clear to me that online courses are not the solution to education inequality because they require technology that perpetuates social inequality—the very problem they strive to address.

6 Supporters also claim online courses are the best way to transform current educational practices. From this point of view, advocates like Hershey Friedman believe that online courses can produce deeper-level thinking because they appeal to different learning styles and enhance creativity by using "numerous teaching tools that include animations, videos, wikis, and virtual labs" (n. pag.). According to this argument, online courses provide an atmosphere conducive to the development of critical thinking skills just as effectively as conventional courses do.

7 While I cannot deny that online courses employ innovative tools with the potential to engage students, the virtual nature of the classes simply cannot recreate the environment of intellectual and interpersonal challenge that is necessary for fully developing critical thinking skills. The importance of critical thinking has been emphasized by many people, from the great American philosopher John Dewey (Michael Roth) to current educational leaders like Tony Wagner. To people like Dewey and Wagner, critical thinking skills are a prerequisite for being an engaged member of society. I would add that critical thinking is also crucial if we are going to creatively and successfully address the wicked problems that face our world, from poverty, to water shortages, to toxic environments, to global climate change.

8 In light of this importance, I believe that critical thinking skills are too vital to entrust to a purely virtual environment. The weaknesses of online courses in promoting critical thinking are highlighted by Rick Roth, who has worked as an academic adviser for over twenty-four years and taught at the University of Washington and Skidmore College. Roth argues that online education is in fact detrimental to the growth of our critical thinking skills. He states that virtual learning through online classes strips education of its context and interdisciplinary nature: "[B]y demanding answers every few minutes in the form of quizzes, …they can't provide enough reflective time or space for those all-important 'it all depends on what you mean by' realizations." Furthermore, he explains that online courses deprive us of the learning that occurs when we become stuck and have to use reason and creativity to find a solution. Roth believes that "profoundly challenging learning needs the oxygen of uncertainty and ambiguity" that arises from the challenges posed by our professors and peers. This direct interaction is critical to engaging with the world and simply cannot be facilitated in a virtual environment where the ability to respond with a right or wrong answer is reinforced through repetitive quizzes and evaluations. This impersonal and simplistic way of learning lacks the challenging interactions that develop our ability to reason, to think creatively, and to work collaboratively—important skills we need in order to address the social and environmental problems we face as a global community.

9 Finally, advocates of virtual learning claim that online courses prepare students for the future by developing technological proficiency, which is needed in most occupations and even in many job applications (Schultz). The problem with this point of view, however, is that it ignores the many other skills that we need to succeed in the world, and does not acknowledge the consequences of relying on technology. I am not saying that all technology is bad and should be abandoned, but that the modern

reliance on computers and superfluous gadgets may be more detrimental than helpful. This concept is captured nicely by the Dutch social critic Michiel Schwarz, who believes that "technology has become our environment as well as our ideology...we no longer use technology, we live it" (qtd. in Glendinning 45). These views suggest that the proliferation of technology (including online courses) may have far reaching negative effects on our lives and the entire global community.

10 Additionally, the dependence on technology in virtual classes merely supports and further promotes, in the words of ecopsychologists Allen Kanner and Mary Gomes, "an almost religious belief among Americans in the ultimate good of all technological progress, through its claim that there is a product to solve each of life's problems" (84). From the perspective of Kanner and Gomes, however, these hopes are merely part of the larger misplaced faith in the power of technology to cure all of the world's social and environmental ills. This misguided faith in technology encourages misunderstanding of pressing environmental problems, something that especially troubles me because I believe we should devote our resources and brain power to collaboratively solving our problems *now* rather than hoping that future generations will invent new technologies to solve the crises we are creating by living beyond the limits of our planet. Rather than blindly looking to future technology as a savior, we must act now to slow the environmental degradation while we still can.

11 Furthermore, attachment to technology not only affects our physical, social, and cultural futures, but also has huge repercussions for the health of the earth we depend on and must preserve for our own health as well as the well-being of future generations. Recent international research is finding that as the use of technology increases, we are slowly losing our ability to interact with the world through all of our senses because current technology overemphasizes visual information (Sewall 202). Thus, the rise of technology (such as online courses) means that we are interacting with the world through screens rather than enjoying the simple beauty and life that surrounds us, from the movement of clouds on a windy day to the smell of the first spring daffodil. This change also has direct impacts on our physical, mental, and emotional health, as Richard Louv explains in his work *Last Child in the Woods*. He cites studies that link a lack of play in nature with higher rates of ADHD, depression, and other mental disorders, especially pronounced in children. But these same patterns are also seen in adults in study after study (Louv 107-110). For everyone's health, we need nature. We must spend time outside, whether it is watching a sunset from a high-rise or helping kids plant seeds and get their hands dirty in rich soil. Online courses may help us become more technologically adept, but they will also keep us more isolated behind computer screens. This gain is not worth the cost of becoming further alienated from the endangered natural world and from other people who need our compassion and understanding.

12 While I admit that online courses have many strong advocates and some potential to make positive change in the world, these changes simply come at too high a price. Credit-bearing virtual courses are expensive and require a technology not everyone can access. They also create an environment devoid of the necessary challenges and interactions that foster complex critical thinking. The online courses also entrench our dangerous reliance on technology and perpetuate unsustainable attitudes about how

we should interact with the natural world. Amidst the current intense societal pressure to develop and employ ever more technology in every aspect of life, we must decide whether this is a direction our education should also follow. At a time when the polar ice is melting at unprecedented rates, species are becoming extinct every day, and the very air we breathe is toxic from the pollution of industrialization, entrusting our education to technology is not the answer.

Works Cited

Brodkin, Jon. "119 Million Americans Lack Broadband Internet, FCC Reports." *ArsTechnica*. Conde Nast, 21 Aug. 2012. Web. 1 Mar. 2013.

Battaglino, Tamara Butler, Matt Haldeman, and Eleanor Laurans. "The Costs of Online Learning: Creating Sound Policy for Digital Learning." Working Paper Series. Thomas B. Fordham Institute, 11 Feb. 2013. *ERIC*. Web. 23 Feb. 2013.

Friedman, Hershey H., and Linda Weiser Friedman. "Crises in Education: Online Learning as a Solution." *Creative Education* 2.3 (2011): 156-63. *ProQuest Research Library*. Web. 12 Feb. 2013.

Friedman, Thomas L. "Revolution Hits the Universities." *The New York Times*. New York Times, 26 Jan. 2013. Web. 5 Feb. 2013.

Glendinning, Chellis. "Technology, Trauma, and the Wild." *Ecopsychology: Restoring the Earth, Healing the Mind*. Ed. Theodore Roszak, Mary E. Gomes, and Allen D. Kanner. San Francisco: Sierra Club, 1995. 41-54. Print.

Kanner, Allen D., and Mary E. Gomes. "The All-Consuming Self." *Ecopsychology: Restoring the Earth, Healing the Mind*. Ed. Theodore Roszak, Mary E. Gomes, and Allen D. Kanner. San Francisco: Sierra Club Books, 1995. 77-91. Print.

Lagos, Taso. "Pro: Are Online Courses Good for Higher Education?" *The Seattle Times*. Seattle Times, 18 Aug. 2012. Web. 23 Feb. 2013.

Louv, Richard. *Last Child in the Woods: Saving Our Children from Nature-deficit Disorder*. Chapel Hill, NC: Algonquin, 2006.

Roth, Michael S. "Learning as Freedom." *The New York Times* 6 Sept. 2012, sec. A: 23. Print.

Roth, Rick. "Assembly-Line Approach Could End Up Killing Nation's Research Engine." *The Seattle Times*. Seattle Times, 19 Aug. 2012. Web. 10 Feb. 2013.

Schultz, Terrie. "The Importance of Technology Literacy." *Yahoo News*. Yahoo, 5 Aug. 2010. Web. 23 Feb. 2013.

Selfe, Cynthia L. *Technology and Literacy in the Twenty-First Century: The Importance of Paying Attention*. Carbondale: Southern Illinois UP, 1999. eBook file.

Sewall, Laura. "The Skill of Ecological Perception." *Ecopsychology: Restoring the Earth, Healing the Mind*. Ed. Theodore Roszak, Mary E. Gomes, and Allen D. Kanner. San Francisco: Sierra Club, 1995. 201-15. Print.

The Sloan Consortium. Press Release. "Changing Course: Ten Years of Tracking Online Education in the United States." Jan. 2013. Web. 13 Feb. 2013.

Toppo, Greg. "Kids' Electronic Media Use Jumps to 53 Hours a Week." *USA Today*. Gannett, 20 Jan. 2010. Web. 12 Mar. 2013.

Wagner, Tony. *The Global Achievement Gap: Why Even Our Best Schools Don't Teach the New Survival Skills Our Children Need – and What We Can Do About It*. New York: Basic, 2008. Print.

THINKING CRITICALLY

about "Virtual Promise: Why Online Courses Will Not Adequately Prepare Us for the Future"

1. What is Claire Giordano's main claim and what are her reasons for opposing online courses?
2. While some classical arguments group alternative views after the writer's development of the reasons, others structure the whole argument as a rebuttal with the writer's reasons in effect answering the opposing views. What choice has Claire made? Why do you think she chose to organize her argument this way? What alternative or opposing views does she address?
3. What audience do you think Claire is trying to reach with this argument? How well does she use appeals to *pathos* to connect with readers' values, beliefs, and emotions?
4. How effectively does Claire create appeals to *ethos* in this argument? Where does her evidence draw on her experience and knowledge as an Environmental Studies major?
5. How would you assess the appeals to *logos* in this argument? Consider the range, quality, and depth of her supporting evidence.
6. What do you see as the major strengths and weaknesses of this argument?

MAKING AN EVALUATION

14

WHAT YOU WILL LEARN

14.1 To explain the criteria-match structure and other rhetorical principles that underlie effective evaluation arguments.

14.2 To write an evaluation argument for an audience of skeptical readers.

Because evaluation arguments have a persuasive rather than a purely informational aim, they differ from typical movie or restaurant reviews that simply note the good points and bad points of the thing being evaluated. Evaluations usually involve a two-step critical thinking process: (1) deciding on the appropriate criteria to use when evaluating something and (2) deciding whether a particular case meets the criteria. Thus when you decide what courses to take next term, you must first decide the criteria you will apply, such as your interest in the subject, the reputation of the instructor, the required workload, or the time of day. Once you establish criteria, you will probably rank-order them and then begin seeing what available courses best meet them. In both your professional and your academic life, you will often have to write evaluations. According to a study by Barbara Walvoord and Lucille McCarthy, college assignments often take the form of "good/better/best" evaluation questions. For example, a history professor might ask: "Was Queen Elizabeth I of England a good ruler?" Or in an environmental studies course, you might be asked to evaluate the features of a successful campaign to encourage water conservation.

Engaging Evaluative Writing

The following exercise will introduce you to the kind of thinking demanded by evaluative writing.

Many people face an evaluation question whenever they purchase a cell phone. What criteria are most important? Note that these criteria will vary depending on each purchaser's needs, desires, and financial situation.

FIGURE 14.1 Variations in Cell Phones

ON YOUR OWN

1. If you currently have a cell phone, do you like it? Why or why not?
2. Suppose you want to change or upgrade your phone. What criteria are most important to you? Why?
3. Suppose that a friend or relative asks you for advice on choosing a cell phone. Keeping in mind the variations of cell phone types (see Figure 14.1), how would the criteria for your evaluation change in each of the following cases?
   a. A friend who wants to use the device primarily to play games, stream movies, and surf the Web and has an unlimited budget.
   b. A friend who can't afford a smartphone but is an avid texter who also likes to take and send photographs.
   c. An older technophobic relative who wants a cell phone for emergencies or occasional calls to family or friends but has a limited budget and doesn't have any interest in texting.

IN CONVERSATION

As a class, brainstorm the possible criteria people might use to evaluate cell phones. Reach consensus on how the criteria may vary depending on the user's budget, purposes, and comfort with techology. Note: Don't talk about specific brands or models of phones. Stay focused on criteria.

Understanding Evaluation Arguments

14.1 Explain the criteria-match structure and other rhetorical principles that underlie effective evaluation arguments.

Now that you have been introduced to evaluative thinking, we'll explain in more detail how to think and write about evaluation issues.

The Criteria-Match Process

Evaluation arguments involve what we call a **criteria-match process**. The first step in this process is to establish criteria; the second step is to show how well your subject matches these criteria. Here are several examples:

- Which students should be awarded the prestigious presidential scholarship?
  Criteria task: What are the criteria for the presidential scholarship?
  Match task: Which of the candidates best meet the criteria?

- Is hospitalization a good treatment for anorexia?
  Criteria task: What are the criteria for a good treatment for anorexia?
  Match task: Does hospitalization meet these criteria?
- Environmentalists have proposed three political actions for combating climate change: (a) a carbon tax; (b) public subsidies for installing solar panels; (c) divestment of oil company stock. Of these three, which is the best approach?
  Criteria task: What are the criteria for an effective way to fight climate change?
  Match task: Which of the three proposals best meets these criteria?
- What is the best cell phone for a technophobic older relative?
  Criteria task: What are the criteria for a good cell phone for a technophobic older person?
  Match task: Which phone best meets the criteria?

In each of these cases, we can see that different stakeholders might pose different criteria and thus make different evaluative claims. To see how an evaluative argument depends on the initial criteria, consider again the opening exercise on evaluating cell phones. Your claim about the best cell phone depends on the criteria determined by the needs and purposes of the user. The following table provides examples of how different criteria will lead to different evaluation arguments (names of phones are fictional):

User's Needs and Purposes	Evaluation Claim	Reasons (Matched to Criteria)	Implied Criteria
Person who uses the device primarily to play games, stream movies, and surf the Web	The best cell phone is the Harpy 500 smartphone	• Because the Harpy 500 has a large, luminous screen • Because the interface makes gaming and video streaming easy • Because its high speed processor is lightning fast	• Large screen size • Easy interface for gaming • High-speed processor NOTE: Cost is not a criterion for this person
Person who can't afford a smartphone but is an avid texter who also likes to take and send photographs	The best cell phone is the Minotaur 200	• Because the Minotaur 200 has a tactile slide keyboard for error-free texting • Because it has an excellent camera • Because it is relatively low-cost	• Slide keyboard • Quality of camera • Low cost
An older, technophobic person who wants to have a cell phone for emergencies or occasional calls to family or a friend	Best cell phone is a flip-top Arachne 100	• Because this phone has a large numeric physical keyboard for easy visibility and touch dialing • Because it has a large-screen display • Because it provides reliable phone service with a minimum of bells and whistles	• Large keyboard for easy visibility and touch dialing • Large-screen display • Reliable but simple

The preceding arguments show how evaluation claims depend on the establishment of criteria. But just as stakeholders can disagree about the critieria, they can also disagree about the match. For example, consider a family deciding what used car to buy. They might agree on the criteria—let's say, (1) low cost, (2) safety, and (3) reliability. But they might disagree whether a specific car meets the criteria. In terms of cost, Car A may be initially cheaper than Car B but may get lower gas mileage and have a higher frequency-of-repair record. In this match argument, the family would be arguing over whether Car A or Car B best meets the low-cost criterion.

FOR WRITING AND DISCUSSION

Establishing and Applying Criteria

Whenever you evaluate something, you first need to establish criteria—that is, for any given class of items, you have to determine the qualities, traits, behaviors, or features that constitute excellence for members of that class. Then you need to match those criteria to a single member of that class—the thing you are evaluating. The following simple exercise will give you practice in thinking in this systematic, two-stage way:

1. Working individually, make a list of criteria that are important to you in choosing a career. These criteria are bound to differ from person to person. Some people might place "high income" at the top of their list, while others might put "prestige," "leadership opportunities," "adventure," "being outdoors," or "time for family and leisure" at the top. Then rank your criteria from highest to lowest priority.
2. Share your criteria lists in small groups or as a whole class. Then write on the chalkboard two or three representative lists of criteria.
3. Finally, write several different careers on the board and match them to the lists of criteria. Which possible careers come out on top for you? Which ones come out on top based on the criteria lists placed on the board? Possible careers to consider include these: grade school/high school teacher, lawyer, auto mechanic, airplane pilot, bus driver, military officer, hedge fund manager, engineer, computer technician, insurance salesperson, accountant, small business owner, plumber, commercial artist, homemaker, nurse/physician/ dentist, chiropractor/optometrist, social worker, police officer.
4. When disagreements arise, try to identify whether they are disagreements about criteria or disagreements about the facts of a given career.

The Role of Purpose and Context in Determining Criteria

Ordinarily, criteria are based on the purpose of the class to which the thing being evaluated belongs. For example, if you asked a professor to write a recommendation for you, he or she would need to know what you were applying for—A scholarship? Internship in a law office? Peace Corps volunteer? Summer job in a national park? The qualities of a successful law office intern differ substantially from those of a successful Peace Corps worker in Uganda. The recommendation isn't about you in the abstract but about your fulfilling the purposes of the class "law office intern" or "Peace Corps volunteer." Similarly, if you were evaluating a car, you would need to ask, "a car for what purpose?"—Reliable family transportation? Social status (if so, what social group?)? Environmental friendliness?

Decisions about purpose are often affected by context. For example, a union member, in buying a car, might specify an American-made car while a subscriber to *Mother Jones* magazine might specify high gas mileage and low pollution. To see how context influences criteria, consider a recent review of Seattle's soup kitchens appearing in a newspaper produced by homeless people. In most contexts, restaurant reviews focus on the quality of food. But in this review the highest criterion was the sense of dignity and love extended to homeless people by the staff.

FOR WRITING AND DISCUSSION

Working with Purpose and Criteria

1. Working in small groups or as a whole class, decide how you would evaluate a local eatery as a place to study. How would you evaluate it as a place to take a date, a place to hang out with friends, or a place to buy a nutritious meal?
2. As a whole class or in small groups, discuss how this individual exercise helped you realize how criteria for excellence vary when you place the same item into different classes with different purposes.

Special Problems in Establishing Criteria

Establishing the criteria for evaluation arguments can entail other considerations besides purpose and context. Sometimes it is difficult to establish criteria because of special problems connected to evaluation. The following chart explains four typical kinds of problems and their solutions.

Problems and Solutions in Establishing Criteria

Problem	Explanation	Solution
Different classes: Apples and oranges	It is harder to establish criteria for a good fruit than it is for a good apple or a good orange.	Comparative evaluations should focus on members of the same class. So, compare one kind of apple against another kind, but not against oranges or bananas. Compare Chris Paul to other basketball players, not to golfers or swimmers. Even better, compare him to other basketball guards.
Competing standards: The ideal versus the doable/achievable	This problem is illustrated by the aphorism "Don't let the perfect be enemy to the good." Sometimes we have to evaluate something highly if it is "good enough" or "better than what we have now" rather than ideal.	Clarify whether you are using an ideal standard or the lesser standard of "achievable." In the debate on Obamacare, many Democrats preferred a Canadian style single-payer system as ideal while others accepted a more achievable Massachusetts style private insurance with an individual mandate. (Meanwhile, Republicans applied different criteria and rejected the bill entirely.)

(*continued*)

Problem	Explanation	Solution
Seductive empirical measures: The power of numbers	We may be tempted to evaluate something based on traits that can be quantified: highest GPA or SAT scores for scholarships; the amount of revenue generated for the best tax policy. Because numbers rank-order themselves, they can hold huge sway in evaluations.	Although numbers can be persuasive, they often don't measure the nonquantifiable things that we really value. Always ask what the numbers do *not* measure and seek ways to evaluate the traits that might be more important.
Tyranny of cost: Can we afford it?	Sometimes the things we evaluate highest simply cost too much. (Note: Cost may be measured by money, time, emotional stress, or other factors.)	You may have to eliminate the top choices in your evaluation because they cost too much. Recognize the inhibiting factor of cost from the start. You may need to evaluate only those items in your cost range.

Distinguishing Necessary, Sufficient, and Accidental Criteria

Still another factor in establishing criteria is recognizing that some criteria are more important than others. Suppose you said, "I will be happy with any job as long as it puts food on my table and gives me time for my family." In this case the criteria "adequate income" and "time for family," taken together, are **sufficient**, meaning that once these criteria are met, the job being rated meets your standard for excellence. Suppose you said instead, "I am hard to please in my choice of a career, which must meet many criteria. But I definitely will reject any career that doesn't put enough food on my table or allow me time for my family." In this case the criteria of "adequate income" and "time for family" are **necessary but not sufficient**, meaning that these two criteria have to be met for a career to meet your standards, but that other criteria must be met also.

Besides necessary and sufficient criteria, there are **accidental** criteria, which are added bonuses but not essential. For example, you might say, "Although it's not essential, having a career that would allow me to be outside a lot would be nice." In this case "being outside" is an accidental criterion (nice but not required).

Using a Planning Schema to Develop Evaluation Arguments

In Chapter 13, we showed you how to use a planning schema to develop ideas for an argument (pp. 322–323). The schema encourages writers to articulate their argument frame (each reason and the underlying assumption that links the reason back to the claim) and then to imagine what kinds of evidence could be used to support both the reason and the underlying assumption. Equally important, the schema encourages writers to anticipate counterarguments by imagining how skeptical readers might object to the writers' reasons or underlying assumptions or both.

Let's say that you are the student member of a committee to select a professor for an outstanding teaching award. Several members of the committee want to give the award to Professor M. Mouse, a popular sociology professor at your institution. You are opposed. One of your lines of reasoning is that Professor Mouse's courses aren't rigorous. Here is how you could develop this line of reasoning using the planning schema explained in Chapter 13.

CLAIM WITH REASON

Professor Mouse does not deserve the teaching award because his courses aren't rigorous.

EVIDENCE TO SUPPORT THE REASON

I need to provide evidence that his courses aren't rigorous. From the dean's office records, I have discovered that 80 percent of his students get As or high Bs; a review of his syllabi shows that he requires little outside reading and only one short paper; he has a reputation in my dorm of being fun and easy.

UNDERLYING ASSUMPTION (CRITERION)

Having rigorous academic standards is a necessary criterion for the university teaching award.

EVIDENCE/ARGUMENTS TO SUPPORT THE ASSUMPTION

I need to show why I think rigorous academic standards are necessary. Quality of teaching should be measured by the amount that students learn. Good teaching is more than a popularity contest. Good teachers draw high-level performance from their students and motivate them to put time and energy into learning. High standards lead to the development of skills that are demanded in society.

WAYS SKEPTICS MIGHT OBJECT

How could someone attack my reason and evidence? Might a person say that Mouse has high standards? Could someone show that students really earned the high grades? Are the students I talked to not representative? Could someone say that Mouse's workload and grading patterns meet or exceed the commonplace behavior of faculty in his department?

How could someone attack my underlying assumption? Could someone argue that rigorous academic standards aren't as important as other criteria—that this is an accidental not a necessary criterion? Could a person say that Mouse's goal—to inspire interest in sociology—is best achieved by not loading students down with too many papers and too much reading, which can appear to be busywork? (I'll need to refute this argument.) Could someone say that the purpose of giving the university teaching award is public relations and it is therefore important to recognize widely popular teachers who will be excellent speakers at banquets and other public forums?

Conducting an Evaluation Argument: An Extended Example

Now that we have explored some potential difficulties in establishing and defending criteria for an evaluation, let's consider in more detail the process of making an evaluation argument.

FIGURE 14.2 Experience Music Project, Seattle, Washington

The student examples in this section focus on the evaluation of a rock and roll museum in Seattle, Washington, called Experience Music Project (EMP). Designed by architect Frank Gehry (who is known for his creation of the Guggenheim Museum in Bilbao, Spain, the Aerospace Hall in Los Angeles, and other famous buildings around the world), EMP was sponsored by Microsoft cofounder Paul Allen as a tribute to rock singer Jimi Hendrix and to rock music itself. In Figure 14.2, you can see this innovative structure, which sparked much controversy (is it a wonder or an eyesore?). Sharing some characteristics with the Rock and Roll Hall of Fame and Museum in Cleveland, Ohio, EMP features some permanent exhibits—the Hendrix Gallery, the Guitar Gallery (tracing the development of guitars from the 1500s to the electric guitars of today), Milestones (including displays from rhythm and blues to hip-hop and current rap artists), and Northwest Passage (focusing on popular music in Seattle, from jazz and rhythm and blues to heavy metal, punk, grunge, and the contemporary music scene). EMP also includes Sound Lab (where visitors can play instruments using interactive technology), On Stage (where visitors can pretend to be rock stars playing before a cheering crowd), Artist's Journey (a ride involving motion platform technology), three restaurants, and a store. (To see for yourself what EMP is and how it looks on the inside, you can go to its Web site.)

Let's now turn to the specific steps of making an evaluation argument.

Step 1: Determining the Class to Which X Belongs and the Purposes of That Class When you conduct an evaluation argument, you must first assign your person/object/phenomenon (the X you are evaluating) to a category or class and then determine the purposes of that class. Often people disagree about an evaluation because they disagree about the arguer's choice of category for X. EMP, as students soon discovered, could be placed in several different categories, leading to different criteria for evaluation. Here are typical classes proposed by students:

- A tourist attraction (for an audience of visitors to Seattle)
- A museum of rock history (for people interested in the development of rock as an art form)
- A rock and roll shrine (for rock fans who want to revere their favorite artists and feel part of the rock scene for a day)

Clearly these classes have different purposes. The purpose of a tourist attraction is to offer a unique, fun place to spend the day during a visit to Seattle. The purpose of a rock museum is to teach about the history of its subject in an informative, interesting, and accessible way. The purpose of a rock and roll shrine is to honor famous rock stars, bring visitors into their lives and work, and let them experience the music scene.

Step 2: Determining and Weighting Criteria The criteria for your evaluation are directly connected to the purposes of the class to which X belongs. The following lists show typical criteria chosen by different students for each of the classes listed in Step 1:

A good *tourist attraction* should

- be entertaining and enjoyable.
- be affordable and worth the price, not simply out to gouge tourists' wallets.
- be unique—something tourists wouldn't find in another city.

A good *museum of rock history* should

- have a clear, well-organized layout that is easy to navigate.
- display objects of clear aesthetic or historical significance.
- teach the public by providing clear, meaningful information about rock music.
- arouse interest in rock as an art form and encourage the public's appreciation and involvement.

A good *rock and roll shrine* should

- take fans up close and personal into the lives of major artists.
- encourage fans to appreciate the complexity of rock and the skills of artists.
- help fans experience the rock scene and fantasize about being rock stars themselves.

In addition to identifying criteria, you should arrange them in order of importance so that you build to your most important criterion. In each of the preceding examples, students placed their most important criterion last.

Step 3: Determining the Extent to Which X Meets Your Criteria for the Class A third step in constructing an evaluation argument is to make your match argument: To what extent does X meet or not meet the criteria you have formulated? The following examples show how three students framed the match part of their evaluation arguments on EMP. Note how each student matches EMP to the specific criteria he or she has selected.

Experience Music Project is a tourist trap rather than an attraction because
- the headphones and heavy computerized MEGs (Museum Exhibit Guides) keep everyone isolated, making companionship difficult.
- the arrangement of exhibits is chaotic, leading to frustration and repetition of the same experiences.
- it doesn't give any substance, just endless music trivia.
- it's too expensive and commercial, leaving the tourist feeling ripped-off.

Experience Music Project is a good museum of rock and roll history because
- it covers a range of popular music styles from jazz and blues to reggae, punk, grunge, and hip-hop.
- it provides interesting information on musicians, musical styles, and key moments in popular music history.
- it makes people excited about popular music and its history through the museum's interactive exhibits and technologically advanced museum guide devices.

For rock fans, Experience Music Project is a good rock and roll shrine because
- it gives illuminating insights into the lives and artistry of many rock musicians.
- it gives an in-depth look at some of the greats like Jimi Hendrix and helps fans really appreciate the talent of these musicians.
- the "onstage" room lets fans fulfill a fantasy by pretending they are rock stars.

Step 4: Determining What Alternative Views You Must Respond to in Your Evaluation Argument Finally, in constructing your evaluation argument you need to determine whether your intended audience is likely to object to (1) the class in which you have placed your object; (2) the criteria you have developed for assessing your object; or (3) the degree to which your object matches the criteria you have chosen. You have numerous options for accommodating your audience's doubts or objections. For example, if your proposed class is controversial, you might choose to justify it in your introduction. If your criteria might be controversial, you could address objections before you start the match part of your argument. If you think your match argument will raise doubts, you could intersperse alternative views throughout or treat them separately near the end of your argument. Any of these methods can work.

In the Readings section of this chapter, we include a student writer's complete evaluation argument on the Experience Music Project.

FOR WRITING AND DISCUSSION

Responding to Objections

Consider how student writer Katie Tiehen confronts and responds to alternative views. After reading this typical passage from her argument, answer the questions that follow:

> ...Some may challenge my contention that EMP is an ineffective museum of rock history by arguing that a day spent at EMP is entertaining and fun. I'll

be the first to admit that EMP is fun. From a rock and roll fan's perspective, EMP is nonstop entertainment, a musical paradise. I felt like a five-year-old on Christmas morning when I saw Eric Clapton's guitar, Jimi Hendrix's personal journals, and walls plastered in punk memorabilia. These items, coupled with video documentaries and hands-on activities, provided hours of enjoyment. Because of the fun factor, it's easy for people to jump to EMP's defense. However, it is not the entertainment value of EMP that I am questioning. There's no doubt that it is a fun and amusing place to visit. The problem arises when one tries to classify EMP as an historical museum, which should provide visitors with access to objects of lasting historical significance. Some entertainment is fine, but not to the point that it clouds the true purpose of the museum as it does in EMP's case. After two visits, I still couldn't tell you where rock and roll originated, but I could tell you that the line to play the drums in Sound Lab is really long. Entertainment is the main purpose of EMP and it shouldn't be.

1. What objections to her argument does Katie anticipate (doubts about her proposed class for EMP, her criteria, or her match argument)?
2. How does Katie respond to alternative views—by conceding points and shifting back to her own perspective or by refuting alternative views with counterreasons and counterexamples?

An Evaluation Argument

WRITING PROJECT

14.2
Write an evaluation argument for an audience of skeptical readers.

Write an argument in which you use evaluative thinking to persuade your audience to see the value (or lack of value) of the person, place, thing, event, or phenomenon that you are evaluating. The introduction to your argument should hook your audience's interest in your evaluation question. The body of your argument should establish criteria for evaluating your chosen subject, and then show how your subject meets or does not meet those criteria. Depending on the degree of controversy surrounding your subject, follow the procedure for other arguments by summarizing alternative views and responding to them through either concession or refutation.

For this assignment you need to pose an evaluative question that is important to your audience and invites multiple views. In some cases, you may choose to evaluate a controversial person, event, thing, or phenomenon—something that engenders lively disagreement within a particular community. (For example: Is "Nimbletoes" Nelson a good quarterback? Is establishing a national ID system or profiling airline passengers a good way to combat terrorism?) When your subject is controversial, you need to consider alternative evaluations and show why yours is better.

In other cases, you may choose to evaluate something that is not itself controversial. Your purpose might be to help a specific audience determine how to spend their time or money. For example, is taking an art gallery walk a good way for students to spend a Saturday afternoon in your city? Or, you might consider writing your evaluation for a specific forum. For example, you might write a review for a parents' magazine or Web site evaluating whether the *Twilight* movies are good family films. Or you might write an editorial for your school newspaper explaining why tutoring with the local children's literacy project is a good experience for education majors.

Generating and Exploring Ideas

For your evaluation essay, you will try either to change your readers' assessment of a controversial person, event, thing, or phenomenon or help your readers decide whether an event or thing is worth their time or money.

If you have not already chosen an evaluation issue, try thinking about evaluative questions within the various communities to which you belong:

Local civic community: evaluative questions about transportation, land use, historical monuments, current leaders, political bills or petitions, housing, parking policies, effectiveness of police

National civic community: evaluative questions about public education, environmental concerns, economic policies, responses to terrorism, Supreme Court decisions, foreign policies, political leaders

Your university community: evaluative questions about academic or sports programs, campus life programs, first-year or transfer student orientation, clubs, dorm life, campus facilities, financial-aid programs, campus security, parking, cultural programs

Your scholarly community or disciplinary community in your major: evaluative questions about internships, study abroad programs, general studies programs, course requirements, first-year studies, major curriculum, advising, course sequences, teaching methods, homework requirements, academic standards, recent books or articles, new theories in a field, library resources, laboratory facilities, Web site sources of primary documents or numerical data in a field

Culture and entertainment issues within your social or family communities: evaluative questions about restaurants, movies, plays, museums, TV shows, musicians, video games, entertainment Web sites, concerts, books, paintings, sports figures, buildings

Consumer issues within your social or family communities: evalutive questions about computer systems, CDs, cars, clothing brands, stores, products, e-commerce

Work communities: evaluative questions about supervisors or subordinates, office efficiency, customer relations, advertising and marketing, production or sales, record keeping and finance, personnel policies

Another good strategy for finding a topic is to think about a recent review or critique with which you disagree—a movie or restaurant review, a sportswriter's assessment of a team or player, an op-ed column or blog assessing a government official or proposed legislation. How would you evaluate this controversial subject differently?

Once you have chosen a possible controversial topic, use the following strategies to help you explore and develop ideas for your evaluation argument.

Strategies for Developing an Evaluative Claim

Strategies	Questions to Ask and Steps to Follow
Place the X you will evaluate in the smallest and most meaningful category for your intended audience.	For the audience you have in mind, what is the smallest, most relevant class in which to place your X? For example, Is Super Eye 2000 a good digital camera *for novices on a low-cost budget* (not simply, is it a good digital camera)?
Determine the criteria you will use to make your evaluation meaningful and helpful to your audience.	What are the purposes of the class in which you have placed your subject? Use freewriting or idea mapping to explore the qualities a member of that class needs to have to achieve those purposes.
Think about the objections to your criteria your audience might raise.	How will you justify your criteria? What reasoning and evidence will you use?
Think about how you will weight or rank your criteria.	Which of your criteria is most important and why?
Evaluate your subject by matching it to each of your criteria.	Why does your subject match or not match each of the criteria? Freewrite to find examples and counterexamples.

Shaping and Drafting

In drafting your evaluation argument, you have two key developmental and organizational questions to consider: (1) Will you have to defend your choice of criteria as well as complete the match part of your argument? (2) Where should you locate and respond to alternative views? Your answers to these questions will depend on your specific evaluation claim and on your audience. In the readings at the end of this chapter, you will notice that student writers Jackie Wyngaard (pp. 376–377) and Teresa Filice (pp. 381–383) chose different approaches to handling alternative views. Although there are many ways to organize an evaluation argument, the framework chart shown in Figure 14.3 is a good place to start.

FIGURE 14.3 Framework for an Evaluation Argument

Introduction	• Presents your issue • Shows why evaluating X is problematic or controversial • Presents your evaluation claim and your criteria
Argument	• States criterion 1 and defends it if necessary • Shows that X meets/does not meet criterion 1 • States criterion 2 and defends it if necessary • Shows that X meets/does not meet criterion 2 • Continues with additional criteria and match arguments
Treatment of alternative or opposing views	• Summarizes objections to your criteria or your match • Responds to these objections
Conclusion	• Sums up your evaluation

Revising

As you revise, think of ways that you can make your evaluation clearer and more useful for your audience. Consider ways to sharpen your criteria and build up the match part of your argument to make your evaluation more persuasive.

Questions for Peer Review

In addition to the generic peer review questions explained in Skill 16.4, ask your peer reviewers to address these questions:

INTRODUCTION

1. How well do the title and introduction capture your interest, provide needed background, identify the controversy, and show importance of the subject?
2. How well has the writer established the evaluative question, the claim, and the criteria? How could these be improved?

THE CRITERIA-MATCH ARGUMENT

3. How fitting and persuasive is the writer's choice of criteria for evaluating this subject? How could the writer support or defend his/her criteria and the weighting of those criteria more clearly or persuasively?
4. How does the writer support and develop the match part of the argument? What evidence helps readers see that the X being evaluated meets or fails to meet each criterion? How could the writer improve the match argument?
5. Where does the writer summarize and address alternative views? How could this treatment of alternative views be improved?

Multimodal or Online Options

1. ***Online Evaluation*** Write an online evaluation of a product, device, store, restaurant, book, film, agency, or something equivalent. Your evaluation should be suitable for posting on Yelp, Angie's List, Amazon, or other Web site that posts user or consumer reviews. In your evaluation, make your criteria clear and relevant to your chosen audience and site. Use specific examples to show how your item under review measures up to your criteria. Try to make this evaluation useful to the audience you have in mind. Also appreciate that evaluative reviews have business consequences. Make sure that your evaluation is respectful, fair, and well supported.
2. ***Speech with Visual Aids (Flip Chart, PowerPoint, Prezi)*** Choose as your subject to be evaluated a proposed policy, action, candidate for office, or other situation or phenomenon that is open to civic debate. Deliver your evaluation argument as a formal speech supported by visual aids and limited to five minutes (modeled, say, after public hearings about a proposed action). Pay attention to the construction and delivery of your speech and to the multimodal design of your visual aids.

WRITING Project

For advice on producing multimedia compositions, see Chapter 19. For an example of a student speech with PowerPoint slides, see Chapter 15, pp. 402–404.

Readings

The first reading is a student essay by Jackie Wyngaard evaluating the Experience Music Project in Seattle, Washington.

Jackie Wyngaard (student)

EMP:

Music History or Music Trivia?

1 Along with other college students new to Seattle, I wanted to see what cultural opportunities the area offers. I especially wanted to see billionaire Paul Allen's controversial Experience Music Project (known as EMP), a huge, bizarre, shiny, multicolored structure that is supposed to resemble a smashed guitar. Brochures say that EMP celebrates the creativity of American popular music, but it has prompted heated discussions among architects, Seattle residents, museumgoers, and music lovers, who have questioned its commercialism and the real value of its exhibits. My sister recommended this museum to me because she knows I am a big music lover and a rock and roll fan. Also, as an active choir member since the sixth grade, I have always been intrigued by the history of music. I went to EMP expecting to learn more about music history from exhibits that showed a range of popular musical styles, that traced historical connections and influences, and that enjoyably conveyed useful information. However, as a museum of rock history, EMP is a disappointing failure.

2 EMP claims that it covers the history of rock and roll from its roots to the styles of today, but it fails at this task because it isolates musicians and styles without explaining historical progressions or cultural influences. For instance, the museum doesn't show how Elvis Presley's musical style was influenced by his predecessors like Chuck Berry and Muddy Waters. It doesn't show how early folk and blues influenced Bob Dylan's music. It doesn't show how early jazz paved the way for rock and roll. How are these isolated and separate EMP exhibits connected? How did rock and roll progress from the '50s "Let's Go to the Hop" beats to the laid-back guitar riffs of the '60s and '70s? How did '70s music become the heavy metal, head-banger rock of the '80s and '90s? How did these styles lead to rap? The exhibits show the existence of these different styles, but they don't help viewers understand the historical developments or historical context. While it is interesting to see a peace patch once owned by Janis Joplin, this exhibit does not explain either the social and political events of the time or Joplin's political views.

3 Another fault of EMP is that it omits many influential groups and musicians, particularly women. For example, there is no display about the Beatles, the Rolling Stones, Led Zeppelin, or the Doors. The exhibits also exclude many major female artists who made substantial contributions to popular music. I found nothing about Joan Baez, Ella Fitzgerald, Aretha Franklin, Carly Simon, or Joni Mitchell. I was also surprised that there were few women mentioned in the Northwest Passage exhibit. Weren't more women involved in the Seattle music scene? As a woman interested in music, I felt left out by EMP's overall neglect of women musicians.

4 Perhaps most frustrating about EMP is the way exhibits are explained through the awkward, difficult-to-use handheld computer called a Museum Exhibit Guide (MEG).

The explanations are hard to access and then disappointing in their content. I wanted to hear a landmark song that an artist wrote or an interesting analysis of the artist's musical style. Instead, I listened to "how Elvis made the leather jacket famous" and other random trivia. The MEG also offers too many choices for each exhibit, like a Web page with a dozen links. But after all the time and effort, you learn nothing that increases your understanding or stimulates your thinking about music history. The MEGs themselves are very heavy, clunky, and inconvenient. If you don't point this gadget exactly at the activator, nothing happens. It took me a good ten minutes to figure out how to get the device to play information for me, and many of my classmates had to keep going back to the booth to get new batteries or other repairs. The museum would be much more effective if visitors had the option of just reading about the displays from plaques on the walls.

5 I know that many people will disagree with my assessment of EMP. They'll point to the fun of the interactive exhibits and the interesting collection of album covers, crushed velvet costumes, concert clips, famous guitars, and old jukeboxes. But a good museum has to be more than a display of artifacts and an array of hands-on activities. Pretending you're a rock star by performing on stage with instruments doesn't tell you how a certain style of music came about. Displaying trivial information about Elvis's leather jacket or Janis Joplin's feather boa doesn't help you appreciate the importance of their music. Devoting half an exhibit to punk rock without any analysis of that style doesn't teach you anything. In short, the museum displays frivolous trivia tidbits without educational substance.

6 Music lovers hoping for an educational experience about the rock and roll era of musical history will be disappointed by EMP. And this is without the additional insult of having to shell out $19.95 to get in the door. Speaking for serious music lovers and students of music history, I have to say that EMP is a failure.

THINKING CRITICALLY

about "EMP: Music History or Music Trivia?"

1. What strategies particularly appropriate for evaluation arguments does Jackie Wyngaard use in her introduction?
2. How has Jackie chosen to classify Experience Music Project? What criteria does she choose?
3. In the match part of her argument, what evidence does Jackie use to support her assessment of Experience Music Project?
4. What alternative views does she acknowledge and where in her argument does she choose to treat them? Does she anticipate objections to her criteria or to the match part of her argument? What other objections might people raise to her argument?
5. What do you find persuasive about her arguments? How might this evaluation argument be improved?

The second reading raises questions about how viewers should evaluate film dramas that claim to represent history. Think of the recent films *Argo* and *Zero Dark Thirty*, and the classic *Apollo 13* and *Glory*. In this evaluation argument about the film *Lincoln*, published in the *New York Times*, Gary Gutting, a professor of philosophy at the University of Notre Dame, challenges the ability of such films to give us accurate understandings of history.

Gary Gutting*

Learning History at the Movies

1 Movies are the source of much of what we know—or think we know—about history. Currently, Steven Spielberg's "Lincoln" is being recommended as a source of knowledge not just about Lincoln and the Civil War but also about politics in general. For example, Ruth Marcus, writing in The Washington Post, has praised the "instructional value" of the film for both President Obama and the current lame-duck Congress. "It presents," she says, "useful lessons in the subtle arts of presidential leadership and the practice of politics, at once grimy and sublime." David Brooks has similarly endorsed the film, and in a post in the Civil War series Disunion, the historian Philip Zelikow explains how the film may have actually put forward its own plausible interpretation of the events surrounding the passage of the 13th Amendment. But there are limits to the extent that we can rely on movies to convey historical truth.

2 Like most popular historical movies, "Lincoln" is not a documentary, but a dramatic presentation. It tells an engaging story, depicts fascinating characters, and has sets and costumes that seem to take us back to Washington in 1865. But to what extent can we trust "Lincoln" (or any other dramatization of history for popular entertainment) as a source of historical fact and understanding? A film drama can present historical events, vividly and movingly perhaps, but it has no place for evidence supporting the truth of the presentation. As a result, simply looking at the movie, we have no way of knowing to what extent "Lincoln" is accurate. This applies to particular details (did Thaddeus Stephens actually wear a wig and have a black mistress?) but most important to the overall interpretation: was Lincoln really a noble politician, reluctantly using patronage and countenancing bribery to achieve a greater good?

3 We might think that questions about the accuracy of "Lincoln" are resolved once we learn that, unlike many historical films, it makes serious use of historical sources and historians' interpretations of them. We're told in the credits that the film is to an important extent based on Doris Kearns Goodwin's well-regarded history, "Team of Rivals: The Political Genius of Abraham Lincoln," and an array of prominent historians are listed as consultants. Still, the film, unlike a historian's book, cannot provide the sources and arguments that might support the countless decisions of its makers about controversial claims and interpretations. Further, since it is a dramatization, the

*Gary Gutting."Learning History at the Movies" from The New York Times, November 29, 2012.

filmmakers—even rigorously faithful ones—are very likely at points within the film to exercise their right to override historical accuracy for the sake of better theater.

4 To pursue the problem of the film's historical value, it will help to reflect on one of the highlights: Daniel Day-Lewis's portrayal of Abraham Lincoln. In The New Yorker, Anthony Lane tells us, "What we derive from Day-Lewis, though, is the mysterious—and accurate—sense of a man who by instinct and by expertise reaches out to the people he leads while seeming lost in himself." Similarly, Kenneth Turan in The Los Angeles Times comments on "the marvelously relaxed way [Day-Lewis] morphs into this character and simply becomes Lincoln. While his heroic qualities are visible when they're needed, Day-Lewis' Lincoln is a deeply human individual, stooped and weary after four years of civil war but endowed with a palpable largeness of spirit and a genuine sense of humor." The performance "rings true," as we say, and it's satisfying to believe that Lincoln was so complex, so human, but finally so great.

5 But how can Lane and Turan have reason to believe that Day-Lewis's portrayal is "accurate"? They would have had to — as Zelikow did in his focused analysis — refer to history books (Goodwin's and others) that sift through the evidence and painstakingly construct a plausible account of Lincoln's character. As I've emphasized, no dramatic presentation in itself provides a basis for accepting its view as even close to the truth.

6 Another problem is that any historical film, particularly one so richly and meticulously realized, will be misleadingly complete and concrete. For example, in the movie, Lincoln orders two congressmen to do what needs to be done to pass the 13th Amendment: "I am president of the United States, clothed in immense power, and I expect to you procure those votes." Goodwin's history cites a memoir that quotes Lincoln as saying this. But no source could give us the volume, tone, facial expression, or contextual nuance that characterized his actual statement. Acting in a movie, however, Day-Lewis has to utter the words in one specific way in one specific situation, and he does so to great effect, conveying a moving interpretation of Lincoln's complex state of mind at the time and of his overall personality. But what Day-Lewis conveys inevitably goes far beyond what our sources tell us Lincoln said and did. His performance may be highly realistic, but we cannot know how close it is to what really happened.

7 But Day-Lewis worked from Tony Kushner's thoroughly researched script, read Goodwin's book (and much else), and discussed details with her. It may well be, then, that his portrayal in this scene gives us an "essential truth" about Lincoln's mental state and character, even if what the movie presents is in fact quite different from what those at the actual scene saw and heard.

8 A similar point applies to the excitingly orchestrated climactic vote on the 13th Amendment in the House of Representatives. We no doubt have records of how people voted, perhaps even of what they said, and of how the crowd reacted. But none of this could underwrite the authenticity of the film's concrete re-enactment, which sweeps us up into its overpowering feeling of justified triumph. But if Kushner and Spielberg have done their historical homework, it may well be that this portrayal expresses the real meaning of the House vote, even if it falls far short as a depiction of what literally happened.

9 The Times's film critic A. O. Scott notes that "some of the ambition of 'Lincoln' seems to be to answer the omissions and distortions of the cinematic past, represented by great films like D. W. Griffith's 'Birth of a Nation,' which glorified the violent

disenfranchisement of African-Americans as a heroic second founding, and 'Gone With the Wind,' with its romantic view of the old South." In purely cinematic terms these two movies may be as compelling as "Lincoln." We resist their force only if we have historical information that undermines their narratives. Apart from such an intellectual substructure, "Lincoln" is no less propaganda than these classics. But once we know that "Lincoln" has superior historical grounding, doesn't that give reason to believe what it presents?

10 Still, merely seeing the movie — even if we know that it is based on a great deal of sound historical research — does not allow us to tell which details are accurate or even which aspects of its interpretation are plausible. To learn this, we need to put the movie in dialogue with the work of historians, as Zelikow has done in his post. (A recent interview with James McPherson, an eminent biographer of Lincoln, also gives a preliminary idea of what can be gained from such an approach.) Without the active engagement of such dialogue, our experience of "Lincoln" will be entertaining but not instructive.

11 But, particularly with a film as well done as "Lincoln," the dialogue will be a genuine two-way exchange. In the end, of course, any truth the film presents needs to be grounded in the meticulous work of historians. But good historians do not merely accumulate data. They need sympathetic perception and imaginative interpretation to turn their data into a plausible historical story. The sympathy and imagination of creative artists can also operate on the materials historians supply. This is why a good historical film (or novel or play) can make its own contribution to our historical understanding. Actors, writers and directors who have immersed themselves in the history can provide their own distinctive insights into its meaning. But to benefit from these insights, we need to make our own connection with the historians' work. It's not nearly enough just to go see the movie.

THINKING CRITICALLY
about "Learning History at the Movies"

1. Gary Gutting's article addresses these questions: Are historical film dramas a good source of knowledge about history? Is the film *Lincoln* a good source of knowledge about Lincoln as president and about the historical events of his presidency? What claims does Gutting make in response to these questions?
2. What criteria does Gutting use to evaluate historical films as a category and the film *Lincoln* in particular? To what extent does Gutting make his evaluation of Lincoln his main argument and to what extent does he use this film as a major illustration of his case against historical film dramas?
3. Where does Gutting explain and justify his criteria?
4. What concessions does Gutting make to alternative views?
5. Gutting concludes his evaluation with a statement about the place and value of films that recreate history. What approach does he recommend for enjoying historical film dramas?
6. How rhetorically effective is Gutting's perspective on historical film dramas?

The final reading, an essay by student writer Teresa Filice, uses the criteria for evaluating Web sites found in Skill 21.3—authority, objectivity or clear disclosure of advocacy, coverage, accuracy, and currency—to evaluate the site Parents: The Anti-Drug (www.theantidrug.com). Although an evaluation of material on the Internet could focus on the home page or even on one link of a Web site, Teresa has chosen to examine whether this advocacy site as a whole accomplishes its purposes effectively.

Teresa Filice

Parents: The Anti-Drug:

A Useful Site

1 The United States' War on Drugs seems to make little progress, and the drug use of American teenagers remains a rampant problem; however, positive, forward-thinking groups have risen to the occasion and sought to meet the challenge, as anyone who listens to radio ads or reads popular news magazines will testify. While the Reagan-sponsored "Just say no" mantra toward drugs still prevails in some households, some anti-drug organizations are promoting open and honest communication between parents and their teens. These groups offer information and fresh perspectives on helping parents talk to their children about illegal substances. In my exploration of how the Web has been enlisted in this campaign against teen drug use, I chose to analyze the site of *Parents: The Anti-Drug* to determine if it is a good advocacy Web site. My evaluation employed the following well-accepted criteria: the breadth of coverage, the accuracy and currency of the information provided, and the site's openness about its mission, goals, and supporters. Despite some strong misgivings in the disclosure area of the Web site, I concluded that it is still a worthwhile advocacy site on the topic of teens and drug prevention, specifically in regards to the current, extensive information it provides on teens and drug use.

2 Initially, I had difficulty discovering what organizations and special interest groups were sponsoring this site, so the site failed to meet the criterion of clear disclosure of advocacy or objectivity. After clicking on the "About Us" link (which was fairly difficult to find), I found out that the site jumps to another Web site for the *Media Campaign*, sponsored by the Office of National Drug Control Policy (http://www.mediacampaign.org). The Office of National Drug Control Policy is a government-sponsored organization, and the Media Campaign site contains links to the White House Web site. Though *Parents: The Anti-Drug* and the *Media Campaign* Web sites are not outrightly politically biased, further scrutiny reveals glimpses of the current conservative political administration in both sites. There is an entire section of *Parents: The Anti-Drug* dedicated to faith leaders and faith-based activities to keep teens away from illegal substances.

3 In addition, I noticed that this advocacy organization's site speaks about and to parents and teens in a traditional, middle-class family setting and therefore limits its coverage and usefulness. Most of the advice the site offers is based on the fact that

teens will have parents with enough time (which often means money as well) to spend with them. While most parents may want to spend quality time with their children, many American parents literally cannot afford time for their children. The site also constantly refers to life in the suburbs and suburban values. One of the boys in the Prescription video states, "I couldn't be a drug addict … I'm from the suburbs." In addition, some of the advice given to parents seems simplistic and unrealistic. For example, the site offers somewhat unrealistic suggestions for "summer activities" for parents to keep their children out of dangerous situations where drugs might be present: "Encourage them to write a song, and then let them record it; build, and maintain a birdfeeder; encourage them to paint a mural; and make homemade ice cream together" (http://www.theantidrug.com/SchoolsOut/activity_checklist.asp?action=form). This site seems to be imagining a specific, limited audience with somewhat old-fashioned values.

4 Despite these flaws and this one area of narrowness, *Parents: The Anti-Drug* has a wide range of information and appears committed to transmitting important factual material to viewers. The site provides an extensive breadth of coverage and accurate information on teen behavior, recreational drugs, and motivating factors for teen drug use. The home page of the site is divided into three panels: "Learn," "Evaluate," and "Take Action," each of which offers numerous links such as "Signs & Symptoms," "Hear Real Stories and Advice," and "Find Help Locally." The "Drug Information" page (http://www.theantidrug.com/drug_info/), which is easily accessible from the home page, offers comprehensive information on a wide variety of drugs, including more recent offenders such as prescription drugs and Ecstasy. In each subsequent section, the site presents basic drug information, the health risks, and the signs that a person might be using that drug. Additionally, each link for the various drugs offers further links with specifics about that drug. The site also has specific "Feature Articles" on topics such as "Keep Your Teen Athlete Drug-Free" and "Teens, Drugs, and Violence." The section on "Teens, Drugs, and Violence" contains documented scientific and social development statistics on the rates of teen drug use and violence. It also has links to other advocacy sites that target gang activity and bullying at school. The "Studies and Research" section (http://www.theantidrug.com/news/studies-and-research.aspx) lists several articles from well-respected medical journals such as the *Journal of Preventative Medicine* and the *American Journal of Public Health*, as well as presenting the authors' credentials. I concluded that the entire site provides well-documented sources for the statistics it uses.

5 *Parents: The Anti-Drug* also shows its worth by meeting the important criterion of currency. The site is surprisingly current and exemplifies a fairly progressive attitude toward and direct approach to drug prevention. *Parents: The Anti-Drug* favors discussion and open communication with teens, as opposed to criticizing their beliefs. The "Teens Today" section cheekily reminds parents that "teens today are less likely to drink, smoke, commit a crime, or get pregnant or drop out of school, compared to their parents' generation" (http://www.theantidrug.com/advice/inside-teens-today.asp). The "Kids Eye View" section provides a voice for the teens themselves, offers a glimpse as to why certain teenagers choose to engage in this activity, and includes video diaries. The site also uses videos to give it a sense of immediacy. For example, on the "Prescription

Drug Abuse" video, a teenage girl with brown curly hair comes into focus on the screen. Her name is Sara and she is nineteen years old. She recalls for the camera her path toward prescription drug addiction that began in her own home. She says, "I could find them [prescriptions] in my kitchen cupboard … My parents wouldn't notice it, without the smell of marijuana" (http://www.theantidrug.com/drug_info/prescription_video.asp). Most parents never want to see their children share this young woman's struggles with addiction, rehab, and the subsequent consequences of both. With material like these videos, this site shows its relevance and awareness of the urgency of the problem and offers helpful advice.

6 Although the site *Parents: The Anti-Drug* has some weaknesses, its strengths compensate well for these deficiencies. I spent many hours poring over the *Parents: The Anti-Drug* Web site. It bothered me greatly that the site emphasized middle-class values and did not fully disclose its government sponsorship. However, after taking some time away from viewing the Web site, I decided to imagine what a visit to this site would mean to parents desperate to communicate with their child. This Web site provides numerous valuable recommendations and, most importantly, provides credible and ample information on a subject that many parents need to understand. Though the site may appear unrealistic in places to older teens, I think it does effectively reach its target group and does qualify as a good advocacy Web site.

Work Cited

Parents: The Anti-Drug. The National Youth Anti-Drug Media Campaign, n.d. Web. 20 May 2007.

THINKING CRITICALLY

about "*Parents: The Anti-Drug*: A Useful Site"

1. In her evaluation argument, Teresa Filice evaluates the advocacy site Parents: The Anti-Drug for its usefulness for parents. How might her evaluation criteria vary if she were evaluating this site for a different audience—for example, teens or the medical profession?
2. What opposing views does Teresa Filice acknowledge in her argument? How does she respond to them?
3. Where do examples work well to support the match part of her argument?
4. From your own use of advocacy Web sites, what evaluation criteria would you add to the typical ones listed here in the headnote, applied in this argument, and presented in more detail in Skill 21.3?

15 PROPOSING A SOLUTION

WHAT YOU WILL LEARN

15.1 To convince your audience that a problem exists and to propose a solution to the problem.

15.2 To use multimodal strategies to create effective proposal arguments.

15.3 To persuade your audience by writing an effective proposal argument.

Proposal arguments call an audience to action. They make a claim that some action should or ought to be taken. Sometimes referred to informally as *should arguments,* proposals are among the most common kinds of arguments that you will write or read.

Practical proposals focus on local, practical problems and generally target a specific audience (usually the person with the power to act on the proposal). For example, Lucy Morsen's proposal in this chapter advocates banning laptops and cell phones in classrooms (pp. 396–399). In the work world, many individuals and businesses generate new revenues by writing competitive proposals to solve a prospective client's practical problem.

Another kind of proposal, a **policy proposal**, addresses public policy issues with the aim of swaying public support toward the writer's proposed solution. Student writer Kent Ansen's proposal to institute mandatory public service for young adults illustrates a researched policy proposal (pp. 405–414).

The power of proposal arguments is often enhanced with images, which can appeal to both *logos* and *pathos.* In fact, proposal arguments sometimes take the form of striking multimodal texts such as **posters** or **advocacy advertisements** calling an audience to action. Additionally, proposal arguments can be delivered as **oral presentations** when, for example, a citizen presents a proposal at an open-mike public hearing.

Engaging Proposal Writing

This activity introduces you to the thinking processes involved in writing a proposal argument.

ON YOUR OWN

Identify and list several major problems facing students in your college or university. Then decide which problems are most important and rank them in order of importance.

IN CONVERSATION

Working in groups, share your lists and decide on your group's number-one problem.

1. Use that problem to explore answers to the following questions. Group recorders should be prepared to present answers to the class as a whole.
   a. Why is the problem a problem?
   b. For whom is the problem a problem?
   c. How will these people suffer if the problem is not solved? Give specific examples.
   d. Who has the power to solve the problem?
   e. Why hasn't the problem been solved up to this point?
   f. How can the problem be solved? Create a proposal for a solution.
   g. What are the probable benefits of acting on your proposal?
   h. What costs are associated with your proposal?
   i. Who will bear these costs?
   j. Why should this proposal be enacted?
   k. What makes this proposal better than alternative proposals?
2. As a group, draft an outline for a proposal argument in which you:
   a. Describe the problem and its significance.
   b. Propose your solution to the problem.
   c. Justify your proposal by showing how the benefits outweigh the costs.
3. Recorders for each group should write the group's outline on the board and be prepared to present the group's argument orally to the class.

Understanding Proposal Writing

15.1
Convince your audience that a problem exists and propose a solution to the problem.

All proposals have one feature in common—they offer a solution to a problem. For every proposed solution, there are always alternative solutions, including doing nothing. Your task therefore is to convince readers that the problem is worth solving, that your proposed solution will actually work, and that the benefits outweigh the costs. Accordingly, a proposal argument typically has three main parts:

1. ***Description of the problem.*** You must first demonstrate that a significant problem exists. Your goal is to make the problem vivid and real for your readers. Who is affected by the problem? What are its causes? Why hasn't it been solved before? What are the negative consequences of not solving the problem?
2. ***Proposal for a solution.*** This section describes your solution with enough detail to show how it would work and what it would cost. If you don't have a solution, you may choose to generate a planning proposal calling for a committee to propose solutions at a later date.
3. ***Justification.*** Here you persuade your audience that your proposal should be enacted. Typically you show that the benefits of your proposal outweigh the costs. You also need to show why your proposed solution is better than alternative solutions. Point out why other possible approaches would not solve the problem, would provide fewer benefits, or would cost significantly more than your proposed solution.

In the following sections, we examine the special challenges of proposal arguments and then show you a powerful strategy for developing the justification section of a proposal.

Special Challenges of Proposal Arguments

To get your readers to take action—the ultimate purpose of a proposal—you must overcome some difficult challenges. In the following chart, we examine the special difficulties people encounter when writing proposal arguments and offer strategies for overcoming them.

Strategies for Overcoming the Special Challenges of Proposal Arguments

Challenge	Explanation	What to Do
Giving the problem presence	To convince readers that a problem exists, you must make them *see* and *feel* the problem—give the problem *presence.*	• Use anecdotes or examples of people suffering from the problem. • Provide startling facts or statistics to dramatize the problem. • Include a photograph or other image that conveys the problem. • Use other appeals to *pathos*.
Appealing to the interests and values of decision makers	A proposal that benefits one group often creates costs for others. Decision makers may not share the sufferers' perspective on a problem. Solving your problem may simply cause more problems for the decision maker.	• Show decision makers how acting on your proposal will benefit *them* directly. • Use audience-based reasons. • If appropriate, appeal to idealism and principle (do the right thing, even if it will cause temporary grief). • Show how benefits to the sufferers outweigh costs to others.
Overcoming inherent conservatism	People are inherently resistant to change, often willing to live with a flawed but bearable situation rather than risk change that could make the situation worse. "Better the devil you know than the one you don't know."	• Emphasize the seriousness of the problem (give it *presence*). • Stress the benefits of solving the problem. • Emphasize the lost potential in not acting. • Show that the risks are minimal. • Show that negative consequences are unlikely.

Challenge	Explanation	What to Do
Predicting consequences	Often readers distrust the proposal writer's rosy scenario. They doubt that the predicted benefits will occur, or they fear negative consequences.	• Take care not to overpromise benefits. • Persuade readers that your predictions are realistic—show how the links in the chain lead directly from the solution to the benefits. • Cite cases where a similar proposal led to real benefits.
Evaluating consequences	Any solution that benefits one group may bring costs to another group. It is difficult to establish a common principle of measurement for weighing costs against benefits.	• In some cases, you can use money as measurement—the savings from this proposal will be more than the initial costs. • In other cases, emphasize that the benefits of increased happiness, less suffering, or saved time outweigh the initial dollar costs. • Emphasize the greatest good for the greatest number (more people will have benefits; fewer will bear costs). • Emphasize idealism and principle (this is the right thing to do despite the cost).

With these particular challenges in mind, we now set forth some strategies for making proposals as effective as possible.

Developing an Effective Justification Section

The distinctions between proposals and other kinds of arguments invite particular kinds of support for proposals. Writers often develop support for their proposals by using the three-strategy approach, which focuses sequentially on principles, consequences, and precedents or analogies, as explained here.

Strategies for Developing a Justification Section

Strategies	What to Do	Templates and Comments	Examples
Argument from principle	Argue that an action should (should not) be taken because it is right (wrong) according to some value, assumption, principle, or belief you share with your audience.	We should (should not) do (this action) because (this action) is ________. Fill in the blank with a belief or value that the audience holds: *good, honest, fair,* and so on.	"We should create publicly financed jobs for poor people because doing so is both charitable and just."

(*continued*)

Strategies	What to Do	Templates and Comments	Examples
Argument from consequence	Argue that an action should (should not) be taken because doing so will lead to consequences that you and your audience think are good (bad).	We should (should not) do (this action) because (this action) will lead to these good (bad) consequences: ________, ________, and ________. Use consequences that your audience will agree are good or bad, as needed.	"We should create publicly financed jobs for poor people because doing so will provide them with money for food and housing, promote a work ethic, and produce needed goods and services."
Argument from precedent or analogy	Argue that an action should (should not) be taken because doing so is similar to what was done in another case, which turned out well (badly).	We should (should not) do (this action) because doing (this action) is like ________, which turned out to be good (bad). Use precedents or analogies that are similar to your proposed action and that will have good (bad) associations for your audience.	*Precedent:* "We should create publicly financed jobs for poor people because doing so will alleviate poverty just as a similar program has helped the poor in Upper Magnesia." *Analogy:* "...because doing so is like teaching the poor how to fish rather than giving them fish."

Each of these argumentation strategies was clearly evident in a public debate in Seattle, Washington, over a proposal to raise county sales taxes to build a new baseball stadium. Those favoring the stadium put forth arguments such as these:

> We should build the new stadium because preserving our national pastime for our children is important (*argument from principle*), because building the stadium will create new jobs and revitalize the adjacent Pioneer Square district (*argument from consequence*), and because building the stadium will have the same beneficial effects on the city that building Camden Yards had in Baltimore (*argument from precedent*).

Those opposing the stadium created arguments using the same strategies:

> We should not build the stadium because it is wrong to subsidize rich owners and players with tax dollars (*argument from principle*), because building a stadium diverts tax money from more important concerns such as low-income housing (*argument from consequence*), and because Toronto's experience with Skydome shows that once the novelty of a new stadium wears off, attendance declines dramatically (*argument from precedent*).

FOR WRITING AND DISCUSSION

Using Different Strategies to Develop Support

Working individually or in small groups, use the strategies of principle, consequence, and precedent/analogy to create *because* clauses that support (or oppose) the following proposals. Try to have at least one *because* clause from each of the strategies, but generate as many reasons as possible. Here is an example:

Claim	Spanking children should be made illegal.
Principle	Because it is wrong to cause bodily pain to children.
Consequence	Because it teaches children that it is okay to hit someone out of anger; because it causes children to obey rules out of fear rather than respect; because it can lead children to be abusive parents.
Precedent/analogy	Because spanking a child is like throwing dishes or banging your fists against a wall—it relieves your anger but turns the child into an object.

1. The school year for grades K–12 should/should not be extended to eleven months.
2. Our city should/should not require all restaurants to post the calorie content of every menu item.
3. Federal law should/should not ban assault weapons and large ammunition clips.
4. The federal government should/should not legalize marijuana.
5. The federal government should/should not enact a substantially increased tax on gasoline.

Multimodal Proposal Arguments

15.2 Use multimodal strategies to create effective proposal arguments.

Proposal arguments can be particularly powerful in multimodal forms. In nonmotion or print formats, verbal text can be enhanced by photographs, drawings, graphs, or other images. Frequently we encounter multimodal proposal arguments in the form of posters or flyers, paid advertisements in newspapers or magazines, brochures, or Web pages in advocacy Web sites. Their creators know the arguments must work fast to capture our attention, give presence to a problem, advocate a solution, and enlist our support. These multimodal proposals frequently use photographs, images, or icons that are arresting or in some way memorable and that appeal to a reader's emotions and imagination. Such arguments can be enhanced further in digital environments where videos or podcasts can employ the narrative power of sound and motion. Multimodal arguments can also be presented orally as speeches, often supplemented with presentation slides in PowerPoint or Prezi.

Advice for creating effective multimodal arguments is provided in Chapter 19.

As an example of a one-page advocacy ad, consider Figure 15.1, which is sponsored by the organization Common Sense for Drug Policy. Note how the advocacy advertisement makes its view of the problem real and urgent to readers

WHITE KIDS ARE MUCH MORE LIKELY TO BE USING (AND SELLING) DRUGS!

According to the federal Centers for Disease Control, he's 4 times more likely than his African-American classmate to be a regular cocaine user.

White high-school students who are current users of cocaine: 4.1%[1]

Chance of a white person ever trying an illicit drug in their lifetime: 42%[2]

Percent of felony drug defendants in state courts who are white: 37%[3]

Percent of white drug felons given probation or nonincarceration sentence by state courts: 32%[4]

Percent of white drug felons sentenced to prison by state courts each year: 27%[5]

According to the Justice Department, if he's arrested on drug charges, he's 1-1/2 times more likely than his white classmate to be sent to prison.

African-American high-school students who are current users of cocaine: 1.1%[1]

Chance of an African-American person ever trying an illicit drug in their lifetime: 37.7%[2]

Percent of felony drug defendants in state courts who are black: 61%[3]

Percent of black drug felons given probation or nonincarceration sentence by state courts: 25%[4]

Percent of black drug felons sentenced to prison by state courts each year: 43%[5]

BLACK KIDS ARE MORE LIKELY TO GO TO PRISON!

Note:
According to the US Justice Department and the Office of National Drug Control Policy, drug users typically buy their drugs from sellers of their own racial or ethnic background. Research of Ethnicity & Race of Drug Sellers and Users: US Dept. of Justice National Institute of Justice & the Office of National Drug Control Policy, "Crack, Powder Cocaine, and Heroin: Drug Purchase and Use Patterns in Six U.S. Cities, " December 1997, p.1, 16, and p. 15, Table 16.

Sources:
[1] Data on drug use by high-school students: Youth Risk Behavior Survey 1999, Centers for Disease Control, reported in Morbidity and Mortality Weekly Report, Vol. 49, No. SS-5, p. 66, Table 24.
[2] Data on lifetime prevalence of drug use: US Dept. of HHS Substance Abuse and Mental Health Services Administration, "Summary of Findings from the 1999 National Household Survey on Drug Abuse," August 2000, p. G-13, Table G-13.
[3] Demographic data on felony drug defendants in state courts: US Dept. of Justice Bureau of Justice Statistics. "Felony Defendants in Large Urban Counties, 1996," October 1999, p.4, Table 3
[4] Demographic data on felony drug defendants in state courts: US Dept. of Justice Bureau of Justice Statistics, "State Court Sentencing of Convicted Felons, 1996," February 2000, p. 13, Table 2.5
[5] Demographic data on felony drug defendants in state courts: US Dept. of Justice Bureau of Justice Statistics, "State Court Sentencing of Convicted Felons, 1996," February 2000, p. 13, Table 2.5

Kevin B. Zeese, President, Common Sense for Drug Policy
3220 "N" Street, NW, #141, Washington, D.C. 20007 * 703-354-9050 * fax 703-354-5695 * info@csdp.org
For more information, visit www.csdp.org and www.drugwarfacts.org

FIGURE 15.1 A One-Page Advocacy Advertisement from a Magazine

by using disturbing black-and-white drawings, varied type sizes and fonts, and powerful lists of evidence. It also gains credibility through its documentation of sources, presented at the bottom of the page. For a multimodal argument with a stronger visceral impact, consider the part opener image shown on page 585. This poster, "BEWARE...Drink Only Approved Water" produced by the United States War Department in 1944, employs a visual shock technique through its horrific image of a reflected skull to warn against dinking infected water.

Further discussion of this image is found in Chapter 19, page 491.

To show how a student writer can use multimodal strategies to enhance a proposal argument, consider Joyce Keeley's PowerPoint slide on African refugee camps (Chapter 19, page 495). Early in her speech, she wants to give "presence" to her problem—the transient and unstable life of African refugees who must flee their homeland either to urban slums without any humanitarian support or to refugee camps where they have support but no economic opportunity or freedom of movement. To dramatize this problem visually, Joyce selected three Web images—a photograph of refugees on the road carrying their life's possessions on their backs, an aerial photograph of an urban slum, and a photograph of a refugee camp. Each image appeals to *pathos* through its heartbreaking connotations of disrupted life, poverty, and hopelessness.

For further discussion of Joyce's PowerPoint slide, see Chapter 19, page 492–49.

A Proposal Argument

WRITING PROJECT

15.3
Persuade your audience by writing an effective proposal argument.

Call your audience's attention to a problem, propose a solution to that problem, and present a justification for your solution. You have two choices (or your instructor may limit you to just one): (a) create a practical proposal, with a letter of transmittal, proposing a nuts-and-bolts solution to a local problem; or (b) write a more general policy proposal, addressing a public issue, in the form of a feature editorial for a particular (state, local, or college) newspaper. If you choose (b), your instructor might ask you to do research and model your proposal after a magazine or journal article.

Generating and Exploring Ideas

If you have trouble thinking of a proposal topic, try making an idea map of local problems you would like to see solved. Consider some of the following starting points:

Finding a Proposal Issue

Problems at your university: parking, registration system, absence of recycling options, hours of cafeterias and eating facilities, too many activities on campus during the week, poor school spirit, problems with residence halls, availability of internships

Problems in your city or town: lack of bike paths, inadequate lighting, unattractive public parks or lack of public parks, zoning problems, inadequate support for public education, need for public transportation, conservation of water

Problems at your place of work: flow of customer traffic, inadequate staffing during peak times, unclear division of responsibilities, no policies for raises or training new employees, health care coverage, safety issues

Social problems and problems related to other aspects of your life: problems with credit card debt, need for financial literacy, physical fitness in the public schools, aid for victims of disasters, employment opportunities for college students, media consumption and awareness of current events

Another approach is to freewrite your response to these trigger statements:

I would really like to solve the problem of ________________.

I believe that X should________________. (Substitute for X words such as *my instructor, the president, the school administration, Congress, my boss,* and so forth.)

Note that the problem you pose for this paper can be personal, but shouldn't be private; that is, others should be able to benefit from a solution to your personal problem. For example, your inability to find child care for your daughter is a private problem. But if you focus your proposal on how zoning laws discourage development of in-home day care—and propose a change in those zoning laws to permit more in-home day care centers—then your proposal will benefit others.

Using Stock Issues to Explore Your Problem

Once you have decided on a proposal issue, explore it by freewriting your responses to the following questions. These questions are often called *stock issues,* since they represent generic, or stock, questions that apply to almost any kind of proposal.

1. Is there a problem here that has to be solved?
2. Will the proposed solution really solve this problem?
3. Can the problem be solved in a simpler way without disturbing the status quo?
4. Is the proposed solution practical enough that it really stands a chance of being implemented?
5. What will be the positive and negative consequences of the proposal?

You might also try freewriting your responses to the questions in the "In Conversation" exercise on page 385. Although these questions cover much the same territory as the stock issues, their different presentation might stimulate additional thought.

Finally, try thinking of justifications for your solution by using the principles/consequences/precedents or analogies strategy described on pages 387–388.

Avoiding Presupposing Your Solution in Your Problem Statement

A common mistake of inexperienced proposal writers is to write problem statements that presuppose their solutions. As a restaurant server, suppose you notice that customers want coffee refills faster than servers can provide them. To solve this problem, you propose placing carafes of hot coffee at each table. When describing your problem, don't presuppose your solution: "The problem is that we don't have carafes of hot coffee at the tables." Rather, describe the problematic situation itself: annoyed customers clamoring for coffee and harassed servers trying to bring around refills. Only by giving presence to the original problem can you interest readers in your proposed solution, which readers will compare to other possible approaches (including doing nothing).

Here is another example:

> **Weak:** The problem is that the Student Union doesn't stay open late enough at night.
>
> **Better:** The problem is that students who study late at night don't have an attractive, convenient place to socialize or study; off-campus coffee houses are too far to walk to at night; dorm lounges aren't attractive or conducive to studying; late-nighters make noise in the dorms instead of going to a convenient place.

Shaping and Drafting

In Figure 15.2, we show a typical organizational plan for a proposal argument that you might use if you get stuck while composing the first draft of your essay.

FIGURE 15.2 Framework of a Proposal Argument

Introduction	• Presents and describes a problem that needs solving, giving it presence • Gives background including previous attempts to solve the problem • Argues that the problem is solvable (optional)
Presentation of the proposed solution	• States the solution succinctly • Explains the specifics of the solution
Justification	• Persuades readers that the proposal should be implemented • Presents and develops Reasons 1, 2, and so forth (Reasons to support the proposed solution may be arguments from principle, consequence, and precedent or analogy)
Summary and rebuttal of opposing views	*Policy proposal:* • Presents opposing view(s) • Rebuts opposing view(s) *Practical proposal:* • Presents alternative solution(s) • Explains why alternative solution(s) are inferior
Conclusion	• Asks readers to act (sometimes incorporated into the last sentences of the final supporting reason)

Revising

After you have completed your first draft and begun to clarify your argument for yourself, you are ready to start making your argument clear and persuasive for your readers. Use the strategies for clear closed-form prose outlined in Chapter 17. At this stage, feedback from peer readers can be very helpful.

Questions for Peer Review

In addition to the generic peer review questions explained in Skill 16.4, ask your peer reviewers to address these questions:

INTRODUCTION AND STATEMENT OF PROBLEM:

1. How could the title more effectively focus the paper and pique your interest?
2. Where does the writer convince you that a problem exists and that it is significant (worth solving) and solvable? Where does the writer give the problem presence? How could the writer improve the presentation of the problem?

PROPOSED SOLUTION:

3. Does the writer's thesis clearly propose a solution to the problem? Could the thesis be made more precise?
4. Could the writer give you more details about the solution so that you can understand it and see how it works? How could the writer make the solution clearer?

JUSTIFICATION:

5. In the justification section, how could the writer provide stronger reasons for acting on the proposal? Where could the reasons be better supported with more details and evidence? How could the reasons appeal more to the values and beliefs of the audience?
6. Can you help the writer think of additional justifying arguments (arguments from principle, from consequences, from precedent or analogy)? How else could the writer improve support for the proposal?
7. Where does the writer anticipate and address opposing views or alternative solutions? How does the writer convince you that the proposed solution is superior to alternative solutions?
8. Has the writer persuaded you that the benefits of this proposal will outweigh the costs? Who will pay the costs and who will get the benefits? What do you think the gut reaction of a typical decision maker would be to the writer's proposal?
9. Can you think of other, unforeseen costs that the writer should acknowledge and address? What unforeseen benefits could the writer mention?
10. How might the writer improve the structure and clarity of the argument? Where might the writer better apply the principles of clarity from Chapter 17?

Multimodal or Online Options

WRITING PROJECT

1. ***Advocacy Ad or Poster*** Create a one-page advocacy ad or poster that presents a controversial public problem and calls for action and support. Consider how you will use all the features of visual arguments—type sizes and fonts, layout, color, and images and graphics—to grab the attention of your audience, construct a compelling sketch of the problem, and inform your audience what course of action you want them to take. In this advocacy piece, you need to capture your proposal argument in a highly condensed form, while making it visually clear and memorable. Your instructor might ask you instead to create a longer brochure-length handout or a Web page. Advice on creating advocacy posters is found in Chapter 19, pages 496–497.
2. ***Proposal Speech with Visual Aids*** Deliver a proposal argument as a prepared but extemporaneous speech of approximately five to eight minutes supported with visual aids created on presentation software such as PowerPoint or Prezi. Your speech should present a problem, propose a solution, justify the solution with reasons and evidence, and defend it against objections or alternative solutions. As you deliver your speech, use appropriate visual aids to give presence to the problem, highlight points, provide memorable data or evidence, or otherwise enhance appeals to *logos, ethos,* and *pathos*. Although presentation software is commonly used in oral presentations, low-tech visual aids (for example, overhead transparencies or flip charts) can also be effective. Follow the guidelines provided by your instructor. As you contemplate this project, consider its three different components: creating the speech itself, designing the visuals, and delivering the speech. Advice on giving oral presentations and designing presentation slides is provided in Chapter 19, pages 498–502.

Readings

Our first reading, by student writer Lucy Morsen, is a practical proposal entitled "A Proposal to Improve the Campus Learning Environment by Banning Laptops and Cell Phones from Class." Because practical proposals are aimed at a specific audience, they are often accompanied by a letter of transmittal that introduces the writer, sets the context, and summarizes the proposal. We reproduce here Lucy's transmittal letter followed by her proposal. We also show you the appearance of her title page.

April 26, 2010

Professor Ralph Sorento
Chair, Faculty Senate
____________ University
Street
City, State, Zip

Dear Professor Sorento:

1 Enclosed is a proposal that I hope you will present to the Faculty Senate. It asks the university to ban all laptops and cell phones from classes in consideration of those many students like myself whose educational experience is diminished by classmates who surf the Web or send text messages during lectures or class discussion. As I try to show in this proposal, the effect of laptops and cell phones in class is distracting to many students and may hurt the academic performance of students who think they can multitask without any negative effects. I use both personal experience and recent research reports on multitasking as support for my argument.

2 Banning laptops and cell phones from class would deepen students' engagement with course material and make for more lively and energetic class discussions. I argue that an outright campus ban would be more effective than leaving the decision up to individual instructors.

3 Thank you for considering my proposal. I am happy that this university has a Faculty Senate that welcomes ideas from students on how to make teaching and learning more effective.

Sincerely,
Lucy Morsen,
First-Year Student

A PROPOSAL TO IMPROVE THE CAMPUS LEARNING ENVIRONMENT BY BANNING LAPTOPS AND CELL PHONES FROM CLASS

Submitted to Professor Ralph Sorento
Chair of the Faculty Senate

Lucy Morsen
First-Year Student, Williamson Hall

If this were the actual proposal, it would begin on a new page following the cover page.

1 Although I am generally happy as a first-year student at this university, I wish to call the Faculty Senate's attention to a distracting problem: classmates' frequent use of laptops and cell phones during class. In many classes more than half the students have open laptops on their desks or are openly text-messaging on cell phones. Inevitably, laptop users multitask between taking notes and checking email, perusing Facebook, surfing the Web, looking at YouTube videos, playing a game, or working on an assignment for another class. (I have yet to see a student use his or her laptop solely for note-taking.) Even though I try to focus on class lectures and discussion, I find myself missing key points and ideas as my eyes are drawn to the animations and flashing colors on neighboring laptop screens. Other distractions come from the clicking of cell phone keypads—or the momentary vibration of a phone on a desktop—which can seem surprisingly loud in an otherwise quiet environment. When the person next to me continually picks up and sets down her phone to send and receive text messages, she not only distracts me from the lecture but also lets me know that she is not engaged in class, and seemingly has no interest in being so. My annoyance at my classmates and my frustration at not being able to focus undercut my enjoyment of class.

2 Given the extensive use of laptops and cell phones in class, I question the academic motivation of my classmates. As a student, I most enjoy classes when I and my classmates are actively interested and engaged in class lecture and discussion. Collective interest has a way of feeding on itself. I mean, we as students do not operate in isolation from one another, but instead we affect and influence one another in gross and subtle ways. Together with our professor we create a collective environment in the classroom, and just as we as individuals affect this collective environment, this collective environment influences us as individuals. The broad effects and consequences of this dynamic interplay should not be underestimated. Humans are highly social beings; we have the power to influence each other in both positive and negative ways. I believe that the distracting nature of laptops and cell phones is negatively affecting classroom environments. Any steps we can take collectively to help each other learn and succeed should be considered.

3 To address this problem, I propose a campus-wide ban on laptops and cell phones during class. I believe a campus-wide ban would be more effective than more limited measures some institutions have adopted, such as blocking wireless access from classrooms or allowing each professor to choose whether or not to ban laptops in his or her classroom. Blocking wireless access does not address the problem of cell phones or non-Web-based laptop distractions (such as computer games or other class work). Leaving the decision up to professors creates an added difficulty for them. I can imagine that professors, fearing resentment and poor evaluations from their students, would be reluctant to enforce a ban in their classrooms, even if they feel it would improve the classroom experience.

4 A campus-wide ban, on the other hand, would be easy to enforce, and students would more easily establish new habits—namely, not using laptops and cell phones during class. Over time, this could become the new campus norm.

5 Although many students might at first object to a ban, the decision to ban all laptops and cell phones in class would bring benefits not only to distracted students like me but also to current users of laptops and cell phones as well as to professors.

6 For one thing, the banning of laptops and cell phones would improve the learning atmosphere of a classroom. These technologies simply create too many distractions for students, and the negative consequences of these distractions are significant enough to call for institutional intervention. While some of my classmates may begrudge the ban, I believe they would quickly get used to it and notice improvements in their own classroom interest and performance. Many of my classmates may actually welcome the ban because they—like myself—are aware of the negative distractions laptops and cell phones create. In fact, an informal survey by a Georgetown University law professor who bans laptops in his classroom indicated that 70% of his students welcomed the ban (Cole, 2008).

7 Second, a ban might directly improve academic performance of current users of laptops and cell phones. A recent study at the University of Winona (Fried, 2008) found that laptop use in the classroom had a significant negative effect on class performance. In Fried's study, students who brought laptops to class received lower grades than their classmates who did not bring laptops to class. Moreover, those who brought laptops to class reported using their laptops for non-class purposes for nearly a quarter of class time.

8 Many of my classmates will likely argue that this study doesn't apply to them. They believe that they are skilled multitaskers who can continue to pay attention to a lecture while also engaging in these other activities. There is empirical evidence that they are in fact mistaken about their ability to multitask. A study by three Stanford University researchers found that persons who self-reported being heavy multitaskers were *more* easily distracted from a primary task than those who reported themselves as light multitaskers (Ophir, Nass, & Wagner, 2009). The researchers conducted this study in a lab by giving multitasking tasks to a group of self-identified heavy multitaskers and then to a group of light multitaskers. This study suggests that a person's own perception of how well he or she multitasks may not be reliable. Moreover it suggests that large amounts of daily multitasking may actually decrease a person's ability to concentrate on a single task and suppress irrelevant information.

9 A handful of students will likely argue that they only use their laptops for class-related purposes, and that an outright ban on laptops in the classroom would be unfair because they would be prohibited from using them for note-taking. However, I am skeptical of any claims that students make of only using laptops for class-related purposes. I personally have never seen any evidence of this, and research is indicating that multitasking is overwhelmingly the common norm among laptop users in the classroom. In a study by Benbunan-Fich and Truman (2009), student laptop use was monitored for 28 classroom sessions of 80 minutes (with students' permission). The researchers analyzed how often the students toggled between screens, and whether the screens were class-related or non-class-related. They found that 76% of the time students toggled between screens that were non-class-related. On average, students toggled between computer-based activities 37.5 times per 80-minute session. This research suggests that the temptations of non-class-related activities are simply too

great for students *not* to engage in multitasking in class—it is just too easy to do a brief check of email or a quick Facebook scan with a swift click of a mouse.

10 University institutions may feel reluctant to propose a campus-wide ban on laptops and cell phones in the classroom for fear of seeming overly authoritative and unnecessarily limiting student freedom. After all, students might rightly claim that they have a right to do whatever they want in the classroom as long as they aren't harming anyone else. (I have already shown they actually are harming others.) While I believe that individual rights are an important concern—in general I believe university institutions should allow for a great amount of autonomy for their students—I think that laptop use has too many negative consequences to be allowed simply in the name of student freedom. (Of course, a professor can always allow laptop use for students with special needs.)

11 For these reasons, I propose that a campus-wide ban on laptops and cell phones in the classroom should be considered. A campus-wide ban would help to create more positive, cohesive classroom experiences, and it would provide a reprieve for students from the myriad of distractions this modern technological age presents us. A campus-wide ban would be easier on professors to enforce, and it would help to establish a new (and improved) norm.

References

Benbunan-Fich, R., & Truman, G. E. (2009). Multitasking with laptops during meetings. *Communications of the ACM, 52*(2), 139–141. doi:10.1145/1461928.1461963

Cole, D. (2008, October 23). Why I ban laptops in my classroom [Web log post]. Retrieved from http://www.britannica.com/blogs/2008/10/why-i-ban-laptops-in-my-classroom

Fried, C. B. (2008). In-class laptop use and its effects on student learning. *Computers and Education, 50,* 906–914. Retrieved from www.elsevier.com

Ophir, E., Nass, C., & Wagner, A. D. (2009). Cognitive control in media multitaskers. *Proceedings of the National Academy of Sciences.* PNAS Early Edition. Retrieved from www.pnas.org

THINKING CRITICALLY

about "A Proposal to Improve the Campus Learning Environment by Banning Laptops and Cell Phones from Class"

1. What strategies does Lucy Morsen use to convince the Faculty Senate that a problem exists?
2. What strategies does Lucy employ to persuade the Faculty Senate that her proposal is worth enacting and that it is more effective than alternative solutions?
3. How does Lucy tie her proposal to the values and beliefs of her audience—college professors who are members of the Faculty Senate?
4. How effective is Lucy's use of research evidence to support her proposal?
5. If you were a faculty member, how effective would you find Lucy's proposal? How effective do you find it as a student? What are its chief strengths and weaknesses?

Our second reading, an op-ed from the *New York Times*, proposes that competitive cheerleading be recognized as a varsity sport. Jennifer Allen is the daughter of former Washington Redskins football coach George Allen and author of the memoir, *Fifth Quarter: The Scrimmage of a Football Coach's Daughter.*

Jennifer Allen*

The Athlete on the Sidelines

1 It's midseason in cheer nation. This winter, thousands of girls will travel on college all-star teams to take part in competitions across the country. Practicing more than 20 hours a week, they will refine a routine of back flips, handsprings, round-offs and splits—all perfectly synchronized and timed to an Olympic second. Their goal: first place. Their game: competitive cheerleading, one of the fastest-growing sports for women in America.

2 Last year, the University of Maryland became the first Division I N.C.A.A. institution to recognize competitive cheerleading as a varsity sport. That means team members are accorded the same benefits as other campus athletes—a coaching and medical staff; locker rooms; help with academics; help dealing with the press. By the 2005–06 academic year, Maryland will provide 12 full scholarships to competitive cheerleaders. The question is this: What took so long?

3 (Time out for a definition. Competitive cheerleading overlaps with but is not identical to the spirit squads you see, say, on the sidelines of a Saturday afternoon college football game. The teams we're talking about do cheer at school games, but they also compete against other schools in cheerleading competitions where they perform high-risk routines under high-pressure circumstances.)

4 For too many years, cheerleading has been the subject of derision. *Sports Illustrated* has lampooned it. Many Americans fail to distinguish it from the sideline shows the Dallas Cowboys cheerleaders put on. Back when I was a cheerleader in high school in the late 70s, we were called a sideshow. In those days, we performed at every sporting event—football, basketball and baseball. We practiced three days a week; purchased our own uniforms (skirts, sweaters, trunks, socks, saddle shoes) and were responsible for our own steady supply of bandages. Ace bandages. There were plenty of injuries, mostly to ligaments. After a big game, my knee would swell. My dad would offer a diagnosis—water on the knee—bandage it up, and then prescribe 50 reps on the knee machine. But cheerleaders weren't allowed in the school weight room.

5 Today, more than 200,000 high-school and college students attend cheerleading camps each year; at least 15 percent of them participate in competitions. The Universal Cheerleading Association feeds its competitions to ESPN for lively weekend fare. When these events were televised last year, they drew an average audience of 334,000 homes.

6 For all its popularity, though, the sport is governed—or not governed—by a patchwork of entities. Schools may treat cheerleaders as athletes—but they don't have to. Some offer little more than a uniform and a game-day parking pass; others offer scholarships; none offer the full range of support and benefit that Maryland does for competitive cheerleading. What's more, cheerleading is not even recognized by the N.C.A.A. as a sport.

7 Given the nature of competitive cheerleading, this seems like a risky proposition. Think about it: in what other sport is an athlete tossed more than 30 feet in the air—smiling—before spiraling down into the arms of a trusted teammate? Lifts and tosses and catches are the mainstay of competitive cheerleading. "Fliers" do not wear hip pads or kneepads or helmets. There is little to protect a cheerleader from awkward or poor landings on the gym floor.

8 Not surprisingly, cheerleading is the No. 1 cause of serious sports injuries to women, according to the National Center for Catastrophic Sport Injury Research, ahead of gymnastics and track. From 1980 to 2001, emergency room visits for cheerleading injuries rose fivefold.

9 Pushing colleges to recognize competitive cheerleading as a sport will surely help to cut down on injuries. Right now, the American Association of Cheering Coaches and Advisers publishes a manual and administers a safety certification program, but only a fraction of coaches have been certified. Many cheerleaders try dangerous stunts without proper training, coaching and supervision.

10 Of course, convincing other schools to make competitive cheerleading an official sport won't be easy. According to Deborah Yow, Maryland's athletic director, it took more than a year to make sure that the university's cheerleading squad would meet all the guidelines set forth by the Department of Education's Office of Civil Rights. While the department does not define what is or is not a "sport," it does determine whether a university's given activity—such as cheerleading—can be considered a sport in order to comply with Title IX.

11 Is Maryland's action entirely altruistic? Probably not. It doubtless relieves some Title IX pressure. But what's wrong with that? And would it be so wrong to ask the N.C.A.A. to sponsor and govern the sport? After all, when the big collegiate cheerleading competitions begin next month, hundreds of thousands of people will tune in, acknowledging the importance of cheerleading. More N.C.A.A. colleges would be wise to follow suit.

THINKING CRITICALLY

about "The Athlete on the Sidelines"

1. As in most proposal arguments, Allen's first task is to convince readers that a problem exists. She has to persuade readers to take competitive cheerleading seriously and to show them why it is problematic for competitive cheerleaders not to be granted varsity sport status. What are her strategies for convincing us that a problem exists? How effective is she?

2. How does Allen justify her claim that cheerleading should be recognized as a sport? According to her argument, what are the benefits that will come from making cheerleading a varsity sport? What costs does she acknowledge? What additional costs might you point to if you were skeptical of her claim?
3. Overall, how persuasive is her argument? In your response to this question, focus on the strengths and weaknesses of her appeals to *logos, ethos,* and *pathos*.
4. If you are persuaded by her argument and if you are attending an institution where competitive cheerleading could exist, how might you persuade the administration on your campus to make cheerleading a varsity sport? (Who are the decision makers for this issue? What arguments would most motivate them? What are the constraints that must be overcome?)

Our third reading, by student writer Sam Rothchild, illustrates a multimodal argument—a speech supported with visual aids. We have reproduced Sam's outline for his speech along with six of his PowerPoint slides. His final slide was a bibliography of the sources used in the speech and the slides. Note how Sam has constructed the slides as visual arguments to support specific points in the speech as opposed to using his slides to reproduce his speech outline. In Chapter 19, we offer advice on preparing and delivering speeches and creating presentation slides.

Sam Rothchild (Student)

Reward Work Not Wealth:

A Proposal to Increase Income Tax Rates for the Richest 1 Percent of Americans

Problem

1. Since 1980 the gap between rich and poor has increased enormously.
   a. Statistical evidence demonstrates the gap.
      (i) The rich have gotten richer.
      (ii) The poor have gotten poorer.
      (iii) The middle class are treading water.
   b. A primary cause of the income gap is the Bush-era tax cuts that benefited the rich more than the poor.
   c. Income gap leads to an unhealthy middle class and increased poverty, hurting all Americans.

Solution

2. The solution is to raise the income tax rates on the ultra-rich back to 1980 levels.

FIGURE 15.3 Sam's Title Slide Using an Image for *Pathos*

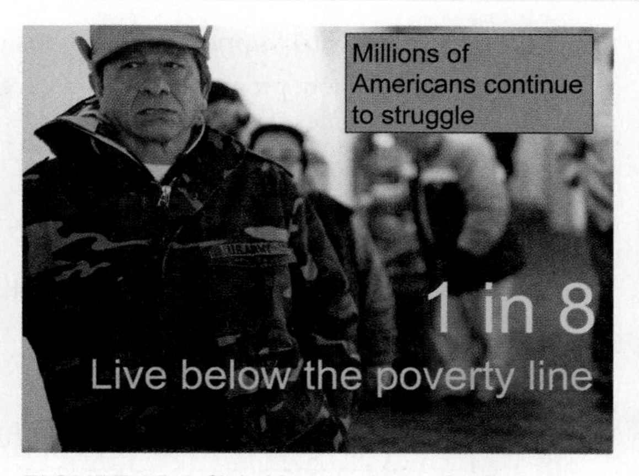

FIGURE 15.4 Slide Using an Image for Pathos

FIGURE 15.5 First of a Two-Slide Sequence Using Images to Illustrate Income Gap

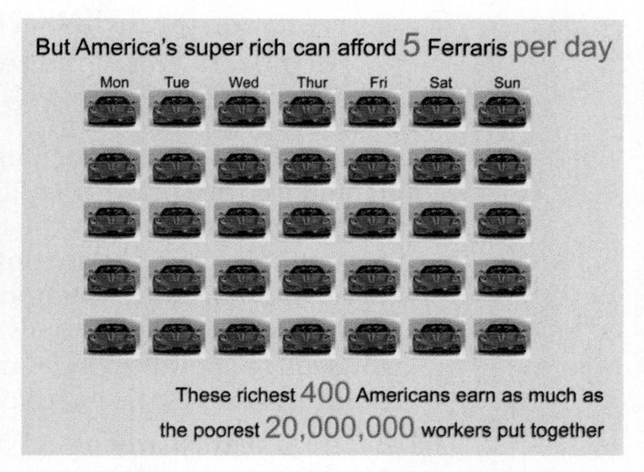

FIGURE 15.6 Second Slide in Sequence, Designed by Sam to Dramatize Wealth

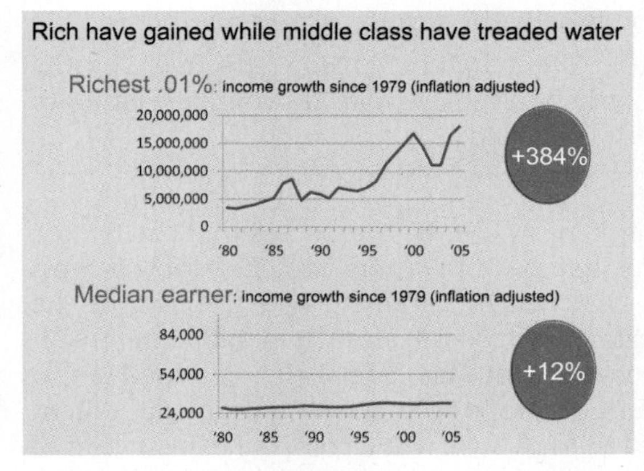

FIGURE 15.7 Slide with Point Title and Graphics for Evidence

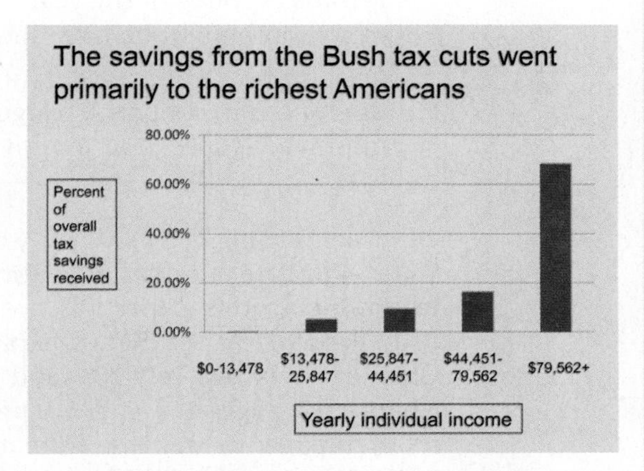

FIGURE 15.8 Another Slide with Point Title and Graphics for Evidence

Reasons to Support this Proposal

3. A more progressive income tax structure promotes a more just society.
   a. Sales taxes and payroll taxes (Social Security, Medicare) take a high-percentage chunk out of low-income salaries and a tiny percentage out of high-income salaries.
   b. Progressive income tax balances the regressive effect of sales taxes and payroll taxes.
4. Reducing the gap between rich and poor creates a stronger middle class and reduces poverty.
5. Increasing tax rates on the very rich will not hurt the incentive to work or the entrepreneurial spirit.
6. The ultra-rich will still be ultra-rich.

THINKING CRITICALLY ABOUT

"Reward Work Not Wealth: A Proposal to Increase Income Tax Rates for the Richest 1 Percent of Americans"

1. Although it is common to design PowerPoint slides using topics and bullets to reproduce the speaker's outline, many media specialists prefer the approach Sam uses here in which the titles of slides are complete sentences that make a point. (See our explanation of "assertion/evidence" slides in Chapter 19, pp. 498–501). Sam's intention is to use the slide title to make a point and then use photographs, drawings, or graphics to support the point through immediate appeals to *logos* and *pathos*. How does each of Sam's slides make a point? How does the image on each slide support the point?
2. Sam was particularly proud of the way he constructed his two Ferrari slides. He wanted to create a startling way to show his audience the extreme wealth of the super-rich: "Not only can they afford a Ferrari. They can afford five Ferraris ever day of the year!" Do you find these Ferrari slides effective? What other ways might he have shown visually the wealth of the super-rich?
3. Overall, how effective do you find Sam's argument? How effectively has he used slides to support his argument? What suggestions do you have either to improve his speech or improve his visual aids?

Our final reading is by student writer Kent Ansen, who proposes that the United States institute mandatory national service for young adults. Kent's process in producing this paper has been discussed in various places throughout the text. Particularly see Kent's exploratory paper and annotated bibliography in Chapter 7, pages 160–164 and 165–167 and his "nutshell" and outline in Chapter 17, pages 440–443. We present his proposal as an illustration of a student research paper written and formatted in MLA style. For a compete explanation of MLA style, see Chapter 23.

Ansen 1

Put last name and page number in header on each page.

Kent Ansen

Professor Johnson

Writing Seminar

15 Mar. 2013

Place name, course information, and date on first page.

Engaging Young Adults to Meet America's Challenges:
A Proposal for Mandatory National Service

Center title.

In high school, I volunteered at an afterschool program for elementary school students located in one of the poorest, most dangerous neighborhoods in town, known for high crime and gang activity. I spent a couple hours per week helping kids complete homework and crafts, reading stories, supervising field games, and serving snacks. The kids' snacks—usually a piece of fruit, some crackers, and a carton of milk—often filled in for dinner because there was no food for them at home. The program was run by a team of AmeriCorps members, who also ran a summer program so the kids had supervision, learning opportunities, and food during the long months of summer. In addition to providing tutoring and food, AmeriCorps connected students and their families to resources like clothing, healthcare, and school supplies. They partnered with Habitat for Humanity to repair dilapidated homes, haul trash to garbage pickup sites, and landscape overgrown yards. Over time, the AmeriCorps program gained so much trust and respect that its program expanded to other neighborhoods like this one, mobilizing an even greater number of volunteers and resources to fight poverty and injustice in our town.

Indent paragraphs ½ inch.

Use one-inch margins at top, bottom, and both sides.

Double-space all parts of the text (no single spacing anywhere).

The successes I witnessed in AmeriCorps suggest that volunteer programs can help address problems in our communities. But it is possible that they can also address problems faced by young people, whose job choices are limited by the slow economic recovery, the reduced number of entry-level jobs, and the crushing burden of student loans. A 2012 Pew Research study found that only 54 percent of Americans aged 18-24 were currently employed

Parenthetical citation—for full citation, see entry under "Young . . ." in Works Cited.

(the lowest rate since the government began tracking this data in 1948) and that these young adults experienced the greatest drop in earnings of any age group in the last four years ("Young, Underemployed and Optimistic"). Young Americans have been classified as a "Lost Generation" struggling to overcome these obstacles and find the path to success and achievement.

Problems like these present us with a unique opportunity for creative problem solving. I propose instituting a mandatory year of national service for Americans ages 18-25. A mandatory service program would engage today's underemployed Lost Generation in helping America's vulnerable communities become stable, healthy, vibrant, and self-sufficient. It would also help young adults by nurturing their personal growth and professional development, and it would help our nation by promoting democracy through increased civic engagement.

What would this year of mandatory service look like? It would require all citizens between the ages of 18 and 25 to spend a year in national service. (Alternatively, persons could volunteer for military service.) Some students might choose to serve immediately after high school as a gap year before starting college or a job. Others might take a gap year during college or wait until they graduate. Mandated national service could be built upon the model of AmeriCorps. It would allow volunteers to choose placements in a variety of nonprofit, public, faith-based, and educational organizations including work in schools and after-school programs, employment training organizations, environmental restoration and stewardship, food banks, shelters, and emergency response. It would pay minimum wage, provide health benefits, defer student loan payments, and offer a financial incentive tuition award at the end of service, which could also be taken as a cash stipend. (For an example of how a national mandatory service program might be organized and funded, see Stengel.)

An entry beginning with "Stengel" appears in Works Cited.

Ansen 3

Although there will be costs associated with mandatory public service, these will be far outweighed by the benefits. First, a program of mandatory national service would be an investment in communities by attacking poverty and building social capital. A national service program would build on the documented success of AmeriCorps, which in 2010 received $480 million in donations and mobilized and managed 3.4 million volunteers (*AmeriCorps Impact Guide*). By helping the poor become self-sufficient, mandatory service could help reduce the needs for future expenditures on poverty. According to an Urban Institute research study on childhood poverty (Ratcliffe and McKernan 14), childhood poverty costs $550 billion annually. Whereas current poverty spending largely aims to provide food, clothing, and housing for the poor, projects like AmeriCorps provide people-to-people contact that can help address the root causes of poverty. Particularly, service programs can help communities build social capital to enhance their capacity to solve their own problems. Social capital is the idea that the number of social connections within a community—things like civic participation, organizational membership, degree of trust in neighbors, educational achievement—determine its ability to solve shared problems. According to Lew Feldstein, a United Way director, communities with high social capital tend to have better outcomes in areas like crime, health, and education than do communities with low social capital. Expanding national service will increase people-to-people contact, creating more opportunities to form the connections that build social capital. The power of volunteers to bring people together shines through the testimonial pages of the AmeriCorps Web site, where volunteers explain why they think AmeriCorps is valuable. In the following testimonial, alumna Sarah shows how AmeriCorps volunteers help marginalized people learn the social-interaction skills needed to live successfully in their community.

Use italics for titles of books or Web sites.

"14" indicates page number in pdf document.

MLA Style

Use brackets to summarize material.

Indent longer quotations 1 inch.

Do not use quotation marks with block quotation. Citation comes after the period.

Ansen 4

> The year I served as an AmeriCorps member I lived and learned [in a community] of immigrants, refugees, and people trying to support their families. My job description was to help welfare recipients, people with disabilities, and refugees find and maintain employment; this meant mock interviews, anger-management, helping clients to use public transportation, and arranging interviews.... Through this experience, my clients' challenges became real and experiencing the same circumstances we could work on solutions to problems such as transportation and housing. ("AmeriCorps Testimonials")

Sarah's testimonial focuses on the one-on-one interactions that build social capital to help communities solve their own problems. The skills contributed by people like Sarah will remain in the community, reflecting the lasting effects national service can have on a community's long-term well-being.

Not only can a national service program benefit impoverished communities, but it also benefits the volunteers themselves by fostering their personal growth and professional development. For example, a volunteer named Maia, in her testimonial on the AmeriCorps Web site, calls her volunteer experience "invaluable." She says, "I now have experience with case management and writing curriculums. 1 am much more confident in my skills and abilities especially concerning the professional world." Another volunteer, Mari, says, "I want to build a career working in social services with immigrant communities." She praises her AmeriCorps experience for giving her the skills she needs for this career. "I was able to work closely with Somali refugees to assess their skills and help them find jobs.... After AmeriCorps, I plan to look for a similar job in the nonprofit sector." Another volunteer, Anjanette, goes into more depth to show how volunteer service creates career skills:

> AmeriCorps is a good learning experience because the people in it are often placed in positions within fields where they don't have any previous experience, and yet they are able to achieve great progress in a short period of time. It's a great opportunity to expand knowledge and horizons in ways that few other jobs or opportunities allow. . . . I hoped to gain relevant experience for my future profession, which is being a clinical social worker, before going to graduate school. It was a great opportunity for me to see if working in the field of mental health in general would be a good fit. I plan on going to school to get a Master's degree in social work with a goal of working primarily with GLBTQ youth. ("AmeriCorps Testimonials")

As these testimonials suggest, public service provides hands-on experience that can't be duplicated by academic study. According to AmeriCorps alumnus Ben, "AmeriCorps gives you the experience that you can't find in a textbook" ("AmeriCorps Testimonials").

Of course, these non-random testimonials do not mean that every AmeriCorps volunteer gains these benefits. But they ring true to my own experience as a high school volunteer working within an AmeriCorps program. Further support for the claim that volunteer community service increases career skills comes from a 2007 longitudinal study where researchers found that AmeriCorps alumni experienced statistically significant gains in employment outcomes and job skills compared to peers not enrolled in AmeriCorps (Jastrzab et al. 45).

The benefits that I have previously mentioned could largely be achieved simply by expanding volunteerism without making national service mandatory. But mandatory national service would bring a vital third benefit: increased civic engagement. When the United States eliminated the draft and moved to an all-volunteer army, it ended the specter of unwanted military service, but it also undermined citizens' sense of being stakeholders in America by allowing citizens to hire volunteers to fight their wars. This vital sense of personal investment in our nation—lost when the draft was eliminated—could be restored through mandatory national service, but in a context of helping our neighbor rather than fighting wars. Currently, low voter turnout and political apathy, especially among young people, suggests that our citizenry is disengaged from government (Bipartisan Policy Center). According to Mark Rosenman, an applied researcher on anti-poverty programs and an opinion writer for the *Chronicle of Philanthropy,* Americans are becoming increasingly passive citizens whose "only obligation is to pay taxes, [reducing Americans to being] little more than consumers of government services, to being government's customers." To form a healthy democracy, Rosenman argues, citizens need to be "more directly and personally involved in working on the problems facing the country and the world." They need to be more "involved in their government and more concerned about public policy."

Use brackets to indicate alteration of quotation to fit grammar of sentence.

For citizens to engage with government on the level advocated by Rosenman, they must first be able to identify community problems, feel a sense of responsibility for those problems, and be compelled to hold elected officials accountable for contributing to solutions. Currently service in AmeriCorps builds these civic skills because volunteers experience first-hand the impact of government failure to serve specific constituencies. For some AmeriCorps teams, a civic engagement project is built into the service experience. Teams follow a six-module civic engagement curriculum in which they work together to identify community needs, prioritize a need, and develop and implement a corresponding service project. The 2007 AmeriCorps alumni study found statistically significant gains in markers of civic engagement among alumni, including increased community-based activism, increased confidence in the ability of communities to identify and solve problems, and increased connection to the community (Jastrzab et al. 45). These markers were present eight years after service was completed, evidence that the impact of mandatory national service will extend far beyond the service year to create a generation of responsive citizens and strengthen the foundation of our democracy.

Of course, there are many objections to mandatory national service. Some fear that mandating a year of national service would harm our democracy by limiting individual freedom. These critics cite the unpopular military draft during the Vietnam War as evidence of public hostility to mandatory service. However, I argue that the unpopularity of the draft reflected the unpopularity of the Vietnam War rather than an objection to serving one's country. Moreover, the personal sacrifice of risking one's life in war is far greater than the sacrifice required for a year of service work on our own soil. Furthermore, individuals will have a greater degree of choice in terms of where, when and how they serve—choices that were not available during the draft. And while freedom is certainly a central American value, it does not mean that our freedom is without limits or that those limits are without benefits. By creating a national culture of service in this country, mandatory national service will engage young people in solving our communities' pressing problems, create bonds of friendship, and link youth to older citizens, thus creating a powerful cross-generational force of people working together.

One powerful critique of national service comes from Michael Kinsley, a consultant for the conservative think tank Heritage Foundation, in a *Time* magazine online article entitled “National Service? Puh-lease.” Kinsley objects to government bureaucrats drawing on a huge labor pool of minimum wage workers to create largely useless jobs that interfere with market forces and waste taxpayer money. Arguing that people are willing to do any job for a decent enough wage, Kinsley wonders why we would force conscripted laborers to work for minimum wage when there is already a supply of workers in the market willing to do the same job for reasonable pay. Kinsley uses George Orwell’s novel *1984* to paint a picture of workers forced to do jobs that they would otherwise not take. Furthermore, Kinsley believes that most of these jobs would be “make-work” activities, meaning that bureaucrats would have to spend their time finding trivial ways to keep all the volunteers busy.

Kinsley’s argument is provocative, but it fails to recognize the documented valuable work already provided by AmeriCorps—work that could be scaled up nationally without leading to “make-work” jobs. Kinsley fails to acknowledge that the kind of work provided by AmeriCorps does not compete with market forces. AmeriCorps jobs supplement the work of the nonprofit sector; they do not displace market-sector jobs such as garbage haulers or carpenters. The best response to Kinsley’s fear of make-work jobs created by bureaucrats is to recognize that the organizational structures for a national service program are already in place through AmeriCorps. Relying on AmeriCorps would ease the transition to mandatory national service by providing a foundational, established program from which to grow and model additional partnerships. An expansion of national service is already underway through 2009’s Generations Invigorating Volunteerism and Education (GIVE) Act (Robertson). This legislation is intended to expand participation in national service from 75,000 to 250,000 by 2014 and diversifies the focus of programs to include disaster relief, urban and rural development, infrastructure improvement, and energy conservation. Building on GIVE Act's public and congressional support could boost momentum for the transition to mandatory national service.

The point to emphasize, then, is that the money used to fund mandatory national service is money directly reinvested in our communities. Our country is currently facing numerous challenges: increasing inequality, expansive poverty, slow economic recovery, environmental and educational crises, and a disengaged citizenry. But we also have a remarkable opportunity to involve our young adults in meeting these challenges. By taking bold action to create a system of mandatory national service built on the AmeriCorps model, we have the chance to fulfill our potential as a nation.

MLA Style

Start Works Cited on a new page.

List sources alphabetically by author's last name or by title if there is no named author.

Use hanging indentation.

Double space throughout.

Use day-month-year format for dates.

Use quotation marks for article titles.

Use italics for book, periodical, and Web site titles.

Ansen 10

Works Cited

AmeriCorps Impact Guide. Corporation for National and Community Service, n.d. Web. 23 Feb. 2013.

"AmeriCorps Testimonials." *Rise: A Partnership that Works.* Rise, 2012. Web. 24 Feb. 2013.

Bipartisan Policy Center. "2012 Voter Turnout." *Bipartisan Policy Center.* 8 Nov. 2012. Web. 23 Feb. 2013.

Feldstein, Lew. "The Importance of Strengthening Social Capital in Communities." United Way of King County, Seattle, WA. 18 Dec. 2012. Guest Lecture.

Jastrzab, JoAnn et al. "Serving Country and Community: A Longitudinal Study of Service in AmeriCorps." *Corporation for National and Community Service.* Abt Associates, Apr. 2007. Web. 23 Feb. 2013.

Kinsley, Michael. "National Service? Puh-lease." *Time Lists.* Time, 30 Aug. 2007. Web. 8 Feb.2013.

Ratcliffe, Caroline E. and Signe-Mary McKernan. "Childhood Poverty and Its Lasting Consequences." Paper 21. *Low-Income Working Families.* The Urban Institute, Sept. 2012. Web. 23 Feb. 2013.

Robertson, Lori. "Mandatory Public Service." *FactCheck.org*. Annenberg Public Policy Center, 31 Mar. 2009. Web. 6 Feb. 2013.

Rosenman, Mark. "A Call for National Service." *Chronicle of Philanthropy* 20.1 (18 Oct. 2007). *Academic Search Complete.* Web. 12 Feb. 2013.

Stengel, Richard. "A Time to Serve." *Time* 10 Sept. 2007: 48-67. Print.

"Young, Underemployed and Optimistic." *Pew Research Social & Demographic Trends.* Pew Research Center, 9 Feb. 2012. Web. 12 Feb. 2013.

THINKING CRITICALLY

about "Engaging Young Adults to Meet America's Challenges: A Proposal for Mandatory National Service"

1. Proposal arguments typically begin with the problem that the proposed solution is intended to address. How effectively does Ansen introduce the problems that mandatory national service might solve? What are these problems?
2. Where does Ansen present his solution to the problem? How effective is he at explaining the details of the solution and convincing the audience that the solution is doable?
3. Where does Ansen justify his solution by presenting reasons for enacting it? What are his primary reasons in favor of the proposal? Which of these reasons do you find particularly strong or particularly weak?
4. Where does Ansen summarize objections to his proposal? If you have objections to his proposal, are your reservations or doubts adequately summarized and addressed? Why or why not?
5. How effective is Ansen's attempt to rebut the objections?
6. Overall, how would you evaluate the *logos* of Ansen's argument? How effectively does he use reasons and evidence to move his audience toward his views? How effective are Ansen's appeals to *ethos* and *pathos*? Does he project a credible and trustworthy persona? To what extent does he connect his argument to the values or beliefs of his audience or otherwise appeal to their emotions?

A GUIDE TO COMPOSING AND REVISING

PART 3

This recent photo depicts the receding Athabasca Glacier in Alberta, Canada, in the Canadian Rockies. A multimodel text, this photo uses words and image to convey its appeals to *logos, ethos,* and *pathos.* The sign informs visitors of the change in the glacier in the last thirty years. The visual impact of the photo with the people hiking up the mountain to get to the glacier, once much closer to the road, dramatically confirms the message of change and loss. You might contrast this photo with the image of the vast iceberg on page 58. Which photo do you think would be more effective in conveying the extent and urgency of global warming?

16 WRITING AS A PROBLEM-SOLVING PROCESS

WHAT YOU WILL LEARN

16.1 To follow the experts' practice of using multiple drafts.
16.2 To revise globally as well as locally.
16.3 To develop ten expert habits to improve your writing processes.
16.4 To use peer reviews to help you think like an expert.

Throughout this text, we have emphasized writing as a critical thinking process requiring writers to "wallow in complexity." This opening chapter of Part 3 explains how experienced writers use multiple drafts to manage the complexities of writing.

16.1 Follow the experts's practice of using multiple drafts.

SKILL 16.1 Follow the experts' practice of using multiple drafts.

We begin this chapter with a close look at why expert writers use multiple drafts to move from an initial exploration of ideas to a finished product. As composition theorist Peter Elbow has asserted about the writing process, "meaning is not what you start out with" but "what you end up with." In the early stages of writing, experienced writers typically discover, deepen, and complicate their ideas before they can clarify them and arrange them effectively. Only in the last drafts will expert writers be in sufficient control of their ideas to shape them elegantly for readers.

What most distinguishes expert from novice writers is the experts' willingness to keep revising their work until they feel it is ready to go public. They typically work much harder at drafting and revising than do novice writers, taking more runs at their subject. Expert writers also make more substantial alterations in their drafts during revision—what we call "global" rather than "local" revision. This difference between expert and novice writers might seem counterintuitive. One might think that novices would need to revise more than experts. But decades of research on the writing process of experts reveals how extensively experts revise. The experienced writer crosses out pages and starts over while the inexperienced writer crosses out a word or two. The experienced writer feels cognitive overload while drafting, having to attend to many different "levels and agendas" at once.

First Draft with Revisions

sticks of our favorite flavors in the bottom of the bag. That discovery was, by far, the best discovery that could ever be made, week after week. So, as you can probably guess, my opinion of farmer's markets has always been very high as they were what fulfilled my sugar fix.

~~However, another important point can come out of that story. That point being about~~ the man who sold us our precious honey sticks. He was kind, patient, and genuinely happy to have our business. In contrast to ~~Not quite the same vibe that one would expect to get from~~ the supermarket employee who often doesn't ~~even really~~ know what isle you need in order to find the peanut butter. Another ~~A~~ huge selling point of farmer's markets, for me, is that you can go and talk to people who know about the food they are selling. It is so refreshing to go

Revised Draft

sticks of our favorite flavors in the bottom of the bag.

Another huge selling point of farmer's markets, for me, is that you can go and talk to people who know about the food they are selling. The man who sold us our precious honey sticks was kind, patient, and genuinely happy to have our business, in contrast to the supermarket employee who often doesn't ~~even really~~ know what aisle you need in order to find the peanut butter.

FIGURE 16.1 A First-Year Student's Substantial Revisions

In contrast, the inexperienced writer seems to think only of replacing words or adding an occasional transition. Learning to revise extensively is thus a hallmark of a maturing writer.

Figure 16.1 shows how a first-year college student demonstrates expert writing behavior when she makes a substantial revision of an early draft. Note that she crosses out several sentences at the end of one paragraph, creates a new topic sentence for the next paragraph, and moves a detail sentence so that it follows the topic sentence.

Why Expert Writers Revise So Extensively

Our emphasis on experts' substantial revision might have surprised you. If the experts are such good writers, why do they need multiple drafts? Why don't they get it right the first time? Our answer is simply this: Expert writers use multiple drafts to break a complex task into manageable subtasks. Let's look more closely at some of the functions that drafting and revising can perform for writers.

- ***Multiple drafts help writers overcome the limits of short-term memory.*** Cognitive psychologists have shown that working memory—often called short-term memory—has remarkably little storage space. You can picture short-term memory as a small tabletop surrounded by filing cabinets (long-term memory). As you write, you can place on your tabletop (working memory) only a few chunks of material at any given moment—a few sentences of a draft or several ideas in an outline. The remaining portions of your draft-in-progress fall off the table without getting stored in long-term memory. (Think of your horror when your computer eats your draft—proof that you can't rely on long-term memory to restore what you wrote.) Writing a draft captures and stores your ideas as your working memory develops them. When you reread these stored ideas, you can then see your evolving ideas whole, note problem areas, develop more ideas, see material that doesn't fit, recall additional information, and begin extending or improving the draft.
- ***Multiple drafts help accommodate shifts and changes in the writer's ideas.*** Early in the writing process, expert writers often are unsure of where their ideas are leading; they find that their ideas shift and evolve as their drafts progress. An expert writer's finished product often is radically different from the first draft—not simply in form and style but also in actual content.
- ***Multiple drafts help writers clarify audience and purpose.*** While thinking about their subject matter, experienced writers also ask questions about audience and purpose: What do my readers already know and believe about my subject? How am I trying to change their views? In the process of drafting and revising, the answers to these questions may evolve so that each new draft reflects a deeper or clearer understanding of audience and purpose.
- ***Multiple drafts help writers improve structure and coherence for readers.*** Whereas the ideas in early drafts often follow the order in which writers conceived them, later drafts are often restructured—sometimes radically— to meet readers' needs. Writing teachers sometimes call this transformation a movement from writer-based to reader-based prose.* The composing and revising skills taught in Chapter 17 will help you learn how to revise your drafts from a reader's perspective.
- ***Multiple drafts let writers postpone worrying about correctness.*** Late in the revision process, experienced writers turn their energy toward fixing errors and revising sentences for increased cohesion, conciseness, and clarity. Focusing on correctness too soon can shut down the creative process.

*The terms "writer-based" and "reader-based" prose come from Linda Flower, "Writer-Based Prose: A Cognitive Basis for Problems in Writing." *College English*, 1979, 41.1, 19–37.

An Expert's Writing Processes Are Recursive

Given this background on why expert writers revise, we can see that for experts, the writing process is recursive rather than linear. Writers continually cycle back to earlier stages as their thinking evolves. Sometimes writers develop a thesis statement early in the writing process. But just as frequently, they formulate a thesis during an "aha!" moment of discovery later in the process, perhaps after several drafts. ("So *this* is my point! Here is my argument in a nutshell!") Even very late in the process, while checking usage and punctuation, experienced writers are apt to think of new ideas, thus triggering more revision.

SKILL 16.2 **Revise globally as well as locally.**

16.2
Revise globally as well as locally.

To think like an expert writer, you need to appreciate the difference between "global" and "local" revision. You revise **locally** whenever you make changes to a text that affect only the one or two sentences that you are currently working on. In contrast, you revise **globally** when a change in one part of your draft drives changes in other parts of the draft. Global revision focuses on the big-picture concerns of ideas, structure, purpose, audience, and genre. It often involves substantial rewriting, even starting over in places with a newly conceived plan. For example, your revising part of the middle of your essay might cause you to rewrite the whole introduction or to change the tone or point of view throughout the essay.

What follows are some on-the-page strategies that you can adopt to practice the global and local revision strategies of experts:*

On-the-Page Strategies for Doing Global and Local Revision

Strategies to Use on the Page	Reasons
Throw out the whole draft and start again.	• Original draft helped writer discover ideas and see the whole territory. • New draft needs to be substantially refocused and restructured.
Cross out large chunks and rewrite from scratch.	• Original passage was unfocused; ideas have changed. • New sense of purpose or point meant that the whole passage needed reshaping. • Original passage was too confused or jumbled for mere editing.

(*continued*)

*We have chosen to say "on the page" rather than "on the screen" because global revision is often facilitated by a writer's working off double-spaced hard copy rather than a computer screen. See page 424 for our advice on using hard copy for revision.

Strategies to Use on the Page	Reasons
Cut and paste; move parts around; (then write new transitions, mapping statements, and topic sentences).	• Parts didn't follow in logical order. • Parts occurred in the order writer thought of them rather than the order needed by readers. • Conclusion was clearer than introduction; part of conclusion had to be moved to introduction. • Revised thesis statement required different order for parts.
Add/revise topic sentences of paragraphs; insert transitions.	• Reader needs signposts to see how parts connect to previous parts and to whole. • Revision of topic sentences often requires global revision of paragraph.
Make insertions; add new material.	• Supporting particulars needed to be added: examples, facts, illustrations, statistics, other evidence (usually added to bodies of paragraphs). • New section was needed or more explanation was needed for a point. • Gaps in argument needed to be filled in.
Delete material.	• Material is no longer needed or is irrelevant. • Deleted material may have been good but went off on a tangent.
Recast sentences (cross out and rewrite portions; combine sentences; rephrase sentences; start sentences with a different grammatical structure).	• Passage violated old/new contract (see Skill 17.7). • Passage was wordy/choppy or lacked rhythm or voice. • Grammar was tangled, diction odd, or meaning confused. • Passage lost focus of topic sentence of paragraph.
Edit sentences to correct mistakes.	• Writer found comma splices, fragments, dangling modifiers, nonparallel constructions, or other problems of grammar and usage. • Writer found spelling errors, typos, repeated or omitted words.

FOR WRITING AND DISCUSSION

Revising a Paragraph Globally

Choose an important paragraph in the body of a draft you are currently working on. Then write your answers to these questions about that paragraph.

1. Why is this an important paragraph?
2. What is its main point?
3. Where is that main point stated?

Now—as an exercise only—write the main point at the top of a blank sheet of paper, put away your original draft, and, without looking at the original, write a new paragraph with the sole purpose of developing the point you wrote at the top of the page.

When you are finished, compare your new paragraph to the original. What have you learned that might help you revise your original?

Here are some typical responses of writers who have tried this exercise:

> I recognized that my original paragraph was unfocused. I couldn't find a main point.
>
> I recognized that my original paragraph was underdeveloped. I had a main point but not enough details supporting it.
>
> I began to see that my draft was scattered and that I had too many short paragraphs.
>
> I recognized that I was making a couple of different points in my original paragraph and that I needed to break it into separate paragraphs.
>
> I recognized that I hadn't stated my main point (or that I had buried it in the middle of the paragraph).
>
> I recognized that there was a big difference in style between my two versions and that I had to choose which version I liked best. (It's not always the "new" version!)

SKILL 16.3 Develop ten expert habits to improve your writing processes.

16.3 Develop ten expert habits to improve your writing processes.

Now that you understand why experts revise more extensively than novices and what they do on the page, we describe in Skill 16.3 the habitual ways of thinking and acting that experts use when they write. Our hope is that this description will help you develop these same habits for yourself. Because one of the best ways to improve your writing process is to do what the experts do, we offer you the following ten habits of experienced writers, expressed as advice:

1. ***Use exploratory writing and talking to discover and clarify ideas.*** Don't let your first draft be the first occasion when you put your ideas into writing. Use exploratory strategies such as freewriting and idea mapping to generate ideas (see Chapter 2, Concept 2.1). Also seek out opportunities to talk about your ideas with classmates or friends in order to clarify your own thinking and appreciate alternative points of view.
2. ***Schedule your time.*** Don't begin your paper the night before it is due. Plan sufficient time for exploration, drafting, revision, and editing. Recognize that your ideas will shift, branch out, and even turn around as you write. Allow some time off between writing the first draft and beginning revision. For many writers, revision takes considerably longer than

writing the first draft. If your institution has a writing center, consider scheduling a visit.

3. ***Discover what methods of drafting work best for you.*** Some people compose rough drafts directly on the computer; others write longhand. Some make outlines first; others plunge directly into drafting and make outlines later. Some revise extensively on the computer as they are drafting; others plough ahead until they have a complete draft before they start revising. Some people sit at their desk for hours at a time; others need to get up and walk around every couple of minutes. Some people need a quiet room; others work best in a coffee shop. Discover the methods that work best for you.
4. ***Think about audience and purpose from the start.*** Early on, think about the effect you want your writing to have on readers. In formulating a thesis, look to change your readers' view of your subject. ("Before reading my paper, my readers will think X. But after reading my paper, my readers will think Y.")
5. ***For the first draft, reduce your expectations.*** Many novice writers get blocked by trying to make their first draft perfect. In contrast, expert writers expect the first draft to be an unreadable mess. (They often call it a "zero draft" or a "garbage draft" because they don't expect it to be good.) They use the first draft merely to get their ideas flowing, knowing they will revise later. If you get blocked, just keep writing. Get some ideas on paper.
6. ***Revise on double- or triple-spaced hard copy.*** Although many experienced writers revise on the screen without going through paper drafts, there are powerful advantages in printing occasional paper drafts. Research suggests that writers are more apt to make global changes in a draft if they work from hard copy because they can see more easily how the parts connect to the whole. They can refer quickly to page two while revising page six without having to scroll back and forth. We suggest that you occasionally print out a double- or triple-spaced hard copy of your draft and then mark it up aggressively. (See again Figure 16.1, which shows how a first-year student learned the benefits of revising off hard copy.) When your draft gets too messy, keyboard your changes into your computer and begin another round of revision.
7. ***As you revise, think increasingly about the needs of your readers.*** Experts use first drafts to help them clarify their ideas for themselves but not necessarily for readers. In many respects, writers of first drafts are talking to themselves. Through global revision, however, writers gradually convert "writer-based prose" to "reader-based prose." Writers begin to employ consciously the skills of reader-expectation theory that we explain in detail in Chapter 17.
8. ***Exchange drafts with others.*** Get other people's reactions to your work in exchange for your reactions to theirs. Experienced writers regularly seek critiques of their drafts from trusted readers. Later in this chapter we explain procedures for peer review of drafts.

9. ***Save correctness for last.*** To revise productively, concentrate first on the big questions: Do I have good ideas in this draft? Am I responding appropriately to the assignment? Are my ideas adequately organized and developed? Save questions about exact wording, grammar, mechanics, and documentation style for later. These concerns are important, but they cannot be efficiently attended to until after higher-order concerns are met. Your first goal is to create a thoughtful, richly developed draft.
10. ***To meet deadlines and bring the process to a close, learn how to satisfice.*** Our description of the writing process may seem formidable. Technically, it seems, you could go on revising forever. How can you ever know when to stop? There is no ready answer to that question, which is more a psychological than a technical problem. Expert writers have generally learned how to **satisfice**, a term coined by influential social scientist Herbert Simon from two root words, *suffice* and *satisfy*. It means to do the best job you can under the circumstances considering your time constraints, the pressures of other demands on you, and the difficulty of the task. Expert writers begin the writing process early and get as far as they can before their deadline looms. Then they let the deadline give them the energy for intensive revision. From lawyers preparing briefs for court to engineers developing design proposals, writers have used deadlines to help them put aside doubts and anxieties and to conclude their work, as every writer must. "Okay, it's not perfect, but it's the best I can do for now."

FOR WRITING AND DISCUSSION

Analyzing Your Own Writing Process

When you write, do you follow a process resembling the one we just described? Have you ever

- had a writing project grow out of your engagement with a problem or question?
- explored ideas by talking with others or by doing exploratory writing?
- made major changes to a draft because you changed your mind or otherwise discovered new ideas?
- revised a draft from a reader's perspective by consciously trying to imagine and respond to a reader's questions, confusions, and other reactions?
- road tested a draft by trying it out on readers and then revising it as a result of what they told you?

Working in groups or as a whole class, share stories about previous writing experiences that match or do not match the description of experienced writers' processes. To the extent that your present process differs, what strategies of experienced writers might you like to try?

16.4 Use peer reviews to help you think like an expert.

SKILL 16.4 Use peer reviews to help you think like an expert.

One of the best ways to become a better reviser is to see your draft from a *reader*'s rather than a *writer*'s perspective. As a writer, you know what you mean; you are already inside your own head. But you need to see what your draft looks like to readers—that is, to people who are not inside your head.

A good way to learn this skill is to practice reading your classmates' drafts and have them read yours. In this section we offer advice on how to respond candidly to your classmates' drafts and how to participate in peer reviews.

Becoming a Helpful Reader of Classmates' Drafts

When you respond to a writer's draft, learn to make *readerly* rather than *writerly* comments. For example, instead of saying, "Your draft is disorganized," say, "I got lost when...." Instead of saying, "This paragraph needs a topic sentence," say, "I had trouble seeing the point of this paragraph." In other words, describe your mental experience in trying to understand the draft rather than use technical terms to point out problem areas or to identify errors.

When you help a writer with a draft, your goal is both to point out where the draft needs more work and to brainstorm with the writer possible ways to improve the draft. Begin by reading the draft all the way through at a normal reading speed. As you read, make mental notes to help focus your feedback. We recommend that you also mark passages that you find confusing. Write "G!" for "Good" next to parts that you like. Write "?" next to places where you want to ask questions.

After you have read the draft, use the following strategies for making helpful responses, either in writing or in direct conversation with the writer.

Strategies for Responding Helpfully to a Classmate's Draft

Kinds of Problems Noted	Helpful Responses
If the ideas in the draft seem thin or undeveloped, or if the draft is too short	• Help the writer brainstorm for more ideas. • Help the writer add more examples, better details, more supporting data or arguments.
If you get confused or lost in some parts of the draft	• Show the writer where you got confused or miscued in reading the draft ("I started getting lost here because I couldn't see why you were giving me this information" or "I thought you were going to say X, but then you said Y"). • Have the writer talk through ideas to clear up confusing spots.

(continued)

<table>
<tr><th>Kinds of Problems Noted</th><th>Helpful Responses</th></tr>
<tr><td>If you get confused or lost at the "big-picture" level</td><td>• Help the writer sharpen the thesis: suggest that the writer view the thesis as the answer to a controversial or problematic question; ask the writer to articulate the question that the thesis answers.
• Help the writer create an outline, tree diagram, or flowchart (see Skill 17.3).
• Help the writer clarify the focus by asking him or her to complete these statements about purpose:
  • The purpose of this paper is ______________.
  • The purpose of this section (paragraph) is ______________.
  • Before reading my paper, my reader will think X. But after reading my paper, my reader will think Y.</td></tr>
<tr><td>If you can understand the sentences but can't see the point</td><td>• Help the writer articulate the meaning by asking "So what?" questions, making the writer bring the point to the surface. ("I can understand what you are saying here but I don't quite understand why you are saying it. What do these details have to do with the topic sentence of the paragraph? Or what does this paragraph have to do with your thesis?")
• Help the writer create transitions, new topic sentences, or other means of making points clear.</td></tr>
<tr><td>If you disagree with the ideas or think the writer has avoided alternative points of view</td><td>• Play devil's advocate to help the writer deepen and complicate ideas.
• Show the writer specific places where you had queries or doubts.</td></tr>
</table>

Using a Generic Peer Review Guide

When participating in peer reviews, writers and reviewers often appreciate a list of guiding questions or checkpoints. What follows is a list of generic questions that can be used for peer-reviewing many different kinds of drafts. In each assignment chapter for Part 2 of this text, we have created additional peer review questions tailored specifically to that chapter's rhetorical aim and genres. For any given peer review session, your instructor may specify which generic or assignment-specific questions you are to use for the peer review.

Generic Peer Review Guide

For the writer

Give your peer reviewer two or three questions to address while responding to your draft. The questions can focus on some aspect of your draft that you are uncertain about, on one more sections where you particularly seek help or advice, on some feature that you particularly like about your draft, or on some part you especially wrestled with.

For the reviewer

Basic overview: As you read at normal speed do the following:

- Mark a "?" next to any passages that you find confusing, that somehow slow down your reading, or that raise questions in your mind.
- Mark a "G" next to any passages where you think the writing is particularly good, strong, or interesting.

Going into more depth: Prior to discussion with the writer, complete the following tasks:

- Identify at least one place in the draft where you got confused. Note why you got confused, using readerly rather than writerly comments.
- Identify one place in the draft where you think the ideas are thin or need more development. Make discussion notes.
- Identify one place where you might write "So what?" after the passage. These are plaes where you don't understand the significance or importance of the writer's points. These are also places where you can't see how certain sentences connect to a topic sentence or how certain paragraphs or sections connect to the thesis statement.
- Identify at least one place where you could play devil's advocate or otherwise object to the writer's ideas. Make notes on the objections or alternative views that you will raise with the writer.

Evaluating the writer' argument: Look at the draft' effectiveness from the perspective of the classical rhetorical appeals:

- *Logos:* How effectively does the writer use reasons and evidence to support his or her claim? How effectively does the writer use details, particulars, examples, and other means as evidence to support points? How logical are the points and how clearly are they connected?
- *Ethos:* What image does the writer project? How effective is the tone? How trustworthy, reliable, knowledgeable, and fair does this writer seem?
- *Pathos:* How effectively does the writer engage the audiene's interest? How effectively does the writer tie into the audience's beliefs and values? To what extent does the writer make the reader care about the topic?

Noting problems of grammar and editing: Mark problems in grammar, spelling, punctuation, documentation, or other issues of mechanics.

Summing up: Create a consolidated summary of your review:

- Sum up the strengths of the draft.
- Identify two or three main weaknesses or problem areas.
- Make two or three suggestions for revision.

FOR WRITING AND DISCUSSION

Practicing a Peer Review

Background: In the following exercise, we invite you to practice a peer review by responding to a student's draft ("Should the University Carpet the Dorm Rooms?" below) or to another draft provided by your instructor. The "Carpets" assignment asked students to take a stand on a local campus issue. Imagine that you have exchanged drafts with this student and that your task is to help this student improve the draft through both global and local revision.

Individual task: Read the draft carefully following the instructions in the "Generic Peer Review Guide." Write out your responses to the bulleted items under "Going into more depth," "Evaluating the writer's argument," and "Summing up."

Small group or whole class: Share your responses. Then turn to the following additional tasks:

1. With the instructor serving as a guide, practice explaining to the writer where or how you got confused while reading the draft. Readers often have difficulty explaining their reading experience to a writer. Let several class members role-play being the reader. Practice using language such as "I like the way this draft started because. . . ." "I got confused when. . . ." "I had to back up and reread when. . . ." "I saw your point here, but then I got lost again because. . . ." Writing theorist Peter Elbow calls such language a "movie of your mind."
2. Have several class members role-play being devil's advocates by arguing against the writer's thesis. Where are the ideas thin or weak?

SHOULD THE UNIVERSITY CARPET THE DORM ROOMS?

Tricia, a university student, came home exhausted from her work-study job. She took a blueberry pie from the refrigerator to satisfy her hunger and a tall glass of milk to quench her thirst. While trying to get comfortable on her bed, she tipped her snack over onto the floor. She cleaned the mess, but the blueberry and milk stains on her brand-new carpet could not be removed.

Tricia didn't realize how hard it was to clean up stains on a carpet. Luckily this was her own carpet.

A lot of students don't want carpets. Students constantly change rooms. The next person may not want carpet.

Some students say that since they pay to live on campus, the rooms should reflect a comfortable home atmosphere. Carpets will make the dorm more comfortable. The carpet will act as insulation and as a soundproofing system.

Paint stains cannot be removed from carpets. If the university carpets the rooms, the students will lose the privilege they have of painting their rooms any color. This would limit students' self-expression.

The carpets would be an institutional brown or gray. This would be ugly. With tile floors, the students can choose and purchase their own carpets to match their taste. You can't be an individual if you can't decorate your room to fit your personality.

(*continued*)

According to Rachel Jones, Assistant Director of Housing Services, the cost will be $300 per room for the carpet and installation. Also the university will have to buy more vacuum cleaners. But will vacuum cleaners be all that is necessary to keep the carpets clean? We'll need shampoo machines too.

What about those stains that won't come off even with a shampoo machine? That's where the student will have to pay damage deposit costs.

There will be many stains on the carpet due to shaving cream fights, food fights, beverage parties, and smoking, all of which can damage the carpets.

Students don't take care of the dorms now. They don't follow the rules of maintaining their rooms. They drill holes into the walls, break mirrors, beds, and closet doors, and leave their food trays all over the floor.

If the university buys carpets our room rates will skyrocket. In conclusion, it is a bad idea for the university to buy carpets.

Participating in Peer Review Workshops

If you are willing to respond candidly to a classmate's draft—in a readerly rather than a writerly way—you will be a valuable participant in peer review workshops. In a typical workshop, classmates work in groups of two to six to respond to each other's rough drafts and offer suggestions for revisions. These workshops are most helpful when group members have developed sufficient levels of professionalism and trust to exchange candid responses. A frequent problem in peer review workshops is that classmates try so hard to avoid hurting each other's feelings that they provide vague, meaningless feedback. Saying, "Your paper's great. I really liked it. Maybe you could make it flow a little better" is much less helpful than saying, "Your issue about environmental pollution in the Antarctic is well defined in the first paragraph, but I got lost in the second paragraph when you began discussing penguin coloration."

Responsibilities of Peer Reviewers and Writers Learning to respond conscientiously and carefully to others' work may be the single most important thing you can do to improve your own writing. When you review a classmate's draft, you are not acting as a teacher, but simply as a fresh reader. You can help the writer appreciate what it's like to encounter his or her text for the first time. Your primary responsibility is to articulate your understanding of what the writer's words say to you and to identify places where you get confused, where you need more details, where you have doubts or queries, and so on.

When you play the role of writer during a workshop session, your responsibilities parallel those of your peer reviewers. You need to provide a legible rough draft, preferably typed and double-spaced, that doesn't baffle the reader with hard-to-follow corrections and confusing pagination. Your instructor may ask you to bring copies of your draft for all group members. During the workshop, your primary responsibility is to *listen*, taking in how others respond to your draft without becoming defensive. Many instructors also ask writers to formulate two or three specific questions about their drafts—questions they particularly want their reviewers to address. These questions might focus on something writers particularly like about their drafts or on specific problem areas or concerns.

Responding to Peer Reviews

After you and your classmates have gone over each other's papers and walked each other through the responses, everyone should identify two or three things about his or her draft that particularly need work. Before you leave the session, you should have some notion about how you want to revise your paper.

You may get mixed or contradictory responses from different reviewers. One reviewer may praise a passage that another finds confusing or illogical. Conflicting advice is a frustrating fact of life for all writers, whether students or professionals. Such disagreements reveal how readers cocreate a text with a writer: Each brings to the text a different background, set of values, and way of reading.

It is important to remember that you are in charge of your own writing. If several readers offer the same critique of a passage, then no matter how much you love that passage, you probably need to follow their advice. But when readers disagree, you have to make your own best judgment about whom to heed.

Once you have received advice from others, reread your draft again slowly and then develop a revision plan, allowing yourself time to make sweeping, global changes if needed. You also need to remember that you can never make your draft perfect. Plan when you will bring the process to a close so that you can turn in a finished product on time and get on with your other classes and your life.

17 STRATEGIES FOR WRITING CLOSED-FORM PROSE

WHAT YOU WILL LEARN

17.1 To satisfy reader expectations by linking new material to old material.
17.2 To convert loose structures into problem-thesis-support structures.
17.3 To nutshell your argument and visualize its structure.
17.4 To start and end with the "big picture" through effective titles, introductions, and conclusions.
17.5 To keep readers on track through the use of effective topic sentences.
17.6 To guide readers with transitions.
17.7 To link sentences by placing old information before new.
17.8 To use four expert moves for organizing and developing ideas.
17.9 To present numerical data effectively through tables, graphs, and charts.
17.10 To use occasional open-form elements to achieve "voice" in closed-form prose.

This chapter gives nuts-and-bolts advice for writing effective closed-form prose. As explained in Part 1 of this text, **closed-form prose** has an explicit thesis statement that is supported with points, subpoints, and details. Its features include unified and coherent paragraphs headed by topic sentences, good transitions between sentences and paragraphs, and forecasting of the whole before presentation of the parts. The strategies explained in this chapter are organized into ten self-contained lessons, each of which can be read comfortably in twenty minutes or less. The first lesson (Skill 17.1) provides a theoretical overview to the rest of the chapter. The remaining lessons can then be assigned and read in any order your instructor desires. Together these lessons will teach you transferable skills—useful in any academic discipline or professional setting—for producing clear, reader-friendly, and persuasive closed-form prose.

See Chapter 1, Concept 1.3, for a detailed explanation of closed-form versus open-form prose.

17.1 Satisfy reader expectations by linking new material to old material.

SKILL 17.1 Satisfy reader expectations by linking new material to old material.

In this opening lesson, we ask you to imagine how readers make sense of a verbal text and what they do when they get confused. Imagine for a moment that your readers have only so much *reader energy,* which they can use either to follow your ideas or to puzzle over confusing passages.* In order to follow your ideas, readers must see how each new sentence in your essay connects to what has come before. Your goal is to keep your readers' energy focused on your meaning rather than on problems in your structure.

The Principle of Old Before New

What makes closed-form prose "closed" is the way it consistently follows the principle of old before new. Rhetoricians sometimes calls this principle the "**old/new contract**," which refers to the writer's obligation to help readers connect each new sentence in an essay to the previous sentences they have already read. As readers read, they don't memorize your text as if they were memorizing a list of facts. Rather they construct in their heads a big picture of your unfolding meaning, usually organized by points and subpoints. If a new sentence doesn't meaningfully connect to that big picture, they divert their reader energy from following your ideas into puzzling over your structure. "Whoa, you lost me on the turn," your reader might say. "I can't see how this part relates to what you just said."

This principle of old before new is grounded in brain research that investigates the way that the human brain makes sense of new information. For example, the old/new contract can explain the left-to-right order of business names and room or location numbers in a building directory. Suppose that you are meeting a friend at Carol's Coffee Clatch in a newly opened mall, but you don't know its exact location. To use the mall map, you begin with old information (Carol's Coffee Clatch) and seek new information (its location in the mall). Because we read English from left to right, we expect to find the business names in the left column (arranged alphabetically) and the corresponding map location indicators in the right column. If the location indicators were in the left column and the business names in the right, we would have to read backwards, slowing us down.

The principle of old-before-new is equally important when we listen as when we read. Suppose you are a passenger on a flight into Chicago and need to transfer to a flight to Memphis. As you descend into Chicago, the flight attendant announces transfer gates. Which of the following formats is easier for you to process? Why?

Announcement A		**Announcement B**	
Atlanta	Gate C12	Gate C12	Atlanta
Dallas	Gate C25	Gate C25	Dallas
Memphis	Gate B20	Gate B20	Memphis
St. Louis	Gate D15	Gate D15	St. Louis

*For the useful term *reader energy*, we are indebted to George Gopen and Judith Swan, "The Science of Scientific Writing," *American Scientist* 78 (1990): 550–559. In addition, much of our discussion of writing in this chapter is indebted to the work of Joseph Williams, George Gopen, and Gregory Colomb. See especially Gregory G. Colomb and Joseph M. Williams, "Perceiving Structure in Professional Prose: A Multiply Determined Experience," in Lee Odell and Dixie Goswamie (eds.), *Writing in Nonacademic Settings* (New York: The Guilford Press, 1985), pp. 87–128.

If you are like most listeners, you prefer Announcement A, which puts old information before new. In this case, the old/known information is our destination (Memphis), while the new/unknown information is the gate number—in this case, Gate B20. Announcement B causes us to expend more *listener energy* than does A because it forces us to hold each gate number in memory until we hear its corresponding city. (The number of the gate is meaningless until it is linked to the crucial old information, "Memphis.") Whereas A allows us to relax until we hear the word "Memphis," B forces us to concentrate intensely on each gate number until we find the meaningful one.

How the Principle of Old Before New Creates Unified and Coherent Paragraphs

This principle of old-before-new also applies to the way readers make sense of verbal texts. To keep readers on track, writers should begin their sentences with old information that hooks back to the previous material that the reader has already read. The last part of the sentence then contains the new information that drives the argument forward. When writers follow this principle, the result is tightly organized closed-form prose. Such prose is said to have both unity and coherence—two defining features of closed-form prose:

- **Unity** refers to the relationship between each part of an essay and the larger whole.
- **Coherence** refers to the relationship between adjacent sentences and paragraphs.

As an illustration of these terms, consider the differences in the following three passages, each of which begins with the same sentence about the father's role in childrearing. However, the first two of these passages thwart the principle of old before new while the third fulfills it.

PASSAGE 1: EXHIBITS NEITHER UNITY NOR COHERENCE

Recent research has given us much deeper—and more surprising—insights into the father's role in childrearing. My family is typical of the east side in that we never had much money. Their tongues became black and hung out of their mouths. The back-to-basics movement got a lot of press, fueled as it was by fears of growing illiteracy and cultural demise.

PASSAGE 2: EXHIBITS COHERENCE BUT NOT UNITY

Recent research has given us much deeper—and more surprising—insights into the father's role in childrearing. Childrearing is a complex process that is frequently investigated by psychologists. Psychologists have also investigated sleep patterns and dreams. When we are dreaming, psychologists have shown, we are often reviewing recent events in our lives.

PASSAGE 3: EXHIBITS BOTH UNITY AND COHERENCE

Recent research has given us much deeper—and more surprising—insights into the father's role in childrearing. It shows that in almost all of their interactions with children, fathers do things a little differently from mothers. What fathers do—their special parenting style—is not only highly complementary to what mothers do but is by all indications important in its own right. [The passage continues by showing the special ways that fathers contribute to childrearing.]

If you are like most readers, Passage 1 comically frustrates your reader energy because it is a string of random sentences without connections to any point. Passage 2 also frustrates your reader energy but in a more subtle way. If you aren't paying attention, Passage 2 may seem to make sense because each sentence is linked to the one before it. But the individual sentences don't develop a larger whole: The topics switch from a father's role in childrearing to psychology to sleep patterns to the function of dreams. This passage has coherence (links between sentences) but not unity (links to a larger point). In contrast, Passage 3 exhibits both coherence and unity. The passage is unified because it makes a consistent point—that fathers have an important role in childrearing. It is also coherent because the opening of sentences 2 and 3 include words that refer to previous information: The pronoun "it" in sentence 2 refers to "research" in sentence 1. In sentence 3 the word "fathers" links to "fathers" in both sentences 1 and 2. We'll have more to say about the old/new contract at the sentence level in Lesson 17.6.

The Explanatory Power of the Principle of Old before New

As we will see throughout this chapter, the principle of old before new has important explanatory power for writers. At the level of the whole essay, this principle helps writers understand why they need to lay out the "big picture" of an essay before presenting the parts (Skill 17.3) or why they need to determine their audience's initial view of a topic (old information) before they can plan an argument strategy to change the audience's view (new information—Skill 17.2). It also helps writers craft effective transitions and topic sentences for paragraphs (Skills 17.4–17.6). Most importantly, it helps writers understand why clear organization of an essay is so important to readers. The rhetorician Kenneth Burke describes "form" as "arousing and fulfillment of desires." The principle of old before new explains how closed-form prose creates this kind of pleasurable form. When a reader starts a new essay, the reader has no specific expectations: Everything in the essay is "new information." However, once the reader reads the title, the title becomes "old information." If the title is effective, it forecasts what will be new in the essay, arousing the reader's anticipation of what will follow and propelling the reader's desire to continue reading. The first part of the introduction further arouses reader desire by explaining a problem or question or knowledge gap (tying backwards into the reader's interest in the question or problem), while the last part presents the thesis (what's new). Once read, the thesis then becomes old information. Because the thesis summarizes the essay's "big picture," it leads readers to anticipate what is coming in the body of the essay. If the essay does what the thesis forecasts, the reader experiences form as a gratifying sequence of anticipation and fulfillment.

What readers need from a closed-form text, then, is an ability to predict what is coming as well as regular fulfillment of those predictions. The rest of this chapter will give you more specific advice on how to keep your reader on track throughout your essay.

FOR WRITING AND DISCUSSION

Explaining Old before New in a Closed-Form Essay

Reread engineer David Rockwood's letter to the editor on page 15 and analyze its structure in terms of old/new contract, unity and coherence, and forecasting and fulfillment.

1. How does the opening sentence refer to old information while forecasting new information?
2. How do the opening and concluding paragraphs create a "big picture" of the writer's argument?
3. How do the body paragraphs relate to the thesis? How does each paragraph reveal unity and coherence?
4. How does the writer use transitions to keep the reader on track?

17.2 Convert loose structures into problem-thesis-support structures.

SKILL 17.2 Convert loose structures into problem-thesis-support structures.

This lesson shows you how to convert loose structures into thesis-support structures that begin with a problem, assert a thesis, and then support that thesis with points and details. Because developing a structure of points and details requires "wallowing in complexity," writers often retreat into simpler structures that avoid this kind of problem-thesis-support thinking. You can better understand thesis-based writing by contrasting it with writing that might seem thesis-based but isn't.

Avoiding "and Then" Writing, or Chronological Structure

One way writers fail to produce a problem-thesis-support structure is to organize primarily by time, arranging sentences and paragraphs in a chronological sequence. Chronological structure, often called "narrative," is the most common organizing principle of open-form prose, but effective open-form writers handle time artistically using literary techniques. In closed-form prose, chronological order is usually ineffective—a strategy for avoiding a thesis. To a large degree, chronological order is the default mode we fall into when we aren't sure how to organize material. For example, if you were asked to analyze a character in a short story, you might slip into a plot summary instead. In much the same way, you might substitute historical chronology ("First A happened, then B happened . . .") for historical analysis ("B happened because A happened . . ."); or you might give a chronological recounting of your research ("First I discovered A, then I discovered B . . .") instead of organizing your material into an argument ("A's account of this phenomenon calls B's account into question because. . . ."). This kind of chronological structure we call **"and then"** writing, meaning the writer strings together one event after another through time.

The tendency toward *and then* writing is revealed in the following example from a student's essay on Shakespeare's *The Tempest*. This excerpt is from the introduction of the student's first draft:

PLOT SUMMARY—*AND THEN* WRITING

> Prospero cares deeply for his daughter. In the middle of the play Prospero acts like a gruff father and makes Ferdinand carry logs in order to test his love for Miranda and Miranda's love for him. In the end, though, Prospero is a loving father who rejoices in his daughter's marriage to a good man.

Here the student seems simply to retell the play's plot without any apparent thesis. (The body of her rough draft primarily retold the same story in more detail.) However, during an office conference, the instructor discovered that the student regarded her sentence about Prospero's being a loving father as her thesis. In fact, the student had gotten in an argument with a classmate over whether Prospero was a good person or an evil one. The instructor helped her convert her draft into a thesis-support structure:

REVISED INTRODUCTION—THESIS-SUPPORT STRUCTURE

> Many persons believe that Prospero is an evil person in the play. They claim that Prospero exhibits a harsh, destructive control over Miranda and also, like Faust, seeks superhuman knowledge through his magic. However, I contend that Prospero is a kind and loving father.

This revised version implies a problem (What kind of father is Prospero?), presents a view that the writer wishes to change (Prospero is harsh and hateful), and asserts a contestable thesis (Prospero is a loving father). The body of her paper can now be converted from plot summary to an argument with reasons and evidence supporting her claim that Prospero is loving.

Avoiding "All about" Writing, or Encyclopedic Structure

Another kind of loose, thesis-less structure is "**all about**" writing, which covers a topic by presenting information organized by categories, like an encyclopedia. When the categories are clearly marked and the information within them is clearly presented, *all about* writing can be organized and interesting, but it doesn't make a thesis-based argument. The categories do not function as points and details in support of a thesis. Rather, like the shelving system in a library, the topic categories are simply ways of arranging information for convenient retrieval.

When students are assigned a research paper or a term paper, they might mistakenly imagine that the task calls for an *all about* report rather than an argument in response to a problem. To illustrate the differences between *all about* writing and *problem-thesis* writing, consider the case of two students choosing to write term papers on the subject of female police officers. One student imagines the task as an *all about* report; the other poses and investigates a problem related to female police officers and writes a thesis-based argument in response. The *all about* writer may produce an initial outline like the following:

I. History of women in police roles
  A. Female police or soldiers in ancient times
  B. 19th century (Calamity Jane)
  C. 1900s–1960
  D. 1960–present

II. How female police officers are selected and trained
III. A typical day in the life of a female police officer
IV. Achievements and acts of heroism of female police officers
V. What the future holds for female police officers

This paper simply presents information about female police officers organized into categories. Several of the categories (particularly I, II, and III) invite chronological order (*and then* writing). Although the information reported in the paper might be interesting, it is riskless. The paper requires the writer simply to gather and report information without doing critical thinking in response to a problem.

In contrast, consider the case of a student, Lynnea, who wrote a research paper entitled "Women Police Officers: Should Size and Strength Be Criteria for Patrol Duty?" Her essay begins with a story reported to her by her boyfriend (a police officer) about being assigned to patrol duty with a new female officer, Connie Jones (not her real name), who is four feet ten inches tall and weighs ninety pounds. Here is the rest of the introduction to Lynnea's essay.

FROM LYNNEA'S INTRODUCTION

> Connie Jones has just completed police academy training and has been assigned to patrol duty in ________________. Because she is so small, she has to have a booster seat in her patrol car and has been given a special gun, since she can barely manage to pull the trigger of a standard police-issue .38 revolver. Although she passed the physical requirements at the academy, which involved speed and endurance running, sit-ups, and monkey bar tests, most of the officers in her department doubt her ability to perform competently as a patrol officer. But nevertheless she is on patrol because men and women receive equal assignments in most of today's police forces. But is this a good policy? Can a person who is significantly smaller and weaker than her peers make an effective patrol officer?

Lynnea examined all the evidence she could find—through library and field research (interviewing police officers)—and arrived at the following thesis: "Because concern for public safety overrides all other concerns, police departments should set stringent size and strength requirements for patrol officers, even if these criteria exclude many women." This thesis has plenty of tension because it sets limits on gender equity. Because Lynnea considers herself a feminist, it distressed her to advocate for public safety over women's rights. The resulting essay was engaging precisely because of the tension it creates and the controversy it engenders.

Avoiding Engfish Writing, or Structure That Doesn't Address a Real Problem

Unlike *and then* papers or *all about* papers, **engfish** papers have a thesis, but the thesis is a riskless truism that doesn't respond to a real problem with stakes.* The writer supports the thesis with predictable reasons—often structured as the three body paragraphs in a traditional five-paragraph theme. It is fill-in-the-blank

*The term *engfish* was coined by the textbook writer Ken Macrorie to describe a fishy kind of canned prose that bright but bored students mechanically produce to please their teachers. See Ken Macrorie, *Telling Writing* (Rochelle Park, NJ: Hayden Press, 1970).

writing: "The food service is bad for three reasons. First, it is bad because the food is not tasty. Blah, blah, blah about tasteless food. Second, it is bad because it is too expensive. Blah, blah, blah about the expense." And so on. The writer is on autopilot and is not contributing to a real conversation about a real question. (Perhaps in this case there would be a real question if the campus were engaged in a genuine argument about switching food services.) *Engfish* writing can therefore be well organized, but it brings no surprise to the reader, nor does it grow out of the writer's "wallowing in complexity." In the end, *engfish* is bad not because what you say is *wrong*, but because what you say couldn't *possibly* be wrong. To avoid *engfish*, stay focused on the need to surprise your reader.

SKILL 17.3 Nutshell your argument and visualize its structure.

17.3
Nutshell your argument and visualize its structure.

The previous lesson showed you how to convert loose structures into problem-thesis-support structures organized by points and details. In this lesson, we provide tips for getting your points and details effectively focused and organized. Particularly we'll show you the value of nutshelling your argument and then visualizing its structure. A chief take-away insight from this lesson is that points need to be stated as complete sentences rather than as topic phrases. A topic phrase by itself—let's say "peanut butter"—invites you to picture (in this case) a tasty substance but not to conceptualize a meaningful point within an argument. To make a point about peanut butter you need to add a predicate (verb): "Peanut butter is surprisingly nutritious." Now you have a point—one that you can support through details about the nutritional content of peanut butter. As we'll show later in this lesson, creating an effective outline for your paper helps you organize *meanings*, not topics, and meanings require complete sentences.

Making a List of "Chunks" and a Scratch Outline Early in the Writing Process

Early in the writing process, while you are still searching for meanings, you probably won't know how to organize your paper. But you may know that you have certain ideas, sections, parts, or "chunks" that you want to include somewhere in your paper. Although you don't yet know where they will go or how long they will be, just listing these chunks will help you get thinking about structure—like placing the pieces of a jigsaw puzzle onto a table top. Here is student writer Kent Ansen's list of chunks early in his process of writing a researched argument on mandatory public service for young adults.

Kent Ansen's final proposal argument is shown on pp. 405–414

KENT'S LIST OF CHUNKS TO INCLUDE

- Section on my own high school experience as a volunteer (perhaps in introduction)
- Testimonies of AmeriCorps volunteers on the value of their experience (from the AmeriCorps Web site)
- Rosenman's argument that national public service would make Americans feel more engaged with their country and be better citizens

- Kinsley's conservative argument against national public service (I'll need to summarize this and refute it)
- A section where I argue that experience with public service would help the "lost generation" improve their resumes and find better jobs

Once you make a list of chunks, you can begin thinking about which of them are high-level points and which are details in support of a point. Before writing a rough draft, many writers like to make a brief scratch outline to help with planning. Here is Kent's initial scratch outline.

KENT'S INITIAL SCRATCH OUTLINE

- Introduction
  - Attention grabber (my volunteer experience—show that it benefited me)
  - Problems with Lost Generation (maybe national service would help them)
  - Thesis—we should institute national public service
- Explain my idea, show what my plan would look like
- Show the benefits of public service
  - Help people in poverty
  - Help people who serve
  - Promote civic engagement
- Summarize Kinsley's opposition
- Try to refute Kinsley

To Achieve Focus, "Nutshell" Your Argument and Create a Working Thesis Statement

Often writers have to go through several drafts to figure out the point of certain sections. See Skills 16.1 and 16.2.

As you begin drafting, you will find your ideas gradually becoming clearer and more focused. At this point, doing the following "nutshell exercise" will ensure that your paper has a *problem-thesis* structure rather than an *and then* or *all about* structure. The six prompts in this exercise will help you focus on the "big picture" of your argument—its main high-level point and purpose. We recommend that you write your responses to each prompt as a way of seeing the "whole" of your paper.

EXERCISE FOR NUTSHELLING YOUR ARGUMENT

1. What puzzle or problem initiated your thinking about X? ___________________
2. *Template: Many people think X, but I am going to argue Y.*
   Before reading my paper, my readers will think X: __________________________. But after reading my paper, my readers will think Y: ______________________________.
3. The purpose of my paper is: ____.
4. My paper addresses the following question: _____________________________.
5. My one-sentence summary answer to this question is this [my thesis statement]: ____.
6. A tentative title for my paper is: ____.

Here are Kent Ansen's responses to these prompts:

1. I was initially puzzled about the value of volunteer work and then wondered if these same values would be obtained if national public service was made mandatory.

2. Before reading my paper, my readers will think that mandatory public service is a bad idea. But after reading my paper my readers will see the benefits of making public service mandatory for young adults.
3. The purpose of my paper is to show the benefits of mandatory public service for young adults.
4. Should the United States institute mandatory public service for young adults?
5. The United States should institute mandatory public service for young adults because such service would help fight poverty, help the young adults themselves, and promote civic engagement.
6. Engaging Young Adults to Meet America's Challenges: A Proposal for Mandatory National Service

Once you have nutshelled your argument, you are ready to create a working thesis statement that includes main supporting points. These supporting points help you visualize an emerging structure. Here is Kent's working thesis statement.

KENT'S WORKING THESIS STATEMENT

The United States should institute mandatory public service for young adults because such service would help impoverished neighborhoods, would nurture the professional growth of young adults, and would promote democracy through increased civic engagement.

Visualize Your Structure

Once you have nutshelled your argument and created a working thesis statement, you can sketch your structure to show how points, subpoints, and details can be arranged hierarchically to support your thesis. We offer you three different ways to visualize your argument: a traditional outline, a verbal/visual tree diagram, or some other kind of visual flowchart that includes both words and images. Use whichever strategy best fits your way of thinking and perceiving.

An effective outline or diagram helps you organize *meanings*, not topics. Note that in the examples that follow, Kent uses *complete sentences* in the high-level slots in order to state meanings rather than identify topics. As we explained in our earlier peanut butter example ("Peanut butter is surprisingly nutritious"), points require both subjects and verbs. Any point—whether a thesis, a main point, or a subpoint—is an assertion that requires elaboration and supporting details. By using complete sentences rather than phrases in an outline, the writer is forced to articulate the point of each section of the emerging argument.

See Skill 17.3, p. 439, for the peanut butter example.

Outlines The most common way of visualizing structure is the traditional outline, which uses numbers and letters to indicate levels of points, subpoints, and details. If this traditional method works for you, we recommend that you use the outlining feature of your word processing program, which allows you to move and insert material and change heading levels with great flexibility. (You can also use bullets and other symbols rather than letters and numbers if you prefer.)

Figure 17.1 shows the first half of Kent's outline for his argument. Note how the outline uses complete sentences in the high-level slots.

Thesis: Despite arguments against the value of public service or against government attempts to mandate "volunteerism," The United States should institute mandatory public service for young adults because such service would help America's vulnerable communities become healthier, would nurture the personal growth and professional development of young adults, and would promote democracy through increased civic engagement

I. Introduction
   A. Attenion grabber (My high school volunteer experience showed me the value of public service.)
   B. Public service might also address problems faced by young people
   C. Thesis paragraph

II. Mandatory public service would have certain features based on the model of AmeriCorps.

III. A mandatory program would invest in communities by attacking poverty and building social captial.
   A. Based on AmeriCorps model of success, national public service would fight poverty by helping the poor become self-sufficient
      1. Data from Ratcliffe and McKernan show social costs of poverty.
      2. Public service provides people-to-people contact, which is better than simply providing money or food.
   B. Testimoney from AmeriCorps volunteers also shows how mandatory public service would build social capital.

IV. A national service program would also benefit the volunteers by fostering personal growth and professional development.
   A. Testimony from AmeriCorps volunteers shows these personal benefits.
   B. These testimonies ring true to my own experience.
   C. Study by Jastrzab provides empirical support for these personal benefits.

FIGURE 17.1 Kent Ansen's Outline for First Half of Paper

Tree Diagrams A tree diagram displays a hierarchical structure visually, using horizontal and vertical space instead of letters and numbers. Figure 17.2 shows how selected points from Kent's argument could be displayed in a tree diagram. His thesis sits at the top of the tree. The main points of his argument appear as branches beneath his claim. Supporting evidence and arguments are subbranches beneath each main point. Unlike outlines, tree diagrams allow us to *see* the hierarchical relationship of points and details. When you develop a point with details, you move vertically down the tree. When you switch to a new point, you move horizontally to make a new branch. Our own teaching experience suggests that for many writers, this visual/spatial technique often produces fuller, more detailed, and more logical arguments than does a traditional outline.

Your Own Methods of Visualizing Structure Many writers develop their own personal ways of visualizing structure. Some create flowcharts with big boxes to represent major parts of the paper and arrows and smaller boxes to show the

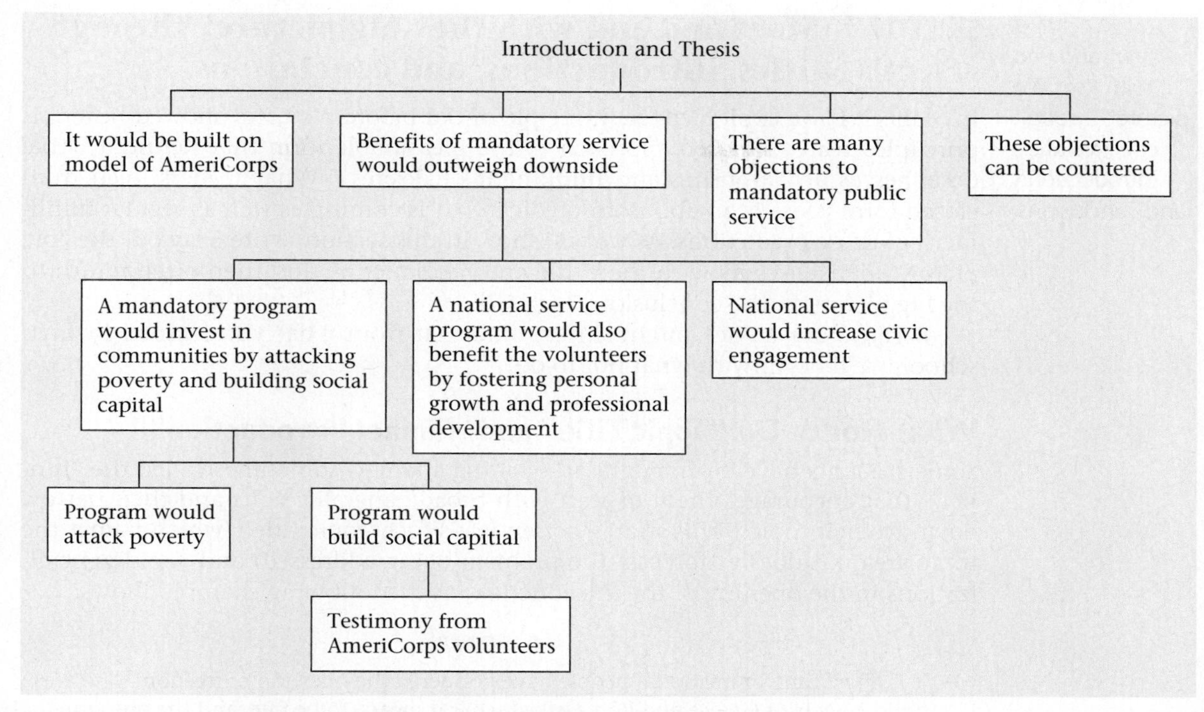

FIGURE 17.2 Tree Diagram of Selected Points from Kent Ansen's Argument

various parts of the big box. Others use the branching methods of a tree diagram but arrange the parts as spokes on a wheel. Still others combine outlines and flow charts in visual ways that work for them. In all cases, the key to organizing meanings is to use complete sentences to state points.

Once you have sketched out an initial outline or structural diagram, you can use it to generate additional ideas. Use question marks on the outline or diagram to "hold open" spots for new points or supporting details. Think of your structural diagrams as evolving sketches rather than rigid blueprints. As your ideas grow and change, revise your outline or diagram, adding or removing points, consolidating and refocusing sections, moving parts around, or filling in details.

FOR WRITING AND DISCUSSION

Nutshelling Your Ideas and Visualizing Your Structure

As you draft a paper, try out the ideas in Skill 17.2 for nutshelling your ideas and visualizing your structure. Then in small groups or as a whole class, share your nutshells and outlines or visual diagrams. What did you find helpful and why?

17.4 Start and end with the "big picture" through effective titles, introductions, and conclusions.

SKILL 17.4 Start and end with the "big picture" through effective titles, introductions, and conclusions.

In Skill 17.1, we explained the principle of old before new and showed how this principle creates a closed approach to the pleasurable form that Kenneth Burke describes as an "arousing and fulfillment of desires." What readers need from closed-form prose is an ability to predict what is coming as well as regular fulfillment of those predictions. As we will show in this section, writers lay out the "big picture" of their essay with their title and introduction and then often return to the big picture in the conclusion.

Because our advice might differ somewhat from what you learned in high school, we'll begin with what not to do.

What Not to Do: "Topic Title" and "Funnel Introduction"

Some students have been taught an opening strategy, sometimes called the "funnel," that encourages them to start with broad generalizations and then narrow down to their topics. This strategy often leads to a "topic title" (which names the topic area but doesn't forecast the problem being addressed) and vapid generalizations in the opening of the introduction, as the following example shows:

> **B. F. SKINNER**
>
> Since time immemorial people have pondered the question of freedom. The great philosophers of Greece and Rome asked what it means to be free, and the question has echoed through the ages up until the present day. One modern psychologist who asked this question was B. F. Skinner, who wanted to study whether humans had free will or were programmed by their environment to act the way they did....

Here the writer eventually gets to his subject, B. F. Skinner, but so far presents no sense of what point the essay will make or why the reader should be interested. A better approach is to hook your readers immediately with an effective title and a problem-posing introduction.

Creating Effective Titles

Good titles follow the principle of old before new information that we introduced in Skill 17.1. A good title needs to have something old (a word or phrase that hooks into a reader's existing interests) and something new (a word or phrase that forecasts the writer's problematic question, thesis, or purpose). Here are examples of effective titles from two student essays in this textbook:

> "Boomerang Kids: What Are the Causes of Generation Y's Growing Pains?"
> "Paintball: Promoter of Violence or Healthy Fun?"

Readers will be attracted to these titles if they already have some background interest in the growing pains of boomerang kids or in controversies about paintball ("old information"). But the titles also promise something "new"—arguments that promise to expand or challenge the readers' views. The first writer will explain what she sees as the causes of these growing pains; the second writer will explore the problem of violence versus fun in paintball.

As these examples show, your title should link your readers' already existing interests with the promise of something new or challenging in your essay. Academic titles are typically longer and more detailed than are titles in popular media. There are three basic approaches that academic writers take, as shown in the following strategies chart.

Strategies for Writing Titles of Academic Papers

What to Do	Examples
State or imply the question that your essay addresses.	• How Clean and Green Are Hydrogen Fuel Cell Cars? • The Impact of Cell Phones on Motor Vehicle Fatalities (Implied question: What is the impact of...?)
State or imply, often in abbreviated form, your essay's thesis.	• Reward Work, Not Wealth • How Foreign Aid Can Foster Democratization in Authoritarian Regimes (Implied thesis: Foreign aid can foster democratization...)
Use a two-part title separated by a colon: • On the left, present key words from your essay's issue or problem or a "mystery phrase" that arouses interest. • On the right, place the essay's question, thesis, or summary of purpose.	• Engaging Young Adults to Meet America's Challenges: A Proposal for Mandatory National Service • Coping with Hurricane Katrina: Psychological Stress and Resilience among African-American Evacuees

Such titles might seem overly formal to you, but they indicate how much the reader of an academic article appreciates a preview of its big picture. Although the titles in popular magazines may be more informal, they often use these same strategies. Here are some titles from popular magazines such as *Redbook* and *Forbes*:

> "Is the Coffee Bar Trend About to Peak?" (question)
> "A Man *Can* Take Maternity Leave—And Love It" (abbreviated thesis)
> "Feed Your Face: Why Your Complexion Needs Vitamins" (two parts linked by colon)

Composing a title for your essay can help you find your focus when you get bogged down in the middle of a draft. Thinking about your title forces you to *nutshell* your ideas by seeing your project's big picture. It causes you to reconsider your purpose and to think about what's old and what's new for your audience.

Writing Good Closed-Form Introductions

Just as effective titles present something old and something new, so do dynamic and powerful introductions. Old information is something your readers already know and find interesting before they start reading your essay. New information is the surprise of your argument, the unfamiliar material that you add to your readers' understanding.

In this section, we elaborate on the rhetorical concept introduced in Chapter 2, Concept 6: "In closed-form prose, an introduction starts with the problem, not the thesis."

Because the writer's thesis statement forecasts the new information the paper will present, a thesis statement for a closed-form essay typically comes *at the end of the introduction.* What precedes the thesis is typically the problem or question that the thesis addresses—the old information that the reader needs in order to understand the conversation that the thesis joins. A typical closed-form introduction has the following shape:

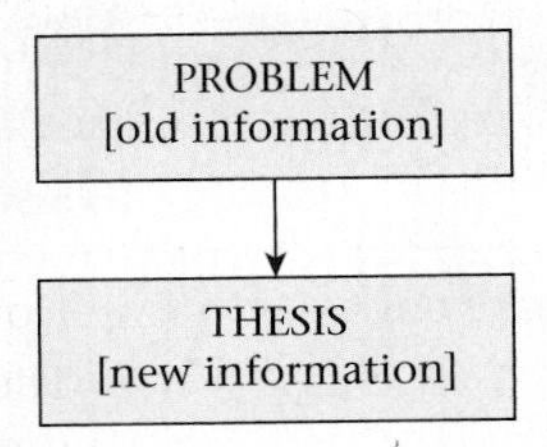

The length and complexity of your introduction is a function of how much your reader already knows and cares about the question or problem your paper addresses. The function of an introduction is to capture the reader's interest in the first few sentences, to identify and explain the question or problem that the essay addresses, to provide any needed background information, and to present the thesis. You can leave out any of the first three elements if the reader is already hooked on your topic and already knows the question you are addressing. For example, in an essay exam you can usually start with your thesis statement because you can assume the instructor already knows the question and finds it interesting.

To illustrate how an effective closed-form introduction takes the reader from the question to the thesis, consider how the following student writer revised his introduction to a paper on Napster.com, one of the earliest music file-sharing sites:

ORIGINAL INTRODUCTION (CONFUSING)

Thesis statement

Background on Napste

Napster is all about sharing, not stealing, as record companies and some musicians would like us to think. Napster is an online program that was released in October of '99. Napster lets users easily search for and trade mp3s—compressed, high-quality music files that can be produced from a CD. Napster is the leading file sharing community; it allows users to locate and share music. It also provides instant messaging, chat rooms, an outlet for fans to identify new artists, and a forum to communicate their interests.

Most readers find this introduction confusing. The writer begins with his thesis statement before the reader is introduced to the question that the thesis addresses. He seems to assume that his reader is already a part of the Napster conversation, and yet in the next sentences, he gives background on Napster. If the reader needs background on Napster, then the reader also needs background on the Napster controversy. In rethinking his assumptions about old-versus-new information for his audience, this writer decided he wants to reach general newspaper readers who may have heard about a lawsuit against Napster and are interested in the issue but aren't sure of what Napster is or how it works. Here is his revised introduction:

REVISED INTRODUCTION (CLEARER)

Several months ago the rock band Metallica filed a lawsuit against Napster.com, an online program that lets users easily search for and trade mp3s—compressed, high-quality music files that can be produced from a CD. Napster.com has been wildly popular among music lovers because it creates a virtual community where users can locate and share music. It also provides instant messaging, chat rooms, an outlet for fans to identify new artists, and a forum to communicate their interests. But big-name bands like Metallica, alarmed at what they see as lost revenues, claim that Napster.com is stealing their royalties. However, Napster is all about sharing, not stealing, as some musicians would like us to think.

Triggers readers' memory of lawsuit

Background on Napster

Clarification of problem (Implied question: Should Napster be shut down?)

Thesis

This revised introduction fills in the old information the reader needs in order to recall and understand the problem; then it presents the thesis.

Typical Elements of a Closed-Form Introduction Now that you understand the general principle of closed-form introductions, let's look more closely at its four typical features or elements:

1. ***An opening attention-grabber.*** If you aren't sure that your reader is already interested in your problem, you can begin with an attention-grabber (what journalists call the "hook" or "lead"), which is typically a dramatic vignette, a startling fact or statistic, an arresting quotation, an interesting scene, or something else that taps into your reader's interests. Attention-grabbers are uncommon in academic prose (where you assume your reader will be initially engaged by the problem itself) but frequently used in popular prose.
2. ***Explanation of the question to be investigated.*** If your reader already knows about the problem and cares about it, then you need merely to summarize it. This problem or question is the starting point of your argument. If you aren't sure whether your audience fully understands the question or fully cares about it, then you need to explain it in more detail, showing why it is both problematic and significant.
3. ***Background information.*** In order to understand the conversation you are joining, readers sometimes need background information such as a definition of key terms, a summary of events leading up to the problem, factual details needed for explaining the context of the problem, and so forth. In academic papers, this background often includes a review of what other scholars have said about the problem.
4. ***A preview of where your paper is heading.*** The final element of a closed-form introduction sketches the big picture of your essay by previewing the kind of surprise or challenge readers can expect and giving them a sense of the whole. This preview is initially new information for your readers (this is why it comes at the end of the introduction). Once stated, however, it becomes old information that readers will use to create a map for their journey through your argument. By predicting what's coming, this preview initiates the pleasurable process of forecasting/fulfillment that we discussed in Skill 17.1. Writers typically forecast the whole by stating their thesis, but they can also use a purpose statement or a blueprint statement to accomplish the same end. These strategies are the subject of the next section.

To see the choice that Ansen actually made, see his paper on pp. 405–414.

Forecasting the Whole with a Thesis Statement, Purpose Statement, or Blueprint Statement The most succinct way to forecast the whole is to state your thesis directly. Student writers often ask how detailed their thesis statements should be and whether it is permissible, sometimes, to delay revealing the thesis until the conclusion—an open-form move that gives papers a more exploratory, mystery-novel feel. It is useful, then, to outline briefly some of your choices as a writer. To illustrate a writer's options for forecasting the whole, we use Kent Ansen's researched proposal argument on mandatory public service.

Strategies for Forecasting the Whole Paper

Options	What to Do	Examples
Short thesis	State claim without summarizing your supporting argument or forecasting your structure.	The United States should institute a mandatory year of national service for Americans ages 18 to 25.
Detailed thesis	Summarize whole argument; may begin with an *although* clause that summarizes the view you are trying to change.	Despite arguments against the value of public service, the United States should institute mandatory public service for young adults because such service would help America's vulnerable communities become healthier, would nurture the personal growth and professional development of young adults, and would promote democracy through increased civic engagement.
Purpose statement	State your purpose or intention without summarizing the argument. A purpose statement typically begins with a phrase such as "My purpose is to . . ." or "In the following paragraphs I wish to . . ."	My purpose is to show the benefits to American society of mandatory public service for young adults.
Blueprint or mapping statement	Describe the structure of your essay by announcing the number of main parts and describing the function or purpose of each one.	First I will explain how mandatory public service could be modeled on the present-day success of AmeriCorps. I will then show the benefits of mandatory public service. Finally, I will summarize the arguments against mandatory public service and respond to them.
Combination of elements	Include two or more of these elements. In long essays, academic writers sometimes have a purpose statement followed by a detailed thesis and blueprint statement.	[Kent's essay is not long enough nor complex enough to need an extensive overview that includes a purpose or blueprint statement along with a thesis.]

Options	What to Do	Examples
Thesis question only *[Implies an exploratory or delayed thesis paper]*	State the question only, without initially implying your answer. This open-form strategy invites the reader to join the writer in a mutual search.	Although volunteer programs like AmeriCorps have been remarkably successful, I wonder if such programs would still work if people were coerced to participate. Would the benefits of a mandatory program outweigh the risks?

Which of these options should a writer choose? There are no firm rules to help you answer this question. How much you forecast in the introduction and where you reveal your thesis is a function of your purpose, audience, and genre. The more you forecast, the clearer your argument is and the easier it is to read quickly. You minimize the demands on readers' time by giving them the gist of your argument in the introduction, making it easier to skim your essay if they don't have time for a thorough reading. The less you forecast, the more demands you make on readers' time: You invite them, in effect, to accompany you through the twists and turns of your own thinking process, and you risk losing them if they become confused, lost, or bored. For these reasons, academic writing is generally closed form and aims at maximum clarity. In many rhetorical contexts, however, more open forms are appropriate.

If you choose a closed-form structure, we can offer some advice on how much to forecast. Readers sometimes feel insulted by too much forecasting, so include only what is needed for clarity. For short papers, readers usually don't need to have the complete supporting argument forecast in the introduction. In longer papers, however, or in especially complex ones, readers appreciate having the whole argument forecast at the outset. Academic writing in particular tends to favor explicit and often detailed forecasting.

FOR WRITING AND DISCUSSION

Revising a Title and Introduction

Individual task: Choose an essay you are currently working on or have recently completed and examine your title and introduction. Ask yourself these questions:

- What audience am I imagining? What do I assume are my readers' initial interests that will lead them to read my essay (the old information I must hook into)? What is new in my essay?
- Do I have an attention-grabber? Why or why not?
- Where do I state or imply the question or problem that my essay addresses?
- Do I explain why the question is problematic and significant? Why or why not?
- For my audience to understand the problem, do I provide too much background information, not enough, or just the right amount?
- What strategies do I use to forecast the whole?

(*continued*)

Based on your analysis of your present title and introduction, revise as appropriate.

Group task: Working with a partner or in small groups, share the changes you made in your title or introduction and explain why you made the changes.

Writing Effective Conclusions

Conclusions can best be understood as complements to introductions. In both the introduction and the conclusion, writers are concerned with the essay as a whole more than with any given part. In a conclusion, the writer is particularly concerned with helping the reader move from the parts back to the big picture and to understand the importance or significance of the essay.

Because many writers find conclusions challenging to write, we offer six possible strategies for ending an essay.

Strategies for Concluding an Essay

Strategies	What to Do	Comments
***Simple summary* conclusion**	Recap what you have said.	This approach is useful in a long or complex essay or in an instructional text that focuses on concepts. However, in a short, easy-to-follow essay, a summary conclusion can be dull and even annoying to readers. A brief summary followed by a more artful concluding strategy can sometimes be effective.
***Larger significance* conclusion**	Draw the reader's attention to the importance or the applications of your argument.	The conclusion is a good place to elaborate on the significance of your problem by showing how your proposed solution to a question leads to understanding a larger, more significant question or brings practical benefits to individuals or society. If you posed a question about values or about the interpretation of a confusing text or phenomenon, you might show how your argument could be applied to related questions, texts, or phenomena.
***Proposal* conclusion**	Call for action.	Often used in analyses and arguments, a *proposal* conclusion states the action that needs to be taken and briefly explains its advantages over alternative actions or describes its beneficial consequences. If your paper analyzes the negative consequences of shifting from a graduated to a flat-rate income tax, your conclusion may recommend an action such as modifying or opposing the flat tax.

Strategies	What to Do	Comments
	Call for future study.	A *call-for-future-study* conclusion indicates what else needs to be known or resolved before a proposal can be offered. Such conclusions are especially common in scientific writing.
***Scenic* or *anecdotal* conclusion**	Use a scene or brief story to illustrate the theme without stating it explicitly.	Often used in popular writing, a scene or anecdote can help the reader experience the emotional significance of the topic. For example, a paper favoring public housing for the homeless may end by describing an itinerant homeless person collecting bottles in a park.
***Hook and return* conclusion**	Return to something mentioned at the beginning of the essay.	If the essay begins with a vivid illustration of a problem, the conclusion can return to the same scene or story but with some variation to indicate the significance of the essay.
***Delayed-thesis* conclusion**	State the thesis for the first time at the end of the essay.	This strategy is effective when you are writing about complex or divisive issues and you don't want to take a stand until you have presented all sides. The introduction of the essay merely states the problem, giving the essay an exploratory feel.

FOR WRITING AND DISCUSSION

Writing Conclusions

Choose a paper you have just written and write an alternative conclusion using one of the strategies discussed in this lesson. Then share your original and revised conclusions in groups. Have group members discuss which one they consider most effective and why.

SKILL 17.5 Create effective topic sentences for paragraphs.

17.5
Keep readers on track through the use of effective topic sentences.

In our lesson on outlining (Skill 17.3) we suggested that you write complete sentences rather than phrases for the high-level slots of the outline in order to articulate the *meaning* or *point* of each section of your argument. In this lesson we show you how to place these points where readers expect them: near the beginning of the sections or paragraphs they govern.

When you place points before particulars, you follow the same principle illustrated in our old-before-new exercise (Skill 17.1) with the flight attendant announcing the name of the city before the departure gate (the city is the old information, the departure gate the new information). When you first state the point, it is the new information that the current paragraph or section will develop. Once you have stated it, it becomes old information that helps readers understand the meaning of the details that follow. If you withhold the point until later, the reader has to keep all the particulars in short-term memory until you finally reveal the point that the particulars are supposed to support or develop.

Placing Topic Sentences at the Beginning of Paragraphs

Readers of closed-form prose need to have point sentences (usually called "topic sentences") at the beginnings of paragraphs. However, writers of rough drafts often don't fulfill this need because, as we explained in Chapter 16, drafting is an exploratory process in which writers are often still searching for their points as they compose. Consequently, in their rough drafts writers often omit topic sentences entirely or place them at the ends of paragraphs, or they write topic sentences that misrepresent what the paragraphs actually say. During revision, then, you should check your body paragraphs carefully to be sure you have placed accurate topic sentences near the beginning.

What follow are examples of the kinds of revisions writers typically make. We have annotated the examples to explain the changes the writer has made to make the paragraphs unified and clear to readers. The first example is from a later draft of the essay on the dorm room carpets from Chapter 16 (pp. 429–430).

Revision–Topic Sentence First

Topic sentence placed first

Another reason for the university not to buy carpets is the cost.
^According to Rachel Jones, Assistant Director of Housing Services, the initial purchase and installation of carpeting would cost $300 per room. Considering the number of rooms in the three residence halls, carpeting amounts to a substantial investment. Additionally, once the carpets are installed, the university would need to maintain them through the purchase of more vacuum cleaners and shampoo machines. This money would be better spent on other dorm improvements that would benefit more residents, such as expanded kitchen facilities and improved recreational space. ~~Thus carpets would be too expensive.~~

In the original draft, the writer states the point at the end of the paragraph. In his revision he states the point in an opening topic sentence that links back to the thesis statement, which promises "several reasons" that the university should not buy carpets for the dorms. The words "Another reason" thus link the topic sentence to the argument's big picture.

Revising Paragraphs for Unity

In addition to placing topic sentences at the heads of paragraphs, writers often need to revise topic sentences to better match what the paragraph actually says, or revise the paragraph to better match the topic sentence. Paragraphs have unity when all their sentences develop the point stated in the topic sentence. Paragraphs in rough drafts are often not unified because they reflect the writer's shifting, evolving, thinking-while-writing process. Consider the following paragraph from an early draft of an argument against euthanasia by student writer Dao Do. Her peer reviewer labeled it "confusing." What makes it confusing?

We look at more examples from Dao's essay later in this chapter.

Early Draft–Confusing

First, euthanasia is wrong because no one has the right to take the life of another person. Some people say that euthanasia or suicide will end suffering and pain. But what proofs do they have for such a claim? Death is still mysterious to us; therefore, we do not know whether death will end suffering and pain or not. What seems to be the real claim is that death to those with illnesses will end *our* pain. Such pain involves worrying over them, paying their medical bills, and giving up so much of our time. Their deaths end our pain rather than theirs. And for that reason, euthanasia is a selfish act, for the outcome of euthanasia benefits us, the nonsufferers, more. Once the sufferers pass away, we can go back to our normal lives.

The paragraph opens with an apparent topic sentence: "Euthanasia is wrong because no one has the right to take the life of another person." But the rest of the paragraph doesn't focus on that point. Instead, it focuses on how euthanasia benefits the survivors more than the sick person. Dao had two choices: to revise the paragraph to fit the topic sentence or to revise the topic sentence to fit the paragraph. Here is her revision, which includes a different topic sentence and an additional sentence midparagraph to keep particulars focused on the opening point. Dao unifies this paragraph by keeping all its parts focused on her main point: "Euthanasia ... benefits the survivors more than the sick person."

Revision for Unity

First, euthanasia is wrong because it benefits the survivors more than the sick person.
^~~First, euthanasia is wrong because no one has the right to take the life of another person~~. Some people say that euthanasia or suicide will end ^*the sick person's* suffering and pain. But what proofs do they have for such a claim?

Revised topic sentence better forecasts focus of paragraph

Keeps focus on "sick person"

Concludes subpoint about sick person

Death is still mysterious to us; therefore, we do not know whether death will end suffering and pain or not. *Moreover, modern pain killers can relieve most of the pain a sick person has to endure.* What seems to be the real claim is that death to those with illnesses will end *our* pain. Such pain involves worrying over them, paying their medical bills, and giving up so much of our time. Their deaths end our pain rather than theirs. And for that reason, euthanasia is a selfish act, for the outcome of euthanasia benefits us, the nonsufferers, more. Once the sufferers pass away, we can go back to our normal lives.

Supports subpoint about how euthanasia benefits survivors

A paragraph may lack unity for a variety of reasons. It may shift to a new direction in the middle, or one or two sentences may simply be irrelevant to the point. The key is to make sure that all the sentences in the paragraph fulfill the reader's expectations based on the topic sentence.

Adding Particulars to Support Points

Just as writers of rough drafts often omit point sentences from paragraphs, they also sometimes leave out the particulars needed to support a point. In such cases, the writer needs to add particulars such as facts, statistics, quotations, research summaries, examples, or further subpoints. Consider how adding additional particulars to the following draft paragraph strengthens a student writer's argument opposing the logging of old-growth forests.

DRAFT PARAGRAPH: PARTICULARS MISSING

One reason that it is not necessary to log old-growth forests is that the timber industry can supply the world's lumber needs without doing so. For example, we have plenty of new-growth forest from which timber can be taken (Sagoff 89). We could also reduce the amount of trees used for paper products by using other materials besides wood for paper pulp. In light of the fact that we have plenty of trees and ways of reducing our wood demands, there is no need to harvest old-growth forests.

REVISED PARAGRAPH: PARTICULARS ADDED

Added particulars support subpoint that we have plenty of new-growth forest

Added particulars support second subpoint that wood alternatives are available

One reason that it is not necessary to log old-growth forests is that the timber industry can supply the world's lumber needs without doing so. For example, we have plenty of new-growth forest from which timber can be taken as a result of major reforestation efforts all over the United States (Sagoff 89). In the Northwest, for instance, Oregon law requires every acre of timber harvested to be replanted. According to Robert Sedjo, a forestry expert, the world's demand for industrial wood could be met by a widely implemented tree farming system (Sagoff 90). We could also reduce the amount of trees used for paper products by using a promising new innovation called Kenaf, a fast-growing annual herb which is fifteen feet tall and is native to Africa. It has been used for making rope for many years, but recently it was found to work just as well for paper pulp. In light of the fact that we have plenty of trees and ways of reducing our wood demands, there is no need to harvest old-growth forests.

FOR WRITING AND DISCUSSION

Revising Paragraphs for Points-First Structure

Individual task: Bring to class a draft-in-progress for a closed-form essay. Pick out several paragraphs in the body of your essay and analyze them for "points-first" structure. For each paragraph, ask the following questions:

- Does my paragraph have a topic sentence near the beginning?
- If so, does my topic sentence accurately forecast what the paragraph says?
- Does my topic sentence link to my thesis statement or to a higher-order point that my paragraph develops?
- Does my paragraph have enough particulars to develop and support my topic sentence?

Group task: Then exchange your draft with a partner and do a similar analysis of your partner's selected paragraphs. Discuss your analyses of each other's paragraphs and then help each other plan appropriate revision strategies. If time permits, revise your paragraphs and show your results to your partner. [Note: Sometimes you can revise simply by adding a topic sentence to a paragraph, rewording a topic sentence, or making other kinds of local revisions. At other times, you may need to cross out whole paragraphs and start over, rewriting from scratch after you rethink your ideas.]

SKILL 17.6 Guide your reader with transitions and other signposts.

17.6
Guide readers with transitions.

As we have explained, when readers read closed-form prose, they expect each new sentence, paragraph, and section to link clearly to what they have already read. They need a well-marked trail with signposts signaling the twists and turns along the way. They also need resting spots at major junctions where they can review where they've been and survey what's coming. In this lesson, we show you how transition words as well as summary and forecasting passages can keep your readers securely on the trail.

Using Common Transition Words to Signal Relationships

Transitions are like signposts that signal where the road is turning and limit the possible directions that an unfolding argument might take. Consider how the use of "therefore" and "nevertheless" limits the range of possibilities in the following examples:

> While on vacation, Suzie caught the chicken pox. Therefore, ________________.
> While on vacation, Suzie caught the chicken pox. Nevertheless, ______________.

"Therefore" signals to the reader that what follows is a consequence. Most readers will imagine a sentence similar to this one:

> Therefore, she spent her vacation lying in bed itchy, feverish, and miserable.

In contrast, "nevertheless" signals an unexpected or denied consequence, so the reader might anticipate a sentence such as this:

> Nevertheless, she enjoyed her two weeks off, thanks to a couple of bottles of calamine lotion, some good books, and a big easy chair overlooking the ocean.

Here is a list of the most common transition words and phrases and what they signal to the reader:*

Words or Phrases	What They Signal
first, second, third, next, finally, earlier, later, meanwhile, afterward	*sequence*—First we went to dinner; then we went to the movies.
that is, in other words, to put it another way, — (dash), : (colon)	*restatement*—He's so hypocritical that you can't trust a word he says. To put it another way, he's a complete phony.
rather, instead	*replacement*—We shouldn't use the money to buy opera tickets; rather, we should use it for a nice gift.
for example, for instance, a case in point	*example*—Mr. Carlyle is very generous. For example, he gave the janitors a special holiday gift.
because, since, for	*reason*—Taxes on cigarettes are unfair because they place a higher tax burden on the working class.
therefore, hence, so, consequently, thus, then, as a result, accordingly, as a consequence	*consequence*—I failed to turn in the essay; therefore I flunked the course.
still, nevertheless	*denied consequence*—The teacher always seemed grumpy in class; nevertheless, I really enjoyed the course.
although, even though, granted that (*with* still)	*concession*—Even though the teacher was always grumpy, I still enjoyed the course.
in comparison, likewise, similarly	*similarity*—Teaching engineering takes a lot of patience. Likewise, so does teaching accounting.
however, in contrast, conversely, on the other hand, but	*contrast*—I disliked my old backpack immensely; however, I really like this new one.
in addition, also, too, moreover, furthermore	*addition*—Today's cars are much safer than those of ten years ago. In addition, they get better gas mileage.
in brief, in sum, in conclusion, finally, to sum up, to conclude	*conclusion or summary*—In sum, the plan presented by Mary is the best choice.

FOR WRITING AND DISCUSSION

Using Transitions

This exercise is designed to show you how transition words govern relationships between ideas. Working in groups or on your own, finish each of the following statements using ideas of your own invention. Make sure what you add fits the logic of the transition word.

1. Writing is difficult; therefore ________________.
2. Writing is difficult; however, ________________.

*Although all the words on the list serve as transitions or connectives, grammatically they are not all equivalent, nor are they all punctuated the same way.

3. Writing is difficult because ________________.
4. Writing is difficult. For example, ________________.
5. Writing is difficult. To put it another way, ________________.
6. Writing is difficult. Likewise, ________________.
7. Although writing is difficult, ________________.

In the following paragraph, various kinds of linking devices have been omitted. Fill in the blanks with words or phrases that would make the paragraph coherent. Clues are provided in brackets.

Writing an essay is a difficult process for most people. ________________ [contrast] the process can be made easier if you learn to practice three simple techniques. ________________ [sequence] learn the technique of nonstop writing. When you are first trying to think of ideas for an essay, put your pen to your paper and write nonstop for ten or fifteen minutes without letting your pen leave the paper. Stay loose and free. Let your pen follow the waves of thought. Don't worry about grammar or spelling. ________________ [concession] this technique won't work for everyone, it helps many people get a good cache of ideas to draw on. A ________________ [sequence] technique is to write your rough draft rapidly without worrying about being perfect. Too many writers try to get their drafts right the first time. ________________ [contrast] by learning to live with imperfection, you will save yourself headaches and a wastepaper basket full of crumpled paper. Think of your first rough draft as a path hacked out of the jungle—as part of an exploration, not as a completed highway. As a ________________ [sequence] technique, try printing out a triple-spaced copy to allow space for revision. Many beginning writers don't leave enough space to revise. ________________ [consequence] these writers never get in the habit of crossing out chunks of their rough draft and writing revisions in the blank spaces. After you have revised your rough draft until it is too messy to work from anymore, you can ________________ [sequence] enter your changes into your word processor and print out a fresh draft, again setting your text on triple-space. The resulting blank space invites you to revise.

Writing Major Transitions between Parts

In long closed-form pieces, writers often put *resting places* between major parts—transitional passages that allow readers to shift their attention momentarily away from the matter at hand to get a sense of where they've been and where they're going. Often such passages sum up the preceding major section, refer back to the essay's thesis statement or opening blueprint plan, and then preview the next major section. Here are three typical examples:

> So far I have looked at a number of techniques that can help people identify debilitating assumptions that block their self-growth. In the next section, I examine ways to question and overcome these assumptions.
>
> Now that the difficulty of the problem is fully apparent, our next step is to examine some of the solutions that have been proposed.
>
> These, then, are the major theories explaining why Hamlet delays. But let's see what happens to Hamlet if we ask the question in a slightly different way. In this next section, we shift our critical focus, looking not at Hamlet's actions, but at his language.

Signaling Major Transitions with Headings

In many genres, particularly scientific and technical reports, government documents, business proposals, textbooks, and long articles in magazines or scholarly journals, writers conventionally break up long stretches of text with headings and subheadings. Headings are often set in different type sizes and fonts and mark transition points between major parts and subparts of the argument.

17.7 Link sentences by placing old information before new.

SKILL 17.7 Bind sentences together by placing old information before new information.

The previous skill focused on marking the reader's trail with transitions. This skill will enable you to build a smooth trail without potholes or washed-out bridges.

The Old/New Contract in Sentences

A powerful way to prevent gaps is to follow the old/new contract—a writing strategy derived from the principle of old before new that we explained and illustrated in Skill 17.1. Simply put, the old/new contract asks writers to begin sentences with something old—something that links to what has gone before—and then to end sentences with new information.

To understand the old/new contract more fully, try the following thought exercise. We'll show you two passages, both of which explain the old/new contract. One of them, however, follows the principle it describes; the other violates it.

THOUGHT EXERCISE

Which of these passages follows the old/new contract?

VERSION 1

The old/new contract is another principle for writing clear closed-form prose. Beginning your sentences with something old—something that links to what has gone before—and then ending your sentences with new information that advances the argument is what the old/new contract asks writers to do. An effect called *coherence,* which is closely related to *unity,* is created by following this principle. Whereas the clear relationship between the topic sentence and the body of the paragraph and between the parts and the whole is what *unity* refers to, the clear relationship between one sentence and the next is what *coherence* relates to.

VERSION 2

Another principle for writing clear closed-form prose is the old/new contract. The old/new contract asks writers to begin sentences with something old—something that links to what has gone before—and then to end sentences with new information that advances the argument. Following this principle creates an effect called *coherence,* which is closely related to unity. Whereas *unity* refers to the clear relationship between the body of a paragraph and its topic sentence and between the parts and the whole, *coherence* refers to the clear relationship between one sentence and the next, between part and part.

If you are like most readers, you have to concentrate much harder to understand Version 1 than Version 2 because Version 1 violates the old-before-new way that our minds normally process information. When a writer doesn't begin a sentence with old material, readers have to hold the new material in suspension until they have figured out how it connects to what has gone before. They can stay on the trail, but they have to keep jumping over the potholes between sentences.

To follow the old/new contract, place old information near the beginning of sentences in what we call the **topic position** and place new information that advances the argument in the predicate or **stress position** at the end of the sentence. We associate topics with the beginnings of sentences simply because in the standard English sentence, the topic (or subject) comes before the predicate—hence the notion of a "contract" by which we agree not to fool or frustrate our readers by breaking with the "normal" order of things. The contract says that the old, backward-linking material comes at the beginning of the sentence and that the new, argument-advancing material comes at the end.

FOR WRITING AND DISCUSSION

Practicing the Old/New Contract

Here are two more passages, one of which obeys the old/new contract while the other violates it. Working in small groups or as a whole class, reach consensus on which of these passages follows the old/new contract. Explain your reasoning by showing how the beginning of each sentence links to something old.

PASSAGE A

Play is an often-overlooked dimension of fathering. From the time a child is born until its adolescence, fathers emphasize caretaking less than play. Egalitarian feminists may be troubled by this, and spending more time in caretaking may be wise for fathers. There seems to be unusual significance in the father's style of play. Physical excitement and stimulation are likely to be part of it. With older children more physical games and teamwork that require the competitive testing of physical and mental skills are also what it involves. Resemblance to an apprenticeship or teaching relationship is also a characteristic of fathers' play: Come on, let me show you how.

PASSAGE B

An often-overlooked dimension of fathering is play. From their children's birth through adolescence, fathers tend to emphasize play more than caretaking. This emphasis may be troubling to egalitarian feminists, and it would indeed be wise for most fathers to spend more time in caretaking. Yet the fathers' style of play seems to have unusual significance. It is likely to be both physically stimulating and exciting. With older children it involves more physical games and teamwork that require the competitive testing of physical and mental skills. It frequently resembles an apprenticeship or teaching relationship: Come on, let me show you how.

How to Make Links to the "Old"

To understand how to link to "old information," you need to understand more fully what we mean by "old" or "familiar." In the context of sentence-level coherence, we mean everything in the text that the reader has read so far. Any upcoming sentence is new information, but once the reader has read it, it becomes old information. For example, when a reader is halfway through a text, everything previously read—the title, the introduction, half the body—is old information to which you can link to meet your readers' expectations for unity and coherence.

In making these backward links, writers have three targets:

1. They can link to a key word or concept in the immediately preceding sentence (creating coherence).
2. They can link to a key word or concept in a preceding point sentence (creating unity).
3. They can link to a preceding forecasting statement about structure (helping readers map their location in the text).

Writers have a number of textual strategies for making these links. In Figure 17.3 our annotations show how a professional writer links to old

FIGURE 17.3 How a Professional Writer Follows the Old/New Contract

Recent research has given us much deeper—and more surprising—insights into the father's role in childrearing. It shows that in almost all of their interactions with children, fathers do things a little differently from mothers. What fathers do—their special parenting style—is not only highly complementary to what mothers do but is by all indications important in its own right.

For example, an often-overlooked dimension of fathering is play. From their children's birth through adolescence, fathers tend to emphasize play more than caretaking. This may be troubling to egalitarian feminists, and it would indeed be wise for most fathers to spend more time in caretaking.

Yet the fathers' style of play seems to have unusual significance. It is likely to be both physically stimulating and exciting. With older children it involves more physical games and teamwork that require the competitive testing of physical and mental skills. It frequently resembles an apprenticeship or teaching relationship: Come on, let me show you how.

David Popenoe, "Where's Papa?" from *Life Without Father: Compelling New Evidence that Fatherhood and Marriage Are Indispensable for the Good of Children and Society.*

Refers to "research" in previous sentence

Refers to "fathers" in previous sentence

Rephrases idea of "childrearing"

Repeats "fathers" from previous sentence

Transition tells us new paragraph will be an example of previous concept

Rephrases concept in previous paragraph

Refers to "fathers"

New information that becomes topic of this paragraph

Pronoun sums up previous concept

Repeats words "father" and "play" from the topic sentence of the preceding paragraph

"It" refers to fathers' style of play

information within the first five or six words of each sentence. What follows is a compendium of these strategies:

Strategies for Linking to the "Old"

What to Do	Example Shown in Figure 17.3
Repeat a key word from the preceding sentence or an earlier point sentence.	Note the number of sentences that open with "father," "father's," or "fathering." Note also the frequent repetitions of "play."
Use a pronoun to substitute for a key word.	In our example, the second sentence opens with the pronouns "It," referring to "research," and "their," referring to "fathers." The last three sentences open with the pronoun "It," referring to "father's style of play."
Summarize, rephrase, or restate earlier concepts.	In the second sentence, "interactions with children" restates the concept of childrearing. Similarly, the phrase "an often-overlooked dimension" sums up a concept implied in the preceding paragraph—that recent research reveals something significant and not widely known about a father's role in childrearing. Finally, note that the pronoun "This" in the second paragraph sums up the main concept of the previous two sentences. (But see our warning on p. 462 about the overuse of "this" as a pronoun.)
Use a transition word such as *first...,second..., third...,* or *therefore* or *however* to cue the reader about the logical relationship between an upcoming sentence and the preceding ones.	Note how the second paragraph opens with "For example," indicating that the upcoming paragraph will illustrate the concept identified in the preceding paragraph.

These strategies give you a powerful way to check and revise your prose. Comb your drafts for gaps between sentences where you have violated the old/new contract. If the opening of a new sentence doesn't refer back to an earlier word, phrase, or concept, your readers could derail, so use what you have learned to repair the tracks.

Applying the Old/New Contract to Your Own Draft

FOR WRITING AND DISC

Individual task: Bring to class a draft-in-progress for a closed-form essay. On a selected page, examine the opening of each sentence. Place a vertical slash in front of any sentence that doesn't contain near the beginning some backward-looking element that links to old, familiar material. Then revise these sentences to follow the old/new contract.

(*continued*)

Group task: Working with a partner, share the changes you each made on your drafts. Then on each other's pages, work together to identify the kinds of links made at the beginning of each sentence. (For example, does the opening of a sentence repeat a key word, use a pronoun to substitute for a key word, rephrase or restate an earlier concept, or use a transition word?)

As we discussed in Skill 17.1, the principle of old before new has great explanatory power in helping writers understand their choices when they compose. In this last section, we give you some further insights into the old/new contract.

Avoiding Ambiguous Use of "This" to Fulfill the Old/New Contract

Some writers try to fulfill the old/new contract by frequent use of the pronoun *this* to sum up a preceding concept. Occasionally such usage is effective, as in our example passage on fathers' style of play when the writer says: "*This* may be troubling to egalitarian feminists." But frequent use of *this* as a pronoun creates lazy and often ambiguous prose. Consider how our example passage might read if many of the explicit links were replaced by *this*:

LAZY USE OF *THIS* AS PRONOUN

Recent research has given us much deeper—and more surprising—insights into **this.** It shows that in doing **this,** fathers do things a little differently from mothers. **This** is not only highly complementary to what mothers do but is by all indications important in its own right.

For example, an often-overlooked dimension of **this** is play.

Perhaps this passage helps you see why we refer to *this* (used by itself as a pronoun) as "the lazy person's all-purpose noun-slot filler."*

17.8 Use four expert moves for organizing and developing ideas.

SKILL 17.8 Learn four expert moves for organizing and developing ideas.

Writers of closed-form prose often employ a conventional set of moves to organize parts of an essay. In using the term *moves*, we are making an analogy with the "set moves" or "set plays" in such sports as basketball, volleyball, and soccer. For example, a common set move in basketball is the "pick," in which an offensive player without the ball stands motionless in order to block the path of

*It's acceptable to use *this* as an adjective, as in "this usage"; we refer here only to *this* used by itself as a pronoun.

a defensive player who is guarding the dribbler. Similarly, certain organizational patterns in writing occur frequently enough to act as set plays for writers. These patterns set up expectations in the reader's mind about the shape of an upcoming stretch of prose, anything from a few sentences to a paragraph to a large block of paragraphs. As you will see, these moves also stimulate the invention of ideas. Next, we describe four of the most powerful set plays.*

The *For Example* Move

Perhaps the most common set play occurs when a writer makes an assertion and then illustrates it with one or more examples, often signaling the move explicitly with transitions such as *for example, for instance,* or *a case in point is*.... Here is how student writer Dao Do used the *for example* move to support her third reason for opposing euthanasia:

FOR EXAMPLE MOVE

My third objection to euthanasia is that it fails to see the value in suffering. Suffering is a part of life. We see the value of suffering only if we look deeply within our suffering. For example, I never thought my crippled uncle from Vietnam was a blessing to my grandmother until I talked to her. My mother's little brother was born prematurely. As a result of oxygen and nutrition deficiency, he was born crippled. His tiny arms and legs were twisted around his body, preventing him from any normal movements such as walking, picking up things, and lying down. He could only sit. Therefore, his world was very limited, for it consisted of his own room and the garden viewed through his window. Because of his disabilities, my grandmother had to wash him, feed him, and watch him constantly. It was hard, but she managed to care for him for forty-three years. He passed away after the death of my grandfather in 1982. Bringing this situation out of Vietnam and into Western society shows the difference between Vietnamese and Western views. In the West, my uncle might have been euthanized as a baby. Supporters of euthanasia would have said he wouldn't have any quality of life and that he would have been a great burden. But he was not a burden on my grandmother. She enjoyed taking care of him, and he was always her company after her other children got married and moved away. Neither one of them saw his defect as meaningless suffering because it brought them closer together.

Topic sentence

Transition signaling the move

Extended example supporting point

This passage uses a single, extended example to support a point. You could also use several shorter examples or other kinds of illustrating evidence such as facts or statistics. In all cases the *for example* move creates a pattern of expectation and fulfillment. This pattern drives the invention of ideas in one of two ways: It urges the writer either to find examples to develop a generalization or to formulate a generalization that shows the point of an example.

*You might find it helpful to follow the set plays we used to write this section. This last sentence is the opening move of a play we call "division into parallel parts." It sets up the expectation that we will develop four set plays in order. Watch for the way we chunk them and signal transitions between them.

FOR WRITING AND DISCUSSION

Practicing the *For Example* Move

Working individually or in groups, develop a plan for supporting one or more of the following generalizations using the *for example* move:

1. Another objection to state sales taxes is that they are so annoying.
2. Although assertiveness training has definite benefits, it can sometimes get you into real trouble.
3. Sometimes effective leaders are indecisive.

The *Summary/However* Move

This move occurs whenever a writer sums up another person's viewpoint in order to qualify or contradict it or to introduce an opposing view. Typically, writers use transition words such as *but, however, in contrast,* or *on the other hand* between the parts of this move. This move is particularly common in academic writing, which often contrasts the writer's new view with prevailing views. Here is how Dao uses a *summary/however* move in the introduction of her essay opposing euthanasia:

***SUMMARY/HOWEVER* MOVE**

Issue over which there is disagreement

Summary of opposing viewpoint

Transition to writer's viewpoint

Statement of writer's view

Should euthanasia be legalized? My classmate Martha and her family think it should be. Martha's aunt was blind from diabetes. For three years she was constantly in and out of the hospital, but then her kidneys shut down and she became a victim of life support. After three months of suffering, she finally gave up. Martha believes this three-month period was unnecessary, for her aunt didn't have to go through all of that suffering. If euthanasia were legalized, her family would have put her to sleep the minute her condition worsened. Then, she wouldn't have had to feel pain, and she would have died in peace and with dignity. However, despite Martha's strong argument for legalizing euthanasia, I find it wrong.

The first sentence of this introduction poses the question that the essay addresses. The main body of the paragraph summarizes Martha's opposing view on euthanasia, and the final sentence, introduced by the transition "However," presents Dao's thesis.

FOR WRITING AND DISCUSSION

Practicing the *Summary/However* Move

For this exercise, assume that you favor development of wind-generated electricity. Use the *summary/however* move to acknowledge the view of civil engineer David Rockwood, whose letter opposing wind-generated electricity you read in Chapter 1 (p. 15). Assume that you are writing the opening paragraph of your own essay. Follow the pattern of Dao's introduction: (a) begin with a one-sentence issue or question; (b) summarize Rockwood's view in approximately one hundred words; and (c) state your own view, using *however* or *in contrast* as a transition. Write out your paragraph on your own, or work in groups to write a consensus paragraph. Then share and critique your paragraphs.

The *Division-into-Parallel-Parts* Move

Among the most frequently encountered and powerful of the set plays is the *division-into-parallel-parts* move. To initiate the move, a writer begins with an umbrella sentence that forecasts the structure and creates a framework. (For example, "Freud's theory differs from Jung's in three essential ways" or "The decline of the U.S. space program can be attributed to several factors.") Typical overview sentences either specify the number of parts that follow by using phrases such as "two ways," "three differences," or "five kinds," or they leave the number unspecified, using words such as *several, a few*, or *many*. Alternatively, the writer may ask a rhetorical question that implies the framework: "What are some main differences, then, between Freud's theory and Jung's? One difference is...."

To signal transitions from one part to the next, writers use two kinds of signposts in tandem. The first is a series of transition words or bullets to introduce each of the parallel parts. Here are typical series of transition words:

First... Second... Third... Finally...
First... Another... Still another... Finally...
One... In addition... Furthermore... Also...

The second kind of signpost, usually used in conjunction with transitions, is an echolike repetition of the same grammatical structure to begin each parallel part.

> I learned several things from this course. First, *I learned that* [development]. Second, *I learned that* [development]. Finally, *I learned that* [development].

The *division-into-parallel-parts* move can be used within a single paragraph, or it can control larger stretches of text in which a dozen or more paragraphs may work together to complete a parallel series of parts. (For example, you are currently in the third part of a parallel series introduced by the mapping sentence on p. 463: "Next, we describe four of the most powerful set plays.") Here is an example of a student paragraph organized by the *division-into-parallel-parts* move.

DIVISION-INTO-PARALLEL-PARTS MOVE

In this paper I will argue that political solutions to homelessness must take into account four categories of homeless people. A first category is persons who are out of work and seek new jobs. Persons in this category may have been recently laid off, unable to meet their rental payments, and forced temporarily to live out of a car or van. They might quickly leave the ranks of the homeless if they can find new jobs. A second category includes the physically disabled or mentally ill. Providing housing addresses only part of their problems since they also need medical care and medication. For many, finding or keeping a job might be impossible. A third category is the street alcoholic or drug addict. These persons need addiction treatment as well as clothing and shelter and will not become productive citizens until they become sober or drug free. The final category includes those who, like the old railroad "hobo," choose homelessness as a way of life.

Mapping statement forecasts "move"

Transition to first parallel part

Transition to second parallel part

Transition to third parallel part

Final transition completes "move"

Instead of transition words, writers can also use bullets followed by indented text:

USE OF BULLETS TO SIGNAL PARALLEL PARTS

The Wolf Recovery Program is rigidly opposed by a vociferous group of ranchers who pose three main objections to increasing wolf populations:

- They perceive wolves as a threat to livestock. [development]
- They fear the wolves will attack humans. [development]
- They believe ranchers will not be compensated by the government for their loss of profits. [development]

FOR WRITING AND DISCUSSION

Practicing the *Division-into-Parallel-Parts* Move

Working individually or in small groups, use the *division-into-parallel-parts* move to create, organize, and develop ideas to support one or more of the following point sentences.

1. To study for an exam effectively, a student should follow these [specify a number] steps.
2. Why do U.S. schoolchildren lag so far behind European and Asian children on standardized tests of mathematics and science? One possible cause is...[continue].
3. Constant dieting is unhealthy for several reasons.

The *Comparison/Contrast* Move

A common variation on the *division-into-parallel-parts* move is the *comparison/ contrast* move. To compare or contrast two items, you must first decide on the points of comparison (or contrast). If you are contrasting the political views of two presidential candidates, you might choose to focus on four points of comparison: differences in their foreign policy, differences in economic policy, differences in social policy, and differences in judicial philosophy. You then have two choices for organizing the parts: the *side-by-side pattern,* in which you discuss all of candidate A's views and then all of candidate B's views; or the *back-and-forth pattern,* in which you discuss foreign policy, contrasting A's views with B's views, then move on to economic policy, then social policy, and then judicial philosophy. Figure 17.4 shows how these two patterns would appear on a tree diagram.

There are no cut-and-dried rules that dictate when to use the *side-by-side pattern* or the *back-and-forth pattern*. However, for lengthy comparisons, the *back-and-forth pattern* is often more effective because the reader doesn't have to store great amounts of information in memory. The *side-by-side pattern* requires readers to remember all the material about A when they get to B, and it is sometimes difficult to keep all the points of comparison clearly in mind.

FIGURE 17.4 Two Ways to Structure a Comparison or Contrast

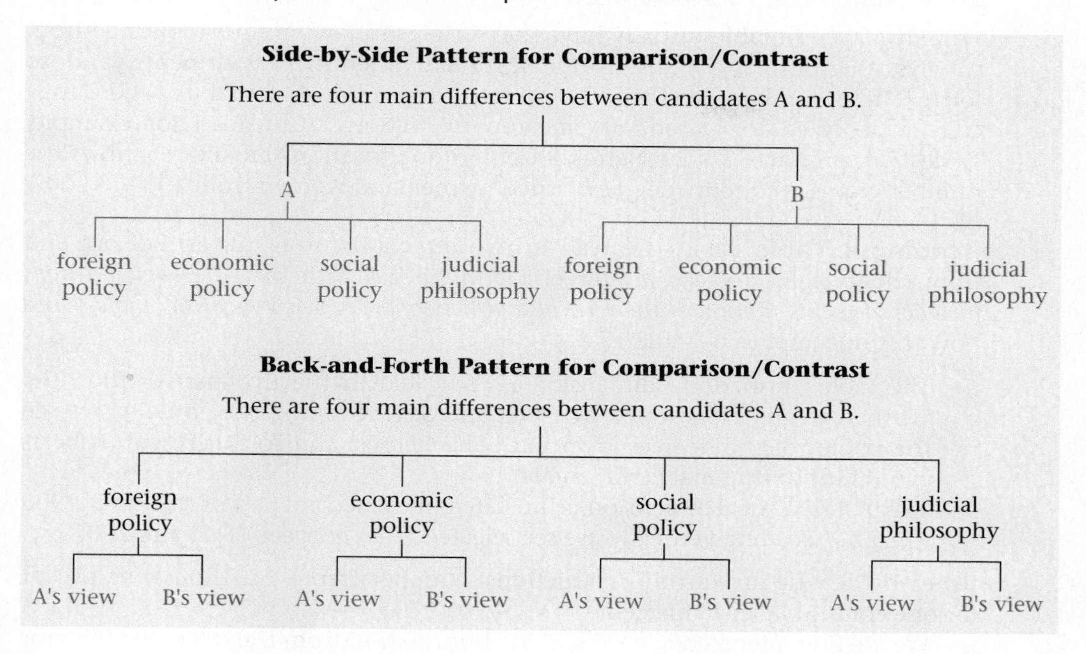

FOR WRITING AND DISCUSSION

Practicing the *Comparison/Contrast* Move

Working individually or in groups, create tree diagrams for stretches of text based on one or more of the following point sentences, all of which call for the *comparison/contrast* move. Make at least one diagram follow the *back-and-forth pattern* and at least one diagram follow the *side-by-side pattern.*

1. To understand U.S. politics, an outsider needs to appreciate some basic differences between Republicans and Democrats.
2. Although they are obviously different on the surface, there are many similarities between the Boy Scouts and a street gang.
3. There are several important differences between closed-form and open-form writing.

SKILL 17.9 Use effective tables, graphs, and charts to present numeric data.

17.9 Present numerical data effectively through tables, graphs, and charts.

In contemporary analyses and arguments, writers often draw on quantitative data to support their points. Writers can make numbers speak powerfully by means of reader-effective graphics including tables, graphs, and charts. Generally, quantitative data displayed in tables invite the reader to tease out many different stories that the numbers might tell. In contrast, line graphs, bar graphs, or pie charts focus vividly on one story.

How Tables Tell Many Stories

This process is explained more fully in Chapter 9 on analyzing field research data.

Data displayed in tables usually have their origins in raw numbers collected from surveys, questionnaires, observational studies, scientific experiments, and so forth. These numbers are then consolidated and arranged in tables where they can be analyzed for potentially meaningful patterns. Consider, for example, Table 17.1, produced by the National Center for Education Statistics. It shows the number of postsecondary degrees earned by men and women from 1960 to 2007.

Reading a Table Tables are read in two directions: from top to bottom and from left to right. To read a table efficiently, begin with the title, *which always includes elements from both the vertical and horizontal dimensions of the table.* Note how this rule applies to Table 17.1.

- The table's horizontal dimension is indicated in the first part of the title: "Earned Degrees Conferred by Level and Sex." Reading horizontally, we see the names of the degrees (associate's, bachelor's, and so forth) with subcategories indicating male and female.
- The table's vertical dimension is indicated in the second part of the title: "1960 to 2007." Reading vertically, we see selected years between 1960 and 2007.

Beneath the title are further instructions: Numbers represent thousands except for one column labeled "percent."

We are now prepared to read specific information from the table. In 1994, for example, colleges and universities in the United States conferred 2,206,000 degrees, of which 45.1 percent were earned by men. In that same year, 532,000 men and 637,000 women earned bachelors's degrees while 27,000 men and 17,000 women earned doctoral degrees.

Discovering Stories in the Data You need to peruse the table carefully before interesting patterns begin to emerge. Among the stories the table tells are these:

- The percent of women receiving postsecondary degrees rose substantially between 1960 and 2007 (with a corresponding fall for men).
- This increased percentage of degrees given to women is more dramatic for associate's and bachelor's degrees than it is for master's, first professional, or doctoral degrees.

As we show in the next section, these two stories, which must be teased out of this table, can be told more dramatically with graphs.

Using a Graphic to Tell a Story

Whereas tables can embed many stories and invite detailed examination of the numbers, a graph or chart makes one selected story immediately visible.

Line Graph A line graph converts numerical data to a series of points on a grid and connects them to create flat, rising, or falling lines. The result gives us a picture of the relationship between the variables represented on the horizontal and vertical axes.

Suppose you wanted to tell the story of the increasing percentage of women receiving bachelor's and doctoral degrees from 1960 to 2007. Using Table 17.1

TABLE 17.1 Earned Degrees Conferred by Level and Sex: 1960 to 2007

[In thousands (477 represents 477,000), except percent. Based on survey; see Appendix III]

Year ending	All degrees		Associate's		Bachelor's		Master's		First professional		Doctoral	
	Total	Percent male	Male	Female	Male	Female	Male	Female	Male	Female	Male	Female
1960[1]	477	65.8	(NA)	(NA)	254	138	51	24	(NA)	(NA)	9	1
1970	1,271	59.2	117	89	451	341	126	83	33	2	26	4
1975	1,666	56.0	191	169	505	418	162	131	49	7	27	7
1980	1,731	51.1	184	217	474	456	151	147	53	17	23	10
1985	1,828	49.3	203	252	483	497	143	143	50	25	22	11
1990	1,940	46.6	191	264	492	560	154	171	44	27	24	14
1991	2,025	45.8	199	283	504	590	156	181	44	25	25	15
1992	2,108	45.6	207	297	521	616	162	191	45	29	26	15
1993	2,167	45.5	212	303	533	632	169	200	45	30	26	16
1994	2,206	45.1	215	315	532	637	176	211	45	31	27	17
1995	2,218	44.9	218	321	526	634	179	219	45	31	27	18
1996[2]	2,248	44.2	220	336	522	642	179	227	45	32	27	18
1997[2]	2,288	43.6	224	347	521	652	181	238	46	33	27	19
1998[2]	2,298	43.2	218	341	520	664	184	246	45	34	27	19
1999[2]	2,323	42.7	218	342	519	682	186	254	44	34	25	19
2000[2]	2,385	42.6	225	340	530	708	192	265	44	36	25	20
2001[2]	2,416	42.4	232	347	532	712	194	274	43	37	25	20
2002[2]	2,494	42.2	238	357	550	742	199	283	43	38	24	20
2003[2]	2,621	42.1	253	380	573	775	211	301	42	39	24	22
2004[2]	2,755	41.8	260	405	595	804	230	329	42	41	25	23
2005[2]	2,850	41.6	268	429	613	826	234	341	44	43	27	26
2006[2]	2,936	41.3	270	443	631	855	238	356	44	44	29	27
2007[2]	3,007	41.2	275	453	650	875	238	366	45	45	30	30

NA Not available.

[1] First-professional degrees are included with bachelor's degrees.

[2] Beginning 1996, data reflect the new classification of institutions.

Source: U.S. National Center for Education Statistics, *Digest of Education Statistics,* annual.

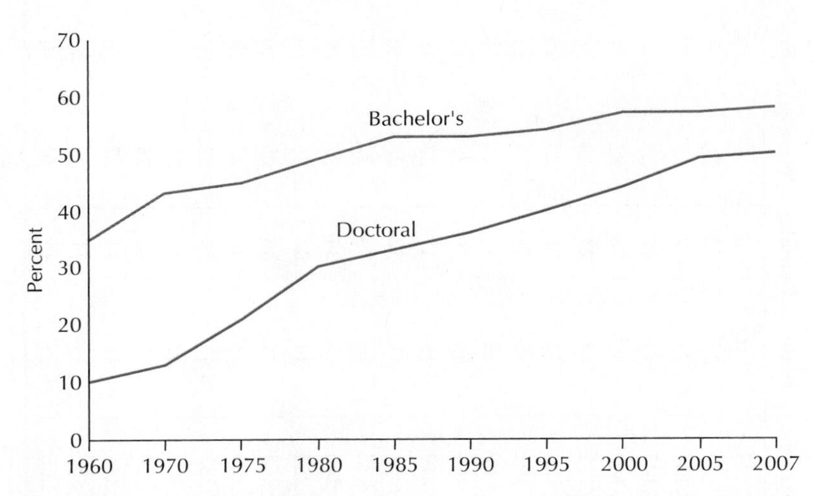

FIGURE 17.5 Percentage of Bachelor's and Doctoral Degrees Conferred on Females: 1960–2007

you can calculate these percentages yourself and display them in a line graph as shown in Figure 17.5. To determine what a graph tells you, you need to clarify what's represented on the two axes. By convention, the horizontal axis of a graph contains the predictable, known variable that has no surprises, such as time or some other sequence—in this case, the years 1960 to 2007 in predictable chronological order. The vertical axis contains the unpredictable variable that tells the graph's story—in this case, the percent of degrees conferred on women in each year on the graph. The ascending lines tell the stories at a glance.

Bar Graph Bar graphs use bars of varying lengths, extending either horizontally or vertically, to contrast two or more quantities. To make the story of women's progress in earning doctoral degrees particularly vivid (the same story told in the "doctoral" line in Figure 17.5), you could use a bar graph as shown in Figure 17.6. To read a bar graph, note carefully the title and the axes to see what is compared to what. Bars are typically distinguished from each other by use of different colors, shades, or patterns of cross-hatching. The special power of bar graphs is that they can help you make quick comparisons. Figure 17.6 tells you at a glance that in 1960, women received far fewer doctoral degrees than men but that in 2007 they received an equal percentage.

Pie Chart A pie chart, also called a circle graph, depicts the different percentages of a total (the pie) represented by variously sized slices. Suppose you wanted to know the most popular undergraduate majors in American colleges and universities. These statistics, which are available in table format from the National Center for Education Statistics, can be quickly converted into a pie chart as shown in Figure 17.7. As you can see, a pie chart shows at a glance how the whole of something is divided into segments. In 2007, for example, 7 percent of graduating seniors majored in education while 22 percent majored in business. The effectiveness of pie charts diminishes as you add more slices. In most cases, you begin to confuse readers if you include more than five or six slices.

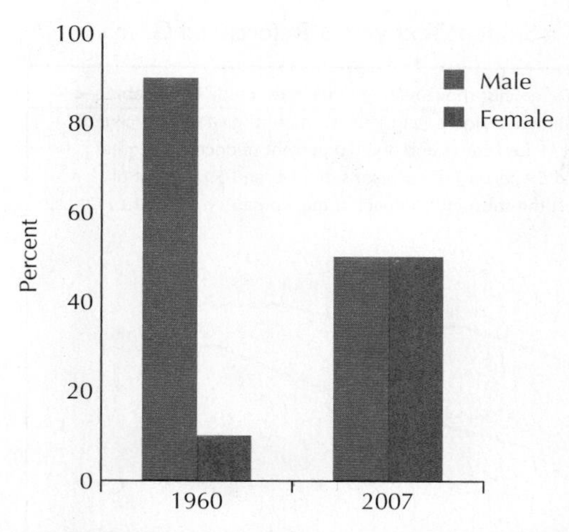

FIGURE 17.6 Percentage of Doctoral Degrees Conferred on Males and Females: 1960 and 2007

Incorporating a Graphic into Your Essay

Today, most word processing programs, often integrated with a spreadsheet, easily allow you to create a graphic and insert it into your document. In some cases, your instructor may give you permission to make a graphic with pen or pencil and paste it into your document.

Designing Your Graphic In academic manuscripts, graphics are designed conservatively without bells and whistles such as three-dimensional effects or special fonts and patterns. Keep the graphic as simple and uncluttered as possible. Also in

FIGURE 17.7 Distribution of Bachelor's Degrees by Majors, 2007

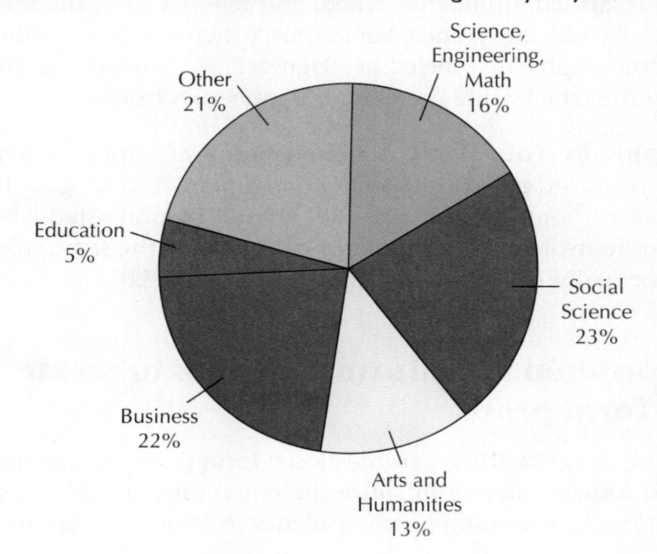

FIGURE 17.8 Example of a Student Text with a Referenced Graph

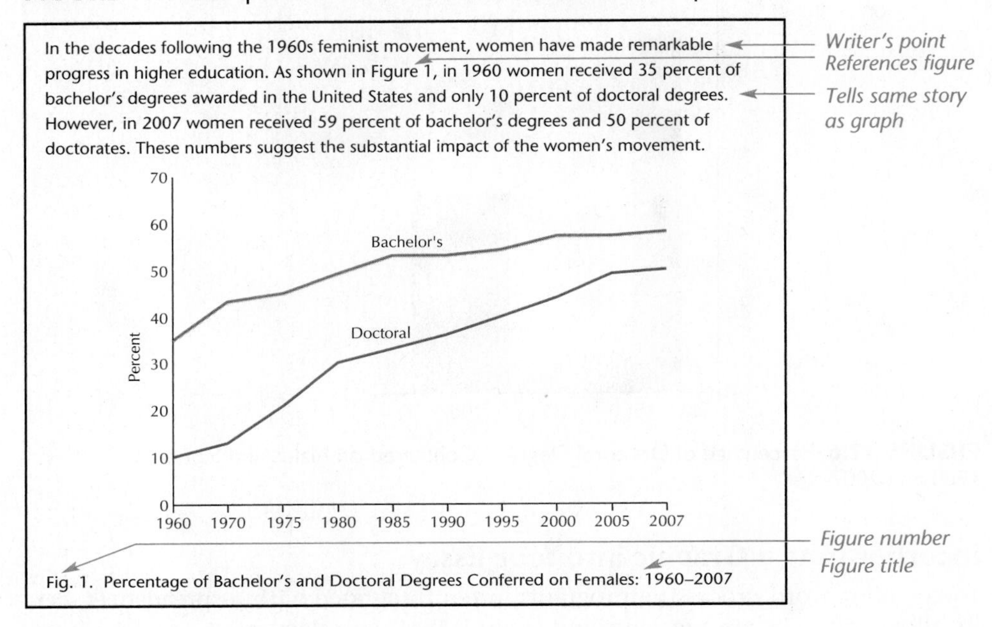

academic manuscripts, do not wrap text around the graphic. In contrast, in popular published work, writers often use flashy fonts, three dimensions, text wrapping, and other effects that would undermine your *ethos* in an academic setting.

Numbering, Labeling, and Titling the Graphic In newspapers and popular magazines, writers often include graphics in boxes or sidebars without specifically referring to them in the text. However, in academic manuscripts or scholarly works, graphics are always labeled, numbered, titled, and referred to in the text. Tables are listed as "Tables," while line graphs, bar graphs, pie charts, or any other kinds of drawings or photographs are labeled as "Figures." By convention, the title for tables goes above the table, while the title for figures goes below.

Referencing the Graphic in Your Text Academic and professional writers follow a referencing convention called independent redundancy. The graphic should be understandable without the text; the text should be understandable without the graphic. In other words, the text should tell in words the same story that the graphic displays visually. An example is shown in Figure 17.8.

SKILL 17.10 Use occasional open-form elements to create "voice" in closed-form prose.

So far we have been talking about tightly organized closed-form prose. Sometimes, however, writers wish to loosen closed-form prose by combining it with some features of open-form prose. If, for example, an academic wanted to share new

17.10
Use occasional open-form elements to achieve "voice" in closed-form prose.

developments in a field with a popular audience, he or she would be well-advised to leaven his or her prose with some elements of open-form writing. For example, writers might use occasional humor or switch from strictly academic language into more popular language with jargon and occasional pop culture references.

Writers who publish regularly for popular audiences develop a vigorous, easy-reading style that differs from the style of much academic writing. The effect of this difference is illustrated by the results of a famous research study conducted by Michael Graves and Wayne Slater at the University of Michigan. For this study, teams of writers revised passages from a high school history textbook.* One team consisted of linguists and technical writers trained in producing closed-form texts using the strategies discussed earlier in this chapter (forecasting structure, putting points first, following the old/new contract, using transitions). A second team consisted of two *Time-Life* book editors.

Whereas the linguists aimed at making the passages clearer, the *Time-Life* writers were more concerned with making them livelier. The result? One hundred eleventh-grade students found the *Time-Life* editors' version both more comprehensible and more memorable. The problem with the original textbook wasn't lack of clarity but rather dryness. According to the researchers, the *Time-Life* editors did not limit themselves to making the passages lucid, well-organized, coherent, and easy to read. Their revisions went beyond such matters and were intended to make the texts interesting, exciting, vivid, rich in human drama, and filled with colorful language.

To see how they achieved this effect, let's look at their revision. Here is a passage about the Vietnam War taken from the original history text:

ORIGINAL HISTORY TEXT

The most serious threat to world peace developed in Southeast Asia. Communist guerrillas threatened the independence of the countries carved out of French Indo-China by the Geneva conference of 1954. In South Vietnam, Communist guerrillas (the Viet Cong) were aided by forces from Communist North Vietnam in a struggle to overthrow the American-supported government....

Shortly after the election of 1964, Communist gains prompted President Johnson to alter his policy concerning Vietnam. American military forces in Vietnam were increased from about 20,000 men in 1964 to more than 500,000 by 1968. Even so, North Vietnamese troops and supplies continued to pour into South Vietnam.

Here is the *Time-Life* editors' revision:

HISTORY PRESENTED IN POPULAR MAGAZINE STYLE

In the early 1960s the greatest threat to world peace was just a small splotch of color on Kennedy's map, one of the fledgling nations sculpted out of French Indo-China by the Geneva peacemakers of 1954. It was a country so tiny and remote that most Americans had never uttered its name: South Vietnam....

Aided by Communist North Vietnam, the Viet Cong guerrillas were eroding the ground beneath South Vietnam's American-backed government. Village by village, road by road, these jungle-wise rebels were waging a war of ambush and mining: They darted out of tunnels to head off patrols, buried exploding booby traps beneath the mud floors of huts, and hid razor-sharp bamboo sticks in holes....

*The study involved three teams, but for purposes of simplification we limit our discussion to two.

> No sooner had Johnson won the election than Communist gains prompted Johnson to go back on his campaign promise. The number of American soldiers in Vietnam skyrocketed from 20,000 in 1964 to more than 500,000 by 1968. But in spite of GI patrols, leech-infested jungles, swarms of buzzing insects, and flash floods that made men cling to trees to escape being washed away—North Vietnamese troops streamed southward without letup along the Ho Chi Minh Trail.

What can this revision teach you about invigorating closed-form prose? What specifically are the editors doing here?

First, notice how far the level of abstraction drops in the revision. The original is barren of sensory words; the revision is alive with them ("South Vietnam" becomes a "small splotch of color on Kennedy's map"; "a struggle to overthrow the American-supported government" becomes "[They] buried exploding booby traps beneath the mud floors of huts, and hid razor-sharp bamboo sticks in holes").

Second, notice how much more dramatic the revision is. Actual scenes, including a vision of men clinging to trees to escape being washed away by flash floods, replace a chronological account of the war's general progress. According to the editors, such scenes, or "nuggets"—vivid events that encapsulate complex processes or principles—are the lifeblood of *Time-Life* prose.

Finally, notice how the revision tends to delay critical information for dramatic effect, moving information you would normally expect to find early on into a later position. In the first paragraph, the *Time-Life* writers talk about "the greatest threat to world peace" in the early 1960s for four lines before revealing the identity of that threat—South Vietnam.

FOR WRITING AND DISCUSSION

Enlivening Closed-Form Prose with Open-Form Elements

Here is a passage from a student argument opposing women's serving on submarines. Working individually or in small groups, enliven this passage by using some of the techniques of the *Time-Life* writers.

> Not only would it be very expensive to refit submarines for women personnel, but having women on submarines would hurt the morale of the sailors. In order for a crew to work effectively, they must have good morale or their discontent begins to show through in their performance. This is especially crucial on submarines, where if any problem occurs, it affects the safety of the whole ship. Women would hurt morale by creating sexual tension. Sexual tension can take many forms. One form is couples' working and living in a close space with all of the crew. When a problem occurs within the relationship, it could affect the morale of those directly involved and in the workplace. This would create an environment that is not conducive to good productivity. Tension would also occur if one of the women became pregnant or if there were complaints of sexual harassment. It would be easier to deal with these problems on a surface ship, but in the small confines of a submarine these problems would cause more trouble.

STRATEGIES FOR WRITING OPEN-FORM PROSE

18

WHAT YOU WILL LEARN

18.1 To make your narrative a story, not an *and then* chronology.
18.2 To evoke images and sensations by writing low on the ladder of abstraction.
18.3 To disrupt your reader's desire for direction and clarity.
18.4 To tap the power of metaphor and other tropes.
18.5 To expand your repertoire of styles.

Although much of this book focuses on points-first, thesis-governed writing, we all share the desire at times to escape the demands of closed-form prose—to read and produce writing that stimulates the imagination and evokes sensations.

In this chapter, we shift our attention to **open-form prose**, which violates the conventions of closed-form prose to establish a different relationship with readers. Open-form prose is often characterized by its aesthetic or beautiful use of language—that is, language used to please and entertain. Because it is not organized as a sequence of points in support of a thesis, it depends on the very specificity of words to create mental pictures and to appeal to readers' senses and emotions. In telling its stories, it uses the literary strategies of plot, characterization, setting, and theme to convey its meanings. It also demands imaginative effort from readers to fill in gaps, make connections, tolerate ambiguity, and apprehend a range of meanings and nuance. For all these reasons, open-form prose is often called *literary nonfiction* or *creative nonfiction.*

See Chapter 1, Concept 1.3, for a detailed explanation of closed-form versus open-form prose.

Of course, it should be remembered that writing exists on a continuum from closed to open forms and that many features of open-form prose can appear in primarily closed-form texts. In fact, many of the example essays in this book combine elements of both open and closed styles. Although at the extremes of the continuum, closed- and open-form writing are markedly different, the styles can be blended in pleasing combinations.

Our goal in this chapter is to give you some practical lessons on how to write effective open-form prose. But we need to acknowledge at the outset that, whereas closed-form prose is governed by a few widely accepted conventions, open-form prose plays freely with conventions in a bewildering variety of ways. Consequently, our discussion of open-form writing seeks more to introduce you to guiding principles than to treat open-form writing exhaustively.

18.1 Make your narrative a story, not an *and then* chronology.

SKILL 18.1 Make your narrative a story, not an *and then* chronology.

We have said that open-form prose is narrative based and uses the strategies of a story. In this first section we want you to think more deeply about the concept of a story—particularly how a story differs from an *and then* chronology. Both a story and an *and then* chronology depict events happening in time. But there are important differences between them. In the following thought exercise, we'd like you to try your own hand at articulating the differences between a story and an *and then* chronology.

THOUGHT EXERCISE ON *AND THEN* CHRONOLOGY VERSUS STORY

1. Read the student autobiographical narrative "No Cats in America?" by Patrick José in Chapter 6, pages 139–140.
2. Then read the following autobiographical narrative entitled "The Stolen Watch," which was submitted by a student as a draft for an assignment on narrative writing.

THE STOLEN WATCH

Last fall and winter I was living in Spokane with my brother, who during this time had a platonic girlfriend come over from Seattle and stay for a weekend. Her name was Karen, and we became interested in each other and I went over to see her at the first of the year. She then invited me to, supposedly, the biggest party of the year, called the Aristocrats' Ball. I said sure and made my way back to Seattle in February. It started out bad on Friday, the day my brother and I left Spokane. We left town an hour late, but what's new. Then my brother had to stop along the way and pick up some parts; we stayed there for an hour trying to find this guy. It all started out bad because we arrived in Seattle and I forgot to call Karen. We were staying at her brother's house and after we brought all our things in, we decided to go to a few bars. Later that night we ran into Karen in one of the bars, and needless to say she was not happy with me. When I got up the next morning I knew I should have stayed in Spokane, because I felt bad vibes. Karen made it over about an hour before the party. By the time we reached the party, which drove me crazy, she wound up with another guy, so her friends and I decided to go to a few bars. The next morning when I was packing, I could not find my watch and decided that someone had to have taken it. We decided that it had to have been the goon that Karen had wound up with the night before, because she was at her brother's house with him before she went home. So how was I going to get my watch back?

We decided the direct and honest approach to the problem would work out the best. We got in contact and confronted him. This turned out to be quite a chore. It turned out that he was visiting some of his family during that weekend and lived in Little Harbor, California. It turned out that Karen knew his half brother and got some information on him, which was not pretty. He had just been released by the army and was trained in a special forces unit, in the field of Martial Arts. He was a trained killer! This information did not help matters at all, but the next bit of information was just as bad if not worse. Believe it or not, he was up on charges of attempted murder and breaking and entering. In a way, it turned out lucky for me, because he was in enough trouble with the police and did not need any more. Karen got in contact with him and threatened him that I would bring him up on charges if he did not return the watch. His mother decided that he was in enough trouble and sent me the watch. I was astounded, it was still working and looked fine. The moral of the story is don't drive 400 miles to see a girl you hardly know, and whatever you do, don't leave your valuables out in the open.

1. How does your experience of reading "No Cats in America?" differ from your experience of reading "The Stolen Watch"? Try to articulate the different ways you reacted to the two pieces while in the process of reading them.
2. Based on the differences between these two pieces, how would you define a "story"? Begin by brainstorming all the ways that the two pieces differ. Then try to identify the essential differences that make one a "story" and the other an *and then* chronology.

Four Criteria for a "Story"

Now that you have tried to define a story for yourselves, we would like to explain our own four criteria for a story: (1) depiction of events through time, (2) connectedness, (3) tension, and (4) resolution. If we combine these criteria into a sentence, it would read like this: A story depicts events that are connected causally or thematically to create a sense of tension that is resolved through action, insight, or understanding. These four criteria occurring together turn a chronology into a story. We will illusrate these criteria by referring to Kris Saknussemm's short autobiographical narrative "Phantom Limb Pain" in Chapter 6 (pp. 137–138).

Depiction of Events Through Time The essence of storytelling is the depiction of events through time. Whereas thesis-based writing descends from problem to thesis to supporting reasons and evidence, stories unfold linearly, temporally, from event to event. You may start in the middle of the action and then jump backward and forward, but you always encounter some sequence of events happening in time. This temporal focus creates a sense of "onceness." Things that happen at a point in time happen only once, as the classic fairy-tale opening "Once upon a time" suggests. When you compose and revise a narrative, you want to try to capture the "onceness" of that experience. Saknussemm's essay contains several different depictions of events through time: the summer when he was thirteen lifting weights and trying to become stronger and more athletic than Miller King; the story of King's accident and the narrator's visit to King's house; the narrator's helping the one-armed King climb down from the Cyclone fence.

Connectedness The events of a story must also be connected, not merely spatially or sequentially, but causally or thematically. When discussing "The Stolen Watch" in the previous exercise, you might have asked yourselves, "What does all that stuff about forgetting to call Karen and stopping for parts, and so forth, have to do with the stolen watch? Is this story about the watch or about confronting a potential killer?" If so, you instinctively understood the concept of connectedness. Stories are more than just chronicles of events. Novelist E. M. Forster offered the simplest definition of a story when he rejected "The king dies and then the queen died," but accepted "The king died and then the queen died...of grief." The words "of grief" connect the two events to each other in a causal relationship, converting a series of events into a patterned, meaningfully related sequence of events. Likewise, we see that all the details in Saknussemm's essay contribute to the thematic intentions of the story. We hear about the narrator's "wearing ankle weights loaded with sand" (connected to his rivalry with Miller King) but not about other things that might have happened during his 13th summer, such as getting a new bike or going on a vacation. Rather than provide an "and then" narrative about his summer, Saknussemm selects only events connected to the rivalry theme.

Tension or Conflict The third criterion for a story—tension or conflict—creates the anticipation and potential significance that keep the reader reading. In whodunit stories, the tension follows from attempts to identify the murderer or to prevent the murderer from doing in yet another victim. In many comic works, the tension is generated by confusion or misunderstanding that drives a wedge between people who would normally be close. Tension always involves contraries, such as those between one belief and another, between opposing values, between the individual and the environment or the social order, between where I am now and where I want to be or used to be. This plot tension in Saknussemm's essay is between himself and his rival Miller King, but the thematic tension is between his "old self" and his "new self."

Resolution, Recognition, or Retrospective Interpretation The final criterion for a story is the resolution or retrospective interpretation of events. The resolution may be stated explicitly or implied. Fables typically sum up the story's significance with an explicit moral at the end. In contrast, the interpretation of events in poetry is almost always implicit. In "Phantom Limb Pain," Saknussemm states part of the resolution explicity: Despite losing his arm, Miller remains more of a leader than the narrator; the amputation has "damaged" King but not "diminished" him. But part of the resolution is also implicit. The narrator has moved from an "old self" to a "new self." He has grown in some way by being "freed from bad dreams," by becoming "a little more real." What exactly Saknussemm means is left up to the reader to ponder.

The typical direction of a story, from singular event(s) to general conclusion, reverses the usual points-first direction of closed-form essays. Stories force readers to read inductively, gathering information and looking for a pattern that's confirmed or unconfirmed by the story's resolution. This resolution is the point *toward* which readers read. It often drives home the significance of the narrative. Typically, a reader's satisfaction or dissatisfaction with a story hinges on how well the resolution manages to explain or justify the events that precede it. Writers need to ask: How does my resolution grow out of my narrative and fit with the resolution the reader has been forming?

FOR WRITING AND DISCUSSION

Identifying Criteria for "Story"

1. Working as a whole class or in small groups, return to Patrick José's essay "No Cats in America?" and explain how it qualifies as a story rather than an *and then* chronology. How does it meet all four of the criteria: depiction of events through time, connectedness, tension, and resolution?
2. Consider again "The Stolen Watch." It seems to meet the criterion of "depiction of events through time," but it is weak in connectedness, tension, and resolution. How could the writer revise the chronology to make it a story? Brainstorm several different ways that this potentially exciting early draft could be rewritten.
3. If you are working on your own open-form narrative, exchange drafts with a classmate. Discuss each other's draft in light of this lesson's focus on story. To what extent do your drafts exhibit the features of a story rather than those of an *and then* chronology? Working together, develop revision plans that might increase the story elements in your narratives.

SKILL 18.2 Evoke images and sensations by writing low on the ladder of abstraction.

18.2 Evoke images and sensations by writing low on the ladder of abstraction.

In Chapter 3 we introduced the concept of "ladder of abstraction," in which words can be arranged from the very abstract (living creatures, clothing) down to the very specific (our hen Lefty, the champion egg layer; my saltwater-stained Birkenstocks). In this lesson we show why and how open-form writers stay low on the ladder of abstraction through their use of concrete words, revelatory words, and memory-soaked words.

The ladder of abstraction is explained in Concept 3.3.

Concrete Words Evoke Images and Sensations

To appreciate the impact of specific, concrete language, look again at a passage from Kris Saknussemm's "Phantom Limb Pain" (pp. 137–138).

> Every morning before sunrise I lumbered around our neighborhood wearing ankle weights loaded with sand. I taught myself how to do Marine push-ups and carried my football everywhere so I'd learn not to fumble.

Here is how that same passage might sound if rewritten a level higher on the ladder of abstraction:

> Each morning I did my exercises and practiced holding the football to prevent fumbling.

This version still makes the same narrative point about exercise, but it loses the power of concrete words to invoke images and sensations. The reader might imagine the narrator doing jumping jacks or spinning on a stationary bicycle. Instead we see ankle weights filled with sand and marine push-ups—all before sunrise. The lower you write on the ladder of abstraction, the more you tap into your readers' storehouse of particular memories and images.

The power of concrete words has been analyzed by writer John McPhee in a widely quoted and cited interview. When asked why he wrote the sentence "Old white oaks are rare because they had a tendency to become bowsprits, barrel staves, and queen-post trusses" instead of a more generic sentence such as, "Old white oaks are rare because they were used as lumber," he responded in a way that reveals his love of the particular:

> There isn't much life in [the alternative version of the sentence]. If you can find a specific, firm, and correct image, it's always going to be better than a generality, and hence I tend, for example, to put in trade names and company names and, in an instance like this, the names of wood products instead of a general term like "lumber." You'd say "Sony" instead of "tape recorder" if the context made it clear you meant to say tape recorder. It's not because you're on the take from Sony, it's because the image, at least to this writer or reader, strikes a clearer note.

Some readers might complain that the particulars "bowsprits, barrel staves, and queen-post trusses" don't help readers' understanding, as do particulars in closed-form prose, but instead give most readers a moment's pause. Today most barrel staves and bowsprits are made of metal, not oak, and few contemporary readers encounter them on a regular basis no matter what they're made of. Furthermore, few readers at any time could readily identify "queen-post trusses," a technical term from the building trade. Instead of smoothly completing the reader's understanding of a point, McPhee's particulars tend to arrest and even sidetrack, sending the reader in pursuit of a dictionary.

But if McPhee's examples momentarily puzzle, it's the sort of puzzlement that can lead to greater understanding. Precisely because they are exotic terms, these words arouse the reader's curiosity and imagination. "Exotic language is of value," says McPhee. "A queen-post truss is great just because of the sound of the words and what they call to mind. The 'queen,' the 'truss'—the ramifications in everything."

For McPhee, the fact that these words trip up the reader is a point in their favor. If McPhee had said that old white oaks are rare these days because they became parts of "ships, barrels, and roofs," no one would blink or notice. If you were to visualize the items, you'd probably call up some ready-made pictures that leave little trace in your mind. You also wouldn't hear the sounds of the words. (In this regard, notice McPhee's emphasis on images sounding "a clearer note.") Your forward progress toward the point would be unimpeded, but what would be lost? A new glimpse into a lost time when oak trees were used to make exotic items that today exist mostly in old books and memories.

Another quality also recommends words that readers trip over, words such as *bowsprit, barrel stave,* and *queen-post truss:* their power to persuade the reader to believe in the world being described. Tripping over things, whether they're made of steel or words, forces the reader to acknowledge their independence, the reality of a world outside the reader's own head. For this reason, writers of formula fiction—thrillers, westerns, romances, and the like—will load their texts with lots of little details and bits of technical information from the time and place they describe. Because their stories are otherwise implausible (e.g., the description of the Evil Empire's doomsday machine), they need all the help they can get from their details (the size of the toggle bolts used to keep the machine in place while it's blasting out intergalactic death rays) to convince readers that the story is real.

Using Revelatory Words and Memory-Soaked Words

As we have seen, concrete language, low on the ladder of abstraction, can evoke imaginative experiences for readers. Two particularly powerful kinds of concrete language are revelatory words and memory-soaked words. By *revelatory* words we mean specific details that reveal the social status, lifestyle, beliefs, and values of people. According to writer Tom Wolfe, carefully chosen details can reveal a person's *status life*—"the entire pattern of behavior and possessions through which people express their position in the world or what they think it is or hope it to be." Wolfe favors writing that records "everyday gestures, habits, manners, customs, styles of furniture, clothing, decoration, styles of traveling, eating, keeping house, modes of behaving toward children, servants, superiors, inferiors, peers, plus the various looks, glances, poses, styles of walking and other symbolic details that might exist within a scene." Thus subtle differences in a person's status life might be revealed in details about fast food (a Big Mac versus a Subway turkey wrap), body piercing (pierced ears versus pierced tongue), a watch (a Timex versus a Rolex), or music (Kenny Chesney versus Busta Rhymes).

Another way to create powerful concrete language is through *memory-soaked* words. Such words trigger a whole complex of ideas, emotions, and sensations in readers who share memories from a particular era. People who grew up in the 1950s, for example, might have deep associations with 45-rpm records, the *Ed Sullivan Show*, or the words "duck tail" or "tail fins." For Vietnam veterans, Nancy Sinatra's "These Boots Were Made for Walking" or the whirr of helicopter blades might evoke strong memories. Persons growing up in the 1970s or 1980s might remember "Cookie Monster," "Pez guns," or 8-track tapes. Kris Saknussemn uses memory-soaked words from the 1960s when he mentions "an Aurora model of Johnny Unitas" or "a poster of Raquel Welch from *One Million Years B.C.*" In recent years, our students have come up with these memory-soaked words from their own childhoods: American Girl dolls, Power Rangers, Ghostbuster action figures, Super Nintendo, Pokemon, *American Idol*, and The Sims.

FOR WRITING AND DISCUSSION

Working Low on the Ladder of Abstraction

1. Working in small groups or as a whole class, try your own hand at using revelatory words to reveal status life. Create a list of specific details that you might associate with each of the following: middle school girls at a slumber party; friends at a tailgate party before a football game; the kitchen of an upscale urban apartment of a two-profession couple who subscribe to *Gourmet* magazine; the kitchen of a middle-class, middle America family with three kids and a collection of *Good Housekeeping* magazines; the kitchen of an apartment shared by college students. (If you are describing

(*continued*)

kitchens, for example, consider the different *status life* signaled by ketchup versus stone-ground mustard or by an iceberg lettuce salad with ranch dressing versus an almond mandarin salad.)

2. Also try your hand at finding memory-soaked words. Make a list of specific words and names associated with your childhood that you now rarely hear or see. Share your list with others in your group and identify the items that have the strongest associations.
3. If you are working on your own open-form narrative, exchange drafts with a classmate and, working together, find specific examples where each of you has successfully used concrete, revelatory, or memory-soaked words. Then find passages that could be profitably revised by moving down a rung on the ladder of abstraction or by adding concrete details that follow the advice in this lesson.

18.3 Disrupt your reader's desire for direction and clarity.

SKILL 18.3 Disrupt your reader's desire for direction and clarity.

The philosopher Kenneth Burke speaks of form as "an arousing and fulfillment of desires." In closed-form prose, we can easily see this process at work: The writer previews what he or she is going to say, arousing the reader's desire to see the general outline fleshed out with specifics, and then fulfills that desire speedily through a presentation of pertinent points and particulars.

In more open-form prose, the fulfillment of desire follows a less straightforward path. Writers offer fewer overviews and clues, leaving readers less sure of where they're headed; or writers mention an idea and then put it aside for a while as they pursue some other point whose relevance may seem tenuous to the reader. Rather than establish the direction or point of their prose, writers suspend that direction, waiting until later in the prose to show how the ideas are meaningfully related. In other words, the period of arousal is longer and more drawn out; the fulfillment of desire is delayed until the end, when the reader finally sees how the pieces fit together.

Open-form prose gives you the opportunity to overlay your narrative core with other patterns of ideas—to move associatively from idea to idea, to weave a complex pattern of meaning in which the complete picture emerges later. Often the way you achieve these surprising twists and turns of structure and meaning is by playing with the conventions of closed-form prose. For example, in the autobiographical narrative "No Cats in America?", Patrick José breaks the cardinal closed-form rule that titles should forecast the essay's thesis: If José's essay were closed form, it should be about some kind of surprising decline of cats in America. However, José's title is metaphoric, and the reader doesn't completely comprehend its significance until the last lines of the essay. This delaying of meaning—requiring the reader to help cocreate the meaning—is typical of open-form prose. Here in this section we describe some of your open-form options for surprising your readers and delaying their fulfillment of desires.

Disrupting Predictions and Making Odd Juxtapositions

Open-form writers frequently violate the principle of forecasting and mapping that we stressed in Chapter 17. Consider the following introduction to an essay:

PASSAGE WITH DISRUPTED PREDICTIONS AND ODD JUXTAPOSITIONS

I suppose their little bones have years ago been lost among the stones and winds of those high glacial pastures. I suppose their feathers blew eventually into the piles of tumbleweed beneath the straggling cattle fences and rotted there in the mountain snows, along with dead steers and all the other things that drift to an end in the corners of the wire. I do not quite know why I should be thinking of birds over the *New York Times* at breakfast, particularly the birds of my youth half a continent away. It is a funny thing what the brain will do with memories and how it will treasure them and finally bring them into odd juxtapositions with other things, as though it wanted to make a design, or get some meaning out of them, whether you want it or not, or even see it.

—Loren Eisley, "The Bird and the Machine"

Whose bones? What feathers?

Birds? What birds?

What do birds have to do with how the brain works? Where is this writer going?

Note the sequence of ideas from bones to birds to breakfast over the *New York Times* to comments about the workings of the brain. In fact, in this essay it takes Eisley six full paragraphs in which he discusses mechanical inventions to return to the birds with the line: " ... or those birds, I'll never forget those birds... . "

Throughout these paragraphs, what drives the reader forward is curiosity to discover the connections between the parts and to understand the meaning of the essay's title, "The Bird and the Machine." Actually, Eisley's comment about the brain's "odd juxtapositions" of memories with "other things, as though it wanted to make a design, or get some meaning out of them" could be a description of this open-form technique we've called "disrupting predictions and making odd juxtapositions." Open-form writers can choose when "odd juxtapositions" are an appropriate strategy for inviting the reader to accompany the discovering, reflecting writer on a journey toward meaning.

Leaving Gaps

An important convention of closed-form prose is the old/new contract, which specifies that the opening of every sentence should link in some way to what has gone before. Open-form prose often violates this convention, leaving *gaps* in the text, forcing the reader to puzzle over the connection between one part and the next.

The following passage clearly violates the old/new contract. This example recounts the writer's thoughts after startling a weasel in the woods and exchanging glances with it.

PASSAGE WITH INTENTIONAL GAPS

What goes on in [a weasel's brain] the rest of the time? What does a weasel think about? He won't say. His journal is tracks in clay, a spray of feathers, mouse blood and bone: uncollected, unconnected, loose-leaf, and blown.

I would like to learn, or remember, how to live. I come to Hollins Pond not so much to learn how to live as, frankly, to forget about it.

—Annie Dillard, "Living Like Weasels"

Gap caused by unexplained or unpredicted shift from weasel to philosophic musing

Dillard suddenly switches, without transition, from musing about the mental life of a weasel to asserting that she would like to learn how to live. What is the connection between her encounter with the weasel and her own search for how to live? Dillard's open-form techniques leave these gaps for readers to ponder and fill in, inviting us to participate in the process of arriving at meaning. Just as open-form writers can deliberately avoid predicting or mapping statements, they also have the liberty to leave gaps in a text when it suits their purpose.

FOR WRITING AND DISCUSSION

Disrupting Reader Expectations

If you are currently working on an open-form narrative, exchange drafts with a classmate. Discuss in what way the strategies explained in this lesson might be appropriate for your purposes. Where might you currently "explain too much" and benefit by juxtaposing scenes without explanatory filler? Where might you use other strategies from this lesson?

18.4 Tap the power of metaphor and other tropes.

SKILL 18.4 Tap the power of metaphor and other tropes.

In situations where closed-form writers might value unambiguous, literal language, open-form writers might value metaphors or other tropes. The term **trope** is a synonym for figurative language. It comes from a Latin word meaning "turning" and refers to language situations where meanings turn suddenly in different directions, immersing the reader in ambiguity or a possible multiplicity of meanings. The word *ambiguous* comes from the Latin "ambi" meaning "both sides" (as in "ambidextrous") and "agere" meaning "to act" or "to go." So ambiguous words, by definition, go two ways. Whereas a closed-form writer might want a word to mean just one thing—to prevent confusion—open form writers often use words that turn two ways at once. In this brief section, we show you some of the power of figurative language.

When journalist Nicholas Tomalin describes a captured Vietnamese prisoner as young and slight, the reader understands him in a literal way, but when, a moment later, he compares the prisoner to "a tiny, fine-boned wild animal," the reader understands him in a different way; the reader understands not only what the subject looks like—his general physical attributes—but how that particular boy appears in that moment to those around him—fierce, frightened, trapped.

Figurative language abounds when literal words fail. Figurative language enables the writer to describe an unfamiliar thing in terms of different, more familiar things. The surprise of yoking two very unlike things evokes from the reader a perception, insight, or emotional experience that could not otherwise be communicated. The originality and vividness of the imaginative comparison frequently resonates with meaning for readers and sticks in their minds long afterward.

Consider the use of metaphors and similes in the following passage in which writer Isak Dinesen describes an experience that most of us have not had—seeing iguanas in the jungle and shooting one.

PASSAGE USING FIGURATIVE LANGUAGE

In the Reserve I have sometimes come upon the Iguana, the big lizards, as they were sunning themselves upon a flat stone in a riverbed. They are not pretty in shape, but nothing can be imagined more beautiful than their coloring. They shine like a heap of precious stones or like a pane cut out of an old church window. When, as you approach, they swish away, there is a flash of azure, green and purple over the stones, the color seems to be standing behind them in the air, like a comet's luminous tail.

Similes heaped up

Simile

Once I shot an Iguana. I thought that I should be able to make some pretty things from his skin. A strange thing happened then, that I have never afterwards forgotten. As I went up to him, where he was lying dead upon his stone, and actually while I was walking a few steps, he faded and grew pale, all color died out of him as in one long sigh, and by the time that I touched him he was gray and dull like a lump of concrete. It was the live impetuous blood pulsating within the animal, which had radiated out all that glow and splendor. Now that the flame was put out, and the soul had flown, the Iguana was as dead as a sandbag.

Metaphor of dying applied to color

Simile

Metaphor

Simile

—Isak Dinesen, "The Iguana"

At a literal level, this passage says simply that an iguana's colorful skin becomes instantly colorless when it dies. But Dinesen's tropes give a deeper, more wonderful, almost spiritual resonance to the phenomonon. The iguana's beautiful color (when alive) is like "precious stone" or "an old church window." Unlike color applied in a literal way like paint, the color of iguanas seems touched with cosmic mystery: It "seems to stand behind them in the air, like a comet's luminous tail." When iguanas die, they don't simply lose their color; they lose a kind of miraculous life principle. They become like an extinguished flame, inanimate, "dull like a lump of concrete," "dead as a sandbag." Dinesen's figurative language opens a multiplicity of meanings that transcend the literal meaning of the passage.

We can also see the possibility of multiple meanings and ambiguous turnings in Saknussemm's title "Phantom Limb Pain." At the literal level, "phantom limb pain" refers to the tingling and often painful sensations that amputees feel out there in the air where their amputated limb used to be. From a literal perspective it should be Miller King who feels phantom limb pain. But as the narrative progresses, we begin to sense more and more that it is Saknussemm who feels phantom limb pain—metaphorically, of course. It was Saknussemm who "performed a ceremony" under the full moon that seemed to curse Miller King. It was Saknussemm who had his bad dreams. The double meaning of "phantom"—either "falsehood" or "imaginary spirit"—begins to transfer from King to Saknussemm, who seems to escape phantoms and become "more real" when the story resolves.

FOR WRITING AND DISCUSSION

Using Figurative Language

1. Figurative language can fall flat when it takes the form of clichés ("I stood transfixed like a bump on a log") or mixed metaphors ("Exposed like a caterpillar on a leaf, he wolfed down his lunch before taking flight"). But when used effectively, figurative language adds powerfully compressed and

(*continued*)

meaningful images to a passage. Working individually or in small groups, find examples of figurative language in one or more of the example passages in this chapter or in Chapter 6 (pp. 125–143). See if you can reach consensus on what makes a particular instance of figurative language effective or ineffective.
2. If you are currently working on an open-form narrative, exchange drafts with a classmate. See if you can find instances of figurative language in your current drafts and analyze their effectiveness. Perhaps you can also discover places where figurative language could be profitably added to the text.

18.5 Expand your repertoire of styles.

SKILL 18.5 Expand your repertoire of styles.

Style is a combination of sentence structure, word choice, and rhythm that allows writers to vary their emphasis and tone in a variety of ways. In this section, we show you how to expand your repertoire of styles through a classic method of teaching in which you try to imitate other writers' styles. This rhetorical practice—called "creative imitation"—has a long history beginning with the rhetoricians of classical Greece and Rome. When you do creative imitation, you examine a passage from an expert stylist and try to emulate it. You substitute your own subject matter, but you try to imitate the exact grammatical structures, lengths and rhythms of the sentences, and the tones of the original passage. The long-range effect of creative imitation is to expand your stylistic choices; the more immediate effect is to increase your skill at analyzing a writer's style. Most practitioners find that creative imitation encourages surprising insights into their own subject matter (when seen through the lens of the original writer's style) as well as a new understanding of how a particular piece of writing creates its special effects.

You begin a creative imitation by asking questions such as these: What is distinctive about the sentences in this passage of writing? How do choices about sentence length and complexity, kinds of words, figures of speech, and so forth create a writer's voice? After close examination of the passage, you then think of your own subject matter that could be appropriately adapted to this writer's style.

To help you understand creative imitation, we provide the following example. In this passage, the writer, Victoria Register-Freeman, is exploring how relations between young men and women today threaten to undo some of the twentieth century's progress toward gender equality. In the section of her article that precedes this passage, Register-Freeman explains how she, as a single mother, taught her boys to cook, sew, do laundry, and "carry their weight domestically." But then, as she explains in this passage, teenage girls undid her attempts at creating gender equality:

REGISTER-FREEMAN PASSAGE

Then came puberty and hunkhood. Over the last few years, the boys' domestic skills have atrophied because handmaidens have appeared en masse. The damsels have driven by, beeped, phoned and faxed. Some appeared so frequently outside the front door they began to remind me of the suction-footed Garfields spread-eagled on car windows. While the girls varied according to height, hair color and basic body type, they shared one characteristic. They were ever eager to help the guys out.

—Victoria Register-Freeman, "My Turn: Hunks and Handmaidens"

Register-Freeman's voice projects the image of a concerned mother and feminist social critic. Her tone includes a range of attitudes: serious, personal, factual, ironic, frustrated. Note how this passage begins and ends with short, clipped sentences. The second sentence states a problem that the next three sentences develop with various kinds of details. The third sentence includes a series of colorful verbs; the fourth uses a metaphor (the ever-present girls compared to Garfields on car windows). The fifth sentence builds to the point in the sixth sentence, which is delivered bluntly and simply.

Here is one writer's attempt at a creative imitation:

CREATIVE IMITATION OF REGISTER-FREEMAN

Then came prosperity and popularity. Over the last ten years, Seattle's special charms have faded because expansion has occurred too rapidly. Traffic has multiplied, thickened, amplified, and slowed. Traffic jams appeared so often on the freeways and arterials they began to remind me of ants swarming over spilled syrup. While the congestion varied according to time, seasons, and weather conditions, it had one dominant effect. It increasingly threatened to spoil the city's beauty.

FOR WRITING AND DISCUSSION

Practicing Style through Creative Imitation

1. Do your own creative imitation of the passage from Register-Freeman.
2. Choose one or both of the following passages for creative imitation. Begin by jotting down all the specific observations you can make about the stylistic features of the passage. Then choose a topic that matches the topic of the original in its degree of lightness or seriousness and its depth. Explore your topic by presenting it using the sentence structures and kinds of words used in the original. Try to imitate the original phrase by phrase and sentence by sentence. You may find it helpful to use a dictionary and thesaurus.

   a. Africa is mystic; it is wild; it is a sweltering inferno; it is a photographer's paradise, a hunter's Valhalla, an escapist's Utopia. It is what you will, and it withstands all interpretations. It is the last vestige of a dead world or the cradle of a shiny new one. To a lot of people, as to myself, it is just "home." It is all of these things but one thing—it is never dull.

   —Beryl Markham, "Flying Elsewhere," West with the Night

   b. The disease was bubonic plague, present in two forms: one that infected the bloodstream, causing the buboes and internal bleeding, and was spread by contact; and a second, more virulent pneumonic type that infected the lungs and was spread by respiratory infection. The presence of both at once caused the high mortality and speed of contagion. So lethal was the disease that cases were known of persons going to bed well and dying before they woke, of doctors catching the illness at bedside and dying before the patient.

   —Barbara Tuchman, "This Is the End of the World," *A Distant Mirror*

19 STRATEGIES FOR COMPOSING MULTIMODAL TEXTS

WHAT YOU WILL LEARN

19.1 To consider a range of multimodal options for accomplishing your rhetorical purpose.

19.2 To design multimodal texts so that each mode contributes its own strengths to the message.

19.3 To design texts in multimodal genres including posters, speeches with visual aids, podcasts, and videos.

This chapter gives practical advice for composing multimodal texts. As we explained in Chapter 4, a **multimodal text** uses two or more "modalities" of communication by variously combining words, images, and sounds. Multimodal productions can be low-tech (a speech with flip charts for visual aids), medium-tech (graphs or photographs embedded into a written text), or high-tech (Web sites, videos, podcasts, desktop published posters or brochures). It is beyond the scope of this text to explain the technological aspects of digital productions. However, many digitally native students already possess technological know-how, and many institutions provide instruction and backup support for multimodal projects. Our purpose in this chapter is to offer rhetorical advice on how to make your multimodal texts as effective as possible for your targeted audience.

19.1 Consider a range of multimodal options for accomplishing your rhetorical purpose.

SKILL 19.1 Consider a range of multimodal options for accomplishing your rhetorical purpose.

One way to appreciate the power of multimedia texts is to imagine how a written text might be transformed or remixed to reach different audiences in different ways. Suppose, for example, that you have written an autobiographical narrative about your recovery from an accident when you were in the 8th grade. That essay might reach a wider audience if you transformed it into a podcast and posted a link to it on your Facebook page or blog. Perhaps you also have relevant and evocative photographs from this period. Instead of a podcast, you might then create a video screencast combining your photographs with a voice-over narrative. Both the podcast and the screencast could be enhanced with music. Or, to take another example, suppose you have written an op-ed piece for your school's newspaper taking a stand on a controversial campus issue. You might widen the reach of your argument through a campaign that includes posters or brochures, a speech supported with PowerPoint or Prezi slides, and a batch of T-shirts embossed with your message in a verbal/visual design.

Of course, not all multimedia texts start off as written arguments. You might upload a funny video to YouTube purely for its entertainment value, or you might post on Flickr a slideshow, set to music, of beautiful photographs of flowers just for the aesthetic or inspirational appeal.

In all cases, when you design a multimodal text, you should think rhetorically about your audience and purpose. In Chapter 1 (Concept 1.2), we identified six common aims or purposes for written texts: to express, to explore, to inform, to analyze/synthesize, to persuade, and to reflect. Table 19.1 provides examples of multimodal texts designed for these aims. As the chart suggests, designing effective multimodal texts requires both purposeful thinking and creative imagination. There is lots of room for trial and error (and fun) when you experiment with multimodal texts.

TABLE 19.1 Rhetorical Purposes and Multimodal Texts

Rhetorical Aim	Subject Matter/Focus of Writing	Possible Multimodal Forms
Express	You share aspects of your life; you invite your audience to walk in your shoes, to experience your insights	Personal story narrated as a podcast or a video with images
Explore	You take your audience on your own intellectual journey by showing your inquiry process (raising questions, seeking evidence, considering alternative views)	A podcast or video that includes interviews with experts who progressively expand your thinking
Inform	You bring to your audience factual knowledge addressing a reader's need or curiosity	An informative poster; a report with graphics; a collaborative wiki article; a how-to video
Analyze/ Synthesize	You provide your audience with deeper insights by breaking an artifact or phenomenon into parts and putting them together in new ways for greater understanding	The text of a poem with marginal drawings that illustrate metaphors; an audioguide analyzing a museum exhibit
Persuade	You try to convince your audience, who may not share your values and beliefs, to accept your stance on an issue	Advocacy poster, podcast, or video; persuasive speech with PowerPoint or Prezi slides
Reflect	You look back retrospectively on an experience or journey and bring to your audience your evaluation of its significance or meaning	A collage of photographs, arranged in a way that represents retrospective thinking about value or meaning; same collage done as a pechakucha presentation

FOR WRITING AND DISCUSSION

Thinking about Your Purpose and Audience

Individually: If you are planning to design a multimodal text, consider your answers to the following questions:

1. What will be the content or subject matter of your text?
2. What is your purpose? Where would you place your imagined text in Table 19.1 on rhetorical aims?
3. Who is your intended audience and what genre or medium will you use to reach them?

In small groups or as a whole class: Share your answers to these questions.

19.2 Design multimodal texts so that each mode contributes its own strengths to the message.

SKILL 19.2 Design multimodal texts so that each mode contributes its own strengths to the message.

The main point of this lesson is intuitively simple: The various elements of a multimodal text should work together to send the same message. In a podcast, the music should match the content. In a poster, the images should work in harmony with the words. In a PowerPoint presentation, the slide on the screen should reinforce the speaker's point. However, the creative opportunities offered by multimodal composing can sometimes lead inadvertently to jumbled multimodal texts, causing audience members to scratch their heads and say "whuuuhh?" In the language of cognitive scientists, the audience members' confusion can be called "cognitive dissonance" or "cognitive overload."

This Design Principle at Work in Successful Multimodal Texts

Let's consider some examples of successful multimodal texts, starting with children's picture books. For many children, their first introduction to multimodal texts comes from being read to while snuggled in a parent's lap. As the child listens to the story of Peter Rabbit, he or she enjoys the pictures, page by page, watching Peter wander into Mr. MacGregor's garden, hide in the watering can, and eventually end up drinking his chamomile tea. Picture books show how our brains can process both auditory information (the story) and visual information (the pictures) at the same time. Some children's books (such as *Pat the Bunny*) even introduce a third communication channel—touch. The child can both see the bunny and feel its cotton-soft ears.

But now imagine how we might create cognitive dissonance for the child. Suppose that we told the child the story of Peter Rabbit (which we had memorized), but actually held in our laps the picture book about Jemima Puddleduck. Suddenly the words she was hearing about Peter Rabbit would no longer match the pictures she was looking at about Jemima Puddleduck. Or suppose we just had the Peter Rabbit story out of sync: While the child looked at Peter drinking his chamomile tea, we told the story of Peter's being chased by Mr. MacGregor. The child would be frustrated by the disconnect between the auditory channel processing words and the visual channel processing images. Our point is that multimodal texts work successfully only when the various modes are in sync with each other.

Function of Images in a Multimodal Text Many multimodal texts rely extensively on images. We examined the power of images in Chapter 3 (Concept 3.4) and then more fully in Chapter 10 on visual rhetoric. As we explained in these chapters, insights that need to be built up slowly through words in the verbal-processing part of our brains might be apprehended almost instantaneously in the visual-processing part of our brains (hence the saying "A picture is worth a thousand words"). An effective image condenses an argument into a memorable scene or symbol that is apprehensible at a glance and taps deeply into our emotions and values. Images make implicit arguments (*logos*) while also appealing directly to our values and emotions (*pathos*). The creative challenge of multimodal composing is to find or design images that tell visually the same story that the words tell verbally. Typical images in a multimodal text (say a poster, brochure, advocacy ad, Web page, PowerPoint slide, cartoon, graphic novel, video) include still or moving photographs, drawings or animations, graphs, charts, maps, or words arranged in meaningful nonlinear designs to show relationships—for example, as components of flow charts, cause-effect diagrams with arrows, circle diagrams showing recursive processes, and so forth.

Function of Words in a Multimodal Text But images by themselves usually need accompanying words to focus the image's point. Because images have open-ended or multiple, ambiguous interpretive possibilities, designers of multimodal texts often use words to crystallize the intended meaning, thereby shaping the audience's response. A successful multimodal text thus usually includes some kind of "nutshell statement" that makes a claim and thereby identifies and sharpens the text's take-away message. This nutshell serves the same function for a multimodal text as a thesis statement serves for an essay or a topic sentence for a paragraph. Consider as an example the classic World War II poster alerting soldiers in jungle warfare to the dangers of unsafe drinking water (see full page poster on page 585 and here in thumbnail).

BEWARE..
Drink only
approved water

The poster shows a soldier, a canteen cup in his hand and a look of horror on his face, peering into a pond in search of drinking water. The poster's message is conveyed visually by the reflection of the soldier's face transfigured into a skull—a powerful appeal to *pathos*. But the same message is also conveyed in the verbal channel through the words: "BEWARE … Drink Only Approved Water. Never give a germ a break." The words, which appeal primarily to *logos*, serve as a "nutshell" for the whole argument, making the poster's message unmistakably clear. But note how the words themselves also register in the visual channel through the effect of layout and font size. In the top half of the poster, the large-font, all-caps "BEWARE" seems to shout a warning to the soldier. In the bottom half of the poster, the text next to the skull—"Drink Only Approved Water"—uses a smaller font and calm sentence case to convey the poster's take-away message. Finally the words along the bottom border of the poster ("Never Give a Germ a Break!") in still a different font offer a cause-and-effect explanation of why the water might kill you. Although the images alone convey the message at a glance, the poster's full punch comes from our registering the argument in both the visual and verbal parts of our brains.

Dual Channel Effect of Words and Images As cognitive scientists researching multimodal learning have shown, multimodal texts achieve their power by combining the strengths of two or more modes of communication. Because each mode or channel is processed in a different area of the brain, each mode contributes its own strengths to the message. This dual-channel effect can be seen in a wide range of multimodal texts. As we have suggested, an effective visual/verbal multimodal text typically has a nutshell claim that summarizes the text's takeaway message combined with images that support the claim through a visual channel. The location of the nutshell claim can vary depending on the design of the text, and it can be emphasized by font size, location on the page, or other means. Table 19.2 shows examples from multimodal posters in this text.

Effect of Sounds in a Multimodal Text Because a print textbook can't accommodate sounds or moving images, our examples have focused primarily on multimodal print genres combining words and images. But sounds can also be a powerful channel for multimedia compositions, particularly the qualities of voice in speeches, podcasts, or videos as well as the special powers of music. In our example of a child listening to Peter Rabbit, the parent's voice coming through the auditory channel is simultaneously an auditory experience and a word/verbal experience. The child sees both the pictures of Peter Rabbit and also the words on the page—an important first step in the process of learning to read. A PowerPoint presentation similarly provides words through both an auditory channel (the speech) but also a visual channel (words on a slide). So sounds in multimodal compositions can range from the language-centered employment of voice to nonlanguage sounds such as street noise, animal sounds, drums, music, and other sounds with powerful emotional and associational effects.

Using This Design Principle to Revise a Jumbled Multimodal Text

Let's contrast effective multimodal texts with a jumbled one, in this case the "first draft" of a PowerPoint slide developed by student writer Joyce Keeley for an oral presentation of her research on the plight of African refugees (Figure 19.1). It is not quite clear what the function or focus of the slide is. The whole

TABLE 19.2 Use of Nutshell Claims and Images in Multimodal Texts

Multimodal text	Verbal nutshell, claim, or key assertion (stated in words)	Images used for visual support
Page 169	Wearing high heel shoes for an extended time can cause leg and heel damage.	Drawing of leg in high heel shoe with callouts explaining damage
 Page 417	This glacier was here in 1982. (Implied claim: Global warming is melting the glaciers.)	Photograph showing at a glance the extent to which the glacier has retreated since 1982
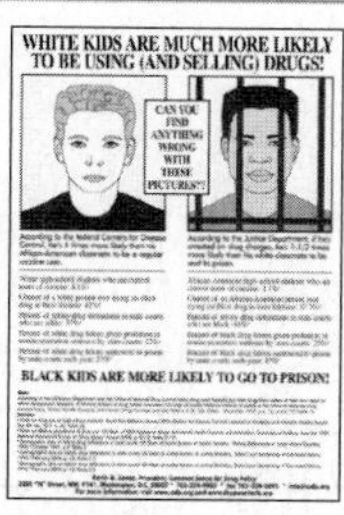 Page 390	Black kids are much more likely to go to prison. The poster uses words interactively to elicit viewer response to the question "What's wrong with these pictures?" White kids are more likely to use and sell drugs, but black kids go to prison more often. Statistical data provides strong appeal to *logos* and *ethos*.	This poster uses simple black and white drawings to appeal to *pathos*: A black kid is shown behind bars while a white kid has no jail time.
	Teach your kids how to be more than a bystander. (Full argument: Kids encounter bullying all the time; parents must teach kids how to respond to it.)	Visual impact comes from layout, font size, and shading. Victims of bullying often feel diminished, their identities blurred and less visible. This feeling is carried metaphorically by the shaded, washed out font of "You're a dumb piece of trash" Adults reading the "piece of trash" text are shocked and turn to the small text in the bottom box for explanation.

slide seems to be about "Life of a Refugee," but it doesn't make a nutshell claim or assertion of the kind we noted previously in the successful posters. The audience might ask, "What is this slide's point about the life of a refugee?" The top right photograph of a refugee camp seems to make the claim that the life of a refugee is harsh or dismal. But it is uncertain what the other photographs

Life of a Refugee
• Political persecution, economic opportunity, flee violence
• Camps (UNHCR supported) or Urban (illegal)
• Resettlement, Repatriation, Integration (Naturalization)

FIGURE 19.1 A Jumbled Multimodal Slide

are doing. The top left photo shows refugees being loaded into the back of a truck while the bottom photo looks like an aerial view of a city, with no apparent connection to the life of a refugee. Additionally, none of the images seems connected to the bulleted list on the left side of the slide about political persecution, economic opportunity, violence, kinds of camps, resettlement, repatriation, integration, and naturalization. The slide is trying to do too many things at once. The words and the images aren't working together to send a single meaningful message.

When her peer reviewers said that they couldn't figure out what her PowerPoint slide was trying to say about the life of a refugee, Joyce decided to redesign it to follow more closely the multimodal principles explained in this lesson. As applied to PowerPoint slides using words and images, we can summarize these principles as follows:

- Make sure that each slide has a point that can be stated in a nutshell claim or assertion
- Make sure the audience knows that point (a presenter can state it in the speech or state it directly on the slide)
- Make sure that the words and images on the slide work together to develop or support that point

For more on oral presentations using PowerPoint, see pp. 498–502.

Figure 19.2 shows Joyce's revision of the slide to focus on just one of the points she originally intended.

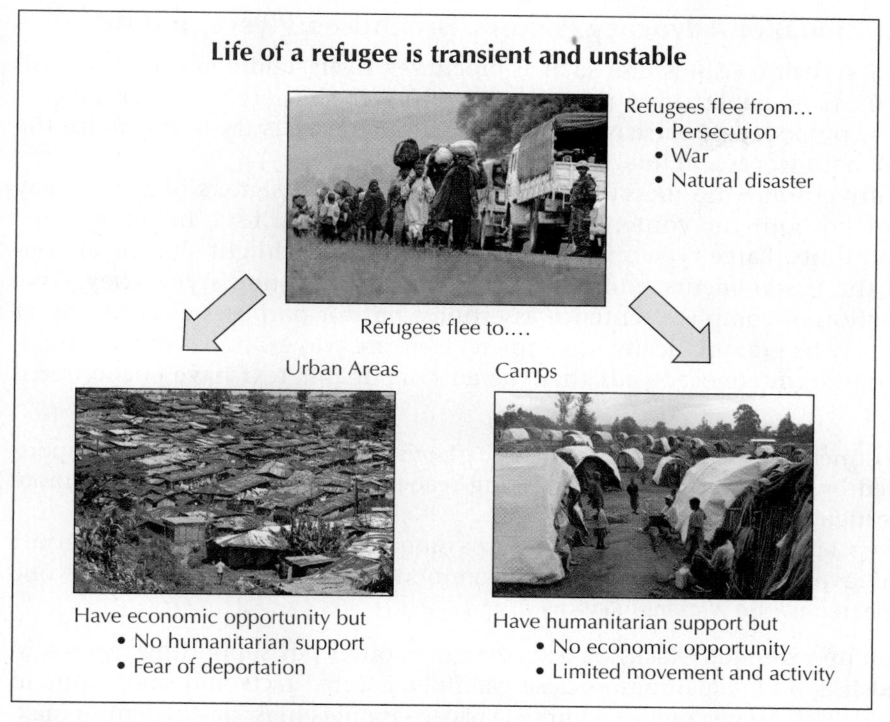

FIGURE 19.2 Joyce's Redesign of Her "Jumbled" Slide

FOR WRITING AND DISCUSSION

Purposeful Design of PowerPoint Slides

1. In small groups or as a whole class, identify the changes that Joyce made when she redesigned her original slide and then speculate on her thinking process. Do you agree that her redesigned slide is more effective than her original one? Why or how? How would you improve it?
2. Examine student writer Sam Rothchild's multimodal PowerPoint slides, which accompanied his speech outline (Chapter 15, p. 403). To what extent do Sam's slides follow the design principles outlined in this chapter? How do you imagine that he used each of these slides in his speech?

19.3 Design multimodal texts in genres including posters, speeches with visual aids, podcasts, and videos.

SKILL 19.3 To design multimodal texts in genres including posters, speeches with visual aids, podcasts, and videos.

In this final lesson, we give some nuts-and-bolts advice connected to specific genres of multimodal texts.

Informational or Advocacy Posters, Brochures, Flyers, and Ads

Posters and their cousin genres such as brochures, flyers, and newspaper ads—all of which can be published in print or posted to Web sites—typically have an informative purpose or a persuasive purpose. Effective posters try to maximize the power of both words and images.

To drive home the message presented in images, designers of posters pay attention to both the content and formatting of verbal text, including type sizes and fonts. Large-type text is frequently used to highlight slogans or condensed thesis statements (nutshells) written in an arresting style. They serve the function of complete sentence assertions, but for purposes of economy or impact may be grammatically incomplete. Here are two examples of large boldfaced copy from advocacy ads that the authors of this text have encountered recently:

- "Abstinence: It works every time.... " (from a newspaper advocacy ad sponsored by Focus on the Family, asking readers to donate money to promote abstinence education)
- "Expectant Mothers Deserve Compassionate Health Care—Not Prison!" (an advocacy advertisement from Common Sense for Drug Policy; this one appeared in the *National Review*)

To break up extended blocks of text, designers often put supporting reasons in bulleted lists and sometimes enclose carefully selected facts and quotations in boxed sidebars. To say a lot in a limited space, designers must be efficient in making words, images, and document design work effectively together. The following strategies will help you design a poster.

Strategies for Designing Posters, Flyers, Brochures, and Ads

Features and Strategies to Consider	Questions to Ask
Purpose, Genre, and Medium Based on your purpose, choose the most appropriate genre and medium for your targeted audience	Will your purpose be informative or persuasive? Should your genre be a poster, a flyer, a one-page advertisement, or a brochure? Should you publish it in print or post it on a Web site?
Giving Visual Presence to Your Message: Choose the most effective visual features to create appeals to *pathos*.	What would be the best visual means to establish the urgency and importance of your subject: graphic elements, cartoon images, photos, drawings?
Presenting the "Nutshell" of Your Message: Decide on how you will condense your argument into an assertion or focused point and convey it clearly.	What type size, font, and layout will be the most powerful in presenting your assertion and supporting it for your intended audience? How much verbal text do you want to use? How much will you rely on images alone?

Features and Strategies to Consider	Questions to Ask
Accentuating Key Phrases: Decide what key phrases could highlight the parts or the main points of this argument.	What memorable phrases or slogans could you use to convey your argument? How condensed or detailed should your argument be?
Clarifying the Call for Action: Decide what you are asking your audience to know or do.	How can document design clarify the takeaway message of your poster?
Using Color for Impact: Decide whether you will use color. Note: For some media, color might be cost-prohibitive.	If color is an option, how could you use color to enhance the overall impact of your advocacy argument? How could you use black-and-white images effectively?

Scientific Posters

A scientific poster is a common means of disseminating research at a conference.* Unlike a fifteen-minute talk (another common means of presentation at a conference), a poster presentation occurs in a large room where dozens of researchers display their work on posters taped to walls or placed upright on tables. As researchers stand next to their displays, conference participants wander around the room, perusing posters and stopping to talk to researchers whose work particularly interests them.

The content of a scientific poster, like an abstract, follows the same structure as the research report. In fact, a poster is sometimes called an "illustrated abstract" that presents at a glance the research question, hypothesis, methods, key results, and significance.

An example of a scientific poster is shown on p. 225.

The function of a scientific poster is to engage viewers' interest in your research project and invite discussion. Professional scientists make posters using special software and plotting printers. A typical poster is thirty-six by fifty-four inches, the largest sheet that most plotting printers can handle. If you don't have access to these professional tools, you can print sections of your poster using regular paper, arrange the sheets on poster board, and tape them in place.

An effective scientific poster has the following features:

- Is readable from four feet away (text fonts should be at least 24 points; heading fonts should be 36 points)
- Uses the least amount of text possible
- Uses lots of white space with content arranged in columns
- Where appropriate, uses headings to tell your story
- Uses effective visual elements to supplement text, to create a balanced appearance, and to tell your story visually
- Has an easy-to-follow structure; readers know where to start and what sequence to follow

*Our discussion of posters is indebted to two excellent Web sites: G. R. Hess, K. Tosney, and L. Liegel. *Creating Effective Poster Presentations*; C. B. Purrington. *Advice on Designing Scientific Posters*.

The most common poster mistake is to use small fonts to cram in more text. An effective poster takes a "sound-bite" approach; it entices viewers into discussion with the research team rather than trying to substitute for the whole paper.

To design a poster, begin by blocking sections for your Title, Introduction, Method, Results, and Discussion. Determine what graphics or drawings will make your poster visually attractive and meaningful. Then create sound-bite headings and text, limiting text blocks to fifty words or fewer. Researchers often reword the title and figure captions of the original research report by turning them from phrases into meaning-making assertions, as we have seen with PowerPoint slides.

	Original Research Report (uses phrases)	**Poster (converts phrases to sentences)**
Title	A Comparison of Gender Stereotypes in *SpongeBob SquarePants* and a 1930s Mickey Mouse Cartoon	*SpongeBob SquarePants* Has Fewer Gender Stereotypes than Mickey Mouse.
Figure caption	Figure 1: Stereotypical Behaviors by Gender in *SpongeBob SquarePants* and Mickey Mouse	Results Show More Non-Stereotypical Behavior for Males and Females in *SpongeBob SquarePants*.

Speeches with Visual Aids (PowerPoint, Prezi, Pechakucha)

Another common multimodal form is a speech supported with visual aids, usually as digitally produced presentation slides. Such presentations are by definition multimodal because the audience receives information through an auditory channel, which processes the speaker's words, and a visual channel, which processes the slides. When the speaker's words and the slides are in sync, they can make the speech memorable and persuasive. But if they are out of sync, the audience is subjected to distracting multitasking.

Although PowerPoint remains the most common form of presentation software, Prezi—with its panning, zooming, and rotating features—is becoming increasingly popular. Also becoming popular is a **Pechakucha 20X20** presentation in which speakers must use exactly 20 slides displayed for 20 seconds each. Developed in Japan and named after the Japanese word for "chit chat," Pechakucha presentations are exactly six minutes and 40 seconds long. Whereas in PowerPoint or Prezi presentations the speaker controls the timing of the slides, in Pechakucha the slides are controlled by the computer timer, ensuring that a speaker can't drone on. Pechakucha evenings are now being sponsored in many cities where individuals can present their carefully timed speeches to welcoming audiences.

In all of these genres, the presenter is expected to speak extemporaneously. To speak **extemporaneously** means to spend ample time preparing the speech, but not to read it from a script or to recite it from memory. Instead, the speaker talks directly to the audience with the aid of an outline or note cards.

Long before the delivery of the speech, the speaker should have engaged in the same sort of composing process that precedes a finished essay. Effective speakers typically spend an hour of preparation time per minute of speaking time. Much of this work focuses on creating a well-developed sentence outline for the speech. Since you won't be writing out the complete argument in prose, this outline will be the written frame for your speech. The following chart suggests strategies for developing your speech outline.

Strategies for Creating an Effective Speech Outline

Strategies	Rationales and Explanations of How They Work
Plan the structure and content of your speech with the needs of your audience in mind.	How can you make the question or problem you are addressing come alive for your audience? What background information or defined terms does your audience need? What kinds of evidence will you need to support your argument? What objections will your listeners be apt to raise? How can you motivate action?
Create a complete-sentence outline of your argument; use parallel structures, coordination, and subordination to clarify relationships among ideas.	See Skill 17.3 for advice about different kinds of outlines, particularly the advantage of complete-sentence outlines, which state meanings rather than topics. Since you won't be writing out the complete argument in prose, this outline will be the written frame for your speech.
Build into your outline places for explicit signposting to help the audience follow your speech.	Indicate where you are in your speech: "My second reason is that...." "As I stated earlier...."
Early on, practice saying your speech in a normally paced speaking voice to determine its length.	Often speeches can cover much less ground than a written argument. By timing the speech when it is still in its rough-draft stage, you will know whether you must cut or add material.

Once you have outlined your speech, you can design slides that follow the design principles that we explain in Skill 19.2 for maximizing the impact of both the auditory and visual channels of your presentation. Common mistakes are to make too many slides, to overdesign them, or to become enamored with special effects rather than with the ideas in the speech. Particularly avoid text-heavy slides that include passages cut and pasted from a print text. Unlike an image, which is apprehended almost instantaneously in the visual processing part of our brains, a text-heavy slide must be read to be understood. Text-heavy slides force the audience to multitask, moving back and forth between trying to listen to the speech and trying to read the slide. The only way to bring the speaker's words and the slide into sync is for the speaker to read the slide directly (boring!).

Another design flaw is to leave your audience confused about the slide's focus or purpose—its nutshell assertion or take-away point. This problem is particularly common with PowerPoint because its software encourages users to create short topic phrases for titles rather than points. This topic/subtopic approach violates the meaning-making principle that we emphasize in Chapter 17 (Skill 17.3), where

The meaning-making function of complete sentence outlines can be found on pp. 439–443.

we advocate complete sentence outlines rather than topic outlines. Meanings are expressed in predicates and thus require complete sentences. In Lesson 17.3, we illustrated this distinction in the contrast between "Peanut butter" (a phrase) and "Peanut butter is nutritious" (an assertion requiring support). From this meaning-making perspective, PowerPoint's focus on topic phrases for titles often leads to slides that don't assert a nutshell point.

One solution to the problem of topic-only titles, advocated by some rhetoricians, is to make the slide's title a complete sentence rather than a phrase. Examples of assertion titles versus topic titles are shown in the following chart:

Slide Title as Topic	Slide Title as a Claim or Assertion
Gender Stereotypes in Children's Birthday Cards	Children's birthday cards revealed extensive gender stereotyping.
Wage Comparison: CEO Versus Worker	Gap between CEO salaries and average worker salaries is increasing rapidly.

Of course, the designer could choose to articulate the slide's point in the speech itself rather than stating it on the slide as a complete sentence title. Sometimes, too, a title can make an assertion or claim without having to be grammatically complete. The key is to make sure that the audience knows what the slide's take-away point is. (Using a grammatically complete sentence for the title is particularly helpful if you want the slide to stand on its own as an independent multimodal argument.)

Here are some additional strategies for creating your visual aids.

Strategies for Creating Effective Visual Aids for a Presentation

Strategies	Rationales and Explanations of How They Work
Limit the number of words per slide; avoid blocks of linear text.	Linear text must be read—a slow process different from the almost instantaneous apprehension of an image. Viewers can't listen to your speech and read the text on the screen simultaneously
Use slides to enhance the points in your speech—either images or very limited number of words.	Effective slides reinforce the aural speech by being apprehended in a visual channel. The meaningful assertion made by the slide should be quickly apparent.
Use visual features that enhance meaning; don't use cutesy bells and whistles.	PowerPoint has special effects like exploding figures, words circling into position, and little buses wheeling across the screen. Using these special effects can distract the audience from the content of your speech, creating the *ethos* of a technical whiz rather than a serious presenter of a proposal.

Strategies	Rationales and Explanations of How They Work
Create your speech first and then design slides to drive home major points. Do not use slides simply to reproduce your speech outline.	If you convert your outline into slides, you simply replicate rather than enhance the speech. Use images (rather than words) wherever possible. Think visually.
Consider using complete sentences for the titles of your slides, particularly if you want them to stand alone as meaning-making arguments.	Complete sentence titles highlight each slide's meaningful point (see Skill 19.2). Note: To have enough room for a complete sentence, you'll need to change the default PowerPoint title font to make room for a complete sentence. It is OK to have a two-line title.
Limit the number of visual aids you use.	Communication experts advise no more than one visual aid per minute of presentation. In many parts of the speech, the screen can be blank.

Once you have outlined your speech and developed your slides, you need to practice delivering your speech. You can stand before a mirror, make a video of a practice session, or practice in front of friends until you are confident about the length of your speech and your ability to deliver it with minimal prompting from your notes. In addition, you should think about these important strategies for successful speechmaking.

Strategies for Successfully Delivering a Speech

Strategies	What to Do
Control your volume and pace.	• Speak loudly enough to be heard and add emphasis by speaking louder or softer. • Speed up to get through details quickly and slow down for points you want to stress.
Use posture and gestures to your advantage.	• Stand straight and tall to help your breathing and projection. • Use natural gestures or a few carefully planned ones. • Avoid distracting or nervous gestures.
Maintain eye contact with your audience and look at every member of your audience.	• Know your speech well enough that you can look at your audience, not read your note cards. • Make steady and even eye contact with your audience.

(continued)

Strategies	What to Do
Show enthusiasm and passion for the issue of your speech.	• Make your audience care about your issue through your own enthusiasm. • Show your audience that your issue is important by the energy you put into your delivery. • Also, use your enthusiasm to help control nervousness.
Use your slides effectively; turn off the screen if you aren't currently referring to a slide.	• Click on slides at the appropriate time. • Give slides air time. Talking through images and graphs is effective. Reading long text passages is not.
Overcome nervousness by controlling your hands, your breathing, and the volume of your voice.	• Take deep breaths and speak slightly louder than usual to help your body relax. • Use a podium if one is available.

Scripted Speech (Podcasts, Video Voiceovers)

When you speak before a live audience, it is best to speak extemporaneously. However, if you are preparing a podcast or the voiceover on a video, you can read from a completed script. Give your script a tone and voice appropriate for your audience and purpose. For example, part of the drafting/revising process is to read your emerging text aloud to make sure the script sounds effective out loud, something you wouldn't necessarily do for a print-only paper. Features that might not be appropriate in an academic paper—slang, street language, or less-than-formal grammar—might be just what you need in your script. You'll also need to practice reading the script so that it sounds spontaneous and natural. If your script includes dialogue, you may need to practice adopting different voices. The most common problems to avoid include reading too rapidly, not enunciating clearly, or swallowing words at the ends of sentences. If you use music in the podcast or video, make sure that it is appropriate to the content of the words and sets an appropriate mood. Don't let the music muffle or overwhelm the words.

Videos

Videos offer a range of production options. At the simplest level, you could make a video of a PowerPoint presentation (yours or a friend's) creating a multimodal text similar to a TED talk or a professor's recorded lecture. You could also make a video that was essentially a screencast of still photos enhanced with background music and voice-over narration. You could even splice in recorded interview segments, captions, or text. At a more complex level, you could make a short documentary or create your own original film with actors and a script. Such productions need to be carefully designed and executed, beginning with preproduction storyboarding, moving through production (where filmmakers often shoot a surprisingly high excess of footage), and concluding with purposeful postproduction editing.

As an example of a simple original production, one of our students, Alex Mullen, was selected to produce a short video to introduce the master of ceremonies at a student award ceremony. He wanted to parody the genre of the humorous "introduction" videos—often used at the Academy Awards or the Grammies—which take the audience backstage to see the Master or Mistress of Ceremonies getting ready. Alex wanted to show the MC getting his official invitation letter, putting on his tux, stopping to talk with friends in a dorm room on his way to the ceremony, forgetting the time, and then racing across campus in goofy circles, arriving breathless at the last moment. Selected scenes from Alex's storyboard are shown in Figure 19.3, and a corresponding screen shot from the video is shown in Figure 19.4. The storyboard, which had more

FIGURE 19.3 Scenes from Alex's Storyboard

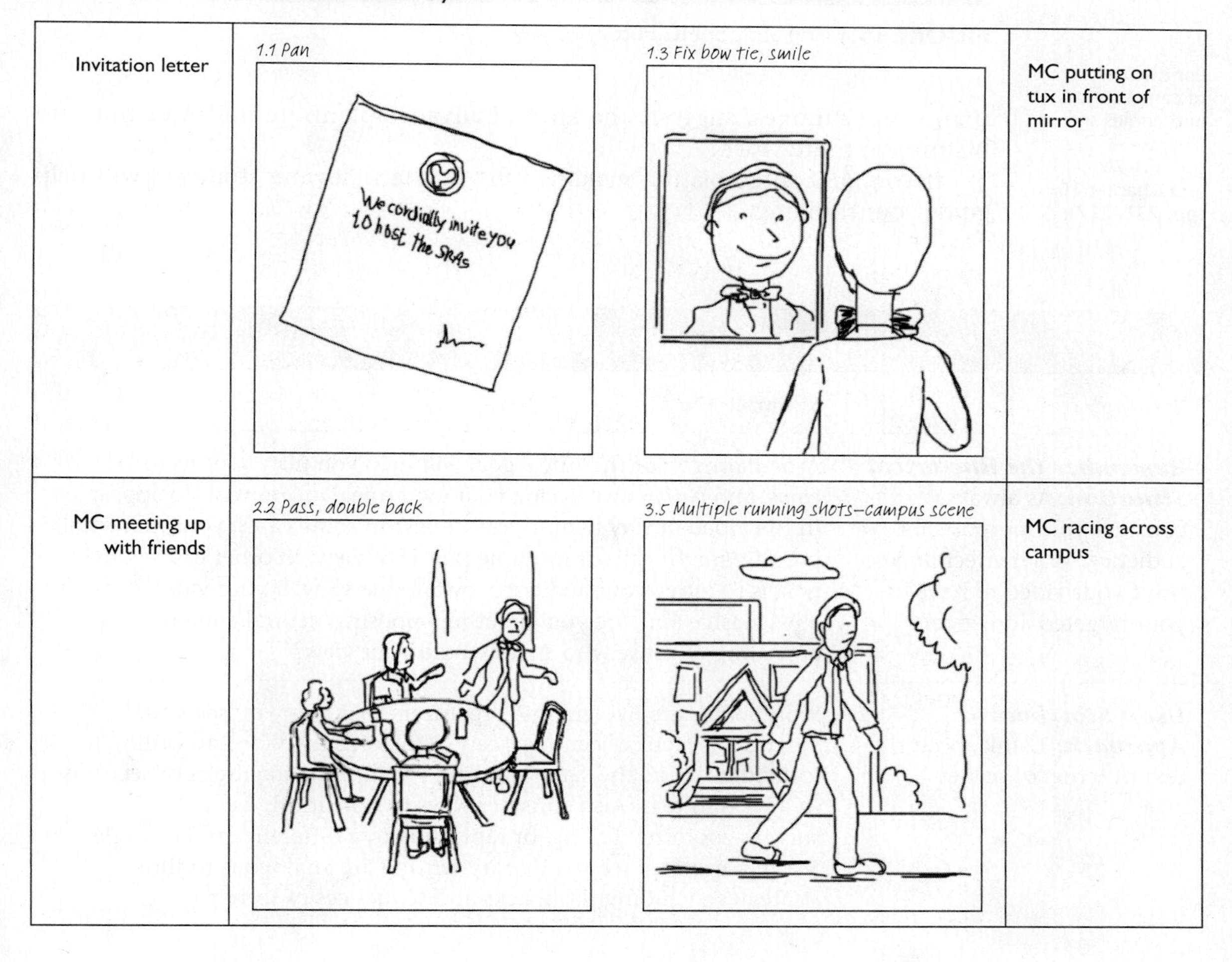

FIGURE 19.4 Still Shot of MC Putting on Tux

For discussion of camera shots and angles see Chapter 4 (pp. 68–70) and Chapter 10 (pp. 231–237).

than twenty frames, suggests the kind of advance planning that Alex put into his three-minute video.

If you are contemplating making a video, the following strategies will help guide your thinking.

Strategies for Creating an Effective Video

Strategy	What to Do
Remember the Rhetorical Situation: As always, consider your purpose and audience. What effect do you want your video to have on your targeted audience?	Articulating your rhetorical goal will help you plan appeals to *logos, ethos,* and *pathos* and decide your own role. Do you wish to appear in the video or stay behind the scenes? In some cases, your rhetorical purpose might call for multiple points of view; in other cases your goal is to move your audience toward one view. If your video has a persuasive aim, are you targeting opposing/neutral audiences or appealing to those who already hold your view?
Use a Storyboard Approach: Think about the text in terms of scenes.	Storyboards are like graphic organizers that help you see your video's big picture scene by scene. Organize the video according to individual shots the same way you might use paragraphs or sections in a written text. Also consider ways to transition, using strategies such as zooming, fading, or rapid cuts to a different camera angle. Many narratives seen in literary writing are analogous to film strategies including flashbacks and sequences of scenes.

Strategy	What to Do
Start with Visual Elements First: The text will be dominated by images.	Audiences of video texts expect to be engaged visually at all times. Avoid using monotonous or uninteresting visuals as filler for stretches of voice-over. Use camera angles to create a narrative "story." Consider particularly the use of establishing shots (medium or long shots), point-of-view shots through a character's eyes, and reaction shots (close-ups of faces). Consider also creative juxtapositions of image with graphics or words.
Incorporate Effective Verbal and Written Text: Use graphic and sound design to emphasize main points.	Video technology allows for more versatile text options than just about any other multimodal form. With the use of graphic design and sound options such as voice-overs and captions, the intended rhetorical impact of images can be underscored with written and spoken words to emphasize main points and highlight important information. Just as in other multimodal texts, be sure to present assertions rather than topics by using complete sentences whenever possible.
Use Musical Elements and Other Sound Options to Emphasize the Effect: As appropriate, underscore important rhetorical goals with auditory effects.	Sound can have a subtle but powerful impact on the viewers of a video text. Effective use of music, background sounds (street noise, café buzz, bird chirps, sudden silence), and qualities of voice (accent, pitch, emotional emphasis) can enhance the key ideas of your video. In shooting scenes, consider the placement of microphones as well as cameras.

A RHETORICAL GUIDE TO RESEARCH

PART 4

These stills from the documentary *Gasland* by Josh Fox (2010) depict a homeowner demonstrating the flow of methane from his water faucet as a result of natural gas wells near his home. This anti-fracking film argues that the process of hydraulic fracturing (commonly called fracking) has not been sufficiently regulated to ensure safety to homeowners and their water supplies. The alarming images of dangerous gas issuing from water faucets elicit a powerful emotional response against fracking. The film builds its authority and credibility by including a number of images like these and interviews with residents around the country, showing fracking's contamination of groundwater with gas and chemicals. Further discussion of the controversy surrounding fracking, including the viewpoints of the gas and oil industry, is found on pages 535–542.

20 ASKING QUESTIONS, FINDING SOURCES

WHAT YOU WILL LEARN

20.1 To argue your own thesis in response to a research question.
20.2 To understand differences among kinds of sources.
20.3 To use purposeful strategies for searching libraries, databases, and Web sites.

Our goal in Part 4 is to explain the skills you'll need for successful college-level research papers. In this opening chapter, we help you start on the right track as a college researcher. The remaining chapters in Part 4 show you how to evaluate research sources (Chapter 21), integrate sources into your own arguments and avoid plagiarism (Chapter 22), and create in-text citations and corresponding bibliographic citations to document your sources (Chapter 23).

An Overview of Research Writing

Although the research paper is a common writing assignment in college, students are often baffled by their professor's expectations. Many students think of research writing as finding information on a topic or as finding quotations to support a thesis rather than as wrestling with a question or problem. One of our colleagues calls these sorts of papers "data dumps": The student dumps a bucket of data on the professor's desk and says, "Here's what I found out about sweatshops, Professor Jones. Enjoy!" Another colleague calls papers full of long quotations "choo-choo train papers": big boxcars of indented block quotations coupled with little patches of a student's own writing.

Characteristics of a Good Research Paper

But a research paper shouldn't be a data dump or a train of boxcar quotations. Instead, it should follow the same principles of writing discussed throughout this text:

- A research paper should pose an interesting and significant problem.
- A research paper should respond to the problem with a contestable thesis.
- In a research paper, sources should be used purposefully and ethically.

An Effective Approach to Research

How does a writer develop a research paper with these characteristics? Early on, your goal is to develop a research question and, through your research process, to begin "wallowing in complexity." You become immersed in alternative points of view, clashing values, different kinds of evidence (often conflicting), and unresolved questions arising from gaps in current knowledge. Relying on your own critical thinking, you eventually refine your research question and begin to formulate your own thesis. In your completed research paper, some of your sources provide background information, others supply supporting evidence, and still others present alternative points of view that you are pushing against. Throughout, your research data should come from credible sources that are documented in a formal, academic style.

The Role of Documentation in College Research

Much of the writing you encounter in popular magazines or online journalism has the characteristics of a research paper—a thesis and support—but not the documentation that college professors expect. By **documentation**, we mean the in-text citations and accompanying bibliography that allow readers to identify and locate your sources for themselves. Such documentation makes all the difference because new knowledge is inevitably built on the work of others. In academic culture, authors who hope to gain acceptance for new findings and ideas must explain the roots of their work as well as show how they reached their conclusions. By documenting their sources according to appropriate conventions, research writers establish a credible *ethos* and provide a valuable resource for others who wish to locate the same sources.

Many of the writing projects in this text invite your use of research sources. In fact, your instructor may pair the material in Part 4 with specific writing projects from Part 2. As you study this material, keep in mind your twofold purpose in reading research sources:

1. To develop your own answer to your research question (your thesis) by bringing your critical thinking to bear on your research sources
2. To position yourself in a conversation with others who have addressed the same question

Throughout, you need to use your research sources responsibly in order to avoid plagiarism and to present yourself as an ethical apprentice scholar joining the academic community. As you begin your research project, make sure that you know your institution's and your teachers' policies on plagiarism and academic honesty. The four chapters in part 4 will explain fully the knowledge and skills needed for confident and ethical research.

SKILL 20.1 Argue your own thesis in response to a research question.

20.1
Argue your own thesis in response to a research question.

The best way to produce effective, engaged, and ethically responsible research papers is to begin with a good research question. A good question keeps you in charge of your writing. It reminds you that your task is to forge an answer to this question yourself, in your own voice, through your own critical thinking. This approach, which follows the principles explained in Chapter 1, Concept 1 ("Subject matter problems are the heart of academic writing") urges you to focus your research on a question rather than a topic. It also helps you avoid the wrong paths of data dumping, strung-together quotations, and uncertainties about why and how you are using sources.

Topic Focus Versus Question Focus

To see the difference between a topic focus and a question focus, suppose a friend asks you what your research paper is about. Consider differences in the following responses:

> Topic Focus: I am writing a paper on eating disorders.
> Question Focus: I'm trying to sort out what the experts say is the best way to treat severe anorexia nervosa. Is inpatient or outpatient treatment more effective?
> Topic Focus: I am writing my paper on gender-specific toys for children.
> Question Focus: I am puzzled about some of the effects of gender-specific toys. Do boys' toys, such as video games, toy weapons, and construction sets, develop intellectual and physical skills more than girls' toys do?

As these scenarios suggest, a topic focus invites you to collect information without a clear purpose—a sure road toward data dumping. In contrast, a question focus requires you to be a critical thinker who must assess and weigh data and understand multiple points of view. A topic focus encourages passive collection of information. A question focus encourages active construction of meaning. The more active your thinking, the more likely you will write in your own voice with no worries about purposeless uses of sources or possible plagiarism.

Formulating a Research Question

How do you arrive at a research question? The concepts discussed in Chapters 1 and 2 about question asking and wallowing in complexity apply to research writing. We invite you to look again at Table 1.1 on pages 5–6 ("How Writers Become Gripped by a Problem") and the strategies chart on pages 35–36 ("Strategies for Creating a Thesis with Tension or Surprise"). Good research questions can emerge from puzzles that you pose for yourself or from controversial questions already "out there" that are being actively debated by others. In most cases your initial research question will evolve as you do your research. You may make it broader or narrower, or refocus it on a newly discovered aspect of your original problem.

You can test the initial feasibility of your research question by considering the following prompts:

- Are you personally interested in this question?
- Is the question both problematic and significant?
- Is the question limited enough for the intended length of your paper?
- Is there a reasonable possibility of finding information on this question based on the time and resources you have available?
- Is the question appropriate for your level of expertise?

Establishing Your Role as a Researcher

After you have formulated your research question, you need to consider the possible roles you might play as a researcher. Your role is connected to the aim or purpose of your paper—to explore, to inform, to analyze, or to persuade. To appreciate your options, consider the following strategies based on typical roles researchers can play:

Strategies for Establishing Your Role as a Researcher

Aims and Roles	What to Do	Examples of Research Questions
Reporter of information that fills a knowledge gap	Find, synthesize, and report data related to an information question.	• How do Japan and France dispose of nuclear waste from nuclear power plants? • What attitude do elementary math teachers have toward the University of Chicago's *Everyday Math* curriculum?
Reporter of the current best thinking on a problem	Research the current thinking of experts on some important problem and report what the experts think.	• What are the views of experts on the causes of homosexuality? • What do researchers consider the possible dangers of online social networks?
Conductor of original field research in response to an empirical question	Pose a problem that requires field research, conduct the research, and present results in a scientific report. Often, include a "review of the literature" section.	• To what extent do pictures of party drinking appear on our students' Facebook profiles? • How do the study habits of humanities majors differ from those of science and engineering majors?
Reviewer of a controversy (primarily an informative aim)	Investigate and report differing arguments on various sides of a controversy.	• What are the arguments for and against granting amnesty and eventual U.S. citizenship to illegal immigrants? • What policy approaches have been proposed to the U.S. government for increasing fuel economy of automobiles?
Advocate for a position in a controversy (primarily an analytic and persuasive aim)	Assert a position using research data for background, for support, or for alternative views.	• Should the United States grant amnesty and eventual citizenship to illegal immigrants? (Writer argues yes or no.) • What is the best way for the U.S. government to ensure that cars achieve higher fuel economy? (Writer argues for a specific approach.)

(continued)

Aims and Roles	What to Do	Examples of Research Questions
Analyzer of an interpretive or evaluative question who also positions himself or herself within a critical conversation	Do your own original analysis of a text, phenomenon, or data source, but also relate your views to what others have said about the same or similar questions.	• To what extent does the film *Avatar* present a Christian worldview? • How effective is microlending at alleviating poverty in third world countries?

FOR WRITING AND DISCUSSION

Using Research Roles to Generate Research Questions

Working individually or in small groups, develop research questions on a general topic such as music, health, sports, use of fossil fuels, a literary work, or some other topic specified by your instructor. Develop research questions that would be appropriate for each of the following roles:

1. Reporter of information to fill a knowledge gap
2. Reporter of the current best thinking of experts on a problem
3. Original field or laboratory researcher
4. Reviewer of a controversy
5. Advocate in a controversy
6. Critical thinker about an interpretive or evaluatve question in conversation with other thinkers
7. Miscellaneous (good questions that don't fit neatly into any of these other roles)

A Case Study: Kent Ansen's Research on Mandatory Public Service

To illustrate how a student writer poses a research question and argues his own thesis, let's return to Kent Ansen's investigation of mandatory public service. We first introduced Kent's research in Chapter 2, where we reprinted his initial musings about community service in the form of a five-minute freewrite (p. 26). Kent's original problem was his uncertainty about requiring all young adults to do public service despite its value to young people and communities. In his original freewrite, he pondered his own positive experience with service learning and volunteering in the community but wondered about the wisdom and public acceptance of mandating such service for all young adults.

Later in the course he decided to investigate mandatory public service for a major research project. His research process is narrated in his exploratory essay in Chapter 7, pages 159–163. As he began reading articles on the value of public service, he noted that many researchers, participants, and advocates spoke highly of serving the community, arguing that both the individuals involved and the communities in which they served experienced significant benefits. However, Kent remained concerned about public resistance to the government's requiring young people to give a year of their lives to working in the community. He became more and more interested in exploring the arguments on different sides of this question. At the conclusion of his exploratory essay, Kent sums up the status of his thinking and mentions a perspective—nurturing engaged citizenship—that he wants to consider further.

> Looking back over my research, I think the rewards of national service to individual volunteers and the communities they serve are clear. However, I continue to worry about the feasibility of making national service a mandatory program. As I end this exploratory paper, I still have some more research and thinking to do before I am ready to start my proposal argument. I am leaning in the direction of supporting mandatory public service. I am convinced that such service will benefit America's communities and also help the "Lost Generation" find themselves through learning more about our country's problems and developing valuable job skills. But the clincher for me—if I go in the direction I am leaning—is that mandatory public service would get Americans more involved in their government.

Kent's exploratory research gave him a solid background on public service, enabling him to bring his own critical thinking to bear on his research sources. In order to convert his exploratory narrative into a closed-form research paper, he eventually created a thesis statement proposing mandatory public service based on its benefits to young adults and the nation. You can read his final paper in Chapter 15, pages 405–414.

FOR WRITING AND DISCUSSION

Following Kent Ansen's Research Process

Working individually, read Kent's exploratory paper (pp. 159–163) and his final research paper (pp. 405–414). Then, working in small groups or as a whole class, try to reach consensus answers to the following questions:

1. Trace the steps in Kent's thinking from the time he first becomes interested in mandatory public service to when he finally settles on his proposal to advocate for it. What were the key moments that shaped his thinking? How did his thinking evolve?
2. We have used Kent's story as an example of a student in charge of his own writing. Where do you see Kent doing active critical thinking? Where do you see instances of what we have called "rhetorical reading"—that is, places where Kent asks questions about an author's purpose, angle of vision, and selection of evidence?
3. How is Kent's final paper different from a data dump or a choo-choo train paper? How does it demonstrate ethical use of sources?

20.2 Understand differences among kinds of sources.

SKILL 20.2 Understand differences among kinds of sources.

To be an effective researcher, you need to understand the differences among the many kinds of sources that you might use while doing your research. These can be classified in different ways, such as primary versus secondary sources (a scheme that focuses on how you'll use the source in your final paper) or as print versus Web sources (a scheme based on its medium of publication). In this section we'll explain a variety of ways to distinguish among different kinds of sources. Your payoff will be an increased ability to read sources rhetorically and to use them purposefully in your research writing.

Primary and Secondary Sources

Researchers often distinguish between primary and secondary sources. **Primary sources** are the original documents, artifacts, or data that you are actively analyzing; **secondary sources** are works by other people who have analyzed the same documents, artifacts, or data. In short, secondary sources comment upon or analyze primary sources. Table 20.1 presents some examples.

The distinction between primary and secondary sources is sometimes slippery and depends on context. In the media studies example from Table 20.1, the parenting Web site is a secondary source if your research question focuses on *South Park*. But if you are investigating the political biases of parenting Web sites, then this site becomes a primary source.

Some research projects use primary sources extensively, while others mainly or exclusively involve secondary sources. You may be asked, for example, to bring your critical thinking to bear on specific primary sources—for example, gender stereotypes in children's birthday cards, political views expressed in old *Archie* comic books, or legal requirements for "proof" in transcripts from witchcraft trials. In these cases, your secondary research would focus on what other

TABLE 20.1 Examples of Primary and Secondary Sources

Field	Examples of Primary Sources	Examples of Secondary Sources
History	Diaries, speeches, newspaper accounts, letters, manuscripts, official records, old photographs, old news reels, archeological sites	• Scholarly book on European fascism in the 1930s • 1970s film about the rise of the Nazis in Germany
Media studies	Rap lyrics, advertisements, graffiti, episodes of *South Park*, bumper stickers, documentary photographs	• Scholarly journal article analyzing racism in *South Park* • Parenting Web site objecting to *South Park*
Nursing	Patient records, direct observation of patients, research findings on transmission of AIDS virus; public health data on swine flu	• Popular magazine article about nurses working in third world hospital • Blog site focusing on nursing issues

scholars have said about these issues in scholarly books or articles. Modern libraries together with the Internet now make available a wealth of primary sources—government documents, historical archives, slide collections, population or ethnographic data, maps, health data, and so forth.

For other kinds of research projects, particularly those connected to civic issues, students often need to work mainly or exclusively with secondary sources. In trying to decide where you stand, say, on nuclear power plants, on a single-payer medical system, or on immigration policy, you will need to enter the civic conversation about these issues carried on in secondary sources. You'll also need to pay attention to what these secondary sources use as evidence in support of their arguments. Were they able to use primary sources for their evidence? Or does their evidence come from other secondary sources? In trying to evaluate each of these secondary sources, you'll need to employ all your rhetorical skills, as we begin to show in the next section.

Reading Secondary Sources Rhetorically

When you look at a secondary source—whether in stable print form or in often unstable Web form—you need to think rhetorically about the kind of source you are perusing and the original author's purpose in producing the source. In this section we'll look specifically at print sources, which are commonly classified either as books or as periodicals (magazines, newspapers, scholarly journals, and so forth), and contrast them with Web sources. Later, in Skill 21.3, we'll look specifically at ways to read Web sources rhetorically.

Table 20.2 shows how these sources can be analyzed according to genre, publisher, author credentials, and angle of vision. The last column in Table 20.2 identifies contextual clues that will help you recognize what category each of these sources belongs to. We suggest that you take a few moments now to peruse the information in these tables so that you can begin to appreciate the distinctions we are making among types of sources.

Print Sources Versus Web-Only Sources New researchers need to appreciate the differences in stability and reliability between print sources and Web-only sources. Print sources (books, journals, magazines, newspapers) are stable in contrast to materials published on Web sites, which might change hourly. If you work from print sources, you can be sure that others will be able to track down your sources for their own projects. Furthermore, print publications generally go through an editorial review process that helps ensure accuracy and reputability. In contrast, Web-only documents from individuals or small organizations may be unedited and thus unreliable. Because the cost of producing, distributing, and storing print materials is high, books and periodicals are now often published in electronic formats, complicating the distinction between print and Web sources.

These changes mean that when evaluating and citing sources, researchers must now pay attention to whether a source retrieved electronically was originally a print source made available electronically (by being posted to a Web site or contained in a database) or is in fact a Web-only source. You'll need

TABLE 20.2 A Rhetorical Overview of Print Books and Periodicals

Genre and Publisher	Author and Angle of Vision	How to Recognize Them
	Books	
SCHOLARLY BOOKS • University/academic presses • Nonprofit • Peer-reviewed	**Author:** Professors, researchers **Angle of vision:** Scholarly advancement of knowledge	• University press on title page • Specialized academic style • Documentation and bibliography • Sometimes available as e-books
TRADE BOOKS (NONFICTION) • Commercial publishers (for example, PenguinPutnam) • Selected for profit potential	**Author:** Journalists, freelancers, scholars aiming at popular audience **Angle of vision:** Varies from informative to persuasive; often well researched and respected, but sometimes shoddy and aimed for quick sale	• Covers designed for marketing appeal • Popular style • Usually documented in an informal rather than an academic style • Sometimes available as e-books
REFERENCE BOOKS • Publishers specializing in reference material • For-profit through library sales	**Author:** Commissioned scholars **Angle of vision:** Balanced, factual overview	• Titles containing words such as *encyclopedia, dictionary,* or *guide* • Found in reference section of library or online through library Web site
	Periodicals	
SCHOLARLY JOURNALS • University/academic presses • Nonprofit • Peer-reviewed • Examples: *Journal of Abnormal Psychology, Review of Metaphysics*	**Author:** Professors, researchers, independent scholars **Angle of vision:** Scholarly advancement of knowledge; presentation of research findings; development of new theories and applications	• Not sold on magazine racks • No commercial advertising • Specialized academic style • Documentation and bibliography • Cover often has table of contents • Often can be found in online databases
PUBLIC AFFAIRS MAGAZINES • Commercial, "for-profit" presses • Manuscripts reviewed by editors • Examples: *Harper's, Commonweal, National Review*	**Author:** Staff writers, freelancers, scholars for general audiences **Angle of vision:** Aims to deepen public understanding of issues; magazines often have political bias of left, center, or right	• Long, well-researched articles • Ads aimed at upscale professionals • Often has reviews of books, theater, film, and the arts • Often can be found in online databases or on the Web

TABLE 20.2 *continued*

Genre and Publisher	Author and Angle of Vision	How to Recognize Them
TRADE MAGAZINES • Commercial, "for-profit" presses • Focused on a profession or trade • Examples: *Advertising Age, Automotive Rebuilder, Farm Journal*	**Author:** Staff writers, industry specialists **Angle of vision:** Informative articles for practitioners; advocacy for the profession or trade	• Title indicating trade or profession • Articles on practical job concerns • Ads geared toward a particular trade or profession
NEWSMAGAZINES AND NEWSPAPERS • Newspaper chains and publishers • Examples: *Time, Washington Post, Los Angeles Times*	**Author:** Staff writers and journalists; occasional freelance pieces **Angle of vision:** News reports aimed at balance and objectivity; editorial pages reflect perspective of editors; op-ed pieces reflect different perspectives	• Readily familiar by name, distinctive cover style • Widely available on newsstands, by subscription, and on the Web • Ads aimed at broad, general audience
POPULAR NICHE MAGAZINES • Large conglomerates or small presses with clear target audience • Focused on special interests of target audience • Examples: *Seventeen, People, TV Guide, Car and Driver, Golf Digest*	**Author:** Staff or freelance writers **Angle of vision:** Varies—in some cases content and point of view are dictated by advertisers or the politics of the publisher	• Glossy paper, extensive ads, lots of visuals • Popular, often distinctive style • Short, undocumented articles • Credentials of writer often not mentioned

to know this information in order to read the source rhetorically, evaluate its trustworthiness, and cite it properly. When you retrieve print sources electronically, be aware that you may lose important contextual clues about the author's purpose and angle of vision—clues that would be immediately apparent in the original print source. These clues come from such things as statements of editorial policy, other articles in the same magazine or journal, or advertisements targeting specific audiences. (The increasing availability of *.pdf* or *portable document format* files, which reproduce the appearance of the original print page, makes understanding publication contexts much easier. When .pdf format is available, take advantage of it.)

Scholarly Books and Journal Articles Versus Trade Books and Magazines Note in Table 20.2 the distinction between scholarly books or journal articles, which are peer-reviewed and published by nonprofit academic presses, and trade books or magazines, which are published by for-profit presses.

By **peer review,** which is a highly prized concept in academia, we mean the selection process by which scholarly manuscripts get chosen for publication. When manuscripts are submitted to an academic publisher, the editor sends them for independent review to experienced scholars who judge the rigor and accuracy of the research and the significance and value of the argument. The process is highly competitive and weeds out much shoddy or trivial work.

In contrast, trade books and magazines are not peer-reviewed by independent scholars. Instead, they are selected for publication by editors whose business is to make a profit. Fortunately, it can be profitable for popular presses to publish superbly researched and argued material because college-educated people, as lifelong learners, create a demand for intellectually satisfying trade books or magazines written for the general reader rather than for the highly specialized reader. These can be excellent sources for undergraduate research, but you need to separate the trash from the treasure. Trade books and magazines are aimed at many different audiences and market segments and can include sloppy, unreliable, and heavily biased material.

Encyclopedias, Wikipedia, and Other Reference Books and Wikis

Another kind of source is an encyclopedia or other kind of reference work. These are sometimes called "tertiary sources" because they provide distilled background information derived from primary and secondary sources. Encyclopedias and reference works are excellent starting places at the beginning of a research project. New researchers, however, should be aware of the difference between a commissioned encyclopedia article and an article in the online source *Wikipedia*. Professional encyclopedia companies such as *Encyclopedia Britannica* commission highly regarded scholars with particular expertise in a subject to write that subject's encyclopedia entry. Usually the entry is signed so that the author can be identified. In contrast, all forms of wikis—including *Wikipedia*—are communal projects using collaborative wiki software. *Wikipedia, the Free Encyclopedia* (its official name) is written communally by volunteers; anyone who follows the site's procedures can edit an entry. The entry's accuracy and angle of vision depend on collective revisions by interested readers.

Wikipedia is a fascinating cultural product that provides rapid overview information, but it is not a reliable academic source. It is often accused of inaccurate information, editorial bias, and shifting content because of constant revisions by readers. Most instructors will not accept *Wikipedia* as a factual or informative source.

FOR WRITING AND DISCUSSION

Identifying Types of Sources

Your instructor will bring to class a variety of sources—different kinds of books, scholarly journals, magazines, and downloaded material. Working individually or in small groups, try to decide which category in Table 20.2 each piece belongs to. Be prepared to justify your decisions on the basis of the cues you used to make your decision.

SKILL 20.3 Use purposeful strategies for searching libraries, databases, and Web sites.

20.3 Use purposeful strategies for searching libraries, databases, and Web sites.

In the previous section, we explained differences among the kinds of sources you may encounter in a research project. In this section, we explain how to find these sources by using your campus library's own collection, library-leased electronic databases, and Web search engines for finding material on the World Wide Web.

Checking Your Library's Home Page

We begin by focusing on the specialized resources provided by your campus library. Your starting place and best initial research tool will be your campus library's home page. This portal will lead you to two important resources: (1) the library's online catalog and (2) direct links to the periodicals and reference databases leased by the library. Here you will find indexes to a wide range of articles in journals and magazines and direct access to frequently used reference materials, including statistical abstracts, biographies, dictionaries, and encyclopedias. Furthermore, many academic library sites post lists of good research starting points, organized by discipline, including Web sites librarians have screened.

In addition to checking your library's home page, make a personal visit to your library to learn its features and especially to note the location of a researcher's best friend and resource: the reference desk. Make use of reference librarians—they are there to help you.

Searching Efficiently: Subject Searches Versus Keyword Searches At the start of a research project, researchers typically search an online catalog or database by subject or by keywords. Your own research process will be speedier if you understand the difference between these kinds of searches.

- ***Subject searches.*** Subject searches use predetermined categories published in the reference work *Library of Congress Subject Headings*. This work informs you that, for example, material on "street people" would be classified under the heading "homeless persons." If the words you use for a subject search don't yield results, seek help from a librarian, who can show you how to use the subject heading guide to find the best word or phrase.
- ***Keyword searches.*** Keyword searches are not based on predetermined subject categories. Rather, the computer locates the keywords you provide in titles, abstracts, introductions, and sometimes bodies of text. Keyword searches in online catalogs are usually limited to finding words and phrases in titles. We explain more about keyword searches in the upcoming section on using licensed databases, whose search engines look for keywords in bodies of text as well as in titles.

Finding Print Articles: Searching a Licensed Database

For many research projects, useful sources are print articles immediately available in your library's periodical collection. You find these articles by searching licensed databases leased by your library.

What Is a Licensed Database? Electronic databases of periodical sources are produced by for-profit companies that index articles in thousands of periodicals and construct engines that can search the database by author, title, subject, keyword, date, genre, and other characteristics. In most cases the database contains an abstract of each article, and in many cases it contains the complete text of the article, which you can download and print. These databases are referred to by several different generic names: "licensed databases" (our preferred term), "periodicals databases," or "subscription services." Because access to these databases is restricted to fee-paying customers, they can't be searched through Web engines like Google. Most university libraries allow students to access these databases from a remote computer by using a password. You can therefore use the Internet to connect your computer to licensed databases as well as to the World Wide Web (see Figure 20.1).

Although the methods of accessing licensed databases vary from institution to institution, we can offer some widely applicable guidelines. Most likely your library has online one or more of the following databases:

- ***EBSCOhost:*** Includes citations and abstracts from journals in most disciplines as well as many full-text articles from thousands of journals.
- ***ProQuest:*** Gives access to full text of articles from magazines and journals in many subject areas; may include full-text articles from newspapers.
- ***FirstSearch Databases:*** Incorporates multiple specialized databases in many subject areas, including WorldCat, which contains records of books, periodicals, and multimedia formats from libraries worldwide.
- ***Lexis-Nexis Academic Universe:*** Is primarily a full-text database covering current events, business, and financial news; includes company profiles and legal, medical, and reference information.
- ***JSTOR:*** Offers full text of scholarly journal articles across many disciplines; you can limit searches to specific disciplines.

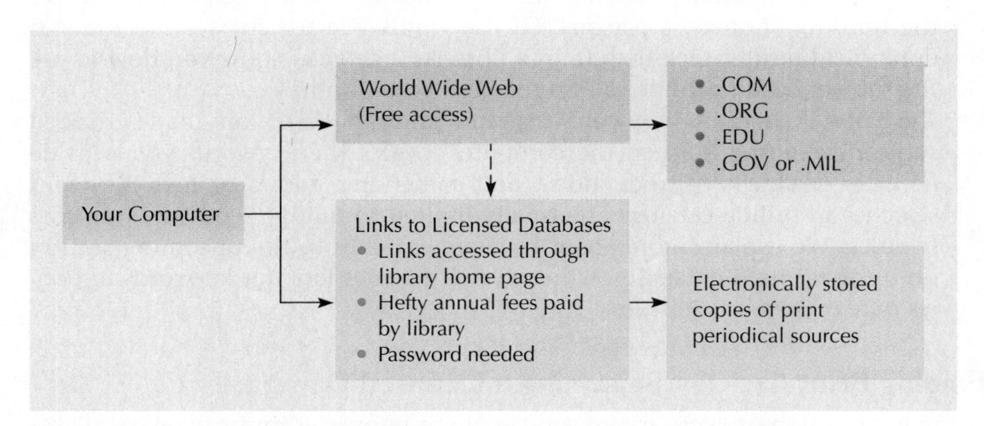

FIGURE 20.1 Licensed Database Versus Free-Access Portions of Internet

Given the variability of these and many other resources, we once again refer you to your campus library's Web site and the librarians at the reference desk (who often answer questions by e-mail). There you will find the best advice about where to look for what. Then, when you decide to use a specific source for your research project, be sure to include in your notes the names of both the database and the database company because, as we explain in Chapter 23, you will need to include that information when you cite your sources.

More on Keyword Searching To use an online database, you need to be adept at keyword searching, which we introduced on page 519. When you type a word or phrase into a search box, the computer will find sources that contain the same words or phrases. If you want the computer to search for a phrase, put it in quotation marks. Thus if you type "*street people*" using quotation marks, the computer will search for those two words occurring together. If you type in *street people* without quotation marks, the computer will look for the word *street* and the word *people* occurring in the same document but not necessarily together. Use your imagination to try a number of related terms. If you are researching gendered toys and you get too many hits using the keyword *toys*, try *gender toys, Barbie, G.I. Joe, girl toys, boy toys, toys psychology*, and so forth. You can increase the flexibility of your searches by using Boolean terms to expand, narrow, or limit your search (see Table 20.3 for an explanation of Boolean searches).

Illustration of a Database Search

As an illustration of a database search, we'll use student writer Kent Ansen's research on mandatory public service. Figure 20.2 shows the results from Kent's

TABLE 20.3 Boolean Search Commands

Command and Function	Research Example	What to Type	Search Result
X OR Y (Expands your search)	You are researching Barbie dolls and decide to include G.I. Joe figures.	"Barbie doll" OR "G.I. Joe"	Articles that contain either phrase
X AND Y (Narrows your search)	You are researching the psychological effects of Barbie dolls and are getting too many hits under *Barbie dolls*.	"Barbie dolls" AND psychology	Articles that include both the phrase "Barbie dolls" and the word *psychology*
X NOT Y (Limits your search)	You are researching girls' toys and are tired of reading about Barbie dolls. You want to look at other popular girls' toys.	"girl toys" NOT Barbie	Articles that include the phrase "girl toys" but exclude *Barbie*

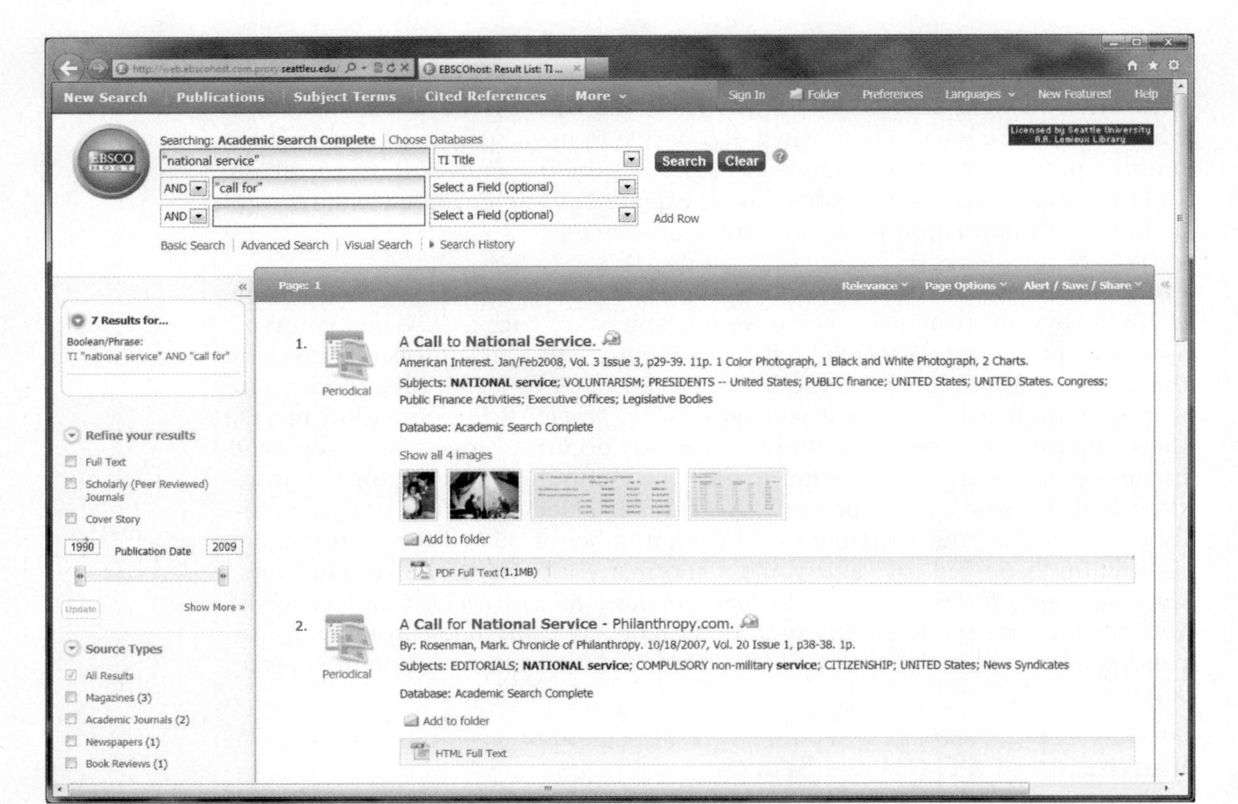

FIGURE 20.2 Sample Results List from a Search Using EBSCOhost

search using the keywords *national service* and *call for* on the database EBSCOhost. EBSCO host returned a number of articles from news commentary and scholarly journals that deal in some way with national service and voluntary service, both civil and military. When Kent experimented with "national service" in the title of the article, he got the two articles shown in Figure 20.2. The first article, "A Call to National Service," comes from the news commentary journal *American Interest*, and a full text of the article is available online in .pdf format. The second article, "A Call for National Service," comes from the biweekly newspaper *Chronicle of Philanthropy* (affiliated with the reputable *Chronicle of Higher Education*) and is available as a full text .html file. When he clicked on that article to get further information, the resulting screen, which is shown in Figure 23.1 (p. 571), gives an abstract of the article as well as complete data about when and where the article was published in print. (We placed this screen in Chapter 23 on documentation, rather than here, to show how it provides the information you'll need for your Works Cited list.) Based on the abstract, Kent downloaded the .html file and eventually used this article in his final research paper. (See the entry under "Rosenman" in his Works Cited list on p. 414.)

A particularly valuable feature of databases is the way that you can limit or expand your searches in a variety of useful ways. Here are some strategies for focusing, narrowing, or expanding your list of sources:

Strategies for Narrowing or Expanding Your Searches on Licensed Databases

What You Want	What to Do
Only scholarly articles in peer-reviewed journals	Check the box for "peer-reviewed" articles in the database search box (different databases have different procedures—ask a librarian).
Only short articles (or only long articles)	Specify length of articles you want in the advanced search feature.
Only magazine articles or only newspaper articles	Specify in the advanced search feature.
Articles within a certain range of dates	Specify the dates in the advanced search feature.
Only articles for which "full text" is available	Check the box for "full text" in the database search box.
Only articles from periodicals carried by your library	Check method used by database. (Most databases accessed through your library will indicate whether your library carries the magazine or journal.)
All articles	Don't check any of the limiting boxes.
To narrow (or expand) the focus of the search	• Experiment with different keywords. • Use Boolean techniques: *online relationships* AND *friendship*; *online relationships* OR Facebook (see Table 20.3). • Try different databases. • Ask your reference librarian for help.

After you've identified articles you'd like to read, locate physically all those available in your library's periodical collection. (This way you won't lose important contextual cues for reading them rhetorically.) For those unavailable in your library, print them from the database (if full text is provided), or order them through interlibrary loan.

Finding Cyberspace Sources: Searching the World Wide Web

Another valuable resource is the World Wide Web. To understand the logic of Web search engines, you need to know that the Internet is divided into restricted sections open only to those with special access rights and a "free-access" section. Web engines such as Google search only the free-access portion of the Internet. When you type keywords into a Web search engine, it searches for matches in material made available on the Web by all the users of the world's network of computers—government agencies, corporations, advocacy groups, information services, individuals with their own Web sites, and many others. You are likely to receive many more hits in a Web search than in a licensed database search, but the quality of sources may vary. For example, when Kent typed *Call for National Service* into Google, he got more than 500,000 hits. Although it would be impossible for any researcher to examine all these hits, the first few screens often turn up valuable leads. Here, for example, are several sources that showed up in the first two screens of Kent's Google search:

- A Web site "United We Serve" from a government Web address (.gov)
- An article entitled "A Call for National Service" from the Web site of a magazine entitled *The American Interest Magazine*
- A news story from the Web site of William and Mary College (an .edu site) titled "W&M joins call for national service initiative"
- An article from the Web site of the Aspen Institute (a .org site) describing the "Franklin Project" devoted to promoting voluntary public service
- An op-ed piece from the *Wall Street Journal* by General Stanley McChrystal calling for national public service
- A blog post entitled "General McChrystal's Un-American Call for Universal National Service" from a blog site entitled "The Objective Standard"

FOR WRITING AND DISCUSSION

Comparing a Licensed Database Search and a Web Search

Working in small groups or as a whole class, see if you can reach consensus on the following questions:

1. How does a licensed database search differ from a Web search? Explain what is being searched in each case.
2. Of the six Web items from the first two screens of Kent's Google search (listed above), which might also show up in a licensed database search? Which would never show up in a licensed database search? (For Web-only sites that would not show up in a licensed database, readers must take particular care to analyze the Web site rhetorically. Skill 21.3 in the next chapter will help you do so.)
3. Which of the six items seem particularly valuable for Kent to examine as part of his initial research? Why?

Using Web Search Engines Different search engines search the Web in different ways, so it is important that you try a variety of search engines when you look for information. For example, a service offered by Google is "Google Scholar," with which you can limit a Web search to academic or scholarly sources. (But you will still need to turn to your library's collection or licensed databases for a full text of the source.) On campus, reference librarians and disciplinary experts can give you good advice about what has worked well in the past for particular kinds of searches. On the Web, an additional resource is NoodleTools.com, which offers lots of good advice for choosing the best search engine.

Determining Where You Are on the Web As you browse the Web looking for resources, clicking from link to link, try to figure out what site you are actually in at any given moment. This information is crucial, both for properly documenting a Web source and for reading the source rhetorically.

To know where you are on the Web, begin by identifying the home page, which is the material to the left of the first single slash in the URL (universal resource locator). The generic structure of a typical URL looks like this: http://www.servername.domain/directory/subdirectory/filename.filetype.

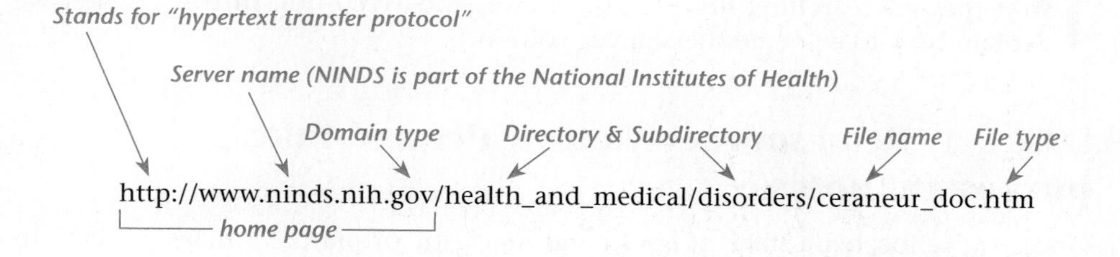

When you click on a link in one site, you may be sent to a totally different site. To determine the home page of a site, simply note the root URL immediately following the "www."* To view the home page directly, delete the codes to the right of the initial home page URL in your computer's location window and hit Enter. You will then be linked directly to the site's home page, where you may be able to find an "About" link through which you can gather information about the purpose and sponsors of the page. As we discuss in later chapters, being able to examine a site's home page helps you read the site rhetorically and document it properly.

*Not all URLs begin with "www" after the first set of double slashes. Our description doesn't include variations of the most typical URL types. You can generally find the home page of a site by eliminating all codes to the right of the first slash mark after the domain or country name.

21 EVALUATING SOURCES

WHAT YOU WILL LEARN

21.1 To read sources rhetorically and take purposeful notes.
21.2 To evaluate sources for reliability, credibility, angle of vision, and degree of advocacy.
21.3 To use your rhetorical knowledge to evaluate Web sources.

In Chapter 20, we explained the importance of posing a good research question, of understanding the different kinds of sources, and of using purposeful strategies for searching libraries, databases, and Web sites. In this chapter we explain how to evaluate the sources you find.

21.1 Read sources rhetorically and take purposeful notes.

SKILL 21.1 **Read sources rhetorically and take purposeful notes.**

Once you've located a stack of books and magazine or journal articles, it's easy to feel overwhelmed. How do you begin reading all this material? There is no one right answer to this question. At times you need to read slowly with analytical closeness. At other times you can skim a source, looking only for its gist or for a needed piece of information. In this section, we offer some advice on how to read your sources with rhetorical savvy and take notes that will help you write your final paper.

Reading with Your Own Goals in Mind

How you read a source depends to a certain extent on where you are in the research process. Early in the process, when you are in the thesis-seeking exploratory stage, your goal is to achieve a basic understanding of your research area. You need to become aware of different points of view, learn what is unknown or controversial about your research question, see what values or assumptions are in conflict, and build up your store of background knowledge. As we saw in the case of Kent Ansen, one's initial research question often evolves as one's knowledge increases and interests shift.

Given these goals, at the early stages of research you should select "overview" kinds of sources to get you into the conversation. In some cases, even an encyclopedia or specialized reference work can be a good start for getting general background.

As you get deeper into your research, your questions become more focused, and the sources you seek out become more specialized. Once you formulate a thesis and plan a structure for your paper, you can determine more clearly the sources you need. For example, after Kent Ansen decided to focus on the beneficial aspects of mandatory public service, he began following up leads on AmeriCorp volunteers, professional training for young adults, and the effects of public service on participation in democracy. At the same time, he remained open-minded about the costs and drawbacks of mandatory national service.

Reading Your Sources Rhetorically

To read your sources rhetorically, you should keep two basic questions in mind:

1. What was the source author's purpose in writing this piece?
2. What might be my purpose in using this piece?

Let's begin with the first question. The following chart sums up the strategies you can use to read your sources rhetorically, along with research tips for answering some of the questions you've posed.

Strategies for Reading Your Sources Rhetorically

Questions to Ask	What to Do	Results
• Who is this author? • What are his or her credentials and affiliations?	• Look for the author's credentials at the end of the article or in the contributors' page. • Google the author's name. • In a database results list, click on the author's name for a list of other articles he/she has written.	• Helps you assess author's *ethos* and credibility. • Helps you establish author's angle of vision.
• What is this source's genre? • Who is the intended audience?	• If the source is downloaded, identify the original publication information. • If the source comes from a periodical, look at the print copy for clues about the audience (titles of other articles, ads, document design). • Use Table 20.2 for further clues about audience and genre. • If a Web-only source, see Skill 21.3.	• Helps you further determine the author's angle of vision as well as the source's reliability and credibility. • Helps explain rhetorical features of the source.

(*continued*)

Questions to Ask	What to Do	Results
• What is this author's purpose? • How is this author trying to change his/her audience's view of the topic?	• Determine whether the piece is primarily expressive, informational, analytical, or persuasive. • If the source comes from the Web, who is the site's sponsor?Read the "About us" material on the site's home page. • If it is a print source, determine the reputation and bias of the journal, magazine, or press (see Table 21.1, pp. 532–533).	• Helps you evaluate the source for angle of vision and degree of advocacy. • Helps you decide how you might use the source in your own argument.
• What is this author's angle of vision or bias? • What facts, data, and other evidence does this author cite and what are the sources for the data? • What are this author's underlying values, assumptions, and beliefs? • What is omitted or censored from this text?	• Apply the rhetorical reading strategies explained in Chapter 5. • Evaluate the source for reliability, credibility, angle of vision, and degree of advocacy as explained in Skill 21.2. • If a Web source, evaluate it using strategies explained in Skill 21.3.	• Helps you bring your own critical thinking to bear on your sources. • Keeps your paper intellectually honest and interesting.

This chart reinforces a point we've made throughout this text: All writing is produced from an angle of vision that privileges some ways of seeing and filters out other ways. You should guard against reading your sources as if they present hard, undisputed facts or universal truths. For example, if one of your sources says that "Saint-John's-wort [an herb] has been shown to be an effective treatment for depression," some of your readers might accept that statement as fact; but many wouldn't. Skeptical readers would want to know who the author is, where his views have been published, and what he uses for evidence. Let's say the author is someone named Samuel Jones. Skeptical readers would ask whether Jones is relying on published research, and if so, whether the studies have been peer-reviewed in reputable, scholarly journals and whether the research has been replicated by other scientists. They would also want to know whether Jones has financial connections to companies that produce herbal remedies and supplements. Rather than settling the question about Saint-John's-wort as a treatment for depression, a quotation from Jones might open up a heated controversy about medical research.

Reading rhetorically is thus a way of thinking critically about your sources. It influences the way you take notes, evaluate sources, and shape your argument.

Taking Purposeful Notes

Many beginning researchers opt not to take notes—a serious mistake, in our view. Instead, they simply photocopy or printout articles, perhaps using a highlighter to mark passages. This practice, which experienced researchers almost never use, reduces your ability to engage the ideas in a source, to synthesize different sources, and to find your own voice in a conversation. When you begin drafting your paper, you'll have no bibliographic information, no notes to refer to, no record of your thinking-in-progress. Your only recourse is to revisit all your sources, thumbing through them one at a time—a practice that leads to passive cutting and pasting (and possible plagiarism).

Recording Bibliographic Information To take good research notes, begin by making a bibliographic entry for the source, following the documentation format assigned by your instructor—usually MLA (Modern Language Association) or APA (American Psychological Association). Although you may be tempted to put off doing this mechanical task ("Hey, boring, I can do this documentation stuff later"), there are two reasons to do it immediately:

Chapter 23 explains in detail how to make a bibliographic entry.

- Doing it now, while the source is in front of you, will save you time in the long run. Otherwise, you'll have to try to retrieve the source, in a late-night panic, just before the paper is due.
- Doing it now will make you look at the source rhetorically. Is this a peer-reviewed journal article? A magazine article? An op-ed piece? A blog? Making the bibliographic entry forces you to identify the source's genre.

Recording Ideas and Information and Responding to Each Source To take good research notes, follow the habits for "strong reading" discussed in Chapter 5 by weaving back and forth between two modes of writing:

- ***Your informational notes on each source:*** Summarize each source's argument and record useful information. To avoid the risk of plagiarizing later, make sure that you put quotation marks around any passages that you copy word for word (be sure to copy *exactly*). When you summarize or paraphrase passages, be sure to put the ideas entirely into your own words.
- ***Your own exploratory notes as you think of ideas:*** Write down your own ideas as they occur to you. Record your thinking-in-progress as you mull over and speak back to your sources.

For more on quoting, summarizing, and paraphrasing sources, see Skill 22.2.

An approach that encourages both modes of writing is to keep a dialectic or double-entry journal. Divide a page in half; enter your informational notes on one side and your exploratory writing on the other. If you use a computer, you can put your informational notes in one font and your own exploratory writing in another.

An example of double-entry notes appears in Chapter 7, pp. 150–151.

Taking effective notes is different from the mechanical process of copying out passages or simply listing facts and information. Rather, make your notes purposeful by imagining how you might use a given source in your research paper. The following chart shows the different functions that research sources might play in your argument and highlights appropriate note-taking strategies for each function.

Strategies for Taking Notes According to Purpose		
Function That Source Might Play in Your Argument	**Strategies for Informational Notes**	**Strategies for Exploratory Notes**
Provides background about your problem or issue	• Summarize the information. • Record specific facts and figures useful for background.	• Speculate on how much background your readers will need.
Gives an alternative view that you will mention briefly	• Summarize the source's argument in a couple of sentences; note its bias and perspective. • Identify brief quotations that sum up the source's perspective.	• Jot down ideas on how and why different sources disagree. • Begin making an idea map of alternative views.
Provides an alternative or opposing view that you might summarize fully and respond to	• Summarize the article fully and fairly (see Chapter 5 on summary writing). • Note the kinds of evidence used.	• Speculate about why you disagree with the source and whether you can refute the argument, concede to it, or compromise with it. • Explore what research you'll need to support your own argument.
Provides information or testimony that you might use as evidence	• Record the data or information. • If using authorities for testimony, quote short passages. • Note the credentials of the writer or person quoted.	• Record new ideas as they occur to you. • Continue to think purposefully about additional research you'll need.
Mentions information or testimony that counters your position or raises doubts about your argument	• Note counterevidence. • Note authorities who disagree with you.	• Speculate how you might respond to counterevidence.
Provides a theory or method that influences your approach to the issue	• Note credentials of the author. • Note passages that sparked ideas.	• Freewrite about how the source influences your method or approach.

Skill 21.2 Evaluate sources for reliability, credibility, angle of vision, and degree of advocacy.

21.2
Evaluate sources for reliability, credibility, angle of vision, and degree of advocacy.

When you read sources for your research project, you need to evaluate them as you go along. As you read each potential source, ask yourself questions about the author's reliability, credibility, angle of vision, and degree of advocacy.

Reliability

"Reliability" refers to the accuracy of factual data in a source. If you check a writer's "facts" against other sources, do you find that the facts are correct? Does the writer distort facts, take them out of context, or otherwise use them unreasonably? In some controversies, key data are highly disputed—for example, the frequency of date rape or the risk factors for many diseases. A reliable writer acknowledges these controversies and doesn't treat disputed data as fact. Furthermore, if you check out the sources used by a reliable writer, they'll reveal accurate and careful research—respected primary sources rather than hearsay or secondhand reports. Journalists of reputable newspapers (not tabloids) pride themselves on meticulously checking out their facts, as do editors of serious popular magazines. Editing is often minimal for Web sources, however, and they can be notoriously unreliable. As you gain knowledge of your research question, you'll develop a good ear for writers who play fast and loose with data.

Credibility

"Credibility" is similar to "reliability" but is based on internal rather than external factors. It refers to the reader's trust in the writer's honesty, goodwill, and trustworthiness and is apparent in the writer's tone, reasonableness, fairness in summarizing opposing views, and respect for different perspectives. Audiences differ in how much credibility they will grant to certain authors. Nevertheless, a writer can achieve a reputation for credibility, even among bitter political opponents, by applying to issues a sense of moral courage, integrity, and consistency of principle.

"Credibility" is synonymous with the classical term ethos. See Concept 3.2, pp. 48–50; see also pp. 326–328.

Angle of Vision and Political Stance

By "angle of vision," we mean the way that a piece of writing is shaped by the underlying values, assumptions, and beliefs of its author, resulting in a text that reflects a certain perspective, worldview, or belief system. Of paramount importance are the underlying values or beliefs that the writer assumes his or her readers will share. You can get useful clues about a writer's angle of vision and intended audience by doing some quick research into the politics and reputation of the author on the Internet or by analyzing the genre, market niche, and political reputation of the publication in which the material appears.

Angle of vision is discussed in detail in Concept 3.1, pp. 42–48. See also Chapter 5, pp. 92–95, which shows how analyzing angle of vision helps you read a text with and against the grain.

Determining Political Stance Your awareness of angle of vision and political stance is especially important if you are doing research on contemporary cultural or political issues. In Table 21.1, we have categorized some well-known political commentators, publications, policy research institutes (commonly known as *think tanks*), and blogs across the political spectrum from left/liberal to right/conservative.

TABLE 21.1 Angles of Vision in U.S. Media and Think Tanks: A Sampling Across the Political Spectrum*

Commentators

Left	Left Center	Center	Right Center	Right
Barbara Ehrenreich	E. J. Dionne	David Ignatius	David Brooks	Charles Krauthammer
Bob Herbert	Leonard Pitts	Thomas Friedman	Peggy Noonan	Cal Thomas
Michael Moore (film-maker)	Eugene Robinson	Kathleen Hall Jamieson	Jonah Goldberg	Glenn Beck (radio/TV)
Bill Moyers (television)	Nicholas Kristof	Kevin Phillips	Andrew Sullivan	Rush Limbaugh (radio/TV)
Paul Krugman	Maureen Dowd	David Broder	George Will	Bill O'Reilly (radio/TV)
Thom Hartman (radio)	Mark Shields	William Saletan	Ruben Navarrette, Jr.	Kathleen Parker
Rachel Maddow (television)	Frank Rich	Mary Sanchez		Thomas Sowell

Newspapers and Magazines**

Left/Liberal	Center	Right/Conservative
The American Prospect	*Atlantic Monthly*	*American Spectator*
Harper's	*Business Week*	*Fortune*
Los Angeles Times	*Commentary*	*National Review*
Mother Jones	*Commonweal*	*Reader's Digest*
The Nation	*Foreign Affairs*	*Reason*
New York Times	*New Republic*	*Wall Street Journal*
New Yorker	*Slate*	*Washington Times*
Salon	*Washington Post*	*Weekly Standard*
Sojourners		

Blogs

Liberal/Left	Center	Right/Conservative
americablog.com	donklephant.com	firstinthenation.us
crooksandliars.com	newmoderate.blogspot.com	instapundit.com
dailykos.com	politics-central.blogspot.com	littlegreenfootballs.com
digbysblog.blogspot.com	rantingbaldhippie.com	michellemalkin.com
firedoglake.com	stevesilver.net	polipundit.com
huffingtonpost.com	themoderatevoice.com	powerlineblog.com
mediamatters.com	washingtonindependent.com	sistertoldjah.com
talkingpointsmemo.com	watchingwashington.blogspot.com	redstate.com
wonkette.com		townhall.com

TABLE 21.1 continued

Think Tanks		
Left/Liberal	**Center**	**Right/Conservative**
Center for American Progress	The Brookings Institution	American Enterprise Institute
Center for Media and Democracy (sponsors Disinfopedia.org)	Carnegie Endowment for International Peace	Cato Institute (Libertarian)
Institute for Policy Studies	Council on Foreign Relations	Center for Strategic and International Studies
Open Society Institute (Soros Foundation)	Jamestown Foundation	Heritage Foundation (sponsors Townhall.com)
Progressive Policy Institute	National Bureau of Economic Research	Project for the New American Century
Urban Institute		

* *For further information about the political leanings of publications or think tanks, ask your librarian about* Gale Directory of Publications and Broadcast Media *or* NIRA World Directory of Think Tanks.
** *Newspapers are categorized according to positions they take on their editorial page; any reputable newspaper strives for objectivity in news reporting and includes a variety of views on its op-ed pages. Magazines do not claim and are not expected to present similar breadth and objectivity.*

Although the terms *liberal* and *conservative* or *left* and *right* often have fuzzy meanings, they provide convenient shorthand for signaling a person's overall views about the proper role of government in relation to the economy and social values. Liberals, tending to sympathize with those potentially harmed by unfettered free markets (workers, consumers, plaintiffs, endangered species), are typically comfortable with government regulation of economic matters while conservatives, who tend to sympathize with business interests, typically assert faith in free markets and favor a limited regulatory role for government. On social issues, conservatives tend to espouse traditional family values and advocate laws that would maintain these values (for example, promoting a Constitutional amendment limiting marriage to a bond between a man and a woman). Liberals, on the other hand, tend to espouse individual choice regarding marital partnerships and a wide range of other issues. Some persons identify themselves as economic conservatives but social liberals; others side with workers' interests on economic issues but are conservative on social issues.

Finally, many persons regard themselves as "centrists." In Table 21.1 the column labeled "Center" includes commentators who seek out common ground between the left and the right and who often believe that the best civic decisions are compromises between opposing views. Likewise, centrist publications and institutes often approach issues from multiple points of view, looking for the most workable solutions.

Degree of Advocacy

By "degree of advocacy" we mean the extent to which an author unabashedly takes a persuasive stance on a contested position as opposed to adopting a more neutral, objective, or exploratory stance. For example, publications affiliated with advocacy organizations (the Sierra Club, the National Rifle Association) will have a clear editorial bias. When a writer has an ax to grind, you need to weigh carefully the writer's selection of evidence, interpretation of data, and fairness to opposing views. Although no one can be completely neutral, it is always useful to seek out authors who offer a balanced assessment of the evidence. Evidence from a more detached and neutral writer may be more trusted by your readers than the arguments of a committed advocate. For example, if you want to persuade corporate executives on the dangers of global warming, evidence from scholarly journals may be more persuasive than evidence from an environmentalist Web site or from a freelance writer for a leftist popular magazine such as *Mother Jones*.

21.3 Use your rhetorical knowledge to evaluate Web sources.

Skill 21.3 Use your rhetorical knowledge to evaluate Web sources.

In the previous section we focused on reading sources rhetorically by asking questions about a source's reliability, credibility, angle of vision, and degree of advocacy. In this section we focus on evaluating sources from the World Wide Web.

The Web As a Unique Rhetorical Environment

Concept 4.1 explains the nonlinear way readers encounter Web content, the short-attention span environment of Web sites, and their potential to present material to attract and move readers.

In addition to familiar entertainment and commercial sites, the Web can be a powerful research tool, providing access to highly specialized databases, historical archives, museum collections, governmental documents, blogosphere commentary, scholarly portals useful for academic researchers, and much more. The Web is also a great vehicle for democracy, giving voice to the otherwise voiceless. Anyone with a cause and a rudimentary knowledge of Web design can create a site. The result is a medium that differs in significant ways from print in its creators, composition, and multimodal content.

Criteria for Evaluating a Web Source

When you evaluate a Web source, we suggest that you ask five different kinds of questions about the site in which the source appeared, as shown in Table 21.2. These questions, developed by scholars and librarians as points to consider when you are evaluating Web sites, will help you determine the usefulness of a site or source for your own purposes.

See Chapter 14, pp. 381–383, for Teresa Filice's essay evaluating the advocacy site "Parents: The Anti-Drug."

As a researcher, the first question you should ask about a potentially useful Web source should be, Who placed this piece on the Web and why? You can begin answering this question by analyzing the site's home page, where you will often find navigational buttons linking to "Mission," "About Us," or other identifying information about the site's sponsors. You can also get hints about the site's purpose by asking, What kind of Web site is it? Different kinds of Web sites have different purposes. You should be conscious of the purpose of

TABLE 21.2 Criteria for Evaluating Web Sites

Criteria	Questions to Ask
1. Authority	• Is the document author or site sponsor clearly identified? • Does the site identify the occupation, position, education, experience, or other credentials of the author? • Does the home page or a clear link from the home page reveal the author's or sponsor's motivation for establishing the site? • Does the site provide contact information for the author or sponsor such as an e-mail or organization address?
2. Objectivity or Clear Disclosure of Advocacy	• Is the site's purpose clear (for example, to inform, entertain, or persuade)? • Is the site explicit about declaring its point of view? • Does the site indicate whether the author is affiliated with a specific organization, institution, or association? • Does the site indicate whether it is directed toward a specific audience?
3. Coverage	• Are the topics covered by the site clear? • Does the site exhibit a suitable depth and comprehensiveness for its purpose? • Is sufficient evidence provided to support the ideas and opinions presented?
4. Accuracy	• Are the sources of information stated? • Do the facts appear to be accurate? • Can you verify this information by comparing this source with other sources in the field?
5. Currency	• Are dates included in the Web site? • Do the dates apply to the material itself, to its placement on the Web, or to the time the site was last revised and updated? • Is the information current, or at least still relevant, for the site's purpose? For your purpose?

the site, often revealed by the domain identifier, such as .com or .org. The most common kinds of sites are as follows:

- **.com** for commercial sites (promoting businesses and marketing services, often with no identified author)
- **.org** sites for nonprofit organizations or advocacy groups (some with balanced coverage but many with distinct angles of vision)
- **.edu** sites for colleges or universities (often complex sites with institutional information as well as scholarly and advocacy links)
- **.gov** or **.mil** sites for government agencies or military units (with a range of data and support for policies)

Analyzing Your Own Purposes for Using Web Sources

Besides analyzing a sponsor's purpose for establishing a Web site, you also need to analyze your own purpose for using the site. To illustrate strategies for evaluating a Web site, we'll use as examples two hypothetical student researchers investigating the civic controversy over hydraulic fracturing (commonly called fracking), an advanced technological process for extracting natural gas from shale buried deep in the earth.

Our first student researcher was interested in doing a rhetorical analysis of arguments for and againt fracking. She did an initial Google search using "fracking" and "natural gas" as her keywords and found dozens of pro-fracking and anti-fracking sites sponsored by the government, energy companies, and advocacy organizations. She found a host of organizations protesting the spread of fracking: Americans Against Fracking, Artists Against Fracking, Students Against Fracking, Farmers Against Fracking, and New Yorkers Against Fracking, among others. She also found a number of sites enthusiastically supporting fracking. One site that caught her attention was EnergyFromShale.org. Fascinated by the way that this organization has chosen to emphasize economic opportunities for local communities with slideshows and videos of happy Americans, our researcher decided to focus her project on the ways that Web sites on fracking frame the issue and the kinds of arguments they make for and against the benefits and dangers of fracking.

Our second researcher was more directly interested in determining her own stance on the fracking debate. She was trying to decide from a citizen's perspective whether to advocate for fracking or to oppose it, or at least to advocate for more regulation of it. As a researcher, her dilemma was to determine how much she could trust data taken from these advocacy sites. For her, the sites were mostly secondary rather than primary sources.

Let's look at each student's research process in turn.

Researcher 1: Using Fracking and Natural Gas Web Sites for Rhetorical Analysis Our first researcher's goal was to analyze fracking sites rhetorically to understand the ways that stakeholders frame their interests and represent themselves. She discovered that the angle of vision of each site—whether pro-fracking or anti-fracking—led to the filtering of evidence in distinctive ways. For example, the pro-fracking and natural gas sites emphasize the economic perspective. Appealing to both *logos* and *pathos,* these sites often feature slideshows and testimonials of smiling people who report that when the oil and shale industry moves into a region, the economic benefits ripple outward, beyond the people who receive royalty checks for wells on their land. These sites claim that the industry brings increased revenue to the government and an infusion of jobs and thus income to boost local businesses such as banks, restaurants, and stores. In addition, the industry draws educational programs to train technicians, providing more jobs. These sites seek to inspire confidence and alleviate fears, minimizing the dangers to the environment. Figure 21.1 is a representative example of a pro-fracking Web site. Presenting a drilling rig as aesthetically beautiful against a dawn sky, this multimodal Web page features links to other pages highlighting the economic and social benefits of fracking.

In contrast, she discovered that anti-fracking sites sponsored by citizen activist groups and environmental advocacy organizations don't mention jobs and the economy (although they do mention the loss of property value from the toxicity of fracking wells) but rather focus on the immediate and long-term dangers to the environment, challenging the idea of "safe" processes. They underscore the lag in federal regulation of this extraction process. In addition to describing the gases released into the air in the process, these sites emphasize the millions of gallons

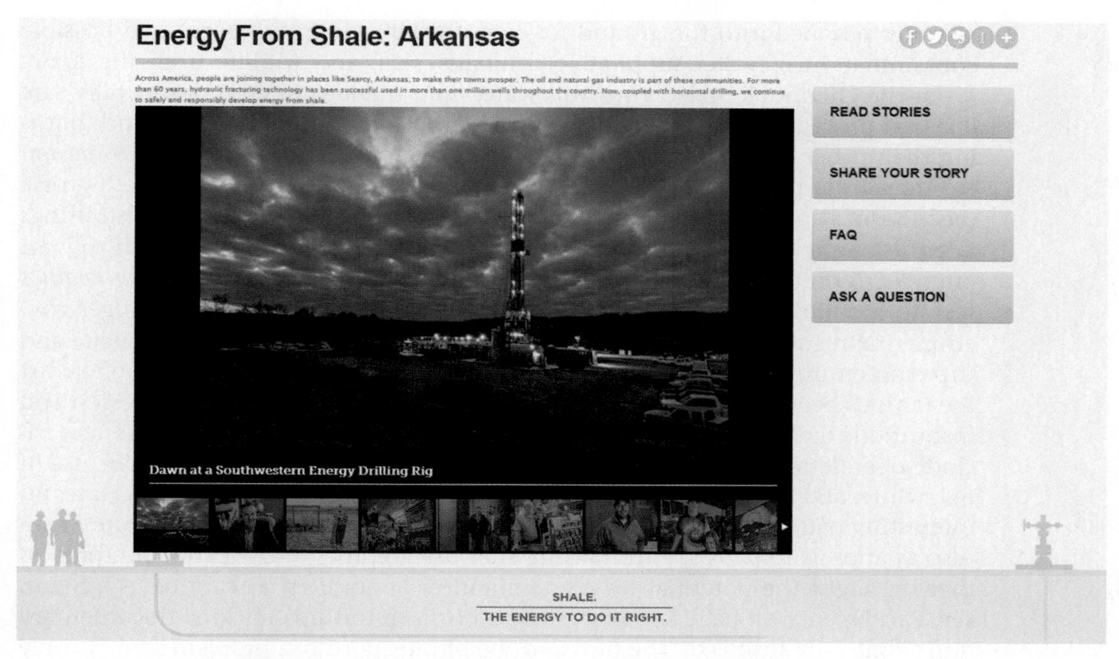

FIGURE 21.1 A Web Site Portraying Fracking Positively (Energy from Shale)

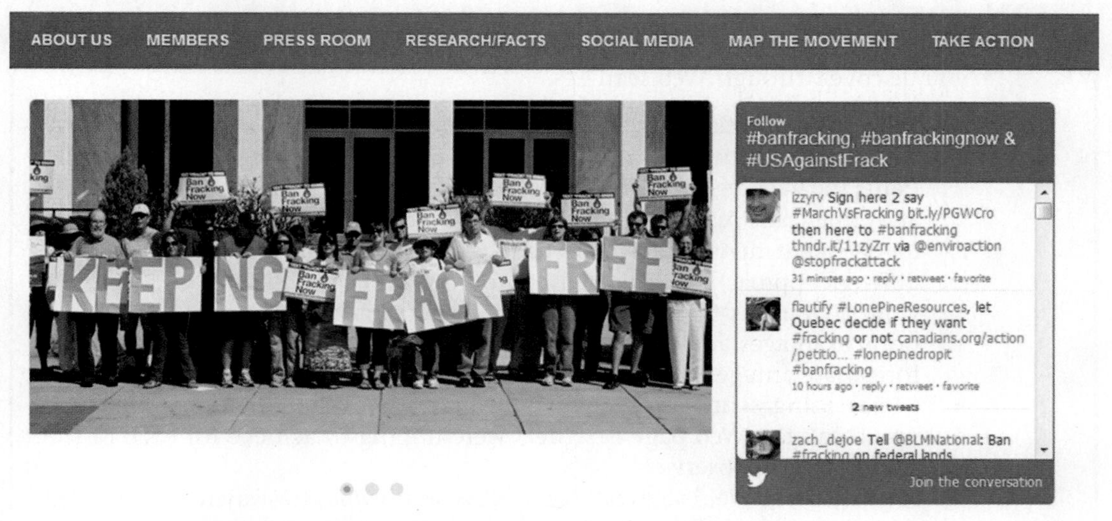

FIGURE 21.2 A Web Site Portraying Fracking Negatively (from Americans Against Fracking)

of water pumped into the ground for each fracking well, the recent and possible contamination of water supplies for humans, fish, and wildlife from the toxicity of the chemicals mixed with this water, and the lack of environmentally safe disposal procedures. Also, while acknowledging that natural gas is cleaner burning than other fossil fuels, they point out that increased commitment to natural gas does little to lessen the climate change threat, and may even make it worse (because of large amounts of methane released during the process). It also brings attention away from the need to develop renewable energy. Their appeals to *logos* often focus on the dangers of pollution from fracking while their appeals to *pathos* seek to mobilize citizens against corporate power and to encourage stronger governmental regulation before it is too late. To convey the urgency of the issue and the momentum of the opposition to fracking, these anti-fracking sites often list the famous people and the numerous organizations, clubs, groups, businesses, and institutions that support a ban on fracking, show photos of recent protests, and include open letters and news about current campaigns against fracking. The use of red, white, and blue in the Americans Against Fracking site, for example, creates an interesting patriotic appeal, a subtle "protect our country" motif. (See Figure 21.2.) Also as appeals to *pathos*, anti-fracking sites use graphics of the extraction process that highlight the potential for contamination of aquifers, a scary development. The Part Opener on page 507 shows two stills from the anti-fracking documentary film *Gasland* by Josh Fox. The film and the photos portray a problem some people have experienced when fracking wells disrupted their water supply, causing both methane and water to come out of their taps. For other strong appeals to *pathos*, see the promotional material for this film and its sequel on the Web.

FOR WRITING AND DISCUSSION

Analyzing the Rhetorical Elements of Fracking Web Pages

Working in small groups or as a whole class, try to reach consensus answers to the following questions about how Web sites seek to draw in readers. Use Figures 21.1 and, 21.2 as well as other pro-fracking and anti-fracking sites that you discover through Web searches.

1. What is your initial impression of the images, information, and layout of the Web pages for the organizations you have found? How do these Web pages frame the fracking issue? In the specific case of Energy from Shale (Figure 21.1) and Americans Against Fracking (Figure 21.2), how are the images of citizen involvement in the fracking debate depicted differently? (For a site with a different approach, investigate New Yorkers Against Fracking.)
2. How do various fracking Web sites use multimodal arguments (combinations of images and text) to make their case? What do you see as the rhetorical advantages of using photographs, including photos of real people, versus using schematic drawings or graphics? What rhetorical effect do you think the Web page designers were hoping to achieve for each of the sites you have observed?
3. How do these Web pages use *logos, ethos,* and *pathos* to sway readers toward their point of view?

Researcher 2: Using Advocacy Web Sites for Data on the Benefits and Dangers of Fracking Researcher 2 is seeking to create her own research-based argument on whether citizens should support or oppose fracking. Her dilemma is to determine to what extent she can use the "facts" presented on these advocacy Web sites. For example, can she trust the pro-fracking sites' statements that drilling companies cooperate with local agencies to protect groundwater and act responsibly in recycling water? On anti-fracking sites, she frequently encountered equivalent statements of fact that raised serious questions about drilling companies' lack of concern for local water, the radioactive and carcinogenic chemicals used, and the failure to clean up water, which is left to seep into the groundwater and eventually into rivers and lakes.

In her initial Web search, she explored the Web site for Energy Citizens, a pro-oil and gas industry site. Searching for information on natural gas and delving into the Web site, she found a pdf article entitled "Freeing Up Energy: Hydraulic Fracturing: Unlocking America's Natural Gas Resources." This article argues that hydraulic fracturing is a process that has been around for decades—although it is improved now—and that it is well monitored by industry itself and by environmental laws. It underscores the lack of confirmed cases of groundwater contamination and the measures involved in the design of wells and the fracking process itself, intended to safeguard groundwater. The purpose of this article and the site is to present fracking as an environmentally safe process, to increase citizens' confidence in the oil and gas industry, and to encourage citizens to relinquish their fears and concerns about the environment and focus on the message of the rest of the article—the benefits of fracking in the form of jobs, revenue, and abundant natural gas resources to last a hundred years.

How should our second researcher proceed in evaluating such an article for her own research purposes? Her first step is to evaluate the site itself. When she reviewed the home page for this site, she found that the site's sponsors targeted a range of energy issues including support for the Keystone XL Pipeline, opposition to the Renewable Fuel Standard, and support for developing domestic oil both on and offshore. The site also emphasized the substantial taxes that that oil and gas companies pay to the federal government. This site obviously advocates a pro-corporation stance and boldly links business growth and prosperity with national well-being. It couples an image of the Statue of Liberty with energy security and a photo of a woman worker with the Keystone XL Pipeline. With this perspective in mind, Researcher 2, reconsidering the article about fracking, could easily evaluate this site against the five criteria:

1. ***Authority:*** She could clearly tell that this site is an advocacy organization affiliated with the petroleum industry; indeed, the article was written by the American Petroleum Institute.
2. ***Advocacy:*** This site clearly promotes removing restrictions from the oil and gas industry and expanding its opportunities for growth, based on the economic philosophy that what is good for American business is good for American citizens.
3. ***Coverage:*** This site does not cover fracking issues in a complex way. Every aspect of the site and the article is filtered to support the growth of the oil and gas industry.

4. ***Accuracy:*** At this point, she was unable to check each of the article's assertions about the safety of the fracking process against other sources, but she assumed that all claims and statistics would be rhetorically filtered and selected to accord with the site's angle of vision.
5. ***Currency:*** Although the article was dated July 19, 2010, one main study cited in it was dated 2004, before recent reports of problems with contamination of water systems by fracking.

Based on this analysis, how might Researcher 2 use the "Freeing Up Energy" article from the Energy Citizens site? Our view is that the article could be very useful as one perspective on the fracking controversy. It is a fairly representative example of the argument that the benefits from exploiting newly discovered natural gas resources far outweigh any possible risk to the environment. It clearly shows the kinds of rhetorical strategies such articles use—claims about the abundance of the resource and the promise of energy independence, the nonexistence of verifiable risks, and the effectiveness of current regulations. A summary of this article's argument could therefore be effective for presenting the pro-fracking point of view.

As a source of factual data, however, this article is unusable. It would be irresponsible for her to use the facts in this article without seeking out other recent sources and reviewing recent legislation regulating fracking. For example, this article includes a chart listing fracturing fluids used in hydraulic fracturing. The chart emphasizes that chemical additives constitute only a minimal 0.5% of the total fluid and labels them common everyday substances such as those used in laundry detergents and antiperspirants, thus masking each chemical's toxicity and carcinogenic properties. Nor does the article mention that the 2005 Bush/Cheney Energy Bill, known as the Halliburton Loophole, exempted petroleum companies from having to reveal the chemicals they use in hydraulic fracturing. Similarly, it would be irresponsible to adopt the anti-fracking advocacy groups' views of the pollution and contamination of water by fracking wells without researching specific claims and state-by-state records. Researcher 2 should instead seek out governmental data, pending legislation, and scientific sources, including peer-reviewed research articles by scholars, to get a current, larger, more accurate perspective and to find neutral studies, not funded by the oil and gas industry, and not featured by anti-fracking documentary films. One purpose of reading sources rhetorically is to appreciate how much advocates for a given position filter data. Finding original data and interpreting it for oneself are two challenges of responsible research.

FOR WRITING AND DISCUSSION

Analyzing the Use of Information Graphics in Advocacy Web Sites

Pro-fracking Web sites take pains to assure their audiences that fracking is environmentally safe. Conversely, anti-fracking Web sites emphasize the environmental dangers of fracking. Figures 21.3 and 21.4 are examples of information graphics, in this case diagrams, that are similar to those found on pro- and anti-fracking advocacy sites. Figure 21.3 is a typical diagram that aims to persuade viewers that fracking poses no dangers to underground aquifers. In contrast, the diagram in Figure 21.4 emphasizes the dangers of fracking to water supplies.

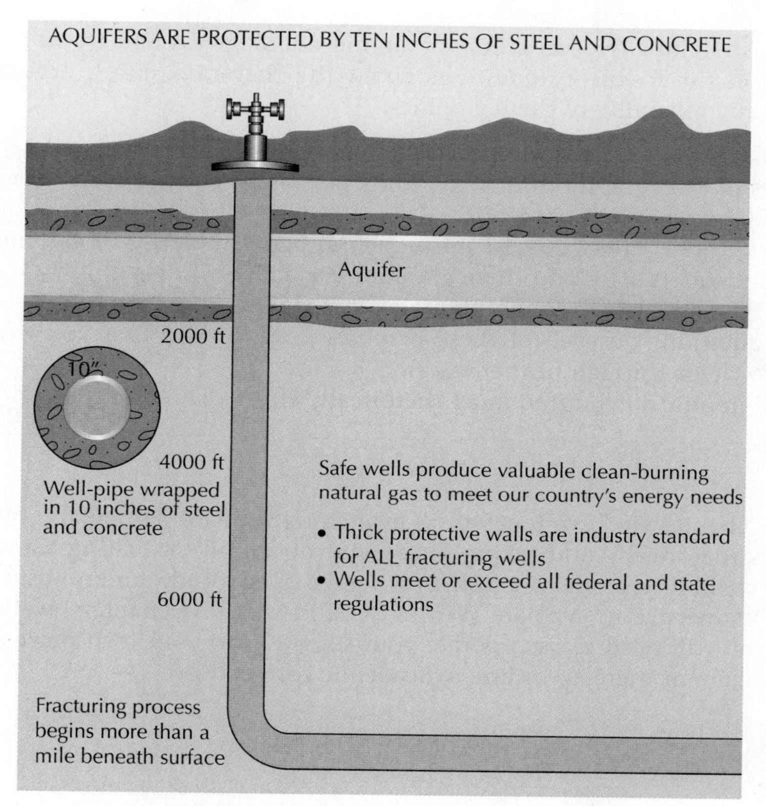

FIGURE 21.3 Typical Diagram Showing Safety of Fracking

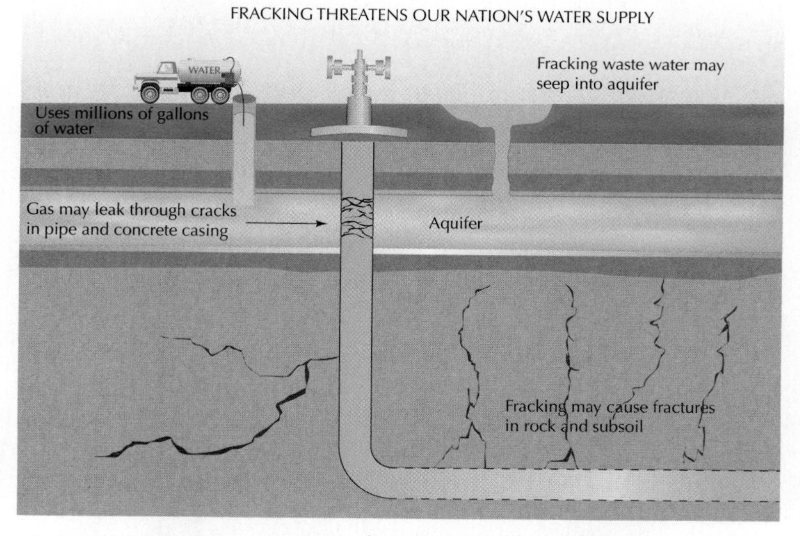

FIGURE 21.4 Typical Diagram Showing Dangers of Fracking

Working individually or in groups, examine the diagrams and try to reach consensus on the following questions about the rhetorical effect, accuracy, credibility, and reliability of these graphics.

1. What is the angle of vision of each graphic? How do the visual and verbal features of each graphic contribute to its purpose? What is "seen" in each graphic and what is "not seen"?
2. What rhetorical effect do you think each designer intends the graphic to have on readers? How do these graphics use appeals to *logos, pathos, and ethos*? How accurate, credible, and reliable do you find each graphic?
3. What questions do each of these graphics raise for you that you would want to check through further research?
4. Which graphic do you find more rhetorically effective and why?

In this chapter we have focused on evaluating sources, particularly on reading sources rhetorically and taking purposeful notes; on evaluating sources for reliability, credibility, angle of vision, and degree of advocacy; and on using your rhetorical knowledge to evaluate Web sources. In the next chapters, we turn to the skills you will need to incorporate your sources into your own prose and to cite and document them according to academic conventions.

INCORPORATING SOURCES INTO YOUR OWN WRITING

22

WHAT YOU WILL LEARN

22.1 To let your own argument determine your use of sources.
22.2 To know when and how to use summary, paraphrase, and quotation.
22.3 To use attributive tags to distinguish your ideas from a source's.
22.4 To avoid plagiarism by following academic conventions for ethical use of sources.

So far, we have covered strategies for finding and evaluating sources. Now we focus on the skills needed for incorporating sources into your own writing. Many of the examples in this chapter will be based on the following short article from the Web site of the American Council on Science and Health (ACSH)—an organization of doctors and scientists devoted to providing scientific information on health issues and to exposing health fads and myths. Please read the argument carefully in preparation for the discussions that follow.

IS VEGETARIANISM HEALTHIER THAN NONVEGETARIANISM?

Many people become vegetarians because they believe, in error, that vegetarianism is uniquely conducive to good health. The findings of several large epidemiologic studies indeed suggest that the death and chronic-disease rates of vegetarians—primarily vegetarians who consume dairy products or both dairy products and eggs—are lower than those of meat eaters....

The health of vegetarians may be better than that of nonvegetarians partly because of nondietary factors: Many vegetarians are health-conscious. They exercise regularly, maintain a desirable body weight, and abstain from smoking. Although most epidemiologists have attempted to take such factors into account in their analyses, it is possible that they did not adequately control their studies for nondietary effects.

People who are vegetarians by choice may differ from the general population in other ways relevant to health. For example, in Western countries most vegetarians are more affluent than nonvegetarians and thus have better living conditions and more access to medical care.

An authoritative review of vegetarianism and chronic diseases classified the evidence for various alleged health benefits of vegetarianism:

- The evidence is "strong" that vegetarians have (a) a lower risk of becoming alcoholic, constipated, or obese and (b) a lower risk of developing lung cancer.

- The evidence is "good" that vegetarians have a lower risk of developing adult-onset diabetes mellitus, coronary artery disease, hypertension, and gallstones.
- The evidence is "fair to poor" that vegetarianism decreases risk of breast cancer, colon cancer, diverticular disease, kidney-stone formation, osteoporosis, and tooth decay.

For some of the diseases mentioned above, the practice of vegetarianism itself probably is the main protective factor. For example, the low incidence of constipation among vegetarians is almost certainly due to their high intakes of fiber-rich foods. For other conditions, nondietary factors may be more important than diet. For example, the low incidence of lung cancer among vegetarians is attributable primarily to their extremely low rate of cigarette smoking. Diet is but one of many risk factors for most chronic diseases.

22.1 Let your own argument determine your use of sources.

SKILL 22.1 Let your own argument determine your use of sources.

How you might use this article in your own writing would depend on your research question and purpose. To illustrate, we'll show you three different hypothetical examples of writers who have reason to cite this article.

Writer 1: An Analysis of Alternative Approaches to Reducing Alcoholism

Writer 1 argues that vegetarianism may be an effective way to resist alcoholism. She uses just one statement from the ACSH article for her own purpose and then moves on to other sources.

Writer's claim

Identification of source

Quotation from ACSH

Another approach to fighting alcoholism is through naturopathy, holistic medicine, and vegetarianism. Vegetarians generally have better health than the rest of the population and particularly have, according to the American Council on Science and Health, "a lower risk of becoming alcoholic." This lower risk has been borne out by other studies showing that the benefits of the holistic health movement are particularly strong for persons with addictive tendencies. ... [goes on to other arguments and sources]

Writer 2: A Proposal Advocating Vegetarianism

Writer 2 proposes that people become vegetarians. Parts of his argument focus on the environmental costs and ethics of eating meat, but he also devotes one paragraph to the health benefits of vegetarianism. As support for this point he summarizes the ACSH article's material on health benefits.

Not only will a vegetarian diet help stop cruelty to animals, but it is also good for your health. According to the American Council on Science and Health, vegetarians have longer life expectancy than nonvegetarians and suffer from fewer chronic diseases. The Council cites "strong" evidence from the scientific literature showing that vegetarians have reduced risk of lung cancer, obesity, constipation, and alcoholism. The Council also cites "good" evidence that they have a reduced risk of adult-onset diabetes, high blood pressure, gallstones, and hardening of the arteries. Although the evidence isn't nearly as strong, vegetarianism may also lower the risk of certain cancers, kidney stones, loss of bone density, and tooth decay.

Writer's claim

Identification of source

Summary of ACSH material

Writer 3: An Evaluation Looking Skeptically at Vegetarianism

Here, Writer 3 uses portions of the same article to make an opposite case from that of Writer 2. She focuses on those parts of the article that Writer 2 consciously excluded.

The link between vegetarianism and death rates is a classic instance of correlation rather than causation. While it is true that vegetarians have a longer life expectancy than nonvegetarians and suffer from fewer chronic diseases, the American Council on Science and Health has shown that the causes can mostly be explained by factors other than diet. As the Council suggests, vegetarians are apt to be more health conscious than nonvegetarians and thus get more exercise, stay slender, and avoid smoking. The Council points out that vegetarians also tend to be wealthier than nonvegetarians and see their doctors more regularly. In short, they live longer because they take better care of themselves, not because they avoid meat.

Writer's claim

Identification of source

Paraphrased points from ACSH

Using a Source for Different Purposes

FOR WRITING AND DISCUSSION

Each of the hypothetical writers uses the short ACSH argument in different ways for different purposes. Working individually or in small groups, respond to the following questions; be prepared to elaborate on and defend your answers.

1. How does each writer use the original article differently and why?
2. If you were the author of the article from the American Council on Science and Health, would you think that your article is used fairly and responsibly in each instance?

(*continued*)

3. Suppose your goal were simply to summarize the argument from the American Council on Science and Health. Write a brief summary of the argument and then explain how your summary is different from the partial summaries by Writers 2 and 3.

22.2
Know when and how to use summary, paraphrase, and quotation.

SKILL 22.2 Know when and how to use summary, paraphrase, and quotation.

For an explanation of avoiding plagiarism in academic writing, see Skill 22.5. For in-text citations, see Chapter 23.

As a research writer, you need to incorporate sources gracefully into your own prose so that you stay focused on your own argument. Depending on your purpose, you might (1) summarize all or part of a source author's argument, (2) paraphrase a relevant portion of a source, or (3) quote small passages from the source directly. Whenever you use a source, you need to avoid plagiarism by referencing the source with an in-text citation, by putting paraphrases and summaries entirely in your own words, and by placing quotation marks around quoted passages. The following strategies chart gives you an overview of summary, paraphrase, and quotation as ways of incorporating sources into your own prose.

Strategies for Incorporating Sources into Your Own Prose

Strategies	What to Do	When to Use These Strategies
Summarize the source.	Condense a source writer's argument by keeping main ideas and omitting details (see Chapter 5, pp. 88–89 and 102–105).	• When the source writer's whole argument is relevant to your purpose • When the source writer presents an alternative or opposing view that you want to push against • When the source writer's argument can be used in support of your own
Paraphrase the source.	Reproduce an idea from a source writer but translate the idea entirely into your own words; a paraphrase should be approximately the same length as the original.	• When you want to incorporate factual information from a source or to use one specific idea from a source • When the source passage is overly complex or technical for your targeted audience • When you want to incorporate a source's point in your own voice without interrupting the flow of your argument

Strategies	What to Do	When to Use These Strategies
Quote short passages from the source using quotation marks.	Work brief quotations from the source smoothly into the grammar of your own sentences (see Skill 22.4 on the mechanics of quoting).	• When you need testimony from an authority (state the authority's credentials in an attributive tag—see Skill 22.3) • In summaries, when you want to reproduce a source's voice, particularly if the language is striking or memorable • In lieu of paraphrase when the source language is memorable
Quote long passages from the source using the block method.	Results in a page with noticeably lengthy block quotations (see Skill 22.4)	• When you intend to analyze or critique the quotation—the quotation is followed by your detailed analysis of its ideas or rhetorical features • When the flavor and language of testimonial evidence is important

With practice, you'll be able to use all these strategies smoothly and effectively.

Summarizing

Detailed instructions on how to write a summary of an article and incorporate it into your own prose are provided in Chapter 5, "Reading Rhetorically" (pp. 88–90 and 102–105). Summaries can be as short as a single sentence or as long as a paragraph. Make the summary as concise as possible so that you don't distract the reader from your own argument. Writer 2's partial summary of the ACSH article (focusing on the benefits of vegetarianism) is a good example of a summary used in support of the writer's own thesis (p. 545).

Paraphrasing

Unlike a summary, which is a condensation of a source's whole argument, a **paraphrase** translates a short passage from a source's words into the writer's own words. Writers often choose to paraphrase when the details of a source passage are particularly important or when the source is overly technical and needs to be simplified for the intended audience. When you paraphrase, be careful to avoid reproducing the original writer's grammatical structure and syntax. If you mirror the original sentence structure while replacing occasional words with synonyms or small structural changes, you will be doing what composition specialists call "**patchwriting**"—that is, patching some of your language into someone else's writing.* Patchwriting is a form of academic dishonesty because you aren't fully composing your own sentences and thus misrepresent both your own work and that of the source writer. An acceptable paraphrase needs to be entirely in your own words. To understand patchwriting more fully, track the differences between unacceptable patchwriting and acceptable paraphrase in the following examples.

ORIGINAL

- The evidence is "strong" that vegetarians have (a) a lower risk of becoming alcoholic, constipated, or obese and (b) a lower risk of developing lung cancer.
- The evidence is "good" that vegetarians have a lower risk of developing adult-onset diabetes mellitus, coronary artery disease, hypertension, and gallstones.

UNACCEPTABLE PATCHWRITING

Identification of source

Note phrases taken word for word from original.

According to the American Council on Science and Health, there is strong evidence that vegetarians have a lower risk of becoming alcoholic, constipated, or obese. The evidence is also strong that they have a lower risk of lung cancer. The evidence is good that vegetarians are less apt to develop adult-onset diabetes, coronary artery disease, hypertension, or gallstones.

ACCEPTABLE PARAPHRASE

Identification of source Doesn't follow original sentence structure

Quotes "strong" and "good" to indicate distinction made in original

The Council summarizes "strong" evidence from the scientific literature showing that vegetarians have reduced risk of lung cancer, obesity, constipation, and alcoholism. The council also cites "good" evidence that they have a reduced risk of adult-onset diabetes, high blood pressure, gallstones, or hardening of the arteries.

Both the patchwriting example and the acceptable paraphrase reproduce the same ideas as the original in approximately the same number of words. But the writer of the acceptable paraphrase has been more careful to change the sentence structure substantially and not copy exact phrases. In contrast, the patchwritten version contains longer strings of borrowed language without quotation marks.

Among novice writers, the ease of copying Web sources can particularly lead to patchwriting. You may be tempted to copy and paste a Web-based passage into your own draft and then revise it slightly by changing some of the words. Such patchwriting won't occur if you write in your own voice—that is, if you convert information from a source into your own words in order to make your own argument.

*We are indebted to the work of Rebecca Moore Howard and others who have led composition researchers to reexamine the use of sources and plagiarism from a cultural and rhetorical perspective. See especially Rebecca Moore Howard, *Standing in the Shadow of Giants: Plagiarists, Authors, Collaborators*. Stamford, CT: Ablex Pub., 1999.

When you first practice paraphrasing, try paraphrasing a passage twice to avoid patchwriting:

- The first time, read the passage carefully and put it into your own words, looking at the source as little as possible.
- The second time, paraphrase your own paraphrase. Then recheck your final version against the original to make sure you have eliminated similar sentence structures or word-for-word strings.

We'll return to the problem of patchwriting in our discussion of plagiarism (Skill 22.4).

Quoting

Besides summary and paraphrase, writers often choose to quote directly in order to give the reader the flavor and style of the source author's prose or to make a memorable point in the source author's own voice. Be careful not to quote a passage that you don't fully understand. (Sometimes novice writers quote a passage because it sounds impressive.) When you quote, you must reproduce the source author's original words exactly without change, unless you indicate changes with ellipses or brackets. Also be careful to represent the author's intention and meaning fairly; don't change the author's meaning by taking quotations out of context.

Because the mechanics of quoting offers its own difficulties, we devote the following sections to it. These sections answer the nuts-and-bolts questions about how to punctuate quotations correctly. Additional explanations covering variations and specific cases can be found in any good handbook.

Quoting a Complete Sentence In some cases, you will want to quote a complete sentence from your source. Typically, you will include an attributive tag that tells the reader who is being quoted (Skill 22.3). At the end of the quotation, you usually indicate its page number in parentheses (see our discussion of in-text citations, Chapter 23).

ORIGINAL PASSAGE

Many people become vegetarians because they believe, in error, that vegetarianism is uniquely conducive to good health. [found on page 543 of source].*

WRITER'S QUOTATION OF THIS PASSAGE

According to the American Council on Science and Health, "Many people become vegetarians because they believe, in error, that vegetarianism is uniquely conducive to good health" (543).

Attributive tag

Quotation introduced with comma. Quotation is a complete sentence, so it starts with a capital letter.

Page number from source; period comes after parentheses.

Final quotation mark goes before parentheses.

*The cited page is from this text. When quoting from print sources or other sources with stable page numbers, you indicate the page number as part of your citation. To illustrate how to punctuate page citations, we'll assume throughout this section that you found the American Council on Science and Health article in this textbook rather than on the Web, in which case it would not be possible to cite page numbers.

Quoting Words and Phrases Instead of quoting a complete sentence, you often want to quote only a few words or phrases from your source and insert them into your own sentence. In these cases, make sure that the grammatical structure of the quotation fits smoothly into the grammar of your own sentence.

ORIGINAL PASSAGE

The health of vegetarians may be better than that of nonvegetarians partly because of nondietary factors: Many vegetarians are health-conscious. They exercise regularly, maintain a desirable body weight, and abstain from smoking. [found on p. 543]

QUOTED PHRASE INSERTED INTO WRITER'S OWN SENTENCE

Attributive tag

Quotation marks show where quotation starts and ends.

No comma or capital letter: Punctuation and capitalization determined by grammar of your own sentence.

Period comes after parentheses containing page number.

The American Council on Science and Health argues that the cause of vegetarians' longer life may be "nondietary factors." The Council claims that vegetarians are more "health-conscious" than meat eaters and that they "exercise regularly, maintain a desirable body weight, and abstain from smoking" (543).

Modifying a Quotation Occasionally you may need to alter a quotation to make it fit your own context. Sometimes the grammar of a desired quotation doesn't match the grammar of your own sentence. At other times, the meaning of a quoted word is unclear when it is removed from its original context. In these cases, use brackets to modify the quotation's grammar or to add a clarifying explanation. Place your changes or additions in brackets to indicate that the bracketed material is not part of the original wording. You should also use brackets to show a change in capitalization.

ORIGINAL PASSAGE

Many vegetarians are health-conscious. They exercise regularly, maintain a desirable body weight, and abstain from smoking. [found on page 543]

QUOTATIONS MODIFIED WITH BRACKETS

Attributive tag

Brackets show change in quotation to fit grammar of writer's sentence.

Page number from source

The American Council on Science and Health hypothesizes that vegetarians maintain better health by "exercis[ing] regularly, maintain[ing] a desirable body weight, and abstain[ing] from smoking" (543).

Attributive tag

Brackets show that writer has added a word to explain what "they" stands for.

According to the American Council on Science and Health, "They [vegetarians] exercise regularly, maintain a desirable body weight, and abstain from smoking" (543).

Omitting Something from a Quoted Passage Another way that writers modify quotations is to leave words out of the quoted passage. To indicate an omission, use three spaced periods called an **ellipsis** (. . .). Placement of the ellipsis depends on where the omitted material occurs. In the middle of a sentence, each of the periods should be preceded and followed by a space. When your ellipsis comes at the boundary between sentences, use an additional period to mark the end of the first sentence. When a parenthetical page number must follow the ellipsis, insert it before the final (fourth) period in the sequence.

ORIGINAL PASSAGE

People who are vegetarians by choice may differ from the general population in other ways relevant to health. For example, in Western countries most vegetarians are more affluent than nonvegetarians and thus have better living conditions and more access to medical care. [found on page 543]

QUOTATIONS WITH OMITTED MATERIAL MARKED BY ELLIPSES

According to the American Council on Science and Health, people who are vegetarians by choice may differ . . . in other ways relevant to health. For example, in Western countries most vegetarians are more affluent than nonvegetarians . . . " (543).

Three spaced periods mark omitted words in middle of sentence. Note spaces between each period.

Three periods form the ellipsis. (Omitted material comes before the end of the sentence.)

This period ends the sentence.

Quoting Something That Contains a Quotation Occasionally a passage that you wish to quote will already contain quotation marks. If you insert the passage within your own quotation marks, change the original double marks (") into single marks (') to indicate the quotation within the quotation. The same procedure works whether the quotation marks are used for quoted words or for a title. Make sure that your attributive tag signals who is being quoted.

ORIGINAL PASSAGE

The evidence is "strong" that vegetarians have (a) a lower risk of becoming alcoholic, constipated, or obese and (b) a lower risk of developing lung cancer. [found on page 543]

USE OF SINGLE QUOTATION MARKS TO IDENTIFY A QUOTATION WITHIN A QUOTATION

According to the American Council on Science and Health, "The evidence is 'strong' that vegetarians have (a) a lower risk of becoming alcoholic, constipated, or obese and (b) a lower risk of developing lung cancer" (543).

Single quotation marks replace the double quotation marks in the original source.

Double quotation marks enclose the material quoted from the source.

Using a Block Quotation for a Long Passage If you quote a long source passage that will take four or more lines in your own paper, use the block indentation method rather than quotation marks. Block quotations are generally introduced with an attributive tag followed by a colon. The indented block of text, rather than quotation marks, signals that the material is a direct quotation. As we explained earlier, block quotations occur rarely in scholarly writing and are used primarily in cases where the writer intends to analyze the text being quoted. If you overuse block quotations, you simply produce a collage of other people's voices.

ORIGINAL PASSAGE

The health of vegetarians may be better than that of nonvegetarians partly because of nondietary factors: Many vegetarians are health-conscious. They exercise regularly, maintain a desirable body weight, and abstain from smoking. Although most epidemiologists have attempted to take such factors into account in their analyses, it is possible that they did not adequately control their studies for nondietary effects. [found on page 543]

BLOCK QUOTATION

Block quotation introduced with a colon

No quotation marks

Block indented 1 inch on left

Page number in parentheses after the closing period preceded by a space.

The American Council on Science and Health suggests that vegetarians may be healthier than nonvegetarians not because of their diet but because of their more healthy lifestyle:

> Many vegetarians are health-conscious. They exercise regularly, maintain a desirable body weight, and abstain from smoking. Although most epidemiologists have attempted to take such factors into account in their analyses, it is possible that they did not adequately control their studies for nondietary effects. (543)

22.3 Use attributive tags to distinguish your ideas from a source's.

SKILL 22.3 Use attributive tags to distinguish your ideas from a source's.

Whenever you use sources in your writing, you need to signal to your reader which words and ideas come from your source and which are your own. There are generally two ways of doing so:

- ***State source author's name in an attributive tag.*** You can identify the source by using a short phrase (called an **attributive tag** or sometimes a **signal phrase** or **signal tag**) such as "according to the American Council on Science and Health," "Kent Ansen says," "in Ansen's view," and so on. In the humanities, the source author's full name is commonly used the first time the author is mentioned. If the tag refers to a specific passage or quotation in the source, then a page number is placed in parentheses at the end of the quotation (see Skill 22.2).

Attributive tag

According to Kent Ansen, a year of public service should be required of all American young adults.

tag

ber of

Ansen explains that "mandated national service could be built upon the model of AmeriCorps" (406).

- ***State source author's name in a parenthetical citation.*** You can identify a source by placing the author's name in parentheses at the end of the material taken from the source (called a **parenthetical citation**).

> A year of public service should be required of all American young adults (Ansen).
>
> "Mandated national service could be built upon the model of AmeriCorps" (Ansen 406).

Source identified in parentheses

Page number of quotation

Of these two methods, attributive tags are generally preferred, especially when you are writing for general rather than specialist audiences. The attributive tag method has three advantages:

- It signals where borrowed material starts and ends.
- It avoids ambiguities about what is "fact" versus what is filtered through a source's angle of vision.
- It allows the writer to frame the borrowed material rhetorically.

Let's look at each of these in turn.

Attributive Tags Mark Where Source Material Starts and Ends

The parenthetical method requires readers to wait until the end of the writer's use of source material before the source is identified. Attributive tags, in contrast, identify the source from the moment it is first used. Here are excerpts from Writer 2's summary of the American Council on Science and Health's article, in which we have highlighted the attributive tags. Note the frequency with which the writer informs the reader that this material comes from the Council. (The complete passage from Writer 2 appears on p. 545.)

USE OF ATTRIBUTIVE TAGS IN WRITER 2'S SUMMARY

> Not only will a vegetarian diet help stop cruelty to animals, but it is also good for your health. According to the American Council on Science and Health, vegetarians have longer life expectancy than nonvegetarians and suffer from fewer chronic diseases. The Council cites "strong" evidence from the scientific literature showing that vegetarians have reduced risk of lung cancer, obesity, constipation, and alcoholism. They also cite "good" evidence that they have a reduced risk of adult-onset diabetes, high blood pressure, gallstones, or hardening of the arteries....

Here the attributive tags signal the use of the Council's ideas throughout the summary. The reader is never confused about which words and ideas come from the original article.

Attributive Tags Avoid Ambiguities that Can Arise with Parenthetical Citations

Not only does the parenthetical method fail to mark where the source material begins, it also tends to imply that the source material is a "fact" rather than the view of the source author. In contrast, attributive tags always call attention to the source's angle of vision. Note this ambiguity in the following passage, where parenthetical citations are used without attributive tags:

AMBIGUOUS ATTRIBUTIONS

> There are many arguments in favor of preserving old-growth forests. First, it is simply unnecessary to log these forests to supply the world's lumber. We have plenty of new-growth forest from which lumber can be taken (Sagoff 89–90). Recently there have been major reforestation efforts all over the United States, and it common practice now for loggers to replant every tree that is harvested. These new-growth forests, combined with extensive planting of tree farms, provide more than enough wood for the world's needs. Tree farms alone can supply the world's demand for industrial lumber (Sedjo 90).

When confronted with this passage, skeptical readers might ask, "Who are Sagoff and Sedjo? I've never heard of them." It is also difficult to tell how much of the passage is the writer's own argument and how much is borrowed from Sagoff and Sedjo. Is this whole passage a paraphrase? Finally, the writer tends to treat Sagoff's and Sedjo's assertions as uncontested facts rather than as professional opinions. Compare the preceding version with this one, in which attributive tags are added:

CLEAR ATTRIBUTION

> There are many arguments in favor of preserving old-growth forests. First, it is simply unnecessary to log these forests to supply the world's lumber. According to environmentalist Carl Sagoff, we have plenty of new-growth forest from which lumber can be taken (89–90). Recently there have been major reforestation efforts all over the United States, and it is common practice now for loggers to replant every tree that is harvested. These new-growth forests, combined with extensive planting of tree farms, provide more than enough wood for the world's needs. According to forestry expert Robert Sedjo, tree farms alone can supply the world's demand for industrial lumber (90).

We can now see that most of the paragraph is the writer's own argument, into which she has inserted the expert testimony of Sagoff and Sedjo, whose views are treated not as indisputable facts but as the opinions of authorities in this field.

Attributive Tags Frame the Source Material Rhetorically

When you introduce a source for the first time, you can use the attributive tag not only to introduce the source but also to shape your readers's attitudes toward the source. In the previous example, the writer wants readers to respect Sagoff and Sedjo, so she identifies Sagoff as an "environmentalist" and Sedjo as a "forestry expert." If the writer favored logging old-growth forests and supported the logging industry's desire to create more jobs, she might have used different tags: "Carl Sagoff, an outspoken advocate for spotted owls over people," or "Robert Sedjo, a forester with limited knowledge of world lumber markets."

When you compose an initial tag, you can add to it any combination of the following kinds of information, depending on your purpose, your audience's values, and your sense of what the audience already knows or doesn't know about the source:

Strategies for Modifying Attributive Tags to Shape Reader Response

Add to Attributive Tags	Examples
Author's credentials or relevant specialty (enhances credibility)	Civil engineer David Rockwood, a noted authority on stream flow in rivers
Author's lack of credentials (decreases credibility)	City Council member Dilbert Weasel, a local politician with no expertise in international affairs
Author's political or social views	Left-wing columnist Alexander Cockburn [has negative feeling]; Alexander Cockburn, a longtime champion of labor [has positive feeling]
Title of source if it provides context	In her book *Fasting Girls: The History of Anorexia Nervosa,* Joan Jacobs Brumberg shows that [establishes credentials for comments on eating disorders]
Publisher of source if it adds prestige or otherwise shapes audience response	Dr. Carl Patrona, in an article published in the prestigious *New England Journal of Medicine*
Historical or cultural information about a source that provides context or background	In his 1960s book popularizing the hippie movement, Charles Reich claims that
Indication of source's purpose or angle of vision	Feminist author Naomi Wolfe, writing a blistering attack on the beauty industry, argues that

Our point here is that you can use attributive tags rhetorically to help your readers understand the significance and context of a source when you first introduce it and to guide your readers' attitudes toward the source.

FOR WRITING AND DISCUSSION

Evaluating Different Ways to Use and Cite a Source

What follow are four different ways that a writer can use the same passage from a source to support a point about the greenhouse effect. Working in groups or as a whole class, rank the four methods from "most effective" to "least effective." Assume that you are writing a researched argument addressed to your college classmates.

1. ***Quotation with parenthetical citation*** The greenhouse effect will have a devastating effect on the earth's environment: "Potential impacts include increased mortality and illness due to heat stress and worsened air pollution, as in the 1995 Chicago heat wave that killed hundreds of people. ... Infants, children and other vulnerable populations—especially in already-stressed regions of the world—would likely suffer disproportionately from these impacts" (Hall 19).
2. ***Quotation with attributive tag*** The greenhouse effect will have a devastating effect on the earth's environment. David C. Hall, president of Physicians for Social Responsibility, claims the following: "Potential impacts include increased mortality and illness due to heat stress and worsened air pollution, as in the 1995 Chicago heat wave that killed hundreds of people. ... Infants, children and other vulnerable populations—especially in already-stressed regions of the world—would likely suffer disproportionately from these impacts" (19).
3. ***Paraphrase with parenthetical citation*** The greenhouse effect will have a devastating effect on the earth's environment. One of the most frightening effects is the threat of diseases stemming from increased air pollution and heat stress. Infants and children would be most at risk (Hall 19).
4. ***Paraphrase with attributive tag*** The greenhouse effect will have a devastating effect on the earth's environment. One of the most frightening effects, according to David C. Hall, president of Physicians for Social Responsibility, is the threat of diseases stemming from increased air pollution and heat stress. Infants and Children would be most at risk (19).

22.4 Avoid plagiarism by following academic conventions for ethical use of sources.

SKILL 22.4 Avoid plagiarism by following academic conventions for ethical use of sources.

In the next chapter, we proceed to the nuts and bolts of citing and documenting sources—a skill that will enhance your *ethos* as a skilled researcher and as a person of integrity. Unethical use of sources—called **plagiarism**—is a major concern not only for writing teachers but for teachers in all disciplines. To combat plagiarism, many instructors across the curriculum use plagiarism-detection software like turnitin.com. Their purpose, of course, is to discourage students from cheating. But sometimes students who have no intention of cheating can fall into producing papers that look like cheating. That is, they produce papers that might be accused of plagiarism even though the students had no intention of deceiving their readers.* Our goal in this section is to explain the concept of plagiarism more fully and to sum up the strategies needed to avoid it.

Why Some Kinds of Plagiarism May Occur Unwittingly

To understand how unwitting plagiarism might occur, consider Table 22.1, where the middle column—"Misuse of Sources"—shows common mistakes of novice writers. Everyone agrees that the behaviors in the "Fraud" column constitute deliberate cheating and deserve appropriate punishment. Everyone also agrees that good scholarly work meets the criteria in the "Ethical Use of Sources" column. Novice researchers, however, may find themselves unwittingly in the middle column until they learn the academic community's conventions for using research sources.

You might appreciate these conventions more fully if you recognize how they have evolved from Western notions of intellectual property and patent law associated with the rise of modern science in the seventeenth and eighteenth centuries. A person not only could own a house or a horse, but also could own an idea and the words used to express that idea. You can see these cultural conventions at work—in the form of laws or professional codes of ethics—whenever a book author is disgraced for lifting words or ideas from another author or whenever an artist or entrepreneur is sued for stealing song lyrics, publishing another person's photographs without permission, or infringing on some inventor's patent.

TABLE 22.1 Plagiarism and the Ethical Use of Sources

Plagiarism		Ethical Use of Sources
Fraud	**Misuse of Sources *(Common Mistakes Made by New Researchers)***	
The writer • buys paper from a paper mill • submits someone else's work as his own • copies chunks of text from sources with obvious intention of not being detected • fabricates data or makes up evidence • intends to deceive	The writer • copies passages directly from a source, references the source with an in-text citation, but fails to use quotation marks or block indentation • in attempting to paraphrase a source, makes some changes, but follows too closely the wording of the original ("patchwriting") • fails to indicate the sources of some ideas or data (often is unsure what needs to be cited or has lost track of sources through poor note taking) • in general, misunderstands the conventions for using sources in academic writing	The writer • writes paper entirely in her own words or uses exact quotations from sources • indicates all quotations with quotation marks or block indentation • indicates her use of all sources through attribution, in-text citation, and an end-of-paper list of works cited

*See Rebecca Moore Howard, *Standing in the Shadow of Giants: Plagiarists, Authors, Collaborators.* Stamford, CT: Ablex Pub., 1999.

This understanding of plagiarism may seem odd in some non-Western cultures where collectivism is valued more than individualism. In these cultures, words written or spoken by ancestors, elders, or other authority figures may be regarded with reverence and shared with others without attribution. Also in these cultures, it might be disrespectful to paraphrase certain passages or to document them in a way that would suggest the audience didn't recognize the ancient wisdom.

However, such collectivist conventions won't work in research communities committed to building new knowledge. In the academic world, the conventions separating ethical from unethical use of sources are essential if research findings are to win the community's confidence. Effective research can occur only within ethical and responsible research communities, where people do not fabricate data and where current researchers respect and acknowledge the work of those who have gone before them.

Strategies for Avoiding Plagiarism

The following chart will help you review the strategies presented throughout Chapters 20 to 23 for using source material ethically and avoiding plagiarism.

Strategies for Avoiding Plagiarism or the Appearance of Plagiarism

What to Do	Why to Do It	Where to Find More Information
	At the beginning	
Read your college's policy on plagiarism as well as statements from your teachers in class or on course syllabi.	Understanding policies on plagiarism and academic integrity will help you research and write ethically.	Chapter 20, p. 509
Pose a research question rather than a topic area.	Arguing your own thesis gives you a voice, establishes your *ethos,* and urges you to write ethically.	Skill 20.1
	At the note-taking stage	
Create a bibliographic entry for each source.	This action makes it easy to create an end-of-paper bibliography and encourages rhetorical reading.	Skill 21.1
When you copy a passage into your notes, copy word for word and enclose it within quotation marks.	It is important to distinguish a source's words from your own words.	Skill 21.1

What to Do	Why to Do It	Where to Find More Information
When you enter summaries or paraphrases into your notes, avoid patchwriting.	If your notes contain any strings of a source's original wording, you might later assume that these words are your own.	Skill 21.1 Skill 22.2
Distinguish your informational notes from your personal exploratory notes.	Keeping these kinds of notes separate will help you identify borrowed ideas when it's time to incorporate the source material into your paper.	Skill 21.1
	When writing your draft	
Except for exact quotations, write the paper entirely in your own words.	This strategy keeps you from patchwriting when you summarize or paraphrase.	Skill 22.2
Indicate all quotations with quotation marks or block indentation. Use ellipses or brackets to make changes to fit your own grammar.	Be careful to represent the author fairly; don't change meaning by taking quotations out of context.	Skill 22.2
When you summarize or paraphrase, avoid patchwriting.	Word-for-word strings from a source must either be avoided or placed in quotation marks. Also avoid mirroring the source's grammatical structure.	Skill 22.2
Never cut and paste a Web passage directly into your draft. Paste it into a separate note file and put quotation marks around it.	Pasted passages are direct invitations to patchwrite.	Skill 22.2
Inside your text, use attributive tags or parenthetical citations to identify all sources. List all sources alphabetically in a concluding works cited or References list.	This strategy makes it easy for readers to know when you are using a source and where to find it.	Skill 22.3 Skill 23.1
Cite with attributive tags or parenthetical citations all quotations, paraphrases, summaries, and any other references to specific sources.	These are the most common in-text citations in a research paper.	Skill 23.1 Skill 23.2

(continued)

What to Do	Why to Do It	Where to Find More Information
Use in-text citations to indicate sources for all visuals and media such as graphs, maps, photographs, films, videos, broadcasts, and recordings.	The rules for citing words and ideas apply equally to visuals and media cited in your paper.	Skill 23.1
Use in-text citations for all ideas and facts that are not common knowledge.	Although you don't need to cite widely accepted and noncontroversial facts and information, it is better to cite them if you are unsure.	Skill 23.1

FOR WRITING AND DISCUSSION

Avoiding Plagiarism

Reread the original article from the American Council on Science and Health (pp. 543–544) and Writer 3's use of this source in her paragraph about how nondietary habits may explain why vegetarians are healthier than nonvegetarians (pp. 545). Then read the paragraph below by Writer 4, who makes the same argument as Writer 3 but crosses the line from ethical to nonethical use of sources. Why might Writer 4 be accused of plagiarism?

WRITER 4'S ARGUMENT (EXAMPLE OF PLAGIARISM)

According to the American Council on Science and Health, the health of vegetarians may be better than that of nonvegetarians partly because of nondietary factors. People who eat only vegetables tend to be very conscious of their health. They exercise regularly, avoid getting fat, and don't smoke. Scientists who examined the data may not have adequately controlled for these nondietary effects. Also in Western countries most vegetarians are more affluent than nonvegetarians and thus have better living conditions and more access to medical care.

Working in small groups or as a whole class, respond to the following questions.

1. How does this passage cross the line into plagiarism?
2. The writer of this passage might say, "How can this be plagiarism? I cited my source." How would you explain the problem to this writer?
3. Psychologically or cognitively, what may have caused Writer 4 to misuse the source? How might this writer's note-taking process or composing process have differed from that of Writer 3 on page 545? In other words, what happened to get this writer into trouble?

CITING AND DOCUMENTING SOURCES

23

WHAT YOU WILL LEARN

23.1 To know what needs to be cited and what doesn't.
23.2 To understand the connection between in-text citations and the end-of-paper list of cited works.
23.3 To cite and document sources using MLA style.
23.4 To cite and document sources using APA style.

In the previous chapter we explained how to incorporate sources into your writing; in this chapter we focus on the nuts and bolts of documenting those sources in a way appropriate to your purpose, audience, and genre, using the systems of the Modern Language Association (MLA) and the American Psychological Association (APA).* Accurate documentation not only helps other researchers locate your sources but also contributes substantially to your own *ethos* as a writer.

SKILL 23.1 Know what needs to be cited and what doesn't.

23.1 Know what needs to be cited and what doesn't.

Beginning researchers are often confused about what needs to be cited and what doesn't. Table 23.1 will help you make this determination. If you are in doubt, it is better to cite than not to cite.

It is often difficult to determine when a given piece of information falls into the "common knowledge" column of Table 23.1. The answer depends both on your target audience's background knowledge and on your own ability to speak as an authority. Consider the statement "Twitter and Facebook are forms of social networking." That information is noncontroversial and well known and so doesn't require citation. But if you added, "Twitter is more popular with middle-aged adults than with teenagers," you would need to cite your source (some newspaper article or poll?) unless you are a teenager speaking with authority from your own experience, in which case you would provide personal-experience examples. If you are uncertain, our best advice is this: When in doubt, cite.

*Our discussion of MLA style is based on the *MLA Handbook for Writers of Research Papers*, 7th ed. (2009). Our discussion of APA style is based on the *Publication Manual of the American Psychological Association*, 6th ed. (2010) and the *APA Style Guide to Electronic References* (2013).

TABLE 23.1 Determining What Needs to Be Cited

What Needs to Be Cited	What Does Not Need to Be Cited
You must cite all uses of your research sources as well as any information that is not commonly known by your targeted audience: • Any quotation • Any passage that you paraphrase • Any passage or source that you summarize or otherwise refer to • Any image, photograph, map, drawing, graph, chart, or other visual that you download from the Web (or find elsewhere) and include in your paper • Any sound or video file that you use in a multimedia project • Any idea, fact, statistic, or other information that you find from a source and that is not commonly known by your targeted audience	You do not need to cite commonly shared, widely known knowledge that will be considered factual and noncontroversial to your targeted audience: • Commonly known facts (Water freezes at 32 degrees Fahrenheit.) • Commonly known dates (Terrorists flew airplanes into New York's World Trade Center on September 11, 2001.) • Commonly known events (Barack Obama defeated Mitt Romney for the presidency.) • Commonly known historical or cultural knowledge (Twitter and Facebook are forms of social networking.)

23.2 Understand the connection between in-text citations and the end-of-paper list of cited works.

SKILL 23.2 Understand the connection between in-text citations and the end-of-paper list of cited works.

The most common forms of documentation use what are called in-text citations that match an end-of-paper list of cited works (as opposed to footnotes or endnotes). An ***in-text citation*** identifies a source in the body of the paper at the point where it is summarized, paraphrased, quoted, inserted, or otherwise referred to. At the end of your paper you include a list—alphabetized by author (or by title if there is no named author)—of all the works you cited. Both the Modern Language Association (MLA) system, used primarily in the humanities, and the American Psychological Association (APA) system, used primarily in the social sciences, follow this procedure. In MLA, your end-of-paper list is called **Works Cited.** In APA it is called **References.**

Whenever you place an in-text citation in the body of your paper, your reader knows to turn to the Works Cited or References list at the end of the paper to get the full bibliographic information. The key to the system's logic is this:

- Every source in Works Cited or References must be mentioned in the body of the paper.
- Conversely, every source mentioned in the body of the paper must be included in the end-of-paper list.
- The first word in each entry of the Works Cited or References list (usually an author's last name) must also appear in the in-text citation. In other words, there must be a one-to-one correspondence between the first word in each entry in the end-of-paper list and the name used to identify the source in the body of the paper.

Suppose a reader sees this phrase in your paper: "According to Debra Goldstein...." The reader should be able to turn to your Works Cited list and find an alphabetized entry beginning with "Goldstein, Debra." Similarly, suppose that in looking over your Works Cited list, your reader sees an article by "Guillen, Manuel." This means that the name "Guillen" has to appear in your paper in one of two ways:

For more on attributive tags, see Skill 22.3.

- As an attributive tag: Economics professor Manuel Guillen argues that....
- As a parenthetical citation, often following a quotation: "...changes in fiscal policy" (Guillen 49).

Because this one-to-one correspondence is so important, let's illustrate it with some complete examples using the MLA formatting style:

If the body of your paper has this:	Then the Works Cited list must have this:
According to linguist Deborah Tannen, political debate in America leaves out the complex middle ground where most solutions must be developed.	Tannen, Deborah. *The Argument Culture: Moving from Debate to Dialogue*. New York: Random, 1998. Print.
In the 1980s, cigarette advertising revealed a noticeable pattern of racial stereotyping (Pollay, Lee, and Carter-Whitney).	Pollay, Richard W., Jung S. Lee, and David Carter-Whitney. "Separate, but Not Equal: Racial Segmentation in Cigarette Advertising." *Journal of Advertising* 21.1 (1992): 45–57. Print.
On its Web site, the National Men's Resource Center offers advice to parents on how to talk with children about alcohol and drugs ("Talking").	"Talking with Kids about Alcohol and Drugs." *Menstuff*. National Men's Resource Center, 1 Mar. 2007. Web. 26 June 2013.

How to format an MLA in-text citation and a Works Cited list entry is the subject of the next section. The APA system is similar except that it emphasizes the date of publication in both the in-text citation and the References entry. APA formatting is the subject of Skill 23.4.

SKILL 23.3 **Cite and document sources using MLA style.**

23.3 Cite and document sources using MLA style.

An in-text citation and its corresponding Works Cited entry are linked in a chicken-and-egg system: You can't cite a source in the text without first knowing how the source's entry will be alphabetized in the Works Cited list. However, since most Works Cited entries are alphabetized by the first author's last name, for convenience we start with in-text citations.

In-Text Citations in MLA Style

A typical in-text citation contains two elements: (1) the last name of the author and (2) the page number of the quoted or paraphrased passage. However, in some cases a work is identified by something other than an author's last name, and sometimes no page number is required. Let's begin with the most common cases.

Typically, an in-text citation uses one of these two methods:

- ***Parenthetical method.*** Place the author's last name and the page number in parentheses immediately after the material being cited.

  > The Spanish tried to reduce the status of Filipina women who had been able to do business, get divorced, and sometimes become village chiefs (Karnow 41).

- ***Attributive tag method.*** Place the author's name in an attributive tag at the beginning of the source material and the page number in parentheses at the end.

  > According to Karnow, the Spanish tried to reduce the status of Filipina women, who had been able to do business, get divorced, and sometimes become village chiefs (41).

Once you have cited an author and it is clear that the same author's material is being used, you need cite only the page numbers in parentheses in subsequent citations. A reader who wishes to look up the source will find the bibliographic information in the Works Cited section by looking for the entry under "Karnow."

Let's now turn to the variations. Table 23.2 identifies the typical variations and shows again the one-to-one connection between the in-text citation and the Works Cited list.

TABLE 23.2 In-Text Citations in MLA Style

Type of Source	Works Cited Entry at End of Paper (*Construct the entry while taking notes on each source.*)	In-Text Citation in Body of Paper (*Use the first word of the Works Cited entry in parentheses or an attributive tag; add page number at end of quoted or paraphrased passage.*)
One author	Pollan, Michael. *The Omnivore's Dilemma: A Natural History of Four Meals*. New York: Penguin, 2006. Print.	...(Pollan 256). OR According to Pollan, ...(256).
More than one author	Pollay, Richard W., Jung S. Lee, and David Carter-Whitney. "Separate, but Not Equal: Racial Segmentation in Cigarette Advertising." *Journal of Advertising* 21.1 (1992): 45–57. Print.	...race" (Pollay, Lee, and Carter-Whitney 52). OR Pollay, Lee, and Carter-Whitney have argued that "advertisers...race" (52). *For the in-text citation, cite the specific page number rather than the whole range of pages given in the Works Cited entry.*

TABLE 23.2 ***continued***

Type of Source	Works Cited Entry at End of Paper (*Construct the entry while taking notes on each source.*)	In-Text Citation in Body of Paper (*Use the first word of the Works Cited entry in parentheses or an attributive tag; add page number at end of quoted or paraphrased passage.*)
Author has more than one work in Works Cited list	Dombrowski, Daniel A. *Babies and Beasts: The Argument from Marginal Cases*. Urbana: U of Illinois P, 1997. Print. ---. *The Philosophy of Vegetarianism*. Amherst: U of Massachusetts P, 1984. Print.	. . . (Dombrowski, *Babies* 207). . . . (Dombrowski, *Philosophy* 328). OR According to Dombrowski, . . . (*Babies* 207). Dombrowski claims that . . . (*Philosophy* 328). *Because author has more than one work in Works Cited, include a short version of title to distinguish between entries.*
Corporate author	American Red Cross. *Standard First Aid*. St. Louis: Mosby Lifeline, 1993. Print.	. . . (American Red Cross 102). OR Snake bite instructions from the American Red Cross show that . . . (102).
No named author (Work is therefore alphabetized by title.)	"Ouch! Body Piercing." *Menstuff*. National Men's Resource Center, n.d. Web. 17 July 2013.	. . . ("Ouch!"). According to the National Men's Resource Center, . . . ("Ouch!"). • *Add "Ouch!" in parentheses to show that work is alphabetized under "Ouch!" not "National."* • *No page numbers are shown because Web site pages aren't stable. "n.d." state for "no date."*
Indirect citation of a source that you found in another source *Suppose you want to use a quotation from Peter Singer that you found in a book by Daniel Dombrowski. Include Dombrowski but not Singer in Works Cited.*	Dombrowski, Daniel A. *Babies and Beasts: The Argument from Marginal Cases*. Urbana: U of Illinois P, 1997. Print.	Animal rights activist Peter Singer argues that . . . (qtd. in Dombrowski 429). • *Singer is used for the attributive tag, but the in-text citation is to Dombrowski.* • *"qtd. in" stands for "quoted in."*

When to Use Page Numbers in In-Text Citations When the materials you are citing are available in print or in .pdf format, you can provide accurate page numbers for parenthetical citations. If you are working with Web sources or HTML files, however, do not use the page numbers obtained from a printout because they will not be consistent from printer to printer. If the item has numbered paragraphs, cite them with the abbreviation *par.* or *pars.*—for example,

"(Jones, pars. 22–24)." In the absence of reliable page numbers for the original material, MLA says to omit page references from the parenthetical citation. The following chart summarizes the use of page numbers in in-text citations.

Include a page number in the in-text citation:	**Do not include a page number:**
If the source has stable page numbers (print source or .pdf version of print source): • If you quote something • If you paraphrase a specific passage • If you refer to data or details from a specific page or range of pages in the source	• If you are referring to the argument of the whole source instead of a specific page or passage • If the source does not have stable page numbers (articles on Web sites, HTML text, and so forth)

Works Cited List in MLA Style

In the MLA system, you place a complete Works Cited list at the end of the paper. The list includes all the sources that you mention in your paper. However, it does *not* include works you read but did not use. Entries in the Works Cited list follow these general guidelines:

- Entries are arranged alphabetically by author, or by title if there is no author.
- Each entry includes the medium of publication of the source you consulted—for example, *Print, Web, DVD, Performance, Oil on canvas,* and so on.
- If there is more than one entry per author, the works are arranged alphabetically by title. For the second and all additional entries, type three hyphens and a period in place of the author's name.

Dombrowski, Daniel A. *Babies and Beasts: The Argument from Marginal Cases.* Urbana: U of Illinois P, 1997. Print.

---. *The Philosophy of Vegetarianism.* Amherst: U of Massachusetts P, 1984. Print.

You can see a complete, properly formatted Works Cited list on the last pages of Kent Ansen's paper (pp. 405–414).

The remaining pages in this section show examples of MLA citation formats for different kinds of sources and provide explanations and illustrations as needed.

MLA Citation Models

To see what citations look like when typed in a research paper, see Kent Ansen's Works Cited list on p. 414.

Print Articles in Scholarly Journals

General Format for Print Article in Scholarly Journal

Author. "Article Title." *Journal Title* volume number.issue number (year): page numbers. Print.

Note that all scholarly journal entries include both volume number and issue number, regardless of how the journal is paginated. For scholarly journal articles retrieved from an online database, see page 570. For articles published in a Web-only e-journal, see page 573.

One author

Herrera-Sobek, Maria. "Border Aesthetics: The Politics of Mexican Immigration in Film and Art." *Western Humanities Review* 60.2 (2006): 60–71. Print.

Two or three authors

Pollay, Richard W., Jung S. Lee, and David Carter-Whitney. "Separate, but Not Equal: Racial Segmentation in Cigarette Advertising." *Journal of Advertising* 21.1 (1992): 45–57. Print.

Four or more authors

Either list all the authors in the order in which they appear, or use "et al." (meaning "and others") to replace all but the first author.

Buck, Gayle A., et al. "Examining the Cognitive Processes Used by Adolescent Girls and Women Scientists in Identifying Science Role Models: A Feminist Approach." *Science Education* 92.4 (2008): 688–707. Print.

Print Articles in Magazines and Newspapers

If no author is identified, begin the entry with the title or headline. Distinguish between news stories and editorials by putting the word "Editorial" after the title. If a magazine comes out weekly or biweekly, include the complete date ("27 Sept. 2013"). If it comes out monthly, then state the month only ("Sept. 2013").

General Format for Magazines and Newspapers

Author. "Article Title." *Magazine Title* day Month year: page numbers. Print.

Note: If the article continues in another part of the magazine or newspaper, add "+" to the number of the first page to indicate the nonsequential pages.

Magazine article with named author

Snyder, Rachel L. "A Daughter of Cambodia Remembers: Loung Ung's Journey." *Ms.* Aug.–Sept. 2001: 62–67. Print.

Magazine article without named author

"Sacred Geese." *Economist* 1 June 2013: 24–25. Print.

Review of book, film, or performance

Schwarz, Benjamin. "A Bit of Bunting: A New History of the British Empire Elevates Expediency to Principle." Rev. of *Ornamentalism: How the British Saw Their Empire*, by David Cannadine. *Atlantic Monthly* Nov. 2001: 126–35. Print.

Kaufman, Stanley. "Polishing a Gem." Rev. of *The Blue Angel*, dir. Josef von Sternberg. *New Republic* 30 July 2001: 28–29. Print.

Lahr, John. "Nobody's Darling: Fascism and the Drama of Human Connection in *Ashes to Ashes*." Rev. of *Ashes to Ashes*, by Harold Pinter. The Roundabout Theater Co. Gramercy Theater, New York. *New Yorker* 22 Feb. 1999: 182–83. Print.

Newspaper article

Dougherty, Conor. "The Latest Urban Trend: Less Elbow Room." *Wall Street Journal* 4 June 2013: A1+. Print.

Page numbers in newspapers are typically indicated by a section letter or number as well as a page number. The "+" indicates that the article continues on one or more pages later in the newspaper.

Newspaper editorial

"Dr. Frankenstein on the Hill." Editorial. *New York Times* 18 May 2002, natl. ed.: A22. Print.

Letter to the editor of a magazine or newspaper

Tomsovic, Kevin. Letter. *New Yorker* 13 July 1998: 7. Print.

Print Books

General Format for Print Books

Author. *Title*. City of publication: Publisher, year of publication. Print.

One author

Pollan, Michael. *The Omnivore's Dilemma: A Natural History of Four Meals*. New York: Penguin, 2006. Print.

Two or more authors

Dombrowski, Daniel A., and Robert J. Deltete. *A Brief, Liberal, Catholic Defense of Abortion*. Urbana: U of Illinois P, 2000. Print.

Belenky, Mary, et al. *Women's Ways of Knowing: The Development of Self, Voice, and Mind*. New York: Basic, 1986. Print.

If there are four or more authors, you have the choice of listing all the authors in the order in which they appear on the title page or using "et al." (meaning "and others") to replace all but the first author. Your Works Cited entry and the parenthetical citation should match.

Second, later, or revised edition

Montagu, Ashley. *Touching: The Human Significance of the Skin*. 3rd ed. New York: Perennial, 1986. Print.

In place of "3rd ed.," you can include abbreviations for other kinds of editions: "Rev. ed." (for "Revised edition") or "Abr. ed." (for "Abridged edition").

Republished book (for example, a paperback published after the original hardback edition or a modern edition of an older work)

Hill, Christopher. *The World Turned Upside Down: Radical Ideas During the English Revolution*. 1972. London: Penguin, 1991. Print.

Wollstonecraft, Mary. *The Vindication of the Rights of Woman, with Strictures on Political and Moral Subjects*. 1792. Rutland: Tuttle, 1995. Print.

The date immediately following the title is the original publication date of the work.

Multivolume work

Churchill, Winston S. *A History of the English-Speaking Peoples*. 4 vols. New York: Dodd, 1956–58. Print.

Churchill, Winston S. *The Great Democracies*. New York: Dodd, 1957. Print. Vol. 4 of *A History of the English-Speaking Peoples*. 4 vols. 1956–58.

Use the first method when you cite the whole work; use the second method when you cite one individually titled volume of the work.

Article in familiar reference work

"Mau Mau." *The New Encyclopaedia Britannica*. 15th ed. 2008. Print.

Article in less familiar reference work

Hirsch, E. D., et al. "Kyoto Protocol." *The New Dictionary of Cultural Literacy*. Boston: Houghton Mifflin, 2002. Print.

Translation

De Beauvoir, Simone. *The Second Sex*. 1949. Trans. H. M. Parshley. New York: Bantam, 1961. Print.

Illustrated book

Jacques, Brian. *The Great Redwall Feast*. Illus. Christopher Denise. New York: Philomel, 1996. Print.

Graphic novel

Miyazaki, Hayao. *Nausicaa of the Valley of Wind*. 4 vols. San Francisco: Viz, 1995–97. Print.

Corporate author (a commission, committee, or other group)

American Red Cross. *Standard First Aid*. St. Louis: Mosby Lifeline, 1993. Print.

No author listed

The Complete Cartoons of The New Yorker. New York: Black Dog & Leventhal, 2004. Print.

Whole anthology

O'Connell, David F., and Charles N. Alexander, eds. *Self Recovery: Treating Addictions Using Transcendental Meditation and Maharishi Ayur-Veda*. New York: Haworth, 1994. Print.

Anthology article

Royer, Ann. "The Role of the Transcendental Meditation Technique in Promoting Smoking Cessation: A Longitudinal Study." *Self Recovery: Treating Addictions Using Transcendental Meditation and Maharishi Ayur-Veda*. Ed. David F. O'Connell and Charles N. Alexander. New York: Haworth, 1994. 221–39. Print.

When you cite an individual article, give the inclusive page numbers for the article at the end of the citation, before the medium of publication.

Articles or Books from an Online Database

General Format for Material from Online Databases

Author. "Title." *Periodical Name* Print publication data including date and volume/ issue numbers: pagination. *Database*. Web. Date of access.

Article from online database

Rosenman, Mark. "A Call for National Service." *Chronicle of Philanthropy* 20.1 (18 Oct. 2007). *Academic Search Complete*. Web. 12 Feb. 2013.

To see where each element in this citation was found, see Figure 23.1, which shows the online database screen from which the Rosenman article was accessed. For articles in databases, follow the formats for print newspapers, magazines, or scholarly journals, as relevant. When the database text provides only the starting page number of a multipage article, insert a plus sign after the number, before the period.

Broadcast transcript from online database

Conan, Neal. "Arab Media." *Talk of the Nation*. With Shibley Telhami. 4 May 2004. Transcript. *LexisNexis*. Web. 31 July 2004.

"Transcript" after the broadcast date indicates a text (not audio) version.

E-book from online database

Hanley, Wayne. *The Genesis of Napoleonic Propaganda, 1796–1799*. New York: Columbia UP, 2002. *Gutenberg-e*. Web. 31 July 2010.

Machiavelli, Niccolo. *The Prince*. 1513. *Bibliomania*. Web. 31 July 2013.

Information about the original print version, including a translator if relevant and available, should be provided.

E-book on Kindle, iPad, or other e-reader

Boyle, T. C. *When the Killing's Done*. New York: Viking Penguin, 2011. Kindle file.

Other Internet Sources

General Format for Web Sources Since Web sources are often unstable, MLA recommends that you download or print your Web sources. The goal in

FIGURE 23.1 Article Downloaded from an Online Database, with Elements Identified for an MLA-Style Citation

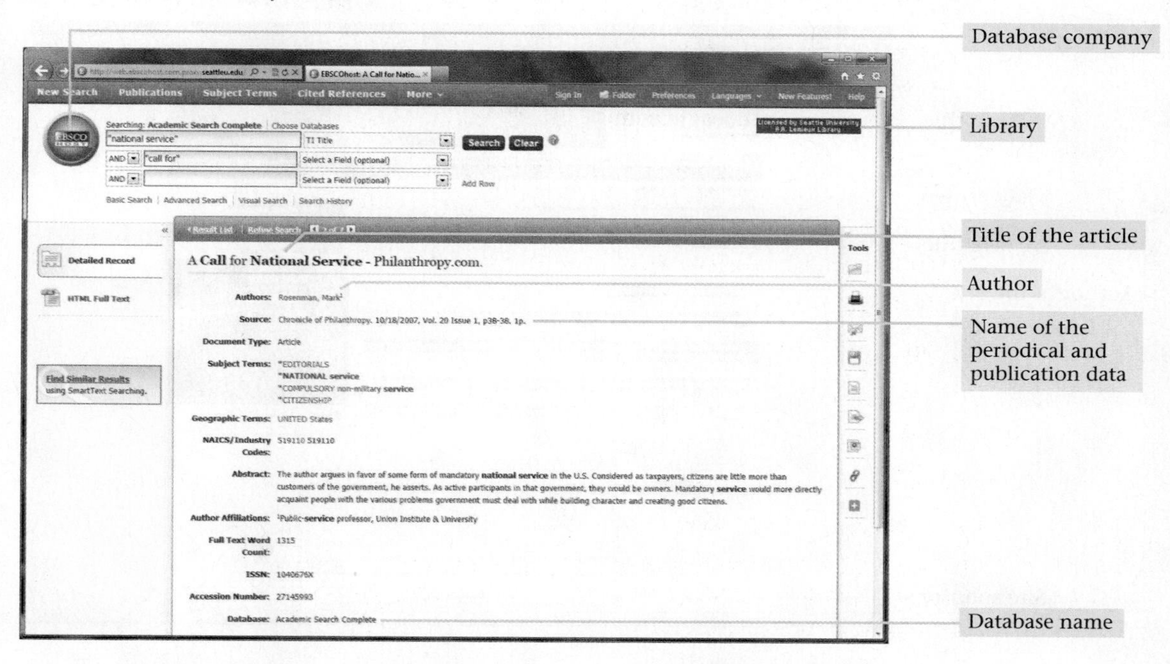

Rosenman, Mark. "A Call for National Service." *Chronicle of Philanthropy* 20.1 (18 Oct. 2007). *Academic Search Complete*. Web. 12 Feb. 2013.

citing these sources is to enable readers to locate the material. To that end, use the basic citation model and adapt it as necessary.

Author, editor, director, narrator, performer, compiler, or producer of the work, if available. *Title of a long work, italicized.* OR "Title of page or document that is part of a larger work, in quotation marks." *Title of the overall site, usually taken from the home page, if this is different from the title of the work*. Publisher or sponsor of the site (if none, use N.p.), day Month year of publication online or last update of the site (if not available, use n.d.). Web. day Month year you accessed the site.

Saucedo, Robert. "A Bad Idea for a Movie." theeagle.com. Bryan College Station Eagle, 1 July 2010. Web. 7 July 2010.

To see where each element of the Saucedo citation comes from, see the Web article in Figure 23.2.

FIGURE 23.2 An Article Published on the Web, with Elements Identified for an MLA-Style Citation

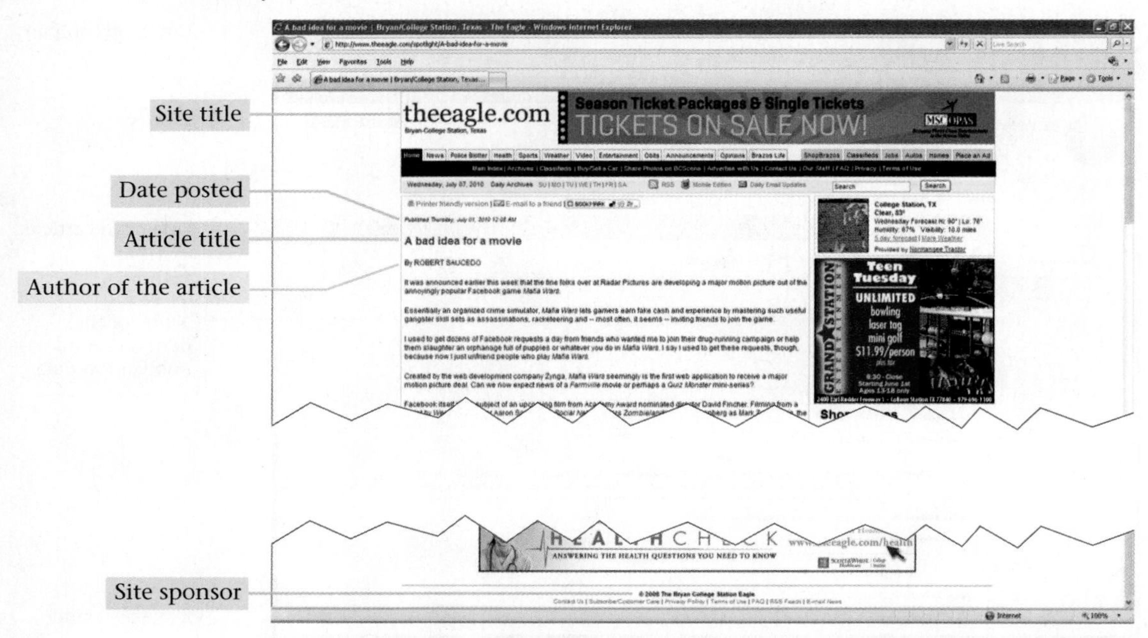

Saucedo, Robert. "A Bad Idea for a Movie." *theeagle.com*. Bryan College Station Eagle, 1 July 2010. Web. 7 July 2010.

MLA assumes that readers will use a search engine to locate a Web source, so do not include a URL *unless* the item would be hard to locate without it. If you do include a URL, it goes at the end of the citation, after the access date. Enclose it in angle brackets <> followed by a period. If you need to break the URL from one line to the next, divide it only after a slash. Do not hyphenate a URL. See the blog entry on page 573 for an example of a citation with a URL.

Entire Web site

BlogPulse. Intelliseek, n.d. Web. 24 July 2012.

Padgett, John B., ed. *William Faulkner on the Web*. U of Mississippi, 26 Mar. 2007. Web. 25 June 2013.

Documents within a Web site

Marks, John. "Overview: Letter from the President." *Search for Common Ground*. Search for Common Ground, n.d. Web. 25 June 2007.

Gourlay, Alexander S. "Glossary." *The William Blake Archive*. Lib. of Cong., 2005. Web. 21 Jan. 2009.

"Ouch! Body Piercing." *Menstuff*. National Men's Resource Center, n.d. Web. 17 July 2013.

Article from a newspaper or newswire site

Bounds, Amy. "Thinking Like Scientists." *Daily Camera* [Boulder]. Scripps Interactive Newspaper Group, 26 June 2007. Web. 26 June 2007.

"Great Lakes: Rwanda Backed Dissident Troops in DRC-UN Panel." *IRIN*. UN Office for the Coordination of Humanitarian Affairs, 21 July 2004. Web. 31 July 2004.

Article from a scholarly e-journal

Welch, John R., and Ramon Riley. "Reclaiming Land and Spirit in the Western Apache Homeland." *American Indian Quarterly* 25.4 (2001): 5–14. Web. 19 Dec. 2012.

Broadcast transcript from a Web site

Woodruff, Judy, Richard Garnett, and Walter Dellinger. "Experts Analyze Supreme Court Free Speech Rulings." Transcript: background and discussion. *Online NewsHour*. PBS, 25 June 2007. Web. 26 June 2007.

Blog posting

Dsyer, Bob, and Ella Barnes. "The 'Greening' of the Arctic." *Greenversations*. U.S. Environmental Protection Agency, 7 Oct. 2008. Web. 11 Oct. 2010. blog.epa.gov/blog/2008/10/07/the-greening-of-the-artic/.

To see where each element of this citation comes from, refer to Figure 23.3.

Social media posting

"Rattlesnake Figure (Aluminum) by Thomas Houseago." *Storm King Art Center*. Facebook, 30 May 2013. Web. 3 June 2013.

Podcast

"The Long and Winding Road: DNA Evidence for Human Migration." *Science Talk*. Scientific American, 7 July 2008. Web. 21 July 2010.

Web video

Beck, Roy. "Immigration Gumballs." *YouTube*. YouTube, 2 Nov. 2006. Web. 23 July 2009.

Home page

African Studies Program. Home page. School of Advanced International Study, Johns Hopkins U, n.d. Web. 31 July 2007.

E-mail

Rubino, Susanna. "Reasons for Unemployment." Message to the author. 12 Dec. 2013. E-mail.

Use the subject line as the title of the e-mail. Use "E-mail" as the medium of publication and omit your access date.

FIGURE 23.3 A Blog Posting from the Web, with Citation Elements Identified

Dyer, Bob, and Ella Barnes. "The 'Greening' of the Arctic." *Greenversations*. U.S. Environmental Protection Agency, 7 Oct. 2008. Web. 11 Oct. 2008. <http://blog.epa.gov/blog/2008/10/07/the-greening-of-the-arctic/>.

Miscellaneous Sources

Television or radio program

Begin with the episode name, if any, in quotation marks, followed by the program name, italicized. Use "Television" or "Radio" as the medium of publication.

"Lie Like a Rug." *NYPD Blue*. Dir. Steven Bochco and David Milch. ABC. KOMO, Seattle. 6 Nov. 2001. Television.

If you accessed a program on the Web, give the basic citation information without the original medium of publication; then include the Web publication information with an access date.

Ashbrook, Tom. "Turf Wars and the American Lawn." *On Point*. Natl. Public Radio, 22 July 2008. Web. 23 July 2009.

For podcasts, see page 573.

Film or video recording

Shakespeare in Love. Dir. John Madden. Perf. Joseph Fiennes and Gwyneth Paltrow. Screenplay by Marc Norman and Tom Stoppard. Universal Miramax, 1998. Film.

Use "DVD" or "Videocassette" rather than "Film" as the medium of publication if that is the medium you consulted. If you accessed a film or video on the Web, omit the original medium of publication, include the Web site or database name (italicized), the sponsor and posting date, "Web" as medium of publication, and the date of access.

Shakespeare in Love. Dir. John Madden. Perf. Joseph Fiennes and Gwyneth Paltrow. Screenplay by Marc Norman and Tom Stoppard. Universal Miramax, 1998. *Netflix*. Netflix, n.d. Web. 9 Mar. 2010.

For videos published originally on the Web, see page 573.

Sound recording

Begin the entry with what your paper emphasizes—for example, the artist's, composer's, or conductor's name—and adjust the elements accordingly. List the medium—CD, LP, Audiocassette—last.

Dylan, Bob. "Rainy Day Women #12." *Blonde on Blonde*. Columbia, 1966. LP.

If you accessed the recording on the Web, drop the original medium of publication and include the Web site or database name (italicized), "Web" as the medium of publication, and the access date.

Dylan, Bob. "Rainy Day Women #12." *Blonde on Blonde*. Columbia, 1966. *Lala*. La La Media, n.d. Web. 10 Mar. 2010.

Cartoon or advertisement

Trudeau, Garry. "Doonesbury." Comic strip. *Seattle Times* 19 Nov. 2001: B4. Print.

Banana Republic. Advertisement. *Details* Oct. 2001: 37. Print.

Interview

Castellucci, Marion. Personal interview. 7 Oct. 2013.

Lecture, speech, or conference presentation

Sharples, Mike. "Authors of the Future." Conference of European Teachers of Academic Writing. U of Groningen. Groningen, Neth. 20 June 2001. Lecture.

Government publications

In general, follow these guidelines:

- Usually cite as author the government agency that produced the document. Begin with the highest level and then branch down to the specific agency:

  United States. Dept. of Justice. FBI.

  Idaho. Dept. of Motor Vehicles.

- Follow this with the title of the document, italicized.
- If a specific person is clearly identified as the author, you may begin the citation with that person's name, or you may list the author (preceded by the word "By") after the title of the document.
- Follow standard procedures for citing publication information for print sources or Web sources.

United States. Dept. of Health and Human Services. Public Health Service. Office of the Surgeon General. *Preventing Tobacco Use Among Youth and Young Adults: A Report of the Surgeon General*. 2012. Web. 26 June 2013.

MLA Format Research Paper

For an illustration of a student research paper written and formatted in MLA style, see "Engaging Young Adults to Meet America's Challenges: A Proposal for Mandatory National Service" by Kent Ansen (Chapter 15, pp. 405–414). Kent's process in producing this paper has been discussed in various places throughout the text.

SKILL 23.4 Cite and document sources using APA style.

23.4 Cite and document sources using APA style.

In many respects, the APA style and the MLA style are similar and the basic logic is the same. In the APA system, the list where readers can find full bibliographic information is titled "References"; as in MLA format, it includes only the sources cited in the body of the paper. The distinguishing features of APA citation style are highlighted in the following sections.

In-Text Citations in APA Style

A typical APA-style in-text citation contains three elements: (1) the last name of the author, (2) the date of the publication, and (3) the page number of the quoted or paraphrased passage. Table 23.3 identifies some typical variations and shows again the one-to-one connection between the in-text citation and the References list.

For an example of as student paper in APA style, see the report by Campbell et al. on pp. 216–223.

TABLE 23.3 In-Text Citations in APA Style

Type of Source	References Entry at End of Paper	In-Text Citation in Body of Paper
One author	Pollan, M. (2006). *The omnivore's dilemma: A natural history of four meals*. New York, NY: Penguin.	...(Pollan, 2006, p. 256). OR According to Pollan (2006),... (p. 256).
Two authors	Kwon, O., & Wen, Y. (2010). An empirical study of the factors affecting social network service use. *Computers in Human Behavior, 26*, 254–263. doi:10.1016/j.chb.2009.04.011	...(Kwon & Wen, 2010, p. 262). OR Kwon and Wen (2010) claim that...(p. 262).
Three to five authors	Pollay, R. W., Lee, J. S., & Carter-Whitney, D. (1992). Separate, but not equal: Racial segmentation in cigarette advertising. *Journal of Advertising, 21*(1), 45–57.	...race" (Pollay, Lee, & Carter-Whitney, 1992, p. 52). OR Pollay, Lee, and Carter-Whitney have argued that "advertisers... race" (1992, p. 52). *For subsequent citations, use* Pollay et al. *For a quotation, use the specific page number, not the whole range of pages.*

(continued)

TABLE 23.3 *continued*

Type of Source	References Entry at End of Paper	In-Text Citation in Body of Paper
Author has more than one work in References list	Dombrowski, D. A. (1984). *The philosophy of vegetarianism.* Amherst, MA: University of Massachusetts Press. Dombrowski, D. A. (1997). *Babies and beasts: The argument from marginal cases.* Urbana: University of Illinois Press.	...(Dombrowski, 1984, p. 207). ...(Dombrowski, 1997, p. 328). OR Dombrowski (1984) claims that...(p. 207). According to Dombrowski (1997),...(p. 328).
Indirect citation of a source that you found in another source *You use a quotation from Peter Singer from a book by Dombrowski. Include Dombrowski, not Singer, in References.*	Dombrowski, D. A. (1997). *Babies and beasts: The argument from marginal cases.* Urbana: University of Illinois Press.	Animal rights activist Peter Singer argues that...(as cited in Dombrowski, 1997, p. 429). *Singer is used for the attributive tag, but the in-text citation is to Dombrowski.*

References List in APA Style

The APA References list at the end of a paper presents entries alphabetically. If you cite more than one item for an author, repeat the author's name each time and arrange the items in chronological order, beginning with the earliest. In cases where two works by an author appeared in the same year, arrange them in the list alphabetically by title, and then add a lowercase "a" or "b" (etc.) after the date so that you can distinguish between them in the in-text citations:

A formatted References list appears on p. 223.

Smith, R. (1999a). *Body image in non-Western cultures, 1750–present.* London, England: Bonanza Press.

Smith, R. (1999b). Eating disorders reconsidered. *Journal of Appetite Studies, 45*, 295–300.

APA Citation Models

Print Articles in Scholarly Journals

General Format for Print Article in Scholarly Journal

Author. (Year of Publication). Article title. *Journal Title, volume number*, page numbers. doi:xx.xxxx/x.xxxx.xx [or] http://dx.doi.org/10.xxxx/xxxxxx

If there is one, include the **DOI** (digital object identifier), a number that is uniquely assigned to many journal article, in numeric or URL form. Note the style for capitalizing article titles and for italicizing the volume number.

One author

Herrera-Sobek, M. (2006). Border aesthetics: The politics of Mexican immigration in film and art. *Western Humanities Review, 60,* 60–71. doi:10.1016/j.chb.2009.04.011

Two to seven authors

McElroy, B. W., & Lubich, B. H. (2013). Predictors of course outcomes: Early indicators of delay in online classrooms. *Distance Education,* 34(1). http://dx.doi.org /10.1080/01587919.2013.770433

When a source has more than seven authors, list the first six and the last one by name. Use ellipses (. . .) to indicate the authors whose names have been omitted.

Scholarly journal that restarts page numbering with each issue

Pollay, R. W., Lee, J. S., & Carter-Whitney, D. (1992). Separate, but not equal: Racial segmentation in cigarette advertising. *Journal of Advertising, 21*(1), 45–57.

Note that the issue number and the parentheses are *not* italicized.

Print Articles in Magazines and Newspapers

General Format for Print Article in Magazine or Newspaper

Author. (Year, Month Day). Article title. *Periodical Title, volume number,* page numbers.

If page numbers are discontinuous, identify every page, separating numbers with a comma.

Magazine article with named author

Hall, S. S. (2001, March 11). Prescription for profit. *The New York Times Magazine,* 40–45, 59, 91–92, 100.

Magazine article without named author

Sacred geese. (2013, June 1). *Economist,* 24–25.

Review of book or film

Schwarz, B. (2001, November). A bit of bunting: A new history of the British empire elevates expediency to principle [Review of the book *Ornamentalism: How the British saw their empire*]. *Atlantic Monthly, 288,* 126–135.

Kaufman, S. (2001, July 30). Polishing a gem [Review of the motion picture *The blue angel*]. *New Republic, 225,* 28–29.

Newspaper article

Dougherty, C. (2013, June 4). The latest urban trend: Less elbow room. *Wall Street Journal,* pp. A1, A12.

Newspaper editorial

Dr. Frankenstein on the hill [Editorial]. (2002, May 18). *The New York Times,* p. A22.

Letter to the editor of a magazine or newspaper

Tomsovic, K. (1998, July 13). Culture clash [Letter to the editor]. *The New Yorker*, 7.

Print Books

General Format for Print Books

Author. (Year of publication). *Book title: Subtitle.* City, State [abbreviated]: Name of Publisher.

Brumberg, J. J. (1997). *The body project: An intimate history of American girls.* New York, NY: Vintage.

If the publisher's name indicates the state in which it is located, list the city but omit the state.

Reid, H., & Taylor, B. (2010). *Recovering the commons: Democracy, place, and global justice.* Champaign: University of Illinois Press.

Second, later, or revised edition

Montagu, A. (1986). *Touching: The human significance of the skin* (3rd ed.). New York, NY: Perennial Press.

Republished book (for example, a paperback published after the original hardback edition or a modern edition of an older work)

Wollstonecraft, M. (1995). *The vindication of the rights of woman, with strictures on political and moral subjects.* Rutland, VT: Tuttle. (Original work published 1792)

The in-text citation should read: (Wollstonecraft, 1792/1995).

Multivolume work

Churchill, W. S. (1956–1958). *A history of the English-speaking peoples* (Vols. 1–4). New York, NY: Dodd, Mead.

Citation for all the volumes together. The in-text citation should read: (Churchill, 1956–1958).

Churchill, W. S. (1957). *A history of the English-speaking peoples: Vol. 4. The great democracies.* New York, NY: Dodd, Mead.

Citation for a specific volume. The in-text citation should read: (Churchill, 1957).

Article in reference work

Hirsch, E. D., Kett, J. F., & Trefil, J. (2002). Kyoto protocol. In *The new dictionary of cultural literacy.* Boston, MA: Houghton Mifflin.

Translation

De Beauvoir, S. (1961). *The second sex* (H. M. Parshley, Trans.). New York, NY: Bantam Books. (Original work published 1949)

The in-text citation should read: (De Beauvoir, 1949/1961).

Corporate author (a commission, committee, or other group)

American Red Cross. (1993). *Standard first aid.* St. Louis, MO: Mosby Lifeline.

Anonymous author

The complete cartoons of The New Yorker. (2004). New York, NY: Black Dog & Leventhal.

The in-text citation is (*Complete cartoons,* 2004).

Whole anthology

O'Connell, D. F., & Alexander, C. N. (Eds.). (1994). *Self recovery: Treating addictions using transcendental meditation and Maharishi Ayur-Veda.* New York, NY: Haworth Press.

Anthology article

Royer, A. (1994). The role of the transcendental meditation technique in promoting smoking cessation: A longitudinal study. In D. F. O'Connell & C. N. Alexander (Eds.), *Self recovery: Treating addictions using transcendental meditation and Maharishi Ayur-Veda* (pp. 221–239). New York, NY: Haworth Press.

Articles or Books from an Online Database

Article from database with a DOI

Scharrer, E., Daniel, K. D., Lin, K.-M., & Liu, Z. (2006). Working hard or hardly working? Gender, humor, and the performance of domestic chores in television commercials. *Mass Communication and Society, 9*(2), 215–238. doi:10.1207/s15327825mcs0902_5

Omit the database name. If an article or other document has been assigned a DOI, include the DOI at the end. To see where the information in the Scharrer citation came from, refer to Figure 23.4.

Article from database without DOI

Highland, R. A., & Dabney, D. A. (2009). Using Adlerian theory to shed light on drug dealer motivations. *Applied Psychology in Criminal Justice, 5*(2), 109–138. Retrieved from http://www.apcj.org

Omit the database name. Instead, use a search engine to locate the publication's home page, and cite that URL. If you need to break a URL at the end of a line, do not use a hyphen. Instead, break it *before* a punctuation mark or *after* http://.

Other Internet Sources

General Format for Web Documents

Author, editor, director, narrator, performer, compiler, or producer of the work, if available. (Year, Month Day of posting). *Title of web document, italicized.* Retrieved from Name of website if different from author or title: URL of home page

Barrett, J. (2007, January 17). *MySpace is a natural monopoly.* Retrieved from ECommerce Times website: http://www.ecommercetimes.com

FIGURE 23.4 Scholarly Journal Article with a Digital Object Identifier (DOI) with Elements Identified for an APA-Style Citations

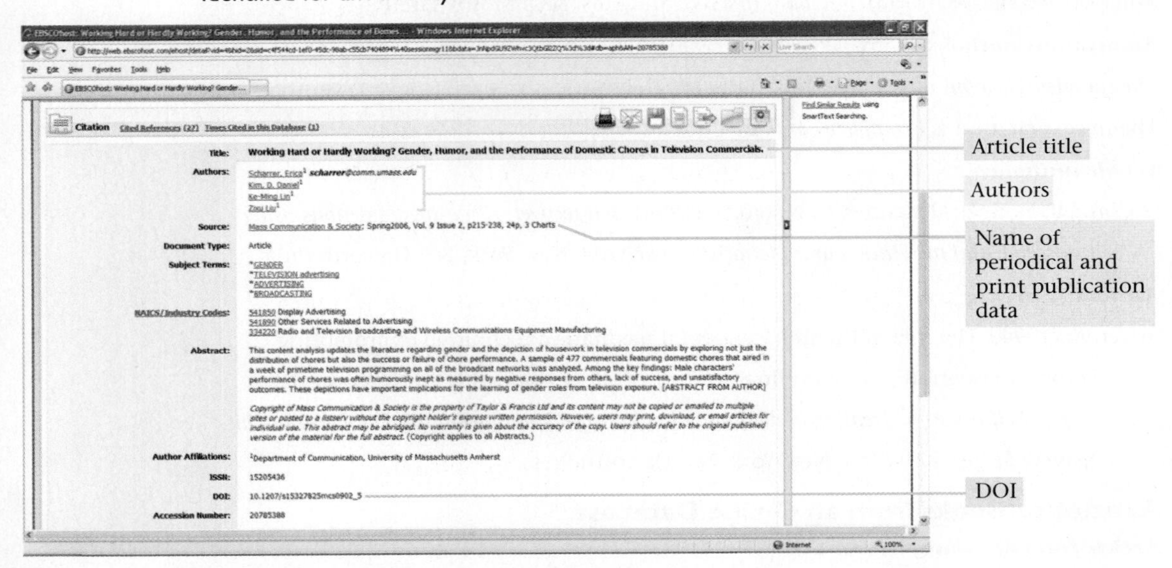

Scharrer, E., Daniel, K. D., Lin, K.-M., & Liu, Z. (2006). Working hard or hardly working? Gender, humor, and the performance of domestic chores in television commericals. *Mass Communication and Society*, *9*(2), 215–238. doi:10.1207/s15327825mcs0902_5

Marks, J. (n.d.). "Overview: Letter from the president." Retrieved June 3, 2010, from the Search for Common Ground website: http://www.sfcg.org

Entire Web site

BlogPulse. (n.d.). Retrieved September 3, 2010, from the Intelliseek website: http://www.intelliseek.com

Article from a newspaper site

Bounds, A. (2007, June 26). Thinking like scientists. *Daily Camera* [Boulder]. Retrieved from http://www.dailycamera.com

Article from a scholarly e-journal

Welch, J. R., & Riley, R. (2001). Reclaiming land and spirit in the western Apache homeland. *American Indian Quarterly, 25*, 5–14. Retrieved from muse.jhu.edu /journals/american_indian_quarterly

Reference material

Cicada. (2004). In *Encyclopaedia Britannica*. Retrieved from http://www.britannica.com

E-book

Hoffman, F. W. (1981). *The literature of rock: 1954–1978*. Retrieved from http:// www.netlibrary.com

E-mail, interviews, and personal correspondence

Cite personal correspondence in the body of your text, but not in the References list: "Rubino (personal communication, December 12, 2013) claims that. . . ."

Blog Posting

Dyer, B., & Barnes, E. (2008, October 7). The "greening" of the Arctic [Web log post]. Retrieved from blog.epa.gov/blog/2008/10/07/the-greening-of-the-arctic

To see where each element of this citation comes from, refer to Figure 23.3.

Social media posting

Storm King Art Centers. (2013, May 30). Rattlesnake figure (aluminums) by Thomas Houseago. [Facebook update]. Retrieved from http://www.facebook.com/StormKingArtCenter

Web video

Beck, R. (2006, November 2). Immigration gumballs [Video file]. Retrieved from http://www.youtube.com/watch?v=n7WJeqxuOfQ

Podcast

Funke, E. (Host). (2007, June 26). *ArtScene* [Audio podcast]. National Public Radio. Retrieved from http://www.npr.org

Miscellaneous Sources

Television program

Bochco, S., & Milch, D. (Directors). (2001, November 6). Lie like a rug [Television series episode]. In *NYPD blue.* New York, NY: American Broadcasting Company.

Film

Madden, J. (Director). (1998). *Shakespeare in love* [Motion picture]. United States: Universal Miramax.

Sound recording

Dylan, B. (1966). Rainy day women #12. On *Blonde on blonde* [Record]. New York, NY: Columbia.

Government publications

U.S. Department of Health and Human Services. (2012). *Preventing tobacco use among youth and young adults: A report of the Surgeon General.* Retrieved from http://www.surgeongeneral.gov/library/reports/preventing-youth-tobacco-use/index.html#Full Report

Student Example of an APA-Style Research Paper

An example of a paper in APA style is shown on pages 216–223.

WRITING FOR ASSESSMENT

PART 5

BEWARE..
Drink only
approved water
NEVER GIVE A GERM A BREAK!

This 1944 War Department poster, now housed in the U.S. National Library of Medicine, warned U.S. soldiers not to drink from jungle streams that could be contaminated with deadly microbes. The skeletal mirror image of the soldier shocks and frightens the soldier away from the danger. Viewers experience the double impact of observing both parts of the image—the horror of the skull and the terror of the soldier. This visual argument, focusing on consequences, is crafted for maximum rhetorical effect in its appeal to both *logos* and *pathos*. This poster is discussed in more detail in Chapter 19, pages 491–92.

24 ESSAY EXAMINATIONS

WHAT YOU WILL LEARN

24.1 To plan and write an essay exam.

24.2 To adapt to the unique requirements of in-class essay writing.

Taking essay exams can be stressful and frustrating. When instructors give essay exams, they want to see how well you can restate, apply, and assess course material. Just as important, they want to see whether you can discuss what you have studied—whether you can participate in that discipline's discourse community. These twin demands make essay exams doubly challenging. Furthermore, not only must you master course material, but you must also write about it quickly.

24.1 Plan and write an essay exam.

How Essay Exams Differ from Other Essays

Essay exams do share similarities with other assignments. Most of the instructions in this book apply to exam writing. For instance, you have learned how to respond to rhetorical context—audience, purpose, and genre—as you write an essay. Your audience for an essay exam is your instructor, so you need to ask yourself what your instructor values and wants. Does your instructor stress analysis of material or application of roles? Does your instructor encourage individual interpretations? Just as analyzing an audience helps you focus an out-of-class essay, so too can analyzing your instructor's expectations help you focus an exam response.

You also know the importance of knowing what you're talking about. Even the most brilliant writers will stumble on a test if they haven't bothered to attend class regularly, take notes, participate in class discussions, and keep up with the reading. Familiarity with the material lays the groundwork for a successful exam performance, just as thorough research and exploratory writing grounds a good paper.

However, not all the writing strategies you use for papers will serve you well in a test situation. Writing researcher Randall Popken, after reviewing more than two hundred sample exams in various disciplines, identified three skills unique to essay exam writing:

1. The ability to store, access, and translate appropriate knowledge into an organized essay
2. The ability to analyze quickly the specific requirements of an exam question and formulate a response to those requirements

3. The ability to deal with time pressure, test anxiety, and other logistical constraints of the exam situation

We examine each of these skills in the next section.

Preparing for an Exam: Learning Subject Matter

Preparing for an exam involves finding efficient ways to organize, recall, and apply your knowledge so that you can easily construct an intelligent discussion on paper.

Identifying and Learning Main Ideas

No instructor will expect you to remember every single piece of information covered in class. Most instructors are happy if you can remember main ideas and theories, key terminology, and a few supporting examples. The best strategy when you study for an essay exam is to figure out what is most important and learn it first.

How do you determine the main ideas and key concepts? Sometimes they're obvious. Many professors outline their lectures on the board or distribute review sheets before each exam. If your professor does not provide explicit instructions, listen for a thesis statement, main points, and transitions in each lecture to determine the key ideas and relationships among them. For example,

> The *most important critics* of the welfare state are ....
>
> *Four developments* contributed to the reemergence of the English after the Norman invasion ....
>
> Hegel's dialectic was *most influenced by* Kant ....

Look for similar signals in your textbook and pay special attention to chapter summaries, subheadings, and highlighted terms. If the course involves a lot of discussion or if your professor prefers informal remarks to highly structured lectures, you may have to work harder to identify major points. But streamlining and organizing your knowledge in this way will keep you from feeling overwhelmed when you sit down to study.

Skill 17.8 explains some of the main organizing moves writers use in the bodies of essays to clarify and develop their points.

Most instructors expect you to master more than the information they cover in class. Essay exams in humanities, social science, and fine arts courses often ask for an individual interpretation, argument, or critique. To prepare for such questions, practice talking back to course readings by developing your own positions on the viewpoints they express. If the professor has lectured on factors involved in mainstreaming schoolchildren with physical disabilities, look at your notes and try to define your own position on mainstreaming. If the textbook identifies salient features of Caravaggio's art, decide how you think his paintings compare to and differ from his contemporaries' work. Questioning texts and lectures in this way will help you personalize the material, expand your understanding, and take ownership of your education. Remember, though, that professors won't be impressed by purely subjective opinions; as you explore your views, search for evidence and arguments, not just from your own experience but from the course as well, that you can use to support your ideas in the exam.

For specific strategies to help you understand and respond to reading material, review Chapter 5 and Chapter 12.

Applying Your Knowledge

In business, science, social science, and education courses, professors may ask you to apply a theory or method to a new situation. For example, they might ask you to show how "first in, last out" accounting might work in bookkeeping for a machine parts factory or how you might use psychodynamic concepts to analyze a hypothetical case study.

If you suspect that such a question might appear, use some study time to practice this kind of thinking. Brainstorm two or three current situations to which you could apply the theories or concepts you've been learning. Check local newspapers or browse the Web for ideas. Then freewrite for a few minutes on how you might organize an essay that puts the theory to work. For instance, if you've studied federal affirmative action law in a public administration course, you might ask the following questions: How did the decision by the U.S. Supreme Court in regard to the University of Michigan's affirmative action policies affect the use of race as a factor in college admissions? How might it apply to a local college trying to attract a diverse student body? You won't be able to predict exactly what will appear on the exam, but you can become skilled at transferring ideas into new settings.

Making a Study Plan

Once you've identified crucial subject matter, you need to develop a study plan. If you're a novice at studying for a major exam, try following some tried-and-true approaches.

- Review your instructor's previous exams. Don't be afraid to ask your instructor for general guidelines about the type, length, and format of questions he or she normally includes on tests.
- Generate your own practice questions and compose responses.
- Organize group study sessions with two to four classmates. Meet regularly to discuss readings, exchange practice questions, test each other informally, and critique each other's essays.

Avoid study techniques that are almost universally ineffective: Don't waste time trying to reread all the material or memorize passages word for word (unless the exam will require you to produce specific formulas or quotations). Don't set an unreasonable schedule. You can seldom learn the material adequately in one or two nights, and the anxiety produced by cramming can hurt your performance even more. Most important, don't stay up all night studying. Doing so can be worse than not studying at all, since sleep deprivation impairs your ability to recall and process information.

24.2 Analyzing Exam Questions

Adapt to the unique requirements of in-class essay writing.

Whereas paper assignments typically ask you to address broad problems that can be solved in numerous possible ways, essay exams usually require much more narrowly focused responses. Essay exams feature well-defined problems with a very narrow range of right answers. They require you to recall a particular body of information and present it in a highly specific way. However, what your instructors are asking you to recall and how they want it presented will not always be clear to you. Exam questions often require interpretation.

Although the language of essay exams varies considerably across disciplines, professors typically draw on a set of conventional moves when they write exam prompts. Consider the following question from an undergraduate course in the history of the English language:

> Walt Whitman once wrote that English was not "an abstract construction of dictionary makers" but a language that had "its basis broad and low, close to the ground." Whitman reminds us that English is a richly expressive language because it comes from a variety of cultural sources. One of these is African-American culture. Write an essay discussing the major ways in which African-American culture and dialect have influenced the English language in the United States. Identify and illustrate at least three important influences: What were the historical circumstances? What important events and people were involved? What were the specific linguistic contributions?

This question presents an intimidating array of instructions, but it becomes manageable if you recognize some standard organizational features.

Understanding the Use of Outside Quotations

First, like many exam questions, this sample opens with a quotation from an author or work not covered in the course. Many students panic when they encounter such questions. "Whitman?! We didn't even study Whitman. What am I supposed to do now?" Don't worry. The primary function of such quotations is to encapsulate a general issue that the instructor wants you to address in your response. When you encounter an unfamiliar quotation, look carefully at the rest of the question for clues about what role the quotation should play in your essay. The point of the Whitman quotation is restated in the very next sentence—English is shaped by numerous cultural influences—and the function of the quotation is simply to reinforce that point. Because the rest of the question tells you specifically what kinds of cultural influences your response should address (African-American culture, three major linguistic contributions), you don't need to consider this quotation when you write your essay.

Sometimes professors will ask you to take a position on an unfamiliar quotation and support your argument with material covered in the course. Suppose that the question was, "What is your position on Whitman's view? Do you believe that English is enriched or corrupted by multicultural influences?" In this case the quotation is presented as the basis for a thesis statement, which you would then explain and support. A successful response might begin, "Whitman believes that multicultural influences make our language better, but this view is hopelessly naive for the following reasons ...." or "Whitman correctly argues that the contributions of different cultures enrich our language. Take these three examples ...."

Recognizing Organizational Cues

The question itself can show you the best way to organize your response. Questions tend to begin with general themes that often suggest a thesis statement. Subsequent divisions tell you how to organize the essay into sections and in what order to introduce supporting points. For example, a successful response that follows the organization of our sample might be arranged as follows:

- A thesis stating that several contributions from African-American language and culture have enriched English
- Three supporting paragraphs, each discussing a different area of influence by
  1. summarizing historical circumstances
  2. noting important people and events
  3. providing one or two examples of linguistic contributions

Interpreting Key Terms

As do all exam questions, this one asks you to write about a specific body of information in a specific way. When you encounter a lengthy question such as this, first pick out the *noun phrases* that direct you to specific areas of knowledge: "African-American culture," "major influences on the English language in the United States," "historical circumstances," "important events and people," "linguistic contributions." Pay careful attention to words that modify these noun phrases. Does the question tell you how many influences to discuss? What kinds of examples to cite? Does the instructor include conjunctions, such as *or*, to give you a choice of topics, or does he or she use words such as *and* or *as well as* that require you to address all areas mentioned? Words such as *who, what, where*, and *why* also point to particular kinds of information.

After you've determined the specific areas you need to address, look for *directive verbs* that tell you what to do: *discuss, identify*, or *illustrate*, for example. These verbs define the horizons of your response. The strategies chart below defines some key directives that frequently appear in essay exams and provides sample questions for each. Meanings vary somewhat according to the course, the context of the question, and the professor's expectations, but you'll feel more confident if you have basic working definitions.

Strategies for Responding to Common Essay-Question Verbs

Verbs	How to Respond	Example Questions
Analyze	Break an argument, concept, or approach into parts and examine the relations among them; discuss causes and effects; evaluate; or explain your interpretation. Look at the rest of the question to determine which strategies to pursue.	*Analyze* the various technical, acoustic, and aesthetic factors that might lead a musician to choose analog over digital recording for a live performance. Be sure to include the strengths and weaknesses of both methods in your discussion.
Apply	Take a concept, formula, theory, or approach and adapt it to another situation.	Imagine that you've been hired to reengineer the operations of a major U.S. automaker. How might you *apply* the principles of Total Quality Management in your recommendations?

Verbs	How to Respond	Example Questions
Argue	Take a position for or against an issue and give reasons and evidence to support that position.	*Argue* whether or not cloning should be pursued as a method of human reproduction. Be sure to account for the relationship between cloning and mitosis in your discussion.
Compare/ Contrast	Note the similarities (compare) or differences (contrast) between two or more objects or ideas.	*Compare* and *contrast* the leadership styles of Franklin Delano Roosevelt, John F. Kennedy, and Ronald Reagan, focusing on their uses of popular media and political rhetoric.
Construct	Assemble a model, diagram, or other organized presentation of your knowledge about a subject.	*Construct* a model of the writing process that illustrates the major stages writers go through when developing an idea into a finished text.
Critique	Analyze and evaluate an argument or idea, explaining both strengths and weaknesses.	Dinesh D'Souza's "Illiberal Education" sparked widespread controversy when it was published in 1991. Write an essay *critiquing* D'Souza's arguments against affirmative action, identifying both the strengths and weaknesses of his position. Use examples from the text, class discussion, and other class readings to illustrate your points.
Define	Provide a clear, concise, authoritative meaning for an object or idea. The response may include describing the object or idea, distinguishing it clearly from other objects or ideas, or providing one or more supporting examples.	How was "equality" *defined* by the Supreme Court in *Plessy v. Ferguson* (1896)? How did that definition influence subsequent educational policy in the United States?
Discuss	Comprehensively present and analyze important concepts, supported by examples or evidence. Cover several key points or examine the topic from several perspectives. Check the question for guidelines about what to include.	*Discuss* the controversy that surrounded Stanley Milgram's studies of authority and state your own position on the relevance and validity of the experiments.
Enumerate (or List)	List steps, components, or events pertaining to a larger phenomenon, perhaps briefly explaining and commenting on each item.	A two-year-old child falls from a swing on the playground and lies unconscious. As the head preschool teacher, *enumerate* the steps you would take from the time of the accident until the ambulance arrives.

(*continued*)

Verbs	How to Respond	Example Questions
Evaluate	Make a judgment about the worth of an object or idea, examining strengths and weaknesses.	*Evaluate* William Whyte's "Street Corner Society" as an ethnographic study. What are its methodological strengths and weaknesses? Do you believe the weaknesses make Whyte's research obsolete?
Explain	Clarify and state reasons to show how some object or idea relates to a more general topic.	*Explain* the relationship of centripetal force to mass and velocity and give an example to illustrate this relationship.
Identify	Describe some object or idea and explain its significance to a larger topic.	*Identify* the major phonetic characteristics of each of the following language groups of Africa, and provide illustrative examples: Koisan, Niger-Kordofanian, and Nilo-Saharan.
Illustrate	Give one or more examples, cases, or other concrete instances to clarify a general concept.	Define "monopoly," "public utility," and "competition," and give specific *illustrations* of each.
Prove	Produce reasons and evidence to establish that a position is logical, supportable, or factual.	Use your knowledge about the findings of the National Assessment of Educational Progress to *prove* that public schools either are or are not doing an adequate job of educating children to become productive U.S. citizens.
Review	Briefly survey or summarize something.	*Review* the major differences between Socrates' conception of ethics and the ethical theories of his contemporaries in the fifth century B.C.E.
Summarize	Lay out the main points of a theory, argument, or event in a concise and organized manner.	*Summarize* Mill's definition of justice and explain how it differs from Kant's. Which definition comes closest to your own,and why?
Trace	Explain chronologically a series of events or the development of an idea.	Write an essay that *traces* the pathway of a nerve impulse through the nervous system, being sure to explain neuron structure, action potential, and the production and reception of neurotransmitters.

Our thanks to Michael C. Flanigan, who suggested some of the terms for this table in his "Processes of Essay Exams" manuscript. University of Oklahoma, 1991.

In some questions, directives are implied rather than stated directly. If a question asks, "Discuss the effects of Ronald Reagan's tax policies on the U.S. economy during the 1980s," you'll need to summarize what those policies were before you can assess their effects. Before you can take a position on an issue, you have to define what the controversy is about. In general, when you answer any question, you should include sufficient background information about the topic to convince your instructor that you're making an informed argument, whether or not the question specifically asks for background information.

FOR WRITING AND DISCUSSION

Analyze Essay Questions

This exercise will hone your ability to analyze essay questions. The following student essay, which received an A, was a response to one of the four closely related questions that follow it. The essay may address issues raised in two or more questions, but it is an A response to only one of them. Your task is to figure out which question the essay answers best.

Decide on your answer independently; then compare answers in small groups. Try to come to a consensus, referring to the strategies chart on pages 590–592 to help resolve disagreements. As you discuss your responses, note any successful strategies that you may be able to adapt to your own writing.

FROM A BRITISH LITERATURE COURSE

Gulliver's Travels and *Frankenstein* portray characters whose adventures bring them face to face with the innate weaknesses and limitations of humankind. Victor Frankenstein and Lemuel Gulliver find out during their travels that humans are limited in reasoning capacity and easily corruptible, traits that cause even their best-intentioned projects to go awry. These characters reflect the critical view that Swift and Shelley take of human nature. Both believe that humans have a "dark side" that leads to disastrous effects.

In *Gulliver's Travels*, Gulliver's sea voyages expose him to the best and worst aspects of human civilization. Through Gulliver's eyes, readers come to share Swift's perception that no matter how good people's original intentions, their innate selfishness corrupts everything they attempt. All the societies Gulliver visits give evidence of this. For example, Lilliput has a system of laws once grounded on justice and morality, but that slowly were perverted by greedy politicians into petty applications. Even the most advanced society, Brobdingnag, has to maintain a militia even though the country is currently peaceful—since they acknowledge that because humans are basically warlike, peace can't last forever. By showing examples of varied cultures with common faults, Swift demonstrates what he believes to be innate human weaknesses. He seems to believe that no matter how much progress we make, human societies will eventually fall back into the same old traps.

(*continued*)

Victor Frankenstein also experiences human limitations, this time in his own personality, as he pushes to gain knowledge beyond what any human has ever possessed. When he first begins his experiments to manufacture life in the laboratory, his goals are noble—to expand scientific knowledge and to help people. As he continues, he becomes more concerned with the power that his discovery will bring him. He desires to be a "god to a new race of men." Later, when the creature he creates wreaks havoc, Frankenstein's pride and selfishness keep him from confessing and preventing further deaths. Like the societies Gulliver observed, Frankenstein is a clear example of how human frailties corrupt potentially good projects.

Even though Swift and Shelley wrote during two different historical periods, they share a critical view of human nature. However, several unambiguously good characters in *Frankenstein*—including the old man and his daughter—suggest that Shelley feels more optimism that people are capable of overcoming their weaknesses, while Swift seems adamant that humans will eternally backslide into greed and violence. Basically, however, both works demonstrate vividly to readers the ever present flaws that prevent people and their societies from ever attaining perfection.

Which of the following questions does this essay address most successfully?

1. Contrast Swift's and Shelley's views of human nature, illustrating your points with specific examples from *Gulliver's Travels* and *Frankenstein*.
2. Analyze the use Swift and Shelley make of scientific knowledge to show the limits of human progress in *Gulliver's Travels* and *Frankenstein*, citing specific illustrations from each work.
3. Discuss the characters of Lemuel Gulliver in *Gulliver's Travels* and Victor Frankenstein in *Frankenstein:* What purpose does each serve in the text? How does each author use the character to illustrate important traits or concepts?
4. Many of the writers we've studied this semester explored the limitations of human potential in their work. Write an essay showing how any two of the following works deal with this idea: William Blake's *Songs of Innocence and Experience*, Jonathan Swift's *Gulliver's Travels*, Mary Shelley's *Frankenstein,* Percy Shelley's "Prometheus Unbound." Does each writer suggest a pessimistic or optimistic view of human nature? Be sure to support your argument with specific illustrations from each text.

Producing an "A" Response

No matter how committed you are to studying, planning, analyzing exam questions, and managing time constraints, your worries about essay tests probably come down to a single, inevitable question: What does an "A" response look like? Research suggests that most professors want closed-form, thesis-based prose that develops key ideas fully, drawing on supporting facts and examples. Although your essay's shape will be influenced by your individual writing style and the particular rhetorical context, the following summary of the points covered in this chapter can serve as a template for a successful essay:

- ***Clear thesis statement.*** Show your professor that you understand the big picture that the question addresses by including a thesis statement early on. Many professors recommend that you state your thesis clearly, though not necessarily stylishly, in the very first sentence.
- ***Coherent organization.*** Although a few instructors will read your essay only to see whether you've included important facts and concepts, most expect a logical presentation. Each paragraph should develop and illustrate one main point. Use transition words and phrases to connect each paragraph clearly to the thesis of the essay: "Another factor that led to the economic decline of the South was ...."; "In contrast to Hegel, Mill believed .... " Show your instructor that you know where the essay's going, that you're developing your thesis.
- ***Support and evidence.*** When the question calls for supporting facts and examples, be specific. Don't assert or generalize unless you present names, dates, studies, examples, diagrams, or quotations from your reading as support.
- ***Independent analysis and argument.*** Your response should not be a pedestrian rehash of the textbook. When the question allows, present your own insights, criticisms, or proposals, making sure to support these statements with course material and relate them clearly to your thesis.
- ***Conclusion.*** Even if you're running short of time, write a sentence or two to tie together main points and restate your thesis. Your conclusion, even if brief, serves an important rhetorical function. It confirms that you've dealt adequately with the question and proved your point.

Clearly we can't teach you everything you need to know about exam writing in one chapter. Becoming comfortable with any genre of writing requires patience and experience. Practicing the suggestions in this chapter for preparing for essay exams, comprehending exam questions, and organizing your answers will help you build your mastery of this kind of writing.

FOR WRITING AND DISCUSSION

Take a Practice Exam

To gain some practical experience, your instructor may ask you to write an essay exam on one of the following topics. Use the preparation and prewriting strategies you've practiced in this chapter and any other strategies you find useful to prepare for the exam. Review the strategies for writing a successful response presented on pages 594–595 and, if possible, organize and conduct group study sessions with your classmates.

(*continued*)

1. Explain the differences between closed-form and open-form prose. as presented in Chapter 1 and Chapters 17 and 18. Illustrate your answer with examples taken from Ross Taylor's "Paintball" (pp. 337–339) and Patrick José's "No Cats in America?" (pp. 139–140). Why does Taylor choose to write near the closed end of the closed-to-open continuum, whereas José chooses to write near the open end?
2. Write an essay on a topic of your instructor's choice.

PORTFOLIOS AND REFLECTIVE ESSAYS

25

WHAT YOU WILL LEARN

25.1 To assemble a portfolio of your writing.
25.2 To write a reflective essay.

Assembling a portfolio of your writing for a composition course, in which you select and present the work that best shows your progress or the work that represents your best writing, engages you deeply in reflective self-evaluation. Sometimes this work includes rough drafts and informal writing such as freewrites and journal entries as well as polished, final drafts; at other times, it includes just the polished, final products. Just as architects select their best designs to put into a portfolio to show a potential employer, so, too, do student writers assemble their best writing to demonstrate to the instructor or portfolio readers what they have learned and accomplished during the term.

Typically, writing portfolios also include a reflective letter or essay in which you discuss your portfolio choices and the learning they represent. The role of the accompanying reflective letter or essay is to offer the author's perspective on the writing in the portfolio, to give a behind-the-scenes account of the thinking and writing that went into the work, and to assess the writer's struggles and achievements during the term. This type of reflective writing, called a **comprehensive reflection,** demonstrates what you have learned from your writing over the course of the term, in order to apply that learning to future writing situations.

Another type of reflective essay focuses on a particular piece of writing. The aim of this type of reflective writing, called a **single reflection,** is to analyze a particular piece of writing in order to understand and often to revise it in the present or near future. When you write a single reflection, you formulate your ideas primarily for yourself and perhaps for a friendly, nonjudgmental audience.

Understanding Portfolios

25.1
Assemble a portfolio of your writing.

Portfolios offer many advantages to writers. The portfolio process gives you more time to revise before presenting your work for evaluation since many instructors who assign portfolios do not assign grades to individual drafts. Through your comprehensive reflection, you can assess and comment on your writing and learning before someone else passes judgment. Further, the portfolio process helps you develop insights about your thinking and writing processes, insights that you can apply to new writing situations. Finally, this experience can prepare you for work-related tasks because portfolios are increasingly required in job applications as well as in assessments for job promotions or merit-based increases.

Specific guidelines for preparing a writing portfolio vary from course to course, so you will need to check with each individual instructor for directions about what to include and how to organize your portfolio. You may be given a lot of leeway in what to include in your portfolio, or you may be required to submit a specific number of assignments or type of work. However, no matter what the specific requirements are, the following general suggestions can help you manage the portfolio process.

Collecting Work

Crucial to your success in assembling a portfolio is careful organization and collection of your work throughout the term. This way, you will avoid the headache and wasted time caused by trying to hunt down lost or misplaced work.

Besides the practical need to keep track of all your work in order to review and select the writing that you will include in your portfolio, the process of saving and organizing your work will cause you to attend to writing processes throughout the term, one of the key goals of portfolio teaching.

Selecting Work for Your Portfolio

Even if you are given explicit instructions about the number and type of writing samples to include in your portfolio, you will still have important choices to make about which completed pieces to include or which pieces to revise for inclusion. We suggest three general guidelines to consider as you review your writing and select work for your portfolio presentation.

- ***Variety:*** One purpose of portfolio assessment is to give a fuller picture of a writer's abilities. Therefore, it is important that you choose work that demonstrates your versatility—your ability to make effective rhetorical choices according to purpose, audience, and genre. What combination of writing samples best illustrates your ability to write effectively for different rhetorical situations and in different genres and media?
- ***Course goals:*** A second consideration is course goals. The goals are likely to be stated in the course syllabus and may include such things as "ability to demonstrate critical thinking in writing"; "ability to use multiple strategies for generating ideas, drafting, revising, and editing"; and "ability to demonstrate control over surface features such as syntax, grammar, punctuation, and spelling." Which pieces of writing most clearly demonstrate the abilities given as your course's goals, or which pieces can be revised to offer such a demonstration?
- ***Personal investment:*** Finally, be sure to consider which pieces of writing best reflect your personal investment and interest. If you are going to be revising the selected pieces multiple times during the last few weeks of class, you will want to make sure you choose work that holds your interest and has ideas you care about. Which pieces are you proudest of? Which were the most challenging or satisfying to write? Which present ideas you'd like to explore further?

Understanding Reflective Writing

Broadly defined, reflective writing is writing that describes, explains, interprets, and evaluates any past performance, action, belief, feeling, or experience. To **reflect** is to turn or look back, to reconsider something thought or done in the past from the perspective of the present.

Whether or not you record your thinking on paper, you think reflectively all the time. Suppose you ask your boss for a raise and get turned down. An hour later, as you cool your anger over coffee and a doughnut, you think of a particular point you could have made more effectively. On a larger scale, this kind of informal reflective thinking can be made more formal, systematic, and purposeful. Consider, for example, a football team that systematically reviews game videos to evaluate their own and their opponents' strategies and patterns of play. The camera's eye offers players and coaches new perspectives on their performance; it enables them to isolate, analyze, and evaluate specific moves that were unconsciously performed in the heat of the game.

Similar ways of thinking can be applied to any past performance. Writing reflectively encourages you to train your own camera's eye, metaphorically speaking, on the past. The following example is from an e-mail message sent by a student writer to her writing instructor concerning his comments on a draft of a paper she had written about the causes of anorexia. On the draft, the instructor had puzzled over a confusing sentence and suggested a revised version. Here is her e-mail response:

EXCERPT FROM A STUDENT REFLECTION ON A DRAFT

> I think that your suggested revision changes what I intended. I'd like that sentence to read: "Perhaps anorexics don't pursue desirability but are rather avoiding it." I am arguing not that anorexics want to be "undesirable" (as your sentence suggests) but rather that they want to avoid the whole issue; they want to be neutral. Sexuality and desire can be tremendously scary if you're in a position that places the value of your body over the value of your self/personage; one can feel that, by entering the sexual world of mature adults, one will lose hold of one's essential self. This is the idea I'm trying to express. Perhaps I should try to draft it some more … . At any rate, thank you for pointing out the inadequacies of the topic sentence of this paragraph. I struggled with it, and I think your impulse is right: it needs to encompass more of a transition.

As this example suggests, reflection involves viewing your writing from different perspectives, looking back on the past from the present, and achieving a critical distance. This process involves dialectial thinking—juxtaposing different, often opposing views, as we discussed in Chapter 7 on exploratory writing. Re-examining your writing from a new perpective yields new insights and an enriched, more complicated understanding of your ideas and your writing choices.

The synthesizing strategies in Chapter 12 for responding to multiple readings and arriving at your own enlarged views can also be applied to your own pieces of writing.

FOR WRITING AND DISCUSSION

Reflecting on a Past Experience

Working individually, think of a past experience that you can evaluate reflectively. This experience could be your performance in a job; participation in a sport, play, music recital, or other activity; development of a skill (learning to play the piano, juggle a soccer ball, perform a complex dance movement); or problem with another person (a coach, your dorm resident assistant, a job supervisor). To encourage you to think about the past from the perspective of the present, try asking yourself the question, "How do I see the experience differently now from the way I saw it then?" Imagine that you are doing a debriefing of your participation in the experience. Working on your own for ten minutes, freewrite reflectively about your performance. What did you do well? What wasn't working for you? What could you have done better?

Then in groups or as a whole class, share what you have learned through your reflective freewrites. How did the process of looking back give you a new perspective on your experience? How might reflective writing help you bring about changes and improvements in future performances?

Why Is Reflective Writing Important?

According to learning theorists, reflective writing can substantially enhance both your learning and your performance.* Reflective writing helps you gain the insights needed to apply current knowledge to new situations. For example, one of our students recently reported that the most important thing she had learned in her first-year writing course was that research could be used in the service of her own argument. In high school, she had thought of research as merely assembling and reporting information she had found in various sources. Now she realized that writers must make their own arguments, and she saw how research could help her do so. Clearly, this new understanding of the relationship between argument and research will help this student do the kind of research writing expected in upper-level college courses.

Learning theorists call this kind of thinking **metacognition:** the ability to monitor consciously one's intellectual processes or, in other words, to be aware of how one "does" intellectual work. Reflection enables you to control more consciously the thinking processes that go into your writing, and it enables you to gain the critical distance you need to evaluate and revise your writing successfully.

*Learning theorists who have made this general claim include J. H. Flavel, "Metacognitive Aspects of Problem-Solving," in L. B. Resnick (ed.), *The Nature of Intelligence* (Hillsdale, NJ: Erlbaum, 1976); Donald Schon, *Educating the Reflective Practitioner* (San Francisco: Jossey-Bass, 1987); and Stephen Brookfield, *Becoming a Critically Reflective Teacher* (San Francisco: Jossey-Bass, 1995). Throughout this chapter we are indebted to Kathleen Blake Yancey, *Reflection in the Writing Classroom* (Logan, UT: Utah State UP, 1998), who has translated and extended this work on reflection for writing instructors. We are also indebted to Donna Qualley, *Turns of Thought: Teaching Composition as Reflexive Inquiry* (Portsmouth, NH: Boynton/Cook, Heinemann, 1997), who draws on feminist and other critical theorists to argue for the value of reflexive approaches to writing instruction.

Reflective Writing Assignments

25.2
Write a reflective essay.

In this section we describe the kinds of reflective writing that your instructors across the disciplines may ask of you.

Single Reflection Assignments

Single reflection assignments are usually informal, exploratory pieces, similar to other kinds of informal writing you have done. Like the exploratory writing described in Chapter 2, Concept 2.1, single reflections are conversational in tone, open in form, and written mainly for yourself and, perhaps, a friendly, nonjudgmental audience. However, single reflections differ from most other kinds of exploratory writing in timing, focus, and purpose.

Whereas exploratory writing helps you generate ideas early in the writing process, single reflection writing is usually assigned between drafts or after you have completed an essay. Its focus is your writing itself, both the draft and the processes that produced it. Its aim is critical understanding, usually for the purpose of revision. In it, you think about what's working or not working in the draft, what thinking and writing processes went into producing it, and what possibilities you see for revising it. An example of a single reflection is Jaime Finger's essay in the Readings section at the end of this chapter (see p. 606).

Instructors use a variety of assignments to prompt single reflections. Some examples of assignments are the following:

- ***Process log:*** Your instructor asks you to keep a process log in which you describe the writing processes and decisions made for each essay you write throughout the term. In particular, you should offer a detailed and specific account of the problems you encountered (your "wallowing in complexity") and the rhetorical and subject-related alternatives considered and choices made.
- ***Writer's memo:*** Your instructor asks you to write a memorandum to turn in with your draft. In it, you answer a series of questions: How did you go about composing this draft? What problems did you encounter? What do you see as this draft's greatest strengths? What are its greatest weaknesses? What questions about your draft would you like the instructor to address?
- ***Companion piece:*** Less structured than a formal memorandum, a companion piece asks you to reflect briefly on one or two questions. A typical assignment might be this: "Please turn in (1) your draft and (2) an additional piece telling me what you would do with this draft if you had more time."
- ***Talk-to:*** In this type of companion piece, your instructor asks you to do four things: (1) believe this is the best paper you've ever written and explain why; (2) doubt that this paper is any good at all and explain why; (3) predict your instructor's response to this paper; and (4) agree or disagree with what you expect your instructor's response to be.

- ***Talk-back:*** In another type of companion piece, the instructor asks you to respond to his or her comments after you get the paper back: (1) What did I value in this text as a reader? (2) Do you agree with my reading? and (3) What else would you like for me to know?*

Guidelines for Writing a Single Reflection

If you are inexperienced with reflective writing, your tendency at first may be to generalize about your writing. That is, you may be tempted to narrate your writing process in generic, blow-by-blow procedural terms ("First I took some notes. Then I wrote a first draft and showed it to my roommate, who gave me some suggestions. Then I revised") or to describe your rhetorical choices in general, prescriptive terms ("I started with a catchy introduction because it's important to grab your reader's attention").

To write an effective single reflection, select only a few ideas to focus on, look at specific aspects of a specific paper, explore dialectically your past thinking versus your present thinking, and support your analysis with adequate details. We suggest the following questions as a guide to producing such reflections. But don't answer them all. Rather, pick out the two or three questions that best apply to your performance and text. (Try to select your questions from at least two different categories.) Your goal should be depth, not a broad survey. The key criteria are these: Be *selective*, be *specific*, show *dialectic thinking*, and include *adequate details*.

Process questions:

- What specific writing strategies did I use to complete this work?
- Which strategies were the most or least productive?
- Did this writing project require new strategies, or did I rely on past strategies?
- What was the biggest problem I faced in writing this piece, and how successful was I in solving that problem?
- What has been my major content-level revision so far?
- What were my favorite sentence- or word-level revisions?
- What did I learn about myself as a writer or about writing in general by writing this paper?

Subject-related questions:

- How did the subject of my writing cause me to "wallow in complexity"?
- What tensions did I encounter between my ideas/experiences and those of others? Between the competing ideas about the subject in my own mind?
- Did I change my mind or come to see something differently as a result of writing this work?
- What passages show my independent thinking about the subject? My unresolved problems or mixed feelings about it?
- What were the major content problems, and how successful was I in resolving them?
- What did writing about this subject teach me?

*We are indebted to Kathleen Blake Yancey and Donna Qualley for a number of the definitions, specific assignments, and suggestions for single and comprehensive reflection tasks that are discussed in the rest of this chapter. Yancey explains the "Talk-To" and "Talk-Back" assignments in her book *Reflection in the Writing Classroom* (Logan, UT: Utah State UP, 1998).

Rhetoric-related questions:

- How did the audience I imagined influence me in writing this paper?
- How did my awareness of genre influence my choices about subject matter and rhetorical features?
- What do I want readers to take away from reading my work?
- What rhetorical strategies please me most (my use of evidence, my examples, my delayed thesis, etc.)? What effect do I hope these strategies have on my audience?
- How would I describe my voice in this work? Is this voice appropriate? Similar to my everyday voice or to the voices I have used in other kinds of writing?
- Did I take any risks in writing this?
- What do readers expect from this genre, and did I fulfill those expectations?

Self-assessment questions:

- What are the most significant strengths and weaknesses in this writing?
- Will others also see these as important strengths or weaknesses? Why or why not?
- What specific ideas and plans do I have for revision?

Comprehensive Reflection Assignments

You may also be asked to write a final, comprehensive reflection on your development as a writer over a whole term. Although end-of-the-term reflective essays differ in scope and audience from single reflections, similar qualities are valued in both: selectivity, specificity, dialectical thinking, and adequate detail.

In some cases, the comprehensive reflective essay will introduce the contents of a final portfolio; in other cases, this will be a stand-alone assignment. Either way, your goal is to help your readers understand more knowledgeably how you developed as a writer. Most important, in explaining what you have learned from this review of your work, you also make new self-discoveries.

Guidelines for Writing a Comprehensive Reflection

Instructors look for four kinds of knowledge in comprehensive reflections: self-knowledge, content knowledge, rhetorical knowledge, and critical knowledge or judgment. Here we suggest questions that you can use to generate ideas for your comprehensive reflective letter or essay. Choose only a few of the questions to respond to, questions that allow you to explain and demonstrate your most important learning in the course. Also, choose experiences to narrate and passages to cite that illustrate more than one kind of knowledge.

Self-Knowledge By *self-knowledge*, we mean your understanding of how you are developing as a writer. Think about the writer you were, are, or hope to be. You can also contemplate how the subjects you have chosen to write about (or the way you have approached your subjects) relate to you personally beyond the scope of your papers. Self-knowledge questions you might ask are the following:

- What knowledge of myself as a writer have I gained from the writing I did in this course?

- What changes, if any, have occurred in my writing practices or my sense of myself as a writer?
- What patterns or discontinuities can I identify between the way I approached one writing project versus the way I approached another?
- How can I best illustrate and explain through reference to specific writing projects the self-knowledge I have gained?

Content Knowledge *Content knowledge* refers to what you have learned by writing about various subjects. It also includes the intellectual work that has gone into the writing and the insights you gained from considering multiple points of view and grappling with your own conflicting ideas. Perhaps you have grasped ideas about your subjects that you have not shown in your papers. These questions about content knowledge can prod your thinking:

- What kinds of content complexities did I grapple with this term?
- What *earned insights** did I arrive at through confronting clashing ideas?
- What new perspectives did I gain about particular subjects from my considerations of multiple or alternate viewpoints?
- What new ideas or perspectives did I gain that may not be evident in the writings themselves?
- What passages from various papers best illustrate the critical thinking I did in my writing projects for this course?

Rhetorical Knowledge Our third category, *rhetorical knowledge*, focuses on your awareness of your rhetorical decisions—how your contemplation of purpose, audience, and genre affected your choices about content, structure, style, and document design. The following questions about rhetorical choices can help you assess this area of your knowledge:

- What important rhetorical choices did I make in various works to accomplish my purpose or to appeal to my audience? What parts of my various works best illustrate these choices? Which of these choices are particularly effective and why? About which choices am I uncertain and why?
- What have I learned about the rhetorical demands of audience, purpose, and genre, and how has that knowledge affected my writing and reading practices?
- How do I expect to use this learning in the future?

*Thomas Newkirk, in *Critical Thinking and Writing: Reclaiming the Essay* (Urbana, IL: NCTE, 1989), coined the phrase "earned insights," a phrase that Donna Qualley also refers to in *Turns of Thought: Teaching Composition as Reflexive Inquiry* (Portsmouth, NH: Boynton/Cook, Heinemann, 1997), pp. 35–37.

Critical Knowledge or Judgment A fourth area of knowledge, *critical knowledge or judgment*, concerns your awareness of significant strengths and weaknesses in your writing. This area also encompasses your ability to identify what you like or value in various pieces of writing and to explain why. You could ask yourself these questions about your critical knowledge:

- Of the works in my portfolio, which is the best and why? Which is the weakest and why?
- How has my ability to identify strengths and weaknesses changed during this course?
- What role has peer, instructor, or other reader feedback had on my assessments of my work?
- What improvements would I make in these works if I had more time?
- How has my writing changed over the term? What new abilities will I take away from this course?
- What are the most important things I still have to work on as a writer?
- What is the most important thing I have learned in this course?
- How do I expect to use what I've learned from this course in the future?

Guidelines for Writing a Comprehensive Reflective Letter

Because the letter (sometimes an essay) that you write to introduce your portfolio shows your insights not only about your writing abilities but also about your abilities as a reflective learner, it may be one of the most important pieces of writing you do for a writing course. Here we offer some additional suggestions geared specifically toward introducing your writing portfolio:

- Review the single reflections you have written about specific writing projects during the term. As you reread these process log entries, writer's memos, companion pieces, and so on, what do you discover about yourself as a writer?
- Consider key rhetorical concepts that you have learned in this course. Use the detailed table of contents of Chapters 1 through 4 to refresh your memory about these concepts. How can you show that you understand these concepts and have applied them in your writing?
- Take notes on your own writing as you review your work and reconstruct your writing processes for particular writing projects. What patterns do you see? What surprises you? How can you show the process behind the product? How can you show your growth as a writer through specific examples?
- Be honest. Identifying weaknesses is as important as identifying strengths. How can you use this opportunity to discover more about yourself as a writer or learner?

Readings

Our first reading is a single reflection by student Jaime Finger. She writes about what she sees as the strengths and weaknesses of an exploratory essay in which she was asked to pose a question raised but not clearly answered in a collection of essays on issues of race and class. (She posed the question, "What motivates people to behave as they do?") She was then asked to investigate various perspectives on the question that were offered by the readings, to consider other perspectives drawn from her own knowledge and experience, and to assess the strengths and weaknesses of differing points of view.

Jaime Finger (student)

A Single Reflection on an Exploratory Essay

1 Although this paper was harder than the first one, I believe I have a good opening question. I like how I divided her [the author of the essays] ideas about motivation into two parts—individual and social. I also like how I used examples from many different essays (this proves I really read the whole book!). Another thing I like about this essay is how I include some examples of my own, like the Michael Jordan example of how he did not make the basketball team in his freshman year and that motivated him to practice every day for a year before making the team his sophomore year. I wonder if he ever would have been as good as he is if he had made the team his freshman year? I wish I could or would have added more of my own examples like this one.

2 What I'm not sure about is if I later ask too many other questions, like when I ask, "If someone is doing something because of society's pressures, is he responsible for that behavior?" and "How much are we responsible to other people like the homeless?" I felt that I piled up questions, and also felt I drifted from my original questions. The paper was confusing for me to write, and I feel that it jumps around. Maybe it doesn't, but I don't know.

3 Since *Alchemy* [the title of the essay collection] was such a hard book, I'm kind of happy with my paper (although after hearing some of the others in my peer group, I don't know if it's up to par!!).

THINKING CRITICALLY

about "A Single Reflection on an Exploratory Essay"

1. To what extent does this reflection show that Jaime has deepened her thinking about the question, "What motivates people to behave as they do?"
2. Where does Jaime show an awareness of audience and purpose in her self-reflection on her essay?
3. To what extent does Jaime show us that she can identify strengths and weaknesses of her essay?
4. What are Jaime's most important insights about her essay?

5. How would you characterize Jaime's voice in this reflection? Does this voice seem appropriate for this kind of reflective writing? Why or why not?
6. What are the greatest strengths and weaknesses in Jaime's single reflection?

Our second reading is the draft of a comprehensive reflective letter written by a student, Bruce Urbanik, for a second-semester composition course that involved a large-scale portfolio assessment. Bruce's portfolio as a whole will be read and scored (Pass or Fail) by two outside readers (and a third if the first two disagree). The contents of Bruce's portfolio include two essays written outside of class and revised extensively and one essay written in class under test conditions. As his letter suggests, his two out-of-class essays were classical arguments (see Chapter 13) written in response to the nonfiction texts that his class read during the semester. The assignment he was given for this comprehensive reflection is similar to the one on pages 603–605.

Bruce Urbanik (student)

A Comprehensive Reflective Letter

Dear Portfolio Reader:

1 This is my first college course in five years. I left school for financial reasons and a career opportunity that I couldn't pass up. I thought of contesting the requirement of this course because I had completed its equivalent five years ago. But, as I reflected on the past few years, I realized that the only books I have read have been manuals for production machinery. My writing has consisted of shorthand, abbreviated notes that summarize a shift's events. Someday, after I finish my degree and move up in my company, I'm going to have to write a presentation to the directors on why we should spend millions of dollars on new machinery to improve productivity. I need this course if I expect to make a persuasive case.

2 I was very intimidated after I read the first book in the course, *No Contest: The Case Against Competition*, by Alfie Kohn. The author used what seemed to me a million outside sources to hammer home his thesis that competition is unhealthy in our society and that cooperation is the correct route. I felt very frustrated with Kohn and found myself disagreeing with him although I wasn't always sure why. I actually liked many of his ideas, but he seemed so detached from his argument. Kohn's sources did all the arguing for him. I tried to take a fresh perspective by writing about my own personal experience. I also used evidence from an interview I conducted with a school psychologist to back up my argument about the validity of my own experiences with cooperative education. The weakness of this paper is my lack of opposing opinions.

3 For my second essay, on Terry Tempest Williams's *Refuge: An Unnatural History of Family and Place*, I certainly could not use any personal experience. Williams, a Mormon woman, writes about the deaths of her mother, grandmother, and other female relatives from breast cancer, believed to be caused by the atomic testing in Utah.

I argued that the author, Williams, unfairly blamed men and the role women play in the Mormon religion for the tragic death of her mother and other relatives. She thinks that if the Mormon Church had not discouraged women from questioning authority, maybe some of them would have protested the nuclear testing. But I think this reasoning ignores the military and government pressures at the time and the fact that women in general didn't have much power back in the '50s. Since I didn't know anything about the subject, I asked a Mormon woman that I know to comment on these ideas. Also, my critique group in class was comprised of myself and three women. I received quite a bit of verbal feedback from them on this essay. I deal with men at work all day. This change, both for this essay and the entire semester, was welcome.

4 In-class, timed essay writing was my biggest downfall. I have not been trained to develop an idea and present support for it on the fly. Thoughts would race through my head as I tried to put them on paper. I thought I was getting better, but the in-class essay in this portfolio is just awful. I really wish I could have had more practice in this area. I'm just not comfortable with my writing unless I've had lots of time to reflect on it.

5 A few weeks ago, I found a disk that had some of my old papers from years ago stored on it. After reading some of them, I feel that the content of my writing has improved since then. I know my writing has leaped huge steps since my first draft back in September. As a student not far from graduation, I know I will value the skills practiced in this course.

THINKING CRITICALLY

about "A Comprehensive Reflective Letter"

1. What kinds of self-knowledge does Bruce display in his reflective letter?
2. Does Bruce demonstrate dialectical thinking about himself as a writer? If so, where? What multiple writing selves does Bruce identify in his letter?
3. What has Bruce learned from writing about *No Contest* and *Refuge*? What specific examples does he give of "earned insights" or dialectical thinking regarding his subjects?
4. Does Bruce demonstrate his ability to make judgments about his essays' strengths and weaknesses?
5. What learning from this course do you think Bruce is likely to use in the future?
6. Which of the four kinds of writer's knowledge would you like Bruce to address more closely in revising this reflective letter? What kinds of questions does he overlook? Which points could he build up more? Where could his comments be more text-specific and detailed?

A GUIDE TO EDITING

PART 6

This poster, sponsored by the Ad Council and StopBullying.gov, is part of an ongoing campaign to curtail bullying among young people. The ad is aimed at parents, urging them to encourage their children to be active in opposing bullying. Although the ad's creators chose to use lettering—not an image—to illustrate bullying, the poster has both visual and verbal rhetorical effects. It makes strong appeals to *pathos* in its use of shocking abusive language and disturbing lettering style. Note how the blurry presentation of the type makes a visual statement about both perception and psychological damage. It reinforces the idea that not everyone is aware of bullying and suggests that bullying dims the personhood of victims. Together with the line about parents' unawareness of the hostility present in their kids' environment, this ad presents a powerful message to parents.

1 IMPROVING YOUR EDITING SKILLS

WHAT YOU WILL LEARN

H1.1 Improve your editing processes.

Why Editing Is Important

In our discussion of the writing process in Chapter 16, we recommend saving editing for last. We do so not because editing is unimportant but because fine-tuning a manuscript requires that the main features of the text—its ideas and organization—be relatively stable. There is no point in correcting mistakes in a passage that is going to be deleted or completely rewritten.

This late-stage concern for clarity and correctness is a crucial part of the writing process because editing and proofreading errors reflect directly on your *ethos*, that is, on the reader's image of you as a writer. The problem with sentence-level errors is that they inevitably show up to embarrass us whenever we let our guard down. If you're writing something with real-world consequences—a job application letter, a grant proposal, a letter to a client, a field report for your boss—then typos, misspellings, sentence fragments, and dangling participles are like a piece of lettuce between your teeth. Instead of focusing on your message, your readers may not even take you seriously enough to finish reading what you have written.

Another reason to edit is more existential than rhetorical. It has to do with the care we devote to the details of something that matters to us. In Robert Pirsig's philosophical novel about writing, *Zen and the Art of Motorcycle Maintenance*, editing and proofreading belong to the "motorcycle maintenance" side of writing, not to the Zen side. For Pirsig, motorcycle maintenance is a metaphor for the unglamorous but essential aspect of any thoughtful enterprise. It requires discipline; you must give yourself up to the object before you, whether it is a motorcycle, a philosophical system, or the draft of an essay. Editing and proofreading, like motorcycle maintenance, require us to focus painstakingly on the parts. It can seem unrelentingly, oppressively nitpicky, but in a complex engine or complex essay, misfires and mistakes among the parts keep the whole from realizing its full potential. Even if you are the only one aware of these failures, you gain an innate satisfaction in making the parts function perfectly—the sort of satisfaction that carries over into larger pursuits.

Improving Your Editing and Proofreading Processes

H1.1
Improve your editing and proofreading processes.

You can become a more attentive editor and proofreader of your own prose if you practice the kinds of editing strategies we suggest in this section.

Keep a List of Your Own Characteristic Errors

When one of your papers is returned, look carefully at the kinds of sentence-level errors noted by your instructor. A paper with numerous errors might actually contain only two or three *kinds* of errors repeated several times. For example, some writers consistently omit apostrophes from possessives or add them to plurals; others regularly create comma splices when they use such words as *therefore* or *however* at the beginning of an independent clause. Try to classify the kinds of errors you made on the paper, and then try to avoid these errors on your next paper.

Do a Self-Assessment of Your Editing Knowledge

Look over the detailed table of contents for this editing guide and note the various topics covered. Which of these topics are familiar to you from previous instruction? In which areas are you most confident? In which areas are you most shaky? We generally recommend that students study the topics in Handbook 3 early in a course because the chapter explains the main punctuation rules that help you avoid fragments and comma splices and that help you make decisions about comma placement within a sentence. The remaining handbook chapters can function as handy references when specific questions arise. Become familiar with the organization of this guide so that you can find information rapidly.

Read Your Draft Aloud

A key to good editing is noting every word. An especially helpful strategy is to read your paper aloud—really aloud, not half-aloud, mumbling to yourself, but at full volume, as if you were reading to a room full of people. When you stumble over a sentence or have to go back to fit sound to sense, mark the spot. Something is probably wrong there and you will want to return to it later. Make sure that the words you read aloud are actually on the page. When reading aloud, people often unconsciously fill in missing words or glide over mispunctuated passages, so check carefully to make sure that what you say matches what you wrote. Some writers like to read aloud into a recorder and then reread their draft silently while playing back the recording. If you haven't tried the recording technique, consider doing so at least once; it is a surprisingly powerful way to improve your editing skills.

Read Your Draft Backward

Another powerful editing technique—strange as it might seem—is to read your paper backward, word by word, from end to beginning. When you read forward, you tend to focus on meaning and often read right past mistakes. Reading backward estranges you from the paper's message and allows you to focus on the details of the essay—the words and sentences. As you read backward, keep a dictionary and this handbook close by. Focus on each word, looking for typos, spelling errors, misused apostrophes, pronoun case errors, and so forth, and attend to each sentence unit, making sure that it is a complete sentence and that its boundaries have been properly marked with punctuation.

Use a Spell-Checker and (Perhaps) Other Editing Programs

With spell-checkers, you have almost no excuse for including misspelled words or typos in a formal paper. Become a skilled operator of your computer's spell-checker, and always run the program before printing your final draft.

Be aware, however, that a spell-checker isn't foolproof. These programs match strings of letters in a document against strings stored in memory. A spell-checker may not contain some of the specialized words you use (authors' names or special course terms), nor can it tell whether a correctly spelled word is used correctly in context (*it's, its; their, there,* or *they're; to, too,* or *two*).

Many writers use "grammar" checkers, also called "style" or "usage" checkers. We place "grammar" in quotation marks because these programs do not really check grammar. They can perform only countable or matchable functions such as identifying *be* verbs and passive constructions, noting extremely long sentences, identifying clichés and wordy expressions, and so forth. Although these programs can be useful by drawing your attention to some areas where you may be able to tighten or enliven your prose, they have to be used with caution. So-called grammar-checkers can't catch most of the most common errors in usage and grammar that writers make, and they often flag nonexistent problems.

Microtheme Projects on Editing

The following microtheme assignments focus on selected problems of editing and style. Since you never know a concept as well as when you have to teach it to someone else, these assignments place you in a teaching role. They ask you to solve an editing problem and to explain your solution in your own words to a hypothetical audience that has turned to you for instruction.

Your instructor can use these microtheme assignments as individual or group writing projects or as prompts for classroom discussion.

Microtheme 1: Apostrophe Madness Your friend Elmer Fuddnick has decided to switch majors from engineering to creative writing. Poor Elmer has a great imagination, but he forgot to study basic punctuation when he was in high school. He's just sent you the first draft of his latest short story, "The Revenge of the Hedgehogs." Here are his opening sentences:

> The hedgehogs' scrambled from behind the rock's at the deserts edge, emitted what sounded like a series of cats scream's and then rolled themselve's into spiny balls. One of the hedgehogs hunched it's back and crept slowly toward a cactus' shadow.

Although you can't wait to finish Elmer's story, you are a bit annoyed by his misuse of apostrophes. Your job is to explain to Elmer how to use apostrophes correctly.

Begin by correcting Elmer's sentences; then explain to Elmer the principles you used to make your corrections. Your explanation of apostrophes should be clear enough so that Elmer can learn their use from your explanation. In other words, you are the teacher. Use your own language and make up your own examples.

Microtheme 2: Stumped by However You are putting yourself through college by operating an online grammar hot line and charging people for your advice. One day you see the following post:

> Dear Grammarperson:
>
> I get really confused on how to punctuate words like "however" and "on the other hand." Sometimes these words have commas on both sides of them, but at other times they have a comma in back and a semicolon in front. What's the deal here? How can I know whether to use a comma or a semicolon in front of a "however"?
>
> Bewildered in Boston

Write a response to Bewildered explaining why words such as *however* are sometimes preceded by a comma and sometimes by a semicolon (or a period, in which case *however* starts with a capital letter). Use your own language and invent your own examples.

Microtheme 3: The Comic Dangler Here is another message received at the grammar hot line (see Microtheme 2):

> Dear Grammarperson:
>
> My history teacher was telling us the other day that editing our papers before we submitted them was really important. And then she mentioned in passing that some editing mistakes often create comic effects. She said that the dangling participle was her favorite because it often produced really funny sentences. Well, maybe so, but I didn't know what she was talking about. What are dangling participles and why are they funny?
>
> Not Laughing in Louisville

Explain to Not Laughing what dangling participles are and why they are often funny. Illustrate with some examples of your own and then show Not Laughing how to correct them.

Microtheme 4: How's That Again? The grammar hot line is doing a great business (see Microtheme 2). Here is another query:

> Dear Grammarperson:
>
> It has often been said by some instructors that I have had in the various educational institutions that I have attended that a deadening effect is achievable in the prose produced by writers through the transformation of verbs into nouns and through the overuse of words that are considered empty in content or otherwise produce a redundant effect by the restating of the same idea in more words than are necessary for the reader's understanding of the aforementioned ideas. Could these teachers' allegations against the sentence structure of many writers be considered to be at least partially applicable to my own style of writing prose?
>
> Verbose in Vermont

Help Verbose out by rewriting his or her post in a crisper style. Then explain briefly, using your own language and examples, the concepts of wordiness and nominalization.

Microtheme 5: The Intentional Fragment Advertisers frequently use sentence fragments purposely. Find an advertisement that makes extensive use of fragments in its copy. Rewrite the copy to eliminate all sentence fragments. Then write a one-paragraph microtheme in which you speculate why the advertiser used fragments rather than complete sentences. Try to suggest at least two possible reasons.

Microtheme 6: Create Your Own Following the model of the five preceding assignments, create your own microtheme assignment on an editing problem related to any section of this handbook (or to a section assigned by your instructor). Then exchange assignments with a classmate and write a microtheme in response to your classmate's assignment. Be prepared to write a microtheme in response to your own assignment also.

UNDERSTANDING SENTENCE STRUCTURE

2

WHAT YOU WILL LEARN

H2.1 To explain what a sentence is.
H2.2 To use basic sentence patterns.
H2.3 To identify parts of speech.
H2.4 To identify types of phrases.
H2.5 To identify types of clauses.
H2.6 To identify simple, compound, complex, and compound-complex sentences.

The Concept of the Sentence

H2.1
Explain what a sentence is.

The *sentence* is perhaps the most crucial grammatical concept for writers to understand. A sentence is a group of related words with a complete subject and a complete predicate. The subject names something, and the predicate makes an assertion about the thing named.

Name Something	Make an Assertion about It
Cheese	tastes good on crackers.
Lizards and snakes	are both kinds of reptiles.
Capital punishment	has been outlawed in many countries.

Every sentence must include at least one subject and one predicate. These components answer two different questions: (1) Who or what is the sentence about? (subject); and (2) What assertion does the sentence make about the subject? (predicate). Consider the following example:

Tree ants in Southeast Asia construct nests by sewing leaves together.

What is this sentence about? *Tree ants in Southeast Asia* (subject). What assertion is made about tree ants? (They) *construct nests by sewing leaves together* (predicate).

Ordinarily a sentence begins with the subject, followed by the verb. Sometimes, however, word order can be changed. In the following examples, the subjects are underlined once and the verbs are underlined twice.

Normal Word Order	The most terrifying insects wander through the countryside seeking prey.
Question	What are the most terrifying insects?
Imperative	Watch for the driver ants. ("You" is understood as the subject.)

"There" Opening	There are various kinds of terrifying insects.
Inverted Order	Across the jungles of Africa marched the driver ants.

Sentences can also have more than one subject or predicate.

Compound Subject	The army ants of South America and the driver ants of Africa march in long columns.
Compound Predicate	The hunters at the head of a column discover a prey, swarm all over it, and eventually cut it apart.

H2.2 Use basic sentence patterns.

Basic Sentence Patterns

All sentences must have a complete subject and a complete predicate. However, the predicates of sentences can take several different shapes, depending on whether the verb needs a following noun, pronoun, or adjective to complete its meaning. These words are called *complements*. The four kinds of complements are *direct objects, indirect objects, subject complements,* and *object complements.*

Pattern One: Subject + Verb (+ Optional Adverb Modifiers)

adverb modifiers

The eagle soared gracefully across the summer sky.

In this pattern, the predicate contains only a verb and optional adverbial modifiers. Because the verb in this pattern does not transfer any action from a doer to a receiver, it is called "intransitive."

Pattern Two: Subject + Verb + Direct Object (DO)

DO

Peter was fixing a flat tire over in Bronco County at the very moment of the crime.

Direct objects occur with *transitive verbs*, which transfer action from a doer (the subject) to a receiver (the direct object). Transitive verbs don't seem complete in themselves; they need a noun or pronoun following the verb to answer the question What? or Whom? Peter was fixing *what*? The *flat tire*.

Pattern Three: Subject + Verb + Subject Complement (SC)

SC

My mother is a professor.

SC

The engine in this car seems sluggish.

In this pattern, verbs are *linking verbs,* which are followed by subject complements rather than direct objects. Unlike direct objects, which receive the action of the verb, subject complements either rename the subject (a noun) or describe the subject (an adjective). You can best understand a subject complement if you think of the linking verb as an equals sign (=).

Pattern Four: Subject + Verb + Direct Object + Object Complement (OC)

DO OC

That woman called me an idiot.

Whereas a subject complement describes the subject of the sentence, an object complement describes the direct object, either by modifying it or by renaming it. Compare the patterns.

SC

Pattern Three I am an idiot.

DO OC

Pattern Four The woman called me an idiot.

Pattern Five: Subject + Verb + Indirect Object (IDO) + Direct Object

IDO DO

My mother sent the professor an angry letter.

IDO DO

My father baked me a cake on Valentine's Day.

Sometimes transitive verbs take an *indirect object* as well as a direct object. Whereas the direct object answers the question What? or Whom? following the verb, the indirect object answers the question To what or whom? or For what or whom? My mother sent *what*? *A letter* (direct object). She sent a letter *to whom*? *The professor* (indirect object). My father baked *what*? *A cake* (direct object). My father baked a cake *for whom*? For *me* (indirect object).

Parts of Speech

H2.3
Identify parts of speech.

Although linguists argue about the best way to classify the functions of words in a sentence, the traditional eight parts of speech listed here are most often used in dictionaries and basic introductions to grammar.

Parts of Speech

nouns (N)	adverbs (Adv)
pronouns (PN)	prepositions (P)
verbs (V)	conjunctions (C)
adjectives (Adj)	interjections (I)

Each part of speech serves a different function in a sentence and also possesses structural features that distinguish it from the other parts of speech. Because many words can serve as different parts of speech in different circumstances, you can determine what part of speech a word plays only within the context of the sentence you are examining.

Nouns

Nouns are the names we give to persons (*Samuel, mechanic*), places (*Yellowstone, the forest*), things (*a rock, potatoes*), and abstract concepts (*love, happiness*). Nouns can be identified by structure as words that follow the articles *a, an,* or *the*; as words that change their form to indicate number; and as words that change their form to indicate possession.

a rock several rock*s* the rock'*s* hardness

But not: a *from*; several *froms*; the *from's* coat.

Pronouns

Pronouns take the place of nouns in sentences. The noun that a pronoun replaces is called the pronoun's *antecedent*. English has the following types of pronouns:

Type of Pronoun	Examples
Personal	I, me, you, he, him, she, her, it, we, us, they, them
Possessive (with Noun)	my, your, his, her, its, our, their
Possessive (no Noun)	mine, yours, his, hers, ours, theirs
Demonstrative	this, that, these, those
Indefinite	any, anybody, someone, everyone, each, nobody
Reflexive/Intensive	myself, yourself, himself, herself, itself, ourselves, yourselves, themselves
Interrogative	who, what, whom, whose, which, whoever, whomever
Relative	who, whom, whose, which, that

Verbs

Verbs are words that express action (*run, laugh*) or state of being (*is, seem*). Structurally, they change form to indicate tense and sometimes to indicate person and number. A word can function as a verb if it can fit the following frames:

I want to ____________. I will ____________.

I want to *throw*. I will *throw*.

But not: I want to *from*; I will *from*.

Verbs are used as complete verbs or as incomplete verbs, often called "verbals." When used as complete verbs, they fill the predicate slot in a sentence. When used as incomplete verbs, they fill a noun's, adjective's, or adverb's slot in a sentence. Verbs often require helping verbs, also called "auxiliary verbs," to fulfill their function.

Principal Parts Verbs have five principal parts, which vary depending on whether the verb is *regular* or *irregular.*

Principal Part	Regular Verb Examples	Irregular Verb Examples
Infinitive or Present Stem (infinitives begin with *to*; the word following the *to* is the *present stem*)	to love to borrow	to begin to get
Present Stem + -s (used for third-person singular, present tense)	loves borrows	begins gets
Past Stem (regular verbs add *-ed* to present stem; irregular verbs have different form)	loved borrowed	began got
Past Participle (same as past stem for regular verbs; usually a different form for irregular verbs)	loved borrowed	begun gotten
Present Participle (add *-ing* to present stem)	loving borrowing	beginning getting

The irregular verb *to be* has more forms than do other verbs.

Infinitive	to be
Present Forms	am, is, are
Past Forms	was, were
Past Participle	been
Present Participle	being

Tenses Verbs change their forms to reflect differences in time. A verb's time is called its "tense." There are six main tenses, each with three forms, sometimes called "aspects"—simple, progressive, and emphatic. For two of the tenses—the simple present and simple past—a complete verb is formed by using one word only. For all other tenses, two or more words are needed to form a complete verb. The additional words are called "helping," or "auxiliary," verbs. In some tenses the main verb or one of the helping verbs changes form to agree with its subject in person and number.

Simple Form. Here are regular and irregular examples of the simple form of the six main tenses:

See pp. 636–639 on subject-verb agreement.

Simple Present	She *enjoys* the pizza. They *begin* the race.
Simple Past	She *enjoyed* the pizza. They *began* the race.
Simple Future	She *will enjoy* the pizza. They *will begin* the race.
Present Perfect	She *has enjoyed* the pizza. They *have begun* the race.
Past Perfect	She *had enjoyed* the pizza. They *had begun* the race.
Future Perfect	She *will have enjoyed* the pizza. They *will have begun* the race.

Progressive Form. Each tense also has a progressive form to indicate actions that are ongoing or in-process.

Present Progressive	Sally *is eating* her sandwich.
Past Progressive	Sally *was eating* her sandwich.
Future Progressive	Sally *will be eating* her sandwich.
Present Perfect Progressive	Sally *has been eating* her sandwich.
Past Perfect Progressive	Sally *had been eating* her sandwich.
Future Perfect Progressive	Sally *will have been eating* her sandwich.

Emphatic Form. Several tenses have an emphatic form, which uses the helping verb *to do* combined with the present stem. The emphatic form is used for giving special stress, for asking questions, and for making negations.

I *do go*. I *did go*.

Did the dog *bark*?

Do you *like* peanuts?

The child *does* not *sit* still.

See the section on subjunctive mood below.

Modal Forms. Additionally, a variety of other helping verbs, often called "modals," can be used to form complete verbs with different senses of time and attitude.

will, would   may, might
can, could   must
shall, should

Mood Verbs have three moods: indicative (by far the most common), subjunctive, and imperative.

Indicative Mood. The indicative mood is used for both statements and questions.

The dog *rode* in the back of the pickup. Where *is* Sally?

Subjunctive Mood. The subjunctive mood is used to indicate that a condition is contrary to fact and, in certain cases, to express desire, hope, or demand. The subjunctive is formed in the present tense by using the infinitive stem.

I request that Joe *pay* the bill.

Compare with the indicative: Joe *pays* the bill.

In the past tense, only the verb *to be* has a distinctive subjunctive form, which is always *were*.

If I *were* the teacher, I would give you an A for that project.

Here the subjunctive *were* means "I am *not* the teacher"; it expresses a condition contrary to fact.

Imperative Mood. Finally, the imperative mood conveys a command or request. For most verbs the imperative form is the same as the second-person present tense. An exception is the verb *to be*, which uses *be*.

Be here by noon. *Pay* the bill immediately.

Voice The voice of a verb indicates whether the subject of the verb acts or is acted on. The concept of voice applies only to *transitive* verbs, which transfer action from a doer to a receiver. In the active voice, the subject is the doer of the action and the direct object is the receiver.

Active Voice The professor graded the paper.

In the passive voice, the subject is the receiver of the action; the actor is either omitted from the sentence or made the object of the preposition *by*. The passive voice is formed with the past participle and some form of the helping verb *to be*. For advice on when to use active and passive voice, see pp. 654–655.

Passive Voice The paper was graded (by the professor).

Adjectives and Adverbs

Adjectives and adverbs describe or *modify* other words.

Adjectives Adjectives modify nouns by answering such questions as Which ones? (*those* rabbits); what kind? (*gentle* rabbits); how many? (*four* rabbits); what size? (*tiny* rabbits); what color? (*white* rabbits); what condition? (*contented* rabbits); and whose? (*Jim's* rabbits).

Articles (*a, an, the*) form a special class of adjectives. *A* and *an* are indefinite and singular, referring to any representative member of a general class of objects.

I would like *an* apple and *a* sandwich.

The is definite and can be singular or plural. It always specifies that a particular object is meant.

I want *the* apple and *the* sandwich that were sitting on my desk a few minutes ago.

Adverbs Adverbs modify verbs, adjectives, or other adverbs. They answer the questions How? (he petted the rabbit *gently*); how often? (he petted the rabbit *frequently*); where? (he petted the rabbit *there* in the corner of the room); when? (he petted the rabbit *early*); and to what degree? (he petted the rabbit *very* gently).

Conjunctive adverbs, such as *therefore, however*, and *moreover*, modify whole clauses by showing logical relationships between clauses or sentences.

Positive, Comparative, and Superlative Forms Adjectives and adverbs have positive, comparative, and superlative forms.

Positive	This is a *quick* turtle. It moves *quickly*.
Comparative	My turtle is *quicker* than yours. It moves *more quickly* than yours.
Superlative	Of the three turtles, mine is the *quickest*. Of all the turtles in the race, mine moves *most quickly*.

Conjunctions

Conjunctions join elements within a sentence. *Coordinating* conjunctions (*and, or, nor, but, for, yet,* and *so*) join elements of equal importance.

John *and* Mary went to town.

The city rejoiced, *for* the rats had finally been exterminated.

Subordinating conjunctions (such as *when, unless, if, because, after, while, although*) turn an independent sentence into a subordinate clause and then join it to an independent clause.

For more on coordinating and subordinating conjunctions, see Handbook Chapter 3.

After I get off work, I will buy you a soda.

She won't show him how to use the TiVo *unless* he apologizes.

If you are going to the city, please get me a magazine at Caesar's.

Prepositions

Prepositions show the relationship between a noun or pronoun (the object of the preposition) and the rest of the sentence. The preposition and its object together are called a "prepositional phrase." Common prepositions include *about, above, across, among, behind, between, from, in, into, of, on, toward,* and *with.*

The cat walked *under* the table.

The vase was *on* the table.

The table is a mixture *of* cherry and walnut woods.

Interjections

Interjections (*Yippee! Sweet! Ouch!*) are forceful expressions, usually followed by exclamation marks, that express emotion.

Hooray, school's out! *Ugh,* that's disgusting!

H2.4 Types of Phrases

Identify types of phrases.

A phrase is a group of related words that does not contain a complete subject and a complete verb. There are four main kinds of phrases:

1. prepositional,
2. appositive,
3. verbal (participial, gerund, and infinitive), and
4. absolute.

Prepositional Phrases

A preposition connects a noun, pronoun, or group of words acting as a noun to the rest of the sentence, thereby creating a prepositional phrase that serves as a modifying element within the sentence. Prepositional phrases usually begin with the preposition and end with the noun or noun substitute, called the "object of the preposition."

We watched the baby crawl *under the table.*

The man *in the gray suit* is my father.

Appositive Phrases

Appositive phrases give additional information about a preceding noun or pronoun. They sometimes consist of only one word.

Jill saw her friend *Susan* in the café.

We stopped for a mocha latte at Adolpho's, *the most famous espresso bar in the city.*

Verbal Phrases

Verbals are incomplete forms of verbs that can't function as predicates in a sentence. Similar to verbs, verbals can show tense and can take complements, but they also function as other parts of speech in that they fill noun, adjective, or adverb slots in a sentence. When a verbal is accompanied by modifiers or complements, the word group is called a "verbal phrase." There are three kinds of verbals and verbal phrases:

1. participial,
2. gerund, and
3. infinitive.

Participial Phrases Participles have two forms: the present participle and the past participle. The present participle is the *-ing* form (*swimming, laughing*); the past participle is the *-ed* form for regular verbs (*laughed*) and an irregular form for irregular verbs (*swum*). Participles and participial phrases always act as adjectives in a sentence. In the following examples, the noun modified by the participle is indicated by an arrow.

I saw some ducks *swimming in the lake.*

Laughing happily, Molly squeezed Jake's arm.

The 100-meter freestyle, a race *swum by more than twenty competitors last year,* was won by a thirteen-year-old boy.

Gerund Phrases Gerunds are always the *-ing* form of the verb, and they always serve as nouns in a sentence.

Swimming is my favorite sport. ***[serves as subject]***

I love *swimming in the lake.* ***[serves as direct object]***

I am not happy about *losing my chemistry notebook in the student union.* ***[serves as object of preposition]***

Infinitive Phrases An infinitive is the dictionary form of a verb preceded by the word *to* (*to run, to swim, to laugh*). Infinitives or infinitive phrases can serve as nouns, adjectives, or adverbs in a sentence.

To complete college with a major in electrical engineering is my primary goal at the moment.

The person *to help you with that math* is Molly Malone.

Absolute Phrases

An absolute phrase is comprised of a noun or noun substitute, followed by a participle. It is *absolute* because it doesn't act as a noun, adverb, or adjective; rather, it modifies the whole clause or sentence to which it is attached.

Her face flushed with sweat, the runner headed down Grant Street.

The assistant hunched over the keyboard, *his fingers typing madly*.

H2.5 Types of Clauses

Identify types of clauses.

Clauses have complete subjects and complete predicates. Some clauses can stand alone as sentences (*independent*, or *main*, clauses), whereas others (*dependent*, or *subordinate*, clauses) cannot stand alone as sentences because they are introduced by a *subordinating conjunction* or a *relative pronoun*.

Here are two independent sentences that could serve as independent clauses:

Sam broke the window.

Lucia studied the violin for thirteen years.

Now here are the same two sentences converted to subordinate clauses:

because Sam broke the window

who studied the violin for thirteen years

In the first example, the subordinating conjunction *because* reduces the independent clause to a subordinate clause. In the second example, the relative pronoun *who*, which replaces *Lucia*, also reduces the independent clause to a subordinate clause.

Finally, here are these subordinated clauses attached to independent clauses to form complete sentences.

Because Sam broke the window, he had to pay for it out of his allowance.

Lucia, who studied the violin for thirteen years, won a music scholarship to a prestigious college.

Subordinate clauses always act as nouns, adjectives, or adverbs in another clause.

Noun Clauses

A noun clause is a subordinate clause that functions as a noun in a sentence. Noun clauses act as subjects, objects, or complements.

He promised *that he would study harder.* **[serves as direct object]**

Why he came here is a mystery. **[serves as subject]**

He lied about *what he did last summer.* **[serves as object of preposition]**

Adjective Clauses

An adjective clause is a subordinate clause that modifies a noun or a pronoun. Adjective clauses are formed with the relative pronouns *who, whom, whose, which,* and *that.* For this reason they are sometimes called "relative clauses."

Peter, *who is a star athlete,* has trouble with reading.

The future threat *that I most fear* is a stock market collapse.

Adverb Clauses

An adverb clause is a subordinate clause that modifies a verb, an adjective, or another adverb. Adverb clauses begin with subordinating conjunctions, such as *although, because, if,* and *when.*

Because he had broken his leg, he danced all night using crutches.

When he got home, he noticed unusual blisters.

Types of Sentences

H2.6
Identify simple, compound, complex, and compound-complex sentences.

Sentences are often classified by the number and kinds of clauses they contain. There are four kinds of sentences:

1. simple,
2. compound,
3. complex, and
4. compound-complex.

Simple Sentences

A sentence is *simple* if it consists of a single independent clause. The clause may contain modifying phrases and have a compound subject and a compound predicate.

John laughed.
John and Mary laughed and sang.

modifying phrase

[Laughing happily and holding hands in the moonlight,] [John and Mary walked

independent clause (with compound subject and predicate)

along the beach, wrote their names in the sand, and threw pebbles into the crashing waves.]

See the discussion of comma splices and run-ons, pp. 631–633.

Compound Sentences

A sentence is *compound* if it consists of two independent clauses linked either by a semicolon or by a comma and a coordinating conjunction. Each clause may contain modifying phrases as well as compound subjects and predicates.

independent clause | independent clause

John laughed, and Mary sang.

modifying phrase | independent clause (with compound subject)

Laughing happily, John and Mary walked hand in hand toward the kitchen, but

independent clause

they weren't prepared for the surprise on the countertop.

Complex Sentences

A sentence is *complex* if it contains one independent clause and one or more subordinate clauses.

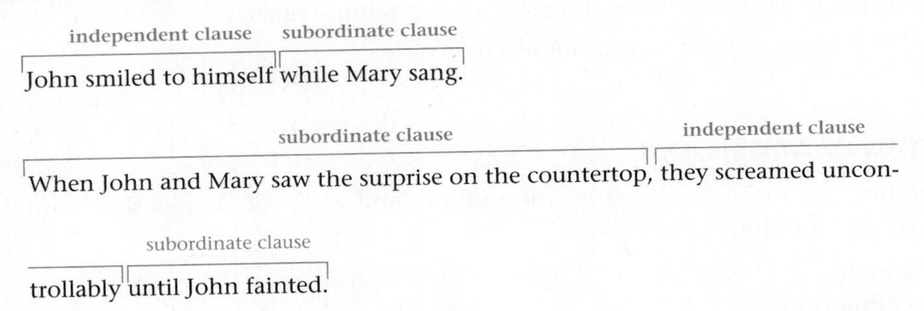
independent clause
subordinate clause
John smiled to himself while Mary sang.
subordinate clause
independent clause
When John and Mary saw the surprise on the countertop, they screamed uncon-
subordinate clause
trollably until John fainted.

Compound-Complex Sentences

A *compound-complex sentence* has at least one subordinate clause and two or more independent clauses joined by a semicolon or by a comma and a coordinating conjunction.

independent clause | subordinate clause | independent clause

John smiled to himself while Mary sang, for he was happy.

subordinate clause | independent clause

When John and Mary saw the surprise on the countertop, they screamed uncon-

independent clause

trollably; soon John collapsed on the floor in a dead faint.

PUNCTUATING BOUNDARIES OF SENTENCES, CLAUSES, AND PHRASES

3

WHAT YOU WILL LEARN

H3.1 To punctuate clauses and phrases in a sentence.
H3.2 To identify and correct sentence fragments.
H3.3 To identify and correct comma splices and run-on sentences.

Rules for Punctuating Clauses and Phrases within a Sentence

H3.1 Punctuate clauses and phrases in a sentence.

This section explains four main punctuation rules for marking the boundaries of clauses and phrases within a sentence. Once you understand these rules, you will find it easier to mark the boundaries of complete sentences and thus to avoid fragments, run-ons, and comma splices.

Rule 1: Join two independent sentences with a semicolon or with a comma and a coordinating conjunction. You can join two complete sentences to form a compound sentence in two ways: (1) with a semicolon, or (2) with a comma and a coordinating conjunction. You should learn the seven coordinating conjunctions:

and   but   or   nor   for   yet   so

When you join two sentences using either of these methods, each sentence becomes an independent clause in the compound sentence; the punctuation signals the joining point.

Two Sentences	Melissa hasn't changed the oil in her car. However, she is still willing to take it to the game.
Joined with Semicolon	Melissa hasn't changed the oil in her car; however, she is still willing to take it to the game.
Joined with Comma and Coordinating Conjunction	Melissa hasn't changed the oil in her car, but she is still willing to take it to the game.

Rule 2: Use a single comma to set off an introductory adverb clause. Another common way to join sentences is to use a subordinating conjunction to convert one sentence to an adverb clause. Subordinating conjunctions are words such as *because, when, if, although*, and *until*. If the resulting adverb clause comes at the start of the sentence, set it off from the independent clause with a comma. If it follows the independent clause, don't set it off.

Adverb Clause Preceding Independent Clause	If the sun is shining in the morning, we'll go for the hike.
Adverb Clause Following Independent Clause	We'll go for the hike if the sun is shining in the morning.

Note that no comma is used in the latter example because the adverb clause follows, rather than precedes, the independent clause.

An exception to this rule occurs with the subordinating conjunction *although*. You should use a comma to set off a clause introduced by *although* even if it comes at the end of a sentence.

The police officer still gave me a ticket, although I explained to her that my speedometer was broken.

Rule 3: Inside a sentence core, use pairs of commas to set off interrupting elements. The core of a sentence consists of the subject, verb, and direct object or subject complement. Within the core of a sentence, never use a single comma; either omit commas or use commas *in pairs* to set off interrupting elements.

Sentence Core	My dog chased the cat around the room.
Interrupting Element Inside the Core	My dog, barking loudly and snapping his teeth, chased the cat around the room.

Note that *a pair* of commas—a comma preceding the element and a comma following the element—marks the boundaries of the interrupting element.

Sentence Core	The police officer still gave me a ticket.
Interrupting Element Inside the Core	The police officer, however, still gave me a ticket.

Rule 4: Use a single comma to set off some introductory or concluding phrases. An introductory phrase often precedes the core of a sentence. Set off an introductory phrase if it is long or if your voice pauses noticeably between the phrase (or single word such as *however*) and the start of the sentence core. Similarly, use a single comma to set off long concluding elements if your voice pauses noticeably after the core. In either case, the comma signals the boundary between the sentence core and the introductory or concluding element.

INTRODUCTORY ELEMENT

Barking loudly and snapping his teeth, my dog chased the cat around the room.

According to many authorities, this author's treatment of women is historically inaccurate.

However, I disagree.

CONCLUDING ELEMENT

My dog chased the cat around the room, his jaws snapping angrily.

The scholar's claim bothered Jensen, leaving him bewildered and possibly angry.

Your familiarity with these four rules will help you understand the logic for punctuating sentences that combine two or more clauses or that include introductory, interrupting, or concluding phrases. Knowing these rules, in turn, will help you learn to signal sentence boundaries to readers.

Exercise

On a separate sheet of paper, create sentences of your own to fill in these sentence pattern templates. Share your sentences with class members.

________________. ________________.

________________; ________________.

________________, however, ________________.

________________; however, ________________.

________________, and ________________.

________________ and ________________.

Because ________________, ________________.

________________ because ________________.

Identifying and Correcting Sentence Fragments

H3.2 Identify and correct sentence fragments.

A sentence fragment is a nonsentence (any structure lacking a complete subject or a complete predicate) that is punctuated either as a sentence or as an independent clause.

Types of Fragments

There are two kinds of sentence fragments.

1. *Phrase fragments* may lack either a subject or a complete predicate or both. In the following passage, the phrase fragments are italicized.

   Caleb and Harper love their mountain home. *Going fishing in the morning. Watching the deer graze in the meadows.* Outside their cabin, a pair of majestic eagles nest in the top of a lone pine; *with only the starry sky as a night roof.*

   The first two fragments are participial phrases punctuated as complete sentences. The last fragment is a prepositional phrase punctuated as an independent clause. The semicolon signals to readers that two independent clauses are joined together.

2. *Subordinate clause fragments* have a subject and a complete predicate, but they begin with either a subordinating conjunction or a relative pronoun, which prevents them from standing alone as a sentence. In the following examples, the subordinate clause fragments are italicized.

   Caleb and Harper often go for a hike. *As soon as the sun comes up.* At night they love to watch the eyes of owls. *Which blink at them from the branches of nearby trees.*

   The first fragment is created by the subordinating conjunction *as soon as*; the second is created by the relative pronoun *which*.

Methods for Correcting Sentence Fragments

There are various ways to correct a fragment; each method produces a slightly different variation in meaning and emphasis.

Method 1: Change a phrase fragment to a complete sentence by converting an incomplete verb into a complete verb or by adding a verb. This method emphasizes the material in the fragment by giving it the weight of a full sentence.

Fragment The buffalo began to stampede. Their heads flailing wildly.

Revised The buffalo began to stampede. Their heads flailed wildly.

The fragment has been converted to a complete sentence by changing the participle *flailing* to the complete verb *flailed*.

Method 2: Change a clause fragment to a complete sentence by removing the subordinator. This method also emphasizes the ideas in the original fragment.

Fragment For Native Americans, killing buffalo was very dangerous. Because the stampeding buffalo herd had to be guided toward the cliff by men shaking wolf skins.

Revised For Native Americans, killing buffalo was very dangerous. The stampeding buffalo herd had to be guided toward the cliff by men shaking wolf skins.

Removing the subordinating conjunction *because* converts the fragment into a complete sentence.

Method 3: Correct the fragment by joining it to the sentence that precedes or follows it, whichever makes more sense. This method subordinates the material in the fragment and can work for either phrase or clause fragments. With this method, you may need to use a comma to signal the joining point.

Fragment The buffalo crashed to their deaths. Although the men killed the animals that were still alive. The women did most of the work in preparing the hides and meat.

Revised The buffalo crashed to their deaths. Although the men killed the animals that were still alive, the women did most of the work in preparing the hides and meat.

The original passage contains a subordinate clause fragment beginning with *although*. The revised passage attaches the *although* clause to the second sentence.

Exercise

Proofread the following passage adapted from a student paper. Underline all of the sentence fragments. Then, on a separate sheet of paper, revise the fragments using one of the main correction methods—turn the fragment into a complete sentence or connect the fragment to a neighboring sentence. Choose the correction method that seems most appropriate for the context of the passage.

> Another difference between a taxi driver and other occupations being the way that taxi drivers interact with people. Driving a taxi is one of the few jobs where you really get to "know the customer." In other service jobs, you rarely get to know the customer's name. Such as waiter or bartender. In those jobs you can wait on one hundred people in a night or mix drinks for two hundred. Without personally talking to five of them. In a taxi, however, each customer spends at least ten to fifteen minutes in a quiet car. Having little to do but talk with the driver.

Identifying and Correcting Run-Ons and Comma Splices

H3.3 Identify and correct comma splices and run-on sentences.

Writers make run-on errors or comma splices whenever they fail to show where one sentence ends and the next begins.

A *run-on error* occurs when two sentences are fused together without any punctuation.

> I explained to the police officer that my speedometer was broken she still gave me a ticket.

> Two sentences come together between *broken* and *she*, but no period and capital letter or semi-colon marks the boundary.

A *comma splice* occurs when a writer marks the end of a sentence with a comma instead of with a period and a capital letter or a semi-colon.

> I explained to the police officer that my speedometer was broken, she still gave me a ticket.

> A comma by itself cannot mark the boundary between two sentences.

Methods for Correcting Run-Ons and Comma Splices

Run-ons and comma splices can be corrected in a variety of ways, depending on the meaning you wish to convey. You may choose to separate the ideas by placing them in two separate sentences, or you may wish to join the ideas into a single sentence. To choose the most appropriate method, consider the rhetorical context of the passage you are writing.

Method 1: Separate the sentences with a period and a capital letter. This method gives equal emphasis to both sentences. If you wish to indicate a logical relationship between the two sentences, you can add a conjunctive adverb (such as *therefore* or *nevertheless*) somewhere in the second sentence.

Revised I explained to the police officer that my speedometer was broken. She still gave me a ticket.

Revised I explained to the police officer that my speedometer was broken. However, she still gave me a ticket.

Method 2: Join the sentences with a semicolon. This method creates a compound sentence with two equally strong independent clauses.

Revised I explained to the police officer that my speedometer was broken; however, she still gave me a ticket.

Method 3: Join the sentences with a comma and a coordinating conjunction. This method also creates a compound sentence with two equally strong independent clauses.

Revised I explained to the police officer that my speedometer was broken, but she still gave me a ticket.

Method 4: Join the sentences with a subordinating conjunction or a relative pronoun. This method creates a complex sentence with an independent clause and a subordinate clause. The material in the independent clause receives more emphasis than the subordinated material does.

Revised Although I explained to the police officer that my speedometer was broken, she still gave me a ticket.

Method 5: Convert one of the sentences into a phrase. This method creates a simple sentence with an added or embedded phrase. The phrase has less importance than the rest of the sentence.

Revised Despite my explanation of the broken speedometer, the police officer gave me a ticket.

Choosing the Most Appropriate Method for Correction Although each of these methods of correcting run-ons and comma splices will produce a grammatically correct solution, the method to be used in a given situation depends on the meaning and emphasis you intend. Consider the following example:

Comma Splice The weather is beautiful, my neighbor is washing her car.

To determine the best way to correct this comma splice, you need to consider the passage in which it occurs. Different correction methods create different effects.

Revised It is a great day. The weather is beautiful. My neighbor is washing her car. Kids are playing in the street. The dog is sleeping in the sun.

Here the focus is on the writer's sense of a great day. The beautiful weather and the neighbor washing her car are only two of four separate pieces of evidence the writer uses to support the feeling. By putting them all in separate sentences, the writer emphasizes each one.

But consider how the comma splice might be corrected in a different context:

Revised I was hoping to invite my neighbor over to watch the football game with me this afternoon. But because the weather is beautiful, she is washing her car.

In this version, the main point is the writer's disappointment that the neighbor isn't coming over to watch football. The beautiful weather is the cause of her washing the car, but the subordinating conjunction *because* makes that information secondary. The writer isn't interested in the beautiful weather for its own sake, so a separate sentence such as the one in the first example would be inappropriate.

These differences illustrate that punctuation is a way of controlling and signaling meaning for readers. As you learn ways of correcting comma splices and run-ons, you will also become aware of the wide variety of options available to convey subtleties of thought and feeling.

Exercise

In the following sentences, underline the comma splices or run-ons (some sentences may be correct). Then revise the underlined sentences.

1. I love to hear coffee perking in the pot on lazy Saturday mornings another of my favorite sounds is rain on a tin roof.
2. When the ice cream wagon begins playing its song in our neighborhood, the children run to greet it, clasping their dimes and quarters in grubby little hands.
3. Freud assumed that the unconscious was the basis for human behavior, therefore, he believed that the pleasure audiences receive from art comes from art's embodiment of unconscious material.
4. Because St. Augustine's conception of God was Neoplatonic, Augustine believed that existence in itself is good.
5. Although scientists don't know for sure how much dinosaurs actually ate, they know that their food intake must have been enormous, a question they ask themselves, therefore, is what the dinosaurs actually ate.
6. The doctor told me that my MRI revealed nothing to be alarmed about, nevertheless, she wants me to come back in six months for another checkup.
7. Juan and Alicia began taking the engine apart they worked diligently for four hours and then discovered that they didn't have the right tools.
8. I should apologize for the snide e-mail I wrote you last week, although I must admit that I am still angry.
9. In a home aquarium fish will sometimes die from overeating the instructions on fish food boxes, therefore, stress that you feed fish a specified amount on a strict schedule.
10. The upgrade on Manuel's antivirus program seems more trouble than it's worth, so he has decided not to install it.

4 EDITING FOR STANDARD ENGLISH USAGE

WHAT YOU WILL LEARN

H4.1 To correct mixed constructions and faulty predication.
H4.2 To avoid shifts in verb tense and person and number of pronouns.
H4.3 To correct subject-verb and pronoun-antecedent agreement errors.
H4.4 To maintain parallel constructions.
H4.5 To avoid dangling or misplaced modifiers.
H4.6 To use correct pronoun cases.
H4.7 To use adjectives and adverbs correctly.

H4.1
Correct mixed constructions and faulty predication.

Fixing Grammatical Tangles

Among the most frequent errors in rough drafts are grammatically tangled sentences that result in *mixed constructions* or *faulty predication.*

Mixed Constructions

In the heat of composing a first draft, a writer sometimes starts a sentence with one kind of construction and shifts midway to another construction.

Faulty By buying a year's supply of laundry soap at one time saves lots of money.

This sentence opens with a prepositional phrase that cannot serve as a sentence subject. The writer can correct the error by eliminating the preposition or by supplying a subject.

Revised Buying a year's supply of laundry soap at one time saves lots of money.

or

By buying a year's supply of laundry soap at one time, the average consumer can save lots of money.

Faulty Predication

Another kind of grammatical tangle, called "faulty predication," occurs when the action specified by the verb can't logically be performed by the subject.

Faulty Throughout *The Scarlet Letter*, Hester Prynne's "A" is imbibed with symbolic significance.

Imbibe means "to drink," so its use makes no sense in this sentence.

Revised Throughout *The Scarlet Letter*, Hester Prynne's "A" is invested with symbolic significance.

Maintaining Consistency

H4.2
Avoid shifts in verb tense and person and number of pronouns.

Consistency errors occur whenever a writer illogically shifts verb tenses or shifts the person or number of pronouns.

Shifts in Tense

Readers can become confused when writers change tenses without explanation. You should avoid shifting verb tenses in a passage unless you mean to signal a shift in time.

Faulty The display cases of the little bakery were filled with cakes, pies, doughnuts, and special pastries. From the heated ovens against the back wall *drifts* the aroma of buttery croissants.

The verbs in the first sentence are all in the past tense. The verb in the second sentence shifts to the present without an explanation.

Revised The display cases of the little bakery were filled with cakes, pies, doughnuts, and special pastries. From the heated ovens against the back wall *drifted* the aroma of buttery croissants.

Shifts in the Person and Number of Pronouns

Pronouns have three persons: first (*I, we*); second (*you*); and third (*he, she, it, one, they*). Keep your point of view consistent by avoiding confusing shifts from one person to another or from singular to plural.

Confusing As readers, we are not prepared for Hamlet's change in the last act. When one sees Hamlet joking with the grave diggers, you forget momentarily about his earlier despair.

For advice on avoiding sexist language when using third-person pronouns, see pp. 655–656.

The pronouns shift from first to third to second person.

Revised As readers, we are not prepared for Hamlet's change in the last act. When we see Hamlet joking with the grave diggers, we forget momentarily about his earlier despair.

Maintaining Agreement

H4.3
Correct subject-verb and pronoun-antecedent agreement errors.

Writers often have to choose between singular and plural forms of verbs and pronouns to ensure that verbs match their subjects and pronouns match their antecedents. In some cases, special rules determine whether a subject or an antecedent is singular or plural.

Subject-Verb Agreement

In most cases, it is easy to determine whether the subject is singular or plural, but some cases are tricky. The following rules cover most of these tricky cases.

Plural Words between Subject and Verb It may be difficult to find the subject when it is separated from the verb by intervening words, phrases, or embedded clauses or when an indefinite word such as *one, each,* or *kind* is followed by a prepositional phrase beginning with *of*. In the latter case the object of the preposition is often mistaken for the subject.

Faulty One of the recent shipments of boxes containing computers, printers, and monitors *were* delayed.

Revised One of the recent shipments of boxes containing computers, printers, and monitors *was* delayed.

In this sentence, *one* is the subject, not any of the intervening plural words.

Similarly, prepositional phrases beginning with *as well as, in addition to, along with*, and *including* can trick writers into thinking that a singular subject is plural.

Faulty My mother, along with several of her coworkers, *are* getting a special award for excellence in customer relations.

Revised My mother, along with several of her coworkers, *is* getting a special award for excellence in customer relations.

In this sentence the subject is *mother*; the intervening prepositional phrase should be ignored.

Compound Subjects Joined by *and* Use a plural verb for singular or plural subjects joined by *and* unless the nouns joined by *and* are thought of as one unit, in which case the verb is singular. Notice the different meanings of the following sentences:

My brother and my best friend *is* with me now.

This sentence means that my brother is with me now and that my brother is my best friend.

My brother and my best friend *are* with me now.

This sentence means that two people are with me—my brother and my best friend.

Compound Subjects Joined by *or, nor, either ... or, neither ... nor* The coordinating conjunctions *or, nor, either ... or*, and *neither ... nor* take singular verbs if they join singular subjects and plural verbs if they join plural subjects. If they join a singular subject to a plural subject, the verb agrees with the nearer subject.

Either a raccoon or a dog *is* getting into the garbage pails.

Both subjects are singular, so the verb is singular.

Either raccoons or dogs *are* getting into the garbage pails.

Both subjects are plural, so the verb is plural.

Either some raccoons or a dog *is* getting into the garbage pails.

The subject closer to the verb is singular, so the verb is singular.

Indefinite Pronoun as Subject Some indefinite pronouns are always singular; others can be singular or plural depending on context.

Always Singular		Singular or Plural
anybody	none	all
anyone	each	any
anything	everybody	some
either	neither	
nobody		

The indefinite pronouns in the left-hand columns are always singular.

Faulty Each of the dogs *are* thirsty.

Revised Each of the dogs *is* thirsty.

The indefinite pronouns in the right-hand column can be singular or plural. These words are generally followed by a prepositional phrase beginning with *of*. The number of the pronoun depends on whether the object of the preposition is singular or plural.

Some of the table *is* sanded.

The object of the preposition (*table*) is singular, so the verb is singular.

Some of the tables *are* sanded.

The object of the preposition (*tables*) is plural, so the verb is plural.

Inversion of Subject and Verb Locating the subject may be tricky in inverted sentences, in which the subject comes after the verb.

Just beyond the fence line on the other side of the road are some pheasants.

The subject is *pheasants*, so the verb is plural.

Be especially careful with inverted sentences that begin with *here, there,* or *where*. Errors occur most frequently when a writer uses these words in contractions or in questions.

Faulty Where's my belt and sweater?

The subject is *belt and sweater*, so the verb should be plural.

Revised Where are my belt and sweater?

Relative Pronoun as Subject Relative pronouns used as subjects (*who, that, which*) are singular or plural depending on their antecedents.

A person who *builds* glass houses shouldn't throw stones.

Who is singular because its antecedent, *person*, is singular; hence the verb should be singular.

People who *build* glass houses shouldn't throw stones.

Who is plural because its antecedent, *people*, is plural; hence the verb should be plural.

Be especially careful when the antecedent is the object of the preposition *of*.

One of the reasons that *are* frequently given is inflation.

The verb of the main clause (*is*) is singular because its subject is the singular pronoun *one*. But the verb of the relative clause (*are*) is plural because its subject (*that*) has a plural antecedent (*reasons*).

Subject Followed by Linking Verb and Subject Complement Linking verbs should agree with the subject of the sentence, not with the subject complement.

Sleeping, eating, and drinking *are* his whole life.

The verb *are* agrees with the plural subject, not with the singular subject complement.

His whole life *is* sleeping, eating, and drinking.

In this case, the verb agrees with the singular subject, not with the plural subjective complement.

Collective Noun as Subject With collective nouns such as *group, committee, crew, crowd, faculty, majority*, and *audience*, use a singular verb if the collective group acts as one unit; use a plural verb if the members of the group act individually.

The faculty at Hogwash College *is* delighted with the new president.

Here the faculty functions as a single unit.

The faculty at Hogwash College *are* arguing at this very moment.

Here *faculty* refers to individuals who act independently.

Some collective nouns present special problems or follow special rules, for instance, *a number* versus *the number. A number* refers to a collection of individual items and takes a plural verb. *The number* refers to a unit and takes a singular verb.

A number of students *are* studying grammar this semester.

The number of students studying grammar *is* declining every year.

Titles or words referred to as words use singular verbs.

Snow White and the Seven Dwarfs is a famous Disney movie.

The italics indicates a title, which takes a singular verb. If you were referring to the characters rather than the title, the verb would be plural: "Snow White and the seven dwarfs are my favorite Disney characters."

Exercise

In the following sentences, underline the true subject or subjects of the verb in parentheses. Then underline the correct verb form twice.

1. Under a pile of old rags in the corner of the basement (is/are) a mother mouse and a squirming family of baby mice.
2. Hard work, together with intelligence, initiative, and a bit of good luck, (explains/explain) the success of many wealthy businesspeople.
3. The first thing she emphasized (was/were) the differences between Pacific and Atlantic breeding patterns of these fish.
4. The myth, legend, prayer, and ritual of primitive religions (contains/contain) many common themes.
5. Unfortunately, neither of the interviewers for the local TV station (has/have) read any of her works.
6. There (is/are) a number of students who (is/are) waiting to see the teacher.
7. (Does/Do) one of the students still have my notebook?
8. One of the students who (is/are) trying out for the play (wants/want) to become a professional actor.
9. He is the only one of all the students in the theater arts class who really (has/have) professional ambitions.
10. The committee (is/are) writing individual letters to the judge.

Pronoun-Antecedent Agreement

Just as a subject must agree in number with its verb, so must a pronoun agree in number with its antecedent (the noun that the pronoun stands for). To apply this rule, you must first determine the antecedent of the pronoun and then decide whether the antecedent is singular or plural, following the rules presented in the previous section. Pronoun-antecedent agreement occasionally presents some difficulties. The following rules cover most cases.

Compound Construction as Antecedent If a compound antecedent is joined by *and*, choose a plural pronoun; if a compound antecedent is joined by *or*, the pronoun should agree in number with the closer antecedent.

Gabriela and Levi invited us to their party.

Either Brian or Luis will bring his volleyball to the party.

Either Brian or his sisters will bring their volleyball.

Collective Noun as Antecedent Use a singular pronoun to refer to a collective noun that acts as one unit; use a plural pronoun if members of the group act individually.

The committee reported its opinion.

The committee began arguing among themselves.

See pp. 655–656 for suggestions on alternative constructions.

Indefinite Pronoun as Antecedent Generally, if the antecedent is an indefinite pronoun such as *either, neither, everyone, everybody, someone, somebody, anyone,* or *anybody*, you use a singular pronoun.

Everybody coming to the party should bring his or her own drinks.

Note: Sentence constructions such as this one can lead to the use of non-inclusive language.

H4.4 Maintaining Parallel Structure

Maintain parallel constructions.

A nonparallel construction occurs whenever a writer fails to maintain the same grammatical structure for each item in a series.

Faulty Shanelle likes playing soccer and to roller-skate.

Here the writer has joined a gerund phrase (*playing soccer*) to an infinitive (*to roller-skate*). The problem can be solved by making both items gerunds or both infinitives.

Revised Shanelle likes playing soccer and roller-skating.

or

Shanelle likes to play soccer and to roller-skate.

Faulty As a teacher, he was a courteous listener, helpful during office hours, and he lectured in an exciting way.

Revised As a teacher, he was a courteous listener, a good helper during office hours, and an exciting lecturer.

In this revision the writer converts all items in the series to nouns.

Faulty This term paper is illogical, poorly documented, and should have used more primary sources.

Here the first two items are parallel (the adjectives *illogical* and *poorly documented*), but the last item is a verb phrase (*should have used more primary sources*).

Revised This term paper is illogical, poorly documented, and poorly researched.

or

This term paper, which should have used more primary sources, is illogical and poorly documented.

To increase clarity, writers often repeat function words such as articles, prepositions, conjunctions, or the infinitive word *to* at the beginning of each item in a parallel series.

Confusing The drill sergeant told the recruits that there would be no weekend passes and they would be on KP instead.

Revised The drill sergeant told the recruits that there would be no weekend passes and that they would be on KP instead.

The repetition of *that* clarifies the writer's intention: to report two things the drill sergeant told the recruits.

Placement of Correlative Conjunctions

When using correlative conjunctions (such as *either ... or, neither ... nor, both ... and,* and *not only ... but also*), make sure that each unit of the correlative precedes the same grammatical structure.

Faulty I not only like ice cream but also root beer.

Here the writer places *not only* in front of a verb (*like*), but places *but also* in front of a noun (*root beer*).

Revised I like not only ice cream but also root beer.

Use of *and which/that* or *and who/whom*

Be sure that a clause beginning with *and which, and that, and who,* or *and whom* is preceded by a parallel clause beginning with *which, that, who,* or *whom.*

Faulty Of all my friends, Jayden is the one with the greatest sense of courage and who most believes in honesty.

The writer links a pronoun (*one*) to a relative clause (*who most believes...*), creating a nonparallel structure.

Revised Of all my friends, Jayden is the one who has the greatest sense of courage and who most believes in honesty.

Exercise

In the following sentences, underline the nonparallel constructions. Then, on a separate sheet of paper, revise the sentences to create parallel structures.

1. We improved our old car's acceleration by resetting the spark plug gaps and also we boiled out the carburetor.
2. Race car driving requires much practical experience, and your reactions must be quick.
3. After reading the events calendar, we decided to go to a festival of Japanese anime and on attending the battle of the bands afterward.
4. I want to read a biography of a flamboyant figure working in volunteer organizations and who has altered history.
5. Sasha not only does volunteer work in the school, but also coaching soccer every fall.
6. Either you must leave early or leave after the major rush hour.
7. The harvest moon shone brightly, pouring its light over the surrounding water, and which made the evening a special moment in their lives.
8. You can avoid a comma splice by joining main clauses with a comma and a coordinating conjunction, with a semicolon, or by changing one of the main clauses to a subordinate clause.
9. Again and again psychologists explore the same questions: Are we shaped by our heredity, by our environment, or do we have free will?
10. To make friends you must first be a friend and then listening carefully.

H4.5 Avoid dangling or misplaced modifiers.

Avoiding Dangling or Misplaced Modifiers

Dangling Modifiers

When a sentence opens with a modifying phrase, the phrase must be followed immediately by the noun it modifies, which is usually the grammatical subject of the sentence; otherwise, the phrase is said to dangle. You can correct a dangling modifier by (a) recasting the sentence so that the subject is the word modified by the opening modifier; or (b) expanding the modifying phrase into a clause that has its own subject.

modifier / subject

Faulty Walking down the street, a flowerpot fell on my head.

This sentence brings to mind a walking flowerpot.

modifier / subject

Revised Walking down the street, I was struck on the head by a flowerpot.

or

modifying clause with subject

While *I* was walking down the street, a flowerpot fell on my head.

modifier / subject

Faulty With only a dollar in change, the meal was too expensive.

Does the meal have only a dollar in change?

modifier / subject

Revised With only a dollar in change, I couldn't afford the meal.

or

modifying clause with subject

Because *I* had only a dollar in change, the meal was too expensive.

Misplaced Modifiers

A modifier is said to be misplaced when a modifying word or phrase is separated from the element it modifies. To correct this type of error, change the location of the modifier so that it is next to the word or phrase it modifies.

Faulty The students gave a present to their teacher in a big box.

This sentence suggests that the teacher is in a big box.

Revised The students gave their teacher a present in a big box.

Note: Be careful to place limiting adverbs, such as *only, just,* and *merely,* next to the words they limit. As the following example shows, changing the location of *only* can often change the meaning of a sentence.

Only I baked the cake. (I am the person solely responsible for baking the cake.)

I only baked the cake. (I baked it, but I didn't put the frosting on it.)

I baked only the cake. (Someone else baked the cookies.)

Place limiting adverbs *directly in front of* the words they modify.

Faulty I should get a higher grade because I only failed one exam.

The writer intends to modify *one exam* rather than *failed* and thus needs to move *only.*

Revised I should get a higher grade because I failed only one exam.

Exercise

In the following sentences, underline the dangling or misplaced modifiers (some sentences may be correct). Then, on a separate sheet of paper, revise the faulty sentences.

1. Feeling cold, tired, and depressed, tears streamed from my friend's eyes.
2. Their heads tilted back in awe, the children on this summer's night began trying to count the stars.
3. Seen through a telescope that magnifies things sixty times, Jupiter appears as big as the moon.
4. By studying the light reflected by Jupiter, its clouds are a poisonous mixture of ammonia floating in hydrogen.
5. Having long expected to return to Harlem after graduation, the young accountant was not prepared for the changes he saw on Lenox Avenue.
6. While cruising at 10,000 feet 45 miles east of Albuquerque, New Mexico, on July 16, 1945, at approximately 5:30 A.M., a brilliant flash of light, brighter than the sun, blazed across the horizon.
7. We were absolutely startled, unable to explain the sunlike flash or to grasp the meaning of the huge mushroom cloud that soon appeared above the desert floor.
8. Reporting what we had seen by radio to ground authorities, no satisfactory explanation could be found.
9. The following morning, still plagued by the event, the newspapers only reported that an ammunition dump had exploded in the approximate area where we had seen the flash.
10. Listening to the radio on August 6, 1945, a similar flash of light occurred over Hiroshima, Japan; then we realized what we had seen several weeks earlier—the first explosion of an atomic bomb.

H4.6 Choosing Correct Pronoun Cases

Use correct pronoun cases.

Many pronouns change their form according to the grammatical slot they fill in a sentence.

Case Name	Used for These Slots	Personal Pronouns	Relative Pronouns
subjective	subject, subject complement	I, we, he, she, they	who, whoever
objective	direct object, indirect object, object of preposition, subject of infinitive	me, us, him, her, them	whom, whomever
possessive	adjective showing possession	my, our, his, her, their	whose

The case of a pronoun is determined by its slot in the sentence.

She and *I* are good friends. ***[subjects]***

Lucas likes *her* and *me*. ***[direct objects]***

Give *her* and *me* the present. ***[indirect objects]***

Lucas did it for *her* and *me*. ***[objects of preposition]***

The winners were *she* and *I*. ***[subject complements]***

Sofia asked *her* and *me* to write the final report. ***[subjects of infinitive]***

Although writers generally handle pronoun cases accurately, the following instances give special trouble.

Cases of Relative Pronouns

In relative or noun clauses, the pronouns *who, whom, whoever*, or *whomever* take their case from their function in their own clause, not from the function of that clause in the rest of the sentence.

Faulty Give the prize to *whomever* says the secret word.

Although *whomever* at first seems to be the object of the preposition *to*, it is actually the subject of the verb *says* and should be in the subjective case. The object of the preposition *to* is actually the whole noun clause.

Revised Give the prize to *whoever* says the secret word.

Faulty I voted against Ralph Winkley, *who* big business especially supports.

In this case the relative pronoun fills a direct object slot in its own clause. Compare: Big business especially supports *him*. The writer should choose *whom*.

Revised I voted against Ralph Winkley, *whom* big business especially supports.

Intervening Parenthetical Clauses

When choosing the case of relative pronouns, don't let such words as *I think* or *he supposes* influence your choice. These are parenthetical expressions that can be discarded from the sentence.

Faulty I voted for Marion Fudge, *whom* I think is the most honest candidate.

Here the relative pronoun is the subject of the verb *is*, not the direct object of *I think*, and hence it should be subjective.

Revised I voted for Marion Fudge, *who* I think is the most honest candidate.

Pronouns as Parts of Compound Constructions

Case errors are especially frequent in compound constructions. Pronouns that fill object slots (or subjects of infinitives) must be in the objective case. You can usually avoid case errors in compound constructions by choosing the same case that you would select if you were using the pronoun alone.

Faulty Isobel appointed Ralph and *I* to the committee.

The pronoun is a direct object and should be in the objective case. Compare: Isobel appointed *me* to the committee.

Revised Isobel appointed Ralph and *me* to the committee.

Note that subjects of infinitives are in the objective case.

Faulty The dean of students wants *she* and *I* to represent the student council at the convention.

Compare: The dean of students wants *me* to represent the student council. …

Revised The dean of students wants *her* and *me* to represent the student council at the convention.

Be especially careful with pronouns appearing in front of infinitives that omit the *to*.

Faulty Let's you and *I* go to the show this evening.

The pronoun is the subject of the infinitive *(to) go* and should be in the objective case. Compare: Let *me* go to the show.

Revised Let's you and *me* go to the show this evening.

Pronouns in Appositive Constructions

In appositive constructions, in which the pronoun is followed by an identifying noun, use the pronoun case that would be correct if the noun were not there:

The principal told *us* boys to go home.

Compare: The principal told us to go home.

We boys hid around the corner until the principal went back to her office.

Compare: We hid around the corner.

Pronouns as Parts of Implied Clauses

When a pronoun occurs after a *than* that is introducing an implied clause, choose the pronoun's case according to the pronoun's use in the implied clause. Both of the following sentences are correct, but their meanings are different.

I like Paul better than he.

This sentence means "I like Paul better than he likes Paul."

I like Paul better than him.

This sentence means "I like Paul better than I like him."

Pronouns Preceding Gerunds or Participles

Use the possessive case before gerunds (*-ing* verbals used as nouns) and the subjective or objective case before present participles (*-ing* verbals used as adjectives).

I saw *him* running away from the police.

In this sentence, *running* is a participle modifying the direct object *him.*

I think *his* running away from the police was his biggest mistake.

Here, *running* is a gerund, the subject of *was.*

Exercise

In the following sentences, underline the correct pronoun from the choices given in parentheses.

1. (We/Us) girls want to bike to the store.
2. Zoe, (who/whom) received the scholarship, will study microbiology.
3. If you and (he/him) can visit Tim and (I/me) next month, we will tour the national park.
4. Jessica and Lin-Ju will bring (her/their) skis.
5. (His/Him) playing loud music annoyed the neighbors.
6. He is the racer (who/whom) I believe fell at the finish line.
7. This vacation was necessary for you and (I/me).
8. A burglar stole our computer, but no one saw (his/him) entering the house.
9. Stephen or Noah will do (his/her/their) practicing before school.
10. Miyuki and Amy do (his/her/their) practicing faithfully every day.

Choosing Correct Adjective and Adverb Forms

H4.7
Use adjectives and adverbs correctly.

For more on adjectives and adverbs, see p. 621.

Although adjectives and adverbs are both modifiers, they cannot be used interchangeably because adjectives modify nouns or pronouns whereas adverbs modify verbs, adjectives, other adverbs, and sometimes whole phrases, clauses, or sentences.

Problems with adjectives and adverbs can occur in the following cases.

Confusion of Adjective and Adverb Forms

Do not use adjectives when adverbs are warranted.

Faulty I did *real good* on that test.

The adverb form is *well*, not *good*. Similarly, *real* is an adjective, which cannot modify an adverb.

Revised I did *really well* on that test.

Be careful to use the appropriate modifier after verbs that can be either linking verbs or action verbs. Linking verbs (such as *is, are,* and *seem*) take subject complements, which are either nouns or adjectives. Certain linking verbs, especially the sense verbs *feel, look, taste, smell,* and *sound* as well as a few others, can also be action verbs. After such verbs, choose an adjective if the word modifies the subject and an adverb if it modifies the verb.

The captain looked *angry*.

Here, *angry* is an adjective modifying *captain*. Compare: The angry captain …

The captain looked *angrily* at the crew.

Here, *angrily* is an adverb telling how the captain did the looking.

Problems with Comparative and Superlative Forms

Short adjectives (with one syllable or two syllables ending in *-y* or *-le*) form their comparative and superlative degrees by adding *-er* and *-est* to the simple form. Other adjectives and most adverbs generally use *more* (or *less*) for the comparative and *most* (or *least*) for the superlative. A few modifiers are irregular.

Choosing Comparatives Versus Superlatives Use the comparative degree for two persons or things and the superlative for three or more.

Of the two players, Maria is the *better*.

Of the whole team, Maria is the *best*.

Misuse of Comparatives with Absolute Adjectives Do not use comparative and superlative degrees with absolute adjectives, such as *unique* or *impossible*.

Faulty Her dress was the *most unique* one I had ever seen.

Unique already means "one of a kind" and can't be further modified.

Revised Her dress was *unique*.

or

Her dress was the *most unusual* one I had ever seen.

Double Comparatives Avoid double comparatives or superlatives.

Faulty Raphael is *more smarter* than George.

Revised Raphael is *smarter* than George.

Illogical Comparisons Avoid making illogical comparisons between items that are not actually comparable. Sometimes illogical comparisons result from a missing word such as *other*.

Faulty Our Volvo is better than any car on the road.

This sentence inadvertently implies that this Volvo isn't on the road.

Revised Our Volvo is better than any *other* car on the road.

At other times an illogical comparison arises when the grammar of the sentence mixes apples and oranges.

Faulty Handwritten papers are harder to read than typing.

Papers cannot be compared with typing.

Revised Handwritten papers are harder to read than typed papers.

EDITING FOR STYLE

5

WHAT YOU WILL LEARN

H5.1 To edit for conciseness.
H5.2 To write lively prose.
H5.3 To avoid unclear pronoun references.
H5.4 To put old information before new.
H5.5 To use the active and passive voices effectively.
H5.6 To use inclusive language.

H5.1
Edit for conciseness.

Pruning Your Prose

In most rhetorical contexts, conciseness is a virtue. Readers like efficient prose that makes its point without padding.

Cutting Out Deadwood

Good writers typically write first drafts that are much longer than their final versions. Eliminating unneeded words and phrases is an essential part of revision.

Wordy At the present time it can be considered a truism that families with incomes neither too far above nor too far below the median income can send their children to expensive colleges with no more out-of-pocket charges and expenses than it would cost to send these same children to colleges whose tuition and related expenses are much lower.

Revised The truth is that for average-income families, an expensive college costs no more than a cheap one.

When eliminating deadwood, watch out for common wordy phrases such as the following:

at the present time (use *now*)

because of the fact that (use *because*)

are of the opinion that (use *believe*)

have the ability to (use *can*)

in spite of the fact that (use *although*)

You can easily delete these expressions—and dozens more like them—without sacrificing meaning.

Combining Sentences

Another cause of wordiness is the inefficient use of short, choppy sentences. Try to recast a choppy passage by combining sentences, thus saving words while creating more complex and graceful structures.

Wordy Jim Maxwell took two years to build his solar building. Building his solar building included nearly one year of planning. His solar building was intended mainly as a grain drier. But it also provided a warm winter shop. Additionally he had the advantage of a machinery shed. This shed kept his machinery dry. His new solar building would pay dividends for years to come.

Revised It took two years to build, including nearly one year of planning, but when Jim Maxwell finished his solar building, he had a grain drier, a warm winter shop, and a dry machinery shed that would pay dividends for years to come.

Exercise

Improve the style of the following sentences by cutting out deadwood, recasting the words, or combining elements to eliminate wordiness.

1. It appears to me that he seems to be an unusually quiet person but also that he is the kind of person who really cares a lot about other people.
2. If a person is the kind of person who hurries rapidly when that person tries to do things, then that person is apt to find that he or she has wasted a lot of valuable time and material by trying to do the events too rapidly.
3. Ilana was interested in finding out the answer to a question that she had recently been puzzling about. The question was this: What is the important and essential difference between a disease that most people would call "mental illness" and a disease that is simply a disease of the brain?
4. It is unfortunate that the mayor acted in this manner. The mayor settled the issue. But before he settled the issue he made a mistake. He fostered a public debate that was very bitter. The debate pitted some of his subordinates against each other (and these were key subordinates, too). It also caused many other people to feel inflamed passions and fears as a result of the way the mayor handled the whole affair.

H5.2 Enlivening Your Prose

Write lively prose.

You can often revise your prose to make the tone livelier and more interesting.

Avoiding Nominalizations

Lively writers express actions with verbs. Lifeless writers often *nominalize* their sentences by converting actions into nouns (for example, by writing, "arrive at a conclusion" rather than "conclude"). A highly nominalized style characterizes much bureaucratic and administrative prose, making it sound stilted, impersonal, and dead.

Nominalized	For the production of effective writing, the expression of an action through the use of a verb is the method most highly preferred.
Revised	Effective writers express actions with verbs.

A nominalized sentence is not only long and dull, but also confusing. Nominalized sentences often include two additional problems: overuse of the verb *to be* and a pileup of prepositional phrases. To revise a nominalized sentence, ask yourself who is doing what; then make the doer of the action the subject and make the action a verb.

Nominalized	Jim's receiving of this low grade was the result of his reading of the material too quickly.
Revised	Jim received a low grade because he read the material too quickly.

By putting *Jim* in the subject slot, the writer eliminates the weak verb *was* as well as three prepositional phrases.

Exercise

Revise the following sentences to eliminate nominalizations.

1. The person who received the rewards is the person who was the victor.
2. The killing of a goose from which the laying of golden eggs is frequent is usually seen to be a mistake.
3. The socialization of children in the avoidance of risky behaviors often results in their timidity as adults.
4. Juanita came to the realization that her preference of major was changing from history to mathematics.
5. The teacher's examination of the student's locker was caused by the teacher's suspicion of the possibility of the hiding of drugs by the student.

Avoiding Noun Pileups

Noun pileups result from the tendency, again common in bureaucratic prose, to use nouns as adjectives.

Noun Pileup	Consideration of an applicant physical disability access plan by the student services reform committee will occur forthwith.
Revised	The committee to reform student services will soon consider a plan for improving access to buildings for physically disabled applicants.

Avoiding Pretentious Language

Unless you are intentionally imitating a long-winded style, strive for language that sounds natural and clear rather than pretentious (or developed through overuse of a thesaurus).

Stilted The tyro in the field of artistic endeavors commenced to ascertain the suitability of different constituencies of pigment.

Revised The student artist began wondering which color paint would be most suitable.

Avoiding Clichés, Jargon, and Slang

Clichés are tired, frequently repeated phrases such as "last but not least," "easier said than done," or "a chill ran up my spine." Replace them with fresh language.

Deciding when to avoid jargon and slang is more problematic because their use may be appropriate depending on your audience, purpose, and genre. Technical jargon is acceptable if you are writing for an audience who understands it within a genre that uses it; slang is also fine if it suits your purpose, audience, and genre. In general, you should avoid jargon that may not be understood by your audience, and you should avoid slang in most formal contexts.

Inappropriate Jargon for a Teacher's Letter to Parents

Your child displays maladaptive socialization behaviors.

Revised **Your** child is sometimes rude to classmates.

Inappropriate Slang for a College Essay

The gods are all bent out of shape because Oedipus killed his dad.

Revised The gods are angry because Oedipus killed his father.

Creating Sentence Variety

Prose can feel wooden or choppy if each sentence has the same construction and length. Skilled writers combine sentences in various ways for emphasis and grace.

Monotonous Martin watched carefully for loose rocks. He picked his way along the edge of the cliff. Martin didn't hear the rattles at first. Then he suddenly froze with fear when he heard them. A timber rattler was about two feet away. It was coiled like a garden hose. The rattler's neck was arched. Its fangs looked like twin needles of death.

In this passage, each sentence starts with the subject, and all the sentences are approximately the same length.

Revised Watching carefully for loose rocks as he picked his way along the edge of the cliff, Martin suddenly froze with fear. At first he didn't hear the rattles. Then he heard them for sure. About two feet away, coiled like a garden hose, was a timber rattler, its neck arched, its fangs looking like twin needles of death.

Here the longest sentence is twenty-four words and the shortest is six words. The two short sentences emphasize dramatically important moments.

Using Specific Details

Except in philosophical or theoretical writing, which uses abstract language precisely, abstract prose can be dull. You can enliven abstract prose by replacing abstract terms with concrete words or by adding specific, colorful details.

Abstract The poor are often stereotyped as beggars, drunks, or people with uncared-for children.

Revised We often stereotype poor people as panhandlers demanding our spare change, as scruffy drunks holding a bottle in a paper bag, or as barefoot children with matted hair, filthy clothes, and tears streaking down their dirty faces as they tug on their mother's arm.

Note that in this example, adding concrete language makes the passage *longer*, whereas pruning deadwood makes a passage shorter. What is the difference between deadwood and detail?

Avoiding Broad or Unclear Pronoun Reference

H5.3
Avoid unclear pronoun references.

Each time you use a pronoun, make sure that the noun to which it refers, its *antecedent*, is clearly apparent. Unclear use of pronouns can confuse readers.

Avoiding Broad Reference

A broad reference occurs whenever a pronoun—usually *this, that*, or *it*—stands for an idea or a whole group of words rather than for a single noun. Although this usage is sometimes acceptable, it is often ambiguous or vague.

For more on *this* as a pronoun, see p. 462.

Broad Reference Harold Krebs in Hemingway's "Soldier's Home" rebels against his parents. He does *this* by refusing to accept their values, and *this* is why his parents are so upset by *it*.

In this sentence the italicized pronouns refer not to specific nouns but to ideas, which shift with each pronoun, confusing the reader.

Revised Harold Krebs in Hemingway's "Soldier's Home" rebels against his parents by refusing to accept their way of life. His rejection of their values explains why his parents are so upset by his later actions.

Do not make broad references with the pronoun *which*, which must have a single noun for its antecedent.

Faulty He drinks a lot, which is something I disapprove of.

Revised I disapprove of his heavy drinking.

In the original sentence, *which* has no noun antecedent.

Avoiding Unclear Antecedents

To avoid confusing your readers, make sure that every pronoun has a clear antecedent. Avoid using pronouns that seem to stand for two different antecedents.

Unclear Antecedent	Chris explained to his son the reasons he couldn't go to the meeting.
Revised	Chris explained the reasons his son couldn't go to the meeting.

In the original sentence, *he* could stand for either *Chris* or *son*, making it unclear whether Chris or his son couldn't go to the meeting.

H5.4 Putting Old Information before New Information

Put old information before new.

In closed-form prose, clear writers begin sentences with old information—a key word or concept from the previous sentence, from the paragraph's topic sentence, or from the essay's thesis statement or purpose—to keep their readers on track. The old/new contract is one of the chief principles of clarity in closed-form prose. See Skills 17.1 and 17.7 for more details.

H5.5 Deciding between Active and Passive Voice

Use the active and passive voices effectively

Experienced writers usually prefer the active voice because it is stronger and more economical. The passive voice requires *to be* helping verbs and prepositional phrases for the doer of the action.

Weak	The cake and ice cream were eaten, and then games were played.
Revised	The children ate the cake and ice cream and then played games.

However, the passive voice isn't always inappropriate. The choice of voice depends on the context of your sentence. Writers sometimes choose the passive voice to create appropriate emphasis or to be intentionally vague.

Passive Voice When Doer Is Unimportant The passive voice is appropriate whenever the receiver of the action is more important than the doer. It is often used in scientific writing, which tends to emphasize the material acted on rather than the doer of the action.

The distillate is then removed from the liquid.

Passive Voice to Place Old Information before New The passive voice is also appropriate when the old information in a sentence is the receiver of the action rather than the doer.

Graphs are essential tools for economic analysis. They *are* commonly *used by* economists to display both concrete economic data and abstract economic concepts.

In the second sentence, the passive voice allows the writer to begin with old information. The pronoun *they* refers to *Graphs* in the previous sentence.

Passive Voice to Create Vagueness Sometimes writers use the passive voice intentionally be vague or evasive rather than direct. This practice is ethically questionable. Avoid it when you can.

Evasive	The decision has been made to raise the dues.
Forthright	The president and the treasurer have decided to raise the dues.

Exercise

On a separate sheet of paper, convert the transitive passive sentences to transitive active, and convert the transitive active sentences to transitive passive. Leave the intransitive sentences unchanged. In converting some transitive passive sentences to transitive active, you may have to add an actor or agent. For each sentence, explain in which rhetorical situations the active-voice version would be better and in which the passive would be better.

1. The wrong carpets were installed by the carpet layers while the owners were away.
2. Smoke rose in thick billows above the burning house.
3. Beth ladled hot liquid blackberry jelly into sterilized jars.
4. The little girl in the green sunsuit slowly covered her sleeping father with piles of sand.
5. Some of the most important scientific principles have been discovered accidentally.
6. The motor was probably ruined by the turbine bearing's being rusted out.

Using Inclusive Language

H5.6 Using Inclusive Language.

For much of the history of the English language, grammarians accepted the use of masculine pronouns ("Everyone should bring *his* own lunch") and the use of *man* ("Peace and goodwill to *men* everywhere") as generic references for both men and women. Many contemporary writers believe that these usages reflect pro-male bias. Many writers are also now aware of other ways in which language subtly reflects attitudes toward gender, culture, and ethnicity. In this section, we offer suggestions that will help you construct sentences free of biased language.

Avoiding Sexist Labels and Stereotypes

Avoid language that labels or stereotypes women. Let the same considerations guide you whether you are describing a man or a woman.

Sexist Janet Peterson, stunning in her new, blue-sequined evening gown, gave the keynote address at the annual mayors' conference.

Would you say, "Robert Peterson, stunning in his new tuxedo, ruffled shirtfront, and cummerbund, gave the keynote address at the annual mayors' conference"?

Revised Janet Peterson, newly elected mayor of the state's third-largest city, gave the keynote address at the annual mayors' conference.

Avoiding Use of Masculine Pronouns to Refer to Both Sexes

Whenever possible, revise sentences to avoid using the masculine pronouns *he, him, his,* and *himself* to refer to people of both sexes. Often you can use plural pronouns (*they, them, their,* and *themselves*), which do not indicate gender.

Problematic If a student wants to bring his text to the exam, he may.

Revised If students want to bring their texts to the exam, they may.

In informal writing, you can also use *you* and *your* to avoid sexist language; in formal prose you can use *one* and *one's*, although this usage sometimes sounds stilted.

Revised If you want to bring your texts to the exam, you may.

Revised If one wants to bring one's text to the exam, one may.

Avoid bureaucratic constructions such as *him/her* or *s/he*, which are cumbersome and inelegant. Occasional use of the combined forms *he or she* or *him or her* is acceptable, but overuse of this construction is tiresome.

Avoiding Inappropriate Use of the Suffix *-man*

Use of *-man* as a suffix in such words as *repairman, mailman,* and *policeman* or as a prefix in *mankind* seems to ignore the presence of women in the workforce and in the human race. The suffix *-person* may be an acceptable substitute; *chairperson* and *salesperson* are common in formal usage. However, *weatherperson* still sounds odd, as does "Joan is a new *freshperson* at state college." Look for alternative expressions.

Avoid	Prefer
congressman	representative, member of Congress
forefathers	ancestors
mailman	mail carrier
man (generic)	person, people, humans, human beings
wives, husbands	spouses
manmade	synthetic

Avoiding Language Biased Against Ethnic or Other Minorities

Avoid language that reflects stereotypes against ethnic or other minorities. Language referring to minorities evolves rapidly. In the 1980s *black* and *Afro-American* were preferred terms, but in the 1990s these largely gave way to *African-American*. Similarly, the terms *Latino* and *Latina* are replacing *Hispanic*. Homosexual people now prefer the terms *gay man* and *lesbian* and in some contexts are reviving the word *queer*. Today the term *people of color* is in favor, but the term *colored person* is an intense insult.

As a writer, you need to be sensitive to the subtle ways in which language can make people feel included and welcomed or excluded and insulted. Nowhere is the evolving and charged nature of language more evident than in the connotations of words referring to cultural minorities.

EDITING FOR PUNCTUATION AND MECHANICS

6

WHAT YOU WILL LEARN

H6.1 To use periods, question marks, and exclamation points correctly.
H6.2 To use commas correctly.
H6.3 To use semicolons correctly.
H6.4 To use colons, dashes, and parentheses correctly.
H6.5 To use apostrophes correctly.
H6.6 To use quotation marks correctly.
H6.7 To use italics (underlining) correctly.
H6.8 To use brackets, ellipses, and slashes correctly.
H6.9 To use capital letters correctly.
H6.10 To use numbers appropriately.
H6.11 To use abbreviations appropriately.

Periods, Question Marks, and Exclamation Points

H6.1 Use periods, question marks, and exclamation points correctly.

Periods, question marks, and exclamation points, sometimes called "terminal punctuation" or "endmarks," signal the end of a sentence. These marks generally raise few problems for writers except in the case of sentence fragments (when an endmark follows a nonsentence), comma splices (when a comma is substituted for an endmark), and run-ons (when two sentences are fused together without an endmark).

A few other situations that sometimes pose problems for writers are discussed next.

Courtesy Questions

Courtesy questions—mild commands phrased politely as questions—normally end with a period.

Would you please return the form in the enclosed envelope.

Indirect Questions

Direct questions require a question mark, but indirect questions end with a period.

Direct Question He asked me, "Where are you going?"

Indirect Question He asked me where I was going.

For a full discussion of sentence boundaries, including advice for avoiding fragments, comma splices, and run-ons, see Handbook 3.

Placement of Question Marks with Quotations

If quotation marks and a question mark appear together, the question mark goes inside the quotation marks when only the quotation is a question and outside when the whole sentence is a question.

QUOTATION IS QUESTION

The professor asked, "Can you solve the fox-and-chicken puzzle?"

ENTIRE SENTENCE IS QUESTION

Did you hear the professor talk about the "fox-and-chicken puzzle"?

Note: When the question mark goes inside the quotation marks, do not follow the question mark with a comma or period.

Faulty "Can we go with you?," she asked.

Revised "Can we go with you?" she asked.

Exclamation Points

An exclamation point is used after a sentence or word group to express strong emotion. Exclamation points are used primarily in dialogue to indicate shouting or an especially strong feeling. Avoid using them in most other instances— especially academic prose—because they rarely have the effect on a reader that the writer intends. Expressing emotion through word choice, sentence structure, and tone is more effective. When an exclamation point goes inside a quotation, do not follow the exclamation point with a comma or period.

H6.2 Commas

Use commas correctly.

The comma is the most frequently used mark of internal punctuation. A comma mistakenly used as an endmark creates a comma splice. The main rules for use of commas to mark the boundaries of phrases, clauses, and sentences are covered in depth in Handbook 3. These rules are reviewed in this section, along with additional guidelines.

Using Commas

Using Commas with Coordinating Conjunctions Use a comma and a coordinating conjunction (*and, or, nor, for, but, yet,* and *so*) to join two independent clauses.

I released the dog's leash, and the dog trotted off across the field.

If the main clauses are very short, it is acceptable to omit the comma before the coordinating conjunction, but it is never acceptable to omit the coordinating conjunction; doing so will create a comma splice.

Comma Splice We crossed the meadow, then we headed toward the mountain.

Revised We crossed the meadow, and then we headed toward the mountain.

Comma after Introductory Adverb Clauses and Long Introductory Phrases Use a comma to set off introductory adverb clauses and long introductory phrases from the rest of the sentence.

Introductory Adverb Clause	When I get home from work, I always fix myself a big sardine sandwich.
Introductory Phrase	Having lost my balance, I began waving my arms frantically.

Note: Initial gerund phrases or infinitive phrases used as sentence subjects should not be set off because they are part of the sentence core.

Faulty To know him, is to love him. Playing her guitar every evening, is Sally's way of relaxing.

These introductory phrases serve as the subjects of their sentences and should not be set off.

Revised To know him is to love him. Playing her guitar every evening is Sally's way of relaxing.

Comma after Introductory Transitional Words and Expressions Set off most introductory transitional words and phrases such as *on the other hand, in sum, however, moreover,* and *for example* with a comma.

On the other hand, bicycle racing involves an astonishing amount of strategy.

Writers often do not use a comma to set off *thus* and *therefore* and some other transitional expressions that do not noticeably interrupt the flow of the sentence. In such cases let your voice be your guide. If you pause noticeably after the transitional expression, set it off with a comma.

Commas to Set Off Absolute Phrases An absolute phrase comprises a noun followed by a participle or participial phrase. These phrases are *absolute* because they are complete in themselves; they modify the entire sentence rather than an individual word within the sentence. Absolute phrases are always set off with commas.

See pp. 623–624 for an explanation of verbal phrases.

His hand wrapped in a blanket, Harvey hobbled toward the ambulance.

The bear reared on its hind legs, *its teeth looking razor sharp in the glaring sun.*

Comma before Concluding Participial Phrases Use commas to set off participial phrases at the ends of sentences if they modify the subjects.

The doctor rushed quickly toward the accident victim, fumbling to open his black bag.

In this example, it is the doctor who fumbles to open his bag. The comma indicates that *fumbling* modifies *doctor* (the sentence subject) and not *victim* (the noun immediately preceding the participle).

Do not use a comma to set off a participial phrase at the end of a sentence if the phrase modifies the immediately preceding noun.

The doctor rushed quickly toward the accident victim lying face forward on the soft shoulder of the road.

Here the participial phrase modifies the preceding noun, *victim*, instead of the sentence subject. It is not set off with commas.

Commas to Avoid Confusion Use commas to separate sentence elements if failure to separate them would create confusion.

Confusing	Every time Manny ate his dog wanted to be fed too.
Revised	Every time Manny ate, his dog wanted to be fed too.

Commas to Set Off Nonrestrictive Clauses and Phrases Adjective modifiers following a noun are either *restrictive* or *nonrestrictive*, depending on whether they are needed to identify the noun they modify. Use commas to set off nonrestrictive clauses and phrases.

Restrictive and Nonrestrictive Clauses. An adjective clause is *nonrestrictive* if it is not needed to identify the noun it modifies. In such cases, set off the clause or phrase with commas.

Nonrestrictive Clause	My father dislikes Bill Jones, who rides a noisy motorcycle.

In this case, you know whom the father dislikes: Bill Jones. The fact that Bill rides a noisy motorcycle is additional information about him.

If the modifying clause is needed to identify the noun it is modifying, then it is *restrictive* and is not set off with commas.

Restrictive Clause	My father dislikes people who ride noisy motorcycles.

Here the meaning is "My father doesn't dislike all people, just those people who ride noisy motorcycles." The adjective clause restricts the meaning of *people*; that is, it narrows down the class "people" to the subclass of "people who ride noisy motorcycles." Because the phrase is needed to identify which people the father dislikes, it is a restrictive clause used *without* commas.

To help you remember this rule, think of this saying: Extra information, extra commas; needed information, no commas.

Nonrestrictive Clause	My grandmother, who graduated from college when she was eighty-two years old, deserves a special award.
Restrictive Clause	Anyone who graduates from college at age eighty-two deserves a special award.

Restrictive and Nonrestrictive Phrases. The same extra information/needed information rule holds for adjective phrases.

Restrictive Phrase	The man wearing the double-breasted suit is an accountant.

Here the phrase *wearing the double-breasted suit* identifies which man is an accountant, it is not set off with commas.

Nonrestrictive Phrase	Elvis Dweezle, wearing a double-breasted suit, looked at himself briefly in the mirror before knocking on his boss's door.

Here the phrase *wearing a double-breasted suit* merely adds extra information about the already-identified Elvis Dweezle.

Commas to Set Off Nonrestrictive Appositives An *appositive* is a noun or noun phrase that immediately follows another noun, renaming it or otherwise referring to it. Appositives also follow the extra information/needed information rule. An appositive is restrictive (needed information) if it serves to identify the preceding noun; it is nonrestrictive (extra information) if it simply contributes additional information to an already-identified noun. As with nonrestrictive adjective clauses and phrases, set off nonrestrictive appositives with commas.

Nonrestrictive Appositive	Angela, a good friend of mine, has just been promoted to chief accountant.

In this example you know who has just been promoted: Angela. The appositive *a good friend of mine* adds extra information about Angela.

Restrictive Appositive	My friend Angela offered to do my income taxes for me.

Here the appositive *Angela* is needed to identify which friend offered to do the taxes. No commas are used.

Commas to Separate Items in a Series Use commas to separate items in a series of three or more words, phrases, or clauses. The first comma leads readers to anticipate a list, with the last two elements joined by *and* or *or*. Place commas after each item in the series except the last.

He especially likes golf, jogging, and swimming.

We went to the movies, had dinner downtown, and then went bowling.

(Note: Although British writers and some American writers omit the comma before the coordinating conjunction in a series, sentences are generally clearer if the comma is included.)

Confusing	I like three kinds of pizza: pepperoni, Canadian bacon and pineapple and Italian sausage.
Clearer	I like three kinds of pizza: pepperoni, Canadian bacon and pineapple, and Italian sausage.

In the first version, the reader initially thinks that the first *and* marks the end of the series when, in fact, it simply joins one of the elements (*Canadian bacon and pineapple*). Placing a comma before the final *and* in the series clarifies the sentence.

Commas to Separate Coordinate Adjectives Preceding a Noun Coordinate adjectives in a series are separated by commas. Adjectives are coordinate if they can be separated by *and* or if they can be placed in a different order.

Coordinate Adjectives	A nearsighted, tall, thin, grumpy-looking man walked slowly down the street.

In this case you could say a "thin and grumpy-looking and nearsighted and tall man," thus separating the elements with *and* and placing them in a different order. These are coordinate adjectives separated by commas.

Noncoordinate Adjectives	Three copper-plated frying pans sat on the shelf.

These adjectives are not coordinate because you cannot say "frying and copper-plated and three pans." Hence these adjectives are not separated by commas.

Commas to Set Off Parenthetical or Interrupting Elements Use commas to set off parenthetical words, phrases, or clauses and other similar elements that interrupt the flow of the sentence. By reading your sentences aloud in a natural voice, you can generally identify parenthetical material that interrupts the flow of a sentence. Such material should be set off by pairs of commas. The following are common examples of interrupting material:

CONTRASTING ELEMENTS INTRODUCED BY BUT, NOT, OR ALTHOUGH

The man at the front desk, not the mechanic, was the one who quoted me the price.

WORDS OF DIRECT ADDRESS, *YES* AND *NO*, AND MILD INTERJECTIONS

I tell you, Jennifer, your plan won't work.

TRANSITION WORDS AND EXPRESSIONS

She will, however, demand more money.

TAG PHRASES CITING SOURCES

This new car, according to the latest government reports, gets below-average mileage.

ATTRIBUTIVE TAGS IDENTIFYING SPEAKERS

"To be a successful student," my adviser told me, "you have to enjoy learning."

Commas to Set Off Elements of Places, Addresses, and Dates Use commas to set off each separate element in a date, place, or address.

He drove to Savannah, Georgia, on July 5, 1971, in an old blue Ford.

Omitting Commas

Many beginning writers tend to use too many commas rather than too few. Do not use a comma unless a specific rule calls for one. "When in doubt, leave commas out" is a good rule of thumb. Learn to recognize the following situations that do *not* require commas. These are frequently sources of error in student papers.

Do Not Use a Comma to Separate a Subject from Its Verb or a Verb from Its Complements

Faulty The man in the apartment next to mine, swallowed a goldfish.

Here a comma mistakenly separates the subject from the verb.

Revised The man in the apartment next to mine swallowed a goldfish.

Do Not Use a Single Comma within a Sentence Core

Faulty My brother, who recently won a pole-sitting contest swallowed a goldfish.

Here a comma occurs on one side of a nonrestrictive clause but not on the other side.

Revised My brother, who recently won a pole-sitting contest, swallowed a goldfish.

Do Not Use a Comma before *and* If It Joins Only Two Words or Phrases

Faulty She pedaled uphill for twenty minutes, and won the race by several lengths.

The *and* joins two verbs rather than two main clauses.

Revised She pedaled uphill for twenty minutes and won the race by several lengths.

Do Not Use a Comma after such *as*

Faulty They forgot some key supplies such as, candles, matches, and trail mix.

Revised They forgot some key supplies such as candles, matches, and trail mix.

Exercise

Insert commas where needed in the following sentences.

1. Whenever I go home to Bismarck North Dakota for Christmas vacation the dinner conversation turns to cross-country skiing.
2. On my last visit during dessert my dad who is an expert skier asked me if I wanted to try dogsled racing.
3. "I've wanted to try dogsledding for years" Dad said "but we've never had the equipment or the dogs. Now however my friend Jake Jackson the new agent for Smith Insurance has just bought a team and wants his friend to give it a try."
4. Rock shrimp unlike some other species have hard shells that make them difficult to peel.

(*continued*)

5. Hiking or biking through southern Germany you will discover a rich mosaic of towns regional foods colors sounds and smells of the rural countryside and historic Black Forest region.
6. Instead of riding on busy boulevards you can pedal on a network of narrow paved roads built for farm vehicles or on graveled paths through lush green forests.
7. According to historian Daniel T. Rodgers a central question that divided workers and employers in the nineteenth and early twentieth centuries was how many hours a day the average worker should work.
8. Believing strongly in tradition the early factory owners thought their workers should follow the old sunrise to sunset work schedule of agricultural laborers.
9. This schedule which meant fourteen-hour workdays during the summer could also be maintained during the winter thanks to the invention of artificial light which owners rapidly installed in their factories.
10. Spurred on by their desire to create a shorter working day laborers began to organize into forerunners of today's labor unions and used their collective powers to strive for change.

H6.3 Semicolons

Use semicolons correctly.

A semicolon is stronger than a comma. It can be used to join two independent clauses to form a single sentence or to separate the main items in a list that already contains commas.

Semicolon to Join Main Clauses

When a semicolon is used to join main clauses, it signals a close relationship between the meanings of the two main clauses and creates a sentence with two balanced, equal parts.

> I asked the professor for an extension on my essay; she told me I was out of luck.

Semicolons are frequently used to connect main clauses when the second clause contains a conjunctive adverb or transitional phrase such as *however, therefore, nevertheless,* and *on the other hand.*

Comma Splice He spent all morning baking the pie, however, nobody seemed to appreciate his efforts.

Revised He spent all morning baking the pie; however, nobody seemed to appreciate his efforts.

For more on comma splices, see pp. 631–633.

Note: Joining two main clauses with only a comma creates a comma splice.

Semicolon in a Series Containing Commas

Use a semicolon to separate elements in a series when some of those elements already contain commas.

> On vacation we went to Laramie, Wyoming; Denver, Colorado; Salt Lake City, Utah; and Boise, Idaho.

Exercise

In the following sentences, insert semicolons and commas as needed. Some sentences may need no additional punctuation. Make sure that your marks of punctuation can be easily read.

1. The two men defended themselves before the justice of the peace in Bilford across the river a similar case was being tried with attorneys and a full jury.
2. She claimed that most teenage shoplifters are never caught moreover those who are caught are seldom punished.
3. I admit that I went to the party I did not however enjoy it.
4. I admit that I went to the party but I did not enjoy it.
5. Although I went to the party I did not enjoy it.
6. When the party ended our apartment was in chaos from one end of the living room to the other end of the bedroom a fine layer of confetti blanketed everything like snow.
7. Within twenty minutes of leaving the trail we saw an antelope two elk one of which had begun to shed the velvet on its antlers an assortment of squirrels gophers and chipmunks and most startling of all a large black bear with two cubs.
8. An effective education does not consist of passive rote learning rather it consists of active problem solving.
9. Failure to introduce and to use calculators and computers in elementary school creates needless barriers for teachers and learners furthermore computer literacy is a basic skill in the new millennium.
10. We watched the slide show of their vacation for what seemed like an eternity—Toledo Ohio Columbus Missouri Topeka Kansas Omaha Nebraska and on and on across the continent.

Colons, Dashes, and Parentheses

H6.4 Use colons, dashes, and parentheses correctly.

Colons

The most frequent uses of a colon are to introduce a list; to announce a word, clause, or phrase predicted in a preceding main clause; or to introduce a block quotation. Colons are generally preceded by main clauses and are not used as internal punctuation within a clause.

Colon to Introduce a List Use a colon to introduce a list when the list follows a grammatically complete independent clause.

We can win in two ways: changing our defense or adding Jones to the offensive lineup.

Do not use a colon in the middle of a clause or after the words *such as, for example,* or *including.*

Faulty The things you should bring to the party are: chips, salsa, and your own drinks.

Revised The things you should bring to the party are chips, salsa, and your own drinks.

or

Please bring to the party the following: chips, salsa, and your own drinks.

In the first example the offending colon is removed. In the second, the structure preceding the colon has been expanded to a main clause by adding *the following,* which serves as the direct object of *bring.*

Faulty We have many opportunities to improve our score, such as: retaking the exam, doing an extra credit project, or doing a longer paper.

Revised We have many opportunities to improve our score, such as retaking the exam, doing an extra credit project, or doing a longer paper.

Colon to Introduce a Predicted Element Following an Independent Clause Following an independent clause, use a colon to introduce a predicted element, which can be a word, a phrase, or a clause.

The professor agreed to something remarkable: grading contracts for all students.

The professor agreed to something remarkable: He allowed Jack to submit a late paper.

Note on capitalization: If what follows the colon is a main clause, you have the option of beginning the clause with a capital letter; if what follows the colon is not a complete sentence, use a lowercase letter.

Colon to Introduce Block Quotations or Quotations Receiving Special Emphasis A colon is used to introduce a block quotation if what precedes the colon is a main clause. You can also use a colon to introduce a short quotation that you want to emphasize.

For an explanation of block quotations, see p. 552.

His father replied slowly, carefully, thoughtfully: "Buying the SUV now, when we are already too deeply in debt, is not a good idea."

A comma could also be used to introduce this quotation; a colon is more formal and emphatic.

Colon in Salutations, Time Notations, Titles, and Biblical Citations

Colons are sometimes used in letter salutations and within titles. They are also used in time expressions and biblical notations.

Salutation	Dear Sarah:
Time Notation	4:30 A.M.
Titles	*Teaching Critical Thinking Skills: Theory and Practice*
Biblical Citations	Proverbs 3:16

Dashes

Think of the dash as a strong comma that gives special emphasis to the material being set off. (To make a dash, type two hyphens; leave no space before, after, or between the hyphens.)

> Sir Walter Raleigh brought the potato—as well as tobacco—to Queen Elizabeth I on his return from Virginia.

In this example a pair of commas could replace the pair of dashes. The dashes emphasize the material between them by calling for a greater pause when reading.

Parentheses

Parentheses are used to enclose nonessential, supplemental information and to enclose citations or list numbers.

Supplemental Information The most common use of parentheses is to enclose supplemental information.

> I wanted to know if my first computer (an old Kaypro from the early 1980s) could be placed in a museum of technology.

Citations and Numbered Items in a List Parentheses are also used to enclose citations in many documentation systems and to enclose numbers or letters identifying parts of a list.

For an explanation of the MLA and APA documentation systems, see Chapter 23.

> To graduate, a student must fill out three forms: (1) the transcript summary, (2) the request form, and (3) the adviser's sign-off sheet (*Junebug State Bulletin* 32).

Punctuating Sentences That Include Parentheses When you place a complete sentence within parentheses, the concluding endmark goes inside the parentheses. When you end a sentence with parenthetical elements, the endmark goes outside the parentheses.

> When visiting England, we watched a lot of cricket. (Cricket is a British game something like American baseball.)

> When visiting England, we watched a lot of cricket (a British game somewhat similar to American baseball).

H6.5 Use apostrophes correctly.

Apostrophes

The apostrophe is used mainly for showing possession, but it is also used to indicate missing letters in contractions and to form special plurals.

Apostrophe to Show Possession

Use the apostrophe to indicate possession of nouns and indefinite pronouns. Possessive constructions show both a possessor and a thing possessed: The thing possessed occurs last in the construction; the person or thing that possesses (the possessor) comes first and contains an apostrophe.

Possessor	Thing Possessed	Alternative Construction
Luciana's	car	car belonging to Luciana
men's	coats	coats for men
cats'	fur	fur of cats
three minutes'	work	work lasting three minutes

Because plurals and possessives both add an *s* sound to words, they are identical to the ear. To the eye, however, they are easily distinguished by the use of the apostrophe in the possessive. Be sure that you don't confuse your reader by mixing possessives and plurals.

Faulty Our neighbor's have two horse's and ten cat's on their grandfathers old farm.

Revised Our neighbors have two horses and ten cats on their grandfather's old farm.

Neighbors, horses, and *cats* are plurals, not possessives; *grandfather's* is a possessive, not a plural.

Forming the Possessive

To make a noun possessive, you must first determine whether it is singular or plural. Add an apostrophe and an *s* (*'s*) to singular nouns and to plural nouns that do not end in *s;* add an apostrophe only (') to plural nouns that end in *s*.

The man's car ***[the car belonging to the man]***

The men's cars ***[the cars belonging to the men]***

The cats' food dish ***[the food dish belonging to the cats]***

The cat's food dish ***[the food dish belonging to the cat]***

To form the possessive of hyphenated words, compound words, and word groups, add an apostrophe and an *s* (*'s*) to the last word only.

her mother-in-law's lawn mower

the ladies-in-waiting's formal gowns

Do Not Use Apostrophes for Possessives of Personal Pronouns Do not use apostrophes with the possessive forms of personal and relative pronouns (*yours, his, hers, ours, theirs, its, whose*). When an apostrophe is used with personal or relative pronouns, it indicates a contraction. Be especially careful to distinguish between *it's* ("it is") and *its* (possessive).

Possessive	Contraction
The dog chases its tail.	It's (it is) a funny dog.
Your tie is crooked.	You're (you are) a sloppy dresser.
Whose dog is that?	Who's (who is) at the door?

Apostrophes with Contractions

Use an apostrophe (') to indicate omitted letters in contractions.

you're (you are)	isn't (is not)
it's (it is)	spring of '34 (spring of 1934)

Note: Be sure to insert the apostrophe exactly where the missing letters would be.

Faulty	is'nt
Revised	isn't

Apostrophes to Form Plurals

Use an apostrophe and an *s* (*'s*) to form the plural of letters and words used as words. Underline (italicize) the letter or word but not the plural ending.

See pp. 672–673 on italics and underlining.

On your test I can't distinguish between your t's and your E's. You also use too many *very*'s and *extremely*'s.

Quotation Marks

H6.6 Use quotation marks correctly.

Use quotation marks to enclose words, phrases, and sentences that are someone's spoken words or that you have copied from a source. Also use quotation marks to set off titles of short works and to indicate words used in a special sense. Quotation marks always occur in pairs, one marking the beginning and the other the ending of the quoted material.

See Chapter 22 for details on how to quote sources and avoid plagiarism.

Punctuating the Start of a Quotation

When a quotation is introduced with an attributive tag (such as "my instructor says" or "Teresa Ortega acknowledges"), the tag can be followed by a comma, a colon, or *that*. If you use a comma or a colon, begin the quotation with a capital letter. If you introduce a quotation with *that*, do not capitalize the first letter of the quotation even if it is capitalized in the original. In this case, you do not precede the quotation with a comma.

Columnist E. J. Dionne says, "Terror is designed to paralyze."

Columnist E. J. Dionne says that "[t]error is designed to paralyze."

For use of brackets, see pp. 673–674.

If you work a short quotation into the structure of your own sentence, use no punctuation other than quotation marks around the quoted passage.

According to E. J. Dionne, all acts of terror are "designed to paralyze."

Placement of Attributive Tags

Attributive tags can be placed before, inside, or after the quotation. When an attributive tag is placed between the two halves of a quotation, the second half is not capitalized unless it begins a new sentence.

Michael Karnok says, "To be a father is to know the meaning of failure."

"To be a father," says Michael Karnok, "is to know the meaning of failure."

"To be a father is to know the meaning of failure," says Michael Karnok.

Punctuating the End of a Quotation

Put commas and periods inside quotation marks.

He told me to "buzz off," and then he went about his business.

He told me to "buzz off." Then he went about his business.

Note that both the comma (first sentence) and the period (second sentence) go inside the quotation marks.

In documented papers that place citations inside parentheses at the end of the quotation, put the comma or period after the parenthetical citation.

According to Immunex Chief Executive Edward Fritzky, "Genetic Institute is doing very, very well" (Lim C5).

Note the order: quotation mark, parenthetical citation, final period.

Place colons and semicolons outside the ending quotation mark.

He told me to "buzz off"; then he went about his business.

My sexist husband wants his "privileges": Monday night football and no household chores.

Note that the semicolon (first sentence) and the colon (second sentence) go outside the quotation marks.

See p. 658 for an example.

Place question marks and exclamation points inside quotation marks if they belong to the quotation; place them outside the ending quotation marks if they belong to the whole sentence.

Indirect Quotations

Use quotation marks for *direct* quotations—the actual words spoken by someone— but not for *indirect* quotations, which report what someone said without using the exact words.

Direct Quotation	"Do you want to go to the library?" Tyler asked Julio.
Indirect Quotation	Tyler asked Julio whether he wanted to go to the library.

Indented Block Method for Long Quotations

When quoting more than four typed lines (MLA style) or forty words (APA style), use the indented block method rather than quotation marks to indicate direct quotations. Double-space the quotation for both styles. For the MLA style, indent each line ten spaces from the left margin. Indent five spaces for the APA style. Do *not* put quotation marks around the blocked passage.

See p. 552 for an example.

Single Quotation Marks

In American practice, use single quotation marks, made with an apostrophe on most keyboards, to enclose a quotation within a quotation.

> Molly angrily told her discussion group, "Every time I ask my husband to help me with the ironing, he says that 'men don't iron clothes' and stalks out of the room in a huff."

> Inside Molly's directly quoted words is a direct quotation from Molly's husband: *men don't iron clothes*. The husband's words in this case are enclosed in single quotation marks.

With the block indentation method, use regular quotation marks to enclose a quotation within a quotation.

Quotation Marks for Titles of Short Works

Use quotation marks for titles of essays, short stories, short poems, songs, book chapters, and other sections that occur within books or periodicals.

> I liked Spenser's sonnet "Most Glorious Lord of Lyfe" better than *The Faerie Queene*.

> In this sentence, both the sonnet and *The Faerie Queene* are poems, but the former is in quotation marks because it is short, and the latter is italicized (underlined) because it is long.

Quotation Marks for Words Used in a Special Sense

Use quotation marks to call attention to a word or phrase used in a special sense. Often your intention is to show that you disagree with how someone else uses the word or phrase.

> My husband refuses to do what he considers "woman's work."

> In this example, the quotation marks indicate that the writer would not use the phrase *woman's work* and that she and her husband have different ideas about what the phrase means.

Although you may set off words used in a special sense with quotation marks, avoid using quotation marks for slang and clichés as an attempt to apologize for them. Rephrase your sentence to eliminate the triteness.

Weak I've been "busy as a bee" all week, so I'm exhausted.

Revised I've been so busy this week that I'm exhausted.

Exercise

In the following sentences, insert apostrophes and single or double quotation marks as needed.

1. My mother told me that she didn't want me to buy a car until I had a permanent part-time job.
2. Jake has his little quirks, as Molly calls them, but he is still lovable.
3. My adviser recently remarked: The nervous student who encounters a professor who states, Twenty percent of this class usually fails, must learn to say, Not I, instead of giving up.
4. Did your friends teacher really say Attendance is mandatory in this class?
5. We are guilty of gross misuse of language, continued the speaker, whenever we use disinterested to mean uninterested.
6. I spent two hours worth of good homework time, complained Thomas friend Karen, trying to invent a tongue twister that would make people stand up and shout, That's a masterpiece.

H6.7 Italics (Underlining)

Use italics (underlining) correctly.

In handwritten papers, indicate italics with underlining. In papers prepared using a computer, italicizing is usually preferable. Check with your instructor.

Italics for Titles of Long Complete Works

Use italics for titles of books, magazines, journals, newspapers, Web sites, plays, films, works of art, long poems, pamphlets, and musical works. Capitalize and italicize *a, an*, and *the* only if they are part of the title.

Moby-Dick	Michaelangelo's *David*	*YouTube*
Newsweek	the *Encyclopaedia Britannica*	*MySpace*
Star Wars	*The Sound and the Fury*	*The Jupiter Symphony*

Note: The Bible and its books, as well as the Qur'an (Koran), are not underlined or italicized.

the Bible   Exodus   Revelations   the Qur'an

Italics for Foreign Words and Phrases

Use italics for foreign words and phrases.

You should avoid the *post hoc ergo propter hoc* fallacy.

Italics for Letters, Numbers, and Words Used as Words

Use italics for letters, for numbers, and for words when they are referred to as words and phrases and not as what they represent.

> To spell the word *separate* correctly, remember there is *a rat* in *separate*.

Brackets, Ellipses, and Slashes

H6.8 Use brackets, ellipses, and slashes correctly.

Brackets and ellipses (three spaced dots) indicate changes within quotations and occasionally have other uses. Slashes are used primarily to indicate line breaks in quoted poetry.

Brackets

Brackets [ ] are made with straight lines and should not be confused with parentheses ( ), which use curved lines.

Brackets to Set Off Explanatory Material Inserted into Quotations Use brackets to set off explanatory material inserted into a quotation.

> According to Joseph Menosky, "Courses offered to teach these skills [computer literacy] have popped up everywhere."

The original source of this quotation did not contain the words *computer literacy*, since the context of the original source explained what *these skills* meant. In this example, *computer literacy* is inserted in brackets to make up for the missing context. The brackets indicate that the material they enclose did not occur in the original version.

Brackets to Indicate the Writer's Alteration of the Grammar of a Quotation Use brackets when you need to change the grammar of a quotation to make it fit the grammar of your own sentence.

Original Source	I see electric cars as our best hope for reducing air pollution. —Jean Haricot
Correct Use of Brackets	Jean Haricot says that "electric cars [are] our best hope for reducing air pollution."

In this example the writer has to change the original *as* to *are* to make the quotation fit the grammar of his or her own sentence. This change is placed in brackets.

Brackets to Enclose *Sic* to Indicate a Mistake in a Quotation If you quote a source that contains an obvious mistake, you can insert *sic* in brackets to indicate that the mistake is in the original source and is not your own.

According to Vernon Tweeble, not your greatest sportswriter, the home-run king is still "Baby [*sic*] Ruth."

Here the *sic* indicates that Tweeble said "Baby Ruth," not "Babe Ruth." The mistake belongs to Tweeble, not to the writer.

Ellipses

An ellipsis, made with three spaced periods, is used to indicate an omission within a quotation. When an ellipsis occurs at the end of a sentence, a period is used before the ellipsis to mark the sentence boundary.

For more on the use of ellipses in quotations, see pp. 550–551.

Original Before the dam, a float trip down the river through Glen Canyon would cost you a minimum of seven days' time, well within anyone's vacation allotment, and a capital outlay of about forty dollars—the prevailing price of a two-man rubber boat with oars, available at any army-navy surplus store. A life jacket might be useful but not required, for there were no dangerous rapids in the 150 miles of Glen Canyon. —Edward Abbey, "The Damnation of a Canyon"

Correct Use of Ellipses According to Edward Abbey, before the dam was built "a float trip down the river through Glen Canyon would cost you a minimum of seven days' time ... and a capital outlay of about forty dollars... . A life jacket might be useful but not required ..." (351).

Here the first ellipsis indicates words omitted in the middle of a sentence. The second ellipsis shows words omitted at the end of a sentence and hence includes a period to mark the sentence boundary. In the last example, the period marking the sentence boundary goes after the parenthetical citation, which indicates the page number of the source.

When quoting poetry, use a line of dots to indicate that one or more full lines of the poem have been omitted, as in this example using Ben Jonson's "Come, My Celia":

Come, my Celia, let us prove,
While we can, the sports of love;
....
Why should we defer our joys?
Fame and rumor are but toys.

Slashes

The main use of the slash is to divide lines of poetry written as a quotation within a sentence.

Ben Jonson evokes the *carpe diem* tradition when he says: "Come, my Celia, let us prove, / While we can, the sports of love."

If you quote more than four lines of poetry, use the indented block method rather than quotation marks with slashes.

Slashes are sometimes used to indicate options, but this use is too informal for most essays.

Informal He told me to take algebra and/or trigonometry.

Formal He told me to take either algebra or trigonometry or both.

Capital Letters

H6.9 Use capital letters correctly.

When in doubt about whether to capitalize a particular word, consult a good dictionary.

Capitals for First Letters of Sentences and Intentional Fragments

Capitalize the first letter of the first word in every sentence and also in sentence fragments used intentionally for effect. In fragmentary questions in a series, initial capital letters are optional.

- That man is a liar and a scoundrel. What do you want me to do? Like him? Invite him to dinner? Offer him my money?

or

What do you want me to do? like him? invite him to dinner? offer him my money?

Capitals for Proper Nouns

Use capitals for all proper nouns. The following rules cover most cases you will encounter.

Capital Letters	Miguel Cabrera, Barack Obama, Jennifer Lawrence
Capitalize titles of people when the title precedes the name or when the title follows the name without an article.	Doctor Teodora Koskov; John Jones, Professor of Mathematics
Do not capitalize titles of people that include an article (*a* or *an*).	Teodora Koskov, a medical doctor; John Jones, a mathematics professor
Capitalize family relationship names (Mother, Uncle) when used with a name. When used in place of a name, capitalization is optional.	Please, Aunt Eloise, tell Grandfather (or grandfather) that dinner is ready.
Do not capitalize relationship words when not used with a name or as a name.	I hear that my uncle and your father are going to visit Tony's grandfather.
Capitalize the names of specific geographic locations, areas, and regions, including compass directions if they are part of a name.	Mount Everest; the Pacific Northwest; Main Street; the Hudson River; the South; Illinois
Do not capitalize geographic locations indicated by compass directions but not considered actual names.	the northeast part of the United States; a mountain south of here

Capitalize historical events, names, movements, and writings.	the Korean War; the Oregon Territory; Articles of Confederation; the Renaissance; the Impressionist Period
Capitalize the names of ships and buildings and capitalize brand names.	USS *Missouri*; the Empire State Building; Pepsi
Capitalize specific academic courses but not academic subject areas, except "English" and foreign languages.	This term I am taking Chemistry 101, Integral Calculus, and French. But: This term I am taking chemistry, calculus, and French. (In the first sentence, the writer names specific courses; in the second sentence, the writer names subject areas only.)
Capitalize specific times, days, months, and holidays, but not names of seasons.	Monday; the Fourth of July; Halloween; last year; autumn; winter
Capitalize abbreviations derived from proper names.	NFL; U.S.A.; RCA; NAFTA; U. of W.

Capitals for Important Words in Titles

In titles of books, articles, plays, musical works, and so forth, capitalize the first and last words, any word following a colon or a semicolon, and all other words except articles, prepositions, and conjunctions of fewer than five letters.

"Ain't No Such Thing as a Montana Cowboy"

Famous Myths and Legends of the World: Stories of Gods and Heroes

Capitals in Quotations and Spoken Dialogue

Capitalize the first word of spoken dialogue, but do not capitalize the first word in the second half of a broken quotation that follows an attributive tag.

She said, "Because it is raining, we won't go."

"Because it is raining," she said, "we won't go."

Do not capitalize indirect quotations.

She said that we wouldn't go because it is raining.

H6.10 Numbers

Use numbers appropriately.

Writers often have to decide whether to write numbers as words (ten) or as numerals (10). Follow the conventions of the genre in which you are writing.

Numbers in Scientific and Technical Writing

Scientific and technical writers generally use numerals for all numbers. Check with your instructor about how to handle numbers in lab reports and other formal papers in science, mathematics, and engineering.

Numbers in Formal Writing for Nontechnical Fields

In the humanities and other nontechnical fields and in most business and professional writing, writers usually adhere to the following conventions:

Use Words Instead of Numerals

For single-word number	eight dogs; a hundred doughnuts
For common fractions	one-third of a cup; half a pie
In the humanities, for two-word numbers	twenty-three students (however, business and professional writers prefer numerals for two-word numbers—23 students)
For numbers greater than a million, use a combination of words and numerals.	72 billion dollars

Use Numerals Instead of Words

For addresses	1420 Heron Street
For times and dates	I'll be there at 10:00 A.M. on November 5th.
For percentages and statistics	At least 30 percent of the students scored above 15 on the standardized test.
With decimals	The average score was 29.63
For amounts of money that include cents	That notebook cost around $3.95.
With symbols	20° C, 5'4"
For scores	The Yankees beat the Indians 5 to 3.
To refer to chapters, pages, and lines	You'll find that statistic in Chapter 12 on page 100 at line 8.

Numbers at the Beginning of a Sentence

Spell out in words any number that begins a sentence. If the result is awkward, rewrite the sentence.

Faulty 375 students showed up for the exam.

Revised Three hundred seventy-five students showed up for the exam.

Or

We counted 375 students at the exam.

Abbreviations

H6.11 Use abbreviations appropriately.

Whenever it is necessary to save space, such as in tables, indexes, and footnotes, you may use abbreviations. In the main text of formal writing, however, you should generally spell out rather than abbreviate words. Abbreviations are acceptable in the following cases.

Abbreviations for Academic Degrees and Titles

Use abbreviations for academic degrees and for the following common titles when used with a person's name: *Mr., Ms., Mrs., Dr., Jr., Sr., St.* (*Saint*). Other titles, such as *governor, colonel, professor*, and *reverend*, are spelled out.

> The doctor asked Colonel Jones, Ms. Hemmings, and Professor Pruitt to present the portrait of St. Thomas to Judge Hogkins on the occasion of her receiving a Ph.D. in religious studies.

Abbreviations for Agencies, Institutions, and Other Entities

Use abbreviations for agencies, groups, people, places, or objects that are commonly known by capitalized initials.

FBI	UCLA
IOOF	DNA molecules
Washington, DC	CD-ROM

If you wish to use a specialized abbreviation that may be unclear to your audience, write out the term in full the first time it appears and place in parentheses the abbreviation that you will use subsequently.

> The Modern Language Association (MLA) recently issued new guidelines for citing electronic sources.

This example indicates that the writer will henceforth use the abbreviation *MLA*.

Abbreviations for Common Latin Terms

Use abbreviations for common Latin terms used in footnotes, bibliographies, or parenthetical comments. In the main text, spell out the English equivalents.

e.g.	for example
i.e.	that is
c.f.	compare

This rule also applies to *etc.* (*et cetera*, meaning "and so forth"). Avoid using *etc.* in formal writing. Instead, use the English *and so forth* or *and so on*, or rewrite your sentence to make it more inclusive, thus eliminating the need for *and so forth*. Never write *and etc.*, because *et* is Latin for "and."

Weak	During my year in London I went to ballets, the opera, Shakespeare plays, etc.
Revised	During my year in London I saw many cultural events, including two ballets, one opera, and four Shakespeare plays.

Plurals of Abbreviations

Do not use an apostrophe when forming the plural of an abbreviation.

Faulty	I've misplaced two of my CD's.
Revised	I've misplaced two of my CDs.

CREDITS

Text

Page 2. Reprinted by permission of Rodney Kilcup.

Page 15. David Rockwood. "Letter to the Editor", *The Oregonian,* January 1, 1993. Reprinted by permission of Rosalie Rockwood Bean.

Page 15. Thomas Merton. From "Rain and the Rhinoceros" from *Raids on the Unspeakable,* copyright © 1966 by The Abbey of Gethsemani, Inc. Reprinted by permission of New Directions Publishing Corp.

Page 22. Walvoord, Barbara E. and McCarthy, Lucile P., "Thinking and Writing in College: A Naturalistic Study of Students in Four Disciplines." Urbana, IL: National Council of Teachers of English (NCTE), 1990, p. 51.

Page 31. "next to of course god america i". Copyright 1926, 1954, © 1991 by the Trustees for the E. E. Cummings Trust. Copyright © 1985 by George James Firmage, from *Complete Poems: 1904-1962* by E. E. Cummings, edited by George J. Firmage. Used by permission of Liveright Publishing Corporation.

Page 42. Kenneth Burke. From *Permanence and Change: An Anatomy of Purpose* by Kenneth Burke, © 1984 by Kenneth Burke. Reprinted by permission of the publisher, University of California Press and The Kenneth Burke Literary Trust.

Page 46. From "Which One is the REAL ANWR?" Arctic Power–Arctic National Wildlife Refuge, p. 1, www.anwr.org. Reprinted by permission of Arctic Power.

Page 66. Kirby Ferguson. From *Everything's a Remix:* The TED Talk, TED.com, June 2012. Reprinted by permission of Kirby Ferguson.

Page 98. Kyle Madsen.

Page 114. "Why Bother" by Michael Pollan from *The New York Times,* April 20, 2008. Copyright (c) 2008 by Michael Pollan for The New York Times. Reprinted by permission of International Creative Management, Inc.

Page 121. Stephanie Malinowski.

Page 128. Excerpt from pp. 216-17 from *Black Boy* by Richard Wright. Copyright, 1937, 1942, 1944, 1945 by Richard Wright; renewed © 1973 by Ellen Wright. Reprinted by permission of HarperCollins Publishers.

Page 131. Meagan Lacy.

Page 132. Jeffrey J. Cain.

Page 139. Patrick J. Ramos.

Page 141. Stephanie Whipple.

Page 160. Kent Ansen (pseudonym) "Should the United States Establish Mandatory Public Service for Young Adults?" Reprinted by permission.

Page 185. Student Writing by Kerri Ann Matsumoto.

Page 186. Student essay by Shannon King.

Page 189. NAACP. "NAACP Report reveals disparate impact of coal-fired power plants," NAACP Press release, November 16, 2012, http://www.naacp.org. Reprinted by permission of the NAACP.

Page 212. LeAnne M. Forquer, Ph.D., et al. "Sleep Patterns of College Students at a Public University" by LeAnne M. Forquer, Ph.D.; Adrain E. Camden, B.S.; Krista M. Gabriau, B.S.; C. Merle Johnson, Ph.D., *Journal of American College Health,* Vol. 56, No. 5, March/April 2008. Reprinted by permission of LeAnne Forquer, Ph.D.

Pages 217, 226. Lauren Campbell.

Page 259. Student Writing by Lydia Wheeler.

Page 265. Alison Townsend, "The Barbie Birthday" from *The Blue Dress*. Copyright © 2003, 2008 by Alison Townsend. Reprinted with the permission of The Permissions Company, Inc., on behalf of White Pine Press, www.whitepine.org.

Page 280. Michelle Eastman. "Unconditional Love and the Function of the Rocking Chair in Kolosov's 'Forsythia'" Reprinted by permission of the author.

Page 282. Bill Konigsberg. "After" from *Sudden Flash Youth,* Christine P. Hazuka, et al., editors. Compilation © 2011 by Christine Perkins-Hazuka, Tom Hazuka, and Mark Budman. Reprinted by permission of The Jennifer DeChiara Literary Agency.

Page 285. Review of "The Accordion Family: Boomerang Kids, Anxious Parents, and the Private Toll of Global Competition" from *Publishers Weekly*, August 29, 2011.

Page 337. Student Essay by Ross Taylor.

Page 341. Megan H. MacKenzie. "Let Women Fight." Reprinted by permission of *Foreign Affairs*, November/December 2012. Copyright 2012 by the Council on Foreign Relations, Inc. www.ForeignAffairs.com

Page 348. Owens, MacKubin Thomas, "Coed Combat Units." This article originally appeared in *The Weekly Standard* on February 4, 2013. Reprinted with permission.

Page 355. Claire Giordano. "Virtual Promise: Why Online Courses Will Not Adequately Prepare Us for the Future." Reprinted by permission of the author.

Page 357. Manoucheka Celeste. "Disturbing Media Images of Haiti Reinforce Stereotypes" from *Seattle Times,* January 26, 2010. Reprinted by permission of the author.

Page 376. Student Writing by Jackie Wyngaard.

Page 381. Student Writing by Teresa Filice

Page 396. Lucy Morsen (pseudonym) "A proposal to improve the campus learning environment." Reprinted by permission.

Page 402. Sam Rothchild (pseudonym) "Reward Work, Not Wealth" Reprinted by permission.

Page 405. Kent Ansen (pseudonym) "Should the United States Establish Mandatory Public Service for Young Adults?" Reprinted by permission.

Page 460. David Popenoe, "Where's Papa?" condensed from *Life Without Father: Compelling New Evidence that Fatherhood and Marriage Are Indispensable for the Good of Children and Society.* Reprinted by permission of the author

Page 463. Student essay by Dao Do.

Page 473. Graves, Michael E., et al., from "Some Characteristics of Memorable Expository Writing: Effects of Revisions by Writers with Different Backgrounds," *Research in the Teaching of English,* 1988, Vol. 22, No. 3, pp. 242–265. Urbana, IL: National Council of Teachers of English, 1988.

Page 522. Reprinted by permission of EBSCO Publishing.

Page 537. "Arkansas" page from Energy for Shale website. © 2013 EnergyFromShale.org. All rights reserved. Reprinted by permission of American Petroleum Institute. (top). Reprinted by permission of Food & Water Watch/Americans Against Fracking (bottom).

Page 571. Academic Search Complete detailed record for "A Call for National Service" opinion piece by Mark Rosenman, *Chronicle of Philanthropy,* October 18, 2007, Vol. 20. No. 1, p. 38. Reprinted by permission of the Chronicle of Philanthropy. Reprinted by permission of EBSCO Publishing.

Page 574. US Environmental Protection Agency (EPA).

Page 582. Scharrer, E.; Kim, D. Daniel; Lin, Ke-Ming and Liu, Zixu. (2006) "Working Hard or Hardly Working: Gender, humor, and the performance of domestic chores in television commercials." *Mass Communication and Society,* 9(2), 215-238, http://www.tandfonline.com/doi/abs/10.1207/s15327825mcs0902_5?tab=permissions#tabModule. doi: 10.1207/s15327825mcs0902_5. Reprinted by permission of EBSCO Publishing.

Page 606. Student Essay by Jamie Finger.

Page 607. Student Writing by Bruce Urbanik.

Images

Page 1. CNAC/MNAM/Dist. RMN-Grand Palais/Art Resource, NY. ©2013 Artists Rights Society (ARS), New York/ADAGP, Paris.

Page 7. Billie G. Lynn

Page 44. Jonathan Carr

Page 58. Peter Sobolev/Shutterstock

Page 60. Montana Fish Wildlife and Parks/AP Images (top left). 4FR/Getty Images (top right). Thomas Kitchin & Victoria Hurst/Design Pics Inc./Alamy (bottom left). Image Source/Getty Images (bottom right).

Page 62. Peter Jordan/Alamy (top left). Digital Vision/Thinkstock (top right). Creatas/Thinkstock (bottom left). Wavebreakmedia/Shutterstock (bottom right).

Page 69. John Bean (3 images)

Page 77. Roz Chast/The Cartoon Bank

Page 81. U.S. Air Force

Page 169, 493. Mary T Nguyen/The Columbus Dispatch

Page 182. Christopher Meder/Fotolia (left). Pyan setia2008/Fotolia (center). Urbanlight/Shutterstock (right).

Page 228. Leslie Stone/The Image Works (top left). Guillermo Arias/AP Images (top right). J. Emilio Flores/Corbis (bottom left). Carlos Barria/Reuters/Corbis (bottom right).

Page 230. Steven James Silva/Reuters/Landov (top left). Det. Greg Semendinger/NYPD/AP Images (top right). David Turnley/Corbis (bottom).

Page 236. Peter Turnley/Corbis

Page 239. Scala/Art Resource, NY

Page 241. Albright-Knox Art Gallery/Art Resource, NY

Page 242. June Johnson (two images)

Page 245. Lars Halbauer/Dpa/Landov

Page 260. Stephen Crowley/The New York Times/Redux

Page 261. Library of Congress Prints and Photographs Division/Lange, Dorothea, [LC-DIG-fsa-8b29516]

Page 349. Sgt. Russell Lee, U.S. Army

Page 352. Mike Kaplan, U.S. Air Force

Page 354. Gary Varvel/Creators Syndicate

Page 362. Altay Kaya/Fotolia (left). Shovalp100/Fotolia (center). Bildagentur-online/Schoening/Alamy (right).

Page 368. David R. Frazier Photolibrary, Inc./Alamy

Page 390, 493. Common Sense for Drug Policy

Page 403. Arinahabich/Fotolia (top left). Liaison Spencer Platt/Getty Images (top right). Don Jon Red/Alamy (center left).

Page 417, 493. Zou Zheng/Xinhua/Landov

Page 493, 609. The Advertising Council

Page 494. Erich Schlegel/Newscom (top left). Cynthia Jones/Getty Images (top right). Dbimages/Alamy (bottom right).

Page 495. Lionel Healing/AFP/Getty Images (top). Dbimages/Alamy (bottom left). Eddie Gerald/Alamy (bottom right).

Page 504. June Johnson

Page 507. International WOW Company

Page 585. National Library of Medicine

INDEX